$73.00

# 2014 NATIONAL PAINTING COST ESTIMATOR

## By Dennis D. Gleason, CPE

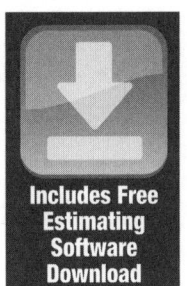

**Includes inside the back cover:**

Inside the back cover of this book you'll find a software download certificate. To access the download, follow the instructions printed there. The download includes the National Estimator, an easy-to-use estimating program with all the cost estimates in this book. The software will run on PCs using Windows XP, Vista, 7 or 8 operating systems.

**Quarterly price updates on the Web are free** and automatic all during 2014. You'll be prompted when it's time to collect the next update. A connection to the Web is required.

Download all of Craftsman's most popular costbooks for one low price with the Craftsman Site License. http://CraftsmanSiteLicense.com

- Turn your estimate into a bid.
- Turn your bid into a contract.
- ConstructionContractWriter.com

**Craftsman Book Company**
6058 Corte del Cedro, Carlsbad, CA 92011

# Acknowledgments

The author thanks the following individuals and organizations for furnishing materials and information used in the preparation of various portions of this book.

**Howard Shahan,** *American Design Painting & Drywall,* Poway, CA
**American Society of Professional Estimators (ASPE),** Wheaton, MD
**Benjamin Moore Paints,** San Diego, CA
**Gordon H. Brevcort,** *Brevcort Consulting Associates,* Ridgewood, NJ
**Scott Williams,** *CSI Paint,* San Francisco, and Napa, CA
**John San Marcos,** *Devoe Coatings,* San Diego Marine Hardware, San Diego, CA
**Ken Hogben,** *Dunn-Edwards Paints & Wallcovering,* Daly City, CA
**Randy Martin,** *Dunn-Edwards Paints & Wallcovering,* San Diego, CA
**Bob Langbein,** *East Bay Paint Center,* Albany, CA
**Mike Barden,** *ICI-Dulux Paints,* San Jose, CA
**Hugh Champeny,** *Kelly-Moore Paint Company,* San Carlos, CA
**Peter Roske,** *Kelly-Moore Paint Company,* Concord, CA
**Dennis Cripe,** *R.W. Little Co, Inc., Sandblasting,* San Diego, CA
**Jim Cornelius,** *Mark's Paint Mart,* Oakland, CA
**Bruce McMullan,** *McMullan & Son Painting,* San Diego, CA
**Joe Garrigan,** *Mr. Paints,* San Diego, CA
**PPG Industries, Inc.,** *Pittsburgh Paints,* Torrance, CA
**Greg Albright,** *Pursel Quality Paints,* Berkeley, CA
**Matt Bond,** *Pursel Quality Paints,* Berkeley, CA
**Keith Braswell,** *Rent-X,* Pleasant Hill, CA
**Richardson Engineering Services, Inc.,** Mesa, AZ
**Rust-Oleum Protective Coatings,** Los Angeles, CA
**Aaron Truit,** *The Sherwin-Williams Company,* Concord, CA
**Ace Harmon,** *The Sherwin-Williams Company,* Berkeley, CA
**Squires-Belt Material Co.,** San Diego, CA
**Steel Structures Painting Council,** Pittsburgh, PA
**John Meyer,** *U.S. Government, Department of the Navy, Public Works,* San Diego, CA
**Sandy Sternberg,** *Vista Paint Centers,* Escondido, CA
**Jerry Rittgarn,** *Waco-Arise Scaffolding & Equipment,* San Diego, CA

Cover design by: *Bill Grote*
Sheila M. Scott, Calligraphy

**©2013 Craftsman Book Company**
**ISBN 978-1-57218-295-0     ISSN 1092-6852**
**Published October 2013 for the year 2014**

# Contents

**Introduction - How to Use This Book** . . . . 5

## Part I - General Painting Costs
- Baseboard ........................... 43
- Beams .............................. 45
- Bookcases and shelves ................ 48
- Cabinets ............................ 52
- Ceilings ............................ 57
- Closets ............................. 88
- Corbels ............................. 92
- Cutting-in .......................... 92
- Decks .............................. 94
- Doors .............................. 95
- Fascia ............................. 118
- Fence .............................. 123
- Fireplaces ......................... 127
- Firewood boxes .................... 128
- Floors ............................. 129
- Garage door backs ................. 137
- Gutters & downspouts .............. 138
- High time difficulty factors ........ 139
- Mail box structures ................ 140
- Masonry ........................... 140
- Molding ........................... 153
- Overhangs ......................... 159
- Pass-through shelves ............... 162
- Plant-on trim ...................... 162
- Plaster or stucco .................. 168
- Pot shelves ........................ 172
- Railings ........................... 173
- Registers, HVAC ................... 182
- Roof jacks ......................... 183
- Roofing ........................... 184
- Sheet metal ....................... 196
- Shutters or blinds ................. 201
- Siding ............................. 202
- Stairs ............................. 219
- Touchup, brush as required ........ 222
- Trellis or lattice ................... 223
- Valances for light fixtures ......... 224
- Walls .............................. 225
- Window screen frames ............. 276
- Window seats ..................... 277
- Window sills ...................... 277
- Windows .......................... 278
- Window conversion factors ........ 292
- Wine racks ........................ 293

## Part II - Preparation Costs
- Acid wash gutters & downspouts .... 296
- Airblast, compressed air ........... 296
- Burn off paint ..................... 297
- Caulk ............................. 298
- Cut cracks ........................ 298
- Fill wood floors ................... 299
- Putty, application ................. 299
- Sand .............................. 299
- Sandblast ......................... 302
- Scribing .......................... 309
- Strip, remove, bleach .............. 311
- Unstick windows .................. 312
- Wash ............................. 313
- Waterblast (Power wash) .......... 315
- Window-protective coating ........ 315
- Wire brush ........................ 316

## Part III - Industrial, Institutional and Heavy Commercial Painting Costs
- Conduit ........................... 318
- Decking and siding ................ 326
- Doors, hollow metal ............... 330
- Ductwork ......................... 331
- Fire escapes ...................... 348
- Fire sprinkler systems ............. 349
- Grates and grilles ................. 350
- Ladders ........................... 354
- Masonry .......................... 354
- Mechanical equipment ............. 356
- Piping ............................ 357
- Radiators ......................... 371
- Structural steel ................... 372
- Tank, silo, vessel, or hopper ...... 400
- Walls, concrete, tilt-up ........... 412
- Windows, steel factory sash ....... 418

## Part IV - Wallcovering Costs
- Adhesive coverage ................. 422
- Wallcovering application .......... 424
- Borders ........................... 424
- Flexible wood sheet and veneer .... 425
- Surface preparation, wallcovering .. 425
- Vinyl wallcovering ................ 426
- Wall fabric ....................... 430
- Wallpaper ........................ 434

**Index** ............................. **440**

# List of Figures

| Figure | Title | Page |
|---|---|---|
| 1 | The basis for cost estimates in this book | 6 |
| 2 | Customize the tables | 7 |
| 3 | Sandblasting pricing table | 11 |
| 4 | Pavement marking pricing table | 12 |
| 5 | Waterblasting pricing table | 13 |
| 6 | Labor productivity categories | 13 |
| 7 | Material coverage rates | 15 |
| 8 | Material price discounts | 16 |
| 9 | Material prices at 20% discount | 17 |
| 10 | Material prices at 30% discount | 20 |
| 11 | Material prices at 40% discount | 23 |
| 12 | Sundry inventory checklist | 27 |
| 13 | Hourly wage rates for wallcovering application | 29 |
| 14 | Labor burden percentages | 30 |
| 15 | Typical equipment purchase and rental prices | 33 |
| 16 | Risk factors and profit margin | 36 |
| 17 | Bidding variables | 36 |
| 18 | Sample painting estimate | 38 |
| 19 | Blank painting estimate | 40 |
| 20 | Interior opening count allowance table | 102 |
| 21 | Conduit/pipe area conversion table | 325 |
| 22 | Square corner decking factors | 327 |
| 23 | Structural steel conversion tables | 391 |
| 24 | Surface area of spheres | 399 |
| 25 | Sample field production times and rates form | 419 |
| 26 | Blank field production times and rates form | 420 |

# How to Use This Book

Paint estimating is more of an art than a science. There's no price that's exactly right for every job and for every bidder. That's because every painting job is unique. No single material cost, no labor estimate, no pricing system fits all types of work. And just as every job varies, so do painting companies. No two painting contractors have the same productivity rates, the same labor burden, the same overhead expense and the same profit requirements.

The best paint estimates are always custom-made for a particular job. They're based on the contractor's actual productivity rate, material cost, labor cost, overhead percentage and profit expectations. No estimating book, no computerized estimating system, no estimating service can possibly account for all the variables that make every job and every painting company different. Only a skilled estimator using professional judgment and a proven estimating system can produce consistently reliable estimates on a wide variety of painting jobs.

## So, Why Buy This Book?

That's easy. This is the most complete, authoritative and reliable unit cost guide ever made available to paint estimators. No matter what types of work you estimate, no matter what your costs are, this book will help produce consistently accurate painting cost estimates in dollars and cents. But it isn't a substitute for expertise. It's not a simple way to do in minutes what an experienced paint estimator might not be able to do in hours. Instead, this unit cost guide will aid you in developing a good estimate of costs for any painting operation on any project. Think of this manual as one good estimating tool. But it's not (or at least shouldn't be) the only estimating tool you'll use.

For most jobs, I expect that the figures you see here will prove to be good estimates. But anyone who understands paint estimating will understand why judgment is needed when applying figures from this manual — or any other paint estimating guide. It's your responsibility to decide which conditions on the job you're bidding are like conditions assumed in this manual, and which conditions are different. Where conditions are different, you'll need good professional judgment to arrive at a realistic estimated cost.

Inside the back cover of this book you'll find a software download certificate. To access the download, follow the instructions printed there. The download includes the National Estimator, an easy-to-use estimating program with all the cost estimates in this book. The software will run on PCs using Windows XP, Vista, 7 or 8 operating systems. When the National Estimator program has been installed, click Help on the menu bar to see a list of topics that will get you up and running. Or, go online to www.costbook.com and click the ShowMe tutorial link to view an interactive tutorial for National Estimator.

National Painting Cost Estimator

|  | Manhour productivity | Labor cost per hour | Labor burden percent | Labor burden dollars | Labor cost plus burden | Material price discount | Overhead percent | Profit |
|---|---|---|---|---|---|---|---|---|
| Slow (1P) | Low | $20.25 | 29.5% | $5.97 | $26.22 | 20% | 19.0% | 16% |
| Medium (2P) | Average | 25.75 | 35.4% | 9.12 | 34.87 | 30% | 25.0% | 12% |
| Fast (3P) | High | 31.50 | 40.8% | 12.85 | 44.35 | 40% | 31.0% | 7% |

Notes: These rates are for painters. Hourly rates for wallcovering are different. See page 29. Slow, Medium and Fast jobs are defined on page 13. Labor burden percentages used in this book are summarized on page 31. National Estimator uses hourly rates in the Labor cost plus burden column. National Estimator shows productivity rates (Slow, Medium and Fast) and copies the words Slow, Medium or Fast to your estimate. It also copies the crew productivity code, either 1P (Slow), 2P (Medium), or 3P (Fast) to your estimating form. National Estimator allows you to enter any percentage you select for overhead and profit.

**Figure 1**
The basis for painting cost estimates in this book

## How to Use the Tables

The estimating tables in this book show typical costs and bid prices for every painting operation you're likely to encounter, whether paint is applied by brush, roller, mitt or spray. Selecting the right cost table and the correct application method is easy. Tables are divided into four parts:

Part I: General Painting Costs

Part II: Preparation Costs

Part III: Industrial, Institutional and Heavy Commercial Painting Costs

Part IV: Wallcovering Costs

Each section is arranged alphabetically by operation. If you have trouble finding the tables you need, use the Table of Contents at the front of the book or the Index at the back of the book.

Once you've found the right table and the appropriate application method, you have to select the correct application rate. For each of the application methods (brush, roll, mitt or spray), the tables show three application rates: "Slow," "Medium," or "Fast." That's a very important decision when using this book, because each application rate assumes different manhour productivity, material coverage, material cost per gallon, hourly labor cost, labor burden, overhead and profit.

Your decision on the application rate to use (or which combination of rates to use) has to be based on your evaluation of the job, your painters and your company. That's where good common sense is needed.

Figure 1 shows crew codes, labor costs, labor burdens, material discounts, and profit for each of the three production rates for painting.

The "Slow" application rate in Figure 1 assumes lower productivity (less area covered per manhour), a lower labor cost (due to a less skilled crew), a lower labor burden (due to lower fringe benefits), a lower discount on materials (because of low volume), higher overhead (due to lower volume) and a higher profit margin (typical on small repaint or custom jobs). Figures in this "Slow" application row will apply where painters with lower skill levels are working on smaller or more difficult repaint jobs.

Look at the "Fast" row in Figure 1. These estimates will apply where a skilled crew (higher hourly rate and larger fringe benefits) is working under good supervision and good conditions (more area covered per manhour) on larger (volume discount on materials) and more competitive jobs (lower profit margin). Figures in the "Fast" application row assume high productivity and lower material coverage, (unpainted surfaces absorb more paint), like that of a residential tract job.

Each of the three application rates is described more completely later in this section.

*How to Use This Book*

|  | Pricing variables ||| Unit cost estimate ||||||
|---|---|---|---|---|---|---|---|---|---|
|  | 1 | 2 | 3 | 4 | 5 | 6 | 7 | 8 | 9 |
|  | Labor SF per manhour | Material coverage SF/gallon | Material cost per gallon | Labor cost per 100 SF | Labor burden 100 SF | Material cost per 100 SF | Overhead per 100 SF | Profit per 100 SF | Total cost per 100 SF |
| **Walls, gypsum drywall, orange peel or knock-down, roll, per 100 SF of wall area** |||||||||
| Flat latex, water base (material #5) |||||||||
| Roll 1st coat |||||||||
| Slow | 400 | 300 | 36.70 | 5.06 | 1.50 | 12.23 | 3.57 | 3.58 | 25.94 |
| Medium | 538 | (275) | (32.10) | 4.79 | 1.70 | (11.67) | 4.54 | 2.72 | 25.42 |
| Fast | (675) | 250 | 27.50 | 4.67 | 1.89 | 11.00 | 5.45 | 1.61 | 24.62 |
| Your customized figures |  |  |  | 3.11 | .92 | 11.67 | 3.93 | 2.36 | 21.99 |

**Figure 2**
Customize the tables

## The Easy Case: No Adjustments

Let's suppose the "Slow" application rate fits the job you're estimating almost perfectly. Your crew's productivity is expected to be low. The labor cost will be $20.25 per hour. Labor burden (fringes, taxes and insurance) will be 29.5 percent. Discount on materials will be 20 percent. Overhead will be 19 percent and profit will be 16 percent. Then your task is easy. All of your costs match the costs in the "Slow" row. No modifications are needed. The same is true if your costs fit the "Medium" or "Fast" rows.

But that's not always going to happen. More often, the job, your crew and your company won't fit exactly into any of the three rows. What then? More evaluation is required. You'll combine costs from several application rate rows to reach an accurate bid price. I call that *customizing your costs* and it's nearly always required for an accurate estimate.

## Customizing Your Costs

Every company has a different combination of worker speed and experience, taxes, benefits, spread rates, equipment needs, percentage for overhead, and profit margin. These are the cost variables in paint estimating. This book is designed so you can quickly and easily adjust estimates to reflect actual costs on the job you're estimating. It's important that you *read the rest of this section before using the cost tables in this book.* That's the only way to get from this manual all the accuracy and flexibility that's built into it.

In the remainder of this section I'll describe the assumptions I've made and the methods I used to compile the cost tables in this manual. Once you understand them, you'll be able to combine and modify costs in the estimating tables so your bids fit the job, your crew and your company as closely as possible.

When you start using the cost tables in this book, I suggest you circle numbers in the "Slow," "Medium," or "Fast" application rate rows that best fit your company and your jobs. To improve accuracy even more, write your own figures in the blank row below the "Fast" row in each table, like I've done in Figure 2.

### A Practical Example

Figure 2 is part of an estimating table taken from Part I of this book, General Painting Costs. I'm going to use it to show how to customize estimates to match

7

your actual costs. In Figure 2 I've circled some of the costs I plan to use in a sample estimate and calculated others.

In column 1, *Labor SF per manhour*, I've circled 675 because I feel the journeyman painter assigned to this job can paint walls at the "Fast" rate of 675 square feet per hour. That's the number I plan to use for my estimate.

In column 2, *Material coverage SF/gallon*, I've reviewed my past performance and I expect coverage will be about 275 square feet per gallon of paint. So I've circled that figure.

In column 3, *Material cost per gallon*, I've circled 32.10 for my cost per gallon for flat water base latex (including tax and an allowance for consumable supplies), based on a 30 percent discount from the retail price.

So far, so good. That completes the first three columns, what I call the *pricing variables*. Now we can begin on the *unit cost estimate*, columns 4 through 9. Each of these columns show a price per 100 square feet of wall.

We'll start with column 4, *Labor cost per 100 SF*. Notice that I've entered 3.11 for this column. Here's why. Look back at Figure 1. Throughout this book the painting labor rate for "Fast" work is assumed to be $31.50 per hour. See page 29 for the wallcovering application rate. I can't use the labor cost per 100 SF for "Fast" work because the journeymen on my job earn $21.00 per hour. That pay rate is a little higher than the "Slow" pay rate as shown in Figure 1. To calculate the labor cost per 100 SF, divide $21.00 by 675 and multiply by 100: 21/675 = .0311 x 100 = 3.11.

In column 5, *Labor burden 100 SF*, I've entered .92. This figure is a result of my labor cost at $3.11 x 29.5 percent, my labor burden (taxes, insurance and benefits) from the "Slow" row of Figure 1. Even though the labor rate is "Fast" and the labor cost is higher than the "Slow" rate, for this example labor burden will be most like work done at the "Slow" rate because this company doesn't offer many benefits.

In column 6, *Material cost per 100 SF*, I've circled 11.67, the number in the "Medium" row. Since I've used numbers in the "Medium" row in both columns 2 and 3, I can take the figure in column 6 for material costs directly from the table, without any calculations.

In column 7, *Overhead per 100 SF*, I've calculated the overhead dollar value by adding the labor cost, labor burden and material cost then multiplying that sum by the "Medium" overhead at 25 percent: $3.11 + $.92 + $11.67 = $15.70 x .25 = $3.93.

In column 8, *Profit per 100 SF*, I've calculated the profit dollar value by adding the labor cost, labor burden, material cost and overhead then multiplying that sum by the "Medium" profit at 12 percent from Figure 1. The result is $3.11 + $.92 + $11.67 + $3.93 = $19.63 x .12 = $2.36.

Column 9, *Total cost per 100 SF*, is the bid price — it's the sum of columns 4 through 8 for each row. Because I've circled costs that fall in more than one row, I can't use any figure in column 9. Instead, I simply add the circled or calculated figures in columns 4 through 8: $3.11 + $.92 + $11.67 + $3.93 + $2.36 = $21.99. That's my bid price per 100 square feet on this job. It's the combination of costs that fit my company, my painters and the job.

### Using Your Good Judgment

Of course, judgment is required when using these tables, as it is when making any estimate. For example, if your journeymen painters earn the top rate of $31.50 but work at the "Medium" production rate or slower, your labor cost per unit will be higher than the highest cost listed in column 4. An adjustment will be required.

Because figures in columns 7 and 8 are percentages of figures in columns 4, 5 and 6, you have to be careful when you blend costs from different rows. Let's look at an extreme (and unlikely) example.

Suppose you use costs from the "Slow" application row for columns 4 (5.06), 5 (1.50) and 6 (12.23) of Figure 2. The total of those three costs is $18.79. Then you decide to use overhead from the "Fast" row because your overhead is about 31 percent of cost, not 19 percent of cost as in the "Slow" row (Figure 1). "Fast" overhead is listed as $5.45 in Figure 2. The correct overhead figure is $5.82, 31 percent of the sum of "Slow" costs in columns 4, 5 and 6. Be aware of this small discrepancy and calculate figures for all the categories yourself if extreme accuracy is essential.

## Converting Unit Prices

The last column in Figure 2 shows the total cost per 100 square feet of wall. Some estimating tables in this book show a total cost per 100 linear feet (such as for baseboard) or total costs per unit (such as for doors). To convert a cost per 100 square feet to a cost per square foot, move the decimal point two places to the left. Thus the cost per 100 square feet for the "Fast" rate in Figure 2 is $24.62 or about 25 cents per square foot.

## General Qualifications

It's important that you understand the conditions the tables are based upon. I call these conditions the job *qualifications*. A qualifications statement follows each estimating table to help you understand what's included and what's excluded. Please read those qualifications before using costs from this manual in your estimates. The following points apply to *all* tables in this book:

### Included Costs

- Minor preparation, both time and material. Normal preparation for new residential construction is included in the "Fast" row and for new commercial jobs in the "Medium" row. Minimal preparation is included for repaint jobs in the "Slow" row.

- Minimum setup and cleanup

- Equipment such as ladders, spray rigs and brushes are included in overhead for the "Fast" rate (residential tracts) or "Medium" (commercial) work. Add equipment costs at their rental rate for "Slow" (repaint) jobs.

### Excluded Costs

- Equipment costs such as ladders, spray rigs, etc. for "Slow" (repaint) jobs. Add these at their rental rate whether or not you own the equipment.

- Extensive surface preparation. Add the cost of time and materials needed for more than "normal" preparation work. Also add time to remove and replace hardware and accessories, protect adjacent surfaces, and do any extensive setup, cleanup, or touchup. (See the discussion of SURRPTUCU on the next page.)

- Mobilization or demobilization

- Supervision

- Material handling, delivery, or storage

- Sample preparation

- Mixing coatings

- Excessive material waste or spillage

- Equipment rental or placement costs

- Scaffolding rental and erection costs

- Subcontract costs

- Contingency allowance

- Owner allowances

- Commissions, bonuses, overtime, premium pay for shift adjustments (evening work), travel time or per diem.

- Bonds, fees, or permits

- Additional insurance to meet owner requirements

- Work at heights above 8 feet or beyond the reach of a wand or extension pole. (See the table for High Time Difficulty Factors on page 139.)

## Surface Preparation

The Preparation estimating tables that follow Part I: General Painting Costs, apply to both interior and exterior surfaces.

Surface preparation is one of the hardest parts of the job to estimate accurately. Any experienced painter can make a reasonably good estimate of the quantity of paint and time needed for application. But the amount of prep work needed will vary widely — especially for repaint jobs. Some will need very little work. Others will take more time for prep than for painting.

Preparation work for new construction jobs is relatively standard and consistent. You'll have to mask cabinets before spraying sealer on wet area walls, caulk at the baseboards, putty the nail holes in wood trim, and occasionally use a wire brush to smooth and clean a surface. The time required for this work is fairly predictable.

Labor cost for normal preparation of unpainted surfaces in new residential construction is included in the "Fast" *labor* costs and for new commercial construction in the "Medium" *labor* cost. The cost of materials for normal surface preparation on unpainted surfaces is included in the sundries allowance that's part of the "Fast" or "Medium" material cost.

But if more than normal surface prep work is needed, estimate the extra manhours and materials required and add these costs to your estimate.

### Add for Repaint Preparation

The "Slow" unit costs include no surface preparation other than a quick wipedown. Preparation on a repaint job may take longer than the painting itself. That's why you have to estimate surface prep as a separate item and add that cost to your estimate.

A misjudgment in estimating preparation work can be very expensive. That's why I recommend that you bid surface preparation by the hour, using your shop rate for "time and material" jobs, or some other specified hourly rate. That protects you against cost overruns if the preparation takes longer than anticipated. But there's a danger here. Owners may be angry about the cost because they don't understand what's involved in preparation and why it takes so long. You can avoid this with a "not to exceed" bid that contains a maximum price for the prep work. Your bid should define the scope of preparation work in detail and list exactly what's included and excluded. Be sure to consider all the labor, material, and equipment costs involved.

If you have to bid repaint work, be sure to include all the miscellaneous costs. The acronym I use to identify these miscellaneous costs is SURRPTUCU: Setup (SU), Remove and Replace (RR), Protection (P), Touchup (TU) and Cleanup (CU). Add these costs to your repaint estimate if they require anything beyond minimum attention.

1) *Setup* includes unloading the vehicle, spreading the tarp and setting up the tools — everything that has to be done before prep or painting can begin.

2) *Remove and replace* everything that will interfere with painting, including door and cabinet hardware, the contents of cabinets, light fixtures, bathroom accessories, switch covers and outlet plates, among others.

3) *Protection* for furniture and adjacent surfaces such as floors, cabinets, plumbing or electrical fixtures, windows, and doors. Protection methods include masking, applying visqueen, laying drop cloths and applying a protective coating on windows.

4) *Touchup* time varies with the speed and quality of the painting job and how fussy the owner is. The more careful your painters are, the less touchup time needed. You can estimate touchup time accurately only if you know how well your crews perform. The Touchup table in this book is based on a percentage of total job cost.

5) *Cleanup* time is usually about the same as setup time, about 20 to 30 minutes each day for repaint jobs. Cleanup time begins when work stops for the day and ends when the crew is back in the truck and ready to go home. It includes cleaning tools, dismantling the paint shop and loading the vehicle.

## Subcontractors

Painting contractors don't hire many subcontractors. But once in a while you'll need a specialist for sandblasting, waterblasting, wallcovering, scaffolding or pavement marking. Subcontract costs are not included in the estimating tables. Add the cost of any subcontract work that will be required.

Figure 3 shows some typical rates quoted by sandblasting subcontractors. Of course, prices in your area will probably be different. You could also figure sandblasting unit costs from the sandblasting estimating tables included in Part II, Preparation Costs, in this book.

| | | | |
|---|---|---|---|
| **Minimum charges:** $582.00, scaffolding not included | | Epoxy coated - add | 1.22 to 1.34/SF |
| **Additional insurance:** May be required to cover adjacent personal and real property which may not be protected. | | With portable equipment - add | .70 to 1.02/SF |
| | | **Commercial blast** - 67% white stage | |
| **Sandblasting water soluble paints** | $1.02 to 1.16/SF | Field welded, new, uncoated | |
| **Sandblasting oil paints** | 1.08 to 1.22/SF | ground runs | 1.08 to 1.28/SF |
| **Sandblasting heavy mastic** | | above ground | 1.34 to 2.11/SF |
| (depends on coating thickness) | 1.40 to 1.53/SF | Previously painted surfaces - add | .65 to 1.16/SF |
| **Sandblasting brick** - light blast | 1.02 to 1.16/SF | Epoxy coated - add | 1.16 to 1.34/SF |
| **Sandblasting masonry block walls** | | With portable equipment - add | .83 to 1.02/SF |
| Clean up & remove grime - light | .96 to 1.02/SF | **Near white blast** - 95% white stage | |
| — heavy | 1.46 to 1.60/SF | Field welded, new, uncoated | |
| **Sandblasting structural steel** | | ground runs | 1.28 to 1.47/SF |
| Pricing rules of thumb: | | above ground | 1.47 to 2.24/SF |
| Pipe up to 12" O.D. | 1.46 to 2.17/SF | Previously painted surfaces - add | .65 to 1.16/SF |
| Structural steel up to 2 SF/LF | 1.34 to 1.55/SF | Epoxy coated - add | 1.16 to 1.34/SF |
| Structural steel from 2 to 5 SF/LF | 1.60 to 1.79/SF | With portable equipment - add | .83 to 1.02/SF |
| Structural steel over 5 SF/LF | (depends on shape) | **White blast** - 100% uniform white stage | |
| Tanks and vessels up to 12'0" O.D. | 2.11 to 2.44/SF | Field welded, new, uncoated | |
| Tanks and vessels over 12'0" O.D. | 2.11 to 2.44/SF | ground runs | 1.92 to 2.24/SF |
| **Brush off blast** - light blast (loose mill scale) | | above ground | 2.11 to 2.49/SF |
| Field welded, new, uncoated | | Previously painted surfaces - add | .65 to 1.08/SF |
| ground runs | .65 to .83/SF | Epoxy coated - add | 1.16 to 1.34/SF |
| above ground | .96 to 1.79/SF | With portable equipment - add | .65 to .96/SF |
| Previously painted surfaces - add | .65 to 1.16/SF | | |

**Figure 3**
Sandblasting pricing table

Figure 4 shows typical subcontract bids for pavement marking. Again, prices in your area may be different.

If you do much repainting, you'll probably want to buy a waterblasting rig. Even if you own the blaster, include a charge in each estimate for the equipment as though you rented it from a rental yard just for that job. Figure the unit costs for waterblasting from Part II of this book, Preparation Costs.

Consider using a waterblasting subcontractor if you don't need the service often. Figure 5 shows some typical rates for waterblasting. Make up a table like this based on quotes from subcontractors in your area. For a more detailed table, see Sandblasting in the Preparation section, page 303.

When you hire a subcontractor, make sure the quoted price includes everything that contractor has to do — all labor, material (with tax, if applicable), equipment, overhead and profit. Add your overhead and profit percentage to the subcontractor's bid price when you enter that item on the estimate.

## Contingencies

Occasionally you'll add a contingency allowance on bids for repaint projects where there are unknowns that can't be forecast before work actually begins. Contingency allowances are rarely needed when estimating new construction. When necessary, the contingency amount is usually from 3 to 5 percent. It can go higher, however, if there are unusual conditions or unknowns that make it hard to produce an accurate estimate. Include a contingency allowance in your estimates only if you have reason to expect:

- An uncertain scope of work (unknown job conditions)
- An inexperienced owner or general contractor
- Incomplete drawings

**Pricing rules of thumb:**

Number of parking spaces: Figure on one space per 300 SF of pavement

| | |
|---|---|
| Single line striping with light graphics application | $10.00 per space |
| Single line striping with heavy graphics application | 17.40 per space |
| Single striping, light graphics and 3' wheel stop | 24.80 per space |
| Single striping, heavy graphics and 3' wheel stop | 32.10 per space |

**Equipment pricing:**

| | |
|---|---|
| Simple "inverted spray can" approximate cost | $225.00 |
| Professional striping machine cost range | 4,631 to 5,093 |
| Professional road/highway striper | 254,000 |

**Subcontractor pricing:**

| | |
|---|---|
| Move on: | $151.00 to 185.00 |

**Striping prices:**

| | |
|---|---|
| Single line striping | $.46 to .59 per lineal foot |
| Bike lane striping | .59 to .69 per lineal foot |
| Fire lane, red curb | .46 to .59 per lineal foot |

**Symbol pricing:**

| | |
|---|---|
| Templates - 8'0" template | $174.00 to 208.00 each |
| Arrows | 39.40 to 46.30 each |
| Handicap symbol, one color | 16.20 to 22.00 each |
| two color | 29.00 to 34.80 each |
| No parking fire lane stencil | 3.13 to 3.82 each |

**Wheel stops:**

| | |
|---|---|
| 3'0" stops | $22.00 to 27.80 each if pinned on asphalt |
| | 29.00 to 34.80 each if glued and pinned |
| 6'0" stops | 34.80 to 41.70 each if pinned on asphalt |
| | 41.70 to 47.60 each if glued and pinned |
| | (add for stops pinned to concrete) |

**Signs and posts:**

| | |
|---|---|
| Sign only 12" x 18" | $48.60 to 68.40 |
| Post mounted 12" x 18" | 128.00 to 176.00 |

**Pavement markers:**

| | |
|---|---|
| One way pavement markers | $10.40 each |
| Two way pavement markers | 13.90 each |

**Figure 4**
Pavement marking pricing table

> **Minimum charges:** $579.00, scaffolding not included
> **Additional insurance:** May be required to cover adjacent personal and real property
> **Pricing rules of thumb:**
>
> | | |
> |---|---|
> | Up to 5,000 PSI blast | 4 hour minimum $128.00/hour |
> | 5,000 to 10,000 PSI blast | 8 hour minimum $185.00/hour |
> | 10,000 PSI blast | 8 hour minimum $229.00/hour |
> | Wet sandblasting | 4 hour minimum $147.00/hour |

**Figure 5**
Waterblasting pricing table

- Delays in beginning the project
- Owner involvement in supervision
- Below-standard working conditions

Don't use contingency allowances as a substitute for complete estimates. Include contingency only to cover what can't be estimated, not what you don't have time to estimate accurately.

## Column Headings Defined

Take another look at Figure 2. The heading describes the surface to be coated: the type, texture, and often, condition. Sections within each surface heading are divided according to coating material, then by application method, and further into the "Slow," "Medium," and "Fast" application rates.

### Column 1: Labor Productivity

This column shows units of work completed per manhour. My estimates assume that painters are experienced and motivated professionals. The labor productivity categories are shown in Figure 6.

My experience is that a painting company that can handle larger projects will have highly skilled, better qualified and more productive painters. The estimating tables also assume that repainting a surface usually takes about 35 percent more time than painting newly constructed surfaces. Much of this extra time is spent protecting adjacent areas.

| Slow | Medium | Fast |
|---|---|---|
| Repaint jobs | New commercial projects | New residential production |
| Custom painting | Industrial painting | Repetitious painting |
| Tenant improvements | — | — |
| Small jobs | Medium-sized jobs | Large projects |
| Single units | Two to four units | Five or more units |
| Low production | Average production | High production |
| High difficulty | Average difficulty | Low difficulty |
| Poor conditions | Average conditions | Good conditions |
| High quality | Average quality | Minimum quality |
| Semi-skilled crew | Skilled crew | Highly skilled crew |
| No supervision | Some supervision | Good supervision |

**Figure 6**
Labor productivity categories

To establish your company's production levels, ask your field superintendent to monitor the time needed to complete each task and to keep records of crew productivity. You can use the Field Production Times and Rates form on pages 419 and 420 to track your painters' productivity. Make copies of the blank form and have your field superintendent or job foreman give one to each painter on every job. Your superintendent should check the forms frequently to insure they are accurate and kept up to date. Your best guide to productivity on future jobs is productivity on jobs already completed, and this form will help you keep track of your production time. Refer back to Figure 2 on page 7. You can use the results collected on these forms to complete the customized figures row under the "Fast" operation in Figure 2 for every operation in the National Painting Cost Estimator. Examples of how to use Figure 2 are on pages 7 through 9. The more you know about your painters' performance, the more accurate your estimates will be. But don't expect your estimates and actual production to always match exactly. Painters are human beings, not robots. You can't expect them to work at the same rate at all times.

## Reduced Productivity

The tables in this book assume no overtime work. Excessive overtime puts a strain on your craftsmen and reduces productivity. A few consecutive days of overtime can drag productivity down to well below average. It's good practice not to assign overtime work on more than two consecutive days.

Work efficiency is also lower when men, materials and equipment are confined in a small area or required to work in cluttered, poorly lit or dirty rooms. Painters need elbow room to work efficiently and get maximum productivity. They're also more productive in a clean environment where they can see what they're doing. It's easier — and safer — to work in a well-lighted area that's relatively clear of debris. If the work area is confined or dirty, reduce estimated productivity accordingly.

## Supervision

Supervision expense is not included in the cost tables. Add the cost of supervision to your estimates.

Most supervision is done by foremen. Every crew should have a project foreman designated, usually the most experienced and reliable painter on the job. When not supervising, project foremen should be painting. Thus the project foreman is a working supervisor. Part of the foreman's time will be productive (applying coatings) and part will be nonproductive (directing the work).

If you have more than three or four jobs going at one time, you need a field superintendent. The field superintendent is the foreman's supervisor. His or her primary responsibility is to be sure that each foreman has the manpower, materials and equipment needed to get the job done. The field superintendent should monitor job progress to be sure manhour productivity and materials used are in line with estimates. Field superintendents usually are not working supervisors; all their time is nonproductive. Figure the field superintendent's salary as overhead expense, because you can't charge his salary to a specific job.

Your project foremen and field superintendent can make or break a job. The better they are, the more work will be done. You want a field superintendent who assigns the right painters to the right foreman, and a foremen who puts the right painters on the right tasks. The most experienced tradesmen should work on tasks that require more skill. Other painters should be used where less skill is needed. The project foreman is also responsible for job safety and quality control.

Your estimates will be more competitive if you can assume high productivity. That's only possible when you have good supervision, from both foremen and superintendent, and motivated crews.

## Allowances for Supervision

Supervision isn't considered productive labor. A foreman isn't painting when he's scheduling, organizing a job and instructing his workers. Here are my rule-of-thumb allowances for nonproductive labor on painting jobs.

*Custom homes.* Allow 2.5 hours of nonproductive supervision for a home up to 1,500 square feet, 3 hours on a home between 1,500 and 2,000 square feet, 4 hours on a custom home between 2,000 and 2,500 square feet, and 5 hours on a larger home.

*Model homes* in a tract. One hour of nonproductive supervision for each day your crew will be on the job.

*Most tract homes.* One hour per house.

*Higher-quality tract homes.* Two hours per house.

| Slow application and light coverage (Repaint jobs) | Medium application and medium coverage (Commercial projects) | Fast application and heavy coverage (Residential tracts) |
|---|---|---|
| Repaint jobs | Commercial projects | Residential production |
| Light usage | Moderate usage | Heavy usage |
| Low absorption | Moderate absorption | High absorption |
| Light application | Medium application | Heavy application |
| Low waste | Moderate waste | High waste |
| Quality paint | Standard paint | Production paint |
| Semi-skilled painters | Skilled crew | Highly skilled crew |

**Figure 7**
Material coverage rates

*Apartments and condos.* Allow 1 hour per unit if there are 10 units or less. For 11 to 30 units, allow 0.75 hours of nonproductive time per unit. If there are more than 30 units, allow 0.5 hour per unit.

Nonproductive labor on commercial, industrial, institutional and government projects varies considerably. More complex jobs will require proportionately more nonproductive labor. Use your knowledge based on past experience to estimate supervision either as a percentage of job cost or by the square foot of floor.

## Column 2: Material Coverage

The second column in the cost tables shows the estimated material coverage in units (usually square feet or linear feet) per gallon. Figure 7 shows the conditions likely to apply for each of the three material coverage rates. Every condition listed in each of these categories won't necessarily occur on every painting operation. For example, it's possible to have high waste and use low quality paint on a repaint job. But it's more likely that waste will be low and paint quality high on jobs like that.

The "Slow" (repaint) application rate assumes light coverage, "Medium" (commercial project) application rate assumes medium coverage and "Fast" (residential tract) application rate assumes heavy coverage. Light coverage is typical on "Slow" (repaint) jobs because previously painted surfaces usually absorb 10 to 15 percent less paint than an unpainted surface. All coverage rates are based on paint that's been thinned according to the manufacturer's recommendations.

Of course, coverage varies with the paint you're using and the surface you're painting. Paint manufacturers usually list the recommended coverage rate on the container label. I've listed estimated coverage rates in the tables throughout this book.

### Calculating Film Thickness

Many project specifications for commercial, industrial and government jobs identify the coating (film) thickness you have to apply to each surface. The thickness is given in *mils*, or thousandths of an inch. One mil is 0.001 inch.

The thickness of the dry paint film depends on the percentage of solids in the paint. If you apply a gallon of paint containing 100 percent solids over 1,600 square feet, the dry film will be 1 mil thick — that is, if 100 percent of the paint adheres to the wall. But if there's 10 percent waste (because of paint that's left in the can, on brushes, or spilled), only 90 percent of the material ends up on the surface.

| Slow application | Medium application | Fast application |
|---|---|---|
| Repaint jobs | Commercial projects | Residential tracts |
| Low volume | Medium volume | High volume |
| 20% discount | 30% discount | 40% discount |

**Figure 8**
Material price discounts

Here's a formula for coverage rates that makes it easy to calculate mil thickness, including the waste factor. Coverage rate equals:

$$\frac{\% \text{ of solids} \times 1600}{\text{mil thickness}} \times (1.00 - \text{waste factor})$$

Here's an example. Assume you're applying paint with 40 percent solids (by volume), using a roller. The waste factor is 10 percent. You need a thickness of 5 mils.

Here's the calculation for the coverage rate:

$$\frac{.40 \times 1600}{5} \times (1.00 - .10) = 115.2 \text{ per gallon}$$

You may have to apply several coats to get a thickness of 5 mils. In any case, you'll have to use one gallon of paint for each 115.2 square feet of surface.

### Waste Factors

Be sure to consider waste and spillage when you figure coverage rates. Professional painters waste very little paint. They rarely kick over a five-gallon paint bucket. But there's always some waste. My material coverage formulas include a typical waste allowance for each application method, whether it's brush, roller or spray. Of course, actual waste depends on the skill of your painters no matter what application method they use.

These are the waste factors I've built into the tables:

Brush . . . . . . . . . . . . . . . . . . . . . . . . . . . . . . . .3 to 5%
Roll . . . . . . . . . . . . . . . . . . . . . . . . . . . . . . . . .5 to 10%
Airless spray . . . . . . . . . . . . . . . . . . . . . . . .20 to 25%
Conventional spray . . . . . . . . . . . . . . . . . . . .25 to 35%

### Changes in Paint Formulation

In the late 1970s, the California State Air Resources Board established a "model rule" for lowering the solvent in oil-based paints. They mandated replacing solvent-based paint with water-based formulas. The objective was to lower the amount of solvents escaping into the air. This change in the formulation of oil-based paints is being adopted nationwide.

Changes in paint formulation will affect coverage rates and the cost for non-flat paints. Review actual coverage rates and paint prices and make adjustments where necessary before using the estimates in this book.

## Column 3: Material Pricing

The third column in the cost tables shows the cost of materials. The "Slow," "Medium," and "Fast" prices in each table are based on the discounts usually offered by suppliers for volume purchases by contractor customers. The material discounts used in this book are defined in Figure 8.

The more paint a contractor buys over a given period, the greater the discount that contractor can expect. Most paint contractors get a discount of at least 20 percent off retail. Contractors buying in heavy volume usually get discounts that approach 40 percent off retail.

### Material Pricing Tables

Figures 9, 10 and 11 show the material prices I've used for each of three application rates throughout this book. In the cost estimating tables each coating is identified by a material number. To find out more about the cost of any of these coatings, refer to the material number listed in Figure 9, 10 or 11.

# Material prices at 20% discount

All pricing is based on production grade material purchased in 5 gallon quantities.

|  | Retail price guide | Contractor price at a 20% discount | Add 15% sundries & 10% escalation | Price with sales tax at 8% | Estimating prices with tax |
|---|---|---|---|---|---|
| **Interior:** | | | | | |
| Sealer, P.V.A., off white (wet area walls & ceilings) | | | | | |
| #1 - Water base | 28.25 | 22.60 | 28.25 | 30.51 | 30.50 |
| #2 - Oil base | 36.80 | 29.44 | 36.80 | 39.74 | 39.70 |
| Undercoat (doors, casings and other paint grade wood) | | | | | |
| #3 - Water base | 30.20 | 24.16 | 30.20 | 32.62 | 32.60 |
| #4 - Oil base | 39.20 | 31.36 | 39.20 | 42.34 | 42.30 |
| Flat latex (walls, ceilings & paint grade baseboard) | | | | | |
| #5 - Water base latex paint | 34.00 | 27.20 | 34.00 | 36.72 | 36.70 |
| Acoustic spray-on texture | | | | | |
| #6 - Primer | 25.00 | 20.00 | 25.00 | 27.00 | 27.00 |
| #7 - Finish | 27.65 | 22.12 | 27.65 | 29.86 | 29.90 |
| #8 - Dripowder mixed (pound) | .85 | .68 | .85 | .92 | .92 |
| Enamel (wet area walls & ceilings and openings) | | | | | |
| #9 - Water base enamel | 43.35 | 34.68 | 43.35 | 46.82 | 46.80 |
| #10- Oil base enamel | 57.15 | 45.72 | 57.15 | 61.72 | 61.70 |
| System estimate (cabinets, bookshelves, molding, interior windows) | | | | | |
| #11a - Wiping stain, oil base | 47.50 | 38.00 | 47.50 | 51.30 | 51.30 |
| #11b - Sanding sealer, lacquer | 38.40 | 30.72 | 38.40 | 41.47 | 41.50 |
| #11c - Lacquer, semi gloss | 42.45 | 33.96 | 42.45 | 45.85 | 45.90 |
| #11 - Stain, seal & 2 coat lacquer system | | | | | |
| Average cost (11a + b + (2 x c)) | 42.70 | 34.16 | 42.70 | 46.12 | 46.10 |
| #12 - Shellac, clear | 67.65 | 54.12 | 67.65 | 73.06 | 73.10 |
| #13 - Penetrating oil stain | 50.45 | 40.36 | 50.45 | 54.49 | 54.50 |
| #14 - Penetrating stain wax (molding) | 43.25 | 34.60 | 43.25 | 46.71 | 46.70 |
| #15 - Wax, per pound (floors) | 14.15 | 11.32 | 14.15 | 15.28 | 15.30 |
| #16 - Glazing (mottling over enamel) | 65.75 | 52.60 | 65.75 | 71.01 | 71.00 |
| #17 - Spray can, each (HVAC registers) | 8.45 | 6.76 | 8.45 | 9.13 | 9.10 |
| **Exterior:** | | | | | |
| Solid body/color stain (beams, light valance, fascia, overhang, siding, plant-on trim, wood shelves) | | | | | |
| #18 - Water base stain | 41.70 | 33.36 | 41.70 | 45.04 | 45.00 |
| #19 - Oil base stain | 50.05 | 40.04 | 50.05 | 54.05 | 54.10 |
| Semi-transparent stain (beams, siding, T & G ceiling) | | | | | |
| #20 - Water base stain | 44.00 | 35.20 | 44.00 | 47.52 | 47.50 |
| #21 - Oil base stain | 45.05 | 36.04 | 45.05 | 48.65 | 48.70 |
| #22 - Polyurethane (exterior doors) | 72.95 | 58.36 | 72.95 | 78.79 | 78.80 |
| #23 - Marine spar varnish, flat or gloss (exterior doors) | | | | | |
| Interior or exterior | 76.95 | 61.56 | 76.95 | 83.11 | 83.10 |

**Figure 9**
Material prices at 20% discount

## Material prices at 20% discount (cont.)

| | Retail price guide | Contractor price at a 20% discount | Add 15% sundries & 10% escalation | Price with sales tax at 8% | Estimating prices with tax |
|---|---|---|---|---|---|
| **Exterior enamel (exterior doors & trim)** | | | | | |
| #24 - Water base | 46.95 | 37.56 | 46.95 | 50.71 | 50.70 |
| #25 - Oil base | 52.25 | 41.80 | 52.25 | 56.43 | 56.40 |
| **Porch & deck enamel - interior or exterior** | | | | | |
| #26 - Water base enamel | 50.35 | 40.28 | 50.35 | 54.38 | 54.40 |
| #27 - Oil base enamel | 62.25 | 49.80 | 62.25 | 67.23 | 67.20 |
| #28 - Epoxy, 1 part, water base | 76.40 | 61.12 | 76.40 | 82.51 | 82.50 |
| #29 - Epoxy, 2 part system | 87.90 | 70.32 | 87.90 | 94.93 | 94.90 |
| **System estimate (exterior windows)** | | | | | |
| #30a - Wiping stain, oil base | 49.40 | 39.52 | 49.40 | 53.35 | 53.40 |
| #30b - Sanding sealer, varnish | 48.15 | 38.52 | 48.15 | 52.00 | 52.00 |
| #30c - Varnish, flat or gloss | 75.65 | 60.52 | 75.65 | 81.70 | 81.70 |
| #30 - Stain, seal & 1 coat varnish system | | | | | |
| Average cost (30a + b + c)) | 57.74 | 46.19 | 57.74 | 62.36 | 62.40 |
| **Masonry paint (masonry, concrete, plaster)** | | | | | |
| #31 - Water base, flat or gloss | 35.40 | 28.32 | 35.40 | 38.23 | 38.20 |
| #32 - Oil base paint | 35.55 | 28.44 | 35.55 | 38.39 | 38.40 |
| #33 - Block filler | 33.90 | 27.12 | 33.90 | 36.61 | 36.60 |
| #34 - Waterproofing, clear hydro seal | 37.55 | 30.04 | 37.55 | 40.55 | 40.60 |
| **Metal primer, rust inhibitor** | | | | | |
| #35 - Clean metal | 55.25 | 44.20 | 55.25 | 59.67 | 59.70 |
| #36 - Rusty metal | 66.95 | 53.56 | 66.95 | 72.31 | 72.30 |
| **Metal finish, synthetic enamel, gloss, interior or exterior** | | | | | |
| #37 - Off white | 55.25 | 44.20 | 55.25 | 59.67 | 59.70 |
| #38 - Colors (except orange/red) | 60.35 | 48.28 | 60.35 | 65.18 | 65.20 |
| **Anti-graffiti stain eliminator** | | | | | |
| #39 - Water base primer & sealer | 46.60 | 37.28 | 46.60 | 50.33 | 50.30 |
| #40 - Oil base primer & sealer | 46.20 | 36.96 | 46.20 | 49.90 | 49.90 |
| #41 - Polyurethane 2 part system | 145.40 | 116.32 | 145.40 | 157.03 | 157.00 |
| **Preparation:** | | | | | |
| #42 - Caulking, per fluid ounce | .32 | .26 | .33 | .36 | .36 |
| **Paint remover, per gallon** | | | | | |
| #43 - Light duty | 34.50 | 27.60 | 34.50 | 37.26 | 37.30 |
| #44 - Heavy duty | 38.80 | 31.04 | 38.80 | 41.90 | 41.90 |
| #45 - Putty, per pound | 6.40 | 5.12 | 6.40 | 6.91 | 6.90 |
| #46 - Silica sand, per pound | .40 | .32 | .40 | .43 | .43 |
| #47 - Visqueen, 1.5 mil, 12' x 200' roll | 37.55 | 30.04 | 37.55 | 40.55 | 40.60 |
| #48 - Wood filler, per gallon | 38.35 | 30.68 | 38.35 | 41.42 | 41.40 |

**Figure 9 (continued)**
Material prices at 20% discount

## Material prices at 20% discount (cont.)

|  | Retail price guide | Contractor price at a 20% discount | Add 15% sundries & 10% escalation | Price with sales tax at 8% | Estimating prices with tax |
|---|---|---|---|---|---|
| **Industrial:** | | | | | |
| #49 - Acid wash (muriatic acid) | 10.65 | 8.52 | 10.65 | 11.50 | 11.50 |
| #50 - Aluminum base paint | 72.60 | 58.08 | 72.60 | 78.41 | 78.40 |
| Epoxy coating, 2 part system | | | | | |
| #51 -  Clear | 136.05 | 108.84 | 136.05 | 146.93 | 146.90 |
| #52 -  White | 163.85 | 131.08 | 163.85 | 176.96 | 177.00 |
| Heat resistant enamel | | | | | |
| #53 -  800 to 1200 degree range | 127.90 | 102.32 | 127.90 | 138.13 | 138.10 |
| #54 -  300 to 800 degree range | 112.40 | 89.92 | 112.40 | 121.39 | 121.40 |
| #55 - Industrial bonding & penetrating oil paint | 45.05 | 36.04 | 45.05 | 48.65 | 48.70 |
| Industrial enamel, oil base, high gloss | | | | | |
| #56 -  Light colors | 56.50 | 45.20 | 56.50 | 61.02 | 61.00 |
| #57 -  Dark (OSHA) colors | 62.55 | 50.04 | 62.55 | 67.55 | 67.60 |
| #58 - Industrial waterproofing | 38.95 | 31.16 | 38.95 | 42.07 | 42.10 |
| #59 - Vinyl coating (tanks) | 98.50 | 78.80 | 98.50 | 106.38 | 106.40 |
| **Wallcovering:** | | | | | |
| Ready-mix: | | | | | |
| #60 -  Light-weight vinyl (gal) | 12.25 | 9.80 | 12.25 | 13.23 | 13.20 |
| #61 -  Heavy weight vinyl (gal) | 13.60 | 10.88 | 13.60 | 14.69 | 14.70 |
| #62 -  Cellulose, clear (gal) | 15.35 | 12.28 | 15.35 | 16.58 | 16.60 |
| #63 -  Vinyl to vinyl (gal) | 22.90 | 18.32 | 22.90 | 24.73 | 24.70 |
| #64 - Powdered cellulose, 2 - 4 ounces | 6.65 | 5.32 | 6.65 | 7.18 | 7.20 |
| #65 - Powdered vinyl, 2 - 4 ounces | 7.75 | 6.20 | 7.75 | 8.37 | 8.40 |
| #66 - Powdered wheat paste, 2-4 ounces | 5.60 | 4.48 | 5.60 | 6.05 | 6.10 |

**Note:** Typically, powdered paste is in 2 to 4 ounce packages which will adhere 6 to 12 rolls of wallcovering.

**Figure 9 (continued)**
Material prices at 20% discount

## Material prices at 30% discount

|  | Retail price guide | Contractor price at a 30% discount | Add 15% sundries & 10% escalation | Price with sales tax at 8% | Estimating prices with tax |
|---|---|---|---|---|---|
| **Interior:** | | | | | |
| *Sealer, P.V.A., off white (wet area walls & ceilings)* | | | | | |
| #1 - Water base | 28.25 | 19.78 | 24.73 | 26.71 | 26.70 |
| #2 - Oil base | 36.80 | 25.76 | 32.20 | 34.78 | 34.80 |
| *Undercoat (doors, casings and other paint grade wood)* | | | | | |
| #3 - Water base | 30.20 | 21.14 | 26.43 | 28.54 | 28.50 |
| #4 - Oil base | 39.20 | 27.44 | 34.30 | 37.04 | 37.00 |
| *Flat latex (walls, ceilings & paint grade baseboard)* | | | | | |
| #5 - Water base latex paint | 34.00 | 23.80 | 29.75 | 32.13 | 32.10 |
| *Acoustic spray-on texture* | | | | | |
| #6 - Primer | 25.00 | 17.50 | 21.88 | 23.63 | 23.60 |
| #7 - Finish | 27.65 | 19.36 | 24.20 | 26.14 | 26.10 |
| #8 - Dripowder mixed (pound) | .85 | .60 | .75 | .81 | .81 |
| *Enamel (wet area walls & ceilings and openings)* | | | | | |
| #9 - Water base enamel | 43.35 | 30.35 | 37.94 | 40.98 | 41.00 |
| #10 - Oil base enamel | 57.15 | 40.01 | 50.01 | 54.01 | 54.00 |
| *System estimate (cabinets, bookshelves, molding, interior windows)* | | | | | |
| #11a - Wiping stain, oil base | 47.50 | 33.25 | 41.56 | 44.88 | 44.90 |
| #11b - Sanding sealer, lacquer | 38.40 | 26.88 | 33.60 | 36.29 | 36.30 |
| #11c - Lacquer, semi gloss | 42.45 | 29.72 | 37.15 | 40.12 | 40.10 |
| #11 - Stain, seal & 2 coat lacquer system Average cost (11a + b + (2 x c)) | 42.70 | 29.89 | 37.36 | 40.35 | 40.40 |
| #12 - Shellac, clear | 67.65 | 47.36 | 59.20 | 63.94 | 63.90 |
| #13 - Penetrating oil stain | 50.45 | 35.32 | 44.15 | 47.68 | 47.70 |
| #14 - Penetrating stain wax (molding) | 43.25 | 30.28 | 37.85 | 40.88 | 40.90 |
| #15 - Wax, per pound (floors) | 14.15 | 9.91 | 12.39 | 13.38 | 13.40 |
| #16 - Glazing (mottling over enamel) | 65.75 | 46.03 | 57.54 | 62.14 | 62.10 |
| #17 - Spray can, each (HVAC registers) | 8.45 | 5.92 | 7.40 | 7.99 | 8.00 |
| **Exterior:** | | | | | |
| *Solid body/color stain (beams, light valance, fascia, overhang, siding, plant-on trim, wood shelves)* | | | | | |
| #18 - Water base stain | 41.70 | 29.19 | 36.49 | 39.41 | 39.40 |
| #19 - Oil base stain | 50.05 | 35.04 | 43.80 | 47.30 | 47.30 |
| *Semi-transparent stain (beams, siding, T & G ceiling)* | | | | | |
| #20 - Water base stain | 44.00 | 30.80 | 38.50 | 41.58 | 41.60 |
| #21 - Oil base stain | 45.05 | 31.54 | 39.43 | 42.58 | 42.60 |
| #22 - Polyurethane (exterior doors) | 72.95 | 51.07 | 63.84 | 68.95 | 69.00 |
| #23 - Marine spar varnish, flat or gloss (exterior doors) Interior or exterior | 76.95 | 53.87 | 67.34 | 72.73 | 72.70 |

**Figure 10**
Material prices at 30% discount

## Material prices at 30% discount (cont.)

|  |  | Retail price guide | Contractor price at a 30% discount | Add 15% sundries & 10% escalation | Price with sales tax at 8% | Estimating prices with tax |
|---|---|---|---|---|---|---|
|  | Exterior enamel (exterior doors & trim) | | | | | |
| #24 - | Water base | 46.95 | 32.87 | 41.09 | 44.38 | 44.40 |
| #25 - | Oil base | 52.25 | 36.58 | 45.73 | 49.39 | 49.40 |
|  | Porch & deck enamel - interior or exterior | | | | | |
| #26 - | Water base enamel | 50.35 | 35.25 | 44.06 | 47.58 | 47.60 |
| #27 - | Oil base enamel | 62.25 | 43.58 | 54.48 | 58.84 | 58.80 |
| #28 - | Epoxy, 1 part, water base | 76.40 | 53.48 | 66.85 | 72.20 | 72.20 |
| #29 - | Epoxy, 2 part system | 87.90 | 61.53 | 76.91 | 83.06 | 83.10 |
|  | System estimate (exterior windows) | | | | | |
| #30a - | Wiping stain, oil base | 49.40 | 34.58 | 43.23 | 46.69 | 46.70 |
| #30b - | Sanding sealer, varnish | 48.15 | 33.71 | 42.14 | 45.51 | 45.50 |
| #30c - | Varnish, flat or gloss | 75.65 | 52.96 | 66.20 | 71.50 | 71.50 |
| #30 - | Stain, seal & 1 coat varnish system Average cost (30a + b + c) | 57.74 | 40.42 | 50.53 | 54.57 | 54.60 |
|  | Masonry paint (masonry, concrete, plaster) | | | | | |
| #31 - | Water base, flat or gloss | 35.40 | 24.78 | 30.98 | 33.46 | 33.50 |
| #32 - | Oil base paint | 35.55 | 24.89 | 31.11 | 33.60 | 33.60 |
| #33 - | Block filler | 33.90 | 23.73 | 29.66 | 32.03 | 32.00 |
| #34 - | Waterproofing, clear hydro seal | 37.55 | 26.29 | 32.86 | 35.49 | 35.50 |
|  | Metal primer, rust inhibitor | | | | | |
| #35 - | Clean metal | 55.25 | 38.68 | 48.35 | 52.22 | 52.20 |
| #36 - | Rusty metal | 66.95 | 46.87 | 58.59 | 63.28 | 63.30 |
|  | Metal finish, synthetic enamel, gloss, interior or exterior | | | | | |
| #37 - | Off white | 55.25 | 38.68 | 48.35 | 52.22 | 52.20 |
| #38 - | Colors (except orange/red) | 60.35 | 42.25 | 52.81 | 57.03 | 57.00 |
|  | Anti-graffiti stain eliminator | | | | | |
| #39 - | Water base primer & sealer | 46.60 | 32.62 | 40.78 | 44.04 | 44.00 |
| #40 - | Oil base primer & sealer | 46.20 | 32.34 | 40.43 | 43.66 | 43.70 |
| #41 - | Polyurethane 2 part system | 145.40 | 101.78 | 127.23 | 137.41 | 137.40 |

### Preparation:

|  |  |  |  |  |  |  |
|---|---|---|---|---|---|---|
| #42 - | Caulking, per fluid ounce | .32 | .22 | .28 | .30 | .30 |
|  | Paint remover, per gallon | | | | | |
| #43 - | Light duty | 34.50 | 24.15 | 30.19 | 32.61 | 32.60 |
| #44 - | Heavy duty | 38.80 | 27.16 | 33.95 | 36.67 | 36.70 |
| #45 - | Putty, per pound | 6.40 | 4.48 | 5.60 | 6.05 | 6.10 |
| #46 - | Silica sand, per pound | .40 | .28 | .35 | .38 | .38 |
| #47 - | Visqueen, 1.5 mil, 12' x 200' roll | 37.55 | 26.29 | 32.86 | 35.49 | 35.50 |
| #48 - | Wood filler, per gallon | 38.35 | 26.85 | 33.56 | 36.24 | 36.20 |

**Figure 10 (continued)**
Material prices at 30% discount

## Material prices at 30% discount (cont.)

|  | Retail price guide | Contractor price at a 30% discount | Add 15% sundries & 10% escalation | Price with sales tax at 8% | Estimating prices with tax |
|---|---|---|---|---|---|
| **Industrial:** | | | | | |
| #49 - Acid wash (muriatic acid) | 10.65 | 7.46 | 9.33 | 10.08 | 10.10 |
| #50 - Aluminum base paint | 72.60 | 50.82 | 63.53 | 68.61 | 68.60 |
| Epoxy coating, 2 part system | | | | | |
| #51 - Clear | 136.05 | 95.24 | 119.05 | 128.57 | 128.60 |
| #52 - White | 163.85 | 114.70 | 143.38 | 154.85 | 154.90 |
| Heat resistant enamel | | | | | |
| #53 - 800 to 1200 degree range | 127.90 | 89.53 | 111.91 | 120.86 | 120.90 |
| #54 - 300 to 800 degree range | 112.40 | 78.68 | 98.35 | 106.22 | 106.20 |
| #55 - Industrial bonding & penetrating oil paint | 45.05 | 31.54 | 39.43 | 42.58 | 42.60 |
| Industrial enamel, oil base, high gloss | | | | | |
| #56 - Light colors | 56.50 | 39.55 | 49.44 | 53.40 | 53.40 |
| #57 - Dark (OSHA) colors | 62.55 | 43.79 | 54.74 | 59.12 | 59.10 |
| #58 - Industrial waterproofing | 38.95 | 27.27 | 34.09 | 36.82 | 36.80 |
| #59 - Vinyl coating (tanks) | 98.50 | 68.95 | 86.19 | 93.09 | 93.10 |
| **Wallcovering:** | | | | | |
| Ready-mix: | | | | | |
| #60 - Light-weight vinyl (gal) | 12.25 | 8.58 | 10.73 | 11.59 | 11.60 |
| #61 - Heavy weight vinyl (gal) | 13.60 | 9.52 | 11.90 | 12.85 | 12.90 |
| #62 - Cellulose, clear (gal) | 15.35 | 10.75 | 13.44 | 14.52 | 14.50 |
| #63 - Vinyl to vinyl (gal) | 22.90 | 16.03 | 20.04 | 21.64 | 21.60 |
| #64 - Powdered cellulose, 2 - 4 ounces | 6.65 | 4.66 | 5.83 | 6.30 | 6.30 |
| #65 - Powdered vinyl, 2 - 4 ounces | 7.75 | 5.43 | 6.79 | 7.33 | 7.30 |
| #66 - Powdered wheat paste, 2-4 ounces | 5.60 | 3.92 | 4.90 | 5.29 | 5.30 |

**Note:** Typically, powdered paste is in 2 to 4 ounce packages which will adhere 6 to 12 rolls of wallcovering.

**Figure 10 (continued)**
Material prices at 30% discount

# Material prices at 40% discount

| | Retail price guide | Contractor price at a 40% discount | Add 15% sundries & 10% escalation | Price with sales tax at 8% | Estimating prices with tax |
|---|---|---|---|---|---|
| **Interior:** | | | | | |
| Sealer, P.V.A., off white (wet area walls & ceilings) | | | | | |
| #1 -   Water base | 28.25 | 16.95 | 21.19 | 22.89 | 22.90 |
| #2 -   Oil base | 36.80 | 22.08 | 27.60 | 29.81 | 29.80 |
| Undercoat (doors, casings and other paint grade wood) | | | | | |
| #3 -   Water base | 30.20 | 18.12 | 22.65 | 24.46 | 24.50 |
| #4 -   Oil base | 39.20 | 23.52 | 29.40 | 31.75 | 31.80 |
| Flat latex (walls, ceilings & paint grade baseboard) | | | | | |
| #5 -   Water base latex paint | 34.00 | 20.40 | 25.50 | 27.54 | 27.50 |
| Acoustic spray-on texture | | | | | |
| #6 -   Primer | 25.00 | 15.00 | 18.75 | 20.25 | 20.30 |
| #7 -   Finish | 27.65 | 16.59 | 20.74 | 22.40 | 22.40 |
| #8 -   Dripowder mixed (pound) | .85 | .51 | .64 | .69 | .69 |
| Enamel (wet area walls & ceilings and openings) | | | | | |
| #9 -   Water base enamel | 43.35 | 26.01 | 32.51 | 35.11 | 35.10 |
| #10 -   Oil base enamel | 57.15 | 34.29 | 42.86 | 46.29 | 46.30 |
| System estimate (cabinets, bookshelves, molding, interior windows) | | | | | |
| #11a -   Wiping stain, oil base | 47.50 | 28.50 | 35.63 | 38.48 | 38.50 |
| #11b -   Sanding sealer, lacquer | 38.40 | 23.04 | 28.80 | 31.10 | 31.10 |
| #11c -   Lacquer, semi gloss | 42.45 | 25.47 | 31.84 | 34.39 | 34.40 |
| #11 - Stain, seal & 2 coat lacquer system | | | | | |
| Average cost (11a + b + (2 x c)) | 42.70 | 25.62 | 32.03 | 34.59 | 34.60 |
| #12 - Shellac, clear | 67.65 | 40.59 | 50.74 | 54.80 | 54.80 |
| #13 - Penetrating oil stain | 50.45 | 30.27 | 37.84 | 40.87 | 40.90 |
| #14 - Penetrating stain wax (molding) | 43.25 | 25.95 | 32.44 | 35.04 | 35.00 |
| #15 - Wax, per pound (floors) | 14.15 | 8.49 | 10.61 | 11.46 | 11.50 |
| #16 - Glazing (mottling over enamel) | 65.75 | 39.45 | 49.31 | 53.25 | 53.30 |
| #17 - Spray can, each (HVAC registers) | 8.45 | 5.07 | 6.34 | 6.85 | 6.90 |
| **Exterior:** | | | | | |
| Solid body/color stain (beams, light valance, fascia, overhang, siding, plant-on trim, wood shelves) | | | | | |
| #18 -   Water base stain | 41.70 | 25.02 | 31.28 | 33.78 | 33.80 |
| #19 -   Oil base stain | 50.05 | 30.03 | 37.54 | 40.54 | 40.50 |
| Semi-transparent stain (beams, siding, T & G ceiling) | | | | | |
| #20 -   Water base stain | 44.00 | 26.40 | 33.00 | 35.64 | 35.60 |
| #21 -   Oil base stain | 45.05 | 27.03 | 33.79 | 36.49 | 36.50 |
| #22 - Polyurethane (exterior doors) | 72.95 | 43.77 | 54.71 | 59.09 | 59.10 |
| #23 - Marine spar varnish, flat or gloss (exterior doors) | | | | | |
| Interior or exterior | 76.95 | 46.17 | 57.71 | 62.33 | 62.30 |

**Figure 11**
Material prices at 40% discount

## Material prices at 40% discount (cont.)

|  | Retail price guide | Contractor price at a 40% discount | Add 15% sundries & 10% escalation | Price with sales tax at 8% | Estimating prices with tax |
|---|---|---|---|---|---|
| **Exterior enamel (exterior doors & trim)** | | | | | |
| #24 - Water base | 46.95 | 28.17 | 35.21 | 38.03 | 38.00 |
| #25 - Oil base | 52.25 | 31.35 | 39.19 | 42.33 | 42.30 |
| **Porch & deck enamel - interior or exterior** | | | | | |
| #26 - Water base enamel | 50.35 | 30.21 | 37.76 | 40.78 | 40.80 |
| #27 - Oil base enamel | 62.25 | 37.35 | 46.69 | 50.43 | 50.40 |
| #28 - Epoxy, 1 part, water base | 76.40 | 45.84 | 57.30 | 61.88 | 61.90 |
| #29 - Epoxy, 2 part system | 87.90 | 52.74 | 65.93 | 71.20 | 71.20 |
| **System estimate (exterior windows)** | | | | | |
| #30a - Wiping stain, oil base | 49.40 | 29.64 | 37.05 | 40.01 | 40.00 |
| #30b - Sanding sealer, varnish | 48.15 | 28.89 | 36.11 | 39.00 | 39.00 |
| #30c - Varnish, flat or gloss | 75.65 | 45.39 | 56.74 | 61.28 | 61.30 |
| #30 - Stain, seal & 1 coat varnish system Average cost (30a + b + c)) | 57.74 | 34.64 | 43.30 | 46.76 | 46.80 |
| **Masonry paint (masonry, concrete, plaster)** | | | | | |
| #31 - Water base, flat or gloss | 35.40 | 21.24 | 26.55 | 28.67 | 28.70 |
| #32 - Oil base paint | 35.55 | 21.33 | 26.66 | 28.79 | 28.80 |
| #33 - Block filler | 33.90 | 20.34 | 25.43 | 27.46 | 27.50 |
| #34 - Waterproofing, clear hydro seal | 37.55 | 22.53 | 28.16 | 30.41 | 30.40 |
| **Metal primer, rust inhibitor** | | | | | |
| #35 - Clean metal | 55.25 | 33.15 | 41.44 | 44.76 | 44.80 |
| #36 - Rusty metal | 66.95 | 40.17 | 50.21 | 54.23 | 54.20 |
| **Metal finish, synthetic enamel, gloss, interior or exterior** | | | | | |
| #37 - Off white | 55.25 | 33.15 | 41.44 | 44.76 | 44.80 |
| #38 - Colors (except orange/red) | 60.35 | 36.21 | 45.26 | 48.88 | 48.90 |
| **Anti-graffiti stain eliminator** | | | | | |
| #39 - Water base primer & sealer | 46.60 | 27.96 | 34.95 | 37.75 | 37.80 |
| #40 - Oil base primer & sealer | 46.20 | 27.72 | 34.65 | 37.42 | 37.40 |
| #41 - Polyurethane 2 part system | 145.40 | 87.24 | 109.05 | 117.77 | 117.80 |
| **Preparation:** | | | | | |
| #42 - Caulking, per fluid ounce | .32 | .19 | .24 | .26 | .26 |
| **Paint remover, per gallon** | | | | | |
| #43 - Light duty | 34.50 | 20.70 | 25.88 | 27.95 | 28.00 |
| #44 - Heavy duty | 38.80 | 23.28 | 29.10 | 31.43 | 31.40 |
| #45 - Putty, per pound | 6.40 | 3.84 | 4.80 | 5.18 | 5.20 |
| #46 - Silica sand, per pound | .40 | .24 | .30 | .32 | .32 |
| #47 - Visqueen, 1.5 mil, 12' x 200' roll | 37.55 | 22.53 | 28.16 | 30.41 | 30.40 |
| #48 - Wood filler, per gallon | 38.35 | 23.01 | 28.76 | 31.06 | 31.10 |

**Figure 11 (continued)**
Material prices at 40% discount

## Material prices at 40% discount (cont.)

|  | Retail price guide | Contractor price at a 40% discount | Add 15% sundries & 10% escalation | Price with sales tax at 8% | Estimating prices with tax |
|---|---|---|---|---|---|
| **Industrial:** | | | | | |
| #49 - Acid wash (muriatic acid) | 10.65 | 6.39 | 7.99 | 8.63 | 8.60 |
| #50 - Aluminum base paint | 72.60 | 43.56 | 54.45 | 58.81 | 58.80 |
| Epoxy coating, 2 part system | | | | | |
| #51 - Clear | 136.05 | 81.63 | 102.04 | 110.20 | 110.20 |
| #52 - White | 163.85 | 98.31 | 122.89 | 132.72 | 132.70 |
| Heat resistant enamel | | | | | |
| #53 - 800 to 1200 degree range | 127.90 | 76.74 | 95.93 | 103.60 | 103.60 |
| #54 - 300 to 800 degree range | 112.40 | 67.44 | 84.30 | 91.04 | 91.00 |
| #55 - Industrial bonding & penetrating oil paint | 45.05 | 27.03 | 33.79 | 36.49 | 36.50 |
| Industrial enamel, oil base, high gloss | | | | | |
| #56 - Light colors | 56.50 | 33.90 | 42.38 | 45.77 | 45.80 |
| #57 - Dark (OSHA) colors | 62.55 | 37.53 | 46.91 | 50.66 | 50.70 |
| #58 - Industrial waterproofing | 38.95 | 23.37 | 29.21 | 31.55 | 31.60 |
| #59 - Vinyl coating (tanks) | 98.50 | 59.10 | 73.88 | 79.79 | 79.80 |
| **Wallcovering:** | | | | | |
| Ready-mix: | | | | | |
| #60 - Light-weight vinyl (gal) | 12.25 | 7.35 | 9.19 | 9.93 | 9.90 |
| #61 - Heavy weight vinyl (gal) | 13.60 | 8.16 | 10.20 | 11.02 | 11.00 |
| #62 - Cellulose, clear (gal) | 15.35 | 9.21 | 11.51 | 12.43 | 12.40 |
| #63 - Vinyl to vinyl (gal) | 22.90 | 13.74 | 17.18 | 18.55 | 18.60 |
| #64 - Powdered cellulose, 2 - 4 ounces | 6.65 | 3.99 | 4.99 | 5.39 | 5.40 |
| #65 - Powdered vinyl, 2 - 4 ounces | 7.75 | 4.65 | 5.81 | 6.27 | 6.30 |
| #66 - Powdered wheat paste, 2-4 ounces | 5.60 | 3.36 | 4.20 | 4.54 | 4.50 |

**Note:** Typically, powdered paste is in 2 to 4 ounce packages which will adhere 6 to 12 rolls of wallcovering.

**Figure 11 (continued)**
Material prices at 40% discount

Figure 9 shows prices at a 20 percent discount off retail. It applies to "Slow" work and assumes light coverage on a previously painted surface. These costs would be typical for a lower-volume company handling mostly repaint or custom work.

Figure 10 reflects a 30 percent discount. It applies to "Medium" work and assumes medium coverage, as in commercial work.

Figure 11 is the 40 percent discount table. It applies to "Fast" work and assumes heavier coverage typically required on unpainted surfaces in new construction. This discount is usually available only to large, high-volume painting companies that purchase materials in large quantities.

Here's an explanation of the columns in Tables 9, 10 and 11:

**Retail price guide:** This is an average based on a survey of eleven paint manufacturers or distributors, for standard grade, construction-quality paint, purchased in five gallon quantities.

Material pricing and discount percentages will vary from supplier to supplier and from area to area. Always keep your supplier's current price list handy. It should show your current cost for all the coatings and supplies you use. Also post a list of all suppliers, their phone numbers, and the salesperson's name beside your phone.

Prices change frequently. Paint quality, your supplier's discount programs, their marketing strategy and competition from other paint manufacturers will influence the price you pay. Never guess about paint prices — especially about less commonly used coatings. Don't assume that a product you haven't used before costs about the same as similar products. It might not. A heavy-duty urethane finish, for example, will cost about twice as much as a heavy-duty vinyl coating. If you don't know that, your profit for the job can disappear very quickly.

**Prices at discount:** The retail price, less the appropriate discount.

**Allowance for sundries:** It's not practical to figure the cost of every sheet of sandpaper and every rag you'll use on a job. And there's no way to accurately predict how many jobs you'll get out of each brush or roller pole, roller handle, ladder, or drop cloth. But don't let that keep you from including an allowance for these important costs in your estimates. If you leave them out, it's the same as estimating the cost of those items as *zero*. That's a 100 percent miss. Too many of those, and you're out of the painting business. It's better to estimate any amount than to omit some costs entirely.

Figure 12 is a sundries inventory checklist. Use it to keep track of the actual cost of expendable tools and equipment.

I've added 15 percent to the paint cost to cover expendable tools and supplies. This is enough for sundries on most jobs. There is one exception, however. On repaint jobs where there's extensive prep work, the cost of sundries may be more than 15 percent of the paint cost. When preparation work is extensive, figure the actual cost of supplies. Then add to the estimate that portion of the sundries cost that exceeds 15 percent of the paint cost. You might have to double the normal sundries allowance. When it comes to prep work, make sure your estimate covers all your supplies.

**Price with sales tax at 8 percent:** This column increases the material cost, including sundries, by 8 percent to cover sales tax. If sales tax in your area is more or less than 8 percent, you can adjust the material cost, or use the price that's closest to your actual cost.

In most cases contractors have to pay sales tax. If you don't pay the tax yourself, you may have to collect it from the building owner or general contractor and remit it to the state taxing authority. In either case, include sales tax in your estimate.

**Estimating prices with tax:** The figures in the last column of Figures 9 through 11 are rounded to the nearest dime unless the total is under a dollar. Those prices are rounded to the nearest penny.

This system for pricing materials isn't exact. But it's quick, easy and flexible. Compare your current material costs with costs in Figures 9, 10 and 11. If your costs are more than a few percent higher or lower than my costs, make a note on the blank line below "Fast" in the estimating tables.

# Sundry Inventory Checklist

**Suppliers:** D-Dumphy Paints
F-Fisher Paints
S-Superior Paints
P-Pioneer Paints

| Supplier | Product number | Product | Inventory quantity | Unit | Cost | 7/21 | 7/27 | 8/2 | 8/10 |
|---|---|---|---|---|---|---|---|---|---|
| D | # — | Bender paint pads | 3 | Each | $ 4.75 | | | | |
| D | #792 | Brush - 3" nylon Peacock | 2 | Each | $ 25.20 | | 1 | | |
| D | #783 | Brush - 4" nylon Scooter | 2 | Each | $ 37.30 | | | 1 | |
| D | #115 | Brush - 5" nylon Pacer | 2 | Each | $ 63.40 | | | 1 | |
| D | #784 | Brush - 3" bristle | 2 | Each | $ 23.40 | | | 1 | |
| D | #2170 | Caulking bags | 2 | Each | $ 5.04 | | | | |
| D | Latex | Caulking-DAP Acrylic latex | 12 | Each | $ 2.73 | | 12 | | |
| D | #2172 | Caulking gun (Newborn) | 2 | Each | $ 9.58 | | 1 | | |
| P | # — | Hydraulic fluid | 2 | Qt | $ 10.80 | | | | |
| P | # — | Lemon oil | 2 | Pint | $ 5.41 | | 1 | | |
| F | # — | Masking paper 18" wide | 3 | Roll | $ 27.60 | | | | |
| F | Anchor | Masking tape 1 1/2" | 24 | Roll | $ 4.06 | | 12 | | 12 |
| P | #2176 | Lacquer - 5 gallons | 2 | 5's | $ 123.00 | | | 1 | |
| P | #2173 | Sanding sealer - 5 gallons | 2 | 5's | $ 117.00 | | 1 | | |
| P | #9850 | Resin sealer - 5 gallons | 2 | 5's | $ 105.00 | | | | |
| P | #131 | PVA sealer (clear) - 5 gallons | 2 | 5's | $ 110.00 | | 1 | | |
| F | #8500 | Particle masks 100/box | 1 | Box | $ 18.00 | | | 1 | |
| P | # — | Putty (Crawfords) | 3 | Qt | $ 12.29 | | 2 | | |
| F | #R-10 | Respirators | 1 | Each | $ 50.40 | | | | 1 |
| F | #R-49 | Respirator cartridges 20/box | 2 | Box | $ 58.70 | | | | |
| F | #R-51 | Respirator filters 20/box | 2 | Box | $ 41.90 | | | 1 | |
| P | # — | Rags - 10 pound sack | 2 | Sack | $ 30.10 | | | | |
| F | #AR 691 | Roller covers 9" x 3/4" | 6 | Each | $ 5.58 | | 2 | | |
| F | #AR 692 | Roller covers 9" x 3/8" | 6 | Each | $ 4.73 | 3 | | | 2 |
| F | #AR 671 | Roller covers 7" x 3/4" | 3 | Each | $ 4.61 | | | 1 | |
| F | #AR 672 | Roller covers 7" x 3/8" | 3 | Each | $ 5.04 | | 1 | | |

**Figure 12**
Sundry inventory checklist

National Painting Cost Estimator

| Supplier | Product number | Product | Inventory quantity | Unit | Cost | 7/21 | 7/27 | 8/2 | 8/10 |
|---|---|---|---|---|---|---|---|---|---|
| F | #AR 611 | Roller covers mini | 3 | Each | $ 3.89 | | | 1 | |
| F | #95 | Roller frames 9" | 6 | Each | $ 7.15 | 1 | 2 | | |
| F | #75 | Roller frames 7" | 5 | Each | $ 6.91 | 3 | | 3 | |
| F | #TSR | Roller frames mini | 2 | Each | $ 4.00 | | | | |
| D | #40 | Roller poles 4' wood tip | 3 | Each | $ 3.52 | | 1 | | |
| D | #10 | Roller poles 6' wood tip | 10 | Each | $ 5.46 | | | 2 | |
| P | #1 | Roller pole tips metal | 2 | Each | $ 4.37 | | | 2 | |
| P | #— | Sandpaper (120C production) | 2 | Slve | $ 65.10 | | | | 1 |
| P | #— | Sandpaper (220A trimite) | 2 | Slve | $ 50.60 | | | | |
| P | #— | Sandpaper (220A garnet) | 1 | Slve | $ 46.10 | | 1 | | |
| D | #— | Spackle (Synkloid) | 3 | Qt | $ 7.10 | 1 | | 1 | |
| D | #42/61 | Spray bombs (black^B/white^W) | 12 | Each | $ 4.13 | ᴮ12 | | | ᵂ12 |
| F | #— | Spray gun tips #3 or #4 | 10 | Each | $ 10.30 | | | 3 | |
| F | #2762 | Spray gun couplers | 10 | Each | $ 2.79 | | | 5 | |
| F | #S-71 | Spray socks   48/box | 1 | Box | $ 22.30 | | | | |
| D | #5271 | Stip fill | 1 | Gal | $ 12.00 | | | 1 | |
| D | #5927 | Strainer bags | 2 | Each | $ 1.94 | 1 | | | |
| D | #JT-21 | Staples - 5/16" | 2 | Box | $ 3.15 | | | | |
| P | 50 Gal | Thinner, lacquer | 1 | Drum | $ 561.00 | | | | |
| P | 50 Gal | Thinner, paint | 1 | Drum | $ 279.00 | | | | 1 |
| P | #— | Thinner, shellac (alcohol) | 1 | Gal | $ 13.10 | | | | |
| D | #— | Visqueen 1.5 mil 12' x 200' | 3 | Roll | $ 33.70 | | | | |
| D | #5775 | Work pots (2 gal. plastic) | 3 | Each | $ 3.76 | | 1 | | 2 |
| | # | | | | $ | | | | |
| | # | | | | $ | | | | |
| | # | | | | $ | | | | |
| | # | | | | $ | | | | |
| | | Order date: | | | | 7/21 | 7/27 | 8/2 | 8/10 |
| | | Ordered by:       (initials) | | | | jj | jj | jj | jj |
| | | Purchase order no. | | | | 0352 | 0356 | 0361 | 0371 |

**Figure 12 (continued)**
Sundry inventory checklist

|  | Residential Wallcovering ||| Commercial Wallcovering ||| Flexible Wood Wallcovering |||
|---|---|---|---|---|---|---|---|---|---|
| Production Rate | Computer Program Crew Code | Labor Cost per Hour | Labor Burden per Hour | Labor Cost + Burden | Computer Program Crew Code | Labor Cost per Hour | Labor Burden per Hour | Labor Cost + Burden | Computer Program Crew Code | Labor Cost per Hour | Labor Burden per Hour | Labor Cost + Burden |
| Slow | 1W | $19.25 | $5.68 | $24.93 | 4W | $18.25 | $5.38 | $23.63 | 7W | $18.75 | $5.53 | $24.28 |
| Medium | 2W | 24.50 | 8.67 | 33.17 | 5W | 23.00 | 8.14 | 31.14 | 8W | 23.75 | 8.41 | 32.16 |
| Fast | 3W | 30.25 | 12.34 | 42.59 | 6W | 28.25 | 11.53 | 39.78 | 9W | 29.25 | 11.93 | 41.18 |

**Figure 13**
Hourly wage rates for wallcovering application

## *Price Escalation*

Escalation is the change in prices between the time you bid a job and the time you pay for labor and materials. Painting contractors seldom include escalation clauses in their bids because they don't expect lengthy delays. That's why escalation isn't included as a separate item in the estimating forms, Figures 18 and 19.

Any minor price escalation will be covered by the 15 percent added to material prices for sundries. But don't rely on that small cushion to absorb major inflationary cost increases. Plan ahead if prices are rising. In that case, add 10% of your material costs as an escalation factor and include this figure as a separate line item in the estimate.

Many formal construction contracts include an escalator clause that allows the contractor to recover for cost increases during the time of construction — especially if there was an unreasonable delay through no fault of the subcontractor. This clause may give you the right to collect for increases in both labor and material costs.

If work is delayed after you've been awarded the contract, you may be able to recover for cost increases under the escalator clause. This is more likely on public projects than on private jobs. Also, if there's a significant delay due to weather, you may have a good argument for adjusting the contract amount.

You can protect yourself against escalation if you include an expiration date on your bids. If the contract award is delayed beyond your expiration date, you can review your costs and make necessary adjustments. But be careful here. Increase the bid too much and you'll probably lose the contract. So raise your bid only if necessary, and then only by the amount of the actual cost increases. Don't try to make a killing on the job just because the bid prices have expired.

## Column 4: Labor Cost

Column 4 in Figure 2 on page 7 shows the labor cost per unit. This figure is based on the productivity rate in column 1 and the wage rate in Figure 1. The wage rate for "Slow" (repaint) work is assumed to be $20.25 per hour. The wage rate for "Medium" (commercial) work is $25.75 per hour. The wage rate for "Fast" (residential tract) work is $31.50 per hour. Wage rates for wallcovering are different (Figure 13).

### *Wage Rates Vary*

Wages vary from city to city. Recently I saw a survey of hourly union rates for painters in U.S. cities. The lowest rate shown was $17.91 an hour for painters in Raleigh, North Carolina. The highest rate was $46.15 for painters in Nome, Alaska. You might ask, "Why don't all the painters in Raleigh move to Nome?"

I don't know the answer, except to suggest that painters aren't starving in Raleigh. Nor are they getting rich in Nome. Working conditions and the cost of living are very different in those two cities. However, on private jobs using non-union tradesmen, wage rates usually don't vary as much from city to city. The wage you pay depends on the demand for painting and how many painters are available for work.

Wages also change over time. For example, wage rates increased between 1996 and 2006. The national average union wage (including fringes) for painters in large cities went from $27.60 in 1996 to $35.00 per hour in 2006. In 2011, the average union wage for commercial work increased to as high as $49.00 per hour. Always base your estimates on the actual wages you'll pay your **most experienced** painters.

### Wages for Higher Skilled Specialists

Wages also vary with a workers' skill, dependability and with job difficulty. Generally higher paid painters are more productive than lower paid painters. Here's a chart to determine how much more per hour to estimate for supervision and for painting and surface preparation specialists. These figures are in addition to the basic journeyman rate.

Foremen . . . . . . . . . . . . . . . . . . . . . . . . . $1.00 to 4.00

Field superintendents . . . . . . . . . . . . . . $4.50 to 6.50

Swing stage brush painters,
spray painters, or paperhangers . . . . . . . . . . . . . $.50

Iron, steel and bridge painters
(ground work) . . . . . . . . . . . . . . . . . . . . . . . . . $1.00

Sandblasters, iron, steel, or
bridge painters (swing stage) . . . . . . . . . . . . . $2.00

Steeplejacks . . . . . . . . . . . . . . . . . . . . . . . . . $2.50

Most government and defense painting contracts require compliance with the Davis Bacon Act, which specifies that contractors pay at least the prevailing wage for each trade in the area where the job is located.

### Calculate Your Labor Rate

Use the wage rate in Figure 1 ($20.25, $25.75 or $31.50 for "Slow," "Medium," or "Fast") that's appropriate for your company. Or, use a rate somewhere in between the rates listed. If you use your own wage rate, divide the hourly wage by the labor productivity (such as square feet per manhour in column 1). That's your labor cost per unit. Multiply by 100 if the units used are 100 linear feet or 100 square feet. ($10 ÷ 400 x 100 = $2.50.)

## Column 5: Labor Burden

For each dollar of wages your company pays, at least another 28 cents has to be paid in payroll tax and for insurance. That's part of your labor burden. The rest is fringe benefits such as vacation pay, health benefits and pension plans.

Federal taxes are the same for all employers. State taxes vary from state to state. Fringe benefits vary the most. Generally, larger companies with more skilled painters offer considerably more fringe benefits than smaller companies.

In the estimating tables, the labor burden percentage varies with the application rate. For "Slow" (repaint) work, it's assumed to be 29.5 percent of $20.25 or $5.97 per hour. For "Medium" (commercial) work, the estimating tables use 35.4 percent of $25.75 or $9.12 per hour. For "Fast" (residential tract) work, the labor burden is 40.8 percent of $31.50 or $12.85 per hour.

Figure 14 shows how the labor burden percentages were compiled for each application rate.

**FICA — Social Security tax:** This is the portion paid by employers and is set by federal law. A similar amount is withheld from each employee's wage and deposited with a Federal Reserve bank by the employer.

**FUTA — Federal Unemployment Insurance tax:** Paid entirely by the employer and set by federal law. No portion is deducted from employee wages.

**SUI — State Unemployment Insurance:** Varies from state to state.

**WCI — Workers' Compensation Insurance:** Provides benefits for employees in case of injury on the job. Workers' comp is required by state law. Rates vary by state, job description and the loss experience of the employer.

**Liab. Ins. — Liability Insurance:** Covers injury or damage done to the public by employees. Comprehensive contractor's liability insurance includes current operations, completed operations, bodily injury, property damage, protective and contractual coverages with a $1,000,000 policy limit.

|  | Fixed burden |  |  |  |  | Fringe benefits |  |  |  |  |  |
|---|---|---|---|---|---|---|---|---|---|---|---|
|  | FICA | FUTA | SUI | WCI | Liab. Ins. | Vac | Med | Life | Pension | Training | Total |
| Slow | 7.65% | 0.8% | 3.0% | 10.5% | 6.55% | 0 | 1.0% | 0 | 0 | 0 | 29.50% |
| Medium | 7.65% | 0.8% | 4.5% | 12.5% | 6.95% | .5% | 2.0% | .25% | .25% | 0 | 35.40% |
| Fast | 7.65% | 0.8% | 6.0% | 13.5% | 7.35% | 1.5% | 3.0% | .25% | 0.5% | .25% | 40.80% |

**Figure 14**
Labor burden percentages

**Fringe benefits:** *Vac* is vacation pay. *Med* is medical insurance. *Life* is life insurance contribution. *Pension* is a pension plan contribution. *Training* is an apprentice training fund.

Vacation, life, pension and training payments depend on the agreement between employers and employees. These are voluntary contributions if not required by a collective bargaining agreement. Smaller companies are less likely to provide these benefits. The cost of fringe benefits in a painting company can range from zero to more than 10 percent of wages.

## Column 6: Material Cost per Unit

This column is the result of dividing column 3 (material cost) by column 2 (material coverage) for each application rate. For example, in Figure 2 in the "Medium" row, a material cost of $32.10 is divided by material coverage of 275, then multiplied by 100 to arrive at $11.67 per 100 square feet. That's the figure listed for "Medium" in column 6.

## Column 7: Overhead

The overhead rate for "Slow" (repaint) jobs is assumed to be 19 percent. For "Medium" (commercial projects), overhead is 25 percent. For "Fast" (residential tracts), overhead is 31 percent. The overhead cost per unit in each row is calculated by adding the labor cost per unit, labor burden per unit, and material cost per unit and then multiplying by the appropriate overhead percentage.

There are two types of overhead, direct overhead and indirect overhead. Only indirect overhead is included in the "Overhead" column of the estimating cost tables. Enter your direct overhead costs on a separate line on your take-off sheet.

*Direct overhead* is job site overhead, expenses you charge to a specific job. Examples include performance bonds, special insurance premiums, or rental of a job site storage trailer. These expenses are not included in the estimating tables and have to be added to your estimates. On many jobs, there may be little or no direct overhead.

*Indirect overhead* is office overhead, expenses that aren't related to any particular job and that tend to continue whether the volume of work increases or decreases. Examples are non-trade salaries, office rent, vehicles, sales and financial expenses, insurance, taxes and licenses.

The percentage of income spent on overhead is assumed to be lower for high volume companies and higher for low volume companies. A large company working many projects at the same time can spread overhead costs over many projects — charging a smaller percentage of overhead to each job. The more jobs, the lower the overhead per job — assuming overhead doesn't increase faster than business volume.

On the other hand, a small business may have to absorb all overhead on a single job. Even painting contractors who work out of their homes have overhead expenses.

Here's one overhead expense every paint contractor has and that you might overlook: the cost of estimating jobs. That's part of the salary cost of the employee who does the estimating.

## *Figure Overhead Carefully*

Estimating indirect (office) overhead isn't as easy as estimating labor and material. There aren't as many clear-cut answers. That's why indirect overhead is often underestimated. Don't make that mistake in your estimates. Underestimating overhead is the same as giving up part of your profit. After all, indirect overhead expenses are real costs, just like paint, labor and taxes.

In large painting companies, management accumulates indirect overhead costs and translates them into a percentage the estimator should add to the costs of each job. In smaller companies, the estimator should keep a record of indirect overhead expenses. With a good record of overhead expense, you can calculate your overhead percentage for future periods very accurately. Then it's easy to add a percentage for indirect overhead costs into your estimate.

## *Computing Your Overhead Percentage*

Here's how to decide which overhead rate to use in the cost estimating tables:

1) List all your overhead expenses for at least the last six months; a year would be better. You need overhead cost information that goes back far enough to eliminate the effect of seasonal changes in business volume

If your company is new, estimate your annual overhead by projecting overhead costs for the first full year. For example, if you've been in business for five months and overhead has been $5,500 so far, you can expect annual overhead to be about $13,200 ($5,500 divided by 5 and multiplied by 12).

2) Here's how to calculate your indirect overhead percentage:

$$\frac{\text{Annual indirect overhead}}{\text{Annual job expenses}} = \text{Overhead \%}$$

Calculate your indirect overhead by adding together your real (or anticipated) annual expenses for the following:

*Salaries.* Include what you pay for all employees except trade workers, plus payroll-related expenses for all employees.

*Office and shop expense.* Rent or mortgage, utilities, furniture and equipment, maintenance, office supplies and postage, storage sheds, warehouses, fences or yard maintenance.

*Vehicles.* Lease or purchase payments, maintenance, repairs and fuel.

*Sales promotion.* Advertising, entertainment and sales-related travel.

*Taxes.* Property tax and income tax, and sales tax (if not included in your material prices).

*Licenses.* Contractor's and business licenses.

*Insurance.* General liability, property and vehicle policies.

*Interest expense.* Loan interest and bank charges. Also consider loss of interest on payments retained by the general contractor until the job is finished.

*Miscellaneous expenses.* Depreciation and amortization on building and vehicles, bad debts, legal and accounting fees, and educational expenses.

Direct overhead is easier to figure. It's all job expenses except tradesman labor, payroll taxes and insurance, materials, equipment, subcontracts, and contingency expenses. Permits, bonds, fees and special insurance policies for property owners are also examples of direct overhead. Add the direct overhead expense on the appropriate lines in your estimate. Direct overhead is not included in the estimating tables in this manual.

## *Field Equipment May Be Part of Overhead*

As you may have noticed, there's no equipment cost column in the estimating tables. Instead, field equipment expense is included in the overhead percentage for "Fast" and "Medium" work but not "Slow" work.

## Equipment Rental Rates

Use the following rates only as a guide. They may not be accurate for your area.
Verify equipment rental rates at your local yard.

| | Rental Day | Rental Week | Rental Month | | Rental Day | Rental Week | Rental Month |
|---|---|---|---|---|---|---|---|
| **Acoustical sprayer** | 57.90 | 172.00 | 432.00 | **Dehumidifier** - 5000 Btu, 89 lb, 8.7 amp | 70.70 | 211.00 | 527.00 |
| **Air compressors** | | | | **Ladders** | | | |
| Electric or gasoline, wheel mounted | | | | Aluminum extension | | | |
| 5 CFM, 1.5 HP, electric | 34.80 | 106.00 | 268.00 | 16' to 36' | 38.20 | 114.00 | 287.00 |
| 8 CFM, 1.5 HP, electric | 41.70 | 123.00 | 307.00 | 40' to 60' | 57.90 | 172.00 | 432.00 |
| 10 CFM, 5.5 HP, gasoline | 47.60 | 142.00 | 354.00 | Step - fiberglass or wood | | | |
| 15 CFM, shop type, electric | 53.20 | 161.00 | 402.00 | 6' | 10.20 | 30.70 | 76.40 |
| 50 CFM, shop type, electric | 70.70 | 211.00 | 527.00 | 8' | 12.80 | 38.20 | 96.20 |
| 100 CFM, gasoline | 96.20 | 287.00 | 718.00 | 10' | 15.30 | 46.00 | 114.00 |
| 125 CFM, gasoline | 108.00 | 326.00 | 813.00 | 12' | 17.90 | 53.60 | 134.00 |
| 150 CFM, gasoline | 122.00 | 364.00 | 908.00 | 14' | 20.40 | 61.40 | 153.00 |
| 175 CFM, gasoline | 133.00 | 402.00 | 1,010.00 | 16' | 25.50 | 76.40 | 191.00 |
| 190 CFM, gasoline | 147.00 | 440.00 | 1,100.00 | 20' | 33.20 | 99.50 | 249.00 |
| Diesel, wheel mounted | | | | **Ladder jacks** - No guardrail. | 10.20 | 25.50 | 63.70 |
| to 159 CFM | 108.00 | 326.00 | 975.00 | **Masking paper dispenser** | 25.50 | 63.70 | 160.00 |
| 160 to 249 CFM | 133.00 | 401.00 | 1,200.00 | **Painter's pic** (walkboards); No guardrail. | | | |
| 250 to 449 CFM | 198.00 | 593.00 | 1,780.00 | (Also known as airplane planks, toothpicks and banana boards) | | | |
| 450 to 749 CFM | 294.00 | 881.00 | 2,650.00 | 16' long | 10.20 | 30.70 | 76.40 |
| 750 to 1199 CFM | 402.00 | 1,200.00 | 3,610.00 | 20' long | 20.40 | 61.40 | 153.00 |
| 1200 CFM & over | 587.00 | 1,760.00 | 6,560.00 | 24' long | 25.50 | 76.40 | 191.00 |
| **Air hose** - with coupling, 50' lengths | | | | 28' long | 30.70 | 91.60 | 229.00 |
| 1/4" I.D. | 7.64 | 23.20 | 57.90 | 32' long | 35.90 | 108.00 | 268.00 |
| 3/8" I.D. | 9.03 | 26.70 | 67.10 | **Planks** - plain end microlam scaffold plank | | | |
| 1/2" I.D. | 10.20 | 30.10 | 76.40 | 9" wide | 12.80 | 38.20 | 96.20 |
| 5/8" I.D. | 11.60 | 34.80 | 86.80 | 10" wide | 15.30 | 46.00 | 114.00 |
| 3/4" I.D. | 12.80 | 38.20 | 96.20 | 12" wide | 17.90 | 53.60 | 134.00 |
| 1" I.D. | 14.00 | 41.70 | 105.00 | **Pressure washers** (See Water pressure washers) | | | |
| 1-1/2" I.D. | 20.40 | 61.40 | 153.00 | **Sandblast compressor and hopper** | | | |
| **Boomlifts** | | | | To 250 PSI | 76.40 | 229.00 | 575.00 |
| 3' x 4' to 3' x 8' basket | | | | Over 250 to 300 PSI | 109.00 | 326.00 | 813.00 |
| 20' two wheel drive | 179.00 | 536.00 | 1,610.00 | Over 600 to 1000 PSI | 140.00 | 421.00 | 1,050.00 |
| 30' two wheel drive | 216.00 | 651.00 | 1,950.00 | **Sandblast machines** | | | |
| 40' four wheel drive | 249.00 | 747.00 | 2,240.00 | 150 lb pot with hood, 175 CFM compressor | 294.00 | 881.00 | 2,210.00 |
| 50' - 1000 lb. | 410.00 | 1,230.00 | 3,680.00 | 300 lb pot with hood, 325 CFM compressor | 525.00 | 1,560.00 | 3,930.00 |
| Telescoping and articulating booms, self propelled, gas or diesel powered, 2-wheel drive | | | | 600 lb pot with hood, 600 CFM compressor | 950.00 | 2,860.00 | 7,130.00 |
| 21' to 30' high | 255.00 | 765.00 | 2,290.00 | | | | |
| 31' to 40' high | 320.00 | 957.00 | 2,870.00 | | | | |
| 41' to 50' high | 415.00 | 1,250.00 | 3,740.00 | | | | |
| 51' to 60' high | 509.00 | 1,530.00 | 4,600.00 | | | | |
| **Burner, paint** | 15.30 | 46.30 | 114.00 | | | | |

**Figure 15**
Typical equipment purchase and rental prices

National Painting Cost Estimator

|  | Rental |  |  |
|---|---|---|---|
|  | Day | Week | Month |

**Sandblast hoses** - 50' lengths, coupled
| 3/8" I.D. | 12.80 | 38.20 | 97.20 |
| 3/4" I.D. | 17.90 | 53.60 | 133.00 |
| 1" I.D. | 22.90 | 68.40 | 172.00 |
| 1-1/4" I.D. | 25.50 | 76.40 | 192.00 |
| 1-1/2" I.D. | 28.10 | 84.50 | 211.00 |

**Sandblast accessories**
| Nozzles, all types | 22.90 | 69.50 | 172.00 |
| Hood, air-fed | 35.70 | 108.00 | 269.00 |
| Valves, remote control (deadman, all sizes) | 38.20 | 114.00 | 287.00 |

**Sanders**
| Belt - 3" | 17.90 | 53.60 | 134.00 |
| Belt - 4" x 24" | 21.70 | 64.80 | 163.00 |
| Disc - 7" | 28.10 | 84.50 | 211.00 |
| Finish sander, 6" | 15.30 | 46.00 | 114.00 |
| Floor edger, 7" disk, 29#, 15 amp. | 25.50 | 76.40 | 191.00 |
| Floor sander, 8" drum, 118#, 14 amp. | 57.50 | 171.00 | 432.00 |
| Palm sander, 4" x 4" | 12.80 | 38.20 | 96.20 |
| Palm sander, 4-1/2" x 9-1/4" | 15.30 | 46.00 | 114.00 |

**Scaffolding**, rolling stage, caster mounted, 30" wide by 7' or 10' long
| 4' to 6' reach | 50.90 | 102.00 | 204.00 |
| 7' to 11' reach | 63.70 | 128.00 | 255.00 |
| 12' to 16' reach | 89.10 | 179.00 | 357.00 |
| 17' to 21' reach | 122.00 | 242.00 | 485.00 |
| 22' to 26' reach | 134.00 | 268.00 | 536.00 |
| 27' to 30' reach | 146.00 | 293.00 | 587.00 |
| Casters - each | 12.81 | 25.50 | 38.20 |

**Scissor lifts**
Electric powered, rolling with 2' x 3' platform, 650 lb capacity
| 30' high | 96.20 | 287.00 | 861.00 |
| 40' high | 166.00 | 499.00 | 1,490.00 |
| 50' high | 191.00 | 575.00 | 1,720.00 |

Rolling, self-propelled, hydraulic, electric powered
| to 20' high | 140.00 | 568.00 | 1,270.00 |
| 21' to 30' high | 172.00 | 516.00 | 1,550.00 |
| 31' to 40' high | 216.00 | 651.00 | 1,950.00 |

Rolling, self-propelled, hydraulic, diesel powered
| to 20' high | 160.00 | 480.00 | 1,440.00 |
| 21' to 30' high | 198.00 | 593.00 | 1,770.00 |
| 31' to 40' high | 255.00 | 767.00 | 2,290.00 |

**Spray rigs**
Airless pumps, complete with gun and 50' of line
| Titan 447, 7/8 HP, electric | 89.10 | 269.00 | 805.00 |
| Titan 660, 1 HP, electric | 102.00 | 307.00 | 920.00 |
| Gasoline, .75 gpm | 109.00 | 326.00 | 1,010.00 |

Emulsion pumps
| 65 gal, 5 HP engine | 89.10 | 269.00 | 805.00 |
| 200 gal, 5 HP engine | 102.00 | 303.00 | 920.00 |
| Emulsion airless, 1.25 gpm, gasoline | 109.00 | 326.00 | 1,010.00 |

Conventional pumps, gas, portable
| High pressure, low vol. (HVLP) | 57.90 | 172.00 | 517.00 |
| 8 CFM complete | 76.40 | 229.00 | 689.00 |
| 17 CFM complete | 83.40 | 249.00 | 747.00 |
| 85 CFM complete | 96.20 | 287.00 | 861.00 |
| 150 CFM complete | 140.00 | 421.00 | 1,270.00 |
| Spray rig accessories: 6' wand | 9.03 | 26.90 | 67.10 |

**Striper, paint** (parking lot striping)
| Aerosol | 25.50 | 76.40 | 191.00 |
| Pressure regulated | 37.10 | 108.00 | 269.00 |

**Swing stage, rental**
Any length drop, motor operated, excluding safety gear and installation or dismantling. Note: Must be set up by a professional to ensure safety.
| Swing stage | 128.00 | 382.00 | 1,140.00 |
| Basket | 64.80 | 192.00 | 574.00 |
| Bosun's chair | 64.80 | 192.00 | 574.00 |

**Swing stage safety gear, purchase only**
Safety harness (114.00)
4' lanyard with locking snap at each end (83.40)
DBI rope grab for 5/8" safety line (89.10)
Komet rope grab for 3/4" safety line (128.00)

**Texturing equipment**
Texturing gun - w/ hopper, no compressor
| | 6.48 | 19.20 | 57.90 |
| Texturing mud paddle mixer | 9.03 | 26.80 | 81.10 |
| Texturing outfit - 1 HP w/ gun, 50' hose, 75 PSI | 14.10 | 42.10 | 126.00 |
| **Wallpaper hanging kit** | 21.70 | 64.80 | 195.00 |

**Wallpaper steamer**
| Electric, small, 10 amp | 25.50 | 76.40 | 229.00 |
| Electric, 15 amp | 38.20 | 114.00 | 345.00 |
| Pressurized, electric | 48.50 | 146.00 | 437.00 |

**Water pressure washer** (pressure washer, water blaster, power washer)
| 1000 PSI, electric, 15 amp | 57.90 | 172.00 | 516.00 |
| 2000 PSI, gas | 96.20 | 287.00 | 861.00 |
| 2500 PSI, gas | 102.00 | 307.00 | 920.00 |
| 3500 PSI, gas | 112.00 | 337.00 | 1,010.00 |

**Figure 15 (continued)**
Typical equipment purchase and rental prices

How to Use This Book

**New Construction and Commercial Work:** The overhead percentage for "Fast" (residential tract) work and "Medium" (commercial) projects *includes* equipment costs such as ladders, spray equipment, and masking paper holders. Those items are used on many jobs, not just one specific job. The overhead allowance covers equipment purchase payments, along with maintenance, repairs and fuel. If you have to rent equipment for a specific new construction project, add that rental expense as a separate cost item in your estimate.

**Repaint Jobs:** Overhead rates for "Slow" (repaint) work do *not* include equipment costs. When you estimate a repaint job, any small or short-term job, or a job that uses only a small quantity of materials, *add* the cost of equipment at the rental rate — even if the equipment is owned by your company.

Rental yards quote daily, weekly and monthly equipment rental rates. Figure 15 shows typical rental costs for painting equipment. Your actual equipment costs may be different. Here's a suggestion that can save you more than a few minutes on the telephone collecting rental rates. Make up a blank form like Figure 15 and give it to your favorite rental equipment suppliers. Ask each supplier to fill in current rental costs. Use the completed forms until you notice that rates have changed. Then ask for a new set of rental rates.

### Commissions and Bonuses

Any commissions or bonuses you have to pay on a job aren't included in the estimating tables. You must add these expenses to your bid.

Painting contractors rarely have a sales staff, so there won't be sales commissions to pay on most jobs. There's one exception, however. Most room addition and remodeling contractors have salespeople. And many of their remodeling projects exclude painting. In fact, their contract may specify that the owner is responsible for the painting. These jobs may be a good source of leads for a painting contractor. Develop a relationship with the remodeling contractor's sales staff (with the remodeling contractor's approval, of course). If you have to pay a sales commission for the referral, this is direct overhead and has to be added to the estimate.

Some painting contractors pay their estimators a bonus of 1 to 3 percent per job in addition to their salary. If you offer an incentive like this, add the cost to your estimate, again as a direct overhead item.

### *An Example of Overhead*

Here's an example of how overhead is added into an estimate. A painting company completed 20 new housing projects in the last year. Average revenue per project was $50,000. Gross receipts were $1,000,000 and the company made a 5 percent profit.

| | |
|---|---|
| Gross income | $1,000,000 |
| Less the profit earned (5%) | - 50,000 |
| Gross expenses | 950,000 |
| Less total direct job cost | - 825,000 |
| Indirect overhead expense | 125,000 |

$$\frac{125,000 \text{ (overhead cost)}}{825,000 \text{ (direct job cost)}} = 0.1515 \text{ or } 15.15\%$$

When you've calculated indirect overhead as a percentage of direct job cost, add that percentage to your estimates. If you leave indirect overhead out of your estimates, you've left out some very significant costs.

## Column 8: Profit

The estimating tables assume that profit on "Slow" (repaint) jobs is 16 percent, profit on "Medium" (commercial) projects is 12 percent and profit on "Fast" (residential tract) jobs is 7 percent. Calculate the profit per unit by first adding together the costs in columns 4 (labor cost per unit), column 5 (labor burden per unit), column 6 (material costs per unit), and column 7 (overhead per unit). Then multiply the total by the appropriate profit percentage to find the profit per unit.

It's my experience that larger companies with larger projects can survive with a smaller profit percentage. Stiff competition for high volume tract work forces bidders to trim their profit margin. Many smaller companies doing custom work earn a higher profit margin because they produce better quality work, have fewer jobs, and face less competition.

| Risk factor | Normal profit (assume 10%) | | Difficulty factor | | Proposed profit range |
|---|---|---|---|---|---|
| High risk | 10% | x | 1.5 to 3.5 | = | 15% to 35% |
| Average risk | 10% | x | 1.3 to 1.4 | = | 13% to 14% |
| Moderate risk | 10% | x | 1.0 to 1.2 | = | 10% to 12% |
| Low risk | 10% | x | 0.5 to 0.9 | = | 5% to 9% |

**Figure 16**
Risk factors and profit margin

## Profit and Risk

Profit is usually proportionate to risk. The more risk, the greater the potential profit has to be to attract bidders. Smaller companies handling custom or repaint work have more risk of a major cost overrun because there are many more variables in that type of work. It's usually safe to estimate a smaller profit on new work because new work tends to be more predictable. The risk of loss smaller.

How do you define risk? Here's my definition: Risk is the *headache factor*, the number and size of potential problems you could face in completing the project. Repaint jobs have more unknowns, so they're a greater risk. And dealing with an indecisive or picky homeowner can be the greatest headache of all. You may need to use a profit margin even higher than the 15 to 35 range indicated for high-risk work in Figure 16.

## Tailoring Your Profit Margin

Of course, your profit margin has to be based on the job, your company and the competition. But don't cut your profit to the bone just to get more work. Instead, review your bid to see if there are reasons why the standard costs wouldn't apply.

I use the term *standard base* bid to refer to my usual charge for all the estimated costs, including my standard profit. Before submitting any bid, spend a minute or two deciding whether your standard base bid will apply.

## Risk Factors

Your assessment of the difficulty of the job may favor assigning a risk factor that could be used to modify your profit percentage. The higher the risk, the higher potential profit should be. My suggestions are in Figure 16.

As you might expect, opinions on difficulty factors can vary greatly. There's a lot of knowledge involved. You need experience and good judgment to apply these factors effectively.

## Bidding Variables

Of course, your profit may be affected by an error in evaluating the job risk factor. You can greatly reduce the risk by accurately evaluating the bidding variables in Figure 17. Make adjustments to your standard base bid for example, if you expect your crews to be more or less efficient on this project, or if you expect competition to be intense. If there are logical reasons to modify your standard base bid, make those changes.

But remember, if you adjust your standard base bid, you're not changing your profit margin. You're only allowing for cost variables in the job. Adjust your standard base costs for unusual labor productivity, material or equipment cost changes, or because of unusual overhead conditions. Review the following bidding variables when deciding how to adjust your standard base bid.

| Reputations and Attitudes | The Site |
|---|---|
| ■ Owner | ■ Location (distance from shop and suppliers) |
| ■ Architect | ■ Accessibility |
| ■ General Contractor | ■ Working conditions |
| ■ Lender | ■ Security requirements |
| ■ Inspector | ■ Safety considerations |
| **The Project** | **Competition** |
| ■ Building type | ■ Number bidding |
| ■ Project size | ■ Their strength, size and competence |
| ■ Your financial limits | |
| ■ Start date | |
| ■ Weather conditions | |
| ■ Manpower availability and capability | **Desire for the work** |

**Figure 17**
Bidding variables

## The Bottom Line

The profit margin you include in estimates depends on the way you do business, the kind of work you do, and your competition. Only you can decide what percentage is right for your bids. Don't take another paint estimator's advice on the "correct" profit margin. There's no single correct answer. Use your own judgment. But here are some typical profit margins for the kinds of work most painting contractors do.

| Repaints: | Custom | 20 to 35% |
|---|---|---|
| | Average | 15 to 20% |
| Commercial or industrial | | 10 to 15% |
| New residential: | 1-4 units | 10 to 12% |
| | 5 or more | 5 to 7% |
| Government work | | 5 to 7% |

## Column 9: Total Cost

The costs in Column 9 of Figure 2, and all the estimating tables in this book, are the totals per unit for each application rate in columns 4, 5, 6, 7, and 8. That includes labor, labor burden, material cost, overhead and profit.

## Sample Estimate

Figure 18 is a sample repaint estimate, using the slow production rate, for a small house with many amenities. The final bid total is the bid price. Figure 19 is a blank estimating form for your use.

**Date** 1/7/14　　　　　　　　　　　　　　　　　　　　　　　　　　　　　**Due date** 1/15/14
**Customer** Dan Gleason　　　　　　　　　　　　　　　　　　　　　　　　**Job name** Gleason Repaint
**Address** 3333 A Street　　　　　　　　　　　　　　　　　　　　　　　　**Job location** 3333 A Street
**City/State/Zip** Yourtown, USA 77777　　　　　　　　　　　　　　　　　　**Estimate #** 14-012
**Phone** (619) 555-1212　　　　　　　　　　　　　　　　　　　　　　　　**Total square feet** 1,020 SF (5 rooms)
**Estimated by** CHS　　　　　　　　　　　　　　　　　　　　　　　　　　**Checked by** Jack

## Interior Costs

| # | Operation | Material | Application Method | Dimensions | Quantity SF/LF/Each | | Unit Cost Per SF | | Total Cost | Formula Page |
|---|---|---|---|---|---|---|---|---|---|---|
| 1 | Ceilings - T & G | Semi-Trans-WB | R + B | 17.5 x 15.3 x 1.3 | 348 SF | x | .40 | = $ | 139.00 | 86 |
| 2 | Beams to 13'H | Solid Body-WB | R + B | 17.5 x 7 | 122.5 LF | x | 2.28 | = $ | 279.00 | 45 |
| 3 | Ceilings - GYP. Drywall | Orange Peel-Flat | R | 127 + 127 | 254 SF | x | .28 | = $ | 71.00 | 65 |
| 4 | Ceilings - GYP. Drywall | Sealer-WB | R | 75 + 15 + 40 | 130 SF | x | .24 | = $ | 31.00 | 65 |
| 5 | Ceilings - GYP. Drywall | Enamel-WB | R | 75 + 15 + 40 | 130 SF | x | .31 | = $ | 40.00 | 65 |
| 6 | Walls - GYP. Drywall | Orange Peel-Flat | R | 675 + 392 + 392 | 1,459 SF | x | .26 | = $ | 379.00 | 228 |
| 7 | Walls - Above 8' (clip) | Orange Peel-Flat | R + B | 70 + 85 = 155 x 1.3 | 201.5 SF | x | .26 | = $ | 52.00 | 228 |
| 8 | Walls - GYP. Drywall | Sealer-WB | R | 280 + 128 + 208 | 616 SF | x | .26 | = $ | 160.00 | 228 |
| 9 | Walls - GYP. Drywall | Enamel-WB | R | 280 + 128 + 208 | 616 SF | x | .35 | = $ | 216.00 | 228 |
| 10 | Doors-Flush | Undercoat | R + B | Opening Count | 10 Ea | = | 146.86 | = $ | 147.00 | 108 |
| 11 | Doors-Flush | Enamel-WB | R + B | Opening Count | 10 Ea | = | 165.83 | = $ | 166.00 | 108 |
| 12 | Baseboard - Prime | Flat w/walls | R + B | 64 + 49 + 49 | 162 LF | x | .10 | = $ | 16.00 | 43 |
| 13 | Baseboard - Finish | Enamel | B | 11 + 16 + 35 | 62 LF | x | .45 | = $ | 28.00 | 43 |
| 14 | Railing - W.I.- Preprimed | Enamel/Off-white | B | 42" High | 15 LF | x | 2.13 | = $ | 32.00 | 180 |
| 15 | Valance-Light-2" x 8" | Solid Body Stain | B | 2 x 8 | 10 LF | x | 1.88 | = $ | 19.00 | 224 |
| 16 | Registers | Spray Can | Spray | 1,020 SF Home | 1,020 SF | x | .06 | = $ | 61.00 | 182 |
| 17 | | | | | | x | | = $ | | |
| 18 | | | | | | x | | = $ | | |

Total Interior Costs (includes overhead and profit) = $ 1,836.00

## Exterior Costs

| # | Operation | Material | Application Method | Dimensions | Quantity SF/LF/Each | | Unit Cost Per SF | | Total Cost | Formula Page |
|---|---|---|---|---|---|---|---|---|---|---|
| 1 | Roof Jacks - 1 Story | Finish-enamel | B | 1 Story | 1 House | x | 27.34 | = $ | 27.00 | 183 |
| 2 | S.M. Diverter-3" W | Finish-enamel | B | 14 | 14 LF | x | .25 | = $ | 4.00 | 198 |
| 3 | S.M. Vents & Flashing | Finish-enamel | B | 1 Story | 1 House | x | 58.30 | = $ | 58.00 | 199 |
| 4 | Fascia - 2 x 8 | Solid-water | Roll | 66 + 59 | 125 LF | x | .81 | = $ | 101.00 | 120 |
| 5 | Overhang - 24" | Solid-water | R + B | (132 + 76) x 1.5 | 312 SF | x | .72 | = $ | 225.00 | 160 |
| 6 | Siding - R.S. Wood | Solid-water | Roll | (1/2 x 24 x 4.5) x 2 | 108 SF | x | .51 | = $ | 55.00 | 210 |
| 7 | Plaster / Stucco | Masonry Paint | Roll | 255 + 255 + 204 + 204 | 918 SF | x | .41 | = $ | 376.00 | 169 |
| 8 | Door - Panel (Entry) | Enamel 2 coats | R + B | Entry | 1 Ea | x | 68.17 | = $ | 68.00 | 101 |
| 9 | Door - Flush | Enamel 2 coats | R + B | Exterior | 1 Ea | x | 29.22 | = $ | 29.00 | 98 |
| 10 | Plant-On Trim - 2 x 4 | Solid-water | R + B | 66 + 62 + 52 | 180 LF | x | .66 | = $ | 119.00 | 162 |
| 11 | PassThrough-Preprimed | Finish-enamel | B | 10 | 10 LF | x | 1.93 | = $ | 19.00 | 162 |
| 12 | Pot Shelf | Solid-water | R + B | 27 | 27 LF | x | 2.07 | = $ | 56.00 | 172 |
| 13 | | | | | | x | | = $ | | |
| 14 | | | | | | x | | = $ | | |
| 15 | | | | | | x | | = $ | | |
| 16 | | | | | | x | | = $ | | |
| 17 | | | | | | x | | = $ | | |
| 18 | | | | | | x | | = $ | | |

Total Exterior Costs (includes overhead and profit) = $ 1,137.00

**Figure 18**
Sample painting estimate

## Preparation Costs

| | Operation | Dimensions | Quantity SF/LF/Each | | Unit Per SF | | Total cost | Formula Page |
|---|---|---|---|---|---|---|---|---|
| 1 | Sand/Putty Wood Ceil (Siding x 1.3) | 17.5 x 15.3 x 1.3 | 348 SF | x | .20 | = $ | 70.00 | 300 |
| 2 | Sand and Putty Int. Wall | 675 + 392 + 392 | 1,459 SF | x | .19 | = $ | 277.00 | 300 |
| 3 | Lt. Sand Doors/Frames (Enamel) | 14 Ea x 21 SF x 2 Sides | 588 SF | x | .28 | = $ | 165.00 | 301 |
| 4 | Wash Int. Walls/Ceil-Enamel | 280 + 128 + 208 | 616 SF | x | .19 | = $ | 117.00 | 313 |
| 5 | Waterblast Exterior Stucco | 125 + 210 + 108 + 918 | 1,361 SF | x | .05 | = $ | 68.00 | 315 |
| 6 | Sand and Putty Ext. Trim | 125 + 210 + 108 | 443 SF | x | .36 | = $ | 159.00 | 300 |
| 7 | Caulk Ext. Windows-1/8" gap | 20 + 15 + 10 + 20 + 12 | 77 SF | x | .64 | = $ | 49.00 | 298 |
| 8 | | | | x | | = $ | | |
| 9 | | | | x | | = $ | | |
| 10 | | | | x | | = $ | | |

Total Preparation Costs (includes overhead and profit) = $ 905.00

## SURRPTUCU Costs

| Operation | Description | Labor hours | Labor cost (at $26.22) | Material cost | Totals | Formula Page |
|---|---|---|---|---|---|---|
| **S**et**U**p | 2 Days @ 1/day | 2.0 | 52.44 | — | 52.00 | 6 |
| **R**emove/**R**eplace | Hardware & Plates | 1.25 | 32.78 | — | 33.00 | 6 |
| **P**rotection | Furniture & Floors | 2.0 | 52.44 | 20.00 | 72.00 | 6 |

**T**ouch**U**p is applied as a percentage of the total costs. See *Extensions*

| **C**lean**U**p | 2 Days @ 1/day | 2.0 | 52.44 | — | 52.00 | 6 |

## Equipment Costs

| Equipment description | Rental days | Daily cost | Total cost | Formula Page |
|---|---|---|---|---|
| Pressure Washer | 1 | 96.20 | $ 96.00 | 34 |
| Ladders, 6', 2 Ea | 1 | 10.20 | $ 20.00 | 33 |
| Palm Sander 4" x 4" | 1 | 12.80 | $ 13.00 | 34 |
| | | | $ | |
| | | | $ | |
| | | | $ | |
| | Total Equipment Costs | | $ 129.00 | |

## Subcontractor Costs

| Trade | Bid Amount |
|---|---|
| Pavement marking | $ 0 |
| Sandblasting | $ 0 |
| Scaffolding | $ 0 |
| Wallcovering | $ 0 |
| Waterblasting | $ 0 |
| Other _____ | $ 0 |
| Other _____ | $ 0 |
| Other _____ | $ 0 |
| Total Subcontractor Costs | $ — |

## Extensions

| | |
|---|---|
| Supervision ( 2 Hr. ) | $ 52.00 |
| Setup | $ 52.00 |
| Remove/replace | $ 33.00 |
| Protection | $ 72.00 |
| Cleanup | $ 52.00 |
| Equipment | $ 129.00 |
| Subcontracts | $ 0 |
| Commissions | $ 0 |
| Other costs | $ 0 |
| Subtotal | $ 390.00 |
| Overhead ( 19 %) | $ 74.00 |
| Profit ( 16 %) | $ 74.00 |
| Subtotal | $ 538.00 |
| Preparation | $ 905.00 |
| Interior total | $ 1,836.00 |
| Exterior total | $ 1,137.00 |
| Subtotal | $ 4,416.00 |
| Touchup ( 10 %) | $ 442.00 |
| Contingency ( 0 %) | $ 0 |
| Total base bid | $ 4,858.00 |
| Adjustment ( -2 %) | $ (97.00) |
| Final bid total | $ 4,761.00 |
| Price per SF ( 1020 ) | $ 4.67 |
| Price per room ( 5 ) | $ 952.00 |

**Figure 18 (continued)**
Sample painting estimate

Date _____  Due date _____
Customer _____  Job name _____
Address _____  Job location _____
City/State/Zip _____  Estimate # _____
Phone _____  Total square feet _____
Estimated by _____  Checked by _____

## Interior Costs

| | Operation | Material | Application Method | Dimensions | Quantity SF/LF/Each | | Unit Cost | | Total Cost |
|---|---|---|---|---|---|---|---|---|---|
| 1 | _____ | _____ | _____ | _____ | _____ | x | _____ | = $ | _____ |
| 2 | _____ | _____ | _____ | _____ | _____ | x | _____ | = $ | _____ |
| 3 | _____ | _____ | _____ | _____ | _____ | x | _____ | = $ | _____ |
| 4 | _____ | _____ | _____ | _____ | _____ | x | _____ | = $ | _____ |
| 5 | _____ | _____ | _____ | _____ | _____ | x | _____ | = $ | _____ |
| 6 | _____ | _____ | _____ | _____ | _____ | x | _____ | = $ | _____ |
| 7 | _____ | _____ | _____ | _____ | _____ | x | _____ | = $ | _____ |
| 8 | _____ | _____ | _____ | _____ | _____ | x | _____ | = $ | _____ |
| 9 | _____ | _____ | _____ | _____ | _____ | x | _____ | = $ | _____ |
| 10 | _____ | _____ | _____ | _____ | _____ | x | _____ | = $ | _____ |
| 11 | _____ | _____ | _____ | _____ | _____ | x | _____ | = $ | _____ |
| 12 | _____ | _____ | _____ | _____ | _____ | x | _____ | = $ | _____ |
| 13 | _____ | _____ | _____ | _____ | _____ | x | _____ | = $ | _____ |
| 14 | _____ | _____ | _____ | _____ | _____ | x | _____ | = $ | _____ |
| 15 | _____ | _____ | _____ | _____ | _____ | x | _____ | = $ | _____ |
| 16 | _____ | _____ | _____ | _____ | _____ | x | _____ | = $ | _____ |
| 17 | _____ | _____ | _____ | _____ | _____ | x | _____ | = $ | _____ |
| 18 | _____ | _____ | _____ | _____ | _____ | x | _____ | = $ | _____ |

Total Interior Costs (includes overhead and profit) = $ _____

## Exterior Costs

| | Operation | Material | Application Method | Dimensions | Quantity SF/LF/Each | | Unit Cost | | Total Cost |
|---|---|---|---|---|---|---|---|---|---|
| 1 | _____ | _____ | _____ | _____ | _____ | x | _____ | = $ | _____ |
| 2 | _____ | _____ | _____ | _____ | _____ | x | _____ | = $ | _____ |
| 3 | _____ | _____ | _____ | _____ | _____ | x | _____ | = $ | _____ |
| 4 | _____ | _____ | _____ | _____ | _____ | x | _____ | = $ | _____ |
| 5 | _____ | _____ | _____ | _____ | _____ | x | _____ | = $ | _____ |
| 6 | _____ | _____ | _____ | _____ | _____ | x | _____ | = $ | _____ |
| 7 | _____ | _____ | _____ | _____ | _____ | x | _____ | = $ | _____ |
| 8 | _____ | _____ | _____ | _____ | _____ | x | _____ | = $ | _____ |
| 9 | _____ | _____ | _____ | _____ | _____ | x | _____ | = $ | _____ |
| 10 | _____ | _____ | _____ | _____ | _____ | x | _____ | = $ | _____ |
| 11 | _____ | _____ | _____ | _____ | _____ | x | _____ | = $ | _____ |
| 12 | _____ | _____ | _____ | _____ | _____ | x | _____ | = $ | _____ |
| 13 | _____ | _____ | _____ | _____ | _____ | x | _____ | = $ | _____ |
| 14 | _____ | _____ | _____ | _____ | _____ | x | _____ | = $ | _____ |
| 15 | _____ | _____ | _____ | _____ | _____ | x | _____ | = $ | _____ |
| 16 | _____ | _____ | _____ | _____ | _____ | x | _____ | = $ | _____ |
| 17 | _____ | _____ | _____ | _____ | _____ | x | _____ | = $ | _____ |
| 18 | _____ | _____ | _____ | _____ | _____ | x | _____ | = $ | _____ |

Total Exterior Costs (includes overhead and profit) = $ _____

**Figure 19**
Blank painting estimate

## Preparation Costs

| | Operation | Dimensions | Quantity SF/LF/Each | Unit cost | Total cost |
|---|---|---|---|---|---|
| 1 | _____ | _____ | _____ x | _____ | = $ _____ |
| 2 | _____ | _____ | _____ x | _____ | = $ _____ |
| 3 | _____ | _____ | _____ x | _____ | = $ _____ |
| 4 | _____ | _____ | _____ x | _____ | = $ _____ |
| 5 | _____ | _____ | _____ x | _____ | = $ _____ |
| 6 | _____ | _____ | _____ x | _____ | = $ _____ |
| 7 | _____ | _____ | _____ x | _____ | = $ _____ |
| 8 | _____ | _____ | _____ x | _____ | = $ _____ |
| 9 | _____ | _____ | _____ x | _____ | = $ _____ |
| 10 | _____ | _____ | _____ x | _____ | = $ _____ |

Total Preparation Costs (includes overhead and profit) = $ _____

## SURRPTUCU Costs

| Operation | Description | Labor hours | Labor cost (at ____) | Material cost | Totals |
|---|---|---|---|---|---|
| **S**et**U**p | _____ | _____ | _____ | _____ | _____ |
| **R**emove/**R**eplace | _____ | _____ | _____ | _____ | _____ |
| **P**rotection | _____ | _____ | _____ | _____ | _____ |

**T**ouch**U**p is applied as a percentage of the total costs. See *Extensions*

**C**lean**U**p _____ _____ _____ _____ _____

## Equipment Costs

| Equipment description | Rental days | Daily cost | Total cost |
|---|---|---|---|
| _____ | _____ | _____ | $ _____ |
| _____ | _____ | _____ | $ _____ |
| _____ | _____ | _____ | $ _____ |
| _____ | _____ | _____ | $ _____ |
| _____ | _____ | _____ | $ _____ |
| _____ | _____ | _____ | $ _____ |

Total Equipment Costs $ _____

## Subcontractor Costs

| Trade | Bid Amount |
|---|---|
| Pavement marking | $ _____ |
| Sandblasting | $ _____ |
| Scaffolding | $ _____ |
| Wallcovering | $ _____ |
| Waterblasting | $ _____ |
| Other _____ | $ _____ |
| Other _____ | $ _____ |
| Other _____ | $ _____ |
| Total Subcontractor Costs | $ _____ |

## Extensions

| | |
|---|---|
| Supervision (____) | $ _____ |
| Setup | $ _____ |
| Remove/replace | $ _____ |
| Protection | $ _____ |
| Cleanup | $ _____ |
| Equipment | $ _____ |
| Subcontracts | $ _____ |
| Commissions | $ _____ |
| Other costs | $ _____ |
| Subtotals | $ _____ |
| Overhead (____%) | $ _____ |
| Profit (____%) | $ _____ |
| Subtotal | $ _____ |
| Preparation | $ _____ |
| Interior total | $ _____ |
| Exterior total | $ _____ |
| Subtotal | $ _____ |
| Touchup (____%) | $ _____ |
| Contingency (____%) | $ _____ |
| Total base bid | $ _____ |
| Adjustment (____%) | $ _____ |
| Final bid total | $ _____ |
| Price per SF (____) | $ _____ |
| Price per room (____) | $ _____ |

**Figure 19 (continued)**
Blank painting estimate

# Part I

# GENERAL *Painting* COSTS

*General Painting Costs*

|  | Labor LF per manhour | Material coverage LF/gallon | Material cost per gallon | Labor cost per 100 LF | Labor burden 100 LF | Material cost per 100 LF | Overhead per 100 LF | Profit per 100 LF | Total price per 100 LF |
|---|---|---|---|---|---|---|---|---|---|
| **Baseboard, per linear foot** | | | | | | | | | |
| Roll 1 coat with walls, brush touchup, paint grade base | | | | | | | | | |
| Flat latex, water base, (material #5) | | | | | | | | | |
| Slow | 900 | 800 | 36.70 | 2.25 | .66 | 4.59 | 1.43 | 1.43 | 10.36 |
| Medium | 1200 | 750 | 32.10 | 2.15 | .74 | 4.28 | 1.80 | 1.08 | 10.05 |
| Fast | 1500 | 700 | 27.50 | 2.10 | .87 | 3.93 | 2.14 | .63 | 9.67 |
| Enamel, water base (material #9) | | | | | | | | | |
| Slow | 600 | 750 | 46.80 | 3.38 | 1.00 | 6.24 | 2.02 | 2.02 | 14.66 |
| Medium | 800 | 725 | 41.00 | 3.22 | 1.14 | 5.66 | 2.51 | 1.50 | 14.03 |
| Fast | 1000 | 700 | 35.10 | 3.15 | 1.29 | 5.01 | 2.93 | .87 | 13.25 |
| Enamel, oil base (material #10) | | | | | | | | | |
| Slow | 600 | 750 | 61.70 | 3.38 | 1.00 | 8.23 | 2.40 | 2.40 | 17.41 |
| Medium | 800 | 725 | 54.00 | 3.22 | 1.14 | 7.45 | 2.95 | 1.77 | 16.53 |
| Fast | 1000 | 700 | 46.30 | 3.15 | 1.29 | 6.61 | 3.43 | 1.01 | 15.49 |
| Brush 1 coat, cut-in, paint grade base | | | | | | | | | |
| Enamel, water base (material #9) | | | | | | | | | |
| Slow | 100 | 700 | 46.80 | 20.25 | 5.97 | 6.69 | 6.25 | 6.27 | 45.43 |
| Medium | 120 | 675 | 41.00 | 21.46 | 7.59 | 6.07 | 8.78 | 5.27 | 49.17 |
| Fast | 140 | 650 | 35.10 | 22.50 | 9.17 | 5.40 | 11.49 | 3.40 | 51.96 |
| Enamel, oil base (material #10) | | | | | | | | | |
| Slow | 100 | 700 | 61.70 | 20.25 | 5.97 | 8.81 | 6.66 | 6.67 | 48.36 |
| Medium | 120 | 675 | 54.00 | 21.46 | 7.59 | 8.00 | 9.27 | 5.56 | 51.88 |
| Fast | 140 | 650 | 46.30 | 22.50 | 9.17 | 7.12 | 12.03 | 3.56 | 54.38 |
| Spray 1 coat, stain in boneyard, stain grade base | | | | | | | | | |
| Wiping stain (material #11a) | | | | | | | | | |
| Slow | -- | -- | -- | -- | -- | -- | -- | -- | -- |
| Medium | 1500 | 1750 | 44.90 | 1.72 | .62 | 2.57 | 1.23 | .74 | 6.88 |
| Fast | 2000 | 1500 | 38.50 | 1.58 | .64 | 2.57 | 1.48 | .44 | 6.71 |

Use these figures for 1-1/2 inch to 3 inch baseboard stock, painted or stained on one side. Measurements are based on linear feet of baseboard. Paint grade base is painted after it is installed but stain grade base is usually stained in a boneyard. Typically, finger joint stock is paint grade and butt joint stock is stain grade. These figures include minimal preparation time and material. Add for extensive preparation. "Slow" work is based on an hourly wage of $20.25, "Medium" work on an hourly wage of $25.75, and "Fast" work on an hourly wage of $31.50. Other qualifications that apply to this table are on page 9.

*National Painting Cost Estimator*

|  | Labor SF per manhour | Material coverage SF/gallon | Material cost per gallon | Labor cost per 100 SF | Labor burden 100 SF | Material cost per 100 SF | Overhead per 100 SF | Profit per 100 SF | Total price per 100 SF |
|---|---|---|---|---|---|---|---|---|---|

## Baseboard, per square foot of floor area

Roll 1 coat with walls, brush touchup, paint grade base
  Flat latex, water base, (material #5)

| | | | | | | | | | |
|---|---|---|---|---|---|---|---|---|---|
| Slow | 2500 | 1500 | 36.70 | .81 | .24 | 2.45 | .67 | .67 | 4.84 |
| Medium | 2750 | 1250 | 32.10 | .94 | .32 | 2.57 | .96 | .58 | 5.37 |
| Fast | 3000 | 1000 | 27.50 | 1.05 | .41 | 2.75 | 1.31 | .39 | 5.91 |

  Enamel, water base (material #9)

| | | | | | | | | | |
|---|---|---|---|---|---|---|---|---|---|
| Slow | 2000 | 1000 | 46.80 | 1.01 | .30 | 4.68 | 1.14 | 1.14 | 8.27 |
| Medium | 2200 | 900 | 41.00 | 1.17 | .40 | 4.56 | 1.54 | .92 | 8.59 |
| Fast | 2400 | 800 | 35.10 | 1.31 | .55 | 4.39 | 1.93 | .57 | 8.75 |

  Enamel, oil base (material #10)

| | | | | | | | | | |
|---|---|---|---|---|---|---|---|---|---|
| Slow | 2000 | 1000 | 61.70 | 1.01 | .30 | 6.17 | 1.42 | 1.42 | 10.32 |
| Medium | 2200 | 900 | 54.00 | 1.17 | .40 | 6.00 | 1.90 | 1.14 | 10.61 |
| Fast | 2400 | 800 | 46.30 | 1.31 | .55 | 5.79 | 2.37 | .70 | 10.72 |

Brush 1 coat, cut-in, paint grade base
  Enamel, water base (material #9)

| | | | | | | | | | |
|---|---|---|---|---|---|---|---|---|---|
| Slow | 500 | 1500 | 46.80 | 4.05 | 1.19 | 3.12 | 1.59 | 1.59 | 11.54 |
| Medium | 550 | 1350 | 41.00 | 4.68 | 1.67 | 3.04 | 2.35 | 1.41 | 13.15 |
| Fast | 600 | 1200 | 35.10 | 5.25 | 2.16 | 2.93 | 3.20 | .95 | 14.49 |

  Enamel, oil base (material #10)

| | | | | | | | | | |
|---|---|---|---|---|---|---|---|---|---|
| Slow | 500 | 1500 | 61.70 | 4.05 | 1.19 | 4.11 | 1.78 | 1.78 | 12.91 |
| Medium | 550 | 1350 | 54.00 | 4.68 | 1.67 | 4.00 | 2.59 | 1.55 | 14.49 |
| Fast | 600 | 1200 | 46.30 | 5.25 | 2.16 | 3.86 | 3.49 | 1.03 | 15.79 |

Spray 1 coat, stain in boneyard, stain grade base
  Wiping stain (material #11a)

| | | | | | | | | | |
|---|---|---|---|---|---|---|---|---|---|
| Slow | -- | -- | -- | -- | -- | -- | -- | -- | -- |
| Medium | 4000 | 1350 | 44.90 | .64 | .23 | 3.33 | 1.05 | .63 | 5.88 |
| Fast | 5000 | 1200 | 38.50 | .63 | .26 | 3.21 | 1.27 | .38 | 5.75 |

Baseboard measurements are based on square feet of floor area. Use these figures for 1-1/2 inch to 3 inch stock, painted or stained on one side. Stain grade base is to be stained in a boneyard. Typically, finger joint stock is paint grade and butt joint stock is stain grade. These figures include minimal preparation time and material. Add for extensive preparation. "Slow" work is based on an hourly wage of $20.25, "Medium" work on an hourly wage of $25.75, and "Fast" work on an hourly wage of $31.50. Other qualifications that apply to this table are on page 9.

*General Painting Costs*

|  | Labor LF per manhour | Material coverage LF/gallon | Material cost per gallon | Labor cost per 100 LF | Labor burden 100 LF | Material cost per 100 LF | Overhead per 100 LF | Profit per 100 LF | Total price per 100 LF |
|---|---|---|---|---|---|---|---|---|---|
| **Beams, per linear foot, heights to 13 feet** | | | | | | | | | |
| Solid body stain, water base (material #18) | | | | | | | | | |
| Roll & brush each coat | | | | | | | | | |
| Slow | 35 | 50 | 45.00 | 57.86 | 17.05 | 90.00 | 31.34 | 31.40 | 227.65 |
| Medium | 40 | 45 | 39.40 | 64.38 | 22.80 | 87.56 | 43.68 | 26.21 | 244.63 |
| Fast | 45 | 40 | 33.80 | 70.00 | 28.55 | 84.50 | 56.75 | 16.79 | 256.59 |
| Solid body stain, oil base (material #19) | | | | | | | | | |
| Roll & brush each coat | | | | | | | | | |
| Slow | 35 | 50 | 54.10 | 57.86 | 17.05 | 108.20 | 34.79 | 34.87 | 252.77 |
| Medium | 40 | 45 | 47.30 | 64.38 | 22.80 | 105.11 | 48.07 | 28.84 | 269.20 |
| Fast | 45 | 40 | 40.50 | 70.00 | 28.55 | 101.25 | 61.94 | 18.32 | 280.06 |
| Semi-transparent stain, water base (material #20) | | | | | | | | | |
| Roll & brush each coat | | | | | | | | | |
| Slow | 40 | 55 | 47.50 | 50.63 | 14.92 | 86.36 | 28.87 | 28.93 | 209.71 |
| Medium | 45 | 50 | 41.60 | 57.22 | 20.26 | 83.20 | 40.17 | 24.10 | 224.95 |
| Fast | 50 | 45 | 35.60 | 63.00 | 25.70 | 79.11 | 52.02 | 15.39 | 235.22 |
| Semi-transparent stain, oil base (material #21) | | | | | | | | | |
| Roll & brush each coat | | | | | | | | | |
| Slow | 40 | 55 | 48.70 | 50.63 | 14.92 | 88.55 | 29.28 | 29.34 | 212.72 |
| Medium | 45 | 50 | 42.60 | 57.22 | 20.26 | 85.20 | 40.67 | 24.40 | 227.75 |
| Fast | 50 | 45 | 36.50 | 63.00 | 25.70 | 81.11 | 52.64 | 15.57 | 238.02 |

Beam measurements are based on linear feet of installed 4" x 6" to 8" x 14" beams. High time difficulty factors are already figured into the formulas. "Slow" work is based on an hourly wage of $20.25, "Medium" work on an hourly wage of $25.75, and "Fast" work on an hourly wage of $31.50. Other qualifications that apply to this table are on page 9.

|  | Labor LF per manhour | Material coverage LF/gallon | Material cost per gallon | Labor cost per 100 LF | Labor burden 100 LF | Material cost per 100 LF | Overhead per 100 LF | Profit per 100 LF | Total price per 100 LF |
|---|---|---|---|---|---|---|---|---|---|

## Beams, per linear foot, heights from 13 to 17 feet

Solid body stain, water base (material #18)
  Roll & brush each coat

| | | | | | | | | | |
|---|---|---|---|---|---|---|---|---|---|
| Slow | 24 | 50 | 45.00 | 84.38 | 24.88 | 90.00 | 37.86 | 37.94 | 275.06 |
| Medium | 27 | 45 | 39.40 | 95.37 | 33.79 | 87.56 | 54.17 | 32.50 | 303.39 |
| Fast | 30 | 40 | 33.80 | 105.00 | 42.82 | 84.50 | 72.03 | 21.31 | 325.66 |

Solid body stain, oil base (material #19)
  Roll & brush each coat

| | | | | | | | | | |
|---|---|---|---|---|---|---|---|---|---|
| Slow | 24 | 50 | 54.10 | 84.38 | 24.88 | 108.20 | 41.32 | 41.41 | 300.19 |
| Medium | 27 | 45 | 47.30 | 95.37 | 33.79 | 105.11 | 58.56 | 35.14 | 327.97 |
| Fast | 30 | 40 | 40.50 | 105.00 | 42.82 | 101.25 | 77.22 | 22.84 | 349.13 |

Semi-transparent stain, water base (material #20)
  Roll & brush each coat

| | | | | | | | | | |
|---|---|---|---|---|---|---|---|---|---|
| Slow | 28 | 55 | 47.50 | 72.32 | 21.31 | 86.36 | 34.20 | 34.27 | 248.46 |
| Medium | 31 | 50 | 41.60 | 83.06 | 29.43 | 83.20 | 48.92 | 29.35 | 273.96 |
| Fast | 34 | 45 | 35.60 | 92.65 | 37.78 | 79.11 | 64.96 | 19.22 | 293.72 |

Semi-transparent stain, oil base (material #21)
  Roll & brush each coat

| | | | | | | | | | |
|---|---|---|---|---|---|---|---|---|---|
| Slow | 28 | 55 | 48.70 | 72.32 | 21.31 | 88.55 | 34.62 | 34.69 | 251.49 |
| Medium | 31 | 50 | 42.60 | 83.06 | 29.43 | 85.20 | 49.42 | 29.65 | 276.76 |
| Fast | 34 | 45 | 36.50 | 92.65 | 37.78 | 81.11 | 65.58 | 19.40 | 296.52 |

Beam measurements are based on linear feet of installed 4" x 6" to 8" x 14" beams. High time difficulty factors are already figured into the formulas. "Slow" work is based on an hourly wage of $20.25, "Medium" work on an hourly wage of $25.75, and "Fast" work on an hourly wage of $31.50. Other qualifications that apply to this table are on page 9.

|  | Labor LF per manhour | Material coverage LF/gallon | Material cost per gallon | Labor cost per 100 LF | Labor burden 100 LF | Material cost per 100 LF | Overhead per 100 LF | Profit per 100 LF | Total price per 100 LF |
|---|---|---|---|---|---|---|---|---|---|

## Beams, per linear foot, heights from 18 to 19 feet

Solid body stain, water base (material #18)
  Roll & brush each coat

| | | | | | | | | | |
|---|---|---|---|---|---|---|---|---|---|
| Slow | 16 | 50 | 45.00 | 126.56 | 37.32 | 90.00 | 48.24 | 48.34 | 350.46 |
| Medium | 18 | 45 | 39.40 | 143.06 | 50.68 | 87.56 | 70.32 | 42.19 | 393.81 |
| Fast | 20 | 40 | 33.80 | 157.50 | 64.25 | 84.50 | 94.94 | 28.08 | 429.27 |

Solid body stain, oil base (material #19)
  Roll & brush each coat

| | | | | | | | | | |
|---|---|---|---|---|---|---|---|---|---|
| Slow | 16 | 50 | 54.10 | 126.56 | 37.32 | 108.20 | 51.70 | 51.81 | 375.59 |
| Medium | 18 | 45 | 47.30 | 143.06 | 50.68 | 105.11 | 74.70 | 44.82 | 418.37 |
| Fast | 20 | 40 | 40.50 | 157.50 | 64.25 | 101.25 | 100.13 | 29.62 | 452.75 |

*General Painting Costs*

|  | Labor LF per manhour | Material coverage LF/gallon | Material cost per gallon | Labor cost per 100 LF | Labor burden 100 LF | Material cost per 100 LF | Overhead per 100 LF | Profit per 100 LF | Total price per 100 LF |
|---|---|---|---|---|---|---|---|---|---|

Semi-transparent stain, water base (material #20)
  Roll & brush each coat

| | | | | | | | | | |
|---|---|---|---|---|---|---|---|---|---|
| Slow | 19 | 55 | 47.50 | 106.58 | 31.42 | 86.36 | 42.63 | 42.72 | 309.71 |
| Medium | 21 | 50 | 41.60 | 122.62 | 43.43 | 83.20 | 62.31 | 37.38 | 348.94 |
| Fast | 23 | 45 | 35.60 | 136.96 | 55.87 | 79.11 | 84.30 | 24.94 | 381.18 |

Semi-transparent stain, oil base (material #21)
  Roll & brush each coat

| | | | | | | | | | |
|---|---|---|---|---|---|---|---|---|---|
| Slow | 19 | 55 | 48.70 | 106.58 | 31.42 | 88.55 | 43.05 | 43.14 | 312.74 |
| Medium | 21 | 50 | 42.60 | 122.62 | 43.43 | 85.20 | 62.81 | 37.68 | 351.74 |
| Fast | 23 | 45 | 36.50 | 136.96 | 55.87 | 81.11 | 84.92 | 25.12 | 383.98 |

Beam measurements are based on linear feet of installed 4" x 6" to 8" x 14" beams. High time difficulty factors are already figured into the formulas. "Slow" work is based on an hourly wage of $20.25, "Medium" work on an hourly wage of $25.75, and "Fast" work on an hourly wage of $31.50. Other qualifications that apply to this table are on page 9.

|  | Labor LF per manhour | Material coverage LF/gallon | Material cost per gallon | Labor cost per 100 LF | Labor burden 100 LF | Material cost per 100 LF | Overhead per 100 LF | Profit per 100 LF | Total price per 100 LF |
|---|---|---|---|---|---|---|---|---|---|

## Beams, per linear foot, heights from 20 to 21 feet

Solid body stain, water base (material #18)
  Roll & brush each coat

| | | | | | | | | | |
|---|---|---|---|---|---|---|---|---|---|
| Slow | 12 | 50 | 45.00 | 168.75 | 49.74 | 90.00 | 58.62 | 58.74 | 425.85 |
| Medium | 14 | 45 | 39.40 | 183.93 | 65.15 | 87.56 | 84.15 | 50.49 | 471.28 |
| Fast | 16 | 40 | 33.80 | 196.88 | 80.31 | 84.50 | 112.13 | 33.17 | 506.99 |

Solid body stain, oil base (material #19)
  Roll & brush each coat

| | | | | | | | | | |
|---|---|---|---|---|---|---|---|---|---|
| Slow | 12 | 50 | 54.10 | 168.75 | 49.74 | 108.20 | 62.08 | 62.21 | 450.98 |
| Medium | 14 | 45 | 47.30 | 183.93 | 65.15 | 105.11 | 88.54 | 53.12 | 495.85 |
| Fast | 16 | 40 | 40.50 | 196.88 | 80.31 | 101.25 | 117.32 | 34.70 | 530.46 |

Semi-transparent stain, water base (material #20)
  Roll & brush each coat

| | | | | | | | | | |
|---|---|---|---|---|---|---|---|---|---|
| Slow | 14 | 55 | 47.50 | 144.64 | 42.65 | 86.36 | 52.00 | 52.11 | 377.76 |
| Medium | 16 | 50 | 41.60 | 160.94 | 57.00 | 83.20 | 75.28 | 45.17 | 421.59 |
| Fast | 18 | 45 | 35.60 | 175.00 | 71.41 | 79.11 | 100.91 | 29.85 | 456.28 |

Semi-transparent stain, oil base (material #21)
  Roll & brush each coat

| | | | | | | | | | |
|---|---|---|---|---|---|---|---|---|---|
| Slow | 14 | 55 | 48.70 | 144.64 | 42.65 | 88.55 | 52.41 | 52.52 | 380.77 |
| Medium | 16 | 50 | 42.60 | 160.94 | 57.00 | 85.20 | 75.78 | 45.47 | 424.39 |
| Fast | 18 | 45 | 36.50 | 175.00 | 71.41 | 81.11 | 101.53 | 30.03 | 459.08 |

Beam measurements are based on linear feet of installed 4" x 6" to 8" x 14" beams. High time difficulty factors are already figured into the formulas. "Slow" work is based on an hourly wage of $20.25, "Medium" work on an hourly wage of $25.75, and "Fast" work on an hourly wage of $31.50. Other qualifications that apply to this table are on page 9.

*National Painting Cost Estimator*

|  | Labor SF per manhour | Material coverage SF/gallon | Material cost per gallon | Labor cost per 100 SF | Labor burden 100 SF | Material cost per 100 SF | Overhead per 100 SF | Profit per 100 SF | Total price per 100 SF |
|---|---|---|---|---|---|---|---|---|---|
| **Bookcases and shelves, paint grade, brush application** | | | | | | | | | |
| Undercoat, water base (material #3) | | | | | | | | | |
|   Roll & brush 1 coat | | | | | | | | | |
|     Slow | 25 | 300 | 32.60 | 81.00 | 23.88 | 10.87 | 22.00 | 22.04 | 159.79 |
|     Medium | 30 | 280 | 28.50 | 85.83 | 30.39 | 10.18 | 31.60 | 18.96 | 176.96 |
|     Fast | 35 | 260 | 24.50 | 90.00 | 36.71 | 9.42 | 42.20 | 12.48 | 190.81 |
| Undercoat, oil base (material #4) | | | | | | | | | |
|   Roll & brush 1 coat | | | | | | | | | |
|     Slow | 25 | 340 | 42.30 | 81.00 | 23.88 | 12.44 | 22.29 | 22.34 | 161.95 |
|     Medium | 30 | 318 | 37.00 | 85.83 | 30.39 | 11.64 | 31.96 | 19.18 | 179.00 |
|     Fast | 35 | 295 | 31.80 | 90.00 | 36.71 | 10.78 | 42.63 | 12.61 | 192.73 |
| Split coat (1/2 undercoat + 1/2 enamel), water base (material #3 + #9) | | | | | | | | | |
|   Roll & brush each coat | | | | | | | | | |
|     Slow | 40 | 350 | 39.70 | 50.63 | 14.92 | 11.34 | 14.61 | 14.64 | 106.14 |
|     Medium | 45 | 328 | 34.75 | 57.22 | 20.26 | 10.59 | 22.02 | 13.21 | 123.30 |
|     Fast | 50 | 305 | 29.80 | 63.00 | 25.70 | 9.77 | 30.53 | 9.03 | 138.03 |
| Split coat (1/2 undercoat + 1/2 enamel), oil base (material #4 + #10) | | | | | | | | | |
|   Roll & brush each coat | | | | | | | | | |
|     Slow | 40 | 350 | 52.00 | 50.63 | 14.92 | 14.86 | 15.28 | 15.31 | 111.00 |
|     Medium | 45 | 328 | 34.75 | 57.22 | 20.26 | 10.59 | 22.02 | 13.21 | 123.30 |
|     Fast | 50 | 305 | 29.80 | 63.00 | 25.70 | 9.77 | 30.53 | 9.03 | 138.03 |
| Enamel, water base (material #9) | | | | | | | | | |
|   Roll & brush 1st finish coat | | | | | | | | | |
|     Slow | 35 | 340 | 46.80 | 57.86 | 17.05 | 13.76 | 16.85 | 16.89 | 122.41 |
|     Medium | 40 | 318 | 41.00 | 64.38 | 22.80 | 12.89 | 25.02 | 15.01 | 140.10 |
|     Fast | 45 | 295 | 35.10 | 70.00 | 28.55 | 11.90 | 34.24 | 10.13 | 154.82 |
|   Roll & brush 2nd or additional finish coats | | | | | | | | | |
|     Slow | 40 | 350 | 46.80 | 50.63 | 14.92 | 13.37 | 15.00 | 15.03 | 108.95 |
|     Medium | 45 | 328 | 41.00 | 57.22 | 20.26 | 12.50 | 22.50 | 13.50 | 125.98 |
|     Fast | 50 | 305 | 35.10 | 63.00 | 25.70 | 11.51 | 31.07 | 9.19 | 140.47 |
| Enamel, oil base (material #10) | | | | | | | | | |
|   Roll & brush 1st finish coat | | | | | | | | | |
|     Slow | 35 | 340 | 61.70 | 57.86 | 17.05 | 18.15 | 17.69 | 17.72 | 128.47 |
|     Medium | 40 | 318 | 54.00 | 64.38 | 22.80 | 16.98 | 26.04 | 15.62 | 145.82 |
|     Fast | 45 | 295 | 46.30 | 70.00 | 28.55 | 15.69 | 35.42 | 10.48 | 160.14 |
|   Roll & brush 2nd or additional finish coats | | | | | | | | | |
|     Slow | 40 | 350 | 61.70 | 50.63 | 14.92 | 17.63 | 15.81 | 15.84 | 114.83 |
|     Medium | 45 | 318 | 54.00 | 57.22 | 20.26 | 16.98 | 23.62 | 14.17 | 132.25 |
|     Fast | 50 | 305 | 46.30 | 63.00 | 25.70 | 15.18 | 32.20 | 9.53 | 145.61 |

Bookcase and shelf estimates are based on overall dimensions (length times width) to 8 feet high and include painting all exposed surfaces (including stiles, interior shelves and backs). For heights above 8 feet, use the High Time Difficulty Factors on page 139. "Slow" work is based on an hourly wage of $20.25, "Medium" work on an hourly wage of $25.75, and "Fast" work on an hourly wage of $31.50. Other qualifications that apply to this table are on page 9.

*General Painting Costs*

|  | Labor SF per manhour | Material coverage SF/gallon | Material cost per gallon | Labor cost per 100 SF | Labor burden 100 SF | Material cost per 100 SF | Overhead per 100 SF | Profit per 100 SF | Total price per 100 SF |
|---|---|---|---|---|---|---|---|---|---|

## Bookcases and shelves, paint grade, spray application

Undercoat, water base (material #3)
  Spray 1 coat

|  | | | | | | | | | |
|---|---|---|---|---|---|---|---|---|---|
| Slow | 150 | 145 | 32.60 | 13.50 | 3.99 | 22.48 | 7.59 | 7.61 | 55.17 |
| Medium | 165 | 133 | 28.50 | 15.61 | 5.52 | 21.43 | 10.64 | 6.39 | 59.59 |
| Fast | 175 | 120 | 24.50 | 18.00 | 7.32 | 20.42 | 14.19 | 4.20 | 64.13 |

Undercoat, oil base (material #4)
  Spray 1 coat

|  | | | | | | | | | |
|---|---|---|---|---|---|---|---|---|---|
| Slow | 150 | 145 | 42.30 | 13.50 | 3.99 | 29.17 | 8.86 | 8.88 | 64.40 |
| Medium | 165 | 133 | 37.00 | 15.61 | 5.52 | 27.82 | 12.24 | 7.34 | 68.53 |
| Fast | 175 | 120 | 31.80 | 18.00 | 7.32 | 26.50 | 16.07 | 4.75 | 72.64 |

Split coat (1/2 undercoat + 1/2 enamel), water base (material #3 + #9)
  Spray each coat

|  | | | | | | | | | |
|---|---|---|---|---|---|---|---|---|---|
| Slow | 245 | 195 | 39.70 | 8.27 | 2.43 | 20.36 | 5.90 | 5.92 | 42.88 |
| Medium | 270 | 183 | 34.75 | 9.54 | 3.36 | 18.99 | 7.98 | 4.79 | 44.66 |
| Fast | 295 | 170 | 29.80 | 10.68 | 4.35 | 17.53 | 10.10 | 2.99 | 45.65 |

Split coat (1/2 undercoat + 1/2 enamel), oil base (material #4 + #10)
  Spray each coat

|  | | | | | | | | | |
|---|---|---|---|---|---|---|---|---|---|
| Slow | 245 | 195 | 52.00 | 8.27 | 2.43 | 26.67 | 7.10 | 7.12 | 51.59 |
| Medium | 270 | 183 | 45.50 | 9.54 | 3.36 | 24.86 | 9.45 | 5.67 | 52.88 |
| Fast | 295 | 170 | 39.05 | 10.68 | 4.35 | 22.97 | 11.78 | 3.49 | 53.27 |

Enamel, water base (material #9)
  Spray 1st finish coat

|  | | | | | | | | | |
|---|---|---|---|---|---|---|---|---|---|
| Slow | 225 | 170 | 46.80 | 9.00 | 2.64 | 27.53 | 7.45 | 7.46 | 54.08 |
| Medium | 250 | 158 | 41.00 | 10.30 | 3.65 | 25.95 | 9.98 | 5.99 | 55.87 |
| Fast | 275 | 145 | 35.10 | 11.45 | 4.69 | 24.21 | 12.50 | 3.70 | 56.55 |

  Spray 2nd or additional finish coats

|  | | | | | | | | | |
|---|---|---|---|---|---|---|---|---|---|
| Slow | 245 | 195 | 46.80 | 8.27 | 2.43 | 24.00 | 6.59 | 6.61 | 47.90 |
| Medium | 270 | 183 | 41.00 | 9.54 | 3.36 | 22.40 | 8.83 | 5.30 | 49.43 |
| Fast | 295 | 170 | 35.10 | 10.68 | 4.35 | 20.65 | 11.06 | 3.27 | 50.01 |

Enamel, oil base (material #10)
  Spray 1st finish coat

|  | | | | | | | | | |
|---|---|---|---|---|---|---|---|---|---|
| Slow | 225 | 170 | 61.70 | 9.00 | 2.64 | 36.29 | 9.11 | 9.13 | 66.17 |
| Medium | 250 | 158 | 54.00 | 10.30 | 3.65 | 34.18 | 12.03 | 7.22 | 67.38 |
| Fast | 275 | 145 | 46.30 | 11.45 | 4.69 | 31.93 | 14.90 | 4.41 | 67.38 |

  Spray 2nd or additional finish coats

|  | | | | | | | | | |
|---|---|---|---|---|---|---|---|---|---|
| Slow | 245 | 195 | 61.70 | 8.27 | 2.43 | 31.64 | 8.05 | 8.06 | 58.45 |
| Medium | 270 | 183 | 54.00 | 9.54 | 3.36 | 29.51 | 10.61 | 6.36 | 59.38 |
| Fast | 295 | 170 | 46.30 | 10.68 | 4.35 | 27.24 | 13.11 | 3.88 | 59.26 |

Bookcase and shelf estimates are based on overall dimensions (length times width) to 8 feet high and include painting all exposed surfaces (including stiles, interior shelves and backs). For heights above 8 feet, use the High Time Difficulty Factors on page 139. "Slow" work is based on an hourly wage of $20.25, "Medium" work on an hourly wage of $25.75, and "Fast" work on an hourly wage of $31.50. Other qualifications that apply to this table are on page 9.

*National Painting Cost Estimator*

|  | Labor SF per manhour | Material coverage SF/gallon | Material cost per gallon | Labor cost per 100 SF | Labor burden 100 SF | Material cost per 100 SF | Overhead per 100 SF | Profit per 100 SF | Total price per 100 SF |
|---|---|---|---|---|---|---|---|---|---|

## Bookcases and shelves, stain grade

**Stain, seal & lacquer (7 step process)**

STEP 1: Sand & putty;
| | | | | | | | | | |
|---|---|---|---|---|---|---|---|---|---|
| Slow | 100 | -- | -- | 20.25 | 5.97 | -- | 4.98 | 4.99 | 36.19 |
| Medium | 125 | -- | -- | 20.60 | 7.30 | -- | 6.97 | 4.18 | 39.05 |
| Fast | 150 | -- | -- | 21.00 | 8.58 | -- | 9.17 | 2.71 | 41.46 |

STEP 2 & 3: Stain (material #11a) & wipe
Brush 1 coat & wipe
| | | | | | | | | | |
|---|---|---|---|---|---|---|---|---|---|
| Slow | 75 | 500 | 51.30 | 27.00 | 7.95 | 10.26 | 8.59 | 8.61 | 62.41 |
| Medium | 85 | 475 | 44.90 | 30.29 | 10.72 | 9.45 | 12.62 | 7.57 | 70.65 |
| Fast | 95 | 450 | 38.50 | 33.16 | 13.54 | 8.56 | 17.13 | 5.07 | 77.46 |

Spray 1 coat & wipe
| | | | | | | | | | |
|---|---|---|---|---|---|---|---|---|---|
| Slow | 300 | 175 | 51.30 | 6.75 | 1.98 | 29.31 | 7.23 | 7.24 | 52.51 |
| Medium | 400 | 138 | 44.90 | 6.44 | 2.28 | 32.54 | 10.32 | 6.19 | 57.77 |
| Fast | 500 | 100 | 38.50 | 6.30 | 2.57 | 38.50 | 14.68 | 4.34 | 66.39 |

STEP 4: Sanding sealer (material #11b)
Brush 1 coat
| | | | | | | | | | |
|---|---|---|---|---|---|---|---|---|---|
| Slow | 130 | 550 | 41.50 | 15.58 | 4.58 | 7.55 | 5.27 | 5.28 | 38.26 |
| Medium | 140 | 525 | 36.30 | 18.39 | 6.51 | 6.91 | 7.95 | 4.77 | 44.53 |
| Fast | 150 | 500 | 31.10 | 21.00 | 8.58 | 6.22 | 11.09 | 3.28 | 50.17 |

Spray 1 coat
| | | | | | | | | | |
|---|---|---|---|---|---|---|---|---|---|
| Slow | 375 | 175 | 41.50 | 5.40 | 1.60 | 23.71 | 5.83 | 5.84 | 42.38 |
| Medium | 475 | 138 | 36.30 | 5.42 | 1.94 | 26.30 | 8.41 | 5.05 | 47.12 |
| Fast | 575 | 100 | 31.10 | 5.48 | 2.24 | 31.10 | 12.03 | 3.56 | 54.41 |

STEP 5: Sand lightly
| | | | | | | | | | |
|---|---|---|---|---|---|---|---|---|---|
| Slow | 175 | -- | -- | 11.57 | 3.40 | -- | 2.85 | 2.85 | 20.67 |
| Medium | 225 | -- | -- | 11.44 | 4.04 | -- | 3.87 | 2.32 | 21.67 |
| Fast | 275 | -- | -- | 11.45 | 4.69 | -- | 5.00 | 1.48 | 22.62 |

STEP 6 & 7: Lacquer (material #11c), 2 coats
Brush 1st coat
| | | | | | | | | | |
|---|---|---|---|---|---|---|---|---|---|
| Slow | 140 | 400 | 45.90 | 14.46 | 4.26 | 11.48 | 5.74 | 5.75 | 41.69 |
| Medium | 185 | 375 | 40.10 | 13.92 | 4.94 | 10.69 | 7.39 | 4.43 | 41.37 |
| Fast | 245 | 350 | 34.40 | 12.86 | 5.23 | 9.83 | 8.66 | 2.56 | 39.14 |

Brush 2nd coat
| | | | | | | | | | |
|---|---|---|---|---|---|---|---|---|---|
| Slow | 155 | 425 | 45.90 | 13.06 | 3.85 | 10.80 | 5.26 | 5.28 | 38.25 |
| Medium | 208 | 413 | 40.10 | 12.38 | 4.39 | 9.71 | 6.62 | 3.97 | 37.07 |
| Fast | 260 | 400 | 34.40 | 12.12 | 4.95 | 8.60 | 7.95 | 2.35 | 35.97 |

Spray 1st coat
| | | | | | | | | | |
|---|---|---|---|---|---|---|---|---|---|
| Slow | 340 | 175 | 45.90 | 5.96 | 1.75 | 26.23 | 6.45 | 6.46 | 46.85 |
| Medium | 458 | 138 | 40.10 | 5.62 | 1.98 | 29.06 | 9.17 | 5.50 | 51.33 |
| Fast | 575 | 100 | 34.40 | 5.48 | 2.24 | 34.40 | 13.06 | 3.86 | 59.04 |

*General Painting Costs*

|  | Labor SF per manhour | Material coverage SF/gallon | Material cost per gallon | Labor cost per 100 SF | Labor burden 100 SF | Material cost per 100 SF | Overhead per 100 SF | Profit per 100 SF | Total price per 100 SF |
|---|---|---|---|---|---|---|---|---|---|
| **Spray 2nd coat** | | | | | | | | | |
| Slow | 430 | 200 | 45.90 | 4.71 | 1.40 | 22.95 | 5.52 | 5.53 | 40.11 |
| Medium | 530 | 163 | 40.10 | 4.86 | 1.73 | 24.60 | 7.80 | 4.68 | 43.67 |
| Fast | 630 | 125 | 34.40 | 5.00 | 2.05 | 27.52 | 6.57 | 6.58 | 47.72 |
| **Complete 7 step stain, seal & lacquer process (material #11)** | | | | | | | | | |
| *Brush all coats* | | | | | | | | | |
| Slow | 30 | 160 | 46.10 | 67.50 | 19.89 | 28.81 | 22.08 | 22.13 | 160.41 |
| Medium | 35 | 150 | 40.40 | 73.57 | 26.05 | 26.93 | 24.04 | 24.09 | 174.68 |
| Fast | 40 | 140 | 34.60 | 78.75 | 32.13 | 24.71 | 33.90 | 20.34 | 189.83 |
| *Spray all coats* | | | | | | | | | |
| Slow | 65 | 60 | 46.10 | 31.15 | 9.18 | 76.83 | 29.29 | 17.58 | 164.03 |
| Medium | 83 | 48 | 40.40 | 31.02 | 11.00 | 84.17 | 23.97 | 24.02 | 174.18 |
| Fast | 100 | 35 | 34.60 | 31.50 | 12.85 | 98.86 | 35.80 | 21.48 | 200.49 |
| **Shellac, clear (material #12)** | | | | | | | | | |
| *Brush each coat* | | | | | | | | | |
| Slow | 205 | 570 | 73.10 | 9.88 | 2.92 | 12.82 | 4.87 | 4.88 | 35.37 |
| Medium | 230 | 545 | 63.90 | 11.20 | 3.97 | 11.72 | 6.72 | 4.03 | 37.64 |
| Fast | 255 | 520 | 54.80 | 12.35 | 5.04 | 10.54 | 8.66 | 2.56 | 39.15 |
| **Varnish, flat or gloss (material #30c)** | | | | | | | | | |
| *Brush each coat* | | | | | | | | | |
| Slow | 175 | 450 | 81.70 | 11.57 | 3.40 | 18.16 | 6.30 | 6.31 | 45.74 |
| Medium | 200 | 438 | 71.50 | 12.88 | 4.56 | 16.32 | 8.44 | 5.06 | 47.26 |
| Fast | 225 | 425 | 61.30 | 14.00 | 5.69 | 14.42 | 10.58 | 3.13 | 47.82 |
| **Penetrating stain wax (material #14) & polish** | | | | | | | | | |
| *Brush 1st coat* | | | | | | | | | |
| Slow | 150 | 595 | 46.70 | 13.50 | 3.99 | 7.85 | 4.81 | 4.82 | 34.97 |
| Medium | 175 | 558 | 40.90 | 14.71 | 5.20 | 7.33 | 6.81 | 4.09 | 38.14 |
| Fast | 200 | 520 | 35.00 | 15.75 | 6.43 | 6.73 | 8.96 | 2.65 | 40.52 |
| *Brush 2nd or additional coats* | | | | | | | | | |
| Slow | 175 | 600 | 46.70 | 11.57 | 3.40 | 7.78 | 5.69 | 3.41 | 31.85 |
| Medium | 200 | 575 | 40.90 | 12.88 | 4.56 | 7.11 | 4.66 | 4.67 | 33.88 |
| Fast | 225 | 550 | 35.00 | 14.00 | 5.69 | 6.36 | 6.52 | 3.91 | 36.48 |

Bookcase and shelf estimates are based on overall dimensions (length times width) to 8 feet high and include painting all exposed surfaces (including stiles, interior shelves and backs). For heights above 8 feet, use the High Time Difficulty Factors on page 139. "Slow" work is based on an hourly wage of $20.25, "Medium" work on an hourly wage of $25.75, and "Fast" work on an hourly wage of $31.50. Other qualifications that apply to this table are on page 9.

*National Painting Cost Estimator*

|  | Labor SF per manhour | Material coverage SF/gallon | Material cost per gallon | Labor cost per 100 SF | Labor burden 100 SF | Material cost per 100 SF | Overhead per 100 SF | Profit per 100 SF | Total price per 100 SF |
|---|---|---|---|---|---|---|---|---|---|
| **Cabinet backs, paint grade, brush** | | | | | | | | | |
| *Flat latex, water base (material #5)* | | | | | | | | | |
| Brush each coat | | | | | | | | | |
| Slow | 100 | 300 | 36.70 | 20.25 | 5.97 | 12.23 | 7.31 | 7.32 | 53.08 |
| Medium | 150 | 275 | 32.10 | 17.17 | 6.09 | 11.67 | 8.73 | 5.24 | 48.90 |
| Fast | 200 | 250 | 27.50 | 15.75 | 6.43 | 11.00 | 10.29 | 3.04 | 46.51 |
| *Enamel, water base (material #9)* | | | | | | | | | |
| Brush each coat | | | | | | | | | |
| Slow | 80 | 275 | 46.80 | 25.31 | 7.47 | 17.02 | 9.46 | 9.48 | 68.74 |
| Medium | 130 | 250 | 41.00 | 19.81 | 7.01 | 16.40 | 10.81 | 6.48 | 60.51 |
| Fast | 175 | 225 | 35.10 | 18.00 | 7.32 | 15.60 | 12.69 | 3.75 | 57.36 |
| *Enamel, oil base (material #10)* | | | | | | | | | |
| Brush each coat | | | | | | | | | |
| Slow | 80 | 275 | 61.70 | 25.31 | 7.47 | 22.44 | 10.49 | 10.51 | 76.22 |
| Medium | 130 | 250 | 54.00 | 19.81 | 7.01 | 21.60 | 12.11 | 7.26 | 67.79 |
| Fast | 175 | 225 | 46.30 | 18.00 | 7.32 | 20.58 | 14.24 | 4.21 | 64.35 |

Cabinet back estimates are based on overall dimensions (length times width) to 8 feet high and include painting the inside back wall of paint grade or stain grade cabinets. ADD for preparation time. For heights above 8 feet, use the High Time Difficulty Factors on page 139. Measurements are based on total area of cabinet faces. "Slow" work is based on an hourly wage of $20.25, "Medium" work on an hourly wage of $25.75, and "Fast" work on an hourly wage of $31.50. Other qualifications that apply to this table are on page 9.

|  | Labor SF per manhour | Material coverage SF/gallon | Material cost per gallon | Labor cost per 100 SF | Labor burden 100 SF | Material cost per 100 SF | Overhead per 100 SF | Profit per 100 SF | Total price per 100 SF |
|---|---|---|---|---|---|---|---|---|---|
| **Cabinet faces, stain grade** | | | | | | | | | |
| *Complete 7 step stain, seal & 2 coat lacquer system (material #11)* | | | | | | | | | |
| Brush all coats | | | | | | | | | |
| Slow | 20 | 190 | 46.10 | 101.25 | 29.85 | 24.26 | 29.52 | 29.58 | 214.46 |
| Medium | 35 | 178 | 40.40 | 73.57 | 26.05 | 22.70 | 30.58 | 18.35 | 171.25 |
| Fast | 50 | 165 | 34.60 | 63.00 | 25.70 | 20.97 | 34.00 | 10.06 | 153.73 |
| Spray all coats | | | | | | | | | |
| Slow | 85 | 67 | 46.10 | 23.82 | 7.01 | 68.81 | 18.94 | 18.98 | 137.56 |
| Medium | 110 | 51 | 40.40 | 23.41 | 8.29 | 79.22 | 27.73 | 16.64 | 155.29 |
| Fast | 135 | 35 | 34.60 | 23.33 | 9.53 | 98.86 | 40.83 | 12.08 | 184.63 |

Cabinet face estimates are based on overall dimensions (length times width) to 8 feet high. Use these figures to estimate finishing the faces of stain grade kitchen, bar, linen, pullman or vanity cabinets. ADD for preparation time. For heights above 8 feet, use the High Time Difficulty Factors on page 139. Measurements are based on total area of cabinet faces. "Slow" work is based on an hourly wage of $20.25, "Medium" work on an hourly wage of $25.75, and "Fast" work on an hourly wage of $31.50. Other qualifications that apply to this table are on page 9.

*General Painting Costs*

|  | Labor SF per manhour | Material coverage SF/gallon | Material cost per gallon | Labor cost per 100 SF | Labor burden 100 SF | Material cost per 100 SF | Overhead per 100 SF | Profit per 100 SF | Total price per 100 SF |
|---|---|---|---|---|---|---|---|---|---|
| **Cabinets, paint grade, roll and brush** | | | | | | | | | |
| Undercoat, water base (material #3) | | | | | | | | | |
|   Roll & brush, 1 coat | | | | | | | | | |
|     Slow | 75 | 260 | 32.60 | 27.00 | 7.95 | 12.54 | 9.03 | 9.05 | 65.57 |
|     Medium | 93 | 250 | 28.50 | 27.69 | 9.80 | 11.40 | 12.22 | 7.33 | 68.44 |
|     Fast | 110 | 240 | 24.50 | 28.64 | 11.67 | 10.21 | 15.67 | 4.63 | 70.82 |
| Undercoat, oil base (material #4) | | | | | | | | | |
|   Roll & brush, 1 coat | | | | | | | | | |
|     Slow | 75 | 275 | 42.30 | 27.00 | 7.95 | 15.38 | 9.57 | 9.59 | 69.49 |
|     Medium | 93 | 268 | 37.00 | 27.69 | 9.80 | 13.81 | 12.83 | 7.70 | 71.83 |
|     Fast | 110 | 250 | 31.80 | 28.64 | 11.67 | 12.72 | 16.45 | 4.87 | 74.35 |
| Split coat (1/2 undercoat + 1/2 enamel), water base (material #3 + #9) | | | | | | | | | |
|   Roll & brush each coat | | | | | | | | | |
|     Slow | 95 | 310 | 39.70 | 21.32 | 6.29 | 12.81 | 7.68 | 7.70 | 55.80 |
|     Medium | 113 | 298 | 34.75 | 22.79 | 8.07 | 11.66 | 10.63 | 6.38 | 59.53 |
|     Fast | 130 | 285 | 29.80 | 24.23 | 9.88 | 10.46 | 13.82 | 4.09 | 62.48 |
| Split coat (1/2 undercoat + 1/2 enamel), oil base (material #4 + #10) | | | | | | | | | |
|   Roll & brush each coat | | | | | | | | | |
|     Slow | 95 | 310 | 52.00 | 21.32 | 6.29 | 16.77 | 8.43 | 8.45 | 61.26 |
|     Medium | 113 | 298 | 45.50 | 22.79 | 8.07 | 15.27 | 11.53 | 6.92 | 64.58 |
|     Fast | 130 | 285 | 39.05 | 24.23 | 9.88 | 13.70 | 14.82 | 4.38 | 67.01 |
| Enamel, water base (material #9) | | | | | | | | | |
|   Roll & brush 1st finish coat | | | | | | | | | |
|     Slow | 85 | 300 | 46.80 | 23.82 | 7.01 | 15.60 | 8.83 | 8.84 | 64.10 |
|     Medium | 103 | 288 | 41.00 | 25.00 | 8.86 | 14.24 | 12.02 | 7.21 | 67.33 |
|     Fast | 120 | 275 | 35.10 | 26.25 | 10.69 | 12.76 | 15.41 | 4.56 | 69.67 |
|   Roll & brush 2nd or additional finish coats | | | | | | | | | |
|     Slow | 95 | 310 | 46.80 | 21.32 | 6.29 | 15.10 | 8.11 | 8.13 | 58.95 |
|     Medium | 113 | 298 | 41.00 | 22.79 | 8.07 | 13.76 | 11.16 | 6.69 | 62.47 |
|     Fast | 130 | 285 | 35.10 | 24.23 | 9.88 | 12.32 | 14.40 | 4.26 | 65.09 |
| Enamel, oil base (material #10) | | | | | | | | | |
|   Roll & brush 1st finish coat | | | | | | | | | |
|     Slow | 85 | 300 | 61.70 | 23.82 | 7.01 | 20.57 | 9.77 | 9.79 | 70.96 |
|     Medium | 103 | 288 | 54.00 | 25.00 | 8.86 | 18.75 | 13.15 | 7.89 | 73.65 |
|     Fast | 120 | 275 | 46.30 | 26.25 | 10.69 | 16.84 | 16.68 | 4.93 | 75.39 |
|   Roll & brush 2nd or additional finish coats | | | | | | | | | |
|     Slow | 95 | 310 | 61.70 | 21.32 | 6.29 | 19.90 | 9.03 | 9.05 | 65.59 |
|     Medium | 113 | 298 | 54.00 | 22.79 | 8.07 | 18.12 | 12.25 | 7.35 | 68.58 |
|     Fast | 130 | 285 | 46.30 | 24.23 | 9.88 | 16.25 | 15.61 | 4.62 | 70.59 |

Cabinet estimates are based on overall dimensions (length times width) to 8 feet high and include painting the cabinet face, back of doors, stiles and rails. See Cabinet backs for painting the inside back wall of the cabinets. Use these figures to estimate paint grade kitchen cabinets. Use the Opening Count Method to estimate paint grade pullmans, vanities, bars or linen cabinets. For heights above 8 feet, apply the High Time Difficulty Factors to labor costs and the labor burden cost categories and add these figures to the total cost. Measurements are based on total area of cabinet faces. "Slow" work is based on an hourly wage of $20.25, "Medium" work on an hourly wage of $25.75, and "Fast" work on an hourly wage of $31.50. Other qualifications that apply to this table are on page 9.

*National Painting Cost Estimator*

|  | Labor SF per manhour | Material coverage SF/gallon | Material cost per gallon | Labor cost per 100 SF | Labor burden 100 SF | Material cost per 100 SF | Overhead per 100 SF | Profit per 100 SF | Total price per 100 SF |
|---|---|---|---|---|---|---|---|---|---|
| **Cabinets, paint grade, spray application** | | | | | | | | | |
| Undercoat, water base (material #3) | | | | | | | | | |
| Spray 1 coat | | | | | | | | | |
| Slow | 125 | 125 | 32.60 | 16.20 | 4.78 | 26.08 | 8.94 | 8.96 | 64.96 |
| Medium | 140 | 113 | 28.50 | 18.39 | 6.51 | 25.22 | 12.53 | 7.52 | 70.17 |
| Fast | 155 | 100 | 24.50 | 20.32 | 8.29 | 24.50 | 16.46 | 4.87 | 74.44 |
| Undercoat, oil base (material #4) | | | | | | | | | |
| Spray 1 coat | | | | | | | | | |
| Slow | 125 | 135 | 42.30 | 16.20 | 4.78 | 31.33 | 9.94 | 9.96 | 72.21 |
| Medium | 140 | 123 | 37.00 | 18.39 | 6.51 | 30.08 | 13.75 | 8.25 | 76.98 |
| Fast | 155 | 110 | 31.80 | 20.32 | 8.29 | 28.91 | 17.83 | 5.27 | 80.62 |
| Split coat (1/2 undercoat + 1/2 enamel), water base (material #3 + #9) | | | | | | | | | |
| Spray each coat | | | | | | | | | |
| Slow | 200 | 175 | 39.70 | 10.13 | 2.98 | 22.69 | 6.80 | 6.82 | 49.42 |
| Medium | 225 | 163 | 34.75 | 11.44 | 4.04 | 21.32 | 9.20 | 5.52 | 51.52 |
| Fast | 250 | 150 | 29.80 | 12.60 | 5.14 | 19.87 | 11.66 | 3.45 | 52.72 |
| Split coat (1/2 undercoat + 1/2 enamel), oil base (material #4 + #10) | | | | | | | | | |
| Spray each coat | | | | | | | | | |
| Slow | 200 | 175 | 52.00 | 10.13 | 2.98 | 29.71 | 8.14 | 8.16 | 59.12 |
| Medium | 225 | 163 | 45.50 | 11.44 | 4.04 | 27.91 | 10.85 | 6.51 | 60.75 |
| Fast | 250 | 150 | 39.05 | 12.60 | 5.14 | 26.03 | 13.57 | 4.01 | 61.35 |
| Enamel, water base (material #9) | | | | | | | | | |
| Spray 1st finish coat | | | | | | | | | |
| Slow | 185 | 150 | 46.80 | 10.95 | 3.24 | 31.20 | 8.62 | 8.64 | 62.65 |
| Medium | 210 | 138 | 41.00 | 12.26 | 4.34 | 29.71 | 11.58 | 6.95 | 64.84 |
| Fast | 235 | 125 | 35.10 | 13.40 | 5.49 | 28.08 | 14.55 | 4.31 | 65.83 |
| Spray 2nd or additional finish coats | | | | | | | | | |
| Slow | 200 | 175 | 46.80 | 10.13 | 2.98 | 26.74 | 7.57 | 7.59 | 55.01 |
| Medium | 225 | 163 | 41.00 | 11.44 | 4.04 | 25.15 | 10.16 | 6.10 | 56.89 |
| Fast | 250 | 150 | 35.10 | 12.60 | 5.14 | 23.40 | 12.75 | 3.77 | 57.66 |
| Enamel, oil base (material #10) | | | | | | | | | |
| Spray 1st finish coat | | | | | | | | | |
| Slow | 185 | 160 | 61.70 | 10.95 | 3.24 | 38.56 | 10.02 | 10.04 | 72.81 |
| Medium | 210 | 148 | 54.00 | 12.26 | 4.34 | 36.49 | 13.27 | 7.96 | 74.32 |
| Fast | 235 | 135 | 46.30 | 13.40 | 5.49 | 34.30 | 16.48 | 4.88 | 74.55 |
| Spray 2nd or additional finish coats | | | | | | | | | |
| Slow | 200 | 185 | 61.70 | 10.13 | 2.98 | 33.35 | 8.83 | 8.85 | 64.14 |
| Medium | 225 | 173 | 54.00 | 11.44 | 4.04 | 31.21 | 11.68 | 7.01 | 65.38 |
| Fast | 250 | 160 | 46.30 | 12.60 | 5.14 | 28.94 | 14.47 | 4.28 | 65.43 |

Cabinet estimates are based on overall dimensions (length times width) to 8 feet high and include painting the cabinet face, back of doors, stiles and rails. See Cabinet backs for painting the inside back wall of the cabinets. Use these figures to estimate paint grade kitchen cabinets. Use the Opening Count Method to estimate paint grade pullmans, vanities, bars or linen cabinets. For heights above 8 feet, apply the High Time Difficulty Factors to labor costs and the labor burden cost categories and add these figures to the total cost. Measurements are based on total area of cabinet faces. "Slow" work is based on an hourly wage of $20.25, "Medium" work on an hourly wage of $25.75, and "Fast" work on an hourly wage of $31.50. Other qualifications that apply to this table are on page 9.

*General Painting Costs*

|  | Labor SF per manhour | Material coverage SF/gallon | Material cost per gallon | Labor cost per 100 SF | Labor burden 100 SF | Material cost per 100 SF | Overhead per 100 SF | Profit per 100 SF | Total price per 100 SF |
|---|---|---|---|---|---|---|---|---|---|

## Cabinets, stain grade
### Stain, seal & 2 coats lacquer system (7 step process)
**STEP 1: Sand & putty;**

| | | | | | | | | | |
|---|---|---|---|---|---|---|---|---|---|
| Slow | 125 | -- | -- | 16.20 | 4.78 | -- | 3.99 | 4.00 | 28.97 |
| Medium | 150 | -- | -- | 17.17 | 6.09 | -- | 5.81 | 3.49 | 32.56 |
| Fast | 175 | -- | -- | 18.00 | 7.32 | -- | 7.86 | 2.32 | 35.50 |

**STEP 2 & 3: Stain (material #11a) & wipe**
Brush 1 coat & wipe

| | | | | | | | | | |
|---|---|---|---|---|---|---|---|---|---|
| Slow | 65 | 450 | 51.30 | 31.15 | 9.18 | 11.40 | 9.83 | 9.85 | 71.41 |
| Medium | 75 | 400 | 44.90 | 34.33 | 12.15 | 11.23 | 14.43 | 8.66 | 80.80 |
| Fast | 85 | 350 | 38.50 | 37.06 | 15.10 | 11.00 | 19.59 | 5.79 | 88.54 |

Spray 1 coat & wipe

| | | | | | | | | | |
|---|---|---|---|---|---|---|---|---|---|
| Slow | 250 | 175 | 51.30 | 8.10 | 2.39 | 29.31 | 7.56 | 7.58 | 54.94 |
| Medium | 350 | 138 | 44.90 | 7.36 | 2.61 | 32.54 | 10.63 | 6.38 | 59.52 |
| Fast | 450 | 100 | 38.50 | 7.00 | 2.85 | 38.50 | 14.99 | 4.43 | 67.77 |

**STEP 4: Sanding sealer (material #11b)**
Brush 1 coat

| | | | | | | | | | |
|---|---|---|---|---|---|---|---|---|---|
| Slow | 110 | 450 | 41.50 | 18.41 | 5.42 | 9.22 | 6.28 | 6.29 | 45.62 |
| Medium | 120 | 425 | 36.30 | 21.46 | 7.59 | 8.54 | 9.40 | 5.64 | 52.63 |
| Fast | 130 | 400 | 31.10 | 24.23 | 9.88 | 7.78 | 12.99 | 3.84 | 58.72 |

Spray 1 coat

| | | | | | | | | | |
|---|---|---|---|---|---|---|---|---|---|
| Slow | 330 | 175 | 41.50 | 6.14 | 1.80 | 23.71 | 6.02 | 6.03 | 43.70 |
| Medium | 430 | 138 | 36.30 | 5.99 | 2.13 | 26.30 | 8.60 | 5.16 | 48.18 |
| Fast | 530 | 100 | 31.10 | 5.94 | 2.44 | 31.10 | 12.23 | 3.62 | 55.33 |

**STEP 5: Sand lightly**

| | | | | | | | | | |
|---|---|---|---|---|---|---|---|---|---|
| Slow | 200 | -- | -- | 10.13 | 2.98 | -- | 2.49 | 2.50 | 18.10 |
| Medium | 250 | -- | -- | 10.30 | 3.65 | -- | 3.49 | 2.09 | 19.53 |
| Fast | 300 | -- | -- | 10.50 | 4.27 | -- | 4.58 | 1.36 | 20.71 |

**STEP 6 & 7: Lacquer (material #11c), 2 coats**
Brush 1st coat

| | | | | | | | | | |
|---|---|---|---|---|---|---|---|---|---|
| Slow | 120 | 375 | 45.90 | 16.88 | 4.96 | 12.24 | 6.48 | 6.49 | 47.05 |
| Medium | 165 | 350 | 40.10 | 15.61 | 5.52 | 11.46 | 8.15 | 4.89 | 45.63 |
| Fast | 215 | 325 | 34.40 | 14.65 | 5.97 | 10.58 | 9.68 | 2.86 | 43.74 |

Brush 2nd coat

| | | | | | | | | | |
|---|---|---|---|---|---|---|---|---|---|
| Slow | 130 | 400 | 45.90 | 15.58 | 4.58 | 11.48 | 6.02 | 6.03 | 43.69 |
| Medium | 173 | 388 | 40.10 | 14.88 | 5.27 | 10.34 | 7.62 | 4.57 | 42.68 |
| Fast | 225 | 375 | 34.40 | 14.00 | 5.69 | 9.17 | 8.95 | 2.65 | 40.46 |

Spray 1st coat

| | | | | | | | | | |
|---|---|---|---|---|---|---|---|---|---|
| Slow | 275 | 150 | 45.90 | 7.36 | 2.18 | 30.60 | 7.62 | 7.64 | 55.40 |
| Medium | 388 | 100 | 40.10 | 6.64 | 2.36 | 40.10 | 12.27 | 7.36 | 68.73 |
| Fast | 500 | 75 | 34.40 | 6.30 | 2.57 | 45.87 | 16.97 | 5.02 | 76.73 |

*National Painting Cost Estimator*

|  | Labor SF per manhour | Material coverage SF/gallon | Material cost per gallon | Labor cost per 100 SF | Labor burden 100 SF | Material cost per 100 SF | Overhead per 100 SF | Profit per 100 SF | Total price per 100 SF |
|---|---|---|---|---|---|---|---|---|---|
| **Spray 2nd coat** | | | | | | | | | |
| Slow | 350 | 200 | 45.90 | 5.79 | 1.71 | 22.95 | 5.79 | 5.80 | 42.04 |
| Medium | 475 | 163 | 40.10 | 5.42 | 1.94 | 24.60 | 7.99 | 4.79 | 44.74 |
| Fast | 600 | 125 | 34.40 | 5.25 | 2.16 | 27.52 | 10.82 | 3.20 | 48.95 |
| **Complete 7 step stain, seal & 2 coat lacquer system (material #11)** | | | | | | | | | |
| *Brush all coats* | | | | | | | | | |
| Slow | 20 | 125 | 46.10 | 101.25 | 29.85 | 36.88 | 31.92 | 31.99 | 231.89 |
| Medium | 25 | 113 | 40.40 | 103.00 | 36.48 | 35.75 | 43.80 | 26.28 | 245.31 |
| Fast | 30 | 100 | 34.60 | 105.00 | 42.82 | 34.60 | 56.56 | 16.73 | 255.71 |
| *Spray all coats* | | | | | | | | | |
| Slow | 40 | 40 | 46.10 | 50.63 | 14.92 | 115.25 | 34.36 | 34.43 | 249.59 |
| Medium | 50 | 30 | 40.40 | 51.50 | 18.24 | 134.67 | 51.10 | 30.66 | 286.17 |
| Fast | 60 | 21 | 34.60 | 52.50 | 21.43 | 164.76 | 73.99 | 21.89 | 334.57 |
| **Shellac, clear (material #12)** | | | | | | | | | |
| *Brush each coat* | | | | | | | | | |
| Slow | 175 | 525 | 73.10 | 11.57 | 3.40 | 13.92 | 7.23 | 4.34 | 40.46 |
| Medium | 200 | 513 | 63.90 | 12.88 | 4.56 | 12.46 | 9.27 | 2.74 | 41.91 |
| Fast | 225 | 500 | 54.80 | 14.00 | 5.69 | 10.96 | 9.51 | 2.81 | 42.97 |
| **Varnish, flat or gloss (material #30c)** | | | | | | | | | |
| *Brush each coat* | | | | | | | | | |
| Slow | 155 | 475 | 81.70 | 13.06 | 3.85 | 17.20 | 10.57 | 3.13 | 47.81 |
| Medium | 180 | 463 | 71.50 | 14.31 | 5.08 | 15.44 | 6.62 | 6.63 | 48.08 |
| Fast | 205 | 450 | 61.30 | 15.37 | 6.27 | 13.62 | 8.82 | 5.29 | 49.37 |
| **Penetrating stain wax (material #14) & polish** | | | | | | | | | |
| *Brush 1st coat* | | | | | | | | | |
| Slow | 125 | 575 | 46.70 | 16.20 | 4.78 | 8.12 | 9.02 | 2.67 | 40.79 |
| Medium | 150 | 538 | 40.90 | 17.17 | 6.09 | 7.60 | 5.86 | 5.87 | 42.59 |
| Fast | 175 | 500 | 35.00 | 18.00 | 7.32 | 7.00 | 8.09 | 4.85 | 45.26 |
| *Brush 2nd or additional coats* | | | | | | | | | |
| Slow | 150 | 600 | 46.70 | 13.50 | 3.99 | 7.78 | 7.83 | 2.32 | 35.42 |
| Medium | 175 | 575 | 40.90 | 14.71 | 5.20 | 7.11 | 8.38 | 2.48 | 37.88 |
| Fast | 200 | 550 | 35.00 | 15.75 | 6.43 | 6.36 | 5.42 | 5.43 | 39.39 |

Cabinet estimates are based on overall dimensions (length times width) to 8 feet high. Use these figures to estimate stain grade kitchen, bar, linen, pullman or vanity cabinets. For the stain, seal and lacquer process, the figures include finishing both sides of cabinet doors, stiles and rails with a fog coat of stain on shelves and the wall behind the cabinet (cabinet back). See Cabinet backs for painting the inside back wall of the cabinets. For heights above 8 feet, use the High Time Difficulty Factors on page 139. Measurements are based on total area of cabinet faces. "Slow" work is based on an hourly wage of $20.25, "Medium" work on an hourly wage of $25.75, and "Fast" work on an hourly wage of $31.50. Other qualifications that apply to this table are on page 9.

*General Painting Costs*

|  | Labor SF per manhour | Material coverage SF/gallon | Material cost per gallon | Labor cost per 100 SF | Labor burden 100 SF | Material cost per 100 SF | Overhead per 100 SF | Profit per 100 SF | Total price per 100 SF |
|---|---|---|---|---|---|---|---|---|---|

## Ceiling panels, suspended, fiber panels in T-bar frames, brush application

Flat latex, water base (material #5)
  Brush 1st coat

| | | | | | | | | | |
|---|---|---|---|---|---|---|---|---|---|
| Slow | 80 | 260 | 36.70 | 25.31 | 7.47 | 14.12 | 8.91 | 8.93 | 64.74 |
| Medium | 110 | 230 | 32.10 | 23.41 | 8.29 | 13.96 | 11.42 | 6.85 | 63.93 |
| Fast | 140 | 200 | 27.50 | 22.50 | 9.17 | 13.75 | 14.08 | 4.17 | 63.67 |

  Brush 2nd or additional coats

| | | | | | | | | | |
|---|---|---|---|---|---|---|---|---|---|
| Slow | 130 | 300 | 36.70 | 15.58 | 4.58 | 12.23 | 6.16 | 6.17 | 44.72 |
| Medium | 150 | 275 | 32.10 | 17.17 | 6.09 | 11.67 | 8.73 | 5.24 | 48.90 |
| Fast | 170 | 250 | 27.50 | 18.53 | 7.55 | 11.00 | 11.50 | 3.40 | 51.98 |

Enamel, water base (material #9)
  Brush 1st coat

| | | | | | | | | | |
|---|---|---|---|---|---|---|---|---|---|
| Slow | 65 | 260 | 46.80 | 31.15 | 9.18 | 18.00 | 11.08 | 11.11 | 80.52 |
| Medium | 100 | 230 | 41.00 | 25.75 | 9.12 | 17.83 | 13.18 | 7.91 | 73.79 |
| Fast | 125 | 200 | 35.10 | 25.20 | 10.28 | 17.55 | 16.44 | 4.86 | 74.33 |

  Brush 2nd or additional coats

| | | | | | | | | | |
|---|---|---|---|---|---|---|---|---|---|
| Slow | 115 | 300 | 46.80 | 17.61 | 5.20 | 15.60 | 7.30 | 7.31 | 53.02 |
| Medium | 135 | 275 | 41.00 | 19.07 | 6.77 | 14.91 | 10.18 | 6.11 | 57.04 |
| Fast | 155 | 250 | 35.10 | 20.32 | 8.29 | 14.04 | 13.22 | 3.91 | 59.78 |

Enamel, oil base (material #10)
  Brush 1st coat

| | | | | | | | | | |
|---|---|---|---|---|---|---|---|---|---|
| Slow | 65 | 250 | 61.70 | 31.15 | 9.18 | 24.68 | 12.35 | 12.38 | 89.74 |
| Medium | 95 | 213 | 54.00 | 27.11 | 9.61 | 25.35 | 15.52 | 9.31 | 86.90 |
| Fast | 125 | 175 | 46.30 | 25.20 | 10.28 | 26.46 | 19.20 | 5.68 | 86.82 |

  Brush 2nd or additional coats

| | | | | | | | | | |
|---|---|---|---|---|---|---|---|---|---|
| Slow | 115 | 275 | 61.70 | 17.61 | 5.20 | 22.44 | 8.60 | 8.61 | 62.46 |
| Medium | 135 | 260 | 54.00 | 19.07 | 6.77 | 20.77 | 11.65 | 6.99 | 65.25 |
| Fast | 155 | 240 | 46.30 | 20.32 | 8.29 | 19.29 | 14.85 | 4.39 | 67.14 |

Ceiling panel estimates are based on overall dimensions (length times width) to 8 feet high. Do not make deductions for openings in the ceiling area that are under 100 square feet. For heights above 8 feet, use the High Time Difficulty Factors on page 139. "Slow" work is based on an hourly wage of $20.25, "Medium" work on an hourly wage of $25.75, and "Fast" work on an hourly wage of $31.50. Other qualifications that apply to this table are on page 9.

*National Painting Cost Estimator*

|  | Labor SF per manhour | Material coverage SF/gallon | Material cost per gallon | Labor cost per 100 SF | Labor burden 100 SF | Material cost per 100 SF | Overhead per 100 SF | Profit per 100 SF | Total price per 100 SF |
|---|---|---|---|---|---|---|---|---|---|

## Ceiling panels, suspended, fiber panels in T-bar frame, roll application

Flat latex, water base (material #5)
  Roll 1st coat

| | | | | | | | | | |
|---|---|---|---|---|---|---|---|---|---|
| Slow | 150 | 270 | 36.70 | 13.50 | 3.99 | 13.59 | 5.90 | 5.92 | 42.90 |
| Medium | 215 | 235 | 32.10 | 11.98 | 4.23 | 13.66 | 7.47 | 4.48 | 41.82 |
| Fast | 280 | 200 | 27.50 | 11.25 | 4.58 | 13.75 | 9.17 | 2.71 | 41.46 |

  Roll 2nd or additional coats

| | | | | | | | | | |
|---|---|---|---|---|---|---|---|---|---|
| Slow | 225 | 280 | 36.70 | 9.00 | 2.64 | 13.11 | 4.71 | 4.72 | 34.18 |
| Medium | 288 | 260 | 32.10 | 8.94 | 3.16 | 12.35 | 6.11 | 3.67 | 34.23 |
| Fast | 350 | 240 | 27.50 | 9.00 | 3.68 | 11.46 | 7.48 | 2.21 | 33.83 |

Enamel, water base (material #9)
  Roll 1st coat

| | | | | | | | | | |
|---|---|---|---|---|---|---|---|---|---|
| Slow | 135 | 250 | 46.80 | 15.00 | 4.43 | 18.72 | 7.25 | 7.26 | 52.66 |
| Medium | 200 | 220 | 41.00 | 12.88 | 4.56 | 18.64 | 9.02 | 5.41 | 50.51 |
| Fast | 265 | 190 | 35.10 | 11.89 | 4.83 | 18.47 | 10.92 | 3.23 | 49.34 |

  Roll 2nd or additional finish coats

| | | | | | | | | | |
|---|---|---|---|---|---|---|---|---|---|
| Slow | 210 | 280 | 46.80 | 9.64 | 2.84 | 16.71 | 5.55 | 5.56 | 40.30 |
| Medium | 273 | 260 | 41.00 | 9.43 | 3.33 | 15.77 | 7.14 | 4.28 | 39.95 |
| Fast | 335 | 240 | 35.10 | 9.40 | 3.86 | 14.63 | 8.64 | 2.56 | 39.09 |

Enamel, oil base (material #10)
  Roll 1st coat

| | | | | | | | | | |
|---|---|---|---|---|---|---|---|---|---|
| Slow | 135 | 240 | 61.70 | 15.00 | 4.43 | 25.71 | 8.58 | 8.60 | 62.32 |
| Medium | 200 | 230 | 54.00 | 12.88 | 4.56 | 23.48 | 10.23 | 6.14 | 57.29 |
| Fast | 265 | 210 | 46.30 | 11.89 | 4.83 | 22.05 | 12.02 | 3.56 | 54.35 |

  Roll 2nd or additional finish coats

| | | | | | | | | | |
|---|---|---|---|---|---|---|---|---|---|
| Slow | 210 | 275 | 61.70 | 9.64 | 2.84 | 22.44 | 6.63 | 6.65 | 48.20 |
| Medium | 273 | 250 | 54.00 | 9.43 | 3.33 | 21.60 | 8.59 | 5.16 | 48.11 |
| Fast | 335 | 230 | 46.30 | 9.40 | 3.86 | 20.13 | 10.34 | 3.06 | 46.79 |

Ceiling panel estimates are based on overall dimensions (length times width) to 8 feet high. Do not make deductions for openings in the ceiling area that are under 100 square feet. For heights above 8 feet, use the High Time Difficulty Factors on page 139. "Slow" work is based on an hourly wage of $20.25, "Medium" work on an hourly wage of $25.75, and "Fast" work on an hourly wage of $31.50. Other qualifications that apply to this table are on page 9.

*General Painting Costs*

|  | Labor SF per manhour | Material coverage SF/gallon | Material cost per gallon | Labor cost per 100 SF | Labor burden 100 SF | Material cost per 100 SF | Overhead per 100 SF | Profit per 100 SF | Total price per 100 SF |
|---|---|---|---|---|---|---|---|---|---|

## Ceiling panels, suspended, fiber panels in T-bar frame, spray application

Flat latex, water base (material #5)
  Spray 1st coat

|  | | | | | | | | | |
|---|---|---|---|---|---|---|---|---|---|
| Slow | 300 | 250 | 36.70 | 6.75 | 1.98 | 14.68 | 4.45 | 4.46 | 32.32 |
| Medium | 345 | 238 | 32.10 | 7.46 | 2.65 | 13.49 | 5.90 | 3.54 | 33.04 |
| Fast | 390 | 225 | 27.50 | 8.08 | 3.27 | 12.22 | 7.32 | 2.16 | 33.05 |

  Spray 2nd or additional coats

|  | | | | | | | | | |
|---|---|---|---|---|---|---|---|---|---|
| Slow | 500 | 270 | 36.70 | 4.05 | 1.19 | 13.59 | 3.58 | 3.59 | 26.00 |
| Medium | 545 | 260 | 32.10 | 4.72 | 1.66 | 12.35 | 4.69 | 2.81 | 26.23 |
| Fast | 590 | 250 | 27.50 | 5.34 | 2.16 | 11.00 | 5.74 | 1.70 | 25.94 |

Enamel, water base (material #9)
  Spray 1st coat

|  | | | | | | | | | |
|---|---|---|---|---|---|---|---|---|---|
| Slow | 275 | 250 | 46.80 | 7.36 | 2.18 | 18.72 | 5.37 | 5.38 | 39.01 |
| Medium | 325 | 238 | 41.00 | 7.92 | 2.82 | 17.23 | 6.99 | 4.19 | 39.15 |
| Fast | 375 | 225 | 35.10 | 8.40 | 3.44 | 15.60 | 8.50 | 2.52 | 38.46 |

  Spray 2nd or additional coats

|  | | | | | | | | | |
|---|---|---|---|---|---|---|---|---|---|
| Slow | 450 | 275 | 46.80 | 4.50 | 1.32 | 17.02 | 4.34 | 4.35 | 31.53 |
| Medium | 500 | 263 | 41.00 | 5.15 | 1.82 | 15.59 | 5.64 | 3.38 | 31.58 |
| Fast | 550 | 250 | 35.10 | 5.73 | 2.34 | 14.04 | 6.85 | 2.03 | 30.99 |

Enamel, oil base (material #10)
  Spray 1st coat

|  | | | | | | | | | |
|---|---|---|---|---|---|---|---|---|---|
| Slow | 275 | 240 | 61.70 | 7.36 | 2.18 | 25.71 | 6.70 | 6.71 | 48.66 |
| Medium | 325 | 220 | 54.00 | 7.92 | 2.82 | 24.55 | 8.82 | 5.29 | 49.40 |
| Fast | 375 | 200 | 46.30 | 8.40 | 3.44 | 23.15 | 10.84 | 3.21 | 49.04 |

  Spray 2nd or additional coats

|  | | | | | | | | | |
|---|---|---|---|---|---|---|---|---|---|
| Slow | 450 | 250 | 61.70 | 4.50 | 1.32 | 24.68 | 5.80 | 5.81 | 42.11 |
| Medium | 500 | 238 | 54.00 | 5.15 | 1.82 | 22.69 | 7.42 | 4.45 | 41.53 |
| Fast | 550 | 225 | 46.30 | 5.73 | 2.34 | 20.58 | 8.88 | 2.63 | 40.16 |

Ceiling panel estimates are based on overall dimensions (length times width) to 8 feet high. Do not make deductions for openings in the ceiling area that are under 100 square feet. For heights above 8 feet, use the High Time Difficulty Factors on page 139. "Slow" work is based on an hourly wage of $20.25, "Medium" work on an hourly wage of $25.75, and "Fast" work on an hourly wage of $31.50. Other qualifications that apply to this table are on page 9.

*National Painting Cost Estimator*

|  | Labor SF per manhour | Material coverage SF/gallon | Material cost per gallon | Labor cost per 100 SF | Labor burden 100 SF | Material cost per 100 SF | Overhead per 100 SF | Profit per 100 SF | Total price per 100 SF |
|---|---|---|---|---|---|---|---|---|---|
| **Ceiling pans, metal, exterior enamel finish** | | | | | | | | | |
| Enamel, water base (material #24) | | | | | | | | | |
| Brush each coat | | | | | | | | | |
| Slow | 80 | 450 | 50.70 | 25.31 | 7.47 | 11.27 | 8.37 | 8.39 | 60.81 |
| Medium | 100 | 388 | 44.40 | 25.75 | 9.12 | 11.44 | 11.58 | 6.95 | 64.84 |
| Fast | 125 | 325 | 38.00 | 25.20 | 10.28 | 11.69 | 14.62 | 4.33 | 66.12 |
| Enamel, oil base (material #25) | | | | | | | | | |
| Brush each coat | | | | | | | | | |
| Slow | 80 | 400 | 56.40 | 25.31 | 7.47 | 14.10 | 8.91 | 8.93 | 64.72 |
| Medium | 103 | 338 | 49.40 | 25.00 | 8.86 | 14.62 | 12.12 | 7.27 | 67.87 |
| Fast | 125 | 275 | 42.30 | 25.20 | 10.28 | 15.38 | 15.77 | 4.66 | 71.29 |
| Enamel, water base (material #24) | | | | | | | | | |
| Roll each coat | | | | | | | | | |
| Slow | 175 | 425 | 50.70 | 11.57 | 3.40 | 11.93 | 5.11 | 5.12 | 37.13 |
| Medium | 200 | 368 | 44.40 | 12.88 | 4.56 | 12.07 | 7.38 | 4.43 | 41.32 |
| Fast | 225 | 300 | 38.00 | 14.00 | 5.69 | 12.67 | 10.04 | 2.97 | 45.37 |
| Enamel, oil base (material #25) | | | | | | | | | |
| Roll each coat | | | | | | | | | |
| Slow | 175 | 375 | 56.40 | 11.57 | 3.40 | 15.04 | 5.70 | 5.72 | 41.43 |
| Medium | 200 | 313 | 49.40 | 12.88 | 4.56 | 15.78 | 8.31 | 4.98 | 46.51 |
| Fast | 225 | 250 | 42.30 | 14.00 | 5.69 | 16.92 | 11.36 | 3.36 | 51.33 |
| Enamel, water base (material #24) | | | | | | | | | |
| Spray each coat | | | | | | | | | |
| Slow | 550 | 380 | 50.70 | 3.68 | 1.09 | 13.34 | 3.44 | 3.45 | 25.00 |
| Medium | 600 | 370 | 44.40 | 4.29 | 1.53 | 12.00 | 4.45 | 2.67 | 24.94 |
| Fast | 650 | 260 | 38.00 | 4.85 | 1.98 | 14.62 | 6.65 | 1.97 | 30.07 |
| Enamel, oil base (material #25) | | | | | | | | | |
| Spray each coat | | | | | | | | | |
| Slow | 550 | 330 | 56.40 | 3.68 | 1.09 | 17.09 | 4.15 | 4.16 | 30.17 |
| Medium | 600 | 270 | 49.40 | 4.29 | 1.53 | 18.30 | 6.03 | 3.62 | 33.77 |
| Fast | 650 | 210 | 42.30 | 4.85 | 1.98 | 20.14 | 8.36 | 2.47 | 37.80 |

Ceiling panel estimates are based on overall dimensions (length times width) to 8 feet high. Do not make deductions for openings in the ceiling area that are under 100 square feet. For heights above 8 feet, use the High Time Difficulty Factors on page 139. "Slow" work is based on an hourly wage of $20.25, "Medium" work on an hourly wage of $25.75, and "Fast" work on an hourly wage of $31.50. Other qualifications that apply to this table are on page 9.

*General Painting Costs*

|  | Labor SF per manhour | Material coverage SF/gallon | Material cost per gallon | Labor cost per 100 SF | Labor burden 100 SF | Material cost per 100 SF | Overhead per 100 SF | Profit per 100 SF | Total price per 100 SF |
|---|---|---|---|---|---|---|---|---|---|

### Ceilings, acoustic spray-on texture on gypsum drywall

Acoustic spray-on texture, primer (material #6)
  Spray prime coat

| | | | | | | | | | |
|---|---|---|---|---|---|---|---|---|---|
| Slow | 250 | 100 | 27.00 | 8.10 | 2.39 | 27.00 | 7.12 | 7.14 | 51.75 |
| Medium | 300 | 90 | 23.60 | 8.58 | 3.03 | 26.22 | 9.46 | 5.68 | 52.97 |
| Fast | 350 | 80 | 20.30 | 9.00 | 3.68 | 25.38 | 11.80 | 3.49 | 53.35 |

Acoustic spray-on texture, finish (material #7)
  Spray 1st finish coat

| | | | | | | | | | |
|---|---|---|---|---|---|---|---|---|---|
| Slow | 400 | 180 | 29.90 | 5.06 | 1.50 | 16.61 | 4.40 | 4.41 | 31.98 |
| Medium | 450 | 170 | 26.10 | 5.72 | 2.02 | 15.35 | 5.77 | 3.46 | 32.32 |
| Fast | 500 | 160 | 22.40 | 6.30 | 2.57 | 14.00 | 7.09 | 2.10 | 32.06 |

  Spray 2nd or additional finish coats

| | | | | | | | | | |
|---|---|---|---|---|---|---|---|---|---|
| Slow | 500 | 200 | 29.90 | 4.05 | 1.19 | 14.95 | 3.84 | 3.84 | 27.87 |
| Medium | 550 | 188 | 26.10 | 4.68 | 1.67 | 13.88 | 5.06 | 3.03 | 28.32 |
| Fast | 600 | 175 | 22.40 | 5.25 | 2.16 | 12.80 | 6.26 | 1.85 | 28.32 |

Ceiling texture estimates are based on overall dimensions (length times width) to 8 feet high. Do not make deductions for openings in the ceiling area that are under 100 square feet. For heights above 8 feet, use the High Time Difficulty Factors on page 139. "Slow" work is based on an hourly wage of $20.25, "Medium" work on an hourly wage of $25.75, and "Fast" work on an hourly wage of $31.50. Other qualifications that apply to this table are on page 9.

|  | Labor SF per manhour | Material coverage SF/pound | Material cost per pound | Labor cost per 100 SF | Labor burden 100 SF | Material cost per 100 SF | Overhead per 100 SF | Profit per 100 SF | Total price per 100 SF |
|---|---|---|---|---|---|---|---|---|---|

### Ceilings, stipple finish texture paint, light, on drywall

Stipple finish texture paint, Drypowder mix, light coverage (material #8)
  Spray each coat

| | | | | | | | | | |
|---|---|---|---|---|---|---|---|---|---|
| Slow | 225 | 10.0 | .92 | 9.00 | 2.64 | 9.20 | 3.96 | 3.97 | 28.77 |
| Medium | 250 | 7.5 | .81 | 10.30 | 3.65 | 10.80 | 6.19 | 3.71 | 34.65 |
| Fast | 275 | 5.0 | .69 | 11.45 | 4.69 | 13.80 | 9.28 | 2.74 | 41.96 |

Estimates for stipple finish texture paint are based on overall dimensions (length times width) to 8 feet high. Do not make deductions for openings in the ceiling area that are under 100 square feet. For heights above 8 feet, use the High Time Difficulty Factors on page 139. "Slow" work is based on an hourly wage of $20.25, "Medium" work on an hourly wage of $25.75, and "Fast" work on an hourly wage of $31.50. Other qualifications that apply to this table are on page 9.

|  | Labor SF per manhour | Material coverage SF/gallon | Material cost per gallon | Labor cost per 100 SF | Labor burden 100 SF | Material cost per 100 SF | Overhead per 100 SF | Profit per 100 SF | Total price per 100 SF |
|---|---|---|---|---|---|---|---|---|---|

### Ceilings, gypsum drywall, anti-graffiti stain eliminator

Water base primer and pigmented sealer (material #39)
   Roll & brush each coat

|  |  |  |  |  |  |  |  |  |  |
|---|---|---|---|---|---|---|---|---|---|
| Slow | 350 | 450 | 50.30 | 5.79 | 1.71 | 11.18 | 3.55 | 3.56 | 25.79 |
| Medium | 375 | 425 | 44.00 | 6.87 | 2.44 | 10.35 | 4.91 | 2.95 | 27.52 |
| Fast | 400 | 400 | 37.80 | 7.88 | 3.21 | 9.45 | 6.37 | 1.88 | 28.79 |

Oil base primer and pigmented sealer (material #40)
   Roll & brush each coat

|  |  |  |  |  |  |  |  |  |  |
|---|---|---|---|---|---|---|---|---|---|
| Slow | 350 | 400 | 49.90 | 5.79 | 1.71 | 12.48 | 3.80 | 3.80 | 27.58 |
| Medium | 375 | 388 | 43.70 | 6.87 | 2.44 | 11.26 | 5.14 | 3.08 | 28.79 |
| Fast | 400 | 375 | 37.40 | 7.88 | 3.21 | 9.97 | 6.53 | 1.93 | 29.52 |

Polyurethane 2 part system (material #41)
   Roll & brush each coat

|  |  |  |  |  |  |  |  |  |  |
|---|---|---|---|---|---|---|---|---|---|
| Slow | 300 | 400 | 157.00 | 6.75 | 1.98 | 39.25 | 9.12 | 9.14 | 66.24 |
| Medium | 325 | 375 | 137.40 | 7.92 | 2.82 | 36.64 | 11.84 | 7.10 | 66.32 |
| Fast | 350 | 350 | 117.80 | 9.00 | 3.68 | 33.66 | 14.36 | 4.25 | 64.95 |

Ceiling estimates are based on overall dimensions (length times width) to 8 feet high. Do not make deductions for openings in the ceiling area that are under 100 square feet. For heights above 8 feet, use the High Time Difficulty Factors on page 139. "Slow" work is based on an hourly wage of $20.25, "Medium" work on an hourly wage of $25.75, and "Fast" work on an hourly wage of $31.50. Other qualifications that apply to this table are on page 9.

*General Painting Costs*

|  | Labor SF per manhour | Material coverage SF/gallon | Material cost per gallon | Labor cost per 100 SF | Labor burden 100 SF | Material cost per 100 SF | Overhead per 100 SF | Profit per 100 SF | Total price per 100 SF |
|---|---|---|---|---|---|---|---|---|---|

## Ceilings, gypsum drywall, orange peel or knock-down texture, brush

Flat latex, water base (material #5)
  Brush 1st coat

| | | | | | | | | | |
|---|---|---|---|---|---|---|---|---|---|
| Slow | 150 | 300 | 36.70 | 13.50 | 3.99 | 12.23 | 5.64 | 5.66 | 41.02 |
| Medium | 175 | 288 | 32.10 | 14.71 | 5.20 | 11.15 | 7.77 | 4.66 | 43.49 |
| Fast | 200 | 275 | 27.50 | 15.75 | 6.43 | 10.00 | 9.98 | 2.95 | 45.11 |

  Brush 2nd coat

| | | | | | | | | | |
|---|---|---|---|---|---|---|---|---|---|
| Slow | 175 | 350 | 36.70 | 11.57 | 3.40 | 10.49 | 4.84 | 4.85 | 35.15 |
| Medium | 200 | 338 | 32.10 | 12.88 | 4.56 | 9.50 | 6.74 | 4.04 | 37.72 |
| Fast | 225 | 325 | 27.50 | 14.00 | 5.69 | 8.46 | 8.73 | 2.58 | 39.46 |

  Brush 3rd or additional coats

| | | | | | | | | | |
|---|---|---|---|---|---|---|---|---|---|
| Slow | 200 | 400 | 36.70 | 10.13 | 2.98 | 9.18 | 4.24 | 4.25 | 30.78 |
| Medium | 225 | 375 | 32.10 | 11.44 | 4.04 | 8.56 | 6.01 | 3.61 | 33.66 |
| Fast | 250 | 350 | 27.50 | 12.60 | 5.14 | 7.86 | 7.94 | 2.35 | 35.89 |

Sealer, water base (material #1)
  Brush prime coat

| | | | | | | | | | |
|---|---|---|---|---|---|---|---|---|---|
| Slow | 175 | 300 | 30.50 | 11.57 | 3.40 | 10.17 | 4.78 | 4.79 | 34.71 |
| Medium | 200 | 288 | 26.70 | 12.88 | 4.56 | 9.27 | 6.68 | 4.01 | 37.40 |
| Fast | 225 | 275 | 22.90 | 14.00 | 5.69 | 8.33 | 8.69 | 2.57 | 39.28 |

Sealer, oil base (material #2)
  Brush prime coat

| | | | | | | | | | |
|---|---|---|---|---|---|---|---|---|---|
| Slow | 175 | 250 | 39.70 | 11.57 | 3.40 | 15.88 | 5.86 | 5.88 | 42.59 |
| Medium | 200 | 238 | 34.80 | 12.88 | 4.56 | 14.62 | 8.02 | 4.81 | 44.89 |
| Fast | 225 | 225 | 29.80 | 14.00 | 5.69 | 13.24 | 10.21 | 3.02 | 46.16 |

Enamel, water base (material #9)
  Brush 1st finish coat

| | | | | | | | | | |
|---|---|---|---|---|---|---|---|---|---|
| Slow | 150 | 350 | 46.80 | 13.50 | 3.99 | 13.37 | 5.86 | 5.87 | 42.59 |
| Medium | 175 | 338 | 41.00 | 14.71 | 5.20 | 12.13 | 8.01 | 4.81 | 44.86 |
| Fast | 200 | 325 | 35.10 | 15.75 | 6.43 | 10.80 | 10.22 | 3.02 | 46.22 |

  Brush 2nd or additional finish coats

| | | | | | | | | | |
|---|---|---|---|---|---|---|---|---|---|
| Slow | 175 | 400 | 46.80 | 11.57 | 3.40 | 11.70 | 5.07 | 5.08 | 36.82 |
| Medium | 200 | 375 | 41.00 | 12.88 | 4.56 | 10.93 | 7.09 | 4.26 | 39.72 |
| Fast | 225 | 350 | 35.10 | 14.00 | 5.69 | 10.03 | 9.22 | 2.73 | 41.67 |

*National Painting Cost Estimator*

|  | Labor SF per manhour | Material coverage SF/gallon | Material cost per gallon | Labor cost per 100 SF | Labor burden 100 SF | Material cost per 100 SF | Overhead per 100 SF | Profit per 100 SF | Total price per 100 SF |
|---|---|---|---|---|---|---|---|---|---|
| **Enamel, oil base (material #10)** | | | | | | | | | |
| Brush 1st finish coat | | | | | | | | | |
| Slow | 150 | 325 | 61.70 | 13.50 | 3.99 | 18.98 | 6.93 | 6.94 | 50.34 |
| Medium | 175 | 313 | 54.00 | 14.71 | 5.20 | 17.25 | 9.29 | 5.58 | 52.03 |
| Fast | 200 | 300 | 46.30 | 15.75 | 6.43 | 15.43 | 11.66 | 3.45 | 52.72 |
| Brush 2nd or additional finish coats | | | | | | | | | |
| Slow | 150 | 400 | 61.70 | 13.50 | 3.99 | 15.43 | 6.25 | 6.27 | 45.44 |
| Medium | 175 | 375 | 54.00 | 14.71 | 5.20 | 14.40 | 8.58 | 5.15 | 48.04 |
| Fast | 200 | 350 | 46.30 | 15.75 | 6.43 | 13.23 | 10.98 | 3.25 | 49.64 |
| **Epoxy coating, white (material #52)** | | | | | | | | | |
| Brush 1st coat | | | | | | | | | |
| Slow | 125 | 350 | 177.00 | 16.20 | 4.78 | 50.57 | 13.59 | 13.62 | 98.76 |
| Medium | 150 | 325 | 154.90 | 17.17 | 6.09 | 47.66 | 17.73 | 10.64 | 99.29 |
| Fast | 175 | 300 | 132.70 | 18.00 | 7.32 | 44.23 | 21.57 | 6.38 | 97.50 |
| Brush 2nd or additional coats | | | | | | | | | |
| Slow | 175 | 375 | 177.00 | 11.57 | 3.40 | 47.20 | 11.81 | 11.84 | 85.82 |
| Medium | 200 | 350 | 154.90 | 12.88 | 4.56 | 44.26 | 15.43 | 9.26 | 86.39 |
| Fast | 225 | 325 | 132.70 | 14.00 | 5.69 | 40.83 | 18.77 | 5.55 | 84.84 |

Ceiling estimates are based on overall dimensions (length times width) to 8 feet high. Do not make deductions for openings in the ceiling area that are under 100 square feet. For heights above 8 feet, use the High Time Difficulty Factors on page 139. ADD for cutting-in at ceilings and protecting adjacent surfaces if ceilings alone are being painted, not walls. Otherwise, figure any cutting-in time with walls. See the notes under the wall formulas for clarification. "Slow" work is based on an hourly wage of $20.25, "Medium" work on an hourly wage of $25.75, and "Fast" work on an hourly wage of $31.50. Other qualifications that apply to this table are on page 9.

*General Painting Costs*

|  | Labor SF per manhour | Material coverage SF/gallon | Material cost per gallon | Labor cost per 100 SF | Labor burden 100 SF | Material cost per 100 SF | Overhead per 100 SF | Profit per 100 SF | Total price per 100 SF |
|---|---|---|---|---|---|---|---|---|---|

## Ceilings, gypsum drywall, orange peel or knock-down texture, roll

### Flat latex, water base (material #5)
**Roll 1st coat**
| | | | | | | | | | |
|---|---|---|---|---|---|---|---|---|---|
| Slow | 325 | 300 | 36.70 | 6.23 | 1.85 | 12.23 | 3.86 | 3.87 | 28.04 |
| Medium | 350 | 275 | 32.10 | 7.36 | 2.61 | 11.67 | 5.41 | 3.25 | 30.30 |
| Fast | 375 | 250 | 27.50 | 8.40 | 3.44 | 11.00 | 7.08 | 2.09 | 32.01 |

**Roll 2nd coat**
| | | | | | | | | | |
|---|---|---|---|---|---|---|---|---|---|
| Slow | 350 | 325 | 36.70 | 5.79 | 1.71 | 11.29 | 3.57 | 3.58 | 25.94 |
| Medium | 375 | 313 | 32.10 | 6.87 | 2.44 | 10.26 | 4.89 | 2.93 | 27.39 |
| Fast | 400 | 300 | 27.50 | 7.88 | 3.21 | 9.17 | 6.28 | 1.86 | 28.40 |

**Roll 3rd or additional coats**
| | | | | | | | | | |
|---|---|---|---|---|---|---|---|---|---|
| Slow | 400 | 350 | 36.70 | 5.06 | 1.50 | 10.49 | 3.24 | 3.24 | 23.53 |
| Medium | 425 | 338 | 32.10 | 6.06 | 2.13 | 9.50 | 4.43 | 2.66 | 24.78 |
| Fast | 450 | 325 | 27.50 | 7.00 | 2.85 | 8.46 | 5.68 | 1.68 | 25.67 |

### Sealer, water base (material #1)
**Roll prime coat**
| | | | | | | | | | |
|---|---|---|---|---|---|---|---|---|---|
| Slow | 350 | 300 | 30.50 | 5.79 | 1.71 | 10.17 | 3.36 | 3.36 | 24.39 |
| Medium | 375 | 275 | 26.70 | 6.87 | 2.44 | 9.71 | 4.75 | 2.85 | 26.62 |
| Fast | 400 | 250 | 22.90 | 7.88 | 3.21 | 9.16 | 6.28 | 1.86 | 28.39 |

### Sealer, oil base (material #2)
**Roll prime coat**
| | | | | | | | | | |
|---|---|---|---|---|---|---|---|---|---|
| Slow | 350 | 275 | 39.70 | 5.79 | 1.71 | 14.44 | 4.17 | 4.18 | 30.29 |
| Medium | 375 | 250 | 34.80 | 6.87 | 2.44 | 13.92 | 5.81 | 3.48 | 32.52 |
| Fast | 400 | 225 | 29.80 | 7.88 | 3.21 | 13.24 | 7.55 | 2.23 | 34.11 |

### Enamel, water base (material #9)
**Roll 1st finish coat**
| | | | | | | | | | |
|---|---|---|---|---|---|---|---|---|---|
| Slow | 325 | 325 | 46.80 | 6.23 | 1.85 | 14.40 | 4.27 | 4.28 | 31.03 |
| Medium | 350 | 313 | 41.00 | 7.36 | 2.61 | 13.10 | 5.77 | 3.46 | 32.30 |
| Fast | 375 | 300 | 35.10 | 8.40 | 3.44 | 11.70 | 7.29 | 2.16 | 32.99 |

**Roll 2nd or additional finish coats**
| | | | | | | | | | |
|---|---|---|---|---|---|---|---|---|---|
| Slow | 375 | 350 | 46.80 | 5.40 | 1.60 | 13.37 | 3.87 | 3.88 | 28.12 |
| Medium | 400 | 338 | 41.00 | 6.44 | 2.28 | 12.13 | 5.21 | 3.13 | 29.19 |
| Fast | 425 | 325 | 35.10 | 7.41 | 3.01 | 10.80 | 6.58 | 1.95 | 29.75 |

*National Painting Cost Estimator*

|  | Labor SF per manhour | Material coverage SF/gallon | Material cost per gallon | Labor cost per 100 SF | Labor burden 100 SF | Material cost per 100 SF | Overhead per 100 SF | Profit per 100 SF | Total price per 100 SF |
|---|---|---|---|---|---|---|---|---|---|
| **Enamel, oil base (material #10)** | | | | | | | | | |
| Roll 1st finish coat | | | | | | | | | |
| Slow | 325 | 300 | 61.70 | 6.23 | 1.85 | 20.57 | 5.44 | 5.45 | 39.54 |
| Medium | 350 | 275 | 54.00 | 7.36 | 2.61 | 19.64 | 7.40 | 4.44 | 41.45 |
| Fast | 375 | 250 | 46.30 | 8.40 | 3.44 | 18.52 | 9.41 | 2.78 | 42.55 |
| Roll 2nd or additional finish coats | | | | | | | | | |
| Slow | 375 | 300 | 61.70 | 5.40 | 1.60 | 20.57 | 5.24 | 5.25 | 38.06 |
| Medium | 400 | 288 | 54.00 | 6.44 | 2.28 | 18.75 | 6.87 | 4.12 | 38.46 |
| Fast | 425 | 275 | 46.30 | 7.41 | 3.01 | 16.84 | 8.45 | 2.50 | 38.21 |
| **Epoxy coating, white (material #52)** | | | | | | | | | |
| Roll 1st coat | | | | | | | | | |
| Slow | 300 | 300 | 177.00 | 6.75 | 1.98 | 59.00 | 12.87 | 12.90 | 93.50 |
| Medium | 325 | 288 | 154.90 | 7.92 | 2.82 | 53.78 | 16.13 | 9.68 | 90.33 |
| Fast | 350 | 275 | 132.70 | 9.00 | 3.68 | 48.25 | 18.89 | 5.59 | 85.41 |
| Roll 2nd or additional coats | | | | | | | | | |
| Slow | 350 | 300 | 177.00 | 5.79 | 1.71 | 59.00 | 12.64 | 12.66 | 91.80 |
| Medium | 375 | 288 | 154.90 | 6.87 | 2.44 | 53.78 | 15.77 | 9.46 | 88.32 |
| Fast | 400 | 275 | 132.70 | 7.88 | 3.21 | 48.25 | 18.40 | 5.44 | 83.18 |

Ceiling estimates are based on overall dimensions (length times width) to 8 feet high. Do not make deductions for openings in the ceiling area that are under 100 square feet. For heights above 8 feet, use the High Time Difficulty Factors on page 139. ADD for cutting-in at ceilings and protecting adjacent surfaces if ceilings alone are being painted, not walls. Otherwise, figure any cutting-in time with walls. See the notes under the wall formulas for clarification. "Slow" work is based on an hourly wage of $20.25, "Medium" work on an hourly wage of $25.75, and "Fast" work on an hourly wage of $31.50. Other qualifications that apply to this table are on page 9.

*General Painting Costs*

|  | Labor SF per manhour | Material coverage SF/gallon | Material cost per gallon | Labor cost per 100 SF | Labor burden 100 SF | Material cost per 100 SF | Overhead per 100 SF | Profit per 100 SF | Total price per 100 SF |
|---|---|---|---|---|---|---|---|---|---|

## Ceilings, gypsum drywall, orange peel or knock-down texture, spray

**Flat latex, water base (material #5)**
Spray 1st coat
| Slow | 650 | 225 | 36.70 | 3.12 | .92 | 16.31 | 3.87 | 3.88 | 28.10 |
| Medium | 750 | 200 | 32.10 | 3.43 | 1.21 | 16.05 | 5.17 | 3.10 | 28.96 |
| Fast | 850 | 175 | 27.50 | 3.71 | 1.52 | 15.71 | 6.49 | 1.92 | 29.35 |

Spray 2nd coat
| Slow | 775 | 250 | 36.70 | 2.61 | .77 | 14.68 | 3.43 | 3.44 | 24.93 |
| Medium | 875 | 225 | 32.10 | 2.94 | 1.04 | 14.27 | 4.56 | 2.74 | 25.55 |
| Fast | 975 | 200 | 27.50 | 3.23 | 1.34 | 13.75 | 5.67 | 1.68 | 25.67 |

Spray 3rd or additional coats
| Slow | 825 | 275 | 36.70 | 2.45 | .72 | 13.35 | 3.14 | 3.15 | 22.81 |
| Medium | 925 | 250 | 32.10 | 2.78 | .99 | 12.84 | 4.15 | 2.49 | 23.25 |
| Fast | 1025 | 225 | 27.50 | 3.07 | 1.28 | 12.22 | 5.13 | 1.52 | 23.22 |

**Sealer, water base (material #1)**
Spray prime coat
| Slow | 700 | 225 | 30.50 | 2.89 | .86 | 13.56 | 3.29 | 3.29 | 23.89 |
| Medium | 800 | 200 | 26.70 | 3.22 | 1.14 | 13.35 | 4.43 | 2.66 | 24.80 |
| Fast | 900 | 175 | 22.90 | 3.50 | 1.42 | 13.09 | 5.59 | 1.65 | 25.25 |

**Sealer, oil base (material #2)**
Spray prime coat
| Slow | 700 | 200 | 39.70 | 2.89 | .86 | 19.85 | 4.48 | 4.49 | 32.57 |
| Medium | 800 | 188 | 34.80 | 3.22 | 1.14 | 18.51 | 5.72 | 3.43 | 32.02 |
| Fast | 900 | 175 | 29.80 | 3.50 | 1.42 | 17.03 | 6.81 | 2.01 | 30.77 |

**Enamel, water base (material #9)**
Spray 1st finish coat
| Slow | 725 | 250 | 46.80 | 2.79 | .83 | 18.72 | 4.24 | 4.25 | 30.83 |
| Medium | 825 | 225 | 41.00 | 3.12 | 1.10 | 18.22 | 5.61 | 3.37 | 31.42 |
| Fast | 925 | 200 | 35.10 | 3.41 | 1.38 | 17.55 | 6.93 | 2.05 | 31.32 |

Spray 2nd or additional finish coat
| Slow | 775 | 275 | 46.80 | 2.61 | .77 | 17.02 | 3.88 | 3.88 | 28.16 |
| Medium | 875 | 250 | 41.00 | 2.94 | 1.04 | 16.40 | 5.10 | 3.06 | 28.54 |
| Fast | 975 | 225 | 35.10 | 3.23 | 1.34 | 15.60 | 6.25 | 1.85 | 28.27 |

*National Painting Cost Estimator*

|  | Labor SF per manhour | Material coverage SF/gallon | Material cost per gallon | Labor cost per 100 SF | Labor burden 100 SF | Material cost per 100 SF | Overhead per 100 SF | Profit per 100 SF | Total price per 100 SF |
|---|---|---|---|---|---|---|---|---|---|
| **Enamel, oil base (material #10)** | | | | | | | | | |
| *Spray 1st finish coat* | | | | | | | | | |
| Slow | 725 | 225 | 61.70 | 2.79 | .83 | 27.42 | 5.90 | 5.91 | 42.85 |
| Medium | 825 | 213 | 54.00 | 3.12 | 1.10 | 25.35 | 7.39 | 4.44 | 41.40 |
| Fast | 925 | 200 | 46.30 | 3.41 | 1.38 | 23.15 | 8.66 | 2.56 | 39.16 |
| *Spray 2nd or additional finish coat* | | | | | | | | | |
| Slow | 775 | 250 | 61.70 | 2.61 | .77 | 24.68 | 5.33 | 5.34 | 38.73 |
| Medium | 875 | 238 | 54.00 | 2.94 | 1.04 | 22.69 | 6.67 | 4.00 | 37.34 |
| Fast | 975 | 225 | 46.30 | 3.23 | 1.34 | 20.58 | 7.79 | 2.30 | 35.24 |

Ceiling estimates are based on overall dimensions (length times width) to 8 feet high. Do not make deductions for openings in the ceiling area that are under 100 square feet. For heights above 8 feet, use the High Time Difficulty Factors on page 139. ADD for cutting-in at ceilings and protecting adjacent surfaces if ceilings alone are being painted, not walls. Otherwise, figure any cutting-in and protection time with the walls. See the notes under the wall formulas for clarification. "Slow" work is based on an hourly wage of $20.25, "Medium" work on an hourly wage of $25.75, and "Fast" work on an hourly wage of $31.50. Other qualifications that apply to this table are on page 9.

*General Painting Costs*

|  | Labor SF per manhour | Material coverage SF/gallon | Material cost per gallon | Labor cost per 100 SF | Labor burden 100 SF | Material cost per 100 SF | Overhead per 100 SF | Profit per 100 SF | Total price per 100 SF |
|---|---|---|---|---|---|---|---|---|---|

## Ceilings, gypsum drywall, sand finish or skip trowel texture, brush

### Flat latex, water base (material #5)
**Brush 1st coat**
| | | | | | | | | | |
|---|---|---|---|---|---|---|---|---|---|
| Slow | 175 | 325 | 36.70 | 11.57 | 3.40 | 11.29 | 4.99 | 5.00 | 36.25 |
| Medium | 200 | 313 | 32.10 | 12.88 | 4.56 | 10.26 | 6.93 | 4.16 | 38.79 |
| Fast | 225 | 300 | 27.50 | 14.00 | 5.69 | 9.17 | 8.95 | 2.65 | 40.46 |

**Brush 2nd coat**
| | | | | | | | | | |
|---|---|---|---|---|---|---|---|---|---|
| Slow | 200 | 400 | 36.70 | 10.13 | 2.98 | 9.18 | 4.24 | 4.25 | 30.78 |
| Medium | 238 | 375 | 32.10 | 10.82 | 3.83 | 8.56 | 5.80 | 3.48 | 32.49 |
| Fast | 275 | 350 | 27.50 | 11.45 | 4.69 | 7.86 | 7.43 | 2.20 | 33.63 |

**Brush 3rd or additional coats**
| | | | | | | | | | |
|---|---|---|---|---|---|---|---|---|---|
| Slow | 225 | 425 | 36.70 | 9.00 | 2.64 | 8.64 | 3.86 | 3.87 | 28.01 |
| Medium | 263 | 400 | 32.10 | 9.79 | 3.46 | 8.03 | 5.32 | 3.19 | 29.79 |
| Fast | 300 | 375 | 27.50 | 10.50 | 4.27 | 7.33 | 6.85 | 2.03 | 30.98 |

### Sealer, water base (material #1)
**Brush prime coat**
| | | | | | | | | | |
|---|---|---|---|---|---|---|---|---|---|
| Slow | 200 | 325 | 30.50 | 10.13 | 2.98 | 9.38 | 4.28 | 4.28 | 31.05 |
| Medium | 225 | 313 | 26.70 | 11.44 | 4.04 | 8.53 | 6.01 | 3.60 | 33.62 |
| Fast | 250 | 300 | 22.90 | 12.60 | 5.14 | 7.63 | 7.86 | 2.33 | 35.56 |

### Sealer, oil base (material #2)
**Brush prime coat**
| | | | | | | | | | |
|---|---|---|---|---|---|---|---|---|---|
| Slow | 200 | 325 | 39.70 | 10.13 | 2.98 | 12.22 | 4.81 | 4.82 | 34.96 |
| Medium | 225 | 313 | 34.80 | 11.44 | 4.04 | 11.12 | 6.65 | 3.99 | 37.24 |
| Fast | 250 | 300 | 29.80 | 12.60 | 5.14 | 9.93 | 8.58 | 2.54 | 38.79 |

### Enamel, water base (material #9)
**Brush 1st finish coat**
| | | | | | | | | | |
|---|---|---|---|---|---|---|---|---|---|
| Slow | 200 | 400 | 46.80 | 10.13 | 2.98 | 11.70 | 4.72 | 4.73 | 34.26 |
| Medium | 225 | 375 | 41.00 | 11.44 | 4.04 | 10.93 | 6.61 | 3.96 | 36.98 |
| Fast | 250 | 350 | 35.10 | 12.60 | 5.14 | 10.03 | 8.61 | 2.55 | 38.93 |

**Brush 2nd or additional finish coats**
| | | | | | | | | | |
|---|---|---|---|---|---|---|---|---|---|
| Slow | 225 | 425 | 46.80 | 9.00 | 2.64 | 11.01 | 4.31 | 4.32 | 31.28 |
| Medium | 263 | 400 | 41.00 | 9.79 | 3.46 | 10.25 | 5.88 | 3.53 | 32.91 |
| Fast | 300 | 375 | 35.10 | 10.50 | 4.27 | 9.36 | 7.48 | 2.21 | 33.82 |

|  | Labor SF per manhour | Material coverage SF/gallon | Material cost per gallon | Labor cost per 100 SF | Labor burden 100 SF | Material cost per 100 SF | Overhead per 100 SF | Profit per 100 SF | Total price per 100 SF |
|---|---|---|---|---|---|---|---|---|---|
| **Enamel, oil base (material #10)** | | | | | | | | | |
| Brush 1st finish coat | | | | | | | | | |
| Slow | 200 | 375 | 61.70 | 10.13 | 2.98 | 16.45 | 5.62 | 5.63 | 40.81 |
| Medium | 225 | 350 | 54.00 | 11.44 | 4.04 | 15.43 | 7.73 | 4.64 | 43.28 |
| Fast | 250 | 325 | 46.30 | 12.60 | 5.14 | 14.25 | 9.92 | 2.93 | 44.84 |
| Brush 2nd or additional finish coats | | | | | | | | | |
| Slow | 225 | 400 | 61.70 | 9.00 | 2.64 | 15.43 | 5.15 | 5.16 | 37.38 |
| Medium | 263 | 375 | 54.00 | 9.79 | 3.46 | 14.40 | 6.92 | 4.15 | 38.72 |
| Fast | 300 | 350 | 46.30 | 10.50 | 4.27 | 13.23 | 8.68 | 2.57 | 39.25 |
| **Epoxy coating, white (material #52)** | | | | | | | | | |
| Brush 1st coat | | | | | | | | | |
| Slow | 150 | 375 | 177.00 | 13.50 | 3.99 | 47.20 | 12.29 | 12.32 | 89.30 |
| Medium | 175 | 350 | 154.90 | 14.71 | 5.20 | 44.26 | 16.05 | 9.63 | 89.85 |
| Fast | 225 | 325 | 132.70 | 14.00 | 5.69 | 40.83 | 18.77 | 5.55 | 84.84 |
| Brush 2nd or additional coats | | | | | | | | | |
| Slow | 175 | 400 | 177.00 | 11.57 | 3.40 | 44.25 | 11.25 | 11.28 | 81.75 |
| Medium | 200 | 375 | 154.90 | 12.88 | 4.56 | 41.31 | 14.69 | 8.81 | 82.25 |
| Fast | 225 | 350 | 132.70 | 14.00 | 5.69 | 37.91 | 17.86 | 5.28 | 80.74 |

Ceiling estimates are based on overall dimensions (length times width) to 8 feet high. Do not make deductions for openings in the ceiling area that are under 100 square feet. For heights above 8 feet, use the High Time Difficulty Factors on page 139. ADD for cutting-in at ceilings and protecting adjacent surfaces if ceilings alone are being painted, not walls. Otherwise, figure any cutting-in time with walls. See the notes under the wall formulas for clarification. "Slow" work is based on an hourly wage of $20.25, "Medium" work on an hourly wage of $25.75, and "Fast" work on an hourly wage of $31.50. Other qualifications that apply to this table are on page 9.

*General Painting Costs*

|  | Labor SF per manhour | Material coverage SF/gallon | Material cost per gallon | Labor cost per 100 SF | Labor burden 100 SF | Material cost per 100 SF | Overhead per 100 SF | Profit per 100 SF | Total price per 100 SF |
|---|---|---|---|---|---|---|---|---|---|

## Ceilings, gypsum drywall, sand finish or skip trowel texture, roll

### Flat latex, water base (material #5)
**Roll 1st coat**
| | | | | | | | | | |
|---|---|---|---|---|---|---|---|---|---|
| Slow | 300 | 325 | 36.70 | 6.75 | 1.98 | 11.29 | 3.81 | 3.81 | 27.64 |
| Medium | 350 | 300 | 32.10 | 7.36 | 2.61 | 10.70 | 5.17 | 3.10 | 28.94 |
| Fast | 400 | 275 | 27.50 | 7.88 | 3.21 | 10.00 | 6.54 | 1.93 | 29.56 |

**Roll 2nd coat**
| | | | | | | | | | |
|---|---|---|---|---|---|---|---|---|---|
| Slow | 350 | 350 | 36.70 | 5.79 | 1.71 | 10.49 | 3.42 | 3.43 | 24.84 |
| Medium | 388 | 338 | 32.10 | 6.64 | 2.36 | 9.50 | 4.62 | 2.77 | 25.89 |
| Fast | 425 | 325 | 27.50 | 7.41 | 3.01 | 8.46 | 5.86 | 1.73 | 26.47 |

**Roll 3rd or additional coats**
| | | | | | | | | | |
|---|---|---|---|---|---|---|---|---|---|
| Slow | 425 | 350 | 36.70 | 4.76 | 1.40 | 10.49 | 3.16 | 3.17 | 22.98 |
| Medium | 450 | 338 | 32.10 | 5.72 | 2.02 | 9.50 | 4.31 | 2.59 | 24.14 |
| Fast | 475 | 325 | 27.50 | 6.63 | 2.73 | 8.46 | 5.52 | 1.63 | 24.97 |

### Sealer, water base (material #1)
**Roll prime coat**
| | | | | | | | | | |
|---|---|---|---|---|---|---|---|---|---|
| Slow | 325 | 325 | 30.50 | 6.23 | 1.85 | 9.38 | 3.32 | 3.32 | 24.10 |
| Medium | 375 | 300 | 26.70 | 6.87 | 2.44 | 8.90 | 4.55 | 2.73 | 25.49 |
| Fast | 425 | 275 | 22.90 | 7.41 | 3.01 | 8.33 | 5.82 | 1.72 | 26.29 |

### Sealer, oil base (material #2)
**Roll prime coat**
| | | | | | | | | | |
|---|---|---|---|---|---|---|---|---|---|
| Slow | 325 | 300 | 39.70 | 6.23 | 1.85 | 13.23 | 4.05 | 4.06 | 29.42 |
| Medium | 375 | 275 | 34.80 | 6.87 | 2.44 | 12.65 | 5.49 | 3.29 | 30.74 |
| Fast | 425 | 250 | 29.80 | 7.41 | 3.01 | 11.92 | 6.93 | 2.05 | 31.32 |

### Enamel, water base (material #9)
**Roll 1st finish coat**
| | | | | | | | | | |
|---|---|---|---|---|---|---|---|---|---|
| Slow | 325 | 350 | 46.80 | 6.23 | 1.85 | 13.37 | 4.07 | 4.08 | 29.60 |
| Medium | 363 | 338 | 41.00 | 7.09 | 2.50 | 12.13 | 5.43 | 3.26 | 30.41 |
| Fast | 400 | 325 | 35.10 | 7.88 | 3.21 | 10.80 | 6.79 | 2.01 | 30.69 |

**Roll 2nd or additional finish coats**
| | | | | | | | | | |
|---|---|---|---|---|---|---|---|---|---|
| Slow | 400 | 350 | 46.80 | 5.06 | 1.50 | 13.37 | 3.78 | 3.79 | 27.50 |
| Medium | 425 | 338 | 41.00 | 6.06 | 2.13 | 12.13 | 5.09 | 3.05 | 28.46 |
| Fast | 450 | 325 | 35.10 | 7.00 | 2.85 | 10.80 | 6.40 | 1.89 | 28.94 |

### Enamel, oil base (material #10)
**Roll 1st finish coat**
| | | | | | | | | | |
|---|---|---|---|---|---|---|---|---|---|
| Slow | 325 | 325 | 61.70 | 6.23 | 1.85 | 18.98 | 5.14 | 5.15 | 37.35 |
| Medium | 363 | 313 | 54.00 | 7.09 | 2.50 | 17.25 | 6.71 | 4.03 | 37.58 |
| Fast | 400 | 300 | 46.30 | 7.88 | 3.21 | 15.43 | 8.22 | 2.43 | 37.17 |

*National Painting Cost Estimator*

|  | Labor SF per manhour | Material coverage SF/gallon | Material cost per gallon | Labor cost per 100 SF | Labor burden 100 SF | Material cost per 100 SF | Overhead per 100 SF | Profit per 100 SF | Total price per 100 SF |
|---|---|---|---|---|---|---|---|---|---|
| Roll 2nd or additional finish coats | | | | | | | | | |
| Slow | 400 | 350 | 61.70 | 5.06 | 1.50 | 17.63 | 4.59 | 4.60 | 33.38 |
| Medium | 425 | 338 | 54.00 | 6.06 | 2.13 | 15.98 | 6.05 | 3.63 | 33.85 |
| Fast | 450 | 325 | 46.30 | 7.00 | 2.85 | 14.25 | 7.47 | 2.21 | 33.78 |
| Epoxy coating, white (material #52) | | | | | | | | | |
| Roll 1st coat | | | | | | | | | |
| Slow | 300 | 350 | 177.00 | 6.75 | 1.98 | 50.57 | 11.27 | 11.29 | 81.86 |
| Medium | 350 | 325 | 154.90 | 7.36 | 2.61 | 47.66 | 14.41 | 8.64 | 80.68 |
| Fast | 375 | 300 | 132.70 | 8.40 | 3.44 | 44.23 | 17.38 | 5.14 | 78.59 |
| Roll 2nd or additional coats | | | | | | | | | |
| Slow | 375 | 375 | 177.00 | 5.40 | 1.60 | 47.20 | 10.30 | 10.32 | 74.82 |
| Medium | 400 | 350 | 154.90 | 6.44 | 2.28 | 44.26 | 13.25 | 7.95 | 74.18 |
| Fast | 425 | 325 | 132.70 | 7.41 | 3.01 | 40.83 | 15.89 | 4.70 | 71.84 |

Ceiling estimates are based on overall dimensions (length times width) to 8 feet high. Do not make deductions for openings in the ceiling area that are under 100 square feet. For heights above 8 feet, use the High Time Difficulty Factors on page 139. ADD for cutting-in at ceilings and protecting adjacent surfaces if ceilings alone are being painted, not walls. Otherwise, figure any cutting-in time with walls. See the notes under the wall formulas for clarification. "Slow" work is based on an hourly wage of $20.25, "Medium" work on an hourly wage of $25.75, and "Fast" work on an hourly wage of $31.50. Other qualifications that apply to this table are on page 9.

*General Painting Costs*

|  | Labor SF per manhour | Material coverage SF/gallon | Material cost per gallon | Labor cost per 100 SF | Labor burden 100 SF | Material cost per 100 SF | Overhead per 100 SF | Profit per 100 SF | Total price per 100 SF |
|---|---|---|---|---|---|---|---|---|---|

## Ceilings, gypsum drywall, sand finish or skip trowel texture, spray

Flat latex, water base (material #5)
  Spray 1st coat

| | | | | | | | | | |
|---|---|---|---|---|---|---|---|---|---|
| Slow | 700 | 275 | 36.70 | 2.89 | .86 | 13.35 | 3.25 | 3.25 | 23.60 |
| Medium | 800 | 250 | 32.10 | 3.22 | 1.14 | 12.84 | 4.30 | 2.58 | 24.08 |
| Fast | 900 | 225 | 27.50 | 3.50 | 1.42 | 12.22 | 5.32 | 1.57 | 24.03 |

  Spray 2nd coat

| | | | | | | | | | |
|---|---|---|---|---|---|---|---|---|---|
| Slow | 800 | 325 | 36.70 | 2.53 | .75 | 11.29 | 2.77 | 2.77 | 20.11 |
| Medium | 900 | 300 | 32.10 | 2.86 | 1.01 | 10.70 | 3.64 | 2.19 | 20.40 |
| Fast | 1000 | 275 | 27.50 | 3.15 | 1.29 | 10.00 | 4.48 | 1.32 | 20.24 |

  Spray 3rd or additional coats

| | | | | | | | | | |
|---|---|---|---|---|---|---|---|---|---|
| Slow | 850 | 325 | 36.70 | 2.38 | .71 | 11.29 | 2.73 | 2.74 | 19.85 |
| Medium | 950 | 313 | 32.10 | 2.71 | .95 | 10.26 | 3.48 | 2.09 | 19.49 |
| Fast | 1050 | 300 | 27.50 | 3.00 | 1.21 | 9.17 | 4.15 | 1.23 | 18.76 |

Sealer, water base (material #1)
  Spray prime coat

| | | | | | | | | | |
|---|---|---|---|---|---|---|---|---|---|
| Slow | 750 | 275 | 30.50 | 2.70 | .79 | 11.09 | 2.77 | 2.78 | 20.13 |
| Medium | 850 | 250 | 26.70 | 3.03 | 1.08 | 10.68 | 3.70 | 2.22 | 20.71 |
| Fast | 950 | 225 | 22.90 | 3.32 | 1.34 | 10.18 | 4.60 | 1.36 | 20.80 |

Sealer, oil base (material #2)
  Spray prime coat

| | | | | | | | | | |
|---|---|---|---|---|---|---|---|---|---|
| Slow | 750 | 225 | 39.70 | 2.70 | .79 | 17.64 | 4.02 | 4.03 | 29.18 |
| Medium | 850 | 213 | 34.80 | 3.03 | 1.08 | 16.34 | 5.11 | 3.07 | 28.63 |
| Fast | 950 | 200 | 29.80 | 3.32 | 1.34 | 14.90 | 6.07 | 1.79 | 27.42 |

Enamel, water base (material #9)
  Spray 1st finish coat

| | | | | | | | | | |
|---|---|---|---|---|---|---|---|---|---|
| Slow | 750 | 325 | 46.80 | 2.70 | .79 | 14.40 | 3.40 | 3.41 | 24.70 |
| Medium | 850 | 300 | 41.00 | 3.03 | 1.08 | 13.67 | 4.44 | 2.67 | 24.89 |
| Fast | 950 | 275 | 35.10 | 3.32 | 1.34 | 12.76 | 5.40 | 1.60 | 24.42 |

  Spray 2nd or additional finish coat

| | | | | | | | | | |
|---|---|---|---|---|---|---|---|---|---|
| Slow | 800 | 325 | 46.80 | 2.53 | .75 | 14.40 | 3.36 | 3.37 | 24.41 |
| Medium | 900 | 313 | 41.00 | 2.86 | 1.01 | 13.10 | 4.24 | 2.55 | 23.76 |
| Fast | 1000 | 300 | 35.10 | 3.15 | 1.29 | 11.70 | 5.00 | 1.48 | 22.62 |

*National Painting Cost Estimator*

|  | Labor SF per manhour | Material coverage SF/gallon | Material cost per gallon | Labor cost per 100 SF | Labor burden 100 SF | Material cost per 100 SF | Overhead per 100 SF | Profit per 100 SF | Total price per 100 SF |
|---|---|---|---|---|---|---|---|---|---|
| **Enamel, oil base (material #10)** | | | | | | | | | |
| *Spray 1st finish coat* | | | | | | | | | |
| Slow | 750 | 300 | 61.70 | 2.70 | .79 | 20.57 | 4.57 | 4.58 | 33.21 |
| Medium | 850 | 288 | 54.00 | 3.03 | 1.08 | 18.75 | 5.71 | 3.43 | 32.00 |
| Fast | 950 | 275 | 46.30 | 3.32 | 1.34 | 16.84 | 6.67 | 1.97 | 30.14 |
| *Spray 2nd or additional finish coat* | | | | | | | | | |
| Slow | 800 | 325 | 61.70 | 2.53 | .75 | 18.98 | 4.23 | 4.24 | 30.73 |
| Medium | 900 | 313 | 54.00 | 2.86 | 1.01 | 17.25 | 5.28 | 3.17 | 29.57 |
| Fast | 1000 | 300 | 46.30 | 3.15 | 1.29 | 15.43 | 6.16 | 1.82 | 27.85 |

Ceiling estimates are based on overall dimensions (length times width) to 8 feet high. Do not make deductions for openings in the ceiling area that are under 100 square feet. For heights above 8 feet, use the High Time Difficulty Factors on page 139. ADD for cutting-in at ceilings and protecting adjacent surfaces if ceilings alone are being painted, not walls. Otherwise, figure any cutting-in and protection time with the walls. See the notes under the wall formulas for clarification. "Slow" work is based on an hourly wage of $20.25, "Medium" work on an hourly wage of $25.75, and "Fast" work on an hourly wage of $31.50. Other qualifications that apply to this table are on page 9.

*General Painting Costs*

|  | Labor SF per manhour | Material coverage SF/gallon | Material cost per gallon | Labor cost per 100 SF | Labor burden 100 SF | Material cost per 100 SF | Overhead per 100 SF | Profit per 100 SF | Total price per 100 SF |
|---|---|---|---|---|---|---|---|---|---|
| **Ceilings, gypsum drywall, smooth finish, brush** | | | | | | | | | |
| Flat latex, water base (material #5) | | | | | | | | | |
|   Brush 1st coat | | | | | | | | | |
|     Slow | 175 | 325 | 36.70 | 11.57 | 3.40 | 11.29 | 4.99 | 5.00 | 36.25 |
|     Medium | 200 | 313 | 32.10 | 12.88 | 4.56 | 10.26 | 6.93 | 4.16 | 38.79 |
|     Fast | 225 | 300 | 27.50 | 14.00 | 5.69 | 9.17 | 8.95 | 2.65 | 40.46 |
|   Brush 2nd coat | | | | | | | | | |
|     Slow | 225 | 400 | 36.70 | 9.00 | 2.64 | 9.18 | 3.96 | 3.97 | 28.75 |
|     Medium | 250 | 375 | 32.10 | 10.30 | 3.65 | 8.56 | 5.63 | 3.38 | 31.52 |
|     Fast | 275 | 350 | 27.50 | 11.45 | 4.69 | 7.86 | 7.43 | 2.20 | 33.63 |
|   Brush 3rd or additional coats | | | | | | | | | |
|     Slow | 250 | 425 | 36.70 | 8.10 | 2.39 | 8.64 | 3.63 | 3.64 | 26.40 |
|     Medium | 275 | 400 | 32.10 | 9.36 | 3.33 | 8.03 | 5.18 | 3.11 | 29.01 |
|     Fast | 300 | 375 | 27.50 | 10.50 | 4.27 | 7.33 | 6.85 | 2.03 | 30.98 |
| Sealer, water base (material #1) | | | | | | | | | |
|   Brush prime coat | | | | | | | | | |
|     Slow | 200 | 325 | 30.50 | 10.13 | 2.98 | 9.38 | 4.28 | 4.28 | 31.05 |
|     Medium | 225 | 313 | 26.70 | 11.44 | 4.04 | 8.53 | 6.01 | 3.60 | 33.62 |
|     Fast | 250 | 300 | 22.90 | 12.60 | 5.14 | 7.63 | 7.86 | 2.33 | 35.56 |
| Sealer, oil base (material #2) | | | | | | | | | |
|   Brush prime coat | | | | | | | | | |
|     Slow | 200 | 350 | 39.70 | 10.13 | 2.98 | 11.34 | 4.65 | 4.66 | 33.76 |
|     Medium | 225 | 338 | 34.80 | 11.44 | 4.04 | 10.30 | 6.45 | 3.87 | 36.10 |
|     Fast | 250 | 325 | 29.80 | 12.60 | 5.14 | 9.17 | 8.34 | 2.47 | 37.72 |
| Enamel, water base (material #9) | | | | | | | | | |
|   Brush 1st finish coat | | | | | | | | | |
|     Slow | 200 | 400 | 46.80 | 10.13 | 2.98 | 11.70 | 4.72 | 4.73 | 34.26 |
|     Medium | 225 | 375 | 41.00 | 11.44 | 4.04 | 10.93 | 6.61 | 3.96 | 36.98 |
|     Fast | 250 | 350 | 35.10 | 12.60 | 5.14 | 10.03 | 8.61 | 2.55 | 38.93 |
|   Brush 2nd and additional finish coats | | | | | | | | | |
|     Slow | 225 | 425 | 46.80 | 9.00 | 2.64 | 11.01 | 4.31 | 4.32 | 31.28 |
|     Medium | 250 | 400 | 41.00 | 10.30 | 3.65 | 10.25 | 6.05 | 3.63 | 33.88 |
|     Fast | 275 | 375 | 35.10 | 11.45 | 4.69 | 9.36 | 7.90 | 2.34 | 35.74 |
| Enamel, oil base (material #10) | | | | | | | | | |
|   Brush 1st finish coat | | | | | | | | | |
|     Slow | 200 | 400 | 61.70 | 10.13 | 2.98 | 15.43 | 5.42 | 5.44 | 39.40 |
|     Medium | 225 | 388 | 54.00 | 11.44 | 4.04 | 13.92 | 7.35 | 4.41 | 41.16 |
|     Fast | 250 | 375 | 46.30 | 12.60 | 5.14 | 12.35 | 9.33 | 2.76 | 42.18 |

*National Painting Cost Estimator*

|  | Labor SF per manhour | Material coverage SF/gallon | Material cost per gallon | Labor cost per 100 SF | Labor burden 100 SF | Material cost per 100 SF | Overhead per 100 SF | Profit per 100 SF | Total price per 100 SF |
|---|---|---|---|---|---|---|---|---|---|
| **Brush 2nd or additional finish coats** | | | | | | | | | |
| Slow | 225 | 425 | 61.70 | 9.00 | 2.64 | 14.52 | 4.97 | 4.98 | 36.11 |
| Medium | 250 | 413 | 54.00 | 10.30 | 3.65 | 13.08 | 6.76 | 4.05 | 37.84 |
| Fast | 275 | 400 | 46.30 | 11.45 | 4.69 | 11.58 | 8.59 | 2.54 | 38.85 |
| **Epoxy coating, white (material #52)** | | | | | | | | | |
| **Brush 1st coat** | | | | | | | | | |
| Slow | 175 | 425 | 177.00 | 11.57 | 3.40 | 41.65 | 10.76 | 10.78 | 78.16 |
| Medium | 200 | 400 | 154.90 | 12.88 | 4.56 | 38.73 | 14.04 | 8.43 | 78.64 |
| Fast | 225 | 375 | 132.70 | 14.00 | 5.69 | 35.39 | 17.08 | 5.05 | 77.21 |
| **Brush 2nd or additional coats** | | | | | | | | | |
| Slow | 200 | 450 | 177.00 | 10.13 | 2.98 | 39.33 | 9.97 | 9.99 | 72.40 |
| Medium | 225 | 425 | 154.90 | 11.44 | 4.04 | 36.45 | 12.99 | 7.79 | 72.71 |
| Fast | 250 | 400 | 132.70 | 12.60 | 5.14 | 33.18 | 15.79 | 4.67 | 71.38 |

Ceiling estimates are based on overall dimensions (length times width) to 8 feet high. Do not make deductions for openings in the ceiling area that are under 100 square feet. For heights above 8 feet, use the High Time Difficulty Factors on page 139. ADD for cutting-in at ceilings and protecting adjacent surfaces if ceilings alone are being painted, not walls. Otherwise, figure any cutting-in time with walls. See the notes under the wall formulas for clarification. "Slow" work is based on an hourly wage of $20.25, "Medium" work on an hourly wage of $25.75, and "Fast" work on an hourly wage of $31.50. Other qualifications that apply to this table are on page 9.

*General Painting Costs*

|  | Labor SF per manhour | Material coverage SF/gallon | Material cost per gallon | Labor cost per 100 SF | Labor burden 100 SF | Material cost per 100 SF | Overhead per 100 SF | Profit per 100 SF | Total price per 100 SF |
|---|---|---|---|---|---|---|---|---|---|
| **Ceilings, gypsum drywall, smooth finish, roll** | | | | | | | | | |
| Flat latex, water base (material #5) | | | | | | | | | |
| Roll 1st coat | | | | | | | | | |
| Slow | 325 | 350 | 36.70 | 6.23 | 1.85 | 10.49 | 3.53 | 3.53 | 25.63 |
| Medium | 375 | 325 | 32.10 | 6.87 | 2.44 | 9.88 | 4.80 | 2.88 | 26.87 |
| Fast | 425 | 300 | 27.50 | 7.41 | 3.01 | 9.17 | 6.08 | 1.80 | 27.47 |
| Roll 2nd coat | | | | | | | | | |
| Slow | 375 | 375 | 36.70 | 5.40 | 1.60 | 9.79 | 3.19 | 3.20 | 23.18 |
| Medium | 413 | 363 | 32.10 | 6.23 | 2.21 | 8.84 | 4.32 | 2.59 | 24.19 |
| Fast | 450 | 350 | 27.50 | 7.00 | 2.85 | 7.86 | 5.49 | 1.62 | 24.82 |
| Roll 3rd or additional coats | | | | | | | | | |
| Slow | 425 | 400 | 36.70 | 4.76 | 1.40 | 9.18 | 2.91 | 2.92 | 21.17 |
| Medium | 450 | 388 | 32.10 | 5.72 | 2.02 | 8.27 | 4.00 | 2.40 | 22.41 |
| Fast | 475 | 375 | 27.50 | 6.63 | 2.73 | 7.33 | 5.17 | 1.53 | 23.39 |
| Sealer, water base (material #1) | | | | | | | | | |
| Roll prime coat | | | | | | | | | |
| Slow | 350 | 350 | 30.50 | 5.79 | 1.71 | 8.71 | 3.08 | 3.09 | 22.38 |
| Medium | 400 | 325 | 26.70 | 6.44 | 2.28 | 8.22 | 4.24 | 2.54 | 23.72 |
| Fast | 450 | 300 | 22.90 | 7.00 | 2.85 | 7.63 | 5.42 | 1.60 | 24.50 |
| Sealer, oil base (material #2) | | | | | | | | | |
| Roll prime coat | | | | | | | | | |
| Slow | 350 | 300 | 39.70 | 5.79 | 1.71 | 13.23 | 3.94 | 3.95 | 28.62 |
| Medium | 400 | 288 | 34.80 | 6.44 | 2.28 | 12.08 | 5.20 | 3.12 | 29.12 |
| Fast | 450 | 275 | 29.80 | 7.00 | 2.85 | 10.84 | 6.42 | 1.90 | 29.01 |
| Enamel, water base, (material #9) | | | | | | | | | |
| Roll 1st finish coat | | | | | | | | | |
| Slow | 350 | 375 | 46.80 | 5.79 | 1.71 | 12.48 | 3.80 | 3.80 | 27.58 |
| Medium | 400 | 363 | 41.00 | 6.44 | 2.28 | 11.29 | 5.00 | 3.00 | 28.01 |
| Fast | 450 | 350 | 35.10 | 7.00 | 2.85 | 10.03 | 6.17 | 1.82 | 27.87 |
| Roll 2nd or additional finish coats | | | | | | | | | |
| Slow | 425 | 400 | 46.80 | 4.76 | 1.40 | 11.70 | 3.39 | 3.40 | 24.65 |
| Medium | 450 | 388 | 41.00 | 5.72 | 2.02 | 10.57 | 4.58 | 2.75 | 25.64 |
| Fast | 475 | 375 | 35.10 | 6.63 | 2.73 | 9.36 | 5.80 | 1.72 | 26.24 |
| Enamel, oil base (material #10) | | | | | | | | | |
| Roll 1st finish coat | | | | | | | | | |
| Slow | 350 | 350 | 61.70 | 5.79 | 1.71 | 17.63 | 4.77 | 4.78 | 34.68 |
| Medium | 400 | 338 | 54.00 | 6.44 | 2.28 | 15.98 | 6.18 | 3.71 | 34.59 |
| Fast | 450 | 325 | 46.30 | 7.00 | 2.85 | 14.25 | 7.47 | 2.21 | 33.78 |

*National Painting Cost Estimator*

|  | Labor SF per manhour | Material coverage SF/gallon | Material cost per gallon | Labor cost per 100 SF | Labor burden 100 SF | Material cost per 100 SF | Overhead per 100 SF | Profit per 100 SF | Total price per 100 SF |
|---|---|---|---|---|---|---|---|---|---|
| **Roll 2nd or additional finish coats** | | | | | | | | | |
| Slow | 425 | 375 | 61.70 | 4.76 | 1.40 | 16.45 | 4.30 | 4.31 | 31.22 |
| Medium | 450 | 363 | 54.00 | 5.72 | 2.02 | 14.88 | 5.66 | 3.39 | 31.67 |
| Fast | 475 | 350 | 46.30 | 6.63 | 2.73 | 13.23 | 7.00 | 2.07 | 31.66 |
| **Epoxy coating, white (material #52)** | | | | | | | | | |
| **Roll 1st finish coat** | | | | | | | | | |
| Slow | 325 | 400 | 177.00 | 6.23 | 1.85 | 44.25 | 9.94 | 9.96 | 72.23 |
| Medium | 363 | 375 | 154.90 | 7.09 | 2.50 | 41.31 | 12.73 | 7.64 | 71.27 |
| Fast | 400 | 350 | 132.70 | 7.88 | 3.21 | 37.91 | 15.19 | 4.49 | 68.68 |
| **Roll 2nd or additional finish coats** | | | | | | | | | |
| Slow | 400 | 425 | 177.00 | 5.06 | 1.50 | 41.65 | 9.16 | 9.18 | 66.55 |
| Medium | 425 | 400 | 154.90 | 6.06 | 2.13 | 38.73 | 11.74 | 7.04 | 65.70 |
| Fast | 450 | 375 | 132.70 | 7.00 | 2.85 | 35.39 | 14.03 | 4.15 | 63.42 |
| **Stipple finish** | | | | | | | | | |
| Slow | 200 | -- | -- | 10.13 | 2.98 | -- | 2.49 | 2.50 | 18.10 |
| Medium | 225 | -- | -- | 11.44 | 4.04 | -- | 3.87 | 2.32 | 21.67 |
| Fast | 250 | -- | -- | 12.60 | 5.14 | -- | 5.50 | 1.63 | 24.87 |

Ceiling estimates are based on overall dimensions (length times width) to 8 feet high. Do not make deductions for openings in the ceiling area that are under 100 square feet. For heights above 8 feet, use the High Time Difficulty Factors on page 139. ADD for cutting-in at ceilings and protecting adjacent surfaces if ceilings alone are being painted, not walls. Otherwise, figure any cutting-in time with walls. See the notes under the wall formulas for clarification. "Slow" work is based on an hourly wage of $20.25, "Medium" work on an hourly wage of $25.75, and "Fast" work on an hourly wage of $31.50. Other qualifications that apply to this table are on page 9.

*General Painting Costs*

|  | Labor SF per manhour | Material coverage SF/gallon | Material cost per gallon | Labor cost per 100 SF | Labor burden 100 SF | Material cost per 100 SF | Overhead per 100 SF | Profit per 100 SF | Total price per 100 SF |
|---|---|---|---|---|---|---|---|---|---|

## Ceilings, gypsum drywall, smooth finish, spray

**Flat latex, water base (material #5)**

*Spray 1st coat*
| | | | | | | | | | |
|---|---|---|---|---|---|---|---|---|---|
| Slow | 750 | 300 | 36.70 | 2.70 | .79 | 12.23 | 2.99 | 3.00 | 21.71 |
| Medium | 850 | 275 | 32.10 | 3.03 | 1.08 | 11.67 | 3.94 | 2.37 | 22.09 |
| Fast | 950 | 250 | 27.50 | 3.32 | 1.34 | 11.00 | 4.86 | 1.44 | 21.96 |

*Spray 2nd coat*
| | | | | | | | | | |
|---|---|---|---|---|---|---|---|---|---|
| Slow | 850 | 350 | 36.70 | 2.38 | .71 | 10.49 | 2.58 | 2.58 | 18.74 |
| Medium | 950 | 325 | 32.10 | 2.71 | .95 | 9.88 | 3.39 | 2.03 | 18.96 |
| Fast | 1050 | 300 | 27.50 | 3.00 | 1.21 | 9.17 | 4.15 | 1.23 | 18.76 |

*Spray 3rd or additional coats*
| | | | | | | | | | |
|---|---|---|---|---|---|---|---|---|---|
| Slow | 900 | 350 | 36.70 | 2.25 | .66 | 10.49 | 2.55 | 2.55 | 18.50 |
| Medium | 1000 | 338 | 32.10 | 2.58 | .91 | 9.50 | 3.25 | 1.95 | 18.19 |
| Fast | 1100 | 325 | 27.50 | 2.86 | 1.18 | 8.46 | 3.87 | 1.15 | 17.52 |

**Sealer, water base (material #1)**

*Spray prime coat*
| | | | | | | | | | |
|---|---|---|---|---|---|---|---|---|---|
| Slow | 800 | 300 | 30.50 | 2.53 | .75 | 10.17 | 2.56 | 2.56 | 18.57 |
| Medium | 900 | 275 | 26.70 | 2.86 | 1.01 | 9.71 | 3.40 | 2.04 | 19.02 |
| Fast | 1000 | 250 | 22.90 | 3.15 | 1.29 | 9.16 | 4.22 | 1.25 | 19.07 |

**Sealer, oil base (material #2)**

*Spray prime coat*
| | | | | | | | | | |
|---|---|---|---|---|---|---|---|---|---|
| Slow | 800 | 250 | 39.70 | 2.53 | .75 | 15.88 | 3.64 | 3.65 | 26.45 |
| Medium | 900 | 238 | 34.80 | 2.86 | 1.01 | 14.62 | 4.62 | 2.77 | 25.88 |
| Fast | 1000 | 225 | 29.80 | 3.15 | 1.29 | 13.24 | 5.48 | 1.62 | 24.78 |

**Enamel, water base (material #9)**

*Spray 1st finish coat*
| | | | | | | | | | |
|---|---|---|---|---|---|---|---|---|---|
| Slow | 800 | 350 | 46.80 | 2.53 | .75 | 13.37 | 3.16 | 3.17 | 22.98 |
| Medium | 900 | 325 | 41.00 | 2.86 | 1.01 | 12.62 | 4.12 | 2.47 | 23.08 |
| Fast | 1000 | 300 | 35.10 | 3.15 | 1.29 | 11.70 | 5.00 | 1.48 | 22.62 |

*Spray 2nd or additional finish coats*
| | | | | | | | | | |
|---|---|---|---|---|---|---|---|---|---|
| Slow | 850 | 350 | 46.80 | 2.38 | .71 | 13.37 | 3.13 | 3.13 | 22.72 |
| Medium | 950 | 338 | 41.00 | 2.71 | .95 | 12.13 | 3.95 | 2.37 | 22.11 |
| Fast | 1050 | 325 | 35.10 | 3.00 | 1.21 | 10.80 | 4.66 | 1.38 | 21.05 |

**Enamel, oil base (material #10)**

*Spray 1st finish coat*
| | | | | | | | | | |
|---|---|---|---|---|---|---|---|---|---|
| Slow | 800 | 300 | 61.70 | 2.53 | .75 | 20.57 | 4.53 | 4.54 | 32.92 |
| Medium | 900 | 280 | 54.00 | 2.86 | 1.01 | 19.29 | 5.79 | 3.47 | 32.42 |
| Fast | 1000 | 260 | 46.30 | 3.15 | 1.29 | 17.81 | 6.90 | 2.04 | 31.19 |

*Spray 2nd or additional finish coats*
| | | | | | | | | | |
|---|---|---|---|---|---|---|---|---|---|
| Slow | 850 | 325 | 61.70 | 2.38 | .71 | 18.98 | 4.19 | 4.20 | 30.46 |
| Medium | 950 | 313 | 54.00 | 2.71 | .95 | 17.25 | 5.23 | 3.14 | 29.28 |
| Fast | 1050 | 300 | 46.30 | 3.00 | 1.21 | 15.43 | 6.09 | 1.80 | 27.53 |

Ceiling estimates are based on overall dimensions (length times width) to 8 feet high. Do not make deductions for openings in the ceiling area that are under 100 square feet. For heights above 8 feet, use the High Time Difficulty Factors on page 139. ADD for cutting-in at ceilings and protecting adjacent surfaces if ceilings alone are being painted, not walls. Otherwise, figure any cutting-in and protection time with the walls. "Slow" work is based on an hourly wage of $20.25, "Medium" work on an hourly wage of $25.75, and "Fast" work on an hourly wage of $31.50. Other qualifications that apply to this table are on page 9.

*National Painting Cost Estimator*

|  | Labor SF per manhour | Material coverage SF/gallon | Material cost per gallon | Labor cost per 100 SF | Labor burden 100 SF | Material cost per 100 SF | Overhead per 100 SF | Profit per 100 SF | Total price per 100 SF |
|---|---|---|---|---|---|---|---|---|---|
| **Ceilings, tongue & groove, paint grade, brush** | | | | | | | | | |
| Flat latex, water base (material #5) | | | | | | | | | |
| Brush 1st coat | | | | | | | | | |
| Slow | 55 | 300 | 36.70 | 36.82 | 10.85 | 12.23 | 11.38 | 11.41 | 82.69 |
| Medium | 65 | 288 | 32.10 | 39.62 | 14.01 | 11.15 | 16.20 | 9.72 | 90.70 |
| Fast | 75 | 275 | 27.50 | 42.00 | 17.12 | 10.00 | 21.43 | 6.34 | 96.89 |
| Brush 2nd coat | | | | | | | | | |
| Slow | 65 | 350 | 36.70 | 31.15 | 9.18 | 10.49 | 9.66 | 9.68 | 70.16 |
| Medium | 75 | 338 | 32.10 | 34.33 | 12.15 | 9.50 | 14.00 | 8.40 | 78.38 |
| Fast | 85 | 325 | 27.50 | 37.06 | 15.10 | 8.46 | 18.80 | 5.56 | 84.98 |
| Brush 3rd or additional coats | | | | | | | | | |
| Slow | 80 | 375 | 36.70 | 25.31 | 7.47 | 9.79 | 8.09 | 8.11 | 58.77 |
| Medium | 90 | 363 | 32.10 | 28.61 | 10.13 | 8.84 | 11.90 | 7.14 | 66.62 |
| Fast | 100 | 350 | 27.50 | 31.50 | 12.85 | 7.86 | 16.19 | 4.79 | 73.19 |
| Sealer, water base (material #1) | | | | | | | | | |
| Brush prime coat | | | | | | | | | |
| Slow | 60 | 300 | 30.50 | 33.75 | 9.96 | 10.17 | 10.24 | 10.26 | 74.38 |
| Medium | 70 | 288 | 26.70 | 36.79 | 13.04 | 9.27 | 14.77 | 8.86 | 82.73 |
| Fast | 80 | 275 | 22.90 | 39.38 | 16.06 | 8.33 | 19.77 | 5.85 | 89.39 |
| Sealer, oil base (material #2) | | | | | | | | | |
| Brush prime coat | | | | | | | | | |
| Slow | 60 | 350 | 39.70 | 33.75 | 9.96 | 11.34 | 10.46 | 10.48 | 75.99 |
| Medium | 70 | 338 | 34.80 | 36.79 | 13.04 | 10.30 | 15.03 | 9.02 | 84.18 |
| Fast | 80 | 325 | 29.80 | 39.38 | 16.06 | 9.17 | 20.03 | 5.93 | 90.57 |
| Enamel, water base (material #9) | | | | | | | | | |
| Brush 1st finish coat | | | | | | | | | |
| Slow | 65 | 300 | 46.80 | 31.15 | 9.18 | 15.60 | 10.63 | 10.65 | 77.21 |
| Medium | 75 | 288 | 41.00 | 34.33 | 12.15 | 14.24 | 15.18 | 9.11 | 85.01 |
| Fast | 85 | 275 | 35.10 | 37.06 | 15.10 | 12.76 | 20.13 | 5.95 | 91.00 |
| Brush 2nd or additional finish coats | | | | | | | | | |
| Slow | 80 | 375 | 46.80 | 25.31 | 7.47 | 12.48 | 8.60 | 8.62 | 62.48 |
| Medium | 90 | 363 | 41.00 | 28.61 | 10.13 | 11.29 | 12.51 | 7.50 | 70.04 |
| Fast | 100 | 350 | 35.10 | 31.50 | 12.85 | 10.03 | 16.86 | 4.99 | 76.23 |

*General Painting Costs*

|  | Labor SF per manhour | Material coverage SF/gallon | Material cost per gallon | Labor cost per 100 SF | Labor burden 100 SF | Material cost per 100 SF | Overhead per 100 SF | Profit per 100 SF | Total price per 100 SF |
|---|---|---|---|---|---|---|---|---|---|
| **Enamel, oil base (material #10)** | | | | | | | | | |
| **Brush 1st finish coat** | | | | | | | | | |
| Slow | 55 | 375 | 61.70 | 36.82 | 10.85 | 16.45 | 12.18 | 12.21 | 88.51 |
| Medium | 65 | 363 | 54.00 | 39.62 | 14.01 | 14.88 | 17.13 | 10.28 | 95.92 |
| Fast | 75 | 350 | 46.30 | 42.00 | 17.12 | 13.23 | 22.43 | 6.64 | 101.42 |
| **Brush 2nd or additional finish coats** | | | | | | | | | |
| Slow | 70 | 425 | 61.70 | 28.93 | 8.54 | 14.52 | 9.88 | 9.90 | 71.77 |
| Medium | 80 | 413 | 54.00 | 32.19 | 11.40 | 13.08 | 14.17 | 8.50 | 79.34 |
| Fast | 90 | 400 | 46.30 | 35.00 | 14.27 | 11.58 | 18.87 | 5.58 | 85.30 |

Ceiling estimates are based on overall dimensions (length times width) to 8 feet high. Do not make deductions for openings in the ceiling area that are under 100 square feet. Figure painting of wood ceilings separate from wood beams. For heights above 8 feet, use the High Time Difficulty Factors on page 139. ADD for protecting adjacent surfaces if ceilings alone are painted, not the walls. Otherwise, figure any cutting-in and protection time with the walls. "Slow" work is based on an hourly wage of $20.25, "Medium" work on an hourly wage of $25.75, and "Fast" work on an hourly wage of $31.50. Other qualifications that apply to this table are on page 9.

|  | Labor SF per manhour | Material coverage SF/gallon | Material cost per gallon | Labor cost per 100 SF | Labor burden 100 SF | Material cost per 100 SF | Overhead per 100 SF | Profit per 100 SF | Total price per 100 SF |
|---|---|---|---|---|---|---|---|---|---|
| **Ceilings, tongue & groove, paint grade, roll and brush** | | | | | | | | | |
| Flat latex, water base (material #5) | | | | | | | | | |
|   Roll 1st coat | | | | | | | | | |
|     Slow | 110 | 275 | 36.70 | 18.41 | 5.42 | 13.35 | 7.07 | 7.08 | 51.33 |
|     Medium | 130 | 263 | 32.10 | 19.81 | 7.01 | 12.21 | 9.76 | 5.85 | 54.64 |
|     Fast | 150 | 250 | 27.50 | 21.00 | 8.58 | 11.00 | 12.58 | 3.72 | 56.88 |
|   Roll 2nd coat | | | | | | | | | |
|     Slow | 140 | 325 | 36.70 | 14.46 | 4.26 | 11.29 | 5.70 | 5.72 | 41.43 |
|     Medium | 155 | 313 | 32.10 | 16.61 | 5.88 | 10.26 | 8.19 | 4.91 | 45.85 |
|     Fast | 170 | 300 | 27.50 | 18.53 | 7.55 | 9.17 | 10.93 | 3.23 | 49.41 |
|   Roll 3rd or additional coats | | | | | | | | | |
|     Slow | 190 | 350 | 36.70 | 10.66 | 3.13 | 10.49 | 4.62 | 4.63 | 33.53 |
|     Medium | 200 | 338 | 32.10 | 12.88 | 4.56 | 9.50 | 6.74 | 4.04 | 37.72 |
|     Fast | 210 | 325 | 27.50 | 15.00 | 6.11 | 8.46 | 9.17 | 2.71 | 41.45 |
| Sealer, water base (material #1) | | | | | | | | | |
|   Roll prime coat | | | | | | | | | |
|     Slow | 100 | 275 | 30.50 | 20.25 | 5.97 | 11.09 | 7.09 | 7.10 | 51.50 |
|     Medium | 120 | 263 | 26.70 | 21.46 | 7.59 | 10.15 | 9.80 | 5.88 | 54.88 |
|     Fast | 150 | 250 | 22.90 | 21.00 | 8.58 | 9.16 | 12.01 | 3.55 | 54.30 |
| Sealer, oil base (material #2) | | | | | | | | | |
|   Roll prime coat | | | | | | | | | |
|     Slow | 100 | 350 | 39.70 | 20.25 | 5.97 | 11.34 | 7.14 | 7.15 | 51.85 |
|     Medium | 120 | 325 | 34.80 | 21.46 | 7.59 | 10.71 | 9.94 | 5.97 | 55.67 |
|     Fast | 150 | 300 | 29.80 | 21.00 | 8.58 | 9.93 | 12.25 | 3.62 | 55.38 |
| Enamel, water base (material #9) | | | | | | | | | |
|   Roll 1st finish coat | | | | | | | | | |
|     Slow | 130 | 325 | 46.80 | 15.58 | 4.58 | 14.40 | 6.57 | 6.58 | 47.71 |
|     Medium | 145 | 313 | 41.00 | 17.76 | 6.30 | 13.10 | 9.29 | 5.57 | 52.02 |
|     Fast | 160 | 300 | 35.10 | 19.69 | 8.03 | 11.70 | 12.22 | 3.61 | 55.25 |
|   Roll 2nd or additional finish coats | | | | | | | | | |
|     Slow | 180 | 350 | 46.80 | 11.25 | 3.33 | 13.37 | 5.31 | 5.32 | 38.58 |
|     Medium | 190 | 338 | 41.00 | 13.55 | 4.79 | 12.13 | 7.62 | 4.57 | 42.66 |
|     Fast | 200 | 325 | 35.10 | 15.75 | 6.43 | 10.80 | 10.22 | 3.02 | 46.22 |

*General Painting Costs*

|  | Labor SF per manhour | Material coverage SF/gallon | Material cost per gallon | Labor cost per 100 SF | Labor burden 100 SF | Material cost per 100 SF | Overhead per 100 SF | Profit per 100 SF | Total price per 100 SF |
|---|---|---|---|---|---|---|---|---|---|
| **Enamel, oil base (material #10)** | | | | | | | | | |
| Roll 1st finish coat | | | | | | | | | |
| Slow | 130 | 375 | 61.70 | 15.58 | 4.58 | 16.45 | 6.96 | 6.97 | 50.54 |
| Medium | 145 | 363 | 54.00 | 17.76 | 6.30 | 14.88 | 9.73 | 5.84 | 54.51 |
| Fast | 160 | 350 | 46.30 | 19.69 | 8.03 | 13.23 | 12.69 | 3.75 | 57.39 |
| Roll 2nd or additional finish coats | | | | | | | | | |
| Slow | 180 | 400 | 61.70 | 11.25 | 3.33 | 15.43 | 5.70 | 5.71 | 41.42 |
| Medium | 190 | 388 | 54.00 | 13.55 | 4.79 | 13.92 | 8.07 | 4.84 | 45.17 |
| Fast | 200 | 375 | 46.30 | 15.75 | 6.43 | 12.35 | 10.70 | 3.17 | 48.40 |

Ceiling estimates are based on overall dimensions (length times width) to 8 feet high. Do not make deductions for openings in the ceiling area that are under 100 square feet. Figure painting of wood ceilings separate from wood beams. For heights above 8 feet, use the High Time Difficulty Factors on page 139. ADD for protecting adjacent surfaces if ceilings alone are painted, not the walls. Otherwise, figure any cutting-in and protection time with the walls. "Slow" work is based on an hourly wage of $20.25, "Medium" work on an hourly wage of $25.75, and "Fast" work on an hourly wage of $31.50. Other qualifications that apply to this table are on page 9.

*National Painting Cost Estimator*

|  | Labor SF per manhour | Material coverage SF/gallon | Material cost per gallon | Labor cost per 100 SF | Labor burden 100 SF | Material cost per 100 SF | Overhead per 100 SF | Profit per 100 SF | Total price per 100 SF |
|---|---|---|---|---|---|---|---|---|---|

## Ceilings, tongue & groove, paint grade, spray

Flat latex, water base (material #5)
  Spray 1st coat

|  | | | | | | | | | |
|---|---|---|---|---|---|---|---|---|---|
| Slow | 300 | 180 | 36.70 | 6.75 | 1.98 | 20.39 | 5.53 | 5.55 | 40.20 |
| Medium | 360 | 155 | 32.10 | 7.15 | 2.54 | 20.71 | 7.60 | 4.56 | 42.56 |
| Fast | 420 | 125 | 27.50 | 7.50 | 3.06 | 22.00 | 10.09 | 2.99 | 45.64 |

  Spray 2nd coat

|  | | | | | | | | | |
|---|---|---|---|---|---|---|---|---|---|
| Slow | 420 | 250 | 36.70 | 4.82 | 1.42 | 14.68 | 3.97 | 3.98 | 28.87 |
| Medium | 470 | 225 | 32.10 | 5.48 | 1.95 | 14.27 | 5.42 | 3.25 | 30.37 |
| Fast | 520 | 200 | 27.50 | 6.06 | 2.46 | 13.75 | 6.91 | 2.04 | 31.22 |

  Spray 3rd or additional coats

|  | | | | | | | | | |
|---|---|---|---|---|---|---|---|---|---|
| Slow | 520 | 325 | 36.70 | 3.89 | 1.14 | 11.29 | 3.10 | 3.11 | 22.53 |
| Medium | 570 | 300 | 32.10 | 4.52 | 1.58 | 10.70 | 4.21 | 2.52 | 23.53 |
| Fast | 620 | 275 | 27.50 | 5.08 | 2.06 | 10.00 | 5.32 | 1.57 | 24.03 |

Sealer, water base (material #1)
  Spray prime coat

|  | | | | | | | | | |
|---|---|---|---|---|---|---|---|---|---|
| Slow | 320 | 180 | 30.50 | 6.33 | 1.88 | 16.94 | 4.78 | 4.79 | 34.72 |
| Medium | 380 | 155 | 26.70 | 6.78 | 2.39 | 17.23 | 6.60 | 3.96 | 36.96 |
| Fast | 440 | 125 | 22.90 | 7.16 | 2.91 | 18.32 | 8.80 | 2.60 | 39.79 |

Sealer, oil base (material #2)
  Spray prime coat

|  | | | | | | | | | |
|---|---|---|---|---|---|---|---|---|---|
| Slow | 320 | 200 | 39.70 | 6.33 | 1.88 | 19.85 | 5.33 | 5.34 | 38.73 |
| Medium | 380 | 190 | 34.80 | 6.78 | 2.39 | 18.32 | 6.88 | 4.13 | 38.50 |
| Fast | 440 | 180 | 29.80 | 7.16 | 2.91 | 16.56 | 8.26 | 2.44 | 37.33 |

Enamel, water base (material #9)
  Spray 1st finish coat

|  | | | | | | | | | |
|---|---|---|---|---|---|---|---|---|---|
| Slow | 400 | 250 | 46.80 | 5.06 | 1.50 | 18.72 | 4.80 | 4.81 | 34.89 |
| Medium | 450 | 225 | 41.00 | 5.72 | 2.02 | 18.22 | 6.49 | 3.89 | 36.34 |
| Fast | 500 | 200 | 35.10 | 6.30 | 2.57 | 17.55 | 8.19 | 2.42 | 37.03 |

  Spray 2nd or additional finish coat

|  | | | | | | | | | |
|---|---|---|---|---|---|---|---|---|---|
| Slow | 500 | 325 | 46.80 | 4.05 | 1.19 | 14.40 | 3.73 | 3.74 | 27.11 |
| Medium | 550 | 300 | 41.00 | 4.68 | 1.67 | 13.67 | 5.00 | 3.00 | 28.02 |
| Fast | 600 | 275 | 35.10 | 5.25 | 2.16 | 12.76 | 6.25 | 1.85 | 28.27 |

*General Painting Costs*

|  | Labor SF per manhour | Material coverage SF/gallon | Material cost per gallon | Labor cost per 100 SF | Labor burden 100 SF | Material cost per 100 SF | Overhead per 100 SF | Profit per 100 SF | Total price per 100 SF |
|---|---|---|---|---|---|---|---|---|---|
| **Enamel, oil base (material #10)** | | | | | | | | | |
| Spray 1st finish coat | | | | | | | | | |
|   Slow | 400 | 270 | 61.70 | 5.06 | 1.50 | 22.85 | 5.59 | 5.60 | 40.60 |
|   Medium | 450 | 250 | 54.00 | 5.72 | 2.02 | 21.60 | 7.34 | 4.40 | 41.08 |
|   Fast | 500 | 230 | 46.30 | 6.30 | 2.57 | 20.13 | 8.99 | 2.66 | 40.65 |
| Spray 2nd or additional finish coat | | | | | | | | | |
|   Slow | 500 | 325 | 61.70 | 4.05 | 1.19 | 18.98 | 4.60 | 4.61 | 33.43 |
|   Medium | 550 | 313 | 54.00 | 4.68 | 1.67 | 17.25 | 5.90 | 3.54 | 33.04 |
|   Fast | 600 | 300 | 46.30 | 5.25 | 2.16 | 15.43 | 7.07 | 2.09 | 32.00 |

Ceiling estimates are based on overall dimensions (length times width) to 8 feet high. Do not make deductions for openings in the ceiling area that are under 100 square feet. Figure painting of wood ceilings separate from wood beams. For heights above 8 feet, use the High Time Difficulty Factors on page 139. ADD for masking-off or cutting-in at wall-to-ceiling intersections and for protecting adjacent surfaces as necessary. "Slow" work is based on an hourly wage of $20.25, "Medium" work on an hourly wage of $25.75, and "Fast" work on an hourly wage of $31.50. Other qualifications that apply to this table are on page 9.

*National Painting Cost Estimator*

|  | Labor SF per manhour | Material coverage SF/gallon | Material cost per gallon | Labor cost per 100 SF | Labor burden 100 SF | Material cost per 100 SF | Overhead per 100 SF | Profit per 100 SF | Total price per 100 SF |
|---|---|---|---|---|---|---|---|---|---|

## Ceilings, tongue & groove, stain grade, roll and brush

Semi-transparent stain, water base (material #20)
Roll & brush each coat

| | | | | | | | | | |
|---|---|---|---|---|---|---|---|---|---|
| Slow | 200 | 300 | 47.50 | 10.13 | 2.98 | 15.83 | 5.50 | 5.51 | 39.95 |
| Medium | 240 | 275 | 41.60 | 10.73 | 3.81 | 15.13 | 7.42 | 4.45 | 41.54 |
| Fast | 280 | 250 | 35.60 | 11.25 | 4.58 | 14.24 | 9.32 | 2.76 | 42.15 |

Semi-transparent stain, oil base (material #21)
Roll & brush each coat

| | | | | | | | | | |
|---|---|---|---|---|---|---|---|---|---|
| Slow | 200 | 280 | 48.70 | 10.13 | 2.98 | 17.39 | 5.80 | 5.81 | 42.11 |
| Medium | 240 | 260 | 42.60 | 10.73 | 3.81 | 16.38 | 7.73 | 4.64 | 43.29 |
| Fast | 280 | 240 | 36.50 | 11.25 | 4.58 | 15.21 | 9.63 | 2.85 | 43.52 |

## Ceilings, tongue & groove, stain grade, spray application

Semi-transparent stain, water base (material #20)
Spray each coat

| | | | | | | | | | |
|---|---|---|---|---|---|---|---|---|---|
| Slow | 300 | 220 | 47.50 | 6.75 | 1.98 | 21.59 | 5.76 | 5.77 | 41.85 |
| Medium | 350 | 200 | 41.60 | 7.36 | 2.61 | 20.80 | 7.69 | 4.62 | 43.08 |
| Fast | 400 | 180 | 35.60 | 7.88 | 3.21 | 19.78 | 9.57 | 2.83 | 43.27 |

Semi-transparent stain, oil base (material #21)
Spray each coat

| | | | | | | | | | |
|---|---|---|---|---|---|---|---|---|---|
| Slow | 300 | 200 | 48.70 | 6.75 | 1.98 | 24.35 | 6.29 | 6.30 | 45.67 |
| Medium | 350 | 188 | 42.60 | 7.36 | 2.61 | 22.66 | 8.16 | 4.89 | 45.68 |
| Fast | 400 | 175 | 36.50 | 7.88 | 3.21 | 20.86 | 9.91 | 2.93 | 44.79 |

Stain, seal and 2 coat lacquer system (7 step process)
STEP 1: Sand & putty

| | | | | | | | | | |
|---|---|---|---|---|---|---|---|---|---|
| Slow | 100 | -- | -- | 20.25 | 5.97 | -- | 4.98 | 4.99 | 36.19 |
| Medium | 125 | -- | -- | 20.60 | 7.30 | -- | 6.97 | 4.18 | 39.05 |
| Fast | 150 | -- | -- | 21.00 | 8.58 | -- | 9.17 | 2.71 | 41.46 |

STEP 2 & 3: Wiping stain, oil base (material #11a) & wipe
Roll & brush, 1 coat & wipe

| | | | | | | | | | |
|---|---|---|---|---|---|---|---|---|---|
| Slow | 75 | 300 | 51.30 | 27.00 | 7.95 | 17.10 | 9.89 | 9.91 | 71.85 |
| Medium | 100 | 275 | 44.90 | 25.75 | 9.12 | 16.33 | 12.80 | 7.68 | 71.68 |
| Fast | 125 | 250 | 38.50 | 25.20 | 10.28 | 15.40 | 15.77 | 4.67 | 71.32 |

Spray, 1 coat & wipe

| | | | | | | | | | |
|---|---|---|---|---|---|---|---|---|---|
| Slow | 275 | 150 | 51.30 | 7.36 | 2.18 | 34.20 | 8.31 | 8.33 | 60.38 |
| Medium | 200 | 125 | 44.90 | 12.88 | 4.56 | 35.92 | 13.34 | 8.00 | 74.70 |
| Fast | 325 | 100 | 38.50 | 9.69 | 3.97 | 38.50 | 16.16 | 4.78 | 73.10 |

*General Painting Costs*

| | Labor SF per manhour | Material coverage SF/gallon | Material cost per gallon | Labor cost per 100 SF | Labor burden 100 SF | Material cost per 100 SF | Overhead per 100 SF | Profit per 100 SF | Total price per 100 SF |
|---|---|---|---|---|---|---|---|---|---|
| **STEP 4: Sanding sealer (material #11b)** | | | | | | | | | |
| Brush, 1 coat | | | | | | | | | |
| Slow | 125 | 325 | 41.50 | 16.20 | 4.78 | 12.77 | 6.41 | 6.43 | 46.59 |
| Medium | 150 | 300 | 36.30 | 17.17 | 6.09 | 12.10 | 8.84 | 5.30 | 49.50 |
| Fast | 175 | 275 | 31.10 | 18.00 | 7.32 | 11.31 | 11.36 | 3.36 | 51.35 |
| Spray, 1 coat | | | | | | | | | |
| Slow | 350 | 150 | 41.50 | 5.79 | 1.71 | 27.67 | 6.68 | 6.70 | 48.55 |
| Medium | 400 | 125 | 36.30 | 6.44 | 2.28 | 29.04 | 9.44 | 5.66 | 52.86 |
| Fast | 450 | 100 | 31.10 | 7.00 | 2.85 | 31.10 | 12.70 | 3.76 | 57.41 |
| **STEP 5: Sand lightly** | | | | | | | | | |
| Slow | 175 | -- | -- | 11.57 | 3.40 | -- | 2.85 | 2.85 | 20.67 |
| Medium | 225 | -- | -- | 11.44 | 4.04 | -- | 3.87 | 2.32 | 21.67 |
| Fast | 275 | -- | -- | 11.45 | 4.69 | -- | 5.00 | 1.48 | 22.62 |
| **STEP 6 & 7: Lacquer, 2 coats (material #11c)** | | | | | | | | | |
| Brush, 1st coat | | | | | | | | | |
| Slow | 150 | 350 | 45.90 | 13.50 | 3.99 | 13.11 | 5.81 | 5.82 | 42.23 |
| Medium | 200 | 338 | 40.10 | 12.88 | 4.56 | 11.86 | 7.33 | 4.40 | 41.03 |
| Fast | 275 | 325 | 34.40 | 11.45 | 4.69 | 10.58 | 8.28 | 2.45 | 37.45 |
| Brush, 2nd coat | | | | | | | | | |
| Slow | 200 | 400 | 45.90 | 10.13 | 2.98 | 11.48 | 4.67 | 4.68 | 33.94 |
| Medium | 250 | 375 | 40.10 | 10.30 | 3.65 | 10.69 | 6.16 | 3.70 | 34.50 |
| Fast | 325 | 350 | 34.40 | 9.69 | 3.97 | 9.83 | 7.28 | 2.15 | 32.92 |
| Spray, 1st coat | | | | | | | | | |
| Slow | 425 | 275 | 45.90 | 4.76 | 1.40 | 16.69 | 4.34 | 4.35 | 31.54 |
| Medium | 525 | 250 | 40.10 | 4.90 | 1.73 | 16.04 | 5.67 | 3.40 | 31.74 |
| Fast | 625 | 225 | 34.40 | 5.04 | 2.06 | 15.29 | 6.94 | 2.05 | 31.38 |
| Spray, 2nd coat | | | | | | | | | |
| Slow | 475 | 300 | 45.90 | 4.26 | 1.27 | 15.30 | 3.96 | 3.96 | 28.75 |
| Medium | 588 | 275 | 40.10 | 4.38 | 1.55 | 14.58 | 5.13 | 3.08 | 28.72 |
| Fast | 650 | 250 | 34.40 | 4.85 | 1.98 | 13.76 | 6.38 | 1.89 | 28.86 |

|  | Labor SF per manhour | Material coverage SF/gallon | Material cost per gallon | Labor cost per 100 SF | Labor burden 100 SF | Material cost per 100 SF | Overhead per 100 SF | Profit per 100 SF | Total price per 100 SF |
|---|---|---|---|---|---|---|---|---|---|
| **Complete 7 step stain, seal & 2 coat lacquer system (material #11)** | | | | | | | | | |
| Brush all coats | | | | | | | | | |
| Slow | 30 | 150 | 46.10 | 67.50 | 19.89 | 30.73 | 22.45 | 22.49 | 163.06 |
| Medium | 35 | 138 | 40.40 | 73.57 | 26.05 | 29.28 | 32.22 | 19.33 | 180.45 |
| Fast | 40 | 125 | 34.60 | 78.75 | 32.13 | 27.68 | 42.95 | 12.71 | 194.22 |
| Spray all coats | | | | | | | | | |
| Slow | 60 | 50 | 46.10 | 33.75 | 9.96 | 92.20 | 25.82 | 25.88 | 187.61 |
| Medium | 70 | 40 | 40.40 | 36.79 | 13.04 | 101.00 | 37.70 | 22.62 | 211.15 |
| Fast | 80 | 30 | 34.60 | 39.38 | 16.06 | 115.33 | 52.94 | 15.66 | 239.37 |

Ceiling estimates are based on overall dimensions (length times width) to 8 feet high. Do not make deductions for openings in the ceiling area that are under 100 square feet. Figure painting of wood ceilings separate from wood beams. For heights above 8 feet, use the High Time Difficulty Factors on page 139. ADD for masking-off or cutting-in at wall-to-ceiling intersections and for protecting adjacent surfaces as necessary. "Slow" work is based on an hourly wage of $20.25, "Medium" work on an hourly wage of $25.75, and "Fast" work on an hourly wage of $31.50. Other qualifications that apply to this table are on page 9.

|  | Labor SF per manhour | Material coverage SF/gallon | Material cost per gallon | Labor cost per 100 SF | Labor burden 100 SF | Material cost per 100 SF | Overhead per 100 SF | Profit per 100 SF | Total price per 100 SF |
|---|---|---|---|---|---|---|---|---|---|
| **Closet pole, stain grade** | | | | | | | | | |
| Penetrating oil stain, (material #13) | | | | | | | | | |
| Brush & wipe, 1 coat | | | | | | | | | |
| Slow | 40 | 225 | 54.50 | 50.63 | 14.92 | 24.22 | 17.06 | 17.10 | 123.93 |
| Medium | 50 | 213 | 47.70 | 51.50 | 18.24 | 22.39 | 23.03 | 13.82 | 128.98 |
| Fast | 60 | 200 | 40.90 | 52.50 | 21.43 | 20.45 | 29.25 | 8.65 | 132.28 |

To stain poles in new construction, apply stain before installation. On repaints, remove the pole before staining. When estimating by the Opening Count Method, count one opening for each 10 linear feet of pole. "Slow" work is based on an hourly wage of $20.25, "Medium" work on an hourly wage of $25.75, and "Fast" work on an hourly wage of $31.50. Other qualifications that apply to this table are on page 9.

*General Painting Costs*

|  | Labor LF per manhour | Material coverage LF/gallon | Material cost per gallon | Labor cost per 100 LF | Labor burden 100 LF | Material cost per 100 LF | Overhead per 100 LF | Profit per 100 LF | Total price per 100 LF |
|---|---|---|---|---|---|---|---|---|---|
| **Closet shelf & pole, paint grade** | | | | | | | | | |
| *Undercoat, water base (material #3)* | | | | | | | | | |
|   Brush 1 coat | | | | | | | | | |
|     Slow | 17 | 80 | 32.60 | 119.12 | 35.11 | 40.75 | 37.05 | 37.13 | 269.16 |
|     Medium | 22 | 70 | 28.50 | 117.05 | 41.43 | 40.71 | 49.80 | 29.88 | 278.87 |
|     Fast | 33 | 60 | 24.50 | 95.45 | 38.93 | 40.83 | 54.32 | 16.07 | 245.60 |
| *Undercoat, oil base (material #4)* | | | | | | | | | |
|   Brush 1 coat | | | | | | | | | |
|     Slow | 17 | 90 | 42.30 | 119.12 | 35.11 | 47.00 | 38.24 | 38.32 | 277.79 |
|     Medium | 22 | 80 | 37.00 | 117.05 | 41.43 | 46.25 | 51.19 | 30.71 | 286.63 |
|     Fast | 33 | 65 | 31.80 | 95.45 | 38.93 | 48.92 | 56.83 | 16.81 | 256.94 |
| *Split coat (1/2 undercoat + 1/2 enamel), water base (material #3 & #9)* | | | | | | | | | |
|   Brush 1 coat | | | | | | | | | |
|     Slow | 16 | 80 | 39.70 | 126.56 | 37.32 | 49.63 | 40.57 | 40.66 | 294.74 |
|     Medium | 21 | 70 | 34.75 | 122.62 | 43.43 | 49.64 | 53.92 | 32.35 | 301.96 |
|     Fast | 32 | 60 | 29.80 | 98.44 | 40.15 | 49.67 | 58.36 | 17.26 | 263.88 |
| *Split coat (1/2 undercoat + 1/2 enamel), oil base (material #4 & #10)* | | | | | | | | | |
|   Brush 1 coat | | | | | | | | | |
|     Slow | 16 | 90 | 52.00 | 126.56 | 37.32 | 57.78 | 42.12 | 42.21 | 305.99 |
|     Medium | 21 | 80 | 45.50 | 122.62 | 43.43 | 56.88 | 55.73 | 33.44 | 312.10 |
|     Fast | 32 | 65 | 39.05 | 98.44 | 40.15 | 60.08 | 61.59 | 18.22 | 278.48 |
| *Enamel, water base (material #9)* | | | | | | | | | |
|   Brush each coat | | | | | | | | | |
|     Slow | 15 | 80 | 46.80 | 135.00 | 39.81 | 58.50 | 44.33 | 44.43 | 322.07 |
|     Medium | 20 | 70 | 41.00 | 128.75 | 45.60 | 58.57 | 58.23 | 34.94 | 326.09 |
|     Fast | 30 | 60 | 35.10 | 105.00 | 42.82 | 58.50 | 63.97 | 18.92 | 289.21 |
| *Enamel, oil base (material #10)* | | | | | | | | | |
|   Brush each coat | | | | | | | | | |
|     Slow | 15 | 90 | 61.70 | 135.00 | 39.81 | 68.56 | 46.24 | 46.34 | 335.95 |
|     Medium | 20 | 80 | 54.00 | 128.75 | 45.60 | 67.50 | 60.46 | 36.27 | 338.58 |
|     Fast | 30 | 65 | 46.30 | 105.00 | 42.82 | 71.23 | 67.91 | 20.09 | 307.05 |

Use these costs for painting the wardrobe closet shelves and poles with an undercoat and enamel system. If painting wardrobe closet shelves and poles with flat latex paint along with walls, use the Opening Count Method described under Doors, interior openings. Measurements are based on linear feet (LF) of shelves and poles. "Slow" work is based on an hourly wage of $20.25, "Medium" work on an hourly wage of $25.75, and "Fast" work on an hourly wage of $31.50. Other qualifications that apply to this table are on page 9.

*National Painting Cost Estimator*

|  | Labor LF per manhour | Material coverage LF/gallon | Material cost per gallon | Labor cost per 100 LF | Labor burden 100 LF | Material cost per 100 LF | Overhead per 100 LF | Profit per 100 LF | Total price per 100 LF |
|---|---|---|---|---|---|---|---|---|---|

## Closet shelves, paint grade

Undercoat, water base (material #3)
  Brush 1 coat

| | | | | | | | | | |
|---|---|---|---|---|---|---|---|---|---|
| Slow | 30 | 100 | 32.60 | 67.50 | 19.89 | 32.60 | 22.80 | 22.85 | 165.64 |
| Medium | 37 | 90 | 28.50 | 69.59 | 24.66 | 31.67 | 31.47 | 18.88 | 176.27 |
| Fast | 44 | 80 | 24.50 | 71.59 | 29.22 | 30.63 | 40.74 | 12.05 | 184.23 |

Undercoat, oil base (material #4)
  Brush 1 coat

| | | | | | | | | | |
|---|---|---|---|---|---|---|---|---|---|
| Slow | 30 | 110 | 42.30 | 67.50 | 19.89 | 38.45 | 23.91 | 23.96 | 173.71 |
| Medium | 37 | 100 | 37.00 | 69.59 | 24.66 | 37.00 | 32.81 | 19.68 | 183.74 |
| Fast | 44 | 90 | 31.80 | 71.59 | 29.22 | 35.33 | 42.20 | 12.48 | 190.82 |

Split coat (1/2 undercoat + 1/2 enamel), water base (material #3 & #9)
  Brush 1 coat

| | | | | | | | | | |
|---|---|---|---|---|---|---|---|---|---|
| Slow | 27 | 100 | 39.70 | 75.00 | 22.12 | 39.70 | 26.00 | 26.05 | 188.87 |
| Medium | 35 | 90 | 34.75 | 73.57 | 26.05 | 38.61 | 34.56 | 20.73 | 193.52 |
| Fast | 42 | 80 | 29.80 | 75.00 | 30.60 | 37.25 | 44.28 | 13.10 | 200.23 |

Split coat (1/2 undercoat + 1/2 enamel), oil base (material #4 & #10)
  Brush 1 coat

| | | | | | | | | | |
|---|---|---|---|---|---|---|---|---|---|
| Slow | 27 | 110 | 52.00 | 75.00 | 22.12 | 47.27 | 27.44 | 27.49 | 199.32 |
| Medium | 35 | 100 | 45.50 | 73.57 | 26.05 | 45.50 | 36.28 | 21.77 | 203.17 |
| Fast | 42 | 90 | 39.05 | 75.00 | 30.60 | 43.39 | 46.19 | 13.66 | 208.84 |

Enamel, water base (material #9)
  Brush each coat

| | | | | | | | | | |
|---|---|---|---|---|---|---|---|---|---|
| Slow | 25 | 100 | 46.80 | 81.00 | 23.88 | 46.80 | 28.82 | 28.88 | 209.38 |
| Medium | 33 | 90 | 41.00 | 78.03 | 27.63 | 45.56 | 37.80 | 22.68 | 211.70 |
| Fast | 40 | 80 | 35.10 | 78.75 | 32.13 | 43.88 | 47.98 | 14.19 | 216.93 |

Enamel, oil base (material #10)
  Brush each coat

| | | | | | | | | | |
|---|---|---|---|---|---|---|---|---|---|
| Slow | 25 | 110 | 61.70 | 81.00 | 23.88 | 56.09 | 30.59 | 30.65 | 222.21 |
| Medium | 33 | 100 | 54.00 | 78.03 | 27.63 | 54.00 | 39.91 | 23.95 | 223.52 |
| Fast | 40 | 90 | 46.30 | 78.75 | 32.13 | 51.44 | 50.32 | 14.88 | 227.52 |

Use these costs for painting the wardrobe closet shelves with an undercoat and enamel system. If painting wardrobe closet shelves with flat latex paint along with walls, use the Opening Count Method described under Doors, interior openings. Measurements are based on linear feet (LF) of shelves. "Slow" work is based on an hourly wage of $20.25, "Medium" work on an hourly wage of $25.75, and "Fast" work on an hourly wage of $31.50. Other qualifications that apply to this table are on page 9.

*General Painting Costs*

|  | Labor LF per manhour | Material coverage LF/gallon | Material cost per gallon | Labor cost per 100 LF | Labor burden 100 LF | Material cost per 100 LF | Overhead per 100 LF | Profit per 100 LF | Total price per 100 LF |
|---|---|---|---|---|---|---|---|---|---|
| **Closets, molding at perimeter, paint grade** | | | | | | | | | |
| Undercoat, water base (material #3) | | | | | | | | | |
|   Brush 1 coat | | | | | | | | | |
|     Slow | 80 | 225 | 32.60 | 25.31 | 7.47 | 14.49 | 8.98 | 9.00 | 65.25 |
|     Medium | 95 | 213 | 28.50 | 27.11 | 9.61 | 13.38 | 12.52 | 7.51 | 70.13 |
|     Fast | 110 | 200 | 24.50 | 28.64 | 11.67 | 12.25 | 16.30 | 4.82 | 73.68 |
| Undercoat, oil base (material #4) | | | | | | | | | |
|   Brush 1 coat | | | | | | | | | |
|     Slow | 80 | 250 | 42.30 | 25.31 | 7.47 | 16.92 | 9.44 | 9.46 | 68.60 |
|     Medium | 95 | 238 | 37.00 | 27.11 | 9.61 | 15.55 | 13.07 | 7.84 | 73.18 |
|     Fast | 110 | 220 | 31.80 | 28.64 | 11.67 | 14.45 | 16.98 | 5.02 | 76.76 |
| Split coat (1/2 undercoat + 1/2 enamel), water base (material #3 & #9) | | | | | | | | | |
|   Brush 1 coat | | | | | | | | | |
|     Slow | 75 | 225 | 39.70 | 27.00 | 7.95 | 17.64 | 10.00 | 10.02 | 72.61 |
|     Medium | 90 | 213 | 34.75 | 28.61 | 10.13 | 16.31 | 13.76 | 8.26 | 77.07 |
|     Fast | 105 | 200 | 29.80 | 30.00 | 12.22 | 14.90 | 17.71 | 5.24 | 80.07 |
| Split coat (1/2 undercoat + 1/2 enamel), oil base (material #4 & #10) | | | | | | | | | |
|   Brush 1 coat | | | | | | | | | |
|     Slow | 75 | 250 | 52.00 | 27.00 | 7.95 | 20.80 | 10.60 | 10.62 | 76.97 |
|     Medium | 90 | 238 | 45.50 | 28.61 | 10.13 | 19.12 | 14.47 | 8.68 | 81.01 |
|     Fast | 105 | 220 | 39.05 | 30.00 | 12.22 | 17.75 | 18.60 | 5.50 | 84.07 |
| Enamel, water base (material #9) | | | | | | | | | |
|   Brush each coat | | | | | | | | | |
|     Slow | 70 | 225 | 46.80 | 28.93 | 8.54 | 20.80 | 11.07 | 11.09 | 80.43 |
|     Medium | 85 | 213 | 41.00 | 30.29 | 10.72 | 19.25 | 15.07 | 9.04 | 84.37 |
|     Fast | 100 | 200 | 35.10 | 31.50 | 12.85 | 17.55 | 19.19 | 5.68 | 86.77 |
| Enamel, oil base (material #10) | | | | | | | | | |
|   Brush each coat | | | | | | | | | |
|     Slow | 70 | 250 | 61.70 | 28.93 | 8.54 | 24.68 | 11.81 | 11.83 | 85.79 |
|     Medium | 85 | 238 | 54.00 | 30.29 | 10.72 | 22.69 | 15.93 | 9.56 | 89.19 |
|     Fast | 100 | 220 | 46.30 | 31.50 | 12.85 | 21.05 | 20.27 | 6.00 | 91.67 |

Use these costs for molding around wardrobe closets. Measurements are based on linear feet (LF) of molding. "Slow" work is based on an hourly wage of $20.25, "Medium" work on an hourly wage of $25.75, and "Fast" work on an hourly wage of $31.50. Other qualifications that apply to this table are on page 9.

|  | Labor LF per manhour | Material coverage LF/gallon | Material cost per gallon | Labor cost per 100 LF | Labor burden 100 LF | Material cost per 100 LF | Overhead per 100 LF | Profit per 100 LF | Total price per 100 LF |
|---|---|---|---|---|---|---|---|---|---|

## Corbels, wood trim, stain grade, average size 4" x 8"

Solid body stain, water base (material #18)
Brush each coat

|  | | | | | | | | | |
|---|---|---|---|---|---|---|---|---|---|
| Slow | 15 | 50 | 45.00 | 135.00 | 39.81 | 90.00 | 50.32 | 50.42 | 365.55 |
| Medium | 20 | 48 | 39.40 | 128.75 | 45.60 | 82.08 | 64.10 | 38.46 | 358.99 |
| Fast | 25 | 45 | 33.80 | 126.00 | 51.40 | 75.11 | 78.28 | 23.16 | 353.95 |

Solid body stain, oil base (material #19)
Brush each coat

|  | | | | | | | | | |
|---|---|---|---|---|---|---|---|---|---|
| Slow | 15 | 55 | 54.10 | 135.00 | 39.81 | 98.36 | 51.91 | 52.02 | 377.10 |
| Medium | 20 | 53 | 47.30 | 128.75 | 45.60 | 89.25 | 65.90 | 39.54 | 369.04 |
| Fast | 25 | 50 | 40.50 | 126.00 | 51.40 | 81.00 | 80.11 | 23.70 | 362.21 |

Semi-transparent stain, water base (material #20)
Brush each coat

|  | | | | | | | | | |
|---|---|---|---|---|---|---|---|---|---|
| Slow | 18 | 55 | 47.50 | 112.50 | 33.18 | 86.36 | 44.09 | 44.18 | 320.31 |
| Medium | 22 | 53 | 41.60 | 117.05 | 41.43 | 78.49 | 59.25 | 35.55 | 331.77 |
| Fast | 28 | 50 | 35.60 | 112.50 | 45.87 | 71.20 | 71.18 | 21.05 | 321.80 |

Semi-transparent stain, oil base (material #21)
Brush each coat

|  | | | | | | | | | |
|---|---|---|---|---|---|---|---|---|---|
| Slow | 18 | 60 | 48.70 | 112.50 | 33.18 | 81.17 | 43.10 | 43.19 | 313.14 |
| Medium | 22 | 58 | 42.60 | 117.05 | 41.43 | 73.45 | 57.99 | 34.79 | 324.71 |
| Fast | 28 | 55 | 36.50 | 112.50 | 45.87 | 66.36 | 69.68 | 20.61 | 315.02 |

Use these costs for painting corbels averaging 4" x 8" in size. Measurements are based on linear feet (LF) of corbels that are painted or stained with a different material or color than the surface they extend from. "Slow" work is based on an hourly wage of $20.25, "Medium" work on an hourly wage of $25.75, and "Fast" work on an hourly wage of $31.50. Other qualifications that apply to this table are on page 9.

|  | Labor LF per manhour | Material coverage LF/gallon | Material cost per gallon | Labor cost per 100 LF | Labor burden 100 LF | Material cost per 100 LF | Overhead per 100 LF | Profit per 100 LF | Total price per 100 LF |
|---|---|---|---|---|---|---|---|---|---|

## Cutting-in, horizontal, interior or exterior

Cutting-in, horizontal, heights less than 6'8"
Brush application

|  | | | | | | | | | |
|---|---|---|---|---|---|---|---|---|---|
| Slow | 23 | -- | -- | 88.04 | 25.96 | -- | 21.66 | 21.71 | 157.37 |
| Medium | 35 | -- | -- | 74.64 | 26.45 | -- | 25.27 | 15.16 | 141.52 |
| Fast | 56 | -- | -- | 55.80 | 22.74 | -- | 24.36 | 7.21 | 110.11 |

Cutting-in, horizontal, heights from 6'8" to 9'0"    (1.3 High Time Difficulty Factor included)
Brush application

|  | | | | | | | | | |
|---|---|---|---|---|---|---|---|---|---|
| Slow | 18 | -- | -- | 114.46 | 33.74 | -- | 28.16 | 28.22 | 204.58 |
| Medium | 27 | -- | -- | 97.03 | 34.36 | -- | 32.85 | 19.71 | 183.95 |
| Fast | 43 | -- | -- | 72.54 | 29.60 | -- | 31.66 | 9.37 | 143.17 |

*General Painting Costs*

|  | Labor LF per manhour | Material coverage LF/gallon | Material cost per gallon | Labor cost per 100 LF | Labor burden 100 LF | Material cost per 100 LF | Overhead per 100 LF | Profit per 100 LF | Total price per 100 LF |
|---|---|---|---|---|---|---|---|---|---|

Cutting-in, horizontal, heights from 9'0" to 13'0"    (1.6 High Time Difficulty Factor included)
Brush application

| | | | | | | | | | |
|---|---|---|---|---|---|---|---|---|---|
| Slow | 14 | -- | -- | 140.87 | 41.54 | -- | 34.66 | 34.73 | 251.80 |
| Medium | 22 | -- | -- | 119.42 | 42.31 | -- | 40.42 | 24.25 | 226.40 |
| Fast | 35 | -- | -- | 89.28 | 36.41 | -- | 38.97 | 11.53 | 176.19 |

Cutting-in, horizontal, heights from 13'0" to 17'0"    (1.9 High Time Difficulty Factor included)
Brush application

| | | | | | | | | | |
|---|---|---|---|---|---|---|---|---|---|
| Slow | 12 | -- | -- | 167.28 | 49.32 | -- | 41.16 | 41.25 | 299.01 |
| Medium | 18 | -- | -- | 141.81 | 50.22 | -- | 48.00 | 28.80 | 268.83 |
| Fast | 30 | -- | -- | 106.01 | 43.27 | -- | 46.27 | 13.69 | 209.24 |

Cutting-in, horizontal, heights from 17'0" to 19'0"    (2.2 High Time Difficulty Factor included)
Brush application

| | | | | | | | | | |
|---|---|---|---|---|---|---|---|---|---|
| Slow | 10 | -- | -- | 193.70 | 57.09 | -- | 47.66 | 47.76 | 346.21 |
| Medium | 16 | -- | -- | 164.20 | 58.17 | -- | 55.58 | 33.35 | 311.30 |
| Fast | 26 | -- | -- | 122.75 | 50.08 | -- | 53.58 | 15.85 | 242.26 |

Cutting-in, horizontal, heights from 19'0" to 21'0"    (2.5 High Time Difficulty Factor included)
Brush application

| | | | | | | | | | |
|---|---|---|---|---|---|---|---|---|---|
| Slow | 9 | -- | -- | 220.11 | 64.90 | -- | 54.16 | 54.27 | 393.44 |
| Medium | 14 | -- | -- | 186.59 | 66.08 | -- | 63.16 | 37.90 | 353.73 |
| Fast | 23 | -- | -- | 139.49 | 56.89 | -- | 60.88 | 18.01 | 275.27 |

## Cutting-in, vertical, interior or exterior

Cutting-in, vertical, heights less than 6'8"
Brush application

| | | | | | | | | | |
|---|---|---|---|---|---|---|---|---|---|
| Slow | 29 | -- | -- | 69.83 | 20.58 | -- | 17.18 | 17.22 | 124.81 |
| Medium | 41 | -- | -- | 63.42 | 22.46 | -- | 21.47 | 12.88 | 120.23 |
| Fast | 58 | -- | -- | 54.31 | 22.15 | -- | 23.71 | 7.01 | 107.18 |

Cutting-in, vertical, heights from 6'8" to 9'0"    (1.3 High Time Difficulty Factor included)
Brush application

| | | | | | | | | | |
|---|---|---|---|---|---|---|---|---|---|
| Slow | 22 | -- | -- | 90.78 | 26.76 | -- | 22.34 | 22.38 | 162.26 |
| Medium | 31 | -- | -- | 82.45 | 29.20 | -- | 27.91 | 16.75 | 156.31 |
| Fast | 45 | -- | -- | 70.60 | 28.79 | -- | 30.81 | 9.11 | 139.31 |

Cutting-in, vertical, heights from 9'0" to 13'0"    (1.6 High Time Difficulty Factor included)
Brush application

| | | | | | | | | | |
|---|---|---|---|---|---|---|---|---|---|
| Slow | 18 | -- | -- | 111.72 | 32.94 | -- | 27.49 | 27.55 | 199.70 |
| Medium | 25 | -- | -- | 101.48 | 35.94 | -- | 34.35 | 20.61 | 192.38 |
| Fast | 36 | -- | -- | 86.90 | 35.46 | -- | 37.93 | 11.22 | 171.51 |

Cutting-in, vertical, heights from 13'0" to 17'0"    (1.9 High Time Difficulty Factor included)
Brush application

| | | | | | | | | | |
|---|---|---|---|---|---|---|---|---|---|
| Slow | 15 | -- | -- | 132.67 | 39.12 | -- | 32.64 | 32.71 | 237.14 |
| Medium | 21 | -- | -- | 120.50 | 42.69 | -- | 40.79 | 24.47 | 228.45 |
| Fast | 31 | -- | -- | 103.19 | 42.10 | -- | 45.04 | 13.32 | 203.65 |

*National Painting Cost Estimator*

|  | Labor LF per manhour | Material coverage LF/gallon | Material cost per gallon | Labor cost per 100 LF | Labor burden 100 LF | Material cost per 100 LF | Overhead per 100 LF | Profit per 100 LF | Total price per 100 LF |
|---|---|---|---|---|---|---|---|---|---|
| Cutting-in, vertical, heights from 17'0" to 19'0" | | | (2.2 High Time Difficulty Factor included) | | | | | | |
| Brush application | | | | | | | | | |
| Slow | 13 | -- | -- | 153.62 | 45.28 | -- | 37.80 | 37.88 | 274.58 |
| Medium | 18 | -- | -- | 139.53 | 49.43 | -- | 47.23 | 28.34 | 264.53 |
| Fast | 26 | -- | -- | 119.48 | 48.74 | -- | 52.15 | 15.43 | 235.80 |
| Cutting-in, vertical, heights from 19'0" to 21'0" | | | (2.5 High Time Difficulty Factor included) | | | | | | |
| Brush application | | | | | | | | | |
| Slow | 12 | -- | -- | 174.57 | 51.47 | -- | 42.95 | 43.04 | 312.03 |
| Medium | 16 | -- | -- | 158.56 | 56.17 | -- | 53.67 | 32.20 | 300.60 |
| Fast | 23 | -- | -- | 135.78 | 55.37 | -- | 59.27 | 17.53 | 267.95 |

Use these figures when cutting-in by hand with a brush at vertical walls, horizontal ceilings, at baseboards, around door frames, etc. when different colors or different sheens (i.e. flat vs. semi-gloss) are used on the adjacent surfaces. "Slow" work is based on an hourly wage of $20.25, "Medium" work on an hourly wage of $25.725, and "Fast" work on an hourly wage of $31.50.

"Slow" applies to residential repaints with heavy texture. "Slow" also applies when cutting in freehand, i.e. using a brush to build-up a bead of paint and running the cut line 3/16" to 1/8" from the adjacent surface, typically horizontal cutting-in at ceilings. "Medium" applies to residential or commercial repaints with light to medium texture. "Medium" speed also applies when using masking tape to form the cut line, then using light brush coats so excess paint doesn't seep under the tape. This application is common around doors, windows at woodwork, and can be used vertically at wall to wall intersections. "Fast" applies to new construction with smooth wall or orange peel texture. "Fast" speed also applies when using a paint guide, either metal or plastic. The paint guide is typically used for vertical wall-to-wall applications, but can be used for horizontal use at baseboards, over doors, etc. As when using masking tape at medium speed, a series of light brush coats works best so paint doesn't seep under the guide tool.

**Tip:** At baseboards, it's sometimes best to use a stiff putty knife to pull the baseboard away from the wall, and use a Bender paint pad to paint the wall behind the baseboard. Then, while the base is away from the wall, paint the top edge of the base and reinstall the baseboard.

**Notes:**
1 - Material consumption for cutting-in is minimal or zero (0) since the material cost is actually calculated in the wall painting or ceiling painting line item.

2 - High Time Difficulty Factors are built into these figures to allow for up and down time and moving ladders or scaffolding.

3 - Horizontal cutting-in is typically more difficult and consumes more time than vertical cutting-in, as the figures indicate.

ADD for scribing and back-painting (scraping the texture to achieve a clean line and back-painting to cover the scraped intersection) at a wall-to-ceiling or wall-to-wall corner intersection. See Preparation section of this book.

ADD for time to switch paint if there is more than one color in any room, i.e. ceiling color (1), wall color (2), accent wall color (3). In this example, add time to switch paint twice.

## Deck overhang, wood
Multiply the horizontal surface area by 1.5 to allow for painting floor joists and use the overhang table for areas greater than 2.5 feet wide to determine pricing.

## Deck surfaces, steps, stair treads & porches, wood
Measure the surface area and apply the prices for smooth siding.

*General Painting Costs*

|   | Labor LF per manhour | Material coverage LF/gallon | Material cost per gallon | Labor cost per 100 LF | Labor burden 100 LF | Material cost per 100 LF | Overhead per 100 LF | Profit per 100 LF | Total price per 100 LF |
|---|---|---|---|---|---|---|---|---|---|
| **Door frames and trim only, per 100 linear feet** | | | | | | | | | |
| Undercoat, water base (material #3) | | | | | | | | | |
|   Brush 1 coat | | | | | | | | | |
|     Slow | 220 | 500 | 32.60 | 9.20 | 2.73 | 6.52 | 3.50 | 3.51 | 25.46 |
|     Medium | 270 | 465 | 28.50 | 9.54 | 3.36 | 6.13 | 4.76 | 2.86 | 26.65 |
|     Fast | 320 | 425 | 24.50 | 9.84 | 4.04 | 5.76 | 6.08 | 1.80 | 27.52 |
| Undercoat, oil base (material #4) | | | | | | | | | |
|   Brush 1 coat | | | | | | | | | |
|     Slow | 220 | 550 | 42.30 | 9.20 | 2.73 | 7.69 | 3.72 | 3.73 | 27.07 |
|     Medium | 270 | 510 | 37.00 | 9.54 | 3.36 | 7.25 | 5.04 | 3.03 | 28.22 |
|     Fast | 320 | 465 | 31.80 | 9.84 | 4.04 | 6.84 | 6.41 | 1.90 | 29.03 |
| Split coat (1/2 undercoat + 1/2 enamel), water base (material #3 & #9) | | | | | | | | | |
|   Brush 1 coat | | | | | | | | | |
|     Slow | 205 | 560 | 39.70 | 9.88 | 2.92 | 7.09 | 3.78 | 3.79 | 27.46 |
|     Medium | 240 | 515 | 34.75 | 10.73 | 3.81 | 6.75 | 5.32 | 3.19 | 29.80 |
|     Fast | 275 | 475 | 29.80 | 11.45 | 4.69 | 6.27 | 6.94 | 2.05 | 31.40 |
| Split coat (1/2 undercoat + 1/2 enamel), oil base (material #4 & #10) | | | | | | | | | |
|   Brush 1 coat | | | | | | | | | |
|     Slow | 205 | 610 | 52.00 | 9.88 | 2.92 | 8.52 | 4.05 | 4.06 | 29.43 |
|     Medium | 240 | 565 | 45.50 | 10.73 | 3.81 | 8.05 | 5.65 | 3.39 | 31.63 |
|     Fast | 275 | 525 | 39.05 | 11.45 | 4.69 | 7.44 | 7.30 | 2.16 | 33.04 |
| Enamel, water base (material #9) | | | | | | | | | |
|   Brush each coat | | | | | | | | | |
|     Slow | 185 | 560 | 46.80 | 10.95 | 3.24 | 8.36 | 4.28 | 4.29 | 31.12 |
|     Medium | 220 | 515 | 41.00 | 11.70 | 4.17 | 7.96 | 5.95 | 3.57 | 33.35 |
|     Fast | 255 | 475 | 35.10 | 12.35 | 5.04 | 7.39 | 7.68 | 2.27 | 34.73 |
| Enamel, oil base (material #10) | | | | | | | | | |
|   Brush each coat | | | | | | | | | |
|     Slow | 185 | 610 | 61.70 | 10.95 | 3.24 | 10.11 | 4.62 | 4.63 | 33.55 |
|     Medium | 220 | 565 | 54.00 | 11.70 | 4.17 | 9.56 | 6.35 | 3.81 | 35.59 |
|     Fast | 255 | 525 | 46.30 | 12.35 | 5.04 | 8.82 | 8.13 | 2.40 | 36.74 |

Use these figures for painting door frames and wood trim on all sides when doors are not to be painted. ADD for additional preparation time, as needed, including setup, remove & replace (hardware), protection (mask walls and visqueen floors), putty, caulking, sanding and cleanup. When doors are painted along with the frames and trim, use the Opening Count Method under Doors, interior openings, and/or the exterior door costs under Doors, exterior. Measurements for door frames and trim are based on linear feet (LF) of the frame. Prices are for about 17 linear feet of frame at each opening. "Slow" work is based on an hourly wage of $20.25, "Medium" work on an hourly wage of $25.75, and "Fast" work on an hourly wage of $31.50. Other qualifications that apply to this table are on page 9.

*National Painting Cost Estimator*

|  | Openings per manhour | Openings per gallon | Material cost per gallon | Labor cost per opening | Labor burden opening | Material cost per opening | Overhead per opening | Profit per opening | Total price per opening |
|---|---|---|---|---|---|---|---|---|---|

### Door frames and trim only, per opening

**Undercoat, water base (material #3)**
Brush 1 coat

| | | | | | | | | | |
|---|---|---|---|---|---|---|---|---|---|
| Slow | 13 | 30 | 32.60 | 1.56 | .46 | 1.09 | .59 | .59 | 4.29 |
| Medium | 16 | 28 | 28.50 | 1.61 | .59 | 1.02 | .80 | .48 | 4.50 |
| Fast | 18 | 25 | 24.50 | 1.75 | .73 | .98 | 1.07 | .32 | 4.85 |

**Undercoat, oil base (material #4)**
Brush 1 coat

| | | | | | | | | | |
|---|---|---|---|---|---|---|---|---|---|
| Slow | 13 | 33 | 42.30 | 1.56 | .46 | 1.28 | .63 | .63 | 4.56 |
| Medium | 16 | 31 | 37.00 | 1.61 | .59 | 1.19 | .84 | .51 | 4.74 |
| Fast | 18 | 28 | 31.80 | 1.75 | .73 | 1.14 | 1.12 | .33 | 5.07 |

**Split coat (1/2 undercoat + 1/2 enamel), water base (material #3 & #9)**
Brush 1 coat

| | | | | | | | | | |
|---|---|---|---|---|---|---|---|---|---|
| Slow | 12 | 33 | 39.70 | 1.69 | .49 | 1.20 | .64 | .64 | 4.66 |
| Medium | 14 | 31 | 34.75 | 1.84 | .64 | 1.12 | .90 | .54 | 5.04 |
| Fast | 16 | 28 | 29.80 | 1.97 | .82 | 1.06 | 1.19 | .35 | 5.39 |

**Split coat (1/2 undercoat + 1/2 enamel), oil base (material #4 & #10)**
Brush 1 coat

| | | | | | | | | | |
|---|---|---|---|---|---|---|---|---|---|
| Slow | 12 | 36 | 52.00 | 1.69 | .49 | 1.44 | .69 | .69 | 5.00 |
| Medium | 14 | 34 | 45.50 | 1.84 | .64 | 1.34 | .96 | .57 | 5.35 |
| Fast | 16 | 31 | 39.05 | 1.97 | .82 | 1.26 | 1.25 | .37 | 5.67 |

**Enamel, water base (material #9)**
Brush each coat

| | | | | | | | | | |
|---|---|---|---|---|---|---|---|---|---|
| Slow | 11 | 33 | 46.80 | 1.84 | .55 | 1.42 | .72 | .72 | 5.25 |
| Medium | 13 | 31 | 41.00 | 1.98 | .70 | 1.32 | 1.00 | .60 | 5.60 |
| Fast | 15 | 28 | 35.10 | 2.10 | .87 | 1.25 | 1.31 | .39 | 5.92 |

**Enamel, oil base (material #10)**
Brush each coat

| | | | | | | | | | |
|---|---|---|---|---|---|---|---|---|---|
| Slow | 11 | 36 | 61.70 | 1.84 | .55 | 1.71 | .78 | .78 | 5.66 |
| Medium | 13 | 34 | 54.00 | 1.98 | .70 | 1.59 | 1.07 | .64 | 5.98 |
| Fast | 15 | 31 | 46.30 | 2.10 | .87 | 1.49 | 1.38 | .41 | 6.25 |

Use these figures for painting door frames and wood trim on all sides when doors are not to be painted. ADD for additional preparation time, as needed, including setup, remove & replace (hardware), protection (mask walls and visqueen floors); putty, caulking, sanding and cleanup. When doors are painted along with the frames and trim, use the Opening Count Method under Doors, interior openings, and/or the exterior door costs under Doors, exterior. These costs are based on a count of the openings requiring paint. Prices are for about 17 linear feet of frame at each opening. "Slow" work is based on an hourly wage of $20.25, "Medium" work on an hourly wage of $25.75, and "Fast" work on an hourly wage of $31.50. Other qualifications that apply to this table are on page 9.

*General Painting Costs*

## Doors, exterior

The tables that follow include costs for both time and material needed to apply two coats of a high quality finish to all six sides of each exterior door, finish the jamb and trim, and lay-off each door smoothly. These costs are in addition to those shown under Doors, interior openings, for both the *Opening Count Method* and the *Per Door Method,* which include one coat of undercoat and one coat of enamel for each exterior door along with the interior doors. New exterior paint grade doors actually receive two coats of exterior enamel. New exterior stain grade doors actually receive a coat of stain, sealer, and then a coat of either marine spar varnish or polyurethane finish. The following two examples give total cost to finish a flush or a panel (entry) exterior door with polyurethane, and includes the cost for the two coats from the interior take-off.

### Example #1    Flush Doors
OPENING COUNT METHOD
   Included in the interior take-off
      Opening Count Method, interior undercoat cost - 1 coat, slow      $ 18.08  (page 103)
      Opening Count Method, interior enamel cost - 1 coat, slow        $ 19.64  (page 103)
   Included in the exterior take-off
      Exterior, flush, two coat system, polyurethane cost - 2 coats, slow      $ 47.09  (page 98)
          Total to finish the exterior door      $ 84.81
    **OR**

PER DOOR METHOD
   Included in the interior take-off
      Per Door Method, interior, flush, undercoat cost - 1 coat, slow      $ 17.95  (page 109)
      Per Door Method, interior enamel cost - 1 coat, slow      $ 16.55  (page 109)
   Included in the exterior take-off
      Exterior, flush, two coat system, polyurethane cost - 2 coats, slow      $ 47.09  (page 98)
          Total to finish the exterior door      $ 81.59

Under this system, much of the cost to paint the exterior door is included in the interior take-off. When counting interior doors, be sure you include all the exterior doors whether you use either the *Opening Count Method* or the *Per Door Method* to estimate doors.

### Example #2    Panel (Entry) Doors
OPENING COUNT METHOD
   Included in the interior take-off
      Opening Count Method, interior undercoat cost - 1 coat, slow      $ 18.08  (page 103)
      Opening Count Method, interior enamel cost - 1 coat, slow      $ 19.64  (page 103)
   Included in the exterior take-off
      Exterior, panel (entry) two coat system, polyurethane cost - 2 coats, slow      $ 88.73  (page 101)
          Total to finish the exterior door      $ 126.45
    **OR**

PER DOOR METHOD
   Included in the interior take-off
      Per Door Method, interior, flush, undercoat cost - 1 coat, slow      $ 17.95  (page 109)
      Per Door Method, interior enamel cost - 1 coat, slow      $ 16.55  (page 109)
   Included in the exterior take-off
      Exterior, panel (entry) two coat system, polyurethane cost - 2 coats, slow      $ 88.73  (page 101)
          Total to finish the exterior door      $ 123.23

*National Painting Cost Estimator*

|  | Manhours per door | Doors per gallon | Material cost per gallon | Labor cost per door | Labor burden door | Material cost per door | Overhead per door | Profit per door | Total price per door |
|---|---|---|---|---|---|---|---|---|---|

### Doors, exterior, flush, two coat system

Exterior enamel, 2 coat system, water base (material #24)
  Roll & brush 2 coats
| | | | | | | | | | |
|---|---|---|---|---|---|---|---|---|---|
| Slow | 0.5 | 7 | 50.70 | 10.13 | 2.98 | 7.24 | 3.87 | 3.88 | 28.10 |
| Medium | 0.4 | 6 | 44.40 | 10.30 | 3.65 | 7.40 | 5.34 | 3.20 | 29.89 |
| Fast | 0.3 | 5 | 38.00 | 9.45 | 3.86 | 7.60 | 6.48 | 1.92 | 29.31 |

Exterior enamel, 2 coat system, oil base (material #25)
  Roll & brush 2 coats
| | | | | | | | | | |
|---|---|---|---|---|---|---|---|---|---|
| Slow | 0.5 | 7 | 56.40 | 10.13 | 2.98 | 8.06 | 4.02 | 4.03 | 29.22 |
| Medium | 0.4 | 6 | 49.40 | 10.30 | 3.65 | 8.23 | 5.55 | 3.33 | 31.06 |
| Fast | 0.3 | 5 | 42.30 | 9.45 | 3.86 | 8.46 | 6.75 | 2.00 | 30.52 |

Polyurethane (material #22)
  Brush 2 coats
| | | | | | | | | | |
|---|---|---|---|---|---|---|---|---|---|
| Slow | 0.7 | 5.0 | 78.80 | 14.18 | 4.17 | 15.76 | 6.48 | 6.50 | 47.09 |
| Medium | 0.6 | 4.5 | 69.00 | 15.45 | 5.47 | 15.33 | 9.06 | 5.44 | 50.75 |
| Fast | 0.5 | 4.0 | 59.10 | 15.75 | 6.43 | 14.78 | 11.46 | 3.39 | 51.81 |

Marine spar varnish, flat or gloss (material #23)
  Brush 2 coats
| | | | | | | | | | |
|---|---|---|---|---|---|---|---|---|---|
| Slow | 0.6 | 6 | 83.10 | 12.15 | 3.58 | 13.85 | 5.62 | 5.63 | 40.83 |
| Medium | 0.5 | 5 | 72.70 | 12.88 | 4.56 | 14.54 | 8.00 | 4.80 | 44.78 |
| Fast | 0.4 | 4 | 62.30 | 12.60 | 5.14 | 15.58 | 10.33 | 3.06 | 46.71 |

ADD - Preparation for spar varnish
| | | | | | | | | | |
|---|---|---|---|---|---|---|---|---|---|
| Steel wool buff | 0.2 | -- | -- | 5.15 | 1.82 | -- | 1.74 | 1.05 | 9.76 |
| Wax application | 0.2 | -- | -- | 5.15 | 1.82 | -- | 1.74 | 1.05 | 9.76 |

Use these figures for painting two coats on flush exterior doors, other than entry doors. These costs are to be included with the exterior door take-off and are in addition to the costs that are included in the interior take-off as explained by the example in the previous section. ADD for additional preparation time, as needed, including setup, remove & replace (hardware), protection (mask walls and visqueen floors); putty, caulking, sanding and cleanup. Add minimum preparation time for varnishing as indicated above. "Slow" work is based on an hourly wage of $20.25, "Medium" work on an hourly wage of $25.75, and "Fast" work on an hourly wage of $31.50. Other qualifications that apply to this table are on page 9.

*General Painting Costs*

|  | Manhours per door | Doors per gallon | Material cost per gallon | Labor cost per door | Labor burden door | Material cost per door | Overhead per door | Profit per door | Total price per door |
|---|---|---|---|---|---|---|---|---|---|

## Doors, exterior, French, two coat system

Exterior enamel, 2 coat system, water base (material #24)
  Roll & brush 2 coats
| | | | | | | | | | |
|---|---|---|---|---|---|---|---|---|---|
| Slow | 1.0 | 12 | 50.70 | 20.25 | 5.97 | 4.23 | 5.79 | 5.80 | 42.04 |
| Medium | 0.8 | 10 | 44.40 | 20.60 | 7.30 | 4.44 | 8.08 | 4.85 | 45.27 |
| Fast | 0.6 | 8 | 38.00 | 18.90 | 7.71 | 4.75 | 9.72 | 2.88 | 43.96 |

Exterior enamel, 2 coat system, oil base (material #25)
  Roll & brush 2 coats
| | | | | | | | | | |
|---|---|---|---|---|---|---|---|---|---|
| Slow | 1.0 | 12 | 56.40 | 20.25 | 5.97 | 4.70 | 5.87 | 5.89 | 42.68 |
| Medium | 0.8 | 10 | 49.40 | 20.60 | 7.30 | 4.94 | 8.21 | 4.92 | 45.97 |
| Fast | 0.6 | 8 | 42.30 | 18.90 | 7.71 | 5.29 | 9.89 | 2.93 | 44.72 |

Polyurethane (material #22)
  Brush 2 coats
| | | | | | | | | | |
|---|---|---|---|---|---|---|---|---|---|
| Slow | 1.5 | 8.0 | 78.80 | 30.38 | 8.95 | 9.85 | 9.35 | 9.37 | 67.90 |
| Medium | 1.3 | 7.5 | 69.00 | 33.48 | 11.85 | 9.20 | 13.63 | 8.18 | 76.34 |
| Fast | 1.0 | 7.0 | 59.10 | 31.50 | 12.85 | 8.44 | 16.36 | 4.84 | 73.99 |

Marine spar varnish, flat or gloss (material #23)
  Brush 2 coats
| | | | | | | | | | |
|---|---|---|---|---|---|---|---|---|---|
| Slow | 1.2 | 12 | 83.10 | 24.30 | 7.16 | 6.93 | 7.30 | 7.31 | 53.00 |
| Medium | 1.0 | 10 | 72.70 | 25.75 | 9.12 | 7.27 | 10.54 | 6.32 | 59.00 |
| Fast | 0.8 | 8 | 62.30 | 25.20 | 10.28 | 7.79 | 13.41 | 3.97 | 60.65 |

ADD - Preparation for spar varnish
| | | | | | | | | | |
|---|---|---|---|---|---|---|---|---|---|
| Steel wool buff | 0.3 | -- | -- | 7.73 | 2.73 | -- | 2.62 | 1.57 | 14.65 |
| Wax application | 0.3 | -- | -- | 7.73 | 2.73 | -- | 2.62 | 1.57 | 14.65 |

Use these figures for painting two coats on exterior French doors that have 10 to 15 lites. These costs are to be included with the exterior door take-off and are in addition to the costs that are included in the interior take-off as explained by the example in the previous section. ADD for additional preparation time, as needed, including setup, remove & replace (hardware), protection (mask walls and visqueen floors); putty, caulking, sanding and cleanup. Add minimum preparation time for varnishing as indicated above. "Slow" work is based on an hourly wage of $20.25, "Medium" work on an hourly wage of $25.75, and "Fast" work on an hourly wage of $31.50. Other qualifications that apply to this table are on page 9.

*National Painting Cost Estimator*

|  | Manhours per door | Doors per gallon | Material cost per gallon | Labor cost per door | Labor burden door | Material cost per door | Overhead per door | Profit per door | Total price per door |
|---|---|---|---|---|---|---|---|---|---|

## Doors, exterior, louvered, two coat system

Exterior enamel, 2 coat system, water base (material #24)
  Roll & brush 2 coats

| | | | | | | | | | |
|---|---|---|---|---|---|---|---|---|---|
| Slow | 1.4 | 7 | 50.70 | 28.35 | 8.36 | 7.24 | 8.35 | 8.37 | 60.67 |
| Medium | 1.1 | 6 | 44.40 | 28.33 | 10.03 | 7.40 | 11.44 | 6.86 | 64.06 |
| Fast | 0.7 | 5 | 38.00 | 22.05 | 9.00 | 7.60 | 11.98 | 3.54 | 54.17 |

Exterior enamel, 2 coat system, oil base (material #25)
  Roll & brush 2 coats

| | | | | | | | | | |
|---|---|---|---|---|---|---|---|---|---|
| Slow | 1.4 | 7 | 56.40 | 28.35 | 8.36 | 8.06 | 8.51 | 8.52 | 61.80 |
| Medium | 1.1 | 6 | 49.40 | 28.33 | 10.03 | 8.23 | 11.65 | 6.99 | 65.23 |
| Fast | 0.7 | 5 | 42.30 | 22.05 | 9.00 | 8.46 | 12.25 | 3.62 | 55.38 |

Polyurethane (material #22)
  Brush 2 coats

| | | | | | | | | | |
|---|---|---|---|---|---|---|---|---|---|
| Slow | 1.7 | 5.0 | 78.80 | 34.43 | 10.14 | 15.76 | 11.47 | 11.49 | 83.29 |
| Medium | 1.5 | 4.5 | 69.00 | 38.63 | 13.68 | 15.33 | 16.91 | 10.15 | 94.70 |
| Fast | 1.2 | 4.0 | 59.10 | 37.80 | 15.42 | 14.78 | 21.08 | 6.24 | 95.32 |

Marine spar varnish, flat or gloss (material #23)
  Brush 2 coats

| | | | | | | | | | |
|---|---|---|---|---|---|---|---|---|---|
| Slow | 1.6 | 7 | 83.10 | 32.40 | 9.55 | 11.87 | 10.23 | 10.25 | 74.30 |
| Medium | 1.3 | 6 | 72.70 | 33.48 | 11.85 | 12.12 | 14.36 | 8.62 | 80.43 |
| Fast | 0.9 | 5 | 62.30 | 28.35 | 11.57 | 12.46 | 16.24 | 4.80 | 73.42 |

ADD - Preparation for spar varnish

| | | | | | | | | | |
|---|---|---|---|---|---|---|---|---|---|
| Steel wool buff | 0.4 | -- | -- | 10.30 | 3.65 | -- | 3.49 | 2.09 | 19.53 |
| Wax application | 0.4 | -- | -- | 10.30 | 3.65 | -- | 3.49 | 2.09 | 19.53 |

Use these figures for painting two coats on exterior louvered doors. These costs are to be included with the exterior door take-off and are in addition to the costs that are included in the interior take-off as explained by the example in the previous section. ADD for additional preparation time, as needed, including setup, remove & replace (hardware), protection (mask walls and visqueen floors); putty, caulking, sanding and cleanup. Add minimum preparation time for varnishing as indicated above. "Slow" work is based on an hourly wage of $20.25, "Medium" work on an hourly wage of $25.75, and "Fast" work on an hourly wage of $31.50. Other qualifications that apply to this table are on page 9.

*General Painting Costs*

|  | Manhours per door | Doors per gallon | Material cost per gallon | Labor cost per door | Labor burden door | Material cost per door | Overhead per door | Profit per door | Total price per door |
|---|---|---|---|---|---|---|---|---|---|

## Doors, exterior, panel (entry), two coat system

Exterior enamel, 2 coat system, water base (material #24)
  Roll & brush 2 coats

| | | | | | | | | | |
|---|---|---|---|---|---|---|---|---|---|
| Slow | 1.4 | 4 | 50.70 | 28.35 | 8.36 | 12.68 | 9.38 | 9.40 | 68.17 |
| Medium | 1.1 | 3 | 44.40 | 28.33 | 10.03 | 14.80 | 13.29 | 7.97 | 74.42 |
| Fast | 0.8 | 2 | 38.00 | 25.20 | 10.28 | 19.00 | 16.89 | 5.00 | 76.37 |

Exterior enamel, 2 coat system, oil base (material #25)
  Roll & brush 2 coats

| | | | | | | | | | |
|---|---|---|---|---|---|---|---|---|---|
| Slow | 1.4 | 4 | 56.40 | 28.35 | 8.36 | 14.10 | 9.65 | 9.67 | 70.13 |
| Medium | 1.1 | 3 | 49.40 | 28.33 | 10.03 | 16.47 | 13.71 | 8.22 | 76.76 |
| Fast | 0.8 | 2 | 42.30 | 25.20 | 10.28 | 21.15 | 17.56 | 5.19 | 79.38 |

Polyurethane (material #22)
  Brush 2 coats

| | | | | | | | | | |
|---|---|---|---|---|---|---|---|---|---|
| Slow | 1.7 | 4 | 78.80 | 34.43 | 10.14 | 19.70 | 12.22 | 12.24 | 88.73 |
| Medium | 1.5 | 3 | 69.00 | 38.63 | 13.68 | 23.00 | 18.83 | 11.30 | 105.44 |
| Fast | 1.2 | 2 | 59.10 | 37.80 | 15.42 | 29.55 | 25.66 | 7.59 | 116.02 |

Marine spar varnish, flat or gloss (material #23)
  Brush 2 coats

| | | | | | | | | | |
|---|---|---|---|---|---|---|---|---|---|
| Slow | 1.4 | 4 | 83.10 | 28.35 | 8.36 | 20.78 | 10.92 | 10.95 | 79.36 |
| Medium | 1.1 | 3 | 72.70 | 28.33 | 10.03 | 24.23 | 15.65 | 9.39 | 87.63 |
| Fast | 0.8 | 2 | 35.60 | 25.20 | 10.28 | 17.80 | 16.52 | 4.89 | 74.69 |

ADD - Preparation for spar varnish

| | | | | | | | | | |
|---|---|---|---|---|---|---|---|---|---|
| Steel wool buff | 0.3 | -- | -- | 7.73 | 2.73 | -- | 2.62 | 1.57 | 14.65 |
| Wax application | 0.3 | -- | -- | 7.73 | 2.73 | -- | 2.62 | 1.57 | 14.65 |

Use these figures for painting two coats on typical exterior paneled doors. These costs are included with the exterior door take-off and are in addition to the costs that are included in the interior take-off as explained by the example in the previous section. ADD for additional preparation time, as needed, including setup, remove & replace (hardware), protection (mask walls and visqueen floors); putty, caulking, sanding and cleanup. Add minimum preparation time for varnishing as indicated above. "Slow" work is based on an hourly wage of $20.25, "Medium" work on an hourly wage of $25.75, and "Fast" work on an hourly wage of $31.50. Other qualifications that apply to this table are on page 9.

## Doors, *Opening Count Method*

Many painting companies estimate paint grade doors (including jambs and frames), wood windows, pullmans, linens, bookcases, wine racks and other interior surfaces that take an undercoat and enamel finish by the "opening." Based on Figure 20 below, each opening is considered to take the same time regardless of whether it's a door, window, pullman, etc. These figures are based on the number of openings finished per 8-hour day and the material required per opening. The Opening Count Method of estimating involves counting the quantity of all openings (including all exterior doors) based on the opening allowance table at Figure 20 below. After you determine the number of openings, use the following table in accumulated multiples of 10 for applying undercoat and enamel. The undercoat process is based on 11 to 13 openings per gallon and enamel is based on 10 to 12 openings per gallon. As an example, using the medium rate for water based material on 12 openings with 1 coat of undercoat and 1 coat of enamel, add the 10 opening figures for each coat to the 2 opening figures for each coat as follows:

### Interior Take-off

|  | Undercoat | Enamel |  |
|---|---|---|---|
| 10 openings | 150.68 | 169.97 | (page 108) |
| 2 openings | 31.20 | 34.75 | (page 103) |
| 12 openings | 181.88 | 204.72 |  |

| | Item | Opening Count |
|---|---|---|
| **Closets** | Molding at closet perimeter | Count 1 opening per 25'0" length |
| | Poles, stain | Count 1 opening per 10'0" length |
| | Shelf & pole (undercoat or enamel) | Count 1 opening per 6'0" length |
| | Shelves (undercoat or enamel) | Count 1 opening per 10'0" length |
| **Doors** | Bifold doors & frames | Count 1 opening per door |
| | Dutch doors & frames | Count 2 openings per door |
| | Entry doors & frames | Count 1 opening per door |
| | Forced air unit doors & frames | Count 1 opening per door |
| | French doors & frames | Count 1.5 openings per door |
| | Linen doors with face frame | Count 1 opening per 2'0" width |
| | Louvered bifold doors & frames | Count 1 opening per door panel |
| |   false | Count 1 opening per door panel |
| |   real | Count 1 opening per door or per 1'6" width |
| | Passage doors & frames | |
| |   flush | Count 1 opening per door |
| |   paneled | Count 1.25 openings per door |
| | Wardrobe doors | Count 1 opening per door |
| | Split coat operation, doors & frames | Count 1 opening per door |
| | Tipoff operation (doors only) | Count .5 opening per door |
| **Pullman cabinets** | | Count 1 opening per lavatory or per 4'0" width |
| **Windows, wood** | | Count 1 opening per 6 SF of window |

**Figure 20**
Interior opening count allowance table

*General Painting Costs*

|  | Manhours per opening | Gallons per opening | Material cost per gallon | Labor cost per opening | Labor burden opening | Material cost per opening | Overhead per opening | Profit per opening | Total price per opening |
|---|---|---|---|---|---|---|---|---|---|

## Doors, interior openings, *Opening Count Method*

**1 opening total**

Undercoat, water base (material #3)
  Roll & brush 1 coat

| Slow | 0.4 | 0.080 | 32.60 | 8.10 | 2.39 | 2.61 | 2.49 | 2.49 | 18.08 |
| Medium | 0.3 | 0.085 | 28.50 | 7.73 | 2.73 | 2.42 | 3.22 | 1.93 | 18.03 |
| Fast | 0.2 | 0.090 | 24.50 | 6.30 | 2.57 | 2.21 | 3.43 | 1.02 | 15.53 |

Undercoat, oil base (material #4)
  Roll & brush 1 coat

| Slow | 0.4 | 0.080 | 42.30 | 8.10 | 2.39 | 3.38 | 2.64 | 2.64 | 19.15 |
| Medium | 0.3 | 0.085 | 37.00 | 7.73 | 2.73 | 3.15 | 3.41 | 2.04 | 19.06 |
| Fast | 0.2 | 0.090 | 31.80 | 6.30 | 2.57 | 2.86 | 3.64 | 1.08 | 16.45 |

Enamel, water base (material #9)
  Roll & brush 1 coat

| Slow | 0.4 | 0.08 | 46.80 | 8.10 | 2.39 | 3.74 | 2.70 | 2.71 | 19.64 |
| Medium | 0.3 | 0.09 | 41.00 | 7.73 | 2.73 | 3.69 | 3.54 | 2.12 | 19.81 |
| Fast | 0.2 | 0.10 | 35.10 | 6.30 | 2.57 | 3.51 | 3.84 | 1.14 | 17.36 |

Enamel, oil base (material #10)
  Roll & brush 1 coat

| Slow | 0.4 | 0.08 | 61.70 | 8.10 | 2.39 | 4.94 | 2.93 | 2.94 | 21.30 |
| Medium | 0.3 | 0.09 | 54.00 | 7.73 | 2.73 | 4.86 | 3.83 | 2.30 | 21.45 |
| Fast | 0.2 | 0.10 | 46.30 | 6.30 | 2.57 | 4.63 | 4.19 | 1.24 | 18.93 |

**2 openings total**

Undercoat, water base (material #3)
  Roll & brush 1 coat

| Slow | 0.7 | 0.16 | 32.60 | 14.18 | 4.17 | 5.22 | 4.48 | 4.49 | 32.54 |
| Medium | 0.5 | 0.17 | 28.50 | 12.88 | 4.56 | 4.85 | 5.57 | 3.34 | 31.20 |
| Fast | 0.3 | 0.18 | 24.50 | 9.45 | 3.86 | 4.41 | 5.49 | 1.62 | 24.83 |

Undercoat, oil base (material #4)
  Roll & brush 1 coat

| Slow | 0.7 | 0.16 | 42.30 | 14.18 | 4.17 | 6.77 | 4.77 | 4.78 | 34.67 |
| Medium | 0.5 | 0.17 | 37.00 | 12.88 | 4.56 | 6.29 | 5.93 | 3.56 | 33.22 |
| Fast | 0.3 | 0.18 | 31.80 | 9.45 | 3.86 | 5.72 | 5.90 | 1.75 | 26.68 |

Enamel, water base (material #9)
  Roll & brush 1 coat

| Slow | 0.7 | 0.17 | 46.80 | 14.18 | 4.17 | 7.96 | 5.00 | 5.01 | 36.32 |
| Medium | 0.5 | 0.18 | 41.00 | 12.88 | 4.56 | 7.38 | 6.21 | 3.72 | 34.75 |
| Fast | 0.3 | 0.20 | 35.10 | 9.45 | 3.86 | 7.02 | 6.30 | 1.86 | 28.49 |

*National Painting Cost Estimator*

|  | Manhours per opening | Gallons per opening | Material cost per gallon | Labor cost per opening | Labor burden opening | Material cost per opening | Overhead per opening | Profit per opening | Total price per opening |
|---|---|---|---|---|---|---|---|---|---|
| **Enamel, oil base (material #10)** | | | | | | | | | |
| Roll & brush 1 coat | | | | | | | | | |
| Slow | 0.7 | 0.17 | 61.70 | 14.18 | 4.17 | 10.49 | 5.48 | 5.49 | 39.81 |
| Medium | 0.5 | 0.18 | 54.00 | 12.88 | 4.56 | 9.72 | 6.79 | 4.07 | 38.02 |
| Fast | 0.3 | 0.20 | 46.30 | 9.45 | 3.86 | 9.26 | 7.00 | 2.07 | 31.64 |
| **3 openings total** | | | | | | | | | |
| **Undercoat, water base (material #3)** | | | | | | | | | |
| Roll & brush 1 coat | | | | | | | | | |
| Slow | 1.00 | 0.23 | 32.60 | 20.25 | 5.97 | 7.50 | 6.41 | 6.42 | 46.55 |
| Medium | 0.75 | 0.25 | 28.50 | 19.31 | 6.84 | 7.13 | 8.32 | 4.99 | 46.59 |
| Fast | 0.50 | 0.27 | 24.50 | 15.75 | 6.43 | 6.62 | 8.93 | 2.64 | 40.37 |
| **Undercoat, oil base (material #4)** | | | | | | | | | |
| Roll & brush 1 coat | | | | | | | | | |
| Slow | 1.00 | 0.23 | 42.30 | 20.25 | 5.97 | 9.73 | 6.83 | 6.84 | 49.62 |
| Medium | 0.75 | 0.25 | 37.00 | 19.31 | 6.84 | 9.25 | 8.85 | 5.31 | 49.56 |
| Fast | 0.50 | 0.27 | 31.80 | 15.75 | 6.43 | 8.59 | 9.54 | 2.82 | 43.13 |
| **Enamel, water base (material #9)** | | | | | | | | | |
| Roll & brush 1 coat | | | | | | | | | |
| Slow | 1.00 | 0.25 | 46.80 | 20.25 | 5.97 | 11.70 | 7.20 | 7.22 | 52.34 |
| Medium | 0.75 | 0.27 | 41.00 | 19.31 | 6.84 | 11.07 | 9.31 | 5.58 | 52.11 |
| Fast | 0.50 | 0.30 | 35.10 | 15.75 | 6.43 | 10.53 | 10.14 | 3.00 | 45.85 |
| **Enamel, oil base (material #10)** | | | | | | | | | |
| Roll & brush 1 coat | | | | | | | | | |
| Slow | 1.00 | 0.25 | 61.70 | 20.25 | 5.97 | 15.43 | 7.91 | 7.93 | 57.49 |
| Medium | 0.75 | 0.27 | 54.00 | 19.31 | 6.84 | 14.58 | 10.18 | 6.11 | 57.02 |
| Fast | 0.50 | 0.30 | 46.30 | 15.75 | 6.43 | 13.89 | 11.18 | 3.31 | 50.56 |
| **4 openings total** | | | | | | | | | |
| **Undercoat, water base (material #3)** | | | | | | | | | |
| Roll & brush 1 coat | | | | | | | | | |
| Slow | 1.3 | 0.31 | 32.60 | 26.33 | 7.76 | 10.11 | 8.40 | 8.42 | 61.02 |
| Medium | 1.0 | 0.33 | 28.50 | 25.75 | 9.12 | 9.41 | 11.07 | 6.64 | 61.99 |
| Fast | 0.7 | 0.36 | 24.50 | 22.05 | 9.00 | 8.82 | 12.36 | 3.66 | 55.89 |
| **Undercoat, oil base (material #4)** | | | | | | | | | |
| Roll & brush 1 coat | | | | | | | | | |
| Slow | 1.3 | 0.31 | 42.30 | 26.33 | 7.76 | 13.11 | 8.97 | 8.99 | 65.16 |
| Medium | 1.0 | 0.33 | 37.00 | 25.75 | 9.12 | 12.21 | 11.77 | 7.06 | 65.91 |
| Fast | 0.7 | 0.36 | 31.80 | 22.05 | 9.00 | 11.45 | 13.18 | 3.90 | 59.58 |

*General Painting Costs*

|  | Manhours per opening | Gallons per opening | Material cost per gallon | Labor cost per opening | Labor burden opening | Material cost per opening | Overhead per opening | Profit per opening | Total price per opening |
|---|---|---|---|---|---|---|---|---|---|
| **Enamel, water base (material #9)** | | | | | | | | | |
| Roll & brush 1 coat | | | | | | | | | |
| Slow | 1.3 | 0.33 | 46.80 | 26.33 | 7.76 | 15.44 | 9.41 | 9.43 | 68.37 |
| Medium | 1.0 | 0.36 | 41.00 | 25.75 | 9.12 | 14.76 | 12.41 | 7.44 | 69.48 |
| Fast | 0.7 | 0.40 | 35.10 | 22.05 | 9.00 | 14.04 | 13.98 | 4.13 | 63.20 |
| **Enamel, oil base (material #10)** | | | | | | | | | |
| Roll & brush 1 coat | | | | | | | | | |
| Slow | 1.3 | 0.33 | 61.70 | 26.33 | 7.76 | 20.36 | 10.35 | 10.37 | 75.17 |
| Medium | 1.0 | 0.36 | 54.00 | 25.75 | 9.12 | 19.44 | 13.58 | 8.15 | 76.04 |
| Fast | 0.7 | 0.40 | 46.30 | 22.05 | 9.00 | 18.52 | 15.37 | 4.55 | 69.49 |
| **5 openings total** | | | | | | | | | |
| Undercoat, water base (material #3) | | | | | | | | | |
| Roll & brush 1 coat | | | | | | | | | |
| Slow | 1.6 | 0.38 | 32.60 | 32.40 | 9.55 | 12.39 | 10.33 | 10.35 | 75.02 |
| Medium | 1.3 | 0.41 | 28.50 | 33.48 | 11.85 | 11.69 | 14.26 | 8.55 | 79.83 |
| Fast | 0.9 | 0.45 | 24.50 | 28.35 | 11.57 | 11.03 | 15.79 | 4.67 | 71.41 |
| Undercoat, oil base (material #4) | | | | | | | | | |
| Roll & brush 1 coat | | | | | | | | | |
| Slow | 1.6 | 0.38 | 42.30 | 32.40 | 9.55 | 16.07 | 11.03 | 11.05 | 80.10 |
| Medium | 1.3 | 0.41 | 37.00 | 33.48 | 11.85 | 15.17 | 15.13 | 9.08 | 84.71 |
| Fast | 0.9 | 0.45 | 31.80 | 28.35 | 11.57 | 14.31 | 16.81 | 4.97 | 76.01 |
| Enamel, water base (material #9) | | | | | | | | | |
| Roll & brush 1 coat | | | | | | | | | |
| Slow | 1.6 | 0.42 | 46.80 | 32.40 | 9.55 | 19.66 | 11.71 | 11.73 | 85.05 |
| Medium | 1.3 | 0.46 | 41.00 | 33.48 | 11.85 | 18.86 | 16.05 | 9.63 | 89.87 |
| Fast | 0.9 | 0.50 | 35.10 | 28.35 | 11.57 | 17.55 | 17.82 | 5.27 | 80.56 |
| Enamel, oil base (material #10) | | | | | | | | | |
| Roll & brush 1 coat | | | | | | | | | |
| Slow | 1.6 | 0.42 | 61.70 | 32.40 | 9.55 | 25.91 | 12.90 | 12.92 | 93.68 |
| Medium | 1.3 | 0.46 | 54.00 | 33.48 | 11.85 | 24.84 | 17.54 | 10.53 | 98.24 |
| Fast | 0.9 | 0.50 | 46.30 | 28.35 | 11.57 | 23.15 | 19.55 | 5.78 | 88.40 |
| **6 openings total** | | | | | | | | | |
| Undercoat, water base (material #3) | | | | | | | | | |
| Roll & brush 1 coat | | | | | | | | | |
| Slow | 1.90 | 0.46 | 32.60 | 38.48 | 11.34 | 15.00 | 12.32 | 12.34 | 89.48 |
| Medium | 1.45 | 0.50 | 28.50 | 37.34 | 13.22 | 14.25 | 16.20 | 9.72 | 90.73 |
| Fast | 1.00 | 0.54 | 24.50 | 31.50 | 12.85 | 13.23 | 17.85 | 5.28 | 80.71 |

*National Painting Cost Estimator*

|  | Manhours per opening | Gallons per opening | Material cost per gallon | Labor cost per opening | Labor burden opening | Material cost per opening | Overhead per opening | Profit per opening | Total price per opening |
|---|---|---|---|---|---|---|---|---|---|
| **Undercoat, oil base (material #4)** | | | | | | | | | |
| Roll & brush 1 coat | | | | | | | | | |
| Slow | 1.90 | 0.46 | 42.30 | 38.48 | 11.34 | 19.46 | 13.17 | 13.19 | 95.64 |
| Medium | 1.45 | 0.50 | 37.00 | 37.34 | 13.22 | 18.50 | 17.27 | 10.36 | 96.69 |
| Fast | 1.00 | 0.54 | 31.80 | 31.50 | 12.85 | 17.17 | 19.07 | 5.64 | 86.23 |
| **Enamel, water base (material #9)** | | | | | | | | | |
| Roll & brush 1 coat | | | | | | | | | |
| Slow | 1.90 | 0.50 | 46.80 | 38.48 | 11.34 | 23.40 | 13.91 | 13.94 | 101.07 |
| Medium | 1.45 | 0.55 | 41.00 | 37.34 | 13.22 | 22.55 | 18.28 | 10.97 | 102.36 |
| Fast | 1.00 | 0.60 | 35.10 | 31.50 | 12.85 | 21.06 | 20.28 | 6.00 | 91.69 |
| **Enamel, oil base (material #10)** | | | | | | | | | |
| Roll & brush 1 coat | | | | | | | | | |
| Slow | 1.90 | 0.50 | 61.70 | 38.48 | 11.34 | 30.85 | 15.33 | 15.36 | 111.36 |
| Medium | 1.45 | 0.55 | 54.00 | 37.34 | 13.22 | 29.70 | 20.07 | 12.04 | 112.37 |
| Fast | 1.00 | 0.60 | 46.30 | 31.50 | 12.85 | 27.78 | 22.36 | 6.61 | 101.10 |
| **7 openings total** | | | | | | | | | |
| **Undercoat, water base (material #3)** | | | | | | | | | |
| Roll & brush 1 coat | | | | | | | | | |
| Slow | 2.2 | 0.54 | 32.60 | 44.55 | 13.13 | 17.60 | 14.31 | 14.34 | 103.93 |
| Medium | 1.7 | 0.59 | 28.50 | 43.78 | 15.50 | 16.82 | 19.03 | 11.42 | 106.55 |
| Fast | 1.2 | 0.64 | 24.50 | 37.80 | 15.42 | 15.68 | 21.36 | 6.32 | 96.58 |
| **Undercoat, oil base (material #4)** | | | | | | | | | |
| Roll & brush 1 coat | | | | | | | | | |
| Slow | 2.2 | 0.54 | 42.30 | 44.55 | 13.13 | 22.84 | 15.30 | 15.33 | 111.15 |
| Medium | 1.7 | 0.59 | 37.00 | 43.78 | 15.50 | 21.83 | 20.28 | 12.17 | 113.56 |
| Fast | 1.2 | 0.64 | 31.80 | 37.80 | 15.42 | 20.35 | 22.81 | 6.75 | 103.13 |
| **Enamel, water base (material #9)** | | | | | | | | | |
| Roll & brush 1 coat | | | | | | | | | |
| Slow | 2.2 | 0.58 | 46.80 | 44.55 | 13.13 | 27.14 | 16.12 | 16.15 | 117.09 |
| Medium | 1.7 | 0.64 | 41.00 | 43.78 | 15.50 | 26.24 | 21.38 | 12.83 | 119.73 |
| Fast | 1.2 | 0.70 | 35.10 | 37.80 | 15.42 | 24.57 | 24.11 | 7.13 | 109.03 |
| **Enamel, oil base (material #10)** | | | | | | | | | |
| Roll & brush 1 coat | | | | | | | | | |
| Slow | 2.2 | 0.58 | 61.70 | 44.55 | 13.13 | 35.79 | 17.76 | 17.80 | 129.03 |
| Medium | 1.7 | 0.64 | 54.00 | 43.78 | 15.50 | 34.56 | 23.46 | 14.08 | 131.38 |
| Fast | 1.2 | 0.70 | 46.30 | 37.80 | 15.42 | 32.41 | 26.55 | 7.85 | 120.03 |

*General Painting Costs*

|  | Manhours per opening | Gallons per opening | Material cost per gallon | Labor cost per opening | Labor burden opening | Material cost per opening | Overhead per opening | Profit per opening | Total price per opening |
|---|---|---|---|---|---|---|---|---|---|
| **8 openings total** | | | | | | | | | |
| Undercoat, water base (material #3) | | | | | | | | | |
| Roll & brush 1 coat | | | | | | | | | |
| Slow | 2.50 | 0.62 | 32.60 | 50.63 | 14.92 | 20.21 | 16.30 | 16.33 | 118.39 |
| Medium | 1.95 | 0.67 | 28.50 | 50.21 | 17.79 | 19.10 | 21.77 | 13.06 | 121.93 |
| Fast | 1.40 | 0.73 | 24.50 | 44.10 | 17.99 | 17.89 | 24.79 | 7.33 | 112.10 |
| Undercoat, oil base (material #4) | | | | | | | | | |
| Roll & brush 1 coat | | | | | | | | | |
| Slow | 2.50 | 0.62 | 42.30 | 50.63 | 14.92 | 26.23 | 17.44 | 17.48 | 126.70 |
| Medium | 1.95 | 0.67 | 37.00 | 50.21 | 17.79 | 24.79 | 23.19 | 13.92 | 129.90 |
| Fast | 1.40 | 0.73 | 31.80 | 44.10 | 17.99 | 23.21 | 26.44 | 7.82 | 119.56 |
| Enamel, water base (material #9) | | | | | | | | | |
| Roll & brush 1 coat | | | | | | | | | |
| Slow | 2.50 | 0.67 | 46.80 | 50.63 | 14.92 | 31.36 | 18.42 | 18.46 | 133.79 |
| Medium | 1.95 | 0.74 | 41.00 | 50.21 | 17.79 | 30.34 | 24.58 | 14.75 | 137.67 |
| Fast | 1.40 | 0.80 | 35.10 | 44.10 | 17.99 | 28.08 | 27.95 | 8.27 | 126.39 |
| Enamel, oil base (material #10) | | | | | | | | | |
| Roll & brush 1 coat | | | | | | | | | |
| Slow | 2.50 | 0.67 | 61.70 | 50.63 | 14.92 | 41.34 | 20.31 | 20.36 | 147.56 |
| Medium | 1.95 | 0.74 | 54.00 | 50.21 | 17.79 | 39.96 | 26.99 | 16.19 | 151.14 |
| Fast | 1.40 | 0.80 | 46.30 | 44.10 | 17.99 | 37.04 | 30.73 | 9.09 | 138.95 |
| **9 openings total** | | | | | | | | | |
| Undercoat, water base (material #3) | | | | | | | | | |
| Roll & brush 1 coat | | | | | | | | | |
| Slow | 2.80 | 0.69 | 32.60 | 56.70 | 16.72 | 22.49 | 18.22 | 18.26 | 132.39 |
| Medium | 2.15 | 0.75 | 28.50 | 55.36 | 19.61 | 21.38 | 24.09 | 14.45 | 134.89 |
| Fast | 1.50 | 0.81 | 24.50 | 47.25 | 19.28 | 19.85 | 26.78 | 7.92 | 121.08 |
| Undercoat, oil base (material #4) | | | | | | | | | |
| Roll & brush 1 coat | | | | | | | | | |
| Slow | 2.80 | 0.69 | 42.30 | 56.70 | 16.72 | 29.19 | 19.50 | 19.54 | 141.65 |
| Medium | 2.15 | 0.75 | 37.00 | 55.36 | 19.61 | 27.75 | 25.68 | 15.41 | 143.81 |
| Fast | 1.50 | 0.81 | 31.80 | 47.25 | 19.28 | 25.76 | 28.61 | 8.46 | 129.36 |
| Enamel, water base (material #9) | | | | | | | | | |
| Roll & brush 1 coat | | | | | | | | | |
| Slow | 2.80 | 0.75 | 46.80 | 56.70 | 16.72 | 35.10 | 20.62 | 20.66 | 149.80 |
| Medium | 2.15 | 0.82 | 41.00 | 55.36 | 19.61 | 33.62 | 27.15 | 16.29 | 152.03 |
| Fast | 1.50 | 0.90 | 35.10 | 47.25 | 19.28 | 31.59 | 30.42 | 9.00 | 137.54 |

*National Painting Cost Estimator*

|  | Manhours per opening | Gallons per opening | Material cost per gallon | Labor cost per opening | Labor burden opening | Material cost per opening | Overhead per opening | Profit per opening | Total price per opening |
|---|---|---|---|---|---|---|---|---|---|
| **Enamel, oil base (material #10)** | | | | | | | | | |
| Roll & brush 1 coat | | | | | | | | | |
| Slow | 2.80 | 0.75 | 61.70 | 56.70 | 16.72 | 46.28 | 22.74 | 22.79 | 165.23 |
| Medium | 2.15 | 0.82 | 54.00 | 55.36 | 19.61 | 44.28 | 29.81 | 17.89 | 166.95 |
| Fast | 1.50 | 0.90 | 46.30 | 47.25 | 19.28 | 41.67 | 33.54 | 9.92 | 151.66 |
| **10 openings total** | | | | | | | | | |
| **Undercoat, water base (material #3)** | | | | | | | | | |
| Roll & brush 1 coat | | | | | | | | | |
| Slow | 3.1 | 0.77 | 32.60 | 62.78 | 18.50 | 25.10 | 20.22 | 20.26 | 146.86 |
| Medium | 2.4 | 0.84 | 28.50 | 61.80 | 21.89 | 23.94 | 26.91 | 16.14 | 150.68 |
| Fast | 1.7 | 0.90 | 24.50 | 53.55 | 21.85 | 22.05 | 30.21 | 8.94 | 136.60 |
| **Undercoat, oil base (material #4)** | | | | | | | | | |
| Roll & brush 1 coat | | | | | | | | | |
| Slow | 3.1 | 0.77 | 42.30 | 62.78 | 18.50 | 32.57 | 21.64 | 21.68 | 157.17 |
| Medium | 2.4 | 0.84 | 37.00 | 61.80 | 21.89 | 31.08 | 28.69 | 17.21 | 160.67 |
| Fast | 1.7 | 0.90 | 31.80 | 53.55 | 21.85 | 28.62 | 32.25 | 9.54 | 145.81 |
| **Enamel, water base (material #9)** | | | | | | | | | |
| Slow | 3.1 | 0.83 | 46.80 | 62.78 | 18.50 | 38.84 | 22.83 | 22.88 | 165.83 |
| Medium | 2.4 | 0.92 | 41.00 | 61.80 | 21.89 | 37.72 | 30.35 | 18.21 | 169.97 |
| Fast | 1.7 | 1.00 | 35.10 | 53.55 | 21.85 | 35.10 | 34.26 | 10.13 | 154.89 |
| **Enamel, oil base (material #10)** | | | | | | | | | |
| Roll & brush 1 coat | | | | | | | | | |
| Slow | 3.1 | 0.83 | 61.70 | 62.78 | 18.50 | 51.21 | 25.18 | 25.23 | 182.90 |
| Medium | 2.4 | 0.92 | 54.00 | 61.80 | 21.89 | 49.68 | 33.34 | 20.00 | 186.71 |
| Fast | 1.7 | 1.00 | 46.30 | 53.55 | 21.85 | 46.30 | 37.73 | 11.16 | 170.59 |

Use these figures for painting interior doors, pullmans, linens and other surfaces described in Figure 20 on page 102. ADD for additional preparation time, as needed, including setup, remove & replace (hardware), protection (mask walls and visqueen floors); putty, caulking, sanding and cleanup. "Slow" work is based on an hourly wage of $20.25, "Medium" work on an hourly wage of $25.75, and "Fast" work on an hourly wage of $31.50. Other qualifications that apply to this table are on page 9.

*General Painting Costs*

|  | Manhours per door | Doors per gallon | Material cost per gallon | Labor cost per door | Labor burden door | Material cost per door | Overhead per door | Profit per door | Total price per door |
|---|---|---|---|---|---|---|---|---|---|

## Doors, interior, flush, paint grade, roll & brush, based on per door method

Undercoat, water base (material #3)
  Roll & brush 1 coat

| | | | | | | | | | |
|---|---|---|---|---|---|---|---|---|---|
| Slow | 0.40 | 13.0 | 32.60 | 8.10 | 2.39 | 2.51 | 2.47 | 2.48 | 17.95 |
| Medium | 0.30 | 11.5 | 28.50 | 7.73 | 2.73 | 2.48 | 3.24 | 1.94 | 18.12 |
| Fast | 0.20 | 10.0 | 24.50 | 6.30 | 2.57 | 2.45 | 3.51 | 1.04 | 15.87 |

Undercoat, oil base (material #4)
  Roll & brush 1 coat

| | | | | | | | | | |
|---|---|---|---|---|---|---|---|---|---|
| Slow | 0.40 | 13.0 | 42.30 | 8.10 | 2.39 | 3.25 | 2.61 | 2.62 | 18.97 |
| Medium | 0.30 | 11.5 | 37.00 | 7.73 | 2.73 | 3.22 | 3.42 | 2.05 | 19.15 |
| Fast | 0.20 | 10.0 | 31.80 | 6.30 | 2.57 | 3.18 | 3.74 | 1.11 | 16.90 |

Enamel, water base (material #9)
  Roll & brush 1st finish coat

| | | | | | | | | | |
|---|---|---|---|---|---|---|---|---|---|
| Slow | 0.33 | 14.0 | 46.80 | 6.68 | 1.97 | 3.34 | 2.28 | 2.28 | 16.55 |
| Medium | 0.25 | 12.5 | 41.00 | 6.44 | 2.28 | 3.28 | 3.00 | 1.80 | 16.80 |
| Fast | 0.17 | 11.0 | 35.10 | 5.36 | 2.18 | 3.19 | 3.33 | .98 | 15.04 |

  Roll & brush additional finish coats

| | | | | | | | | | |
|---|---|---|---|---|---|---|---|---|---|
| Slow | 0.25 | 15.0 | 46.80 | 5.06 | 1.50 | 3.12 | 1.84 | 1.84 | 13.36 |
| Medium | 0.20 | 13.5 | 41.00 | 5.15 | 1.82 | 3.04 | 2.50 | 1.50 | 14.01 |
| Fast | 0.15 | 12.0 | 35.10 | 4.73 | 1.92 | 2.93 | 2.97 | .88 | 13.43 |

Enamel, oil base (material #10)
  Roll & brush 1st finish coat

| | | | | | | | | | |
|---|---|---|---|---|---|---|---|---|---|
| Slow | 0.33 | 14.0 | 61.70 | 6.68 | 1.97 | 4.41 | 2.48 | 2.49 | 18.03 |
| Medium | 0.25 | 12.5 | 54.00 | 6.44 | 2.28 | 4.32 | 3.26 | 1.96 | 18.26 |
| Fast | 0.17 | 11.0 | 46.30 | 5.36 | 2.18 | 4.21 | 3.65 | 1.08 | 16.48 |

  Roll & brush additional finish coats

| | | | | | | | | | |
|---|---|---|---|---|---|---|---|---|---|
| Slow | 0.25 | 15.0 | 61.70 | 5.06 | 1.50 | 4.11 | 2.03 | 2.03 | 14.73 |
| Medium | 0.20 | 13.5 | 54.00 | 5.15 | 1.82 | 4.00 | 2.74 | 1.65 | 15.36 |
| Fast | 0.15 | 12.0 | 46.30 | 4.73 | 1.92 | 3.86 | 3.26 | .96 | 14.73 |

This table is not to be confused with the Opening Count Method for estimating doors. Use these figures for painting both interior and exterior doors. These costs are in addition to the costs for applying the finish coats to exterior doors as explained on page 97. These figures include coating all six (6) sides of each door along with the frame and the jamb on both sides. These figures include minimal preparation time. ADD for additional preparation time, as needed, including setup, remove & replace (hardware), protection (mask walls and visqueen floors); putty, caulking, sanding and cleanup. "Slow" work is based on an hourly wage of $20.25, "Medium" work on an hourly wage of $25.75, and "Fast" work on an hourly wage of $31.50. Other qualifications that apply to this table are on page 9.

*National Painting Cost Estimator*

|  | Manhours per door | Doors per gallon | Material cost per gallon | Labor cost per door | Labor burden per door | Material cost per door | Overhead per door | Profit per door | Total price per door |
|---|---|---|---|---|---|---|---|---|---|

## Doors, interior, flush, paint grade, spray application, based on per door method

Undercoat, water base (material #3)
  Spray 1 coat

| | | | | | | | | | |
|---|---|---|---|---|---|---|---|---|---|
| Slow | 0.10 | 17 | 32.60 | 2.03 | .59 | 1.92 | .86 | .87 | 6.27 |
| Medium | 0.09 | 16 | 28.50 | 2.32 | .82 | 1.78 | 1.23 | .74 | 6.89 |
| Fast | 0.08 | 15 | 24.50 | 2.52 | 1.03 | 1.63 | 1.61 | .48 | 7.27 |

Undercoat, oil base (material #4)
  Spray 1 coat

| | | | | | | | | | |
|---|---|---|---|---|---|---|---|---|---|
| Slow | 0.10 | 17 | 42.30 | 2.03 | .59 | 2.49 | .97 | .97 | 7.05 |
| Medium | 0.09 | 16 | 37.00 | 2.32 | .82 | 2.31 | 1.36 | .82 | 7.63 |
| Fast | 0.08 | 15 | 31.80 | 2.52 | 1.03 | 2.12 | 1.76 | .52 | 7.95 |

Enamel, water base (material #9)
  Spray 1st finish coat

| | | | | | | | | | |
|---|---|---|---|---|---|---|---|---|---|
| Slow | 0.09 | 18 | 46.80 | 1.82 | .54 | 2.60 | .94 | .94 | 6.84 |
| Medium | 0.08 | 17 | 41.00 | 2.06 | .73 | 2.41 | 1.30 | .78 | 7.28 |
| Fast | 0.07 | 16 | 35.10 | 2.21 | .89 | 2.19 | 1.64 | .49 | 7.42 |

  Spray 2nd or additional finish coats

| | | | | | | | | | |
|---|---|---|---|---|---|---|---|---|---|
| Slow | 0.08 | 19 | 46.80 | 1.62 | .48 | 2.46 | .87 | .87 | 6.30 |
| Medium | 0.07 | 18 | 41.00 | 1.80 | .64 | 2.28 | 1.18 | .71 | 6.61 |
| Fast | 0.06 | 17 | 35.10 | 1.89 | .77 | 2.06 | 1.46 | .43 | 6.61 |

Enamel, oil base (material #10)
  Spray 1st finish coat

| | | | | | | | | | |
|---|---|---|---|---|---|---|---|---|---|
| Slow | 0.09 | 18 | 61.70 | 1.82 | .54 | 3.43 | 1.10 | 1.10 | 7.99 |
| Medium | 0.08 | 17 | 54.00 | 2.06 | .73 | 3.18 | 1.49 | .90 | 8.36 |
| Fast | 0.07 | 16 | 46.30 | 2.21 | .89 | 2.89 | 1.86 | .55 | 8.40 |

  Spray 2nd or additional finish coats

| | | | | | | | | | |
|---|---|---|---|---|---|---|---|---|---|
| Slow | 0.08 | 19 | 61.70 | 1.62 | .48 | 3.25 | 1.02 | 1.02 | 7.39 |
| Medium | 0.07 | 18 | 54.00 | 1.80 | .64 | 3.00 | 1.36 | .82 | 7.62 |
| Fast | 0.06 | 17 | 46.30 | 1.89 | .77 | 2.72 | 1.67 | .49 | 7.54 |

This table is not to be confused with the Opening Count Method for estimating doors. Use these figures for painting both interior and exterior doors. These costs are in addition to the costs for applying the finish coats to exterior doors as explained on page 97. These figures include coating all six (6) sides of each door along with the frame and the jamb on both sides. These figures include minimal preparation time. ADD for additional preparation time, as needed, including setup, remove & replace (hardware), protection (mask walls and visqueen floors); putty, caulking, sanding and cleanup. "Slow" work is based on an hourly wage of $20.25, "Medium" work on an hourly wage of $25.75, and "Fast" work on an hourly wage of $31.50. Other qualifications that apply to this table are on page 9.

*General Painting Costs*

|  | Manhours per door | Doors per gallon | Material cost per gallon | Labor cost per door | Labor burden door | Material cost per door | Overhead per door | Profit per door | Total price per door |
|---|---|---|---|---|---|---|---|---|---|

### Doors, interior, flush, stain grade, spray application, based on per door method
Complete 7 step stain, seal & 2 coat lacquer system (material #11)
  Spray all coats

| | | | | | | | | | |
|---|---|---|---|---|---|---|---|---|---|
| Slow | 0.90 | 6 | 46.10 | 18.23 | 5.37 | 7.68 | 5.95 | 5.96 | 43.19 |
| Medium | 0.80 | 5 | 40.40 | 20.60 | 7.30 | 8.08 | 8.99 | 5.40 | 50.37 |
| Fast | 0.70 | 4 | 34.60 | 22.05 | 9.00 | 8.65 | 12.31 | 3.64 | 55.65 |

This table is not to be confused with the Opening Count Method for estimating doors. Use these figures for painting both interior and exterior doors. These costs are in addition to the costs for applying the finish coats to exterior doors as explained on page 97. These figures include coating all six (6) sides of each door along with the frame and the jamb on both sides. These figures include minimal preparation time. ADD for preparation time, as needed, including setup, remove & replace (hardware), protection (mask walls and visqueen floors); putty, caulking, sanding and cleanup. "Slow" work is based on an hourly wage of $20.25, "Medium" work on an hourly wage of $25.75, and "Fast" work on an hourly wage of $31.50. Other qualifications that apply to this table are on page 9.

|  | Manhours per door | Doors per gallon | Material cost per gallon | Labor cost per door | Labor burden door | Material cost per door | Overhead per door | Profit per door | Total price per door |
|---|---|---|---|---|---|---|---|---|---|

### Doors, interior, French, paint grade, roll & brush, based on per door method
Undercoat, water base (material #3)
  Roll & brush 1 coat

| | | | | | | | | | |
|---|---|---|---|---|---|---|---|---|---|
| Slow | 0.45 | 14 | 32.60 | 9.11 | 2.69 | 2.33 | 2.68 | 2.69 | 19.50 |
| Medium | 0.38 | 13 | 28.50 | 9.79 | 3.46 | 2.19 | 3.86 | 2.32 | 21.62 |
| Fast | 0.30 | 12 | 24.50 | 9.45 | 3.86 | 2.04 | 4.76 | 1.41 | 21.52 |

Undercoat, oil base (material #4)
  Roll & brush 1 coat

| | | | | | | | | | |
|---|---|---|---|---|---|---|---|---|---|
| Slow | 0.45 | 14 | 42.30 | 9.11 | 2.69 | 3.02 | 2.82 | 2.82 | 20.46 |
| Medium | 0.38 | 13 | 37.00 | 9.79 | 3.46 | 2.85 | 4.03 | 2.42 | 22.55 |
| Fast | 0.30 | 12 | 31.80 | 9.45 | 3.86 | 2.65 | 4.95 | 1.46 | 22.37 |

Enamel, water base (material #9)
  Roll & brush 1st finish coat

| | | | | | | | | | |
|---|---|---|---|---|---|---|---|---|---|
| Slow | 0.43 | 15 | 46.80 | 8.71 | 2.56 | 3.12 | 2.74 | 2.74 | 19.87 |
| Medium | 0.35 | 14 | 41.00 | 9.01 | 3.19 | 2.93 | 3.78 | 2.27 | 21.18 |
| Fast | 0.28 | 13 | 35.10 | 8.82 | 3.60 | 2.70 | 4.69 | 1.39 | 21.20 |

  Roll & brush 2nd or additional finish coats

| | | | | | | | | | |
|---|---|---|---|---|---|---|---|---|---|
| Slow | 0.40 | 16 | 46.80 | 8.10 | 2.39 | 2.93 | 2.55 | 2.56 | 18.53 |
| Medium | 0.33 | 15 | 41.00 | 8.50 | 3.01 | 2.73 | 3.56 | 2.14 | 19.94 |
| Fast | 0.25 | 14 | 35.10 | 7.88 | 3.21 | 2.51 | 4.22 | 1.25 | 19.07 |

|  | Manhours per door | Doors per gallon | Material cost per gallon | Labor cost per door | Labor burden door | Material cost per door | Overhead per door | Profit per door | Total price per door |
|---|---|---|---|---|---|---|---|---|---|
| **Enamel, oil base (material #10)** | | | | | | | | | |
| Roll & brush 1st finish coat | | | | | | | | | |
| Slow | 0.43 | 15 | 61.70 | 8.71 | 2.56 | 4.11 | 2.92 | 2.93 | 21.23 |
| Medium | 0.35 | 14 | 54.00 | 9.01 | 3.19 | 3.86 | 4.02 | 2.41 | 22.49 |
| Fast | 0.28 | 13 | 46.30 | 8.82 | 3.60 | 3.56 | 4.95 | 1.47 | 22.40 |
| Roll & brush 2nd or additional finish coats | | | | | | | | | |
| Slow | 0.40 | 16 | 61.70 | 8.10 | 2.39 | 3.86 | 2.73 | 2.73 | 19.81 |
| Medium | 0.33 | 15 | 54.00 | 8.50 | 3.01 | 3.60 | 3.78 | 2.27 | 21.16 |
| Fast | 0.25 | 14 | 46.30 | 7.88 | 3.21 | 3.31 | 4.47 | 1.32 | 20.19 |

This table is not to be confused with the Opening Count Method for estimating doors. Use these figures for painting both interior and exterior doors. These costs are in addition to the costs for applying the finish coats to exterior doors as explained on page 97. These figures include coating all six (6) sides of each door along with the frame and the jamb on both sides. These figures include minimal preparation time. ADD for additional preparation time, as needed, including setup, remove & replace (hardware), protection (mask walls and visqueen floors); putty, caulking, sanding and cleanup. "Slow" work is based on an hourly wage of $20.25, "Medium" work on an hourly wage of $25.75, and "Fast" work on an hourly wage of $31.50. Other qualifications that apply to this table are on page 9.

|  | Manhours per door | Doors per gallon | Material cost per gallon | Labor cost per door | Labor burden door | Material cost per door | Overhead per door | Profit per door | Total price per door |
|---|---|---|---|---|---|---|---|---|---|

### Doors, interior, French, stain grade, spray application, based on per door method

Complete 7 step stain, seal & 2 coat lacquer system (material #11)

|  | | | | | | | | | |
|---|---|---|---|---|---|---|---|---|---|
| Spray all coats | | | | | | | | | |
| Slow | 1.50 | 12 | 46.10 | 30.38 | 8.95 | 3.84 | 8.20 | 8.22 | 59.59 |
| Medium | 1.25 | 11 | 40.40 | 32.19 | 11.40 | 3.67 | 11.82 | 7.09 | 66.17 |
| Fast | 1.00 | 10 | 34.60 | 31.50 | 12.85 | 3.46 | 14.82 | 4.38 | 67.01 |

This table is not to be confused with the Opening Count Method for estimating doors. Use these figures for painting both interior and exterior doors. These costs are in addition to the costs for applying the finish coats to exterior doors as explained on page 97. These figures include coating all six (6) sides of each door along with the frame and the jamb on both sides. These figures include minimal preparation time. ADD for additional preparation time, as needed, including setup, remove & replace (hardware), protection (mask walls and visqueen floors); putty, caulking, sanding and cleanup. "Slow" work is based on an hourly wage of $20.25, "Medium" work on an hourly wage of $25.75, and "Fast" work on an hourly wage of $31.50. Other qualifications that apply to this table are on page 9.

*General Painting Costs*

|  | Manhours per door | Doors per gallon | Material cost per gallon | Labor cost per door | Labor burden door | Material cost per door | Overhead per door | Profit per door | Total price per door |
|---|---|---|---|---|---|---|---|---|---|

## Doors, interior, louvered, paint grade, roll & brush, based on per door method

**Undercoat, water base (material #3)**
*Roll & brush 1 coat*
| | | | | | | | | | |
|---|---|---|---|---|---|---|---|---|---|
| Slow | 0.67 | 8 | 32.60 | 13.57 | 4.00 | 4.08 | 4.11 | 4.12 | 29.88 |
| Medium | 0.54 | 7 | 28.50 | 13.91 | 4.92 | 4.07 | 5.73 | 3.44 | 32.07 |
| Fast | 0.40 | 6 | 24.50 | 12.60 | 5.14 | 4.08 | 6.76 | 2.00 | 30.58 |

**Undercoat, oil base (material #4)**
*Roll & brush 1 coat*
| | | | | | | | | | |
|---|---|---|---|---|---|---|---|---|---|
| Slow | 0.67 | 8 | 42.30 | 13.57 | 4.00 | 5.29 | 4.34 | 4.35 | 31.55 |
| Medium | 0.54 | 7 | 37.00 | 13.91 | 4.92 | 5.29 | 6.03 | 3.62 | 33.77 |
| Fast | 0.40 | 6 | 31.80 | 12.60 | 5.14 | 5.30 | 7.14 | 2.11 | 32.29 |

**Enamel, water base (material #9)**
*Roll & brush 1st finish coat*
| | | | | | | | | | |
|---|---|---|---|---|---|---|---|---|---|
| Slow | 0.50 | 9 | 46.80 | 10.13 | 2.98 | 5.20 | 3.48 | 3.49 | 25.28 |
| Medium | 0.42 | 8 | 41.00 | 10.82 | 3.83 | 5.13 | 4.95 | 2.97 | 27.70 |
| Fast | 0.33 | 7 | 35.10 | 10.40 | 4.24 | 5.01 | 6.09 | 1.80 | 27.54 |

*Roll & brush 2nd or additional finish coats*
| | | | | | | | | | |
|---|---|---|---|---|---|---|---|---|---|
| Slow | 0.40 | 10 | 46.80 | 8.10 | 2.39 | 4.68 | 2.88 | 2.89 | 20.94 |
| Medium | 0.30 | 9 | 41.00 | 7.73 | 2.73 | 4.56 | 3.76 | 2.25 | 21.03 |
| Fast | 0.20 | 8 | 35.10 | 6.30 | 2.57 | 4.39 | 4.11 | 1.22 | 18.59 |

**Enamel, oil base (material #10)**
*Roll & brush 1st finish coat*
| | | | | | | | | | |
|---|---|---|---|---|---|---|---|---|---|
| Slow | 0.50 | 9 | 61.70 | 10.13 | 2.98 | 6.86 | 3.80 | 3.80 | 27.57 |
| Medium | 0.42 | 8 | 54.00 | 10.82 | 3.83 | 6.75 | 5.35 | 3.21 | 29.96 |
| Fast | 0.33 | 7 | 46.30 | 10.40 | 4.24 | 6.61 | 6.59 | 1.95 | 29.79 |

*Roll & brush 2nd or additional finish coats*
| | | | | | | | | | |
|---|---|---|---|---|---|---|---|---|---|
| Slow | 0.40 | 10 | 61.70 | 8.10 | 2.39 | 6.17 | 3.17 | 3.17 | 23.00 |
| Medium | 0.30 | 9 | 54.00 | 7.73 | 2.73 | 6.00 | 4.12 | 2.47 | 23.05 |
| Fast | 0.20 | 8 | 46.30 | 6.30 | 2.57 | 5.79 | 4.54 | 1.34 | 20.54 |

This table is not to be confused with the Opening Count Method for estimating doors. Use these figures for painting both interior and exterior doors. These costs are in addition to the costs for applying the finish coats to exterior doors as explained on page 97. These figures include coating all six (6) sides of each door along with the frame and the jamb on both sides. These figures include minimal preparation time. ADD for additional preparation time, as needed, including setup, remove & replace (hardware), protection (mask walls and visqueen floors); putty, caulking, sanding and cleanup. "Slow" work is based on an hourly wage of $20.25, "Medium" work on an hourly wage of $25.75, and "Fast" work on an hourly wage of $31.50. Other qualifications that apply to this table are on page 9.

*National Painting Cost Estimator*

|  | Manhours per door | Doors per gallon | Material cost per gallon | Labor cost per door | Labor burden door | Material cost per door | Overhead per door | Profit per door | Total price per door |
|---|---|---|---|---|---|---|---|---|---|

## Doors, interior, louvered, paint grade, spray application, based on per door method

Undercoat, water base (material #3)
  Spray 1 coat

| | | | | | | | | | |
|---|---|---|---|---|---|---|---|---|---|
| Slow | 0.17 | 12 | 32.60 | 3.44 | 1.02 | 2.72 | 1.36 | 1.36 | 9.90 |
| Medium | 0.14 | 11 | 28.50 | 3.61 | 1.27 | 2.59 | 1.87 | 1.12 | 10.46 |
| Fast | 0.12 | 10 | 24.50 | 3.78 | 1.54 | 2.45 | 2.41 | .71 | 10.89 |

Undercoat, oil base (material #4)
  Spray 1 coat

| | | | | | | | | | |
|---|---|---|---|---|---|---|---|---|---|
| Slow | 0.17 | 12 | 42.30 | 3.44 | 1.02 | 3.53 | 1.52 | 1.52 | 11.03 |
| Medium | 0.14 | 11 | 37.00 | 3.61 | 1.27 | 3.36 | 2.06 | 1.24 | 11.54 |
| Fast | 0.12 | 10 | 31.80 | 3.78 | 1.54 | 3.18 | 2.64 | .78 | 11.92 |

Enamel, water base (material #9)
  Spray 1st finish coat

| | | | | | | | | | |
|---|---|---|---|---|---|---|---|---|---|
| Slow | 0.13 | 13 | 46.80 | 2.63 | .78 | 3.60 | 1.33 | 1.33 | 9.67 |
| Medium | 0.11 | 12 | 41.00 | 2.83 | 1.01 | 3.42 | 1.81 | 1.09 | 10.16 |
| Fast | 0.09 | 11 | 35.10 | 2.84 | 1.15 | 3.19 | 2.23 | .66 | 10.07 |

  Spray 2nd or additional finish coats

| | | | | | | | | | |
|---|---|---|---|---|---|---|---|---|---|
| Slow | 0.10 | 14 | 46.80 | 2.03 | .59 | 3.34 | 1.13 | 1.14 | 8.23 |
| Medium | 0.09 | 13 | 41.00 | 2.32 | .82 | 3.15 | 1.57 | .94 | 8.80 |
| Fast | 0.08 | 12 | 35.10 | 2.52 | 1.03 | 2.93 | 2.01 | .59 | 9.08 |

Enamel, oil base (material #10)
  Spray 1st finish coat

| | | | | | | | | | |
|---|---|---|---|---|---|---|---|---|---|
| Slow | 0.13 | 13 | 61.70 | 2.63 | .78 | 4.75 | 1.55 | 1.55 | 11.26 |
| Medium | 0.11 | 12 | 54.00 | 2.83 | 1.01 | 4.50 | 2.08 | 1.25 | 11.67 |
| Fast | 0.09 | 11 | 46.30 | 2.84 | 1.15 | 4.21 | 2.55 | .75 | 11.50 |

  Spray 2nd or additional finish coats

| | | | | | | | | | |
|---|---|---|---|---|---|---|---|---|---|
| Slow | 0.10 | 14 | 61.70 | 2.03 | .59 | 4.41 | 1.34 | 1.34 | 9.71 |
| Medium | 0.09 | 13 | 54.00 | 2.32 | .82 | 4.15 | 1.82 | 1.09 | 10.20 |
| Fast | 0.08 | 12 | 46.30 | 2.52 | 1.03 | 3.86 | 2.30 | .68 | 10.39 |

This table is not to be confused with the Opening Count Method for estimating doors. Use these figures for painting both interior and exterior doors. These costs are in addition to the costs for applying the finish coats to exterior doors as explained on page 97. These figures include coating all six (6) sides of each door along with the frame and the jamb on both sides. These figures include minimal preparation time. ADD for additional preparation time, as needed, including setup, remove & replace (hardware), protection (mask walls and visqueen floors); putty, caulking, sanding and cleanup. "Slow" work is based on an hourly wage of $20.25, "Medium" work on an hourly wage of $25.75, and "Fast" work on an hourly wage of $31.50. Other qualifications that apply to this table are on page 9.

*General Painting Costs*

|  | Manhours per door | Doors per gallon | Material cost per gallon | Labor cost per door | Labor burden door | Material cost per door | Overhead per door | Profit per door | Total price per door |
|---|---|---|---|---|---|---|---|---|---|

### Doors, interior, louvered, stain grade, spray application, based on per door method
Complete 7 step stain, seal & 2 coat lacquer system (material #11)
  Spray all coats

| | | | | | | | | | |
|---|---|---|---|---|---|---|---|---|---|
| Slow | 1.70 | 5 | 46.10 | 34.43 | 10.14 | 9.22 | 10.22 | 10.24 | 74.25 |
| Medium | 1.45 | 4 | 40.40 | 37.34 | 13.22 | 10.10 | 15.17 | 9.10 | 84.93 |
| Fast | 1.20 | 3 | 34.60 | 37.80 | 15.42 | 11.53 | 20.07 | 5.94 | 90.76 |

This table is not to be confused with the Opening Count Method for estimating doors. Use these figures for painting both interior and exterior doors. These costs are in addition to the costs for applying the finish coats to exterior doors as explained on page 97. These figures include coating all six (6) sides of each door along with the frame and the jamb on both sides. These figures include minimal preparation time. ADD for additional preparation time, as needed, including setup, remove & replace (hardware), protection (mask walls and visqueen floors); putty, caulking, sanding and cleanup. "Slow" work is based on an hourly wage of $20.25, "Medium" work on an hourly wage of $25.75, and "Fast" work on an hourly wage of $31.50. Other qualifications that apply to this table are on page 9.

# National Painting Cost Estimator

|  | Manhours per door | Doors per gallon | Material cost per gallon | Labor cost per door | Labor burden door | Material cost per door | Overhead per door | Profit per door | Total price per door |
|---|---|---|---|---|---|---|---|---|---|

## Doors, interior, panel, paint grade, roll & brush, based on per door method

Undercoat, water base (material #3)
  Roll & brush 1 coat

|  |  |  |  |  |  |  |  |  |  |
|---|---|---|---|---|---|---|---|---|---|
| Slow | 0.50 | 8 | 32.60 | 10.13 | 2.98 | 4.08 | 3.27 | 3.28 | 23.74 |
| Medium | 0.33 | 7 | 28.50 | 8.50 | 3.01 | 4.07 | 3.90 | 2.34 | 21.82 |
| Fast | 0.25 | 6 | 24.50 | 7.88 | 3.21 | 4.08 | 4.71 | 1.39 | 21.27 |

Undercoat, oil base (material #4)
  Roll & brush 1 coat

|  |  |  |  |  |  |  |  |  |  |
|---|---|---|---|---|---|---|---|---|---|
| Slow | 0.50 | 8 | 42.30 | 10.13 | 2.98 | 5.29 | 3.50 | 3.51 | 25.41 |
| Medium | 0.33 | 7 | 37.00 | 8.50 | 3.01 | 5.29 | 4.20 | 2.52 | 23.52 |
| Fast | 0.25 | 6 | 31.80 | 7.88 | 3.21 | 5.30 | 5.08 | 1.50 | 22.97 |

Enamel, water base (material #9)
  Roll & brush 1st finish coat

|  |  |  |  |  |  |  |  |  |  |
|---|---|---|---|---|---|---|---|---|---|
| Slow | 0.40 | 11 | 46.80 | 8.10 | 2.39 | 4.25 | 2.80 | 2.81 | 20.35 |
| Medium | 0.30 | 10 | 41.00 | 7.73 | 2.73 | 4.10 | 3.64 | 2.19 | 20.39 |
| Fast | 0.20 | 9 | 35.10 | 6.30 | 2.57 | 3.90 | 3.96 | 1.17 | 17.90 |

  Roll & brush 2nd or additional finish coats

|  |  |  |  |  |  |  |  |  |  |
|---|---|---|---|---|---|---|---|---|---|
| Slow | 0.33 | 12 | 46.80 | 6.68 | 1.97 | 3.90 | 2.38 | 2.39 | 17.32 |
| Medium | 0.25 | 11 | 41.00 | 6.44 | 2.28 | 3.73 | 3.11 | 1.87 | 17.43 |
| Fast | 0.17 | 10 | 35.10 | 5.36 | 2.18 | 3.51 | 3.43 | 1.01 | 15.49 |

Enamel, oil base (material #10)
  Roll & brush 1st finish coat

|  |  |  |  |  |  |  |  |  |  |
|---|---|---|---|---|---|---|---|---|---|
| Slow | 0.40 | 11 | 61.70 | 8.10 | 2.39 | 5.61 | 3.06 | 3.07 | 22.23 |
| Medium | 0.30 | 10 | 54.00 | 7.73 | 2.73 | 5.40 | 3.97 | 2.38 | 22.21 |
| Fast | 0.20 | 9 | 46.30 | 6.30 | 2.57 | 5.14 | 4.34 | 1.28 | 19.63 |

  Roll & brush 2nd or additional finish coats

|  |  |  |  |  |  |  |  |  |  |
|---|---|---|---|---|---|---|---|---|---|
| Slow | 0.33 | 12 | 61.70 | 6.68 | 1.97 | 5.14 | 2.62 | 2.63 | 19.04 |
| Medium | 0.25 | 11 | 54.00 | 6.44 | 2.28 | 4.91 | 3.41 | 2.04 | 19.08 |
| Fast | 0.17 | 10 | 46.30 | 5.36 | 2.18 | 4.63 | 3.78 | 1.12 | 17.07 |

This table is not to be confused with the Opening Count Method for estimating doors. Use these figures for painting both interior and exterior doors. These costs are in addition to the costs for applying the finish coats to exterior doors as explained on page 97. These figures include coating all six (6) sides of each door along with the frame and the jamb on both sides. These figures include minimal preparation time. ADD for additional preparation time, as needed, including setup, remove & replace (hardware), protection (mask walls and visqueen floors); putty, caulking, sanding and cleanup. "Slow" work is based on an hourly wage of $20.25, "Medium" work on an hourly wage of $25.75, and "Fast" work on an hourly wage of $31.50. Other qualifications that apply to this table are on page 9.

*General Painting Costs*

|  | Manhours per door | Doors per gallon | Material cost per gallon | Labor cost per door | Labor burden door | Material cost per door | Overhead per door | Profit per door | Total price per door |
|---|---|---|---|---|---|---|---|---|---|

## Doors, interior, panel, paint grade, spray application, based on per door method

Undercoat, water base (material #3)
  Spray 1 coat

|  |  |  |  |  |  |  |  |  |  |
|---|---|---|---|---|---|---|---|---|---|
| Slow | 0.13 | 15 | 32.60 | 2.63 | .78 | 2.17 | 1.06 | 1.06 | 7.70 |
| Medium | 0.11 | 14 | 28.50 | 2.83 | 1.01 | 2.04 | 1.47 | .88 | 8.23 |
| Fast | 0.10 | 13 | 24.50 | 3.15 | 1.29 | 1.88 | 1.96 | .58 | 8.86 |

Undercoat, oil base (material #4)
  Spray 1 coat

|  |  |  |  |  |  |  |  |  |  |
|---|---|---|---|---|---|---|---|---|---|
| Slow | 0.13 | 15 | 42.30 | 2.63 | .78 | 2.82 | 1.18 | 1.19 | 8.60 |
| Medium | 0.11 | 14 | 37.00 | 2.83 | 1.01 | 2.64 | 1.62 | .97 | 9.07 |
| Fast | 0.10 | 13 | 31.80 | 3.15 | 1.29 | 2.45 | 2.14 | .63 | 9.66 |

Enamel, water base (material #9)
  Spray 1st finish coat

|  |  |  |  |  |  |  |  |  |  |
|---|---|---|---|---|---|---|---|---|---|
| Slow | 0.09 | 16 | 46.80 | 1.82 | .54 | 2.93 | 1.01 | 1.01 | 7.31 |
| Medium | 0.08 | 15 | 41.00 | 2.06 | .73 | 2.73 | 1.38 | .83 | 7.73 |
| Fast | 0.08 | 14 | 35.10 | 2.52 | 1.03 | 2.51 | 1.88 | .56 | 8.50 |

  Spray 2nd or additional finish coats

|  |  |  |  |  |  |  |  |  |  |
|---|---|---|---|---|---|---|---|---|---|
| Slow | 0.08 | 17 | 46.80 | 1.62 | .48 | 2.75 | .92 | .92 | 6.69 |
| Medium | 0.08 | 16 | 41.00 | 2.06 | .73 | 2.56 | 1.34 | .80 | 7.49 |
| Fast | 0.07 | 15 | 35.10 | 2.21 | .89 | 2.34 | 1.69 | .50 | 7.63 |

Enamel, oil base (material #10)
  Spray 1st finish coat

|  |  |  |  |  |  |  |  |  |  |
|---|---|---|---|---|---|---|---|---|---|
| Slow | 0.09 | 16 | 61.70 | 1.82 | .54 | 3.86 | 1.18 | 1.18 | 8.58 |
| Medium | 0.08 | 15 | 54.00 | 2.06 | .73 | 3.60 | 1.60 | .96 | 8.95 |
| Fast | 0.08 | 14 | 46.30 | 2.52 | 1.03 | 3.31 | 2.13 | .63 | 9.62 |

  Spray 2nd or additional finish coats

|  |  |  |  |  |  |  |  |  |  |
|---|---|---|---|---|---|---|---|---|---|
| Slow | 0.08 | 17 | 61.70 | 1.62 | .48 | 3.63 | 1.09 | 1.09 | 7.91 |
| Medium | 0.08 | 16 | 54.00 | 2.06 | .73 | 3.38 | 1.54 | .93 | 8.64 |
| Fast | 0.07 | 15 | 46.30 | 2.21 | .89 | 3.09 | 1.92 | .57 | 8.68 |

This table is not to be confused with the Opening Count Method for estimating doors. Use these figures for painting both interior and exterior doors. These costs are in addition to the costs for applying the finish coats to exterior doors as explained on page 97. These figures include coating all six (6) sides of each door along with the frame and the jamb on both sides. These figures include minimal preparation time. ADD for additional preparation time, as needed, including setup, remove & replace (hardware), protection (mask walls and visqueen floors); putty, caulking, sanding and cleanup. "Slow" work is based on an hourly wage of $20.25, "Medium" work on an hourly wage of $25.75, and "Fast" work on an hourly wage of $31.50. Other qualifications that apply to this table are on page 9.

|  | Manhours per door | Doors per gallon | Material cost per gallon | Labor cost per door | Labor burden door | Material cost per door | Overhead per door | Profit per door | Total price per door |
|---|---|---|---|---|---|---|---|---|---|

### Doors, interior, panel, stain grade, spray application, based on per door method

Complete 7 step stain, seal & 2 coat lacquer system (material #11)
  Spray all coats

| | | | | | | | | | |
|---|---|---|---|---|---|---|---|---|---|
| Slow | 1.25 | 6 | 46.10 | 25.31 | 7.47 | 7.68 | 7.69 | 7.70 | 55.85 |
| Medium | 1.08 | 5 | 40.40 | 27.81 | 9.85 | 8.08 | 11.43 | 6.86 | 64.03 |
| Fast | 0.90 | 4 | 34.60 | 28.35 | 11.57 | 8.65 | 15.06 | 4.45 | 68.08 |

This table is not to be confused with the Opening Count Method for estimating doors. Use these figures for painting both interior and exterior doors. These costs are in addition to the costs for applying the finish coats to exterior doors as explained on page 97. These figures include coating all six (6) sides of each door along with the frame and the jamb on both sides. These figures include minimal preparation time. ADD for additional preparation time, as needed, including setup, remove & replace (hardware), protection (mask walls and visqueen floors); putty, caulking, sanding and cleanup. "Slow" work is based on an hourly wage of $20.25, "Medium" work on an hourly wage of $25.75, and "Fast" work on an hourly wage of $31.50. Other qualifications that apply to this table are on page 9.

|  | Labor LF per manhour | Material coverage LF/gallon | Material cost per gallon | Labor cost per 100 LF | Labor burden 100 LF | Material cost per 100 LF | Overhead per 100 LF | Profit per 100 LF | Total price per 100 LF |
|---|---|---|---|---|---|---|---|---|---|

### Fascia, 2" x 4", brush one coat stain "to cover"

Solid body stain, water or oil base (material #18 or #19)
  Brush each coat

| | | | | | | | | | |
|---|---|---|---|---|---|---|---|---|---|
| Slow | 80 | 170 | 49.55 | 25.31 | 7.47 | 29.15 | 11.77 | 11.79 | 85.49 |
| Medium | 105 | 160 | 43.35 | 24.52 | 8.68 | 27.09 | 15.07 | 9.04 | 84.40 |
| Fast | 130 | 150 | 37.15 | 24.23 | 9.88 | 24.77 | 18.26 | 5.40 | 82.54 |

Semi-transparent stain, water or oil base (material #20 or #21)
  Brush each coat

| | | | | | | | | | |
|---|---|---|---|---|---|---|---|---|---|
| Slow | 95 | 195 | 48.10 | 21.32 | 6.29 | 24.67 | 9.93 | 9.95 | 72.16 |
| Medium | 120 | 185 | 42.10 | 21.46 | 7.59 | 22.76 | 12.96 | 7.77 | 72.54 |
| Fast | 145 | 175 | 36.05 | 21.72 | 8.88 | 20.60 | 15.87 | 4.69 | 71.76 |

Use these figures for brushing stain on 2" x 4" fascia board on two sides - the face and the lower edge. The back side is calculated with the overhang (eaves) operation. These figures include one full coat and any touchup required to meet the "to cover" specification. They also include minimum preparation time. ADD for additional preparation time, as needed, including setup, remove & replace (hardware), protection (masking and visqueen); putty, caulking, sanding and cleanup. Measurements are based on continuous linear feet. "Slow" work is based on an hourly wage of $20.25, "Medium" work on an hourly wage of $25.75, and "Fast" work on an hourly wage of $31.50. Other qualifications that apply to this table are on page 9.

*General Painting Costs*

|  | Labor LF per manhour | Material coverage LF/gallon | Material cost per gallon | Labor cost per 100 LF | Labor burden 100 LF | Material cost per 100 LF | Overhead per 100 LF | Profit per 100 LF | Total price per 100 LF |
|---|---|---|---|---|---|---|---|---|---|

### Fascia, 2" x 4", roll one coat stain "to cover"

**Solid body stain, water or oil base (material #18 or #19)**
Roll each coat

| | | | | | | | | | |
|---|---|---|---|---|---|---|---|---|---|
| Slow | 180 | 140 | 49.55 | 11.25 | 3.33 | 35.39 | 9.49 | 9.51 | 68.97 |
| Medium | 205 | 130 | 43.35 | 12.56 | 4.46 | 33.35 | 12.59 | 7.55 | 70.51 |
| Fast | 230 | 120 | 37.15 | 13.70 | 5.59 | 30.96 | 15.58 | 4.61 | 70.44 |

**Semi-transparent stain, water or oil base (material #20 or #21)**
Roll each coat

| | | | | | | | | | |
|---|---|---|---|---|---|---|---|---|---|
| Slow | 200 | 160 | 48.10 | 10.13 | 2.98 | 30.06 | 8.20 | 8.22 | 59.59 |
| Medium | 225 | 150 | 42.10 | 11.44 | 4.04 | 28.07 | 10.89 | 6.53 | 60.97 |
| Fast | 250 | 140 | 36.05 | 12.60 | 5.14 | 25.75 | 13.48 | 3.99 | 60.96 |

Use these figures for rolling stain on 2" x 4" fascia board on two sides - the face and the lower edge. The back side is calculated with the overhang (eaves) operation. These figures include one full coat and any touchup required to meet the "to cover" specification. They also include minimum preparation time. ADD time for extensive preparation. Measurements are based on continuous linear feet. "Slow" work is based on an hourly wage of $20.25, "Medium" work on an hourly wage of $25.75, and "Fast" work on an hourly wage of $31.50. Other qualifications that apply to this table are on page 9.

|  | Labor LF per manhour | Material coverage LF/gallon | Material cost per gallon | Labor cost per 100 LF | Labor burden 100 LF | Material cost per 100 LF | Overhead per 100 LF | Profit per 100 LF | Total price per 100 LF |
|---|---|---|---|---|---|---|---|---|---|

### Fascia, 2" x 4", spray one coat stain "to cover"

**Solid body stain, water or oil base (material #18 or #19)**
Spray each coat

| | | | | | | | | | |
|---|---|---|---|---|---|---|---|---|---|
| Slow | 275 | 110 | 49.55 | 7.36 | 2.18 | 45.05 | 10.37 | 10.39 | 75.35 |
| Medium | 325 | 100 | 43.35 | 7.92 | 2.82 | 43.35 | 13.52 | 8.11 | 75.72 |
| Fast | 375 | 90 | 37.15 | 8.40 | 3.44 | 41.28 | 16.46 | 4.87 | 74.45 |

**Semi-transparent stain, water or oil base (material #20 or #21)**
Spray each coat

| | | | | | | | | | |
|---|---|---|---|---|---|---|---|---|---|
| Slow | 300 | 125 | 48.10 | 6.75 | 1.98 | 38.48 | 8.97 | 8.99 | 65.17 |
| Medium | 350 | 115 | 42.10 | 7.36 | 2.61 | 36.61 | 11.65 | 6.99 | 65.22 |
| Fast | 400 | 105 | 36.05 | 7.88 | 3.21 | 34.33 | 14.08 | 4.17 | 63.67 |

Use these figures for spraying stain on 2" x 4" fascia board on two sides - the face and the lower edge. The back side is calculated with the overhang (eaves) operation. These figures include one full coat and any touchup required to meet the "to cover" specification. They also include minimum preparation time. ADD time for extensive preparation. Measurements are based on continuous linear feet. "Slow" work is based on an hourly wage of $20.25, "Medium" work on an hourly wage of $25.75, and "Fast" work on an hourly wage of $31.50. Other qualifications that apply to this table are on page 9.

|  | Labor LF per manhour | Material coverage LF/gallon | Material cost per gallon | Labor cost per 100 LF | Labor burden 100 LF | Material cost per 100 LF | Overhead per 100 LF | Profit per 100 LF | Total price per 100 LF |
|---|---|---|---|---|---|---|---|---|---|

### Fascia, 2" x 6" to 2" x 10", brush one coat stain "to cover"

Solid body stain, water or oil base (material #18 or #19)
  Brush each coat

| | | | | | | | | | |
|---|---|---|---|---|---|---|---|---|---|
| Slow | 70 | 140 | 49.55 | 28.93 | 8.54 | 35.39 | 13.84 | 13.87 | 100.57 |
| Medium | 90 | 130 | 43.35 | 28.61 | 10.13 | 33.35 | 18.02 | 10.81 | 100.92 |
| Fast | 110 | 120 | 37.15 | 28.64 | 11.67 | 30.96 | 22.10 | 6.54 | 99.91 |

Semi-transparent stain, water or oil base (material #20 or #21)
  Brush each coat

| | | | | | | | | | |
|---|---|---|---|---|---|---|---|---|---|
| Slow | 85 | 165 | 48.10 | 23.82 | 7.01 | 29.15 | 11.40 | 11.42 | 82.80 |
| Medium | 105 | 155 | 42.10 | 24.52 | 8.68 | 27.16 | 15.09 | 9.05 | 84.50 |
| Fast | 125 | 145 | 36.05 | 25.20 | 10.28 | 24.86 | 18.71 | 5.53 | 84.58 |

Use these figures for brushing stain on 2" x 6" to 2" x 10" fascia board on two sides - the face and the lower edge. The back side is calculated with the overhang (eaves) operation. These figures include one full coat and any touchup required to meet the "to cover" specification. They also include minimum preparation time. ADD time for extensive preparation. Measurements are based on continuous linear feet. "Slow" work is based on an hourly wage of $20.25, "Medium" work on an hourly wage of $25.75, and "Fast" work on an hourly wage of $31.50. Other qualifications that apply to this table are on page 9.

|  | Labor LF per manhour | Material coverage LF/gallon | Material cost per gallon | Labor cost per 100 LF | Labor burden 100 LF | Material cost per 100 LF | Overhead per 100 LF | Profit per 100 LF | Total price per 100 LF |
|---|---|---|---|---|---|---|---|---|---|

### Fascia, 2" x 6" to 2" x 10", roll one coat stain "to cover"

Solid body stain, water or oil base (material #18 or #19)
  Roll each coat

| | | | | | | | | | |
|---|---|---|---|---|---|---|---|---|---|
| Slow | 150 | 120 | 49.55 | 13.50 | 3.99 | 41.29 | 11.17 | 11.19 | 81.14 |
| Medium | 175 | 110 | 43.35 | 14.71 | 5.20 | 39.41 | 14.83 | 8.90 | 83.05 |
| Fast | 200 | 100 | 37.15 | 15.75 | 6.43 | 37.15 | 18.39 | 5.44 | 83.16 |

Semi-transparent stain, water or oil base (material #20 or #21)
  Roll each coat

| | | | | | | | | | |
|---|---|---|---|---|---|---|---|---|---|
| Slow | 170 | 140 | 48.10 | 11.91 | 3.51 | 34.36 | 9.46 | 9.48 | 68.72 |
| Medium | 195 | 130 | 42.10 | 13.21 | 4.68 | 32.38 | 12.57 | 7.54 | 70.38 |
| Fast | 220 | 120 | 36.05 | 14.32 | 5.86 | 30.04 | 15.56 | 4.60 | 70.38 |

Use these figures for rolling stain on 2" x 6" to 2" x 10" fascia board on two sides - the face and the lower edge. The back side is calculated with the overhang (eaves) operation. These figures include one full coat and any touchup required to meet the "to cover" specification. They also include minimum preparation time. ADD time for extensive preparation. Measurements are based on continuous linear feet. "Slow" work is based on an hourly wage of $20.25, "Medium" work on an hourly wage of $25.75, and "Fast" work on an hourly wage of $31.50. Other qualifications that apply to this table are on page 9.

*General Painting Costs*

|  | Labor LF per manhour | Material coverage LF/gallon | Material cost per gallon | Labor cost per 100 LF | Labor burden 100 LF | Material cost per 100 LF | Overhead per 100 LF | Profit per 100 LF | Total price per 100 LF |
|---|---|---|---|---|---|---|---|---|---|

### Fascia, 2" x 6" to 2" x 10", spray one coat stain "to cover"

Solid body stain, water or oil base (material #18 or #19)
Spray each coat

| | | | | | | | | | |
|---|---|---|---|---|---|---|---|---|---|
| Slow | 225 | 90 | 49.55 | 9.00 | 2.64 | 55.06 | 12.68 | 12.70 | 92.08 |
| Medium | 300 | 80 | 43.35 | 8.58 | 3.03 | 54.19 | 16.45 | 9.87 | 92.12 |
| Fast | 350 | 70 | 37.15 | 9.00 | 3.68 | 53.07 | 20.38 | 6.03 | 92.16 |

Semi-transparent stain, water or oil base (material #20 or #21)
Spray each coat

| | | | | | | | | | |
|---|---|---|---|---|---|---|---|---|---|
| Slow | 250 | 105 | 48.10 | 8.10 | 2.39 | 45.81 | 10.70 | 10.72 | 77.72 |
| Medium | 313 | 95 | 42.10 | 8.23 | 2.89 | 44.32 | 13.87 | 8.32 | 77.63 |
| Fast | 375 | 85 | 36.05 | 8.40 | 3.44 | 42.41 | 16.81 | 4.97 | 76.03 |

Use these figures for spraying stain on 2" x 6" to 2" x 10" fascia board on two sides - the face and the lower edge. The back side is calculated with the overhang (eaves) operation. These figures include one full coat and any touchup required to meet the "to cover" specification. They also include minimum preparation. ADD time for extensive preparation. Measurements are based on continuous linear feet. "Slow" work is based on an hourly wage of $20.25, "Medium" work on an hourly wage of $25.75, and "Fast" work on an hourly wage of $31.50. Other qualifications that apply to this table are on page 9.

|  | Labor LF per manhour | Material coverage LF/gallon | Material cost per gallon | Labor cost per 100 LF | Labor burden 100 LF | Material cost per 100 LF | Overhead per 100 LF | Profit per 100 LF | Total price per 100 LF |
|---|---|---|---|---|---|---|---|---|---|

### Fascia, 2" x 12", brush one coat stain "to cover"

Solid body stain, water or oil base (material #18 or #19)
Brush each coat

| | | | | | | | | | |
|---|---|---|---|---|---|---|---|---|---|
| Slow | 60 | 100 | 49.55 | 33.75 | 9.96 | 49.55 | 17.72 | 17.76 | 128.74 |
| Medium | 80 | 90 | 43.35 | 32.19 | 11.40 | 48.17 | 22.94 | 13.76 | 128.46 |
| Fast | 100 | 80 | 37.15 | 31.50 | 12.85 | 46.44 | 28.14 | 8.33 | 127.26 |

Semi-transparent stain, water or oil base (material #20 or #21)
Brush each coat

| | | | | | | | | | |
|---|---|---|---|---|---|---|---|---|---|
| Slow | 75 | 125 | 48.10 | 27.00 | 7.95 | 38.48 | 13.96 | 13.99 | 101.38 |
| Medium | 95 | 115 | 42.10 | 27.11 | 9.61 | 36.61 | 18.33 | 11.00 | 102.66 |
| Fast | 105 | 105 | 36.05 | 30.00 | 12.22 | 34.33 | 23.74 | 7.02 | 107.31 |

Use these figures for brushing stain on 2" x 12" fascia board on two sides - the face and the lower edge. The back side is calculated with the overhang (eaves) operation. These figures include one full coat and any touchup required to meet the "to cover" specification. They also include minimum preparation. ADD time for extensive preparation. Measurements are based on continuous linear feet. "Slow" work is based on an hourly wage of $20.25, "Medium" work on an hourly wage of $25.75, and "Fast" work on an hourly wage of $31.50. Other qualifications that apply to this table are on page 9.

National Painting Cost Estimator

|  | Labor LF per manhour | Material coverage LF/gallon | Material cost per gallon | Labor cost per 100 LF | Labor burden 100 LF | Material cost per 100 LF | Overhead per 100 LF | Profit per 100 LF | Total price per 100 LF |
|---|---|---|---|---|---|---|---|---|---|

### Fascia, 2" x 12", roll one coat stain "to cover"

Solid body stain, water or oil base (material #18 or #19)
Roll each coat

| | | | | | | | | | |
|---|---|---|---|---|---|---|---|---|---|
| Slow | 110 | 90 | 49.55 | 18.41 | 5.42 | 55.06 | 14.99 | 15.02 | 108.90 |
| Medium | 130 | 75 | 43.35 | 19.81 | 7.01 | 57.80 | 21.16 | 12.69 | 118.47 |
| Fast | 150 | 60 | 37.15 | 21.00 | 8.58 | 61.92 | 28.36 | 8.39 | 128.25 |

Semi-transparent stain, water or oil base (material #20 or #21)
Roll each coat

| | | | | | | | | | |
|---|---|---|---|---|---|---|---|---|---|
| Slow | 130 | 110 | 48.10 | 15.58 | 4.58 | 43.73 | 12.14 | 12.17 | 88.20 |
| Medium | 150 | 95 | 42.10 | 17.17 | 6.09 | 44.32 | 16.89 | 10.14 | 94.61 |
| Fast | 170 | 80 | 36.05 | 18.53 | 7.55 | 45.06 | 22.06 | 6.52 | 99.72 |

Use these figures for rolling stain on 2" x 12" fascia board on two sides - the face and the lower edge. The back side is calculated with the overhang (eaves) operation. These figures include one full coat and any touchup required to meet the "to cover" specification. They also include minimum preparation. ADD time for extensive preparation. Measurements are based on continuous linear feet. "Slow" work is based on an hourly wage of $20.25, "Medium" work on an hourly wage of $25.75, and "Fast" work on an hourly wage of $31.50. Other qualifications that apply to this table are on page 9.

|  | Labor LF per manhour | Material coverage LF/gallon | Material cost per gallon | Labor cost per 100 LF | Labor burden 100 LF | Material cost per 100 LF | Overhead per 100 LF | Profit per 100 LF | Total price per 100 LF |
|---|---|---|---|---|---|---|---|---|---|

### Fascia, 2" x 12", spray one coat stain "to cover"

Solid body stain, water or oil base (material #18 or #19)
Spray each coat

| | | | | | | | | | |
|---|---|---|---|---|---|---|---|---|---|
| Slow | 200 | 60 | 49.55 | 10.13 | 2.98 | 82.58 | 18.18 | 18.22 | 132.09 |
| Medium | 263 | 50 | 43.35 | 9.79 | 3.46 | 86.70 | 24.99 | 14.99 | 139.93 |
| Fast | 325 | 40 | 37.15 | 9.69 | 3.97 | 92.88 | 33.02 | 9.77 | 149.33 |

Semi-transparent stain, water or oil base (material #20 or #21)
Spray each coat

| | | | | | | | | | |
|---|---|---|---|---|---|---|---|---|---|
| Slow | 225 | 75 | 48.10 | 9.00 | 2.64 | 64.13 | 14.40 | 14.43 | 104.60 |
| Medium | 288 | 65 | 42.10 | 8.94 | 3.16 | 64.77 | 19.22 | 11.53 | 107.62 |
| Fast | 350 | 55 | 36.05 | 9.00 | 3.68 | 65.55 | 24.25 | 7.17 | 109.65 |

Use these figures for spraying stain on 2" x 12" fascia board on two sides - the face and the lower edge. The back side is calculated with the overhang (eaves) operation. These figures include one full coat and any touchup required to meet the "to cover" specification. They also include minimum preparation. ADD time for extensive preparation. Measurements are based on continuous linear feet. "Slow" work is based on an hourly wage of $20.25, "Medium" work on an hourly wage of $25.75, and "Fast" work on an hourly wage of $31.50. Other qualifications that apply to this table are on page 9.

*General Painting Costs*

|  | Labor SF per manhour | Material coverage SF/gallon | Material cost per gallon | Labor cost per 100 SF | Labor burden 100 SF | Material cost per 100 SF | Overhead per 100 SF | Profit per 100 SF | Total price per 100 SF |
|---|---|---|---|---|---|---|---|---|---|

## Fence, chain link or wire mesh

Solid body stain, water or oil base (material #18 or #19)

Brush 1st coat

| | | | | | | | | | |
|---|---|---|---|---|---|---|---|---|---|
| Slow | 90 | 600 | 49.55 | 22.50 | 6.63 | 8.26 | 7.11 | 7.12 | 51.62 |
| Medium | 110 | 550 | 43.35 | 23.41 | 8.29 | 7.88 | 9.90 | 5.94 | 55.42 |
| Fast | 125 | 500 | 37.15 | 25.20 | 10.28 | 7.43 | 13.30 | 3.93 | 60.14 |

Brush 2nd coat

| | | | | | | | | | |
|---|---|---|---|---|---|---|---|---|---|
| Slow | 130 | 650 | 49.55 | 15.58 | 4.58 | 7.62 | 5.28 | 5.29 | 38.35 |
| Medium | 145 | 600 | 43.35 | 17.76 | 6.30 | 7.23 | 7.82 | 4.69 | 43.80 |
| Fast | 160 | 550 | 37.15 | 19.69 | 8.03 | 6.75 | 10.69 | 3.16 | 48.32 |

Roll 1st coat

| | | | | | | | | | |
|---|---|---|---|---|---|---|---|---|---|
| Slow | 260 | 575 | 49.55 | 7.79 | 2.30 | 8.62 | 3.55 | 3.56 | 25.82 |
| Medium | 275 | 525 | 43.35 | 9.36 | 3.33 | 8.26 | 5.23 | 3.14 | 29.32 |
| Fast | 290 | 475 | 37.15 | 10.86 | 4.44 | 7.82 | 7.16 | 2.12 | 32.40 |

Roll 2nd coat

| | | | | | | | | | |
|---|---|---|---|---|---|---|---|---|---|
| Slow | 280 | 625 | 49.55 | 7.23 | 2.13 | 7.93 | 3.29 | 3.29 | 23.87 |
| Medium | 300 | 575 | 43.35 | 8.58 | 3.03 | 7.54 | 4.79 | 2.87 | 26.81 |
| Fast | 320 | 525 | 37.15 | 9.84 | 4.04 | 7.08 | 6.49 | 1.92 | 29.37 |

Use these figures for chain link or wire mesh fencing. The figures are based on painting both sides to meet the "to cover" specification. These figures include minimum preparation time. ADD time for extensive preparation. To calculate the area, base measurements on the square feet (length times width) of one side of the fence then multiply by a difficulty factor of 3 and use the figures in the above table. For example, if the fence is 100' long x 3' high, the area is 300 SF. Multiply 300 SF x 3 to arrive at 900 SF which is the total to be used with this table. "Slow" work is based on an hourly wage of $20.25, "Medium" work on an hourly wage of $25.75, and "Fast" work on an hourly wage of $31.50. Other qualifications that apply to this table are on page 9.

## Fence, wood

For *solid plank fence*, measure the surface area of one side and multiply by 2 to find the area for both sides. Then use the cost table for Siding, exterior. For good neighbor fence (planks on alternate sides of the rail), measure the surface area of one side and multiply by 2 to find the area for both sides. Then multiply by a difficulty factor of 1.5 and use the pricing table for Siding, exterior.

|  | Labor SF per manhour | Material coverage SF/gallon | Material cost per gallon | Labor cost per 100 SF | Labor burden 100 SF | Material cost per 100 SF | Overhead per 100 SF | Profit per 100 SF | Total price per 100 SF |
|---|---|---|---|---|---|---|---|---|---|

### Fence, picket, brush application

Solid body or semi-transparent stain, water base (material #18 or #20)
  Brush 1st coat

| | | | | | | | | | |
|---|---|---|---|---|---|---|---|---|---|
| Slow | 75 | 400 | 46.25 | 27.00 | 7.95 | 11.56 | 8.84 | 8.86 | 64.21 |
| Medium | 113 | 388 | 40.50 | 22.79 | 8.07 | 10.44 | 10.33 | 6.20 | 57.83 |
| Fast | 150 | 375 | 34.70 | 21.00 | 8.58 | 9.25 | 12.03 | 3.56 | 54.42 |

  Brush 2nd or additional coats

| | | | | | | | | | |
|---|---|---|---|---|---|---|---|---|---|
| Slow | 120 | 450 | 46.25 | 16.88 | 4.96 | 10.28 | 6.11 | 6.12 | 44.35 |
| Medium | 145 | 438 | 40.50 | 17.76 | 6.30 | 9.25 | 8.33 | 5.00 | 46.64 |
| Fast | 170 | 425 | 34.70 | 18.53 | 7.55 | 8.16 | 10.62 | 3.14 | 48.00 |

Solid body or semi-transparent stain, oil base (material #19 or #21)
  Brush 1st coat

| | | | | | | | | | |
|---|---|---|---|---|---|---|---|---|---|
| Slow | 75 | 450 | 51.40 | 27.00 | 7.95 | 11.42 | 8.81 | 8.83 | 64.01 |
| Medium | 113 | 438 | 44.95 | 22.79 | 8.07 | 10.26 | 10.28 | 6.17 | 57.57 |
| Fast | 150 | 425 | 38.50 | 21.00 | 8.58 | 9.06 | 11.98 | 3.54 | 54.16 |

  Brush 2nd or additional coats

| | | | | | | | | | |
|---|---|---|---|---|---|---|---|---|---|
| Slow | 120 | 500 | 51.40 | 16.88 | 4.96 | 10.28 | 6.11 | 6.12 | 44.35 |
| Medium | 145 | 488 | 44.95 | 17.76 | 6.30 | 9.21 | 8.32 | 4.99 | 46.58 |
| Fast | 170 | 475 | 38.50 | 18.53 | 7.55 | 8.11 | 10.60 | 3.14 | 47.93 |

For picket fence, measure the overall area of one side and multiply by 4 for painting both sides. Then apply these cost figures. "Slow" work is based on an hourly wage of $20.25, "Medium" work on an hourly wage of $25.75, and "Fast" work on an hourly wage of $31.50. Other qualifications that apply to this table are on page 9.

*General Painting Costs*

|  | Labor SF per manhour | Material coverage SF/gallon | Material cost per gallon | Labor cost per 100 SF | Labor burden 100 SF | Material cost per 100 SF | Overhead per 100 SF | Profit per 100 SF | Total price per 100 SF |
|---|---|---|---|---|---|---|---|---|---|

**Fence, picket, roll application**

Solid body or semi-transparent stain, water base (material #18 or #20)

Roll 1st coat

| | | | | | | | | | |
|---|---|---|---|---|---|---|---|---|---|
| Slow | 120 | 360 | 46.25 | 16.88 | 4.96 | 12.85 | 6.59 | 6.61 | 47.89 |
| Medium | 145 | 343 | 40.50 | 17.76 | 6.30 | 11.81 | 8.97 | 5.38 | 50.22 |
| Fast | 170 | 325 | 34.70 | 18.53 | 7.55 | 10.68 | 11.40 | 3.37 | 51.53 |

Roll 2nd or additional coats

| | | | | | | | | | |
|---|---|---|---|---|---|---|---|---|---|
| Slow | 200 | 400 | 46.25 | 10.13 | 2.98 | 11.56 | 4.69 | 4.70 | 34.06 |
| Medium | 225 | 388 | 40.50 | 11.44 | 4.04 | 10.44 | 6.48 | 3.89 | 36.29 |
| Fast | 250 | 375 | 34.70 | 12.60 | 5.14 | 9.25 | 8.37 | 2.48 | 37.84 |

Solid body or semi-transparent stain, oil base (material #19 or #21)

Roll 1st coat

| | | | | | | | | | |
|---|---|---|---|---|---|---|---|---|---|
| Slow | 120 | 400 | 51.40 | 16.88 | 4.96 | 12.85 | 6.59 | 6.61 | 47.89 |
| Medium | 145 | 388 | 44.95 | 17.76 | 6.30 | 11.59 | 8.91 | 5.35 | 49.91 |
| Fast | 170 | 375 | 38.50 | 18.53 | 7.55 | 10.27 | 11.27 | 3.33 | 50.95 |

Roll 2nd or additional coats

| | | | | | | | | | |
|---|---|---|---|---|---|---|---|---|---|
| Slow | 200 | 450 | 51.40 | 10.13 | 2.98 | 11.42 | 4.66 | 4.67 | 33.86 |
| Medium | 225 | 438 | 44.95 | 11.44 | 4.04 | 10.26 | 6.44 | 3.86 | 36.04 |
| Fast | 250 | 425 | 38.50 | 12.60 | 5.14 | 9.06 | 8.31 | 2.46 | 37.57 |

For picket fence, measure the overall area of one side and multiply by 4 for painting both sides. Then apply these cost figures. "Slow" work is based on an hourly wage of $20.25, "Medium" work on an hourly wage of $25.75, and "Fast" work on an hourly wage of $31.50. Other qualifications that apply to this table are on page 9.

*National Painting Cost Estimator*

|  | Labor SF per manhour | Material coverage SF/gallon | Material cost per gallon | Labor cost per 100 SF | Labor burden 100 SF | Material cost per 100 SF | Overhead per 100 SF | Profit per 100 SF | Total price per 100 SF |
|---|---|---|---|---|---|---|---|---|---|

### Fence, picket, spray application

Solid body or semi-transparent stain, water base (material #18 or #20)
  Spray 1st coat

| | | | | | | | | | |
|---|---|---|---|---|---|---|---|---|---|
| Slow | 400 | 300 | 46.25 | 5.06 | 1.50 | 15.42 | 4.17 | 4.18 | 30.33 |
| Medium | 500 | 275 | 40.50 | 5.15 | 1.82 | 14.73 | 5.43 | 3.26 | 30.39 |
| Fast | 600 | 250 | 34.70 | 5.25 | 2.16 | 13.88 | 6.59 | 1.95 | 29.83 |

  Spray 2nd or additional coats

| | | | | | | | | | |
|---|---|---|---|---|---|---|---|---|---|
| Slow | 500 | 350 | 46.25 | 4.05 | 1.19 | 13.21 | 3.51 | 3.51 | 25.47 |
| Medium | 600 | 325 | 40.50 | 4.29 | 1.53 | 12.46 | 4.57 | 2.74 | 25.59 |
| Fast | 700 | 300 | 34.70 | 4.50 | 1.84 | 11.57 | 5.55 | 1.64 | 25.10 |

Solid body or semi-transparent stain, oil base (material #19 or #21)
  Spray 1st coat

| | | | | | | | | | |
|---|---|---|---|---|---|---|---|---|---|
| Slow | 400 | 350 | 51.40 | 5.06 | 1.50 | 14.69 | 4.04 | 4.04 | 29.33 |
| Medium | 500 | 325 | 44.95 | 5.15 | 1.82 | 13.83 | 5.20 | 3.12 | 29.12 |
| Fast | 600 | 300 | 38.50 | 5.25 | 2.16 | 12.83 | 6.27 | 1.85 | 28.36 |

  Spray 2nd or additional coats

| | | | | | | | | | |
|---|---|---|---|---|---|---|---|---|---|
| Slow | 500 | 425 | 51.40 | 4.05 | 1.19 | 12.09 | 3.29 | 3.30 | 23.92 |
| Medium | 600 | 400 | 44.95 | 4.29 | 1.53 | 11.24 | 4.26 | 2.56 | 23.88 |
| Fast | 700 | 375 | 38.50 | 4.50 | 1.84 | 10.27 | 5.15 | 1.52 | 23.28 |

For picket fence, measure the overall area of one side and multiply by 4 for painting both sides. Then apply these cost figures. "Slow" work is based on an hourly wage of $20.25, "Medium" work on an hourly wage of $25.75, and "Fast" work on an hourly wage of $31.50. Other qualifications that apply to this table are on page 9.

*General Painting Costs*

|  | Labor SF per manhour | Material coverage SF/gallon | Material cost per gallon | Labor cost per 100 SF | Labor burden 100 SF | Material cost per 100 SF | Overhead per 100 SF | Profit per 100 SF | Total price per 100 SF |
|---|---|---|---|---|---|---|---|---|---|
| **Fireplace masonry, interior, smooth surface masonry** | | | | | | | | | |
| Masonry paint, water base (material #31) | | | | | | | | | |
|   Brush each coat | | | | | | | | | |
|     Slow | 70 | 140 | 38.20 | 28.93 | 8.54 | 27.29 | 12.30 | 12.33 | 89.39 |
|     Medium | 75 | 130 | 33.50 | 34.33 | 12.15 | 25.77 | 18.06 | 10.84 | 101.15 |
|     Fast | 80 | 120 | 28.70 | 39.38 | 16.06 | 23.92 | 24.60 | 7.28 | 111.24 |
| Masonry paint, oil base (material #32) | | | | | | | | | |
|   Brush each coat | | | | | | | | | |
|     Slow | 70 | 165 | 38.40 | 28.93 | 8.54 | 23.27 | 11.54 | 11.56 | 83.84 |
|     Medium | 75 | 155 | 33.60 | 34.33 | 12.15 | 21.68 | 17.04 | 10.22 | 95.42 |
|     Fast | 80 | 145 | 28.80 | 39.38 | 16.06 | 19.86 | 23.35 | 6.91 | 105.56 |
| Masonry paint, water base (material #31) | | | | | | | | | |
|   Roll each coat | | | | | | | | | |
|     Slow | 140 | 120 | 38.20 | 14.46 | 4.26 | 31.83 | 9.61 | 9.63 | 69.79 |
|     Medium | 150 | 110 | 33.50 | 17.17 | 6.09 | 30.45 | 13.43 | 8.06 | 75.20 |
|     Fast | 160 | 100 | 28.70 | 19.69 | 8.03 | 28.70 | 17.49 | 5.17 | 79.08 |
| Masonry paint, oil base (material #32) | | | | | | | | | |
|   Roll each coat | | | | | | | | | |
|     Slow | 140 | 140 | 38.40 | 14.46 | 4.26 | 27.43 | 8.77 | 8.79 | 63.71 |
|     Medium | 150 | 130 | 33.60 | 17.17 | 6.09 | 25.85 | 12.28 | 7.37 | 68.76 |
|     Fast | 160 | 120 | 28.80 | 19.69 | 8.03 | 24.00 | 16.03 | 4.74 | 72.49 |
| Masonry paint, water base (material #31) | | | | | | | | | |
|   Spray each coat | | | | | | | | | |
|     Slow | 400 | 105 | 38.20 | 5.06 | 1.50 | 36.38 | 8.16 | 8.17 | 59.27 |
|     Medium | 450 | 100 | 33.50 | 5.72 | 2.02 | 33.50 | 10.31 | 6.19 | 57.74 |
|     Fast | 500 | 90 | 28.70 | 6.30 | 2.57 | 31.89 | 12.64 | 3.74 | 57.14 |
| Masonry paint, oil base (material #32) | | | | | | | | | |
|   Spray each coat | | | | | | | | | |
|     Slow | 400 | 125 | 38.40 | 5.06 | 1.50 | 30.72 | 7.08 | 7.10 | 51.46 |
|     Medium | 450 | 120 | 33.60 | 5.72 | 2.02 | 28.00 | 8.94 | 5.36 | 50.04 |
|     Fast | 500 | 110 | 28.80 | 6.30 | 2.57 | 26.18 | 10.87 | 3.21 | 49.13 |

Measurements are based on square feet of the surface area (length times width) to be painted. For fireplace exteriors, use the Masonry cost table which applies. "Slow" work is based on an hourly wage of $20.25, "Medium" work on an hourly wage of $25.75, and "Fast" work on an hourly wage of $31.50. Other qualifications that apply to this table are on page 9.

*National Painting Cost Estimator*

|  | Labor LF per manhour | Material coverage LF/gallon | Material cost per gallon | Labor cost per 100 LF | Labor burden 100 LF | Material cost per 100 LF | Overhead per 100 LF | Profit per 100 LF | Total price per 100 LF |
|---|---|---|---|---|---|---|---|---|---|

### Fireplace trim, wood, roll & brush each coat
Mantel, rough sawn 4' x 12"
  Solid body or semi-transparent stain, water or oil base (Material #18 or #19 or #20 or #21)
    Roll & brush each coat

| | | | | | | | | |
|---|---|---|---|---|---|---|---|---|
| Slow | 15 | 50 | 48.83 | 135.00 | 39.81 | 97.66 | 51.77 | 51.88 | 376.12 |
| Medium | 18 | 45 | 42.73 | 143.06 | 50.68 | 94.96 | 72.17 | 43.30 | 404.17 |
| Fast | 20 | 40 | 36.60 | 157.50 | 64.25 | 91.50 | 97.11 | 28.73 | 439.09 |

Plant-on trim, interior
  Solid body or semi-transparent stain, water or oil base (Material #18 or #19 or #20 or #21)
    Roll & brush each coat

| | | | | | | | | |
|---|---|---|---|---|---|---|---|---|
| Slow | 75 | 135 | 48.83 | 27.00 | 7.95 | 36.17 | 13.52 | 13.55 | 98.19 |
| Medium | 80 | 130 | 42.73 | 32.19 | 11.40 | 32.87 | 19.12 | 11.47 | 107.05 |
| Fast | 85 | 125 | 36.60 | 37.06 | 15.10 | 29.28 | 25.25 | 7.47 | 114.16 |

Siding, interior, tongue & groove
  Solid body or semi-transparent stain, water or oil base (Material #18 or #19 or #20 or #21)
    Roll & brush each coat

| | | | | | | | | |
|---|---|---|---|---|---|---|---|---|
| Slow | 50 | 100 | 48.83 | 40.50 | 11.94 | 48.83 | 19.24 | 19.28 | 139.79 |
| Medium | 75 | 95 | 42.73 | 34.33 | 12.15 | 44.98 | 22.87 | 13.72 | 128.05 |
| Fast | 100 | 90 | 36.60 | 31.50 | 12.85 | 40.67 | 26.36 | 7.80 | 119.18 |

"Slow" work is based on an hourly wage of $20.25, "Medium" work on an hourly wage of $25.75, and "Fast" work on an hourly wage of $31.50. Other qualifications that apply to this table are on page 9.

|  | Manhours per box | Material coverage gallons/box | Material cost per gallon | Labor cost per box | Labor burden box | Material cost per box | Overhead per box | Profit per box | Total price per box |
|---|---|---|---|---|---|---|---|---|---|

### Firewood boxes, wood, brush each coat
Boxes of rough sawn wood, 3'0" x 3'0" x 3'0" deep
  Solid body or semi-transparent stain, water or oil base (Material #18 or #19 or #20 or #21)
    Roll & brush each coat

| | | | | | | | | |
|---|---|---|---|---|---|---|---|---|
| Slow | 0.40 | 0.20 | 48.83 | 8.10 | 2.39 | 9.77 | 3.85 | 3.86 | 27.97 |
| Medium | 0.35 | 0.23 | 42.73 | 9.01 | 3.19 | 9.83 | 5.51 | 3.30 | 30.84 |
| Fast | 0.30 | 0.25 | 36.60 | 9.45 | 3.86 | 9.15 | 6.96 | 2.06 | 31.48 |

"Slow" work is based on an hourly wage of $20.25, "Medium" work on an hourly wage of $25.75, and "Fast" work on an hourly wage of $31.50. Other qualifications that apply to this table are on page 9.

*General Painting Costs*

|  | Labor SF per manhour | Material coverage SF/gallon | Material cost per gallon | Labor cost per 100 SF | Labor burden 100 SF | Material cost per 100 SF | Overhead per 100 SF | Profit per 100 SF | Total price per 100 SF |
|---|---|---|---|---|---|---|---|---|---|

## Floors, concrete, brush, interior or exterior

Masonry (concrete) paint, water base (material #31)
  Brush 1st coat

| | | | | | | | | | |
|---|---|---|---|---|---|---|---|---|---|
| Slow | 90 | 250 | 38.20 | 22.50 | 6.63 | 15.28 | 8.44 | 8.46 | 61.31 |
| Medium | 145 | 238 | 33.50 | 17.76 | 6.30 | 14.08 | 9.53 | 5.72 | 53.39 |
| Fast | 200 | 225 | 28.70 | 15.75 | 6.43 | 12.76 | 10.83 | 3.20 | 48.97 |

  Brush 2nd coat

| | | | | | | | | | |
|---|---|---|---|---|---|---|---|---|---|
| Slow | 125 | 375 | 38.20 | 16.20 | 4.78 | 10.19 | 5.92 | 5.93 | 43.02 |
| Medium | 200 | 325 | 33.50 | 12.88 | 4.56 | 10.31 | 6.94 | 4.16 | 38.85 |
| Fast | 275 | 275 | 28.70 | 11.45 | 4.69 | 10.44 | 8.23 | 2.44 | 37.25 |

  Brush 3rd or additional coats

| | | | | | | | | | |
|---|---|---|---|---|---|---|---|---|---|
| Slow | 150 | 335 | 38.20 | 13.50 | 3.99 | 11.40 | 5.49 | 5.50 | 39.88 |
| Medium | 225 | 310 | 33.50 | 11.44 | 4.04 | 10.81 | 6.58 | 3.95 | 36.82 |
| Fast | 300 | 285 | 28.70 | 10.50 | 4.27 | 10.07 | 7.70 | 2.28 | 34.82 |

Masonry (concrete) paint, oil base (material #32)
  Brush 1st coat

| | | | | | | | | | |
|---|---|---|---|---|---|---|---|---|---|
| Slow | 90 | 300 | 38.40 | 22.50 | 6.63 | 12.80 | 7.97 | 7.99 | 57.89 |
| Medium | 145 | 288 | 33.60 | 17.76 | 6.30 | 11.67 | 8.93 | 5.36 | 50.02 |
| Fast | 200 | 275 | 28.80 | 15.75 | 6.43 | 10.47 | 10.12 | 2.99 | 45.76 |

  Brush 2nd coat

| | | | | | | | | | |
|---|---|---|---|---|---|---|---|---|---|
| Slow | 125 | 400 | 38.40 | 16.20 | 4.78 | 9.60 | 5.81 | 5.82 | 42.21 |
| Medium | 200 | 388 | 33.60 | 12.88 | 4.56 | 8.66 | 6.53 | 3.92 | 36.55 |
| Fast | 275 | 375 | 28.80 | 11.45 | 4.69 | 7.68 | 7.38 | 2.18 | 33.38 |

  Brush 3rd or additional coats

| | | | | | | | | | |
|---|---|---|---|---|---|---|---|---|---|
| Slow | 150 | 550 | 38.40 | 13.50 | 3.99 | 6.98 | 4.65 | 4.66 | 33.78 |
| Medium | 225 | 525 | 33.60 | 11.44 | 4.04 | 6.40 | 5.47 | 3.28 | 30.63 |
| Fast | 300 | 500 | 28.80 | 10.50 | 4.27 | 5.76 | 6.37 | 1.88 | 28.78 |

Epoxy, 1 part, water base (material #28)
  Brush each coat

| | | | | | | | | | |
|---|---|---|---|---|---|---|---|---|---|
| Slow | 125 | 400 | 82.50 | 16.20 | 4.78 | 20.63 | 7.91 | 7.92 | 57.44 |
| Medium | 163 | 388 | 72.20 | 15.80 | 5.58 | 18.61 | 10.00 | 6.00 | 55.99 |
| Fast | 200 | 375 | 61.90 | 15.75 | 6.43 | 16.51 | 11.99 | 3.55 | 54.23 |

Epoxy, 2 part system (material #29)
  Brush each coat

| | | | | | | | | | |
|---|---|---|---|---|---|---|---|---|---|
| Slow | 100 | 400 | 94.90 | 20.25 | 5.97 | 23.73 | 9.49 | 9.51 | 68.95 |
| Medium | 138 | 388 | 83.10 | 18.66 | 6.62 | 21.42 | 11.67 | 7.00 | 65.37 |
| Fast | 175 | 375 | 71.20 | 18.00 | 7.32 | 18.99 | 13.74 | 4.06 | 62.11 |

Also use these formulas for concrete steps, stair treads, porches and patios. "Slow" work is based on an hourly wage of $20.25, "Medium" work on an hourly wage of $25.75, and "Fast" work on an hourly wage of $31.50. Other qualifications that apply to this table are on page 9.

*National Painting Cost Estimator*

|  | Labor SF per manhour | Material coverage SF/gallon | Material cost per gallon | Labor cost per 100 SF | Labor burden 100 SF | Material cost per 100 SF | Overhead per 100 SF | Profit per 100 SF | Total price per 100 SF |
|---|---|---|---|---|---|---|---|---|---|
| **Floors, concrete, roll, interior or exterior** | | | | | | | | | |
| Masonry (concrete) paint, water base (material #31) | | | | | | | | | |
| Roll 1st coat | | | | | | | | | |
| Slow | 135 | 275 | 38.20 | 15.00 | 4.43 | 13.89 | 6.33 | 6.34 | 45.99 |
| Medium | 218 | 263 | 33.50 | 11.81 | 4.20 | 12.74 | 7.18 | 4.31 | 40.24 |
| Fast | 300 | 250 | 28.70 | 10.50 | 4.27 | 11.48 | 8.14 | 2.41 | 36.80 |
| Roll 2nd coat | | | | | | | | | |
| Slow | 195 | 350 | 38.20 | 10.38 | 3.07 | 10.91 | 4.63 | 4.64 | 33.63 |
| Medium | 268 | 325 | 33.50 | 9.61 | 3.40 | 10.31 | 5.83 | 3.50 | 32.65 |
| Fast | 340 | 300 | 28.70 | 9.26 | 3.78 | 9.57 | 7.01 | 2.07 | 31.69 |
| Roll 3rd or additional coats | | | | | | | | | |
| Slow | 210 | 375 | 38.20 | 9.64 | 2.84 | 10.19 | 4.31 | 4.32 | 31.30 |
| Medium | 300 | 350 | 33.50 | 8.58 | 3.03 | 9.57 | 5.30 | 3.18 | 29.66 |
| Fast | 390 | 325 | 28.70 | 8.08 | 3.27 | 8.83 | 6.27 | 1.85 | 28.30 |
| Masonry (concrete) paint, oil base (material #32) | | | | | | | | | |
| Roll 1st coat | | | | | | | | | |
| Slow | 135 | 370 | 38.40 | 15.00 | 4.43 | 10.38 | 5.66 | 5.68 | 41.15 |
| Medium | 218 | 345 | 33.60 | 11.81 | 4.20 | 9.74 | 6.43 | 3.86 | 36.04 |
| Fast | 300 | 320 | 28.80 | 10.50 | 4.27 | 9.00 | 7.37 | 2.18 | 33.32 |
| Roll 2nd coat | | | | | | | | | |
| Slow | 195 | 500 | 38.40 | 10.38 | 3.07 | 7.68 | 4.01 | 4.02 | 29.16 |
| Medium | 268 | 475 | 33.60 | 9.61 | 3.40 | 7.07 | 5.02 | 3.01 | 28.11 |
| Fast | 340 | 450 | 28.80 | 9.26 | 3.78 | 6.40 | 6.03 | 1.78 | 27.25 |
| Roll 3rd or additional coats | | | | | | | | | |
| Slow | 210 | 550 | 38.40 | 9.64 | 2.84 | 6.98 | 3.70 | 3.71 | 26.87 |
| Medium | 300 | 525 | 33.60 | 8.58 | 3.03 | 6.40 | 4.51 | 2.70 | 25.22 |
| Fast | 390 | 500 | 28.80 | 8.08 | 3.27 | 5.76 | 5.31 | 1.57 | 23.99 |
| Epoxy, 1 part, water base (material #28) | | | | | | | | | |
| Roll each coat | | | | | | | | | |
| Slow | 150 | 500 | 82.50 | 13.50 | 3.99 | 16.50 | 6.46 | 6.47 | 46.92 |
| Medium | 225 | 488 | 72.20 | 11.44 | 4.04 | 14.80 | 7.57 | 4.54 | 42.39 |
| Fast | 300 | 475 | 61.90 | 10.50 | 4.27 | 13.03 | 8.62 | 2.55 | 38.97 |
| Epoxy, 2 part system (material #29) | | | | | | | | | |
| Roll each coat | | | | | | | | | |
| Slow | 135 | 500 | 94.90 | 15.00 | 4.43 | 18.98 | 7.30 | 7.31 | 53.02 |
| Medium | 208 | 488 | 83.10 | 12.38 | 4.39 | 17.03 | 8.45 | 5.07 | 47.32 |
| Fast | 250 | 475 | 71.20 | 12.60 | 5.14 | 14.99 | 10.15 | 3.00 | 45.88 |

Also use these formulas for concrete steps, stair treads, porches and patios. "Slow" work is based on an hourly wage of $20.25, "Medium" work on an hourly wage of $25.75, and "Fast" work on an hourly wage of $31.50. Other qualifications that apply to this table are on page 9.

*General Painting Costs*

|  | Labor SF per manhour | Material coverage SF/gallon | Material cost per gallon | Labor cost per 100 SF | Labor burden 100 SF | Material cost per 100 SF | Overhead per 100 SF | Profit per 100 SF | Total price per 100 SF |
|---|---|---|---|---|---|---|---|---|---|

## Floors, concrete, spray, interior or exterior

**Masonry (concrete) paint, water base (material #31)**

Spray 1st coat
| | | | | | | | | | |
|---|---|---|---|---|---|---|---|---|---|
| Slow | 800 | 175 | 38.20 | 2.53 | .75 | 21.83 | 4.77 | 4.78 | 34.66 |
| Medium | 900 | 163 | 33.50 | 2.86 | 1.01 | 20.55 | 6.11 | 3.66 | 34.19 |
| Fast | 1000 | 150 | 28.70 | 3.15 | 1.29 | 19.13 | 7.31 | 2.16 | 33.04 |

Spray 2nd coat
| | | | | | | | | | |
|---|---|---|---|---|---|---|---|---|---|
| Slow | 900 | 275 | 38.20 | 2.25 | .66 | 13.89 | 3.19 | 3.20 | 23.19 |
| Medium | 1000 | 263 | 33.50 | 2.58 | .91 | 12.74 | 4.06 | 2.43 | 22.72 |
| Fast | 1100 | 250 | 28.70 | 2.86 | 1.18 | 11.48 | 4.81 | 1.42 | 21.75 |

Spray 3rd or additional coats
| | | | | | | | | | |
|---|---|---|---|---|---|---|---|---|---|
| Slow | 1000 | 325 | 38.20 | 2.03 | .59 | 11.75 | 2.73 | 2.74 | 19.84 |
| Medium | 1100 | 313 | 33.50 | 2.34 | .83 | 10.70 | 3.47 | 2.08 | 19.42 |
| Fast | 1200 | 300 | 28.70 | 2.63 | 1.05 | 9.57 | 4.11 | 1.22 | 18.58 |

**Masonry (concrete) paint, oil base (material #32)**

Spray 1st coat
| | | | | | | | | | |
|---|---|---|---|---|---|---|---|---|---|
| Slow | 800 | 200 | 38.40 | 2.53 | .75 | 19.20 | 4.27 | 4.28 | 31.03 |
| Medium | 900 | 188 | 33.60 | 2.86 | 1.01 | 17.87 | 5.44 | 3.26 | 30.44 |
| Fast | 1000 | 175 | 28.80 | 3.15 | 1.29 | 16.46 | 6.48 | 1.92 | 29.30 |

Spray 2nd coat
| | | | | | | | | | |
|---|---|---|---|---|---|---|---|---|---|
| Slow | 900 | 300 | 38.40 | 2.25 | .66 | 12.80 | 2.98 | 2.99 | 21.68 |
| Medium | 1000 | 288 | 33.60 | 2.58 | .91 | 11.67 | 3.79 | 2.27 | 21.22 |
| Fast | 1100 | 275 | 28.80 | 2.86 | 1.18 | 10.47 | 4.50 | 1.33 | 20.34 |

Spray 3rd or additional coats
| | | | | | | | | | |
|---|---|---|---|---|---|---|---|---|---|
| Slow | 1000 | 350 | 38.40 | 2.03 | .59 | 10.97 | 2.58 | 2.59 | 18.76 |
| Medium | 1100 | 338 | 33.60 | 2.34 | .83 | 9.94 | 3.28 | 1.97 | 18.36 |
| Fast | 1200 | 325 | 28.80 | 2.63 | 1.05 | 8.86 | 3.89 | 1.15 | 17.58 |

Also use these formulas for concrete steps, stair treads, porches and patios. "Slow" work is based on an hourly wage of $20.25, "Medium" work on an hourly wage of $25.75, and "Fast" work on an hourly wage of $31.50. Other qualifications that apply to this table are on page 9.

## Floors, concrete, penetrating stain, interior or exterior

| | Labor SF per manhour | Material coverage SF/gallon | Material cost per gallon | Labor cost per 100 SF | Labor burden 100 SF | Material cost per 100 SF | Overhead per 100 SF | Profit per 100 SF | Total price per 100 SF |
|---|---|---|---|---|---|---|---|---|---|
| **Penetrating oil stain (material #13)** | | | | | | | | | |
| Roll 1st coat | | | | | | | | | |
| Slow | 225 | 450 | 54.50 | 9.00 | 2.64 | 12.11 | 4.52 | 4.53 | 32.80 |
| Medium | 250 | 425 | 47.70 | 10.30 | 3.65 | 11.22 | 6.29 | 3.78 | 35.24 |
| Fast | 275 | 400 | 40.90 | 11.45 | 4.69 | 10.23 | 8.17 | 2.42 | 36.96 |
| Roll 2nd coat | | | | | | | | | |
| Slow | 325 | 500 | 54.50 | 6.23 | 1.85 | 10.90 | 3.60 | 3.61 | 26.19 |
| Medium | 345 | 475 | 47.70 | 7.46 | 2.65 | 10.04 | 5.04 | 3.02 | 28.21 |
| Fast | 365 | 450 | 40.90 | 8.63 | 3.52 | 9.09 | 6.58 | 1.95 | 29.77 |
| Roll 3rd and additional coats | | | | | | | | | |
| Slow | 365 | 525 | 54.50 | 5.55 | 1.63 | 10.38 | 3.34 | 3.35 | 24.25 |
| Medium | 383 | 500 | 47.70 | 6.72 | 2.38 | 9.54 | 4.66 | 2.80 | 26.10 |
| Fast | 400 | 475 | 40.90 | 7.88 | 3.21 | 8.61 | 6.11 | 1.81 | 27.62 |

Also use these formulas for concrete steps, stair treads, porches and patios. "Slow" work is based on an hourly wage of $20.25, "Medium" work on an hourly wage of $25.75, and "Fast" work on an hourly wage of $31.50. Other qualifications that apply to this table are on page 9.

*General Painting Costs*

|  | Labor SF per manhour | Material coverage SF/gallon | Material cost per gallon | Labor cost per 100 SF | Labor burden 100 SF | Material cost per 100 SF | Overhead per 100 SF | Profit per 100 SF | Total price per 100 SF |
|---|---|---|---|---|---|---|---|---|---|
| **Floors, wood, interior or exterior, paint grade, brush application** | | | | | | | | | |
| Undercoat, water base (material #3) | | | | | | | | | |
|   Brush prime coat | | | | | | | | | |
|     Slow | 275 | 450 | 32.60 | 7.36 | 2.18 | 7.24 | 3.19 | 3.19 | 23.16 |
|     Medium | 300 | 425 | 28.50 | 8.58 | 3.03 | 6.71 | 4.58 | 2.75 | 25.65 |
|     Fast | 325 | 400 | 24.50 | 9.69 | 3.97 | 6.13 | 6.13 | 1.81 | 27.73 |
| Undercoat, oil base (material #4) | | | | | | | | | |
|   Brush prime coat | | | | | | | | | |
|     Slow | 275 | 500 | 42.30 | 7.36 | 2.18 | 8.46 | 3.42 | 3.43 | 24.85 |
|     Medium | 300 | 475 | 37.00 | 8.58 | 3.03 | 7.79 | 4.85 | 2.91 | 27.16 |
|     Fast | 325 | 450 | 31.80 | 9.69 | 3.97 | 7.07 | 6.42 | 1.90 | 29.05 |
| Porch & deck enamel, water base (material #26) | | | | | | | | | |
|   Brush 1st and additional finish coats | | | | | | | | | |
|     Slow | 300 | 475 | 54.40 | 6.75 | 1.98 | 11.45 | 3.84 | 3.84 | 27.86 |
|     Medium | 325 | 450 | 47.60 | 7.92 | 2.82 | 10.58 | 5.33 | 3.20 | 29.85 |
|     Fast | 350 | 425 | 40.80 | 9.00 | 3.68 | 9.60 | 6.90 | 2.04 | 31.22 |
| Porch & deck enamel, oil base (material #27) | | | | | | | | | |
|   Brush 1st and additional finish coats | | | | | | | | | |
|     Slow | 300 | 550 | 67.20 | 6.75 | 1.98 | 12.22 | 3.98 | 3.99 | 28.92 |
|     Medium | 325 | 525 | 58.80 | 7.92 | 2.82 | 11.20 | 5.48 | 3.29 | 30.71 |
|     Fast | 350 | 500 | 50.40 | 9.00 | 3.68 | 10.08 | 7.05 | 2.09 | 31.90 |
| Epoxy, 1 part, water base (material #28) | | | | | | | | | |
|   Brush each coat | | | | | | | | | |
|     Slow | 125 | 450 | 82.50 | 16.20 | 4.78 | 18.33 | 7.47 | 7.48 | 54.26 |
|     Medium | 163 | 425 | 72.20 | 15.80 | 5.58 | 16.99 | 9.60 | 5.76 | 53.73 |
|     Fast | 200 | 400 | 61.90 | 15.75 | 6.43 | 15.48 | 11.67 | 3.45 | 52.78 |
| Epoxy, 2 part system (material #29) | | | | | | | | | |
|   Brush each coat | | | | | | | | | |
|     Slow | 100 | 425 | 94.90 | 20.25 | 5.97 | 22.33 | 9.22 | 9.24 | 67.01 |
|     Medium | 138 | 400 | 83.10 | 18.66 | 6.62 | 20.78 | 11.51 | 6.91 | 64.48 |
|     Fast | 175 | 375 | 71.20 | 18.00 | 7.32 | 18.99 | 13.74 | 4.06 | 62.11 |

"Slow" work is based on an hourly wage of $20.25, "Medium" work on an hourly wage of $25.75, and "Fast" work on an hourly wage of $31.50. Other qualifications that apply to this table are on page 9.

*National Painting Cost Estimator*

|  | Labor SF per manhour | Material coverage SF/gallon | Material cost per gallon | Labor cost per 100 SF | Labor burden 100 SF | Material cost per 100 SF | Overhead per 100 SF | Profit per 100 SF | Total price per 100 SF |
|---|---|---|---|---|---|---|---|---|---|
| **Floors, wood, interior or exterior, paint grade, roll application** | | | | | | | | | |
| Undercoat, water base (material #3) | | | | | | | | | |
|   Roll prime coat | | | | | | | | | |
|     Slow | 400 | 425 | 32.60 | 5.06 | 1.50 | 7.67 | 2.70 | 2.71 | 19.64 |
|     Medium | 438 | 400 | 28.50 | 5.88 | 2.07 | 7.13 | 3.77 | 2.26 | 21.11 |
|     Fast | 475 | 375 | 24.50 | 6.63 | 2.73 | 6.53 | 4.92 | 1.46 | 22.27 |
| Undercoat, oil base (material #4) | | | | | | | | | |
|   Roll prime coat | | | | | | | | | |
|     Slow | 400 | 475 | 42.30 | 5.06 | 1.50 | 8.91 | 2.94 | 2.94 | 21.35 |
|     Medium | 438 | 450 | 37.00 | 5.88 | 2.07 | 8.22 | 4.05 | 2.43 | 22.65 |
|     Fast | 475 | 425 | 31.80 | 6.63 | 2.73 | 7.48 | 5.21 | 1.54 | 23.59 |
| Porch & deck enamel, water base (material #26) | | | | | | | | | |
|   Roll 1st or additional finish coats | | | | | | | | | |
|     Slow | 425 | 475 | 54.40 | 4.76 | 1.40 | 11.45 | 3.35 | 3.35 | 24.31 |
|     Medium | 463 | 450 | 47.60 | 5.56 | 1.97 | 10.58 | 4.53 | 2.72 | 25.36 |
|     Fast | 500 | 425 | 40.80 | 6.30 | 2.57 | 9.60 | 5.73 | 1.69 | 25.89 |
| Porch & deck enamel, oil base (material #27) | | | | | | | | | |
|   Roll 1st or additional finish coats | | | | | | | | | |
|     Slow | 425 | 525 | 67.20 | 4.76 | 1.40 | 12.80 | 3.60 | 3.61 | 26.17 |
|     Medium | 463 | 500 | 58.80 | 5.56 | 1.97 | 11.76 | 4.82 | 2.89 | 27.00 |
|     Fast | 500 | 475 | 50.40 | 6.30 | 2.57 | 10.61 | 6.04 | 1.79 | 27.31 |
| Epoxy, 1 part, water base (material #28) | | | | | | | | | |
|   Brush each coat | | | | | | | | | |
|     Slow | 200 | 425 | 82.50 | 10.13 | 2.98 | 19.41 | 6.18 | 6.19 | 44.89 |
|     Medium | 250 | 400 | 72.20 | 10.30 | 3.65 | 18.05 | 8.00 | 4.80 | 44.80 |
|     Fast | 300 | 375 | 61.90 | 10.50 | 4.27 | 16.51 | 9.70 | 2.87 | 43.85 |
| Epoxy, 2 part system (material #29) | | | | | | | | | |
|   Brush each coat | | | | | | | | | |
|     Slow | 175 | 400 | 94.90 | 11.57 | 3.40 | 23.73 | 7.35 | 7.37 | 53.42 |
|     Medium | 225 | 375 | 83.10 | 11.44 | 4.04 | 22.16 | 9.41 | 5.65 | 52.70 |
|     Fast | 275 | 350 | 71.20 | 11.45 | 4.69 | 20.34 | 11.30 | 3.34 | 51.12 |

"Slow" work is based on an hourly wage of $20.25, "Medium" work on an hourly wage of $25.75, and "Fast" work on an hourly wage of $31.50. Other qualifications that apply to this table are on page 9.

*General Painting Costs*

|  | Labor SF per manhour | Material coverage SF/gallon | Material cost per gallon | Labor cost per 100 SF | Labor burden 100 SF | Material cost per 100 SF | Overhead per 100 SF | Profit per 100 SF | Total price per 100 SF |
|---|---|---|---|---|---|---|---|---|---|
| **Floors, wood, interior or exterior, stain grade** | | | | | | | | | |
| Wiping stain, varnish, oil base (material #30a) | | | | | | | | | |
| Stain, brush 1st coat, wipe & fill | | | | | | | | | |
| Slow | 225 | 500 | 53.40 | 9.00 | 2.64 | 10.68 | 4.24 | 4.25 | 30.81 |
| Medium | 250 | 475 | 46.70 | 10.30 | 3.65 | 9.83 | 5.95 | 3.57 | 33.30 |
| Fast | 275 | 450 | 40.00 | 11.45 | 4.69 | 8.89 | 7.75 | 2.29 | 35.07 |
| Stain, brush 2nd coat, wipe & fill | | | | | | | | | |
| Slow | 400 | 525 | 53.40 | 5.06 | 1.50 | 10.17 | 3.18 | 3.18 | 23.09 |
| Medium | 425 | 500 | 46.70 | 6.06 | 2.13 | 9.34 | 4.39 | 2.63 | 24.55 |
| Fast | 450 | 475 | 40.00 | 7.00 | 2.85 | 8.42 | 5.67 | 1.68 | 25.62 |
| Stain, brush 3rd or additional coats, wipe & fill | | | | | | | | | |
| Slow | 425 | 550 | 53.40 | 4.76 | 1.40 | 9.71 | 3.02 | 3.02 | 21.91 |
| Medium | 450 | 525 | 46.70 | 5.72 | 2.02 | 8.90 | 4.16 | 2.50 | 23.30 |
| Fast | 475 | 500 | 40.00 | 6.63 | 2.73 | 8.00 | 5.38 | 1.59 | 24.33 |
| Sanding sealer, varnish (material #30b) | | | | | | | | | |
| Maple or pine, brush 1 coat | | | | | | | | | |
| Slow | 375 | 475 | 52.00 | 5.40 | 1.60 | 10.95 | 3.41 | 3.42 | 24.78 |
| Medium | 400 | 450 | 45.50 | 6.44 | 2.28 | 10.11 | 4.71 | 2.82 | 26.36 |
| Fast | 425 | 425 | 39.00 | 7.41 | 3.01 | 9.18 | 6.08 | 1.80 | 27.48 |
| Maple or pine, brush 2nd or additional coats | | | | | | | | | |
| Slow | 425 | 550 | 52.00 | 4.76 | 1.40 | 9.45 | 2.97 | 2.97 | 21.55 |
| Medium | 450 | 525 | 45.50 | 5.72 | 2.02 | 8.67 | 4.10 | 2.46 | 22.97 |
| Fast | 475 | 500 | 39.00 | 6.63 | 2.73 | 7.80 | 5.31 | 1.57 | 24.04 |
| Oak, brush 1 coat | | | | | | | | | |
| Slow | 400 | 525 | 52.00 | 5.06 | 1.50 | 9.90 | 3.13 | 3.13 | 22.72 |
| Medium | 425 | 500 | 45.50 | 6.06 | 2.13 | 9.10 | 4.33 | 2.60 | 24.22 |
| Fast | 450 | 475 | 39.00 | 7.00 | 2.85 | 8.21 | 5.60 | 1.66 | 25.32 |
| Oak, brush 2nd or additional coats | | | | | | | | | |
| Slow | 500 | 625 | 52.00 | 4.05 | 1.19 | 8.32 | 2.58 | 2.58 | 18.72 |
| Medium | 525 | 600 | 45.50 | 4.90 | 1.73 | 7.58 | 3.55 | 2.13 | 19.89 |
| Fast | 550 | 575 | 39.00 | 5.73 | 2.34 | 6.78 | 4.60 | 1.36 | 20.81 |
| Shellac, clear (material #12) | | | | | | | | | |
| Brush 1st coat | | | | | | | | | |
| Slow | 275 | 475 | 73.10 | 7.36 | 2.18 | 15.39 | 4.73 | 4.74 | 34.40 |
| Medium | 300 | 450 | 63.90 | 8.58 | 3.03 | 14.20 | 6.46 | 3.87 | 36.14 |
| Fast | 325 | 425 | 54.80 | 9.69 | 3.97 | 12.89 | 8.22 | 2.43 | 37.20 |
| Brush 2nd or additional coats | | | | | | | | | |
| Slow | 400 | 500 | 73.10 | 5.06 | 1.50 | 14.62 | 4.02 | 4.03 | 29.23 |
| Medium | 425 | 475 | 63.90 | 6.06 | 2.13 | 13.45 | 5.42 | 3.25 | 30.31 |
| Fast | 450 | 450 | 54.80 | 7.00 | 2.85 | 12.18 | 6.83 | 2.02 | 30.88 |

*National Painting Cost Estimator*

|  | Labor SF per manhour | Material coverage SF/gallon | Material cost per gallon | Labor cost per 100 SF | Labor burden 100 SF | Material cost per 100 SF | Overhead per 100 SF | Profit per 100 SF | Total price per 100 SF |
|---|---|---|---|---|---|---|---|---|---|
| **Varnish, gloss or flat (material #30c)** | | | | | | | | | |
| Brush 1st coat | | | | | | | | | |
| Slow | 275 | 475 | 81.70 | 7.36 | 2.18 | 17.20 | 5.08 | 5.09 | 36.91 |
| Medium | 300 | 450 | 71.50 | 8.58 | 3.03 | 15.89 | 6.88 | 4.13 | 38.51 |
| Fast | 325 | 425 | 61.30 | 9.69 | 3.97 | 14.42 | 8.70 | 2.57 | 39.35 |
| Brush 2nd or additional coats | | | | | | | | | |
| Slow | 350 | 600 | 81.70 | 5.79 | 1.71 | 13.62 | 4.01 | 4.02 | 29.15 |
| Medium | 375 | 575 | 71.50 | 6.87 | 2.44 | 12.43 | 5.43 | 3.26 | 30.43 |
| Fast | 400 | 550 | 61.30 | 7.88 | 3.21 | 11.15 | 6.90 | 2.04 | 31.18 |
| **Penetrating stain wax & wipe (material #14)** | | | | | | | | | |
| Stain, brush 1st coat & wipe | | | | | | | | | |
| Slow | 200 | 550 | 46.70 | 10.13 | 2.98 | 8.49 | 4.11 | 4.12 | 29.83 |
| Medium | 250 | 525 | 40.90 | 10.30 | 3.65 | 7.79 | 5.44 | 3.26 | 30.44 |
| Fast | 300 | 500 | 35.00 | 10.50 | 4.27 | 7.00 | 6.75 | 2.00 | 30.52 |
| Stain, brush 2nd or additional coats & wipe | | | | | | | | | |
| Slow | 250 | 600 | 46.70 | 8.10 | 2.39 | 7.78 | 3.47 | 3.48 | 25.22 |
| Medium | 300 | 575 | 40.90 | 8.58 | 3.03 | 7.11 | 4.68 | 2.81 | 26.21 |
| Fast | 350 | 550 | 35.00 | 9.00 | 3.68 | 6.36 | 5.90 | 1.75 | 26.69 |
| **Wax & polish (material #15)** | | | | | | | | | |
| Hand apply 1 coat | | | | | | | | | |
| Slow | 175 | 1000 | 15.30 | 11.57 | 3.40 | 1.53 | 3.14 | 3.14 | 22.78 |
| Medium | 200 | 950 | 13.40 | 12.88 | 4.56 | 1.41 | 4.71 | 2.83 | 26.39 |
| Fast | 225 | 900 | 11.50 | 14.00 | 5.69 | 1.28 | 6.51 | 1.93 | 29.41 |
| Buffing with machine | | | | | | | | | |
| Slow | 400 | -- | -- | 5.06 | 1.50 | -- | 1.24 | 1.25 | 9.05 |
| Medium | 450 | -- | -- | 5.72 | 2.02 | -- | 1.94 | 1.16 | 10.84 |
| Fast | 500 | -- | -- | 6.30 | 2.57 | -- | 2.75 | .81 | 12.43 |

"Slow" work is based on an hourly wage of $20.25, "Medium" work on an hourly wage of $25.75, and "Fast" work on an hourly wage of $31.50. Other qualifications that apply to this table are on page 9.

*General Painting Costs*

|  | Manhours per door | Gallons per Door | Material cost per gallon | Labor cost per door | Labor burden door | Material cost per door | Overhead per door | Profit per door | Total price per door |
|---|---|---|---|---|---|---|---|---|---|
| **Garage door backs, seal coat, spray one coat** | | | | | | | | | |
| Sanding sealer, lacquer (material #11b) | | | | | | | | | |
| 1 car garage, 8' x 7' | | | | | | | | | |
| Slow | 0.30 | 0.40 | 41.50 | 6.08 | 1.79 | 16.60 | 4.65 | 4.66 | 33.78 |
| Medium | 0.25 | 0.50 | 36.30 | 6.44 | 2.28 | 18.15 | 6.72 | 4.03 | 37.62 |
| Fast | 0.20 | 0.60 | 31.10 | 6.30 | 2.57 | 18.66 | 8.53 | 2.52 | 38.58 |
| 2 car garage, 16' x 7' | | | | | | | | | |
| Slow | 0.40 | 0.80 | 41.50 | 8.10 | 2.39 | 33.20 | 8.30 | 8.32 | 60.31 |
| Medium | 0.35 | 0.90 | 36.30 | 9.01 | 3.19 | 32.67 | 11.22 | 6.73 | 62.82 |
| Fast | 0.30 | 1.00 | 31.10 | 9.45 | 3.86 | 31.10 | 13.77 | 4.07 | 62.25 |
| 3 car garage, 16' x 7' + 8' x 7' | | | | | | | | | |
| Slow | 0.60 | 1.00 | 41.50 | 12.15 | 3.58 | 41.50 | 10.87 | 10.90 | 79.00 |
| Medium | 0.55 | 1.10 | 36.30 | 14.16 | 5.02 | 39.93 | 14.78 | 8.87 | 82.76 |
| Fast | 0.50 | 1.20 | 31.10 | 15.75 | 6.43 | 37.32 | 18.45 | 5.46 | 83.41 |

Use the figures for Siding when estimating the cost of painting garage door fronts. These figures assume a one-car garage door measures 7' x 8' and a two-car garage door measures 7' x 16'. A three-car garage has one single and one double door. Government funded projects (FHA, VA, HUD) usually require sealing the garage door back on new construction projects. The doors are usually sprayed along with the cabinet sealer coat (as used in this table) or stained along with the exterior trim. "Slow" work is based on an hourly wage of $20.25, "Medium" work on an hourly wage of $25.75, and "Fast" work on an hourly wage of $31.50. Other qualifications that apply to this table are on page 9.

*National Painting Cost Estimator*

|  | Labor LF per manhour | Material coverage LF/gallon | Material cost per gallon | Labor cost per 100 LF | Labor burden 100 LF | Material cost per 100 LF | Overhead per 100 LF | Profit per 100 LF | Total price per 100 LF |
|---|---|---|---|---|---|---|---|---|---|

## Gutters and downspouts (galvanized), brush application
Gutters
  Metal prime, rust inhibitor, clean metal (material #35)
    Brush prime coat

|  | | | | | | | | | |
|---|---|---|---|---|---|---|---|---|---|
| Slow | 80 | 400 | 59.70 | 25.31 | 7.47 | 14.93 | 9.06 | 9.08 | 65.85 |
| Medium | 90 | 375 | 52.20 | 28.61 | 10.13 | 13.92 | 13.17 | 7.90 | 73.73 |
| Fast | 100 | 350 | 44.80 | 31.50 | 12.85 | 12.80 | 17.72 | 5.24 | 80.11 |

  Metal prime, rust inhibitor, rusty metal (material #36)
    Brush prime coat

|  | | | | | | | | | |
|---|---|---|---|---|---|---|---|---|---|
| Slow | 80 | 400 | 72.30 | 25.31 | 7.47 | 18.08 | 9.66 | 9.68 | 70.20 |
| Medium | 90 | 375 | 63.30 | 28.61 | 10.13 | 16.88 | 13.91 | 8.34 | 77.87 |
| Fast | 100 | 350 | 54.20 | 31.50 | 12.85 | 15.49 | 18.55 | 5.49 | 83.88 |

  Metal finish - synthetic enamel (off white), gloss (material #37)
    Brush 1st finish coat

|  | | | | | | | | | |
|---|---|---|---|---|---|---|---|---|---|
| Slow | 100 | 425 | 59.70 | 20.25 | 5.97 | 14.05 | 7.65 | 7.67 | 55.59 |
| Medium | 110 | 400 | 52.20 | 23.41 | 8.29 | 13.05 | 11.19 | 6.71 | 62.65 |
| Fast | 120 | 375 | 44.80 | 26.25 | 10.69 | 11.95 | 15.16 | 4.48 | 68.53 |

    Brush 2nd or additional finish coats

|  | | | | | | | | | |
|---|---|---|---|---|---|---|---|---|---|
| Slow | 120 | 450 | 59.70 | 16.88 | 4.96 | 13.27 | 6.67 | 6.69 | 48.47 |
| Medium | 130 | 425 | 52.20 | 19.81 | 7.01 | 12.28 | 9.78 | 5.87 | 54.75 |
| Fast | 140 | 400 | 44.80 | 22.50 | 9.17 | 11.20 | 13.29 | 3.93 | 60.09 |

  Metal finish - synthetic enamel (colors except orange/red), gloss (material #38)
    Brush 1st finish coat

|  | | | | | | | | | |
|---|---|---|---|---|---|---|---|---|---|
| Slow | 100 | 425 | 65.20 | 20.25 | 5.97 | 15.34 | 7.90 | 7.91 | 57.37 |
| Medium | 110 | 400 | 57.00 | 23.41 | 8.29 | 14.25 | 11.49 | 6.89 | 64.33 |
| Fast | 120 | 375 | 48.90 | 26.25 | 10.69 | 13.04 | 15.50 | 4.59 | 70.07 |

    Brush 2nd or additional finish coats

|  | | | | | | | | | |
|---|---|---|---|---|---|---|---|---|---|
| Slow | 120 | 450 | 65.20 | 16.88 | 4.96 | 14.49 | 6.91 | 6.92 | 50.16 |
| Medium | 130 | 425 | 57.00 | 19.81 | 7.01 | 13.41 | 10.06 | 6.03 | 56.32 |
| Fast | 140 | 400 | 48.90 | 22.50 | 9.17 | 12.23 | 13.61 | 4.03 | 61.54 |

Downspouts
  Metal prime, rust inhibitor, clean metal (material #35)
    Brush prime coat

|  | | | | | | | | | |
|---|---|---|---|---|---|---|---|---|---|
| Slow | 30 | 250 | 59.70 | 67.50 | 19.89 | 23.88 | 21.15 | 21.19 | 153.61 |
| Medium | 35 | 225 | 52.20 | 73.57 | 26.05 | 23.20 | 30.70 | 18.42 | 171.94 |
| Fast | 40 | 200 | 44.80 | 78.75 | 32.13 | 22.40 | 41.32 | 12.22 | 186.82 |

  Metal prime, rust inhibitor, rusty metal (material #36)
    Brush prime coat

|  | | | | | | | | | |
|---|---|---|---|---|---|---|---|---|---|
| Slow | 30 | 250 | 72.30 | 67.50 | 19.89 | 28.92 | 22.10 | 22.15 | 160.56 |
| Medium | 35 | 225 | 63.30 | 73.57 | 26.05 | 28.13 | 31.94 | 19.16 | 178.85 |
| Fast | 40 | 200 | 54.20 | 78.75 | 32.13 | 27.10 | 42.77 | 12.65 | 193.40 |

*General Painting Costs*

|  | Labor LF per manhour | Material coverage LF/gallon | Material cost per gallon | Labor cost per 100 LF | Labor burden 100 LF | Material cost per 100 LF | Overhead per 100 LF | Profit per 100 LF | Total price per 100 LF |
|---|---|---|---|---|---|---|---|---|---|
| **Metal finish - synthetic enamel (off white), gloss (material #37)** | | | | | | | | | |
| *Brush 1st finish coat* | | | | | | | | | |
| Slow | 50 | 275 | 59.70 | 40.50 | 11.94 | 21.71 | 14.09 | 14.12 | 102.36 |
| Medium | 60 | 250 | 52.20 | 42.92 | 15.21 | 20.88 | 19.75 | 11.85 | 110.61 |
| Fast | 70 | 225 | 44.80 | 45.00 | 18.38 | 19.91 | 25.81 | 7.64 | 116.74 |
| *Brush 2nd or additional finish coats* | | | | | | | | | |
| Slow | 70 | 300 | 59.70 | 28.93 | 8.54 | 19.90 | 10.90 | 10.92 | 79.19 |
| Medium | 80 | 275 | 52.20 | 32.19 | 11.40 | 18.98 | 15.64 | 9.39 | 87.60 |
| Fast | 90 | 250 | 44.80 | 35.00 | 14.27 | 17.92 | 20.83 | 6.16 | 94.18 |
| **Metal finish - synthetic enamel (colors except orange/red), gloss (material #38)** | | | | | | | | | |
| *Brush 1st finish coat* | | | | | | | | | |
| Slow | 50 | 275 | 65.20 | 40.50 | 11.94 | 23.71 | 14.47 | 14.50 | 105.12 |
| Medium | 60 | 250 | 57.00 | 42.92 | 15.21 | 22.80 | 20.23 | 12.14 | 113.30 |
| Fast | 70 | 225 | 48.90 | 45.00 | 18.38 | 21.73 | 26.38 | 7.80 | 119.29 |
| *Brush 2nd or additional finish coats* | | | | | | | | | |
| Slow | 70 | 300 | 65.20 | 28.93 | 8.54 | 21.73 | 11.25 | 11.27 | 81.72 |
| Medium | 80 | 275 | 57.00 | 32.19 | 11.40 | 20.73 | 16.08 | 9.65 | 90.05 |
| Fast | 90 | 250 | 48.90 | 35.00 | 14.27 | 19.56 | 21.34 | 6.31 | 96.48 |

NOTE: Oil base material is recommended for any metal surface. Although water base material is often used, it may cause oxidation, corrosion and rust. These figures assume that all exposed surfaces of 5" gutters and 4" downspouts are painted. For ornamental gutters and downspouts, multiply the linear feet by 1.5 before using these figures. "Slow" work is based on an hourly wage of $20.25, "Medium" work on an hourly wage of $25.75, and "Fast" work on an hourly wage of $31.50. Other qualifications that apply to this table are on page 9.

## High Time Difficulty Factors

Painting takes longer and may require more material when heights above the floor exceed 8 feet. The additional time and material for working at these heights and using a roller pole or a wand on a spray gun, climbing up and down a ladder or scaffolding is applied by using one of the factors listed below. The wall area above 8 feet is typically referred to as the "Clip." To apply the high time difficulty factor, measure the surface above 8 feet which is to be painted and multiply that figure by the appropriate factor. This measurement can be listed on a separate line of your take-off and the appropriate price can be applied for a total.

For labor calculations only:  Add 30% to the area for heights between 8 and 13 feet (multiply by 1.3)
Add 60% to the area for heights from 13 to 17 feet (multiply by 1.6)
Add 90% to the area for heights from 17 to 19 feet (multiply by 1.9)
Add 120% to the area for heights from 19 to 21 feet (multiply by 2.2)

EXAMPLE: A 17 x 14 living room has a vaulted ceiling 13 feet high. Your take-off sheet might look like this:

Walls to 8 feet: 136 + 112 + 136 + 112 = 496 SF
Clip:         [(5 x 14) / 2] x 2  +  (5 x 17) = 70 + 85 = 155 SF
         area of two triangles  +  rectangular area
         155 SF  x  1.3 (high time difficulty factor)  =  202 SF

Then multiply each SF total by the appropriate price per square foot.

## Mail box structures, wood, apartment type

Measure the length of each board to be painted and use the manhours and material given for Trellis or Plant-on trim or Siding.

|  | Labor SF per manhour | Material coverage SF/gallon | Material cost per gallon | Labor cost per 100 SF | Labor burden 100 SF | Material cost per 100 SF | Overhead per 100 SF | Profit per 100 SF | Total price per 100 SF |
|---|---|---|---|---|---|---|---|---|---|

## Masonry, anti-graffiti stain eliminator on smooth or rough surface

Water base primer and sealer (material #39)
  Roll & brush each coat

|  |  |  |  |  |  |  |  |  |  |
|---|---|---|---|---|---|---|---|---|---|
| Slow | 350 | 400 | 50.30 | 5.79 | 1.71 | 12.58 | 3.82 | 3.82 | 27.72 |
| Medium | 375 | 375 | 44.00 | 6.87 | 2.44 | 11.73 | 5.26 | 3.15 | 29.45 |
| Fast | 400 | 350 | 37.80 | 7.88 | 3.21 | 10.80 | 6.79 | 2.01 | 30.69 |

Oil base primer and sealer (material #40)
  Roll & brush each coat

|  |  |  |  |  |  |  |  |  |  |
|---|---|---|---|---|---|---|---|---|---|
| Slow | 350 | 375 | 49.90 | 5.79 | 1.71 | 13.31 | 3.95 | 3.96 | 28.72 |
| Medium | 375 | 350 | 43.70 | 6.87 | 2.44 | 12.49 | 5.45 | 3.27 | 30.52 |
| Fast | 400 | 325 | 37.40 | 7.88 | 3.21 | 11.51 | 7.01 | 2.07 | 31.68 |

Polyurethane 2 part system (material #41)
  Roll & brush each coat

|  |  |  |  |  |  |  |  |  |  |
|---|---|---|---|---|---|---|---|---|---|
| Slow | 300 | 375 | 157.00 | 6.75 | 1.98 | 41.87 | 9.62 | 9.64 | 69.86 |
| Medium | 325 | 350 | 137.40 | 7.92 | 2.82 | 39.26 | 12.50 | 7.50 | 70.00 |
| Fast | 350 | 325 | 117.80 | 9.00 | 3.68 | 36.25 | 15.17 | 4.49 | 68.59 |

Use these figures for new brick, used brick, or Concrete Masonry Units (CMU) where the block surfaces are either smooth or rough, porous or unfilled, with joints struck to average depth. The more porous the surface, the rougher the texture, the more time and material will be required. "Slow" work is based on an hourly wage of $20.25, "Medium" work on an hourly wage of $25.75, and "Fast" work on an hourly wage of $31.50. Other qualifications that apply to this table are on page 9.

*General Painting Costs*

|  | Labor SF per manhour | Material coverage SF/gallon | Material cost per gallon | Labor cost per 100 SF | Labor burden 100 SF | Material cost per 100 SF | Overhead per 100 SF | Profit per 100 SF | Total price per 100 SF |
|---|---|---|---|---|---|---|---|---|---|
| **Masonry, block filler** | | | | | | | | | |
| Brush 1 coat (material #33) | | | | | | | | | |
|   Slow | 95 | 75 | 36.60 | 21.32 | 6.29 | 48.80 | 14.52 | 14.55 | 105.48 |
|   Medium | 125 | 65 | 32.00 | 20.60 | 7.30 | 49.23 | 19.28 | 11.57 | 107.98 |
|   Fast | 155 | 55 | 27.50 | 20.32 | 8.29 | 50.00 | 24.37 | 7.21 | 110.19 |
| Roll 1 coat (material #33) | | | | | | | | | |
|   Slow | 190 | 70 | 36.60 | 10.66 | 3.13 | 52.29 | 12.56 | 12.58 | 91.22 |
|   Medium | 215 | 60 | 32.00 | 11.98 | 4.23 | 53.33 | 17.39 | 10.43 | 97.36 |
|   Fast | 240 | 50 | 27.50 | 13.13 | 5.36 | 55.00 | 22.78 | 6.74 | 103.01 |
| Spray 1 coat (material #33) | | | | | | | | | |
|   Slow | 425 | 65 | 36.60 | 4.76 | 1.40 | 56.31 | 11.87 | 11.89 | 86.23 |
|   Medium | 525 | 55 | 32.00 | 4.90 | 1.73 | 58.18 | 16.20 | 9.72 | 90.73 |
|   Fast | 625 | 45 | 27.50 | 5.04 | 2.06 | 61.11 | 21.15 | 6.26 | 95.62 |

Use these figures for using block filler on rough or porous masonry with joints struck to average depth. "Slow" work is based on an hourly wage of $20.25, "Medium" work on an hourly wage of $25.75, and "Fast" work on an hourly wage of $31.50. Other qualifications that apply to this table are on page 9.

|  | Labor SF per manhour | Material coverage SF/gallon | Material cost per gallon | Labor cost per 100 SF | Labor burden 100 SF | Material cost per 100 SF | Overhead per 100 SF | Profit per 100 SF | Total price per 100 SF |
|---|---|---|---|---|---|---|---|---|---|
| **Masonry, brick, new, smooth-surface, brush** | | | | | | | | | |
| Masonry paint, water base, flat or gloss (material #31) | | | | | | | | | |
|   Brush 1st coat | | | | | | | | | |
|     Slow | 200 | 300 | 38.20 | 10.13 | 2.98 | 12.73 | 4.91 | 4.92 | 35.67 |
|     Medium | 225 | 275 | 33.50 | 11.44 | 4.04 | 12.18 | 6.92 | 4.15 | 38.73 |
|     Fast | 250 | 250 | 28.70 | 12.60 | 5.14 | 11.48 | 9.06 | 2.68 | 40.96 |
|   Brush 2nd or additional coats | | | | | | | | | |
|     Slow | 250 | 325 | 38.20 | 8.10 | 2.39 | 11.75 | 4.23 | 4.24 | 30.71 |
|     Medium | 275 | 300 | 33.50 | 9.36 | 3.33 | 11.17 | 5.96 | 3.58 | 33.40 |
|     Fast | 300 | 275 | 28.70 | 10.50 | 4.27 | 10.44 | 7.82 | 2.31 | 35.34 |
| Masonry paint, oil base (material #32) | | | | | | | | | |
|   Brush 1st coat | | | | | | | | | |
|     Slow | 200 | 350 | 38.40 | 10.13 | 2.98 | 10.97 | 4.58 | 4.59 | 33.25 |
|     Medium | 225 | 325 | 33.60 | 11.44 | 4.04 | 10.34 | 6.46 | 3.87 | 36.15 |
|     Fast | 250 | 300 | 28.80 | 12.60 | 5.14 | 9.60 | 8.48 | 2.51 | 38.33 |
|   Brush 2nd or additional coats | | | | | | | | | |
|     Slow | 250 | 400 | 38.40 | 8.10 | 2.39 | 9.60 | 3.82 | 3.83 | 27.74 |
|     Medium | 275 | 363 | 33.60 | 9.36 | 3.33 | 9.26 | 5.48 | 3.29 | 30.72 |
|     Fast | 300 | 325 | 28.80 | 10.50 | 4.27 | 8.86 | 7.33 | 2.17 | 33.13 |

Use these figures for new smooth-surface brick with joints struck to average depth. "Slow" work is based on an hourly wage of $20.25, "Medium" work on an hourly wage of $25.75, and "Fast" work on an hourly wage of $31.50. Other qualifications that apply to this table are on page 9.

|  | Labor SF per manhour | Material coverage SF/gallon | Material cost per gallon | Labor cost per 100 SF | Labor burden 100 SF | Material cost per 100 SF | Overhead per 100 SF | Profit per 100 SF | Total price per 100 SF |
|---|---|---|---|---|---|---|---|---|---|
| **Masonry, brick, new, smooth-surface, roll** | | | | | | | | | |
| Masonry paint, water base, flat or gloss (material #31) | | | | | | | | | |
| Roll 1st coat | | | | | | | | | |
| Slow | 325 | 250 | 38.20 | 6.23 | 1.85 | 15.28 | 4.44 | 4.45 | 32.25 |
| Medium | 350 | 213 | 33.50 | 7.36 | 2.61 | 15.73 | 6.43 | 3.86 | 35.99 |
| Fast | 375 | 175 | 28.70 | 8.40 | 3.44 | 16.40 | 8.75 | 2.59 | 39.58 |
| Roll 2nd or additional coats | | | | | | | | | |
| Slow | 375 | 275 | 38.20 | 5.40 | 1.60 | 13.89 | 3.97 | 3.98 | 28.84 |
| Medium | 400 | 250 | 33.50 | 6.44 | 2.28 | 13.40 | 5.53 | 3.32 | 30.97 |
| Fast | 425 | 225 | 28.70 | 7.41 | 3.01 | 12.76 | 7.19 | 2.13 | 32.50 |
| Masonry paint, oil base (material #32) | | | | | | | | | |
| Roll 1st coat | | | | | | | | | |
| Slow | 325 | 325 | 38.40 | 6.23 | 1.85 | 11.82 | 3.78 | 3.79 | 27.47 |
| Medium | 350 | 288 | 33.60 | 7.36 | 2.61 | 11.67 | 5.41 | 3.25 | 30.30 |
| Fast | 375 | 250 | 28.80 | 8.40 | 3.44 | 11.52 | 7.24 | 2.14 | 32.74 |
| Roll 2nd or additional coats | | | | | | | | | |
| Slow | 375 | 350 | 38.40 | 5.40 | 1.60 | 10.97 | 3.41 | 3.42 | 24.80 |
| Medium | 400 | 313 | 33.60 | 6.44 | 2.28 | 10.73 | 4.86 | 2.92 | 27.23 |
| Fast | 425 | 275 | 28.80 | 7.41 | 3.01 | 10.47 | 6.48 | 1.92 | 29.29 |
| Waterproofing, clear hydro sealer, oil base (material #34) | | | | | | | | | |
| Roll 1st coat | | | | | | | | | |
| Slow | 200 | 175 | 40.60 | 10.13 | 2.98 | 23.20 | 6.90 | 6.92 | 50.13 |
| Medium | 225 | 150 | 35.50 | 11.44 | 4.04 | 23.67 | 9.79 | 5.87 | 54.81 |
| Fast | 250 | 125 | 30.40 | 12.60 | 5.14 | 24.32 | 13.04 | 3.86 | 58.96 |
| Roll 2nd or additional coats | | | | | | | | | |
| Slow | 225 | 200 | 40.60 | 9.00 | 2.64 | 20.30 | 6.07 | 6.08 | 44.09 |
| Medium | 250 | 190 | 35.50 | 10.30 | 3.65 | 18.68 | 8.16 | 4.89 | 45.68 |
| Fast | 275 | 180 | 30.40 | 11.45 | 4.69 | 16.89 | 10.23 | 3.03 | 46.29 |

Use these figures for new smooth-surface brick with joints struck to average depth. "Slow" work is based on an hourly wage of $20.25, "Medium" work on an hourly wage of $25.75, and "Fast" work on an hourly wage of $31.50. Other qualifications that apply to this table are on page 9.

## General Painting Costs

|  | Labor SF per manhour | Material coverage SF/gallon | Material cost per gallon | Labor cost per 100 SF | Labor burden 100 SF | Material cost per 100 SF | Overhead per 100 SF | Profit per 100 SF | Total price per 100 SF |
|---|---|---|---|---|---|---|---|---|---|
| **Masonry, brick, new, smooth-surface, spray** | | | | | | | | | |
| Masonry paint, water base, flat or gloss (material #31) | | | | | | | | | |
| Spray 1st coat | | | | | | | | | |
| Slow | 650 | 250 | 38.20 | 3.12 | .92 | 15.28 | 3.67 | 3.68 | 26.67 |
| Medium | 750 | 225 | 33.50 | 3.43 | 1.21 | 14.89 | 4.88 | 2.93 | 27.34 |
| Fast | 850 | 200 | 28.70 | 3.71 | 1.52 | 14.35 | 6.07 | 1.79 | 27.44 |
| Spray 2nd or additional coats | | | | | | | | | |
| Slow | 750 | 275 | 38.20 | 2.70 | .79 | 13.89 | 3.30 | 3.31 | 23.99 |
| Medium | 825 | 238 | 33.50 | 3.12 | 1.10 | 14.08 | 4.58 | 2.75 | 25.63 |
| Fast | 900 | 250 | 28.70 | 3.50 | 1.42 | 11.48 | 5.09 | 1.51 | 23.00 |
| Masonry paint, oil base (material #32) | | | | | | | | | |
| Spray 1st coat | | | | | | | | | |
| Slow | 650 | 275 | 38.40 | 3.12 | .92 | 13.96 | 3.42 | 3.43 | 24.85 |
| Medium | 750 | 250 | 33.60 | 3.43 | 1.21 | 13.44 | 4.52 | 2.71 | 25.31 |
| Fast | 850 | 225 | 28.80 | 3.71 | 1.52 | 12.80 | 5.59 | 1.65 | 25.27 |
| Spray 2nd or additional coats | | | | | | | | | |
| Slow | 750 | 300 | 38.40 | 2.70 | .79 | 12.80 | 3.10 | 3.10 | 22.49 |
| Medium | 825 | 288 | 33.60 | 3.12 | 1.10 | 11.67 | 3.97 | 2.38 | 22.24 |
| Fast | 900 | 275 | 28.80 | 3.50 | 1.42 | 10.47 | 4.77 | 1.41 | 21.57 |
| Waterproofing, clear hydro sealer, oil base (material #34) | | | | | | | | | |
| Spray 1st coat | | | | | | | | | |
| Slow | 700 | 120 | 40.60 | 2.89 | .86 | 33.83 | 7.14 | 7.15 | 51.87 |
| Medium | 800 | 100 | 35.50 | 3.22 | 1.14 | 35.50 | 9.97 | 5.98 | 55.81 |
| Fast | 900 | 80 | 30.40 | 3.50 | 1.42 | 38.00 | 13.31 | 3.94 | 60.17 |
| Spray 2nd or additional coats | | | | | | | | | |
| Slow | 800 | 150 | 40.60 | 2.53 | .75 | 27.07 | 5.77 | 5.78 | 41.90 |
| Medium | 900 | 138 | 35.50 | 2.86 | 1.01 | 25.72 | 7.40 | 4.44 | 41.43 |
| Fast | 1000 | 125 | 30.40 | 3.15 | 1.29 | 24.32 | 8.92 | 2.64 | 40.32 |

Use these figures for new smooth-surface brick with joints struck to average depth. "Slow" work is based on an hourly wage of $20.25, "Medium" work on an hourly wage of $25.75, and "Fast" work on an hourly wage of $31.50. Other qualifications that apply to this table are on page 9.

*National Painting Cost Estimator*

|  | Labor SF per manhour | Material coverage SF/gallon | Material cost per gallon | Labor cost per 100 SF | Labor burden 100 SF | Material cost per 100 SF | Overhead per 100 SF | Profit per 100 SF | Total price per 100 SF |
|---|---|---|---|---|---|---|---|---|---|
| **Masonry, brick, used, rough surface, brush** | | | | | | | | | |
| Masonry paint, water base, flat or gloss (material #31) | | | | | | | | | |
| Brush 1st coat | | | | | | | | | |
| Slow | 150 | 300 | 38.20 | 13.50 | 3.99 | 12.73 | 5.74 | 5.75 | 41.71 |
| Medium | 175 | 275 | 33.50 | 14.71 | 5.20 | 12.18 | 8.03 | 4.82 | 44.94 |
| Fast | 200 | 250 | 28.70 | 15.75 | 6.43 | 11.48 | 10.43 | 3.09 | 47.18 |
| Brush 2nd or additional coats | | | | | | | | | |
| Slow | 200 | 375 | 38.20 | 10.13 | 2.98 | 10.19 | 4.43 | 4.44 | 32.17 |
| Medium | 225 | 350 | 33.50 | 11.44 | 4.04 | 9.57 | 6.27 | 3.76 | 35.08 |
| Fast | 250 | 325 | 28.70 | 12.60 | 5.14 | 8.83 | 8.24 | 2.44 | 37.25 |
| Masonry paint, oil base (material #32) | | | | | | | | | |
| Brush 1st coat | | | | | | | | | |
| Slow | 150 | 325 | 38.40 | 13.50 | 3.99 | 11.82 | 5.57 | 5.58 | 40.46 |
| Medium | 175 | 300 | 33.60 | 14.71 | 5.20 | 11.20 | 7.78 | 4.67 | 43.56 |
| Fast | 200 | 275 | 28.80 | 15.75 | 6.43 | 10.47 | 10.12 | 2.99 | 45.76 |
| Brush 2nd or additional coats | | | | | | | | | |
| Slow | 200 | 400 | 38.40 | 10.13 | 2.98 | 9.60 | 4.32 | 4.33 | 31.36 |
| Medium | 225 | 375 | 33.60 | 11.44 | 4.04 | 8.96 | 6.11 | 3.67 | 34.22 |
| Fast | 250 | 350 | 28.80 | 12.60 | 5.14 | 8.23 | 8.05 | 2.38 | 36.40 |

Use these figures for dry pressed used brick, clay brick tile, or adobe block with joints struck to average depth. "Slow" work is based on an hourly wage of $20.25, "Medium" work on an hourly wage of $25.75, and "Fast" work on an hourly wage of $31.50. Other qualifications that apply to this table are on page 9.

*General Painting Costs*

|  | Labor SF per manhour | Material coverage SF/gallon | Material cost per gallon | Labor cost per 100 SF | Labor burden 100 SF | Material cost per 100 SF | Overhead per 100 SF | Profit per 100 SF | Total price per 100 SF |
|---|---|---|---|---|---|---|---|---|---|

## Masonry, brick, used, rough surface, roll

Masonry paint, water base, flat or gloss (material #31)
  Roll 1st coat

| | | | | | | | | | |
|---|---|---|---|---|---|---|---|---|---|
| Slow | 300 | 250 | 38.20 | 6.75 | 1.98 | 15.28 | 4.56 | 4.57 | 33.14 |
| Medium | 325 | 225 | 33.50 | 7.92 | 2.82 | 14.89 | 6.40 | 3.84 | 35.87 |
| Fast | 350 | 200 | 28.70 | 9.00 | 3.68 | 14.35 | 8.38 | 2.48 | 37.89 |

  Roll 2nd or additional coats

| | | | | | | | | | |
|---|---|---|---|---|---|---|---|---|---|
| Slow | 350 | 325 | 38.20 | 5.79 | 1.71 | 11.75 | 3.66 | 3.67 | 26.58 |
| Medium | 375 | 300 | 33.50 | 6.87 | 2.44 | 11.17 | 5.12 | 3.07 | 28.67 |
| Fast | 400 | 275 | 28.70 | 7.88 | 3.21 | 10.44 | 6.68 | 1.98 | 30.19 |

Masonry paint, oil base (material #32)
  Roll 1st coat

| | | | | | | | | | |
|---|---|---|---|---|---|---|---|---|---|
| Slow | 300 | 275 | 38.40 | 6.75 | 1.98 | 13.96 | 4.31 | 4.32 | 31.32 |
| Medium | 325 | 250 | 33.60 | 7.92 | 2.82 | 13.44 | 6.04 | 3.62 | 33.84 |
| Fast | 350 | 225 | 28.80 | 9.00 | 3.68 | 12.80 | 7.90 | 2.34 | 35.72 |

  Roll 2nd or additional coats

| | | | | | | | | | |
|---|---|---|---|---|---|---|---|---|---|
| Slow | 350 | 350 | 38.40 | 5.79 | 1.71 | 10.97 | 3.51 | 3.52 | 25.50 |
| Medium | 375 | 325 | 33.60 | 6.87 | 2.44 | 10.34 | 4.91 | 2.95 | 27.51 |
| Fast | 400 | 300 | 28.80 | 7.88 | 3.21 | 9.60 | 6.42 | 1.90 | 29.01 |

Waterproofing, clear hydro sealer, oil base (material #34)
  Roll 1st coat

| | | | | | | | | | |
|---|---|---|---|---|---|---|---|---|---|
| Slow | 150 | 125 | 40.60 | 13.50 | 3.99 | 32.48 | 9.49 | 9.51 | 68.97 |
| Medium | 175 | 113 | 35.50 | 14.71 | 5.20 | 31.42 | 12.84 | 7.70 | 71.87 |
| Fast | 200 | 100 | 30.40 | 15.75 | 6.43 | 30.40 | 16.30 | 4.82 | 73.70 |

  Roll 2nd or additional coats

| | | | | | | | | | |
|---|---|---|---|---|---|---|---|---|---|
| Slow | 175 | 150 | 40.60 | 11.57 | 3.40 | 27.07 | 7.99 | 8.01 | 58.04 |
| Medium | 200 | 138 | 35.50 | 12.88 | 4.56 | 25.72 | 10.79 | 6.47 | 60.42 |
| Fast | 225 | 125 | 30.40 | 14.00 | 5.69 | 24.32 | 13.65 | 4.04 | 61.70 |

Use these figures for dry pressed used brick, clay brick tile, or adobe block with joints struck to average depth. "Slow" work is based on an hourly wage of $20.25, "Medium" work on an hourly wage of $25.75, and "Fast" work on an hourly wage of $31.50. Other qualifications that apply to this table are on page 9.

*National Painting Cost Estimator*

|  | Labor SF per manhour | Material coverage SF/gallon | Material cost per gallon | Labor cost per 100 SF | Labor burden 100 SF | Material cost per 100 SF | Overhead per 100 SF | Profit per 100 SF | Total price per 100 SF |
|---|---|---|---|---|---|---|---|---|---|

## Masonry, brick, used, rough surface, spray

Masonry paint, water base, flat or gloss (material #31)
  Spray 1st coat

| | | | | | | | | | |
|---|---|---|---|---|---|---|---|---|---|
| Slow | 600 | 200 | 38.20 | 3.38 | 1.00 | 19.10 | 4.46 | 4.47 | 32.41 |
| Medium | 700 | 175 | 33.50 | 3.68 | 1.31 | 19.14 | 6.03 | 3.62 | 33.78 |
| Fast | 800 | 150 | 28.70 | 3.94 | 1.60 | 19.13 | 7.65 | 2.26 | 34.58 |

  Spray 2nd or additional coats

| | | | | | | | | | |
|---|---|---|---|---|---|---|---|---|---|
| Slow | 700 | 225 | 38.20 | 2.89 | .86 | 16.98 | 3.94 | 3.95 | 28.62 |
| Medium | 800 | 213 | 33.50 | 3.22 | 1.14 | 15.73 | 5.02 | 3.01 | 28.12 |
| Fast | 900 | 200 | 28.70 | 3.50 | 1.42 | 14.35 | 5.98 | 1.77 | 27.02 |

Masonry paint, oil base (material #32)
  Spray 1st coat

| | | | | | | | | | |
|---|---|---|---|---|---|---|---|---|---|
| Slow | 600 | 225 | 38.40 | 3.38 | 1.00 | 17.07 | 4.08 | 4.08 | 29.61 |
| Medium | 700 | 200 | 33.60 | 3.68 | 1.31 | 16.80 | 5.45 | 3.27 | 30.51 |
| Fast | 800 | 175 | 28.80 | 3.94 | 1.60 | 16.46 | 6.82 | 2.02 | 30.84 |

  Spray 2nd or additional coats

| | | | | | | | | | |
|---|---|---|---|---|---|---|---|---|---|
| Slow | 700 | 250 | 38.40 | 2.89 | .86 | 15.36 | 3.63 | 3.64 | 26.38 |
| Medium | 800 | 238 | 33.60 | 3.22 | 1.14 | 14.12 | 4.62 | 2.77 | 25.87 |
| Fast | 900 | 225 | 28.80 | 3.50 | 1.42 | 12.80 | 5.50 | 1.63 | 24.85 |

Waterproofing, clear hydro sealer, oil base (material #34)
  Spray 1st coat

| | | | | | | | | | |
|---|---|---|---|---|---|---|---|---|---|
| Slow | 600 | 80 | 40.60 | 3.38 | 1.00 | 50.75 | 10.47 | 10.50 | 76.10 |
| Medium | 700 | 75 | 35.50 | 3.68 | 1.31 | 47.33 | 13.08 | 7.85 | 73.25 |
| Fast | 800 | 70 | 30.40 | 3.94 | 1.60 | 43.43 | 15.18 | 4.49 | 68.64 |

  Spray 2nd coat

| | | | | | | | | | |
|---|---|---|---|---|---|---|---|---|---|
| Slow | 800 | 100 | 40.60 | 2.53 | .75 | 40.60 | 8.34 | 8.36 | 60.58 |
| Medium | 900 | 90 | 35.50 | 2.86 | 1.01 | 39.44 | 10.83 | 6.50 | 60.64 |
| Fast | 1000 | 80 | 30.40 | 3.15 | 1.29 | 38.00 | 13.16 | 3.89 | 59.49 |

Use these figures for dry pressed used brick, clay brick tile, or adobe block with joints struck to average depth. "Slow" work is based on an hourly wage of $20.25, "Medium" work on an hourly wage of $25.75, and "Fast" work on an hourly wage of $31.50. Other qualifications that apply to this table are on page 9.

*General Painting Costs*

|  | Labor SF per manhour | Material coverage SF/gallon | Material cost per gallon | Labor cost per 100 SF | Labor burden 100 SF | Material cost per 100 SF | Overhead per 100 SF | Profit per 100 SF | Total price per 100 SF |
|---|---|---|---|---|---|---|---|---|---|

## Masonry, Concrete Masonry Units (CMU), rough, porous surface, brush

### Masonry paint, water base, flat or gloss (material #31)
Brush 1st coat

| | | | | | | | | | |
|---|---|---|---|---|---|---|---|---|---|
| Slow | 110 | 100 | 38.20 | 18.41 | 5.42 | 38.20 | 11.79 | 11.81 | 85.63 |
| Medium | 130 | 88 | 33.50 | 19.81 | 7.01 | 38.07 | 16.22 | 9.73 | 90.84 |
| Fast | 150 | 75 | 28.70 | 21.00 | 8.58 | 38.27 | 21.03 | 6.22 | 95.10 |

Brush 2nd or additional coats

| | | | | | | | | | |
|---|---|---|---|---|---|---|---|---|---|
| Slow | 185 | 180 | 38.20 | 10.95 | 3.24 | 21.22 | 6.73 | 6.74 | 48.88 |
| Medium | 210 | 168 | 33.50 | 12.26 | 4.34 | 19.94 | 9.14 | 5.48 | 51.16 |
| Fast | 230 | 155 | 28.70 | 13.70 | 5.59 | 18.52 | 11.72 | 3.47 | 53.00 |

### Masonry paint, oil base (material #32)
Brush 1st coat

| | | | | | | | | | |
|---|---|---|---|---|---|---|---|---|---|
| Slow | 110 | 130 | 38.40 | 18.41 | 5.42 | 29.54 | 10.14 | 10.16 | 73.67 |
| Medium | 130 | 120 | 33.60 | 19.81 | 7.01 | 28.00 | 13.71 | 8.22 | 76.75 |
| Fast | 150 | 110 | 28.80 | 21.00 | 8.58 | 26.18 | 17.28 | 5.11 | 78.15 |

Brush 2nd or additional coats

| | | | | | | | | | |
|---|---|---|---|---|---|---|---|---|---|
| Slow | 185 | 200 | 38.40 | 10.95 | 3.24 | 19.20 | 6.34 | 6.36 | 46.09 |
| Medium | 208 | 180 | 33.60 | 12.38 | 4.39 | 18.67 | 8.86 | 5.31 | 49.61 |
| Fast | 230 | 160 | 28.80 | 13.70 | 5.59 | 18.00 | 11.56 | 3.42 | 52.27 |

### Epoxy coating, 2 part system clear (material #51)
Brush 1st coat

| | | | | | | | | | |
|---|---|---|---|---|---|---|---|---|---|
| Slow | 95 | 110 | 146.90 | 21.32 | 6.29 | 133.55 | 30.62 | 30.68 | 222.46 |
| Medium | 115 | 98 | 128.60 | 22.39 | 7.95 | 131.22 | 40.39 | 24.23 | 226.18 |
| Fast | 135 | 85 | 110.20 | 23.33 | 9.53 | 129.65 | 50.38 | 14.90 | 227.79 |

Brush 2nd or additional coats

| | | | | | | | | | |
|---|---|---|---|---|---|---|---|---|---|
| Slow | 165 | 200 | 146.90 | 12.27 | 3.62 | 73.45 | 16.97 | 17.01 | 123.32 |
| Medium | 190 | 188 | 128.60 | 13.55 | 4.79 | 68.40 | 21.69 | 13.01 | 121.44 |
| Fast | 210 | 175 | 110.20 | 15.00 | 6.11 | 62.97 | 26.07 | 7.71 | 117.86 |

### Waterproofing, clear hydro sealer, oil base (material #34)
Brush 1st coat

| | | | | | | | | | |
|---|---|---|---|---|---|---|---|---|---|
| Slow | 125 | 90 | 40.60 | 16.20 | 4.78 | 45.11 | 12.56 | 12.58 | 91.23 |
| Medium | 150 | 80 | 35.50 | 17.17 | 6.09 | 44.38 | 16.91 | 10.14 | 94.69 |
| Fast | 175 | 70 | 30.40 | 18.00 | 7.32 | 43.43 | 21.32 | 6.31 | 96.38 |

Brush 2nd or additional coats

| | | | | | | | | | |
|---|---|---|---|---|---|---|---|---|---|
| Slow | 230 | 130 | 40.60 | 8.80 | 2.61 | 31.23 | 8.10 | 8.12 | 58.86 |
| Medium | 275 | 110 | 35.50 | 9.36 | 3.33 | 32.27 | 11.24 | 6.74 | 62.94 |
| Fast | 295 | 90 | 30.40 | 10.68 | 4.35 | 33.78 | 15.13 | 4.48 | 68.42 |

Use these figures for Concrete Masonry Units (CMU) such as split face, fluted, or slump block, whose surfaces are rough, porous or unfilled, with joints struck to average depth. The more porous the surface, the rougher the texture, the more time and material will be required. For heavy waterproofing applications, see Masonry under Industrial Painting Operations. "Slow" work is based on an hourly wage of $20.25, "Medium" on an hourly wage of $25.75, and "Fast" work on an hourly wage of $31.50. Other qualifications that apply to this table are on page 9.

*National Painting Cost Estimator*

|  | Labor SF per manhour | Material coverage SF/gallon | Material cost per gallon | Labor cost per 100 SF | Labor burden 100 SF | Material cost per 100 SF | Overhead per 100 SF | Profit per 100 SF | Total price per 100 SF |
|---|---|---|---|---|---|---|---|---|---|

## Masonry, Concrete Masonry Units (CMU), rough, porous surface, roll

**Masonry paint, water base, flat or gloss (material #31)**
Roll 1st coat
| | | | | | | | | | |
|---|---|---|---|---|---|---|---|---|---|
| Slow | 245 | 90 | 38.20 | 8.27 | 2.43 | 42.44 | 10.10 | 10.12 | 73.36 |
| Medium | 300 | 78 | 33.50 | 8.58 | 3.03 | 42.95 | 13.64 | 8.19 | 76.39 |
| Fast | 350 | 65 | 28.70 | 9.00 | 3.68 | 44.15 | 17.61 | 5.21 | 79.65 |

Roll 2nd or additional coats
| | | | | | | | | | |
|---|---|---|---|---|---|---|---|---|---|
| Slow | 275 | 160 | 38.20 | 7.36 | 2.18 | 23.88 | 6.35 | 6.36 | 46.13 |
| Medium | 325 | 143 | 33.50 | 7.92 | 2.82 | 23.43 | 8.54 | 5.12 | 47.83 |
| Fast | 420 | 125 | 28.70 | 7.50 | 3.06 | 22.96 | 10.39 | 3.07 | 46.98 |

**Masonry paint, oil base (material #32)**
Roll 1st coat
| | | | | | | | | | |
|---|---|---|---|---|---|---|---|---|---|
| Slow | 245 | 110 | 38.40 | 8.27 | 2.43 | 34.91 | 8.67 | 8.69 | 62.97 |
| Medium | 300 | 98 | 33.60 | 8.58 | 3.03 | 34.29 | 11.48 | 6.89 | 64.27 |
| Fast | 350 | 85 | 28.80 | 9.00 | 3.68 | 33.88 | 14.43 | 4.27 | 65.26 |

Roll 2nd or additional coats
| | | | | | | | | | |
|---|---|---|---|---|---|---|---|---|---|
| Slow | 275 | 185 | 38.40 | 7.36 | 2.18 | 20.76 | 5.76 | 5.77 | 41.83 |
| Medium | 325 | 170 | 33.60 | 7.92 | 2.82 | 19.76 | 7.62 | 4.57 | 42.69 |
| Fast | 420 | 155 | 28.80 | 7.50 | 3.06 | 18.58 | 9.03 | 2.67 | 40.84 |

**Epoxy coating, 2 part system, clear (material #51)**
Roll 1st coat
| | | | | | | | | | |
|---|---|---|---|---|---|---|---|---|---|
| Slow | 220 | 100 | 146.90 | 9.20 | 2.73 | 146.90 | 30.17 | 30.24 | 219.24 |
| Medium | 275 | 88 | 128.60 | 9.36 | 3.33 | 146.14 | 39.70 | 23.82 | 222.35 |
| Fast | 325 | 75 | 110.20 | 9.69 | 3.97 | 146.93 | 49.78 | 14.72 | 225.09 |

Roll 2nd or additional coats
| | | | | | | | | | |
|---|---|---|---|---|---|---|---|---|---|
| Slow | 250 | 175 | 146.90 | 8.10 | 2.39 | 83.94 | 17.94 | 17.98 | 130.35 |
| Medium | 300 | 160 | 128.60 | 8.58 | 3.03 | 80.38 | 23.00 | 13.80 | 128.79 |
| Fast | 395 | 145 | 110.20 | 7.97 | 3.25 | 76.00 | 27.04 | 8.00 | 122.26 |

**Waterproofing, clear hydro sealer, oil base (material #34)**
Roll 1st coat
| | | | | | | | | | |
|---|---|---|---|---|---|---|---|---|---|
| Slow | 170 | 110 | 40.60 | 11.91 | 3.51 | 36.91 | 9.94 | 9.96 | 72.23 |
| Medium | 200 | 98 | 35.50 | 12.88 | 4.56 | 36.22 | 13.42 | 8.05 | 75.13 |
| Fast | 245 | 85 | 30.40 | 12.86 | 5.23 | 35.76 | 16.70 | 4.94 | 75.49 |

Roll 2nd or additional coats
| | | | | | | | | | |
|---|---|---|---|---|---|---|---|---|---|
| Slow | 275 | 175 | 40.60 | 7.36 | 2.18 | 23.20 | 6.22 | 6.23 | 45.19 |
| Medium | 300 | 145 | 35.50 | 8.58 | 3.03 | 24.48 | 9.03 | 5.42 | 50.54 |
| Fast | 325 | 115 | 30.40 | 9.69 | 3.97 | 26.43 | 12.42 | 3.67 | 56.18 |

Use these figures for Concrete Masonry Units (CMU) such as split face, fluted, or slump block, whose surfaces are rough, porous or unfilled, with joints struck to average depth. The more porous the surface, the rougher the texture, the more time and material will be required. For heavy waterproofing applications, see Masonry under Industrial Painting Operations. "Slow" work is based on an hourly wage of $20.25, "Medium" on an hourly wage of $25.75, and "Fast" work on an hourly wage of $31.50. Other qualifications that apply to this table are on page 9.

*General Painting Costs*

|  | Labor SF per manhour | Material coverage SF/gallon | Material cost per gallon | Labor cost per 100 SF | Labor burden 100 SF | Material cost per 100 SF | Overhead per 100 SF | Profit per 100 SF | Total price per 100 SF |
|---|---|---|---|---|---|---|---|---|---|

## Masonry, Concrete Masonry Units (CMU), rough, porous surface, spray

Masonry paint, water base, flat or gloss (material #31)
  Spray 1st coat

| | | | | | | | | | |
|---|---|---|---|---|---|---|---|---|---|
| Slow | 600 | 100 | 38.20 | 3.38 | 1.00 | 38.20 | 8.09 | 8.11 | 58.78 |
| Medium | 700 | 78 | 33.50 | 3.68 | 1.31 | 42.95 | 11.98 | 7.19 | 67.11 |
| Fast | 800 | 55 | 28.70 | 3.94 | 1.60 | 52.18 | 17.90 | 5.29 | 80.91 |

  Spray 2nd or additional coats

| | | | | | | | | | |
|---|---|---|---|---|---|---|---|---|---|
| Slow | 700 | 155 | 38.20 | 2.89 | .86 | 24.65 | 5.39 | 5.40 | 39.19 |
| Medium | 800 | 133 | 33.50 | 3.22 | 1.14 | 25.19 | 7.39 | 4.43 | 41.37 |
| Fast | 900 | 110 | 28.70 | 3.50 | 1.42 | 26.09 | 9.62 | 2.84 | 43.47 |

Masonry paint, oil base (material #32)
  Spray 1st coat

| | | | | | | | | | |
|---|---|---|---|---|---|---|---|---|---|
| Slow | 600 | 100 | 38.40 | 3.38 | 1.00 | 38.40 | 8.13 | 8.15 | 59.06 |
| Medium | 700 | 83 | 33.60 | 3.68 | 1.31 | 40.48 | 11.37 | 6.82 | 63.66 |
| Fast | 800 | 65 | 28.80 | 3.94 | 1.60 | 44.31 | 15.46 | 4.57 | 69.88 |

  Spray 2nd or additional coats

| | | | | | | | | | |
|---|---|---|---|---|---|---|---|---|---|
| Slow | 700 | 160 | 38.40 | 2.89 | .86 | 24.00 | 5.27 | 5.28 | 38.30 |
| Medium | 800 | 143 | 33.60 | 3.22 | 1.14 | 23.50 | 6.97 | 4.18 | 39.01 |
| Fast | 900 | 125 | 28.80 | 3.50 | 1.42 | 23.04 | 8.67 | 2.56 | 39.19 |

Epoxy coating, 2 part system, clear (material #51)
  Spray 1st coat

| | | | | | | | | | |
|---|---|---|---|---|---|---|---|---|---|
| Slow | 500 | 85 | 146.90 | 4.05 | 1.19 | 172.82 | 33.83 | 33.90 | 245.79 |
| Medium | 600 | 68 | 128.60 | 4.29 | 1.53 | 189.12 | 48.73 | 29.24 | 272.91 |
| Fast | 700 | 50 | 110.20 | 4.50 | 1.84 | 220.40 | 70.29 | 20.79 | 317.82 |

  Spray 2nd or additional coats

| | | | | | | | | | |
|---|---|---|---|---|---|---|---|---|---|
| Slow | 600 | 145 | 146.90 | 3.38 | 1.00 | 101.31 | 20.08 | 20.12 | 145.89 |
| Medium | 700 | 130 | 128.60 | 3.68 | 1.31 | 98.92 | 25.98 | 15.59 | 145.48 |
| Fast | 800 | 115 | 110.20 | 3.94 | 1.60 | 95.83 | 31.43 | 9.30 | 142.10 |

Waterproofing, clear hydro sealer, oil base (material #34)
  Spray 1st coat

| | | | | | | | | | |
|---|---|---|---|---|---|---|---|---|---|
| Slow | 500 | 60 | 40.60 | 4.05 | 1.19 | 67.67 | 13.85 | 13.88 | 100.64 |
| Medium | 700 | 50 | 35.50 | 3.68 | 1.31 | 71.00 | 19.00 | 11.40 | 106.39 |
| Fast | 900 | 40 | 30.40 | 3.50 | 1.42 | 76.00 | 25.09 | 7.42 | 113.43 |

  Spray 2nd or additional coats

| | | | | | | | | | |
|---|---|---|---|---|---|---|---|---|---|
| Slow | 600 | 90 | 40.60 | 3.38 | 1.00 | 45.11 | 9.40 | 9.42 | 68.31 |
| Medium | 800 | 75 | 35.50 | 3.22 | 1.14 | 47.33 | 12.92 | 7.75 | 72.36 |
| Fast | 1000 | 60 | 30.40 | 3.15 | 1.29 | 50.67 | 17.08 | 5.05 | 77.24 |

Use these figures for Concrete Masonry Units (CMU) such as split face, fluted, or slump block, whose surfaces are rough, porous or unfilled, with joints struck to average depth. The more porous the surface, the rougher the texture, the more time and material will be required. For heavy waterproofing applications, see Masonry under Industrial Painting Operations. "Slow" work is based on an hourly wage of $20.25, "Medium" on an hourly wage of $25.75, and "Fast" work on an hourly wage of $31.50. Other qualifications that apply to this table are on page 9.

## National Painting Cost Estimator

|  | Labor SF per manhour | Material coverage SF/gallon | Material cost per gallon | Labor cost per 100 SF | Labor burden 100 SF | Material cost per 100 SF | Overhead per 100 SF | Profit per 100 SF | Total price per 100 SF |
|---|---|---|---|---|---|---|---|---|---|
| **Masonry, Concrete Masonry Units (CMU), smooth-surface, brush** | | | | | | | | | |
| Masonry paint, water base, flat or gloss (material #31) | | | | | | | | | |
| Brush 1st coat | | | | | | | | | |
| Slow | 140 | 310 | 38.20 | 14.46 | 4.26 | 12.32 | 5.90 | 5.91 | 42.85 |
| Medium | 190 | 275 | 33.50 | 13.55 | 4.79 | 12.18 | 7.63 | 4.58 | 42.73 |
| Fast | 230 | 240 | 28.70 | 13.70 | 5.59 | 11.96 | 9.69 | 2.87 | 43.81 |
| Brush 2nd or additional coats | | | | | | | | | |
| Slow | 170 | 410 | 38.20 | 11.91 | 3.51 | 9.32 | 4.70 | 4.71 | 34.15 |
| Medium | 250 | 370 | 33.50 | 10.30 | 3.65 | 9.05 | 5.75 | 3.45 | 32.20 |
| Fast | 325 | 340 | 28.70 | 9.69 | 3.97 | 8.44 | 6.84 | 2.02 | 30.96 |
| Masonry paint, oil base (material #32) | | | | | | | | | |
| Brush 1st coat | | | | | | | | | |
| Slow | 140 | 350 | 38.40 | 14.46 | 4.26 | 10.97 | 5.64 | 5.65 | 40.98 |
| Medium | 190 | 320 | 33.60 | 13.55 | 4.79 | 10.50 | 7.21 | 4.33 | 40.38 |
| Fast | 230 | 290 | 28.80 | 13.70 | 5.59 | 9.93 | 9.06 | 2.68 | 40.96 |
| Brush 2nd or additional coats | | | | | | | | | |
| Slow | 170 | 450 | 38.40 | 11.91 | 3.51 | 8.53 | 4.55 | 4.56 | 33.06 |
| Medium | 250 | 420 | 33.60 | 10.30 | 3.65 | 8.00 | 5.49 | 3.29 | 30.73 |
| Fast | 325 | 390 | 28.80 | 9.69 | 3.97 | 7.38 | 6.52 | 1.93 | 29.49 |
| Epoxy coating, 2 part system clear (material #51) | | | | | | | | | |
| Brush 1st coat | | | | | | | | | |
| Slow | 120 | 325 | 146.90 | 16.88 | 4.96 | 45.20 | 12.74 | 12.77 | 92.55 |
| Medium | 160 | 295 | 128.60 | 16.09 | 5.70 | 43.59 | 16.35 | 9.81 | 91.54 |
| Fast | 200 | 265 | 110.20 | 15.75 | 6.43 | 41.58 | 19.77 | 5.85 | 89.38 |
| Brush 2nd or additional coats | | | | | | | | | |
| Slow | 150 | 425 | 146.90 | 13.50 | 3.99 | 34.56 | 9.89 | 9.91 | 71.85 |
| Medium | 225 | 395 | 128.60 | 11.44 | 4.04 | 32.56 | 12.01 | 7.21 | 67.26 |
| Fast | 300 | 365 | 110.20 | 10.50 | 4.27 | 30.19 | 13.94 | 4.12 | 63.02 |
| Waterproofing, clear hydro sealer, oil base (material #34) | | | | | | | | | |
| Brush 1st coat | | | | | | | | | |
| Slow | 150 | 100 | 40.60 | 13.50 | 3.99 | 40.60 | 11.04 | 11.06 | 80.19 |
| Medium | 175 | 88 | 35.50 | 14.71 | 5.20 | 40.34 | 15.07 | 9.04 | 84.36 |
| Fast | 200 | 75 | 30.40 | 15.75 | 6.43 | 40.53 | 19.44 | 5.75 | 87.90 |
| Brush 2nd or additional coats | | | | | | | | | |
| Slow | 230 | 140 | 40.60 | 8.80 | 2.61 | 29.00 | 7.68 | 7.69 | 55.78 |
| Medium | 275 | 120 | 35.50 | 9.36 | 3.33 | 29.58 | 10.56 | 6.34 | 59.17 |
| Fast | 295 | 100 | 30.40 | 10.68 | 4.35 | 30.40 | 14.09 | 4.17 | 63.69 |

Use these figures for Concrete Masonry Units (CMU) where the block surfaces are smooth with joints struck to average depth. For heavy waterproofing applications, see Masonry under Industrial Painting Operations. "Slow" work is based on an hourly wage of $20.25, "Medium" work on an hourly wage of $25.75, and "Fast" work on an hourly wage of $31.50. Other qualifications that apply to this table are on page 9.

*General Painting Costs*

|  | Labor SF per manhour | Material coverage SF/gallon | Material cost per gallon | Labor cost per 100 SF | Labor burden 100 SF | Material cost per 100 SF | Overhead per 100 SF | Profit per 100 SF | Total price per 100 SF |
|---|---|---|---|---|---|---|---|---|---|
| **Masonry, Concrete Masonry Units (CMU), smooth-surface, roll** | | | | | | | | | |
| Masonry paint, water base, flat or gloss (material #31) | | | | | | | | | |
| Roll 1st coat | | | | | | | | | |
| Slow | 300 | 240 | 38.20 | 6.75 | 1.98 | 15.92 | 4.69 | 4.70 | 34.04 |
| Medium | 350 | 228 | 33.50 | 7.36 | 2.61 | 14.69 | 6.17 | 3.70 | 34.53 |
| Fast | 390 | 215 | 28.70 | 8.08 | 3.27 | 13.35 | 7.67 | 2.27 | 34.64 |
| Roll 2nd or additional coats | | | | | | | | | |
| Slow | 350 | 325 | 38.20 | 5.79 | 1.71 | 11.75 | 3.66 | 3.67 | 26.58 |
| Medium | 400 | 313 | 33.50 | 6.44 | 2.28 | 10.70 | 4.86 | 2.91 | 27.19 |
| Fast | 450 | 300 | 28.70 | 7.00 | 2.85 | 9.57 | 6.02 | 1.78 | 27.22 |
| Masonry paint, oil base (material #32) | | | | | | | | | |
| Roll 1st coat | | | | | | | | | |
| Slow | 300 | 285 | 38.40 | 6.75 | 1.98 | 13.47 | 4.22 | 4.23 | 30.65 |
| Medium | 350 | 273 | 33.60 | 7.36 | 2.61 | 12.31 | 5.57 | 3.34 | 31.19 |
| Fast | 390 | 260 | 28.80 | 8.08 | 3.27 | 11.08 | 6.96 | 2.06 | 31.45 |
| Roll 2nd or additional coats | | | | | | | | | |
| Slow | 350 | 375 | 38.40 | 5.79 | 1.71 | 10.24 | 3.37 | 3.38 | 24.49 |
| Medium | 400 | 358 | 33.60 | 6.44 | 2.28 | 9.39 | 4.53 | 2.72 | 25.36 |
| Fast | 450 | 340 | 28.80 | 7.00 | 2.85 | 8.47 | 5.68 | 1.68 | 25.68 |
| Epoxy coating, 2 part system, clear (material #51) | | | | | | | | | |
| Roll 1st coat | | | | | | | | | |
| Slow | 275 | 265 | 146.90 | 7.36 | 2.18 | 55.43 | 12.34 | 12.37 | 89.68 |
| Medium | 325 | 253 | 128.60 | 7.92 | 2.82 | 50.83 | 15.39 | 9.23 | 86.19 |
| Fast | 375 | 240 | 110.20 | 8.40 | 3.44 | 45.92 | 17.90 | 5.30 | 80.96 |
| Roll 2nd or additional coats | | | | | | | | | |
| Slow | 325 | 355 | 146.90 | 6.23 | 1.85 | 41.38 | 9.40 | 9.42 | 68.28 |
| Medium | 375 | 340 | 128.60 | 6.87 | 2.44 | 37.82 | 11.78 | 7.07 | 65.98 |
| Fast | 425 | 325 | 110.20 | 7.41 | 3.01 | 33.91 | 13.75 | 4.07 | 62.15 |
| Waterproofing, clear hydro sealer, oil base (material #34) | | | | | | | | | |
| Roll 1st coat | | | | | | | | | |
| Slow | 170 | 110 | 40.60 | 11.91 | 3.51 | 36.91 | 9.94 | 9.96 | 72.23 |
| Medium | 200 | 95 | 35.50 | 12.88 | 4.56 | 37.37 | 13.70 | 8.22 | 76.73 |
| Fast | 245 | 80 | 30.40 | 12.86 | 5.23 | 38.00 | 17.39 | 5.15 | 78.63 |
| Roll 2nd or additional coats | | | | | | | | | |
| Slow | 275 | 150 | 40.60 | 7.36 | 2.18 | 27.07 | 6.95 | 6.97 | 50.53 |
| Medium | 300 | 125 | 35.50 | 8.58 | 3.03 | 28.40 | 10.01 | 6.00 | 56.02 |
| Fast | 325 | 100 | 30.40 | 9.69 | 3.97 | 30.40 | 13.65 | 4.04 | 61.75 |

Use these figures for Concrete Masonry Units (CMU) where the block surfaces are smooth with joints struck to average depth. For heavy waterproofing applications, see Masonry under Industrial Painting Operations. "Slow" work is based on an hourly wage of $20.25, "Medium" work on an hourly wage of $25.75, and "Fast" work on an hourly wage of $31.50. Other qualifications that apply to this table are on page 9.

*National Painting Cost Estimator*

|  | Labor SF per manhour | Material coverage SF/gallon | Material cost per gallon | Labor cost per 100 SF | Labor burden 100 SF | Material cost per 100 SF | Overhead per 100 SF | Profit per 100 SF | Total price per 100 SF |
|---|---|---|---|---|---|---|---|---|---|

## Masonry, Concrete Masonry Units (CMU), smooth-surface, spray

Masonry paint, water base, flat or gloss (material #31)
  Spray 1st coat

| | | | | | | | | | |
|---|---|---|---|---|---|---|---|---|---|
| Slow | 725 | 240 | 38.20 | 2.79 | .83 | 15.92 | 3.71 | 3.72 | 26.97 |
| Medium | 788 | 215 | 33.50 | 3.27 | 1.16 | 15.58 | 5.00 | 3.00 | 28.01 |
| Fast | 850 | 190 | 28.70 | 3.71 | 1.52 | 15.11 | 6.30 | 1.86 | 28.50 |

  Spray 2nd or additional coats

| | | | | | | | | | |
|---|---|---|---|---|---|---|---|---|---|
| Slow | 800 | 320 | 38.20 | 2.53 | .75 | 11.94 | 2.89 | 2.90 | 21.01 |
| Medium | 950 | 295 | 33.50 | 2.71 | .95 | 11.36 | 3.76 | 2.25 | 21.03 |
| Fast | 1100 | 270 | 28.70 | 2.86 | 1.18 | 10.63 | 4.54 | 1.34 | 20.55 |

Masonry paint, oil base (material #32)
  Spray 1st coat

| | | | | | | | | | |
|---|---|---|---|---|---|---|---|---|---|
| Slow | 725 | 280 | 38.40 | 2.79 | .83 | 13.71 | 3.29 | 3.30 | 23.92 |
| Medium | 788 | 255 | 33.60 | 3.27 | 1.16 | 13.18 | 4.40 | 2.64 | 24.65 |
| Fast | 850 | 230 | 28.80 | 3.71 | 1.52 | 12.52 | 5.50 | 1.63 | 24.88 |

  Spray 2nd or additional coats

| | | | | | | | | | |
|---|---|---|---|---|---|---|---|---|---|
| Slow | 800 | 345 | 38.40 | 2.53 | .75 | 11.13 | 2.74 | 2.74 | 19.89 |
| Medium | 950 | 328 | 33.60 | 2.71 | .95 | 10.24 | 3.48 | 2.09 | 19.47 |
| Fast | 1100 | 310 | 28.80 | 2.86 | 1.18 | 9.29 | 4.13 | 1.22 | 18.68 |

Epoxy coating, 2 part system clear (material #51)
  Spray 1st coat

| | | | | | | | | | |
|---|---|---|---|---|---|---|---|---|---|
| Slow | 675 | 255 | 146.90 | 3.00 | .88 | 57.61 | 11.69 | 11.71 | 84.89 |
| Medium | 738 | 238 | 128.60 | 3.49 | 1.25 | 54.03 | 14.69 | 8.81 | 82.27 |
| Fast | 800 | 220 | 110.20 | 3.94 | 1.60 | 50.09 | 17.25 | 5.10 | 77.98 |

  Spray 2nd or additional coats

| | | | | | | | | | |
|---|---|---|---|---|---|---|---|---|---|
| Slow | 750 | 325 | 146.90 | 2.70 | .79 | 45.20 | 9.25 | 9.27 | 67.21 |
| Medium | 900 | 308 | 128.60 | 2.86 | 1.01 | 41.75 | 11.41 | 6.84 | 63.87 |
| Fast | 1050 | 290 | 110.20 | 3.00 | 1.21 | 38.00 | 13.09 | 3.87 | 59.17 |

Waterproofing, clear hydro sealer, oil base (material #34)
  Spray 1st coat

| | | | | | | | | | |
|---|---|---|---|---|---|---|---|---|---|
| Slow | 500 | 75 | 40.60 | 4.05 | 1.19 | 54.13 | 11.28 | 11.30 | 81.95 |
| Medium | 750 | 63 | 35.50 | 3.43 | 1.21 | 56.35 | 15.25 | 9.15 | 85.39 |
| Fast | 900 | 50 | 30.40 | 3.50 | 1.42 | 60.80 | 20.38 | 6.03 | 92.13 |

  Spray 2nd or additional coats

| | | | | | | | | | |
|---|---|---|---|---|---|---|---|---|---|
| Slow | 600 | 100 | 40.60 | 3.38 | 1.00 | 40.60 | 8.55 | 8.56 | 62.09 |
| Medium | 800 | 88 | 35.50 | 3.22 | 1.14 | 40.34 | 11.18 | 6.71 | 62.59 |
| Fast | 1000 | 75 | 30.40 | 3.15 | 1.29 | 40.53 | 13.94 | 4.12 | 63.03 |

Use these figures for Concrete Masonry Units (CMU) where the block surfaces are smooth with joints struck to average depth. For heavy waterproofing applications, see Masonry under Industrial Painting Operations. "Slow" work is based on an hourly wage of $20.25, "Medium" work on an hourly wage of $25.75, and "Fast" work on an hourly wage of $31.50. Other qualifications that apply to this table are on page 9.

## General Painting Costs

|  | Labor SF per manhour | Material coverage SF/gallon | Material cost per gallon | Labor cost per 100 SF | Labor burden 100 SF | Material cost per 100 SF | Overhead per 100 SF | Profit per 100 SF | Total price per 100 SF |
|---|---|---|---|---|---|---|---|---|---|
| **Masonry, stone, marble or granite** | | | | | | | | | |
| Waterproof, clear hydro sealer, oil base (material #34) | | | | | | | | | |
| Spray 1st coat | | | | | | | | | |
| Slow | 600 | 220 | 40.60 | 3.38 | 1.00 | 18.45 | 4.34 | 4.35 | 31.52 |
| Medium | 700 | 200 | 35.50 | 3.68 | 1.31 | 17.75 | 5.68 | 3.41 | 31.83 |
| Fast | 800 | 180 | 30.40 | 3.94 | 1.60 | 16.89 | 6.96 | 2.06 | 31.45 |
| Spray 2nd coat | | | | | | | | | |
| Slow | 700 | 225 | 40.60 | 2.89 | .86 | 18.04 | 4.14 | 4.15 | 30.08 |
| Medium | 800 | 213 | 35.50 | 3.22 | 1.14 | 16.67 | 5.26 | 3.15 | 29.44 |
| Fast | 900 | 200 | 30.40 | 3.50 | 1.42 | 15.20 | 6.24 | 1.85 | 28.21 |

Use these figures for the cost to apply waterproof sealer on stone, marble or granite surfaces. "Slow" work is based on an hourly wage of $20.25, "Medium" work on an hourly wage of $25.75, and "Fast" work on an hourly wage of $31.50. Other qualifications that apply to this table are on page 9.

|  | Labor LF per manhour | Material coverage LF/gallon | Material cost per gallon | Labor cost per 100 LF | Labor burden 100 LF | Material cost per 100 LF | Overhead per 100 LF | Profit per 100 LF | Total price per 100 LF |
|---|---|---|---|---|---|---|---|---|---|
| **Molding, interior or exterior, paint grade, smooth-surface** | | | | | | | | | |
| Undercoat, water or oil base (material #3 or #4) | | | | | | | | | |
| Brush prime coat | | | | | | | | | |
| Slow | 135 | 700 | 37.45 | 15.00 | 4.43 | 5.35 | 4.71 | 4.72 | 34.21 |
| Medium | 205 | 600 | 32.75 | 12.56 | 4.46 | 5.46 | 5.62 | 3.37 | 31.47 |
| Fast | 275 | 500 | 28.15 | 11.45 | 4.69 | 5.63 | 6.74 | 1.99 | 30.50 |
| Split coat (1/2 undercoat + 1/2 enamel), water or oil base (material #3 and #9, or material #4 and #10) | | | | | | | | | |
| Brush 1st or additional finish coats | | | | | | | | | |
| Slow | 125 | 750 | 45.85 | 16.20 | 4.78 | 6.11 | 5.15 | 5.16 | 37.40 |
| Medium | 135 | 675 | 40.13 | 19.07 | 6.77 | 5.95 | 7.94 | 4.77 | 44.50 |
| Fast | 145 | 600 | 34.43 | 21.72 | 8.88 | 5.74 | 11.26 | 3.33 | 50.93 |
| Enamel, interior, water or oil base (material #9 or #10) | | | | | | | | | |
| Brush 1st finish coat | | | | | | | | | |
| Slow | 125 | 750 | 54.25 | 16.20 | 4.78 | 7.23 | 5.36 | 5.37 | 38.94 |
| Medium | 160 | 675 | 47.50 | 16.09 | 5.70 | 7.04 | 7.21 | 4.32 | 40.36 |
| Fast | 200 | 600 | 40.70 | 15.75 | 6.43 | 6.78 | 8.98 | 2.66 | 40.60 |
| Brush 2nd or additional finish coats | | | | | | | | | |
| Slow | 115 | 750 | 54.25 | 17.61 | 5.20 | 7.23 | 5.71 | 5.72 | 41.47 |
| Medium | 150 | 675 | 47.50 | 17.17 | 6.09 | 7.04 | 7.57 | 4.54 | 42.41 |
| Fast | 175 | 600 | 40.70 | 18.00 | 7.32 | 6.78 | 9.96 | 2.95 | 45.01 |

*National Painting Cost Estimator*

|  | Labor LF per manhour | Material coverage LF/gallon | Material cost per gallon | Labor cost per 100 LF | Labor burden 100 LF | Material cost per 100 LF | Overhead per 100 LF | Profit per 100 LF | Total price per 100 LF |
|---|---|---|---|---|---|---|---|---|---|
| **Enamel, exterior, water or oil base (material #24 or #25)** | | | | | | | | | |
| *Brush 1st finish coat* | | | | | | | | | |
| Slow | 125 | 750 | 53.55 | 16.20 | 4.78 | 7.14 | 5.34 | 5.35 | 38.81 |
| Medium | 160 | 675 | 46.90 | 16.09 | 5.70 | 6.95 | 7.19 | 4.31 | 40.24 |
| Fast | 200 | 600 | 40.15 | 15.75 | 6.43 | 6.69 | 8.95 | 2.65 | 40.47 |
| *Brush 2nd or additional finish coats* | | | | | | | | | |
| Slow | 115 | 750 | 53.55 | 17.61 | 5.20 | 7.14 | 5.69 | 5.70 | 41.34 |
| Medium | 150 | 675 | 46.90 | 17.17 | 6.09 | 6.95 | 7.55 | 4.53 | 42.29 |
| Fast | 175 | 600 | 40.15 | 18.00 | 7.32 | 6.69 | 9.93 | 2.94 | 44.88 |
| **Stipple finish** | | | | | | | | | |
| Slow | 80 | -- | -- | 25.31 | 7.47 | -- | 6.23 | 6.24 | 45.25 |
| Medium | 90 | -- | -- | 28.61 | 10.13 | -- | 9.69 | 5.81 | 54.24 |
| Fast | 100 | -- | -- | 31.50 | 12.85 | -- | 13.75 | 4.07 | 62.17 |
| **Glazing or mottling over enamel (material #16)** | | | | | | | | | |
| *Glaze & wipe, brush 1 coat* | | | | | | | | | |
| Slow | 55 | 950 | 71.00 | 36.82 | 10.85 | 7.47 | 10.48 | 10.50 | 76.12 |
| Medium | 65 | 900 | 62.10 | 39.62 | 14.01 | 6.90 | 15.14 | 9.08 | 84.75 |
| Fast | 75 | 850 | 53.30 | 42.00 | 17.12 | 6.27 | 20.28 | 6.00 | 91.67 |

Consider all trim to be at least 12" wide (even if it's much less than 12" wide) when calculating the area to be painted. Trim painted the same color as the wall or ceiling behind it may take no more time than painting the wall or ceiling itself. Use the slow rate when cutting-in is required to paint molding that's a different color from the surface behind the molding. "Slow" work is based on an hourly wage of $20.25, "Medium" work on an hourly wage of $25.75, and "Fast" work on an hourly wage of $31.50. Other qualifications that apply to this table are on page 9.

*General Painting Costs*

|  | Labor LF per manhour | Material coverage LF/gallon | Material cost per gallon | Labor cost per 100 LF | Labor burden 100 LF | Material cost per 100 LF | Overhead per 100 LF | Profit per 100 LF | Total price per 100 LF |
|---|---|---|---|---|---|---|---|---|---|

## Molding, interior, stain grade, smooth surface
### Stain, seal and 2 coat lacquer system (7 step process)
**STEP 1: Sand & putty;**

|  |  |  |  |  |  |  |  |  |  |
|---|---|---|---|---|---|---|---|---|---|
| Slow | 150 | -- | -- | 13.50 | 3.99 | -- | 3.32 | 3.33 | 24.14 |
| Medium | 175 | -- | -- | 14.71 | 5.20 | -- | 4.98 | 2.99 | 27.88 |
| Fast | 200 | -- | -- | 15.75 | 6.43 | -- | 6.88 | 2.03 | 31.09 |

**STEP 2 & 3: Wiping stain (material 11a) & wipe**

Brush 1 coat & wipe

|  |  |  |  |  |  |  |  |  |  |
|---|---|---|---|---|---|---|---|---|---|
| Slow | 150 | 550 | 51.30 | 13.50 | 3.99 | 9.33 | 5.09 | 5.10 | 37.01 |
| Medium | 175 | 525 | 44.90 | 14.71 | 5.20 | 8.55 | 7.12 | 4.27 | 39.85 |
| Fast | 200 | 500 | 38.50 | 15.75 | 6.43 | 7.70 | 9.26 | 2.74 | 41.88 |

Spray 1 coat & wipe

|  |  |  |  |  |  |  |  |  |  |
|---|---|---|---|---|---|---|---|---|---|
| Slow | 400 | 250 | 51.30 | 5.06 | 1.50 | 20.52 | 5.14 | 5.15 | 37.37 |
| Medium | 425 | 225 | 44.90 | 6.06 | 2.13 | 19.96 | 7.04 | 4.23 | 39.42 |
| Fast | 450 | 200 | 38.50 | 7.00 | 2.85 | 19.25 | 9.02 | 2.67 | 40.79 |

**STEP 4 & 5: Sanding sealer (material 11b) & light sand**

Brush 1 coat

|  |  |  |  |  |  |  |  |  |  |
|---|---|---|---|---|---|---|---|---|---|
| Slow | 260 | 575 | 41.50 | 7.79 | 2.30 | 7.22 | 3.29 | 3.30 | 23.90 |
| Medium | 280 | 563 | 36.30 | 9.20 | 3.25 | 6.45 | 4.73 | 2.84 | 26.47 |
| Fast | 300 | 550 | 31.10 | 10.50 | 4.27 | 5.65 | 6.33 | 1.87 | 28.62 |

Spray 1 coat

|  |  |  |  |  |  |  |  |  |  |
|---|---|---|---|---|---|---|---|---|---|
| Slow | 450 | 250 | 41.50 | 4.50 | 1.32 | 16.60 | 4.26 | 4.27 | 30.95 |
| Medium | 475 | 225 | 36.30 | 5.42 | 1.94 | 16.13 | 5.87 | 3.52 | 32.88 |
| Fast | 500 | 200 | 31.10 | 6.30 | 2.57 | 15.55 | 7.57 | 2.24 | 34.23 |

**STEP 6 & 7: Lacquer (material 11c), 2 coats**

Brush 1st coat

|  |  |  |  |  |  |  |  |  |  |
|---|---|---|---|---|---|---|---|---|---|
| Slow | 200 | 300 | 45.90 | 10.13 | 2.98 | 15.30 | 5.40 | 5.41 | 39.22 |
| Medium | 275 | 288 | 40.10 | 9.36 | 3.33 | 13.92 | 6.65 | 3.99 | 37.25 |
| Fast | 350 | 275 | 34.40 | 9.00 | 3.68 | 12.51 | 7.81 | 2.31 | 35.31 |

Brush 2nd coat

|  |  |  |  |  |  |  |  |  |  |
|---|---|---|---|---|---|---|---|---|---|
| Slow | 225 | 375 | 45.90 | 9.00 | 2.64 | 12.24 | 4.54 | 4.55 | 32.97 |
| Medium | 300 | 350 | 40.10 | 8.58 | 3.03 | 11.46 | 5.77 | 3.46 | 32.30 |
| Fast | 375 | 325 | 34.40 | 8.40 | 3.44 | 10.58 | 6.95 | 2.06 | 31.43 |

Spray 1st coat

|  |  |  |  |  |  |  |  |  |  |
|---|---|---|---|---|---|---|---|---|---|
| Slow | 250 | 200 | 45.90 | 8.10 | 2.39 | 22.95 | 6.35 | 6.37 | 46.16 |
| Medium | 350 | 188 | 40.10 | 7.36 | 2.61 | 21.33 | 7.83 | 4.70 | 43.83 |
| Fast | 450 | 175 | 34.40 | 7.00 | 2.85 | 19.66 | 9.15 | 2.71 | 41.37 |

Spray 2nd coat

|  |  |  |  |  |  |  |  |  |  |
|---|---|---|---|---|---|---|---|---|---|
| Slow | 300 | 250 | 45.90 | 6.75 | 1.98 | 18.36 | 5.15 | 5.16 | 37.40 |
| Medium | 388 | 225 | 40.10 | 6.64 | 2.36 | 17.82 | 6.70 | 4.02 | 37.54 |
| Fast | 475 | 200 | 34.40 | 6.63 | 2.73 | 17.20 | 8.23 | 2.43 | 37.22 |

*National Painting Cost Estimator*

|  | Labor LF per manhour | Material coverage LF/gallon | Material cost per gallon | Labor cost per 100 LF | Labor burden 100 LF | Material cost per 100 LF | Overhead per 100 LF | Profit per 100 LF | Total price per 100 LF |
|---|---|---|---|---|---|---|---|---|---|
| **Complete 7 step process, stain, seal & 2 coat lacquer system (material #11)** | | | | | | | | | |
| Brush all coats | | | | | | | | | |
| Slow | 50 | 60 | 46.10 | 40.50 | 11.94 | 76.83 | 24.56 | 24.61 | 178.44 |
| Medium | 75 | 50 | 40.40 | 34.33 | 12.15 | 80.80 | 31.82 | 19.09 | 178.19 |
| Fast | 100 | 40 | 34.60 | 31.50 | 12.85 | 86.50 | 40.56 | 12.00 | 183.41 |
| Spray all coats | | | | | | | | | |
| Slow | 100 | 40 | 45.90 | 20.25 | 5.97 | 114.75 | 26.78 | 26.84 | 194.59 |
| Medium | 150 | 30 | 40.10 | 17.17 | 6.09 | 133.67 | 39.23 | 23.54 | 219.70 |
| Fast | 200 | 20 | 34.40 | 15.75 | 6.43 | 172.00 | 60.20 | 17.81 | 272.19 |

These figures are based on linear feet for all molding up to 12" wide. For estimating purposes, consider all molding and trim to be at least 12" wide (even if it's much less than 12") when calculating the area to be finished. The spray figures are based on finishing large quantities of molding in an area set up for spray painting before it's installed. Use the brush figures for small quantities. Use the fast brush rate for molding that's finished before it's installed. If the molding is attached and has to be masked off, use the slow brush figures. Masking time is not included. See the Preparation Operations tables for masking rates. Trim stained the same color as the surface behind it will take no more time than staining the wall itself. "Slow" work is based on an hourly wage of $20.25, "Medium" work on an hourly wage of $25.75, and "Fast" work on an hourly wage of $31.50. Other qualifications that apply to this table are on page 9.

*General Painting Costs*

|  | Labor LF per manhour | Material coverage LF/gallon | Material cost per gallon | Labor cost per 100 LF | Labor burden 100 LF | Material cost per 100 LF | Overhead per 100 LF | Profit per 100 LF | Total price per 100 LF |
|---|---|---|---|---|---|---|---|---|---|
| **Molding, interior or exterior, stain grade, smooth surface** | | | | | | | | | |
| Stain, fill and shellac or varnish | | | | | | | | | |
|   Wiping stain (material #30a) & fill | | | | | | | | | |
|     Brush each coat | | | | | | | | | |
|       Slow | 80 | 550 | 53.40 | 25.31 | 7.47 | 9.71 | 8.07 | 8.09 | 58.65 |
|       Medium | 130 | 525 | 47.60 | 19.81 | 7.01 | 9.07 | 8.97 | 5.38 | 50.24 |
|       Fast | 180 | 500 | 40.80 | 17.50 | 7.16 | 8.16 | 10.17 | 3.01 | 46.00 |
|   Shellac, clear (material #12) | | | | | | | | | |
|     Brush each coat | | | | | | | | | |
|       Slow | 180 | 550 | 73.10 | 11.25 | 3.33 | 13.29 | 5.29 | 5.30 | 38.46 |
|       Medium | 230 | 525 | 63.90 | 11.20 | 3.97 | 12.17 | 6.83 | 4.10 | 38.27 |
|       Fast | 280 | 500 | 54.80 | 11.25 | 4.58 | 10.96 | 8.31 | 2.46 | 37.56 |
|   Varnish, gloss (material #30c) | | | | | | | | | |
|     Brush each coat | | | | | | | | | |
|       Slow | 115 | 550 | 81.70 | 17.61 | 5.20 | 14.85 | 7.15 | 7.17 | 51.98 |
|       Medium | 150 | 525 | 71.50 | 17.17 | 6.09 | 13.62 | 9.22 | 5.53 | 51.63 |
|       Fast | 210 | 500 | 61.30 | 15.00 | 6.11 | 12.26 | 10.35 | 3.06 | 46.78 |
|   Varnish, flat (material #30c) | | | | | | | | | |
|     Brush each coat | | | | | | | | | |
|       Slow | 125 | 550 | 81.70 | 16.20 | 4.78 | 14.85 | 6.81 | 6.82 | 49.46 |
|       Medium | 160 | 525 | 71.50 | 16.09 | 5.70 | 13.62 | 8.85 | 5.31 | 49.57 |
|       Fast | 220 | 500 | 61.30 | 14.32 | 5.86 | 12.26 | 10.05 | 2.97 | 45.46 |
| Penetrating stain wax (material #14) & wipe | | | | | | | | | |
|   Stain, brush each coat & wipe | | | | | | | | | |
|     Slow | 225 | 500 | 46.70 | 9.00 | 2.64 | 9.34 | 3.99 | 4.00 | 28.97 |
|     Medium | 275 | 450 | 40.90 | 9.36 | 3.33 | 9.09 | 5.44 | 3.26 | 30.48 |
|     Fast | 325 | 400 | 35.00 | 9.69 | 3.97 | 8.75 | 6.94 | 2.05 | 31.40 |
| Polish added coats of wax | | | | | | | | | |
|   Slow | 150 | -- | -- | 13.50 | 3.99 | -- | 3.32 | 3.33 | 24.14 |
|   Medium | 175 | -- | -- | 14.71 | 5.20 | -- | 4.98 | 2.99 | 27.88 |
|   Fast | 200 | -- | -- | 15.75 | 6.43 | -- | 6.88 | 2.03 | 31.09 |

*National Painting Cost Estimator*

|  | Labor LF per manhour | Material coverage LF/gallon | Material cost per gallon | Labor cost per 100 LF | Labor burden 100 LF | Material cost per 100 LF | Overhead per 100 LF | Profit per 100 LF | Total price per 100 LF |
|---|---|---|---|---|---|---|---|---|---|
| Steel wool buff by hand | | | | | | | | | |
| Slow | 100 | -- | -- | 20.25 | 5.97 | -- | 4.98 | 4.99 | 36.19 |
| Medium | 110 | -- | -- | 23.41 | 8.29 | -- | 7.93 | 4.76 | 44.39 |
| Fast | 125 | -- | -- | 25.20 | 10.28 | -- | 11.00 | 3.25 | 49.73 |
| Wax application & polish, hand apply 1 coat | | | | | | | | | |
| Slow | 100 | -- | -- | 20.25 | 5.97 | -- | 4.98 | 4.99 | 36.19 |
| Medium | 110 | -- | -- | 23.41 | 8.29 | -- | 7.93 | 4.76 | 44.39 |
| Fast | 125 | -- | -- | 25.20 | 10.28 | -- | 11.00 | 3.25 | 49.73 |

These figures are based on linear feet for all molding up to 12" wide. For estimating purposes, consider all molding and trim to be at least 12" wide (even if it's much less than 12") when calculating the area to be finished. The spray figures are based on finishing large quantities of molding in an area set up for spray painting before it's installed. Use the brush figures for small quantities. Use the fast brush rate for molding that's finished before it's installed. If the molding is attached and has to be masked off, use the slow brush figures. Masking time is not included. See the Preparation Operations tables for masking rates. Trim stained the same color as the surface behind it will take no more time than staining the wall itself. "Slow" work is based on an hourly wage of $20.25, "Medium" work on an hourly wage of $25.75, and "Fast" work on an hourly wage of $31.50. Other qualifications that apply to this table are on page 9.

*General Painting Costs*

|  | Boxed eaves | | Exposed rafters | |
|---|---|---|---|---|
|  | One color | Two color | One color | Two color |

## Overhang difficulty factors, eaves, cornice

| | | | | |
|---|---|---|---|---|
| One story, repaint | | | | |
|   Standard | 1.5 | 2.0 | 2.0 | 2.5 |
|   Ornamental | -- | -- | 2.5 | 3.0 |
| One story, new construction | -- | 1.5 | 1.5 | 2.0 |
| Two story, with scaffolding, repaint | | | | |
|   Standard | 1.5 | 2.0 | 2.0 | 2.5 |
|   Ornamental | -- | -- | 2.5 | 3.0 |
| Two story, without scaffolding, repaint | | | | |
|   Standard | 3.0 | 3.5 | 3.5 | 4.0 |
|   Ornamental | -- | -- | 4.0 | 4.5 |
| Two story, new construction | | | | |
|   With scaffolding | -- | 1.5 | 1.5 | 2.0 |
|   No scaffolding | 2.0 | 2.5 | 2.5 | 3.0 |

Before using the figures in the tables for overhangs, apply these difficulty factors to the surface area (length times width) to be painted. Multiply the factor in this table by the overall surface area of the overhang. This allows for slower work on high eaves and the extra time needed to paint rafter tails. This table adjusts for the kind of eaves, the eave height, the number of colors used, and whether scaffolding is available and erected on site. Boxed eaves have plywood covering the rafter tails.

| | Labor SF per manhour | Material coverage SF/gallon | Material cost per gallon | Labor cost per 100 SF | Labor burden 100 SF | Material cost per 100 SF | Overhead per 100 SF | Profit per 100 SF | Total price per 100 SF |
|---|---|---|---|---|---|---|---|---|---|

## Overhang at carports, large continuous surface areas

Solid body or semi-transparent stain, water or oil base (material #18 or #19 or #20 or #21)

| | | | | | | | | | |
|---|---|---|---|---|---|---|---|---|---|
| Spray 1st coat | | | | | | | | | |
|   Slow | 550 | 95 | 48.83 | 3.68 | 1.09 | 51.40 | 10.67 | 10.69 | 77.53 |
|   Medium | 600 | 90 | 42.73 | 4.29 | 1.53 | 47.48 | 13.32 | 7.99 | 74.61 |
|   Fast | 650 | 85 | 36.60 | 4.85 | 1.98 | 43.06 | 15.47 | 4.58 | 69.94 |
| Spray 2nd coat | | | | | | | | | |
|   Slow | 600 | 175 | 48.83 | 3.38 | 1.00 | 27.90 | 6.13 | 6.15 | 44.56 |
|   Medium | 650 | 163 | 42.73 | 3.96 | 1.41 | 26.21 | 7.89 | 4.74 | 44.21 |
|   Fast | 700 | 150 | 36.60 | 4.50 | 1.84 | 24.40 | 9.53 | 2.82 | 43.09 |
| Spray 3rd or additional coats | | | | | | | | | |
|   Slow | 650 | 225 | 48.83 | 3.12 | .92 | 21.70 | 4.89 | 4.90 | 35.53 |
|   Medium | 700 | 213 | 42.73 | 3.68 | 1.31 | 20.06 | 6.26 | 3.76 | 35.07 |
|   Fast | 750 | 200 | 36.60 | 4.20 | 1.70 | 18.30 | 7.51 | 2.22 | 33.93 |

"Slow" work is based on an hourly wage of $20.25, "Medium" work on an hourly wage of $25.75, and "Fast" work on an hourly wage of $31.50. Other qualifications that apply to this table are on page 9.

*National Painting Cost Estimator*

|  | Labor SF per manhour | Material coverage SF/gallon | Material cost per gallon | Labor cost per 100 SF | Labor burden 100 SF | Material cost per 100 SF | Overhead per 100 SF | Profit per 100 SF | Total price per 100 SF |
|---|---|---|---|---|---|---|---|---|---|
| **Overhang at eaves or rake, widths up to 2.5 feet** | | | | | | | | | |
| Solid body stain, water or oil base (material #18 or #19) | | | | | | | | | |
| Roll & Brush 1st coat | | | | | | | | | |
| Slow | 95 | 200 | 49.55 | 21.32 | 6.29 | 24.78 | 9.95 | 9.97 | 72.31 |
| Medium | 125 | 185 | 43.35 | 20.60 | 7.30 | 23.43 | 12.83 | 7.70 | 71.86 |
| Fast | 150 | 170 | 37.15 | 21.00 | 8.58 | 21.85 | 15.94 | 4.72 | 72.09 |
| Roll & Brush 2nd coat | | | | | | | | | |
| Slow | 140 | 260 | 49.55 | 14.46 | 4.26 | 19.06 | 7.18 | 7.20 | 52.16 |
| Medium | 185 | 240 | 43.35 | 13.92 | 4.94 | 18.06 | 9.23 | 5.54 | 51.69 |
| Fast | 220 | 220 | 37.15 | 14.32 | 5.86 | 16.89 | 11.49 | 3.40 | 51.96 |
| Roll & Brush 3rd or additional coats | | | | | | | | | |
| Slow | 170 | 295 | 49.55 | 11.91 | 3.51 | 16.80 | 6.12 | 6.13 | 44.47 |
| Medium | 225 | 270 | 43.35 | 11.44 | 4.04 | 16.06 | 7.89 | 4.73 | 44.16 |
| Fast | 275 | 245 | 37.15 | 11.45 | 4.69 | 15.16 | 9.70 | 2.87 | 43.87 |
| Solid body stain or semi-transparent stain, water or oil base (material #18 or #19 or #20 or #21) | | | | | | | | | |
| Spray 1st coat | | | | | | | | | |
| Slow | 300 | 150 | 48.83 | 6.75 | 1.98 | 32.55 | 7.85 | 7.86 | 56.99 |
| Medium | 350 | 125 | 42.73 | 7.36 | 2.61 | 34.18 | 11.04 | 6.62 | 61.81 |
| Fast | 400 | 100 | 36.60 | 7.88 | 3.21 | 36.60 | 14.79 | 4.37 | 66.85 |
| Spray 2nd coat | | | | | | | | | |
| Slow | 375 | 175 | 48.83 | 5.40 | 1.60 | 27.90 | 6.63 | 6.64 | 48.17 |
| Medium | 450 | 163 | 42.73 | 5.72 | 2.02 | 26.21 | 8.49 | 5.09 | 47.53 |
| Fast | 540 | 150 | 36.60 | 5.83 | 2.37 | 24.40 | 10.11 | 2.99 | 45.70 |
| Spray 3rd or additional coats | | | | | | | | | |
| Slow | 450 | 225 | 48.83 | 4.50 | 1.32 | 21.70 | 5.23 | 5.24 | 37.99 |
| Medium | 525 | 213 | 42.73 | 4.90 | 1.73 | 20.06 | 6.67 | 4.00 | 37.36 |
| Fast | 600 | 200 | 36.60 | 5.25 | 2.16 | 18.30 | 7.96 | 2.36 | 36.03 |

Use this table after multiplying the overall area (length times width) by the difficulty factor listed under Overhang, difficulty factor. Remember to ADD preparation time for masking, caulking, sanding, waterblasting, etc. "Slow" work is based on an hourly wage of $20.25, "Medium" work on an hourly wage of $25.75, and "Fast" work on an hourly wage of $31.50. Other qualifications that apply to this table are on page 9.

*General Painting Costs*

|  | Labor SF per manhour | Material coverage SF/gallon | Material cost per gallon | Labor cost per 100 SF | Labor burden 100 SF | Material cost per 100 SF | Overhead per 100 SF | Profit per 100 SF | Total price per 100 SF |
|---|---|---|---|---|---|---|---|---|---|

## Overhang at entries or decks, widths greater than 2.5 feet
Solid body stain, water or oil base (material #18 or #19)
  Roll & Brush 1st coat

| | | | | | | | | | |
|---|---|---|---|---|---|---|---|---|---|
| Slow | 125 | 225 | 49.55 | 16.20 | 4.78 | 22.02 | 8.17 | 8.19 | 59.36 |
| Medium | 180 | 210 | 43.35 | 14.31 | 5.08 | 20.64 | 10.01 | 6.00 | 56.04 |
| Fast | 225 | 195 | 37.15 | 14.00 | 5.69 | 19.05 | 12.02 | 3.55 | 54.31 |

  Roll & Brush 2nd coat

| | | | | | | | | | |
|---|---|---|---|---|---|---|---|---|---|
| Slow | 170 | 295 | 49.55 | 11.91 | 3.51 | 16.80 | 6.12 | 6.13 | 44.47 |
| Medium | 225 | 275 | 43.35 | 11.44 | 4.04 | 15.76 | 7.81 | 4.69 | 43.74 |
| Fast | 275 | 255 | 37.15 | 11.45 | 4.69 | 14.57 | 9.51 | 2.81 | 43.03 |

  Roll & Brush 3rd or additional coats

| | | | | | | | | | |
|---|---|---|---|---|---|---|---|---|---|
| Slow | 210 | 340 | 49.55 | 9.64 | 2.84 | 14.57 | 5.14 | 5.15 | 37.34 |
| Medium | 280 | 315 | 43.35 | 9.20 | 3.25 | 13.76 | 6.56 | 3.93 | 36.70 |
| Fast | 345 | 290 | 37.15 | 9.13 | 3.73 | 12.81 | 7.96 | 2.35 | 35.98 |

Solid body stain or semi-transparent stain, water or oil base (material #18 or #19 or #20 or #21)
  Spray 1st coat

| | | | | | | | | | |
|---|---|---|---|---|---|---|---|---|---|
| Slow | 400 | 150 | 48.83 | 5.06 | 1.50 | 32.55 | 7.43 | 7.44 | 53.98 |
| Medium | 463 | 125 | 42.73 | 5.56 | 1.97 | 34.18 | 10.43 | 6.26 | 58.40 |
| Fast | 525 | 100 | 36.60 | 6.00 | 2.43 | 36.60 | 13.97 | 4.13 | 63.13 |

  Spray 2nd coat

| | | | | | | | | | |
|---|---|---|---|---|---|---|---|---|---|
| Slow | 450 | 175 | 48.83 | 4.50 | 1.32 | 27.90 | 6.41 | 6.42 | 46.55 |
| Medium | 550 | 163 | 42.73 | 4.68 | 1.67 | 26.21 | 8.14 | 4.88 | 45.58 |
| Fast | 650 | 150 | 36.60 | 4.85 | 1.98 | 24.40 | 9.68 | 2.86 | 43.77 |

  Spray 3rd or additional coats

| | | | | | | | | | |
|---|---|---|---|---|---|---|---|---|---|
| Slow | 550 | 225 | 48.83 | 3.68 | 1.09 | 21.70 | 5.03 | 5.04 | 36.54 |
| Medium | 625 | 213 | 42.73 | 4.12 | 1.46 | 20.06 | 6.41 | 3.85 | 35.90 |
| Fast | 700 | 200 | 36.60 | 4.50 | 1.84 | 18.30 | 7.64 | 2.26 | 34.54 |

Use this table after multiplying the overall area (length times width) by the difficulty factor listed under Overhang, difficulty factor. Remember to ADD preparation time for masking, caulking, sanding, waterblasting, etc. "Slow" work is based on an hourly wage of $20.25, "Medium" work on an hourly wage of $25.75, and "Fast" work on an hourly wage of $31.50. Other qualifications that apply to this table are on page 9.

National Painting Cost Estimator

|  | Labor LF per manhour | Material coverage LF/gallon | Material cost per gallon | Labor cost per 100 LF | Labor burden 100 LF | Material cost per 100 LF | Overhead per 100 LF | Profit per 100 LF | Total price per 100 LF |
|---|---|---|---|---|---|---|---|---|---|

### Pass-through shelves, wood top & wrought iron support
Metal primer, rust inhibitor, clean metal (material #35)
  Brush 1st coat

| | | | | | | | | | |
|---|---|---|---|---|---|---|---|---|---|
| Slow | 30 | 125 | 59.70 | 67.50 | 19.89 | 47.76 | 25.68 | 25.74 | 186.57 |
| Medium | 35 | 113 | 52.20 | 73.57 | 26.05 | 46.19 | 36.45 | 21.87 | 204.13 |
| Fast | 40 | 100 | 44.80 | 78.75 | 32.13 | 44.80 | 48.26 | 14.28 | 218.22 |

Metal finish - synthetic enamel (colors except orange/red) (material #38)
  Brush 1st coat

| | | | | | | | | | |
|---|---|---|---|---|---|---|---|---|---|
| Slow | 30 | 125 | 65.20 | 67.50 | 19.89 | 52.16 | 26.52 | 26.57 | 192.64 |
| Medium | 35 | 113 | 57.00 | 73.57 | 26.05 | 50.44 | 37.51 | 22.51 | 210.08 |
| Fast | 40 | 100 | 48.90 | 78.75 | 32.13 | 48.90 | 49.53 | 14.65 | 223.96 |

Use these figures to estimate pass-through shelves which are approximately 12" wide and 3'0" long with a wood top and wrought iron supports. The *rule-of-thumb* minimum time and material is .2 hours and $1.00 for material per shelf. A two-coat system using oil based material is recommended for any metal surface. Although water based material is often used, it may cause oxidation, corrosion and rust. One coat of oil based, solid body stain is often used on exterior metal, but it may crack, peel or chip without the proper prime coat application. "Slow" work is based on an hourly wage of $20.25, "Medium" work on an hourly wage of $25.75, and "Fast" work on an hourly wage of $31.50. Other qualifications that apply to this table are on page 9.

|  | Labor LF per manhour | Material coverage LF/gallon | Material cost per gallon | Labor cost per 100 LF | Labor burden 100 LF | Material cost per 100 LF | Overhead per 100 LF | Profit per 100 LF | Total price per 100 LF |
|---|---|---|---|---|---|---|---|---|---|

### Plant-on trim, exterior, 2" x 2" to 2" x 4" wood
2" x 2" to 2" x 4" rough sawn or resawn wood
  Solid body or semi-transparent stain, water base (material #18 or #20)
    Roll & brush 1st coat

| | | | | | | | | | |
|---|---|---|---|---|---|---|---|---|---|
| Slow | 80 | 310 | 46.25 | 25.31 | 7.47 | 14.92 | 9.06 | 9.08 | 65.84 |
| Medium | 100 | 275 | 40.50 | 25.75 | 9.12 | 14.73 | 12.40 | 7.44 | 69.44 |
| Fast | 120 | 240 | 34.70 | 26.25 | 10.69 | 14.46 | 15.94 | 4.72 | 72.06 |

    Roll & brush 2nd coat

| | | | | | | | | | |
|---|---|---|---|---|---|---|---|---|---|
| Slow | 90 | 350 | 46.25 | 22.50 | 6.63 | 13.21 | 8.05 | 8.06 | 58.45 |
| Medium | 120 | 325 | 40.50 | 21.46 | 7.59 | 12.46 | 10.38 | 6.23 | 58.12 |
| Fast | 150 | 300 | 34.70 | 21.00 | 8.58 | 11.57 | 12.75 | 3.77 | 57.67 |

    Roll & brush 3rd or additional coats

| | | | | | | | | | |
|---|---|---|---|---|---|---|---|---|---|
| Slow | 100 | 375 | 46.25 | 20.25 | 5.97 | 12.33 | 7.32 | 7.34 | 53.21 |
| Medium | 140 | 350 | 40.50 | 18.39 | 6.51 | 11.57 | 9.12 | 5.47 | 51.06 |
| Fast | 180 | 325 | 34.70 | 17.50 | 7.16 | 10.68 | 10.95 | 3.24 | 49.53 |

  Solid body or semi-transparent stain, oil base (material #19 or #21)
    Roll & brush 1st coat

| | | | | | | | | | |
|---|---|---|---|---|---|---|---|---|---|
| Slow | 95 | 400 | 51.40 | 21.32 | 6.29 | 12.85 | 7.69 | 7.70 | 55.85 |
| Medium | 115 | 365 | 44.95 | 22.39 | 7.95 | 12.32 | 10.66 | 6.40 | 59.72 |
| Fast | 135 | 330 | 38.50 | 23.33 | 9.53 | 11.67 | 13.80 | 4.08 | 62.41 |

*General Painting Costs*

|  | Labor LF per manhour | Material coverage LF/gallon | Material cost per gallon | Labor cost per 100 LF | Labor burden 100 LF | Material cost per 100 LF | Overhead per 100 LF | Profit per 100 LF | Total price per 100 LF |
|---|---|---|---|---|---|---|---|---|---|
| **Roll & brush 2nd coat** | | | | | | | | | |
| Slow | 105 | 475 | 51.40 | 19.29 | 5.67 | 10.82 | 6.80 | 6.82 | 49.40 |
| Medium | 135 | 438 | 44.95 | 19.07 | 6.77 | 10.26 | 9.02 | 5.41 | 50.53 |
| Fast | 165 | 400 | 38.50 | 19.09 | 7.79 | 9.63 | 11.32 | 3.35 | 51.18 |
| **Roll & brush 3rd or additional coats** | | | | | | | | | |
| Slow | 115 | 500 | 51.40 | 17.61 | 5.20 | 10.28 | 6.29 | 6.30 | 45.68 |
| Medium | 155 | 463 | 44.95 | 16.61 | 5.88 | 9.71 | 8.05 | 4.83 | 45.08 |
| Fast | 195 | 425 | 38.50 | 16.15 | 6.60 | 9.06 | 9.86 | 2.92 | 44.59 |
| **Varnish, flat or gloss (material #30c)** | | | | | | | | | |
| **Roll & brush 1st coat** | | | | | | | | | |
| Slow | 70 | 270 | 52.00 | 28.93 | 8.54 | 19.26 | 10.78 | 10.80 | 78.31 |
| Medium | 90 | 255 | 45.50 | 28.61 | 10.13 | 17.84 | 14.15 | 8.49 | 79.22 |
| Fast | 110 | 240 | 39.00 | 28.64 | 11.67 | 16.25 | 17.54 | 5.19 | 79.29 |
| **Roll & brush 2nd coat** | | | | | | | | | |
| Slow | 80 | 330 | 52.00 | 25.31 | 7.47 | 15.76 | 9.22 | 9.24 | 67.00 |
| Medium | 110 | 315 | 45.50 | 23.41 | 8.29 | 14.44 | 11.54 | 6.92 | 64.60 |
| Fast | 140 | 300 | 39.00 | 22.50 | 9.17 | 13.00 | 13.85 | 4.10 | 62.62 |
| **Roll & brush 3rd or additional coats** | | | | | | | | | |
| Slow | 90 | 350 | 52.00 | 22.50 | 6.63 | 14.86 | 8.36 | 8.38 | 60.73 |
| Medium | 130 | 335 | 45.50 | 19.81 | 7.01 | 13.58 | 10.10 | 6.06 | 56.56 |
| Fast | 170 | 320 | 39.00 | 18.53 | 7.55 | 12.19 | 11.87 | 3.51 | 53.65 |

Don't add additional time for plant-on trim if it's painted with the same coating as the adjacent siding. For heights above 8 feet, use the High Time Difficulty Factors on page 139. Use slow rates when cutting-in or masking adjacent surfaces. ADD preparation time for masking adjacent surfaces or protecting windows. Use fast rates when plant-on trim is finished before it's installed or on new construction projects where a prime coat can be sprayed prior to stucco color coat application. "Slow" work is based on an hourly wage of $20.25, "Medium" work on an hourly wage of $25.75, and "Fast" work on an hourly wage of $31.50. Other qualifications that apply to this table are on page 9.

## Plant-on trim, exterior, 2" x 6" to 2" x 8" wood

2" x 6" to 2" x 8" rough sawn or resawn wood

|  | Labor LF per manhour | Material coverage LF/gallon | Material cost per gallon | Labor cost per 100 LF | Labor burden 100 LF | Material cost per 100 LF | Overhead per 100 LF | Profit per 100 LF | Total price per 100 LF |
|---|---|---|---|---|---|---|---|---|---|
| **Solid body or semi-transparent stain, water base (material #18 or #20)** | | | | | | | | | |
| *Roll & brush 1st coat* | | | | | | | | | |
| Slow | 70 | 210 | 46.25 | 28.93 | 8.54 | 22.02 | 11.30 | 11.32 | 82.11 |
| Medium | 85 | 175 | 40.50 | 30.29 | 10.72 | 23.14 | 16.04 | 9.62 | 89.81 |
| Fast | 100 | 140 | 34.70 | 31.50 | 12.85 | 24.79 | 21.43 | 6.34 | 96.91 |
| *Roll & brush 2nd coat* | | | | | | | | | |
| Slow | 80 | 250 | 46.25 | 25.31 | 7.47 | 18.50 | 9.74 | 9.76 | 70.78 |
| Medium | 110 | 225 | 40.50 | 23.41 | 8.29 | 18.00 | 12.43 | 7.46 | 69.59 |
| Fast | 140 | 200 | 34.70 | 22.50 | 9.17 | 17.35 | 15.20 | 4.50 | 68.72 |
| *Roll & brush 3rd or additional coats* | | | | | | | | | |
| Slow | 90 | 275 | 46.25 | 22.50 | 6.63 | 16.82 | 8.73 | 8.75 | 63.43 |
| Medium | 130 | 250 | 40.50 | 19.81 | 7.01 | 16.20 | 10.76 | 6.45 | 60.23 |
| Fast | 170 | 225 | 34.70 | 18.53 | 7.55 | 15.42 | 12.87 | 3.81 | 58.18 |
| **Solid body or semi-transparent stain, oil base (material #19 or #21)** | | | | | | | | | |
| *Roll & brush 1st coat* | | | | | | | | | |
| Slow | 85 | 300 | 51.40 | 23.82 | 7.01 | 17.13 | 9.12 | 9.14 | 66.22 |
| Medium | 110 | 265 | 44.95 | 23.41 | 8.29 | 16.96 | 12.17 | 7.30 | 68.13 |
| Fast | 135 | 230 | 38.50 | 23.33 | 9.53 | 16.74 | 15.37 | 4.55 | 69.52 |
| *Roll & brush 2nd coat* | | | | | | | | | |
| Slow | 95 | 375 | 51.40 | 21.32 | 6.29 | 13.71 | 7.85 | 7.87 | 57.04 |
| Medium | 125 | 338 | 44.95 | 20.60 | 7.30 | 13.30 | 10.30 | 6.18 | 57.68 |
| Fast | 155 | 300 | 38.50 | 20.32 | 8.29 | 12.83 | 12.85 | 3.80 | 58.09 |
| *Roll & brush 3rd or additional coats* | | | | | | | | | |
| Slow | 105 | 400 | 51.40 | 19.29 | 5.67 | 12.85 | 7.19 | 7.20 | 52.20 |
| Medium | 145 | 363 | 44.95 | 17.76 | 6.30 | 12.38 | 9.11 | 5.46 | 51.01 |
| Fast | 185 | 325 | 38.50 | 17.03 | 6.96 | 11.85 | 11.11 | 3.29 | 50.24 |
| **Varnish, flat or gloss (material #30c)** | | | | | | | | | |
| *Roll & brush 1st coat* | | | | | | | | | |
| Slow | 60 | 170 | 52.00 | 33.75 | 9.96 | 30.59 | 14.12 | 14.15 | 102.57 |
| Medium | 70 | 155 | 45.50 | 36.79 | 13.04 | 29.35 | 19.79 | 11.87 | 110.84 |
| Fast | 90 | 140 | 39.00 | 35.00 | 14.27 | 27.86 | 23.91 | 7.07 | 108.11 |

*General Painting Costs*

|  | Labor LF per manhour | Material coverage LF/gallon | Material cost per gallon | Labor cost per 100 LF | Labor burden 100 LF | Material cost per 100 LF | Overhead per 100 LF | Profit per 100 LF | Total price per 100 LF |
|---|---|---|---|---|---|---|---|---|---|
| **Roll & brush 2nd coat** | | | | | | | | | |
| Slow | 70 | 240 | 52.00 | 28.93 | 8.54 | 21.67 | 11.23 | 11.26 | 81.63 |
| Medium | 100 | 220 | 45.50 | 25.75 | 9.12 | 20.68 | 13.89 | 8.33 | 77.77 |
| Fast | 130 | 200 | 39.00 | 24.23 | 9.88 | 19.50 | 16.62 | 4.92 | 75.15 |
| **Roll & brush 3rd or additional coats** | | | | | | | | | |
| Slow | 80 | 260 | 52.00 | 25.31 | 7.47 | 20.00 | 10.03 | 10.05 | 72.86 |
| Medium | 115 | 240 | 45.50 | 22.39 | 7.95 | 18.96 | 12.32 | 7.39 | 69.01 |
| Fast | 150 | 220 | 39.00 | 21.00 | 8.58 | 17.73 | 14.66 | 4.34 | 66.31 |

Don't add additional time for plant-on trim if it's painted with the same coating as the adjacent siding. For heights above 8 feet, use the High Time Difficulty Factors on page 139. Use slow rates when cutting-in or masking adjacent surfaces. Add preparation time for masking adjacent surfaces or protecting windows. Use fast rates when plant-on trim is finished before it's installed or on new construction projects where a prime coat can be sprayed prior to stucco color coat application. "Slow" work is based on an hourly wage of $20.25, "Medium" work on an hourly wage of $25.75, and "Fast" work on an hourly wage of $31.50. Other qualifications that apply to this table are on page 9.

*National Painting Cost Estimator*

|  | Labor LF per manhour | Material coverage LF/gallon | Material cost per gallon | Labor cost per 100 LF | Labor burden 100 LF | Material cost per 100 LF | Overhead per 100 LF | Profit per 100 LF | Total price per 100 LF |
|---|---|---|---|---|---|---|---|---|---|

## Plant-on trim, exterior, 2" x 10" to 2" x 12" wood
2" x 10" to 2" x 12" rough sawn or resawn wood
  Solid body or semi-transparent stain, water base (material #18 or #20)
    Roll & brush 1st coat

| | | | | | | | | | |
|---|---|---|---|---|---|---|---|---|---|
| Slow | 60 | 150 | 46.25 | 33.75 | 9.96 | 30.83 | 14.16 | 14.19 | 102.89 |
| Medium | 75 | 115 | 40.50 | 34.33 | 12.15 | 35.22 | 20.43 | 12.26 | 114.39 |
| Fast | 90 | 80 | 34.70 | 35.00 | 14.27 | 43.38 | 28.72 | 8.50 | 129.87 |

Roll & brush 2nd coat

| | | | | | | | | | |
|---|---|---|---|---|---|---|---|---|---|
| Slow | 70 | 190 | 46.25 | 28.93 | 8.54 | 24.34 | 11.74 | 11.77 | 85.32 |
| Medium | 110 | 165 | 40.50 | 23.41 | 8.29 | 24.55 | 14.06 | 8.44 | 78.75 |
| Fast | 130 | 140 | 34.70 | 24.23 | 9.88 | 24.79 | 18.26 | 5.40 | 82.56 |

Roll & brush 3rd or additional coats

| | | | | | | | | | |
|---|---|---|---|---|---|---|---|---|---|
| Slow | 80 | 215 | 46.25 | 25.31 | 7.47 | 21.51 | 10.32 | 10.34 | 74.95 |
| Medium | 120 | 190 | 40.50 | 21.46 | 7.59 | 21.32 | 12.60 | 7.56 | 70.53 |
| Fast | 160 | 165 | 34.70 | 19.69 | 8.03 | 21.03 | 15.11 | 4.47 | 68.33 |

  Solid body or semi-transparent stain, oil base (material #19 or #21)
    Roll & brush 1st coat

| | | | | | | | | | |
|---|---|---|---|---|---|---|---|---|---|
| Slow | 70 | 290 | 51.40 | 28.93 | 8.54 | 17.72 | 10.48 | 10.51 | 76.18 |
| Medium | 85 | 255 | 44.95 | 30.29 | 10.72 | 17.63 | 14.66 | 8.80 | 82.10 |
| Fast | 100 | 220 | 38.50 | 31.50 | 12.85 | 17.50 | 19.17 | 5.67 | 86.69 |

Roll & brush 2nd coat

| | | | | | | | | | |
|---|---|---|---|---|---|---|---|---|---|
| Slow | 80 | 315 | 51.40 | 25.31 | 7.47 | 16.32 | 9.33 | 9.35 | 67.78 |
| Medium | 110 | 278 | 44.95 | 23.41 | 8.29 | 16.17 | 11.97 | 7.18 | 67.02 |
| Fast | 140 | 240 | 38.50 | 22.50 | 9.17 | 16.04 | 14.79 | 4.38 | 66.88 |

Roll & brush 3rd or additional coats

| | | | | | | | | | |
|---|---|---|---|---|---|---|---|---|---|
| Slow | 90 | 340 | 51.40 | 22.50 | 6.63 | 15.12 | 8.41 | 8.43 | 61.09 |
| Medium | 130 | 303 | 44.95 | 19.81 | 7.01 | 14.83 | 10.41 | 6.25 | 58.31 |
| Fast | 170 | 265 | 38.50 | 18.53 | 7.55 | 14.53 | 12.59 | 3.72 | 56.92 |

  Varnish, flat or gloss (material #30c)
    Roll & brush 1st coat

| | | | | | | | | | |
|---|---|---|---|---|---|---|---|---|---|
| Slow | 50 | 120 | 52.00 | 40.50 | 11.94 | 43.33 | 18.20 | 18.24 | 132.21 |
| Medium | 65 | 100 | 45.50 | 39.62 | 14.01 | 45.50 | 24.79 | 14.87 | 138.79 |
| Fast | 80 | 80 | 39.00 | 39.38 | 16.06 | 48.75 | 32.30 | 9.56 | 146.05 |

*General Painting Costs*

|  | Labor LF per manhour | Material coverage LF/gallon | Material cost per gallon | Labor cost per 100 LF | Labor burden 100 LF | Material cost per 100 LF | Overhead per 100 LF | Profit per 100 LF | Total price per 100 LF |
|---|---|---|---|---|---|---|---|---|---|
| **Roll & brush 2nd coat** | | | | | | | | | |
| Slow | 60 | 190 | 52.00 | 33.75 | 9.96 | 27.37 | 13.51 | 13.53 | 98.12 |
| Medium | 90 | 165 | 45.50 | 28.61 | 10.13 | 27.58 | 16.58 | 9.95 | 92.85 |
| Fast | 120 | 140 | 39.00 | 26.25 | 10.69 | 27.86 | 20.09 | 5.94 | 90.83 |
| **Roll & brush 3rd or additional coats** | | | | | | | | | |
| Slow | 70 | 200 | 52.00 | 28.93 | 8.54 | 26.00 | 12.06 | 12.08 | 87.61 |
| Medium | 110 | 175 | 45.50 | 23.41 | 8.29 | 26.00 | 14.43 | 8.66 | 80.79 |
| Fast | 150 | 150 | 39.00 | 21.00 | 8.58 | 26.00 | 17.23 | 5.10 | 77.91 |

Don't add additional time for plant-on trim if it's painted with the same coating as the adjacent siding. For heights above 8 feet, use the High Time Difficulty Factors on page 139. Use slow rates when cutting-in or masking adjacent surfaces. Add preparation time for masking adjacent surfaces or protecting windows. Use fast rates when plant-on trim is finished before it's installed or on new construction projects where a prime coat can be sprayed prior to stucco color coat application. "Slow" work is based on an hourly wage of $20.25, "Medium" work on an hourly wage of $25.75, and "Fast" work on an hourly wage of $31.50. Other qualifications that apply to this table are on page 9.

*National Painting Cost Estimator*

|  | Labor SF per manhour | Material coverage SF/gallon | Material cost per gallon | Labor cost per 100 SF | Labor burden 100 SF | Material cost per 100 SF | Overhead per 100 SF | Profit per 100 SF | Total price per 100 SF |
|---|---|---|---|---|---|---|---|---|---|

### Plaster or stucco, exterior, medium texture, brush application

Masonry paint, water base, flat or gloss (material #31)
Brush 1st coat

| | | | | | | | | | |
|---|---|---|---|---|---|---|---|---|---|
| Slow | 100 | 225 | 38.20 | 20.25 | 5.97 | 16.98 | 8.21 | 8.23 | 59.64 |
| Medium | 120 | 213 | 33.50 | 21.46 | 7.59 | 15.73 | 11.20 | 6.72 | 62.70 |
| Fast | 140 | 200 | 28.70 | 22.50 | 9.17 | 14.35 | 14.27 | 4.22 | 64.51 |

Brush 2nd coat

| | | | | | | | | | |
|---|---|---|---|---|---|---|---|---|---|
| Slow | 150 | 250 | 38.20 | 13.50 | 3.99 | 15.28 | 6.22 | 6.24 | 45.23 |
| Medium | 163 | 230 | 33.50 | 15.80 | 5.58 | 14.57 | 8.99 | 5.39 | 50.33 |
| Fast | 175 | 210 | 28.70 | 18.00 | 7.32 | 13.67 | 12.09 | 3.58 | 54.66 |

Brush 3rd or additional coats

| | | | | | | | | | |
|---|---|---|---|---|---|---|---|---|---|
| Slow | 160 | 270 | 38.20 | 12.66 | 3.73 | 14.15 | 5.80 | 5.81 | 42.15 |
| Medium | 173 | 245 | 33.50 | 14.88 | 5.27 | 13.67 | 8.46 | 5.07 | 47.35 |
| Fast | 185 | 220 | 28.70 | 17.03 | 6.96 | 13.05 | 11.48 | 3.40 | 51.92 |

Masonry paint, oil base (material #32)
Brush 1st coat

| | | | | | | | | | |
|---|---|---|---|---|---|---|---|---|---|
| Slow | 80 | 265 | 38.40 | 25.31 | 7.47 | 14.49 | 8.98 | 9.00 | 65.25 |
| Medium | 100 | 250 | 33.60 | 25.75 | 9.12 | 13.44 | 12.08 | 7.25 | 67.64 |
| Fast | 120 | 235 | 28.80 | 26.25 | 10.69 | 12.26 | 15.26 | 4.51 | 68.97 |

Brush 2nd coat

| | | | | | | | | | |
|---|---|---|---|---|---|---|---|---|---|
| Slow | 145 | 300 | 38.40 | 13.97 | 4.12 | 12.80 | 5.87 | 5.88 | 42.64 |
| Medium | 165 | 275 | 33.60 | 15.61 | 5.52 | 12.22 | 8.34 | 5.00 | 46.69 |
| Fast | 185 | 250 | 28.80 | 17.03 | 6.96 | 11.52 | 11.01 | 3.26 | 49.78 |

Brush 3rd or additional coats

| | | | | | | | | | |
|---|---|---|---|---|---|---|---|---|---|
| Slow | 155 | 350 | 38.40 | 13.06 | 3.85 | 10.97 | 5.30 | 5.31 | 38.49 |
| Medium | 175 | 325 | 33.60 | 14.71 | 5.20 | 10.34 | 7.57 | 4.54 | 42.36 |
| Fast | 195 | 300 | 28.80 | 16.15 | 6.60 | 9.60 | 10.03 | 2.97 | 45.35 |

For heights above 8 feet, use the High Time Difficulty Factors on page 139. For oil base paint and clear hydro sealer, I recommend spraying. For painting interior plaster, see Walls, plaster. "Slow" work is based on an hourly wage of $20.25, "Medium" work on an hourly wage of $25.75, and "Fast" work on an hourly wage of $31.50. Other qualifications that apply to this table are on page 9.

*General Painting Costs*

| | Labor SF per manhour | Material coverage SF/gallon | Material cost per gallon | Labor cost per 100 SF | Labor burden 100 SF | Material cost per 100 SF | Overhead per 100 SF | Profit per 100 SF | Total price per 100 SF |
|---|---|---|---|---|---|---|---|---|---|

## Plaster or stucco, exterior, medium texture, roll application

**Masonry paint, water base, flat or gloss (material #31)**

Roll 1st coat
| | | | | | | | | | |
|---|---|---|---|---|---|---|---|---|---|
| Slow | 245 | 200 | 38.20 | 8.27 | 2.43 | 19.10 | 5.66 | 5.68 | 41.14 |
| Medium | 273 | 175 | 33.50 | 9.43 | 3.33 | 19.14 | 7.98 | 4.79 | 44.67 |
| Fast | 300 | 150 | 28.70 | 10.50 | 4.27 | 19.13 | 10.51 | 3.11 | 47.52 |

Roll 2nd coat
| | | | | | | | | | |
|---|---|---|---|---|---|---|---|---|---|
| Slow | 300 | 225 | 38.20 | 6.75 | 1.98 | 16.98 | 4.89 | 4.90 | 35.50 |
| Medium | 320 | 200 | 33.50 | 8.05 | 2.86 | 16.75 | 6.91 | 4.15 | 38.72 |
| Fast | 340 | 175 | 28.70 | 9.26 | 3.78 | 16.40 | 9.13 | 2.70 | 41.27 |

Roll 3rd or additional coats
| | | | | | | | | | |
|---|---|---|---|---|---|---|---|---|---|
| Slow | 320 | 250 | 38.20 | 6.33 | 1.88 | 15.28 | 4.46 | 4.47 | 32.42 |
| Medium | 340 | 225 | 33.50 | 7.57 | 2.68 | 14.89 | 6.29 | 3.77 | 35.20 |
| Fast | 360 | 200 | 28.70 | 8.75 | 3.58 | 14.35 | 8.27 | 2.45 | 37.40 |

**Masonry paint, oil base (material #32)**

Roll 1st coat
| | | | | | | | | | |
|---|---|---|---|---|---|---|---|---|---|
| Slow | 200 | 250 | 38.40 | 10.13 | 2.98 | 15.36 | 5.41 | 5.42 | 39.30 |
| Medium | 240 | 225 | 33.60 | 10.73 | 3.81 | 14.93 | 7.37 | 4.42 | 41.26 |
| Fast | 280 | 200 | 28.80 | 11.25 | 4.58 | 14.40 | 9.37 | 2.77 | 42.37 |

Roll 2nd coat
| | | | | | | | | | |
|---|---|---|---|---|---|---|---|---|---|
| Slow | 220 | 275 | 38.40 | 9.20 | 2.73 | 13.96 | 4.92 | 4.93 | 35.74 |
| Medium | 265 | 250 | 33.60 | 9.72 | 3.43 | 13.44 | 6.65 | 3.99 | 37.23 |
| Fast | 305 | 225 | 28.80 | 10.33 | 4.22 | 12.80 | 8.48 | 2.51 | 38.34 |

Roll 3rd or additional coats
| | | | | | | | | | |
|---|---|---|---|---|---|---|---|---|---|
| Slow | 235 | 300 | 38.40 | 8.62 | 2.55 | 12.80 | 4.55 | 4.56 | 33.08 |
| Medium | 285 | 275 | 33.60 | 9.04 | 3.20 | 12.22 | 6.12 | 3.67 | 34.25 |
| Fast | 335 | 250 | 28.80 | 9.40 | 3.86 | 11.52 | 7.68 | 2.27 | 34.73 |

For heights above 8 feet, use the High Time Difficulty Factors on page 139. For oil base paint and clear hydro sealer, I recommend spraying. For painting interior plaster, see Walls, plaster. "Slow" work is based on an hourly wage of $20.25, "Medium" work on an hourly wage of $25.75, and "Fast" work on an hourly wage of $31.50. Other qualifications that apply to this table are on page 9.

## Plaster or stucco, exterior, medium texture, spray application

|  | Labor SF per manhour | Material coverage SF/gallon | Material cost per gallon | Labor cost per 100 SF | Labor burden 100 SF | Material cost per 100 SF | Overhead per 100 SF | Profit per 100 SF | Total price per 100 SF |
|---|---|---|---|---|---|---|---|---|---|
| **Masonry paint, water base, flat or gloss (material #31)** | | | | | | | | | |
| *Spray prime coat* | | | | | | | | | |
| Slow | 600 | 150 | 38.20 | 3.38 | 1.00 | 25.47 | 5.67 | 5.68 | 41.20 |
| Medium | 675 | 120 | 33.50 | 3.81 | 1.35 | 27.92 | 8.27 | 4.96 | 46.31 |
| Fast | 750 | 90 | 28.70 | 4.20 | 1.70 | 31.89 | 11.72 | 3.47 | 52.98 |
| *Spray 2nd coat* | | | | | | | | | |
| Slow | 700 | 175 | 38.20 | 2.89 | .86 | 21.83 | 4.86 | 4.87 | 35.31 |
| Medium | 800 | 150 | 33.50 | 3.22 | 1.14 | 22.33 | 6.67 | 4.00 | 37.36 |
| Fast | 900 | 125 | 28.70 | 3.50 | 1.42 | 22.96 | 8.65 | 2.56 | 39.09 |
| *Spray 3rd or additional coats* | | | | | | | | | |
| Slow | 750 | 200 | 38.20 | 2.70 | .79 | 19.10 | 4.29 | 4.30 | 31.18 |
| Medium | 850 | 168 | 33.50 | 3.03 | 1.08 | 19.94 | 6.01 | 3.61 | 33.67 |
| Fast | 950 | 135 | 28.70 | 3.32 | 1.34 | 21.26 | 8.04 | 2.38 | 36.34 |
| **Masonry paint, oil base (material #32)** | | | | | | | | | |
| *Spray prime coat* | | | | | | | | | |
| Slow | 550 | 200 | 38.40 | 3.68 | 1.09 | 19.20 | 4.55 | 4.56 | 33.08 |
| Medium | 600 | 145 | 33.60 | 4.29 | 1.53 | 23.17 | 7.25 | 4.35 | 40.59 |
| Fast | 650 | 90 | 28.80 | 4.85 | 1.98 | 32.00 | 12.04 | 3.56 | 54.43 |
| *Spray 2nd coat* | | | | | | | | | |
| Slow | 650 | 225 | 38.40 | 3.12 | .92 | 17.07 | 4.01 | 4.02 | 29.14 |
| Medium | 700 | 175 | 33.60 | 3.68 | 1.31 | 19.20 | 6.05 | 3.63 | 33.87 |
| Fast | 750 | 125 | 28.80 | 4.20 | 1.70 | 23.04 | 8.97 | 2.65 | 40.56 |
| *Spray 3rd or additional coats* | | | | | | | | | |
| Slow | 700 | 250 | 38.40 | 2.89 | .86 | 15.36 | 3.63 | 3.64 | 26.38 |
| Medium | 750 | 193 | 33.60 | 3.43 | 1.21 | 17.41 | 5.51 | 3.31 | 30.87 |
| Fast | 800 | 135 | 28.80 | 3.94 | 1.60 | 21.33 | 8.33 | 2.46 | 37.66 |

For heights above 8 feet, use the High Time Difficulty Factors on page 139. For oil base paint and clear hydro sealer, I recommend spraying. For painting interior plaster, see Walls, plaster. "Slow" work is based on an hourly wage of $20.25, "Medium" work on an hourly wage of $25.75, and "Fast" work on an hourly wage of $31.50. Other qualifications that apply to this table are on page 9.

*General Painting Costs*

|  | Labor SF per manhour | Material coverage SF/gallon | Material cost per gallon | Labor cost per 100 SF | Labor burden 100 SF | Material cost per 100 SF | Overhead per 100 SF | Profit per 100 SF | Total price per 100 SF |
|---|---|---|---|---|---|---|---|---|---|

## Plaster or stucco, exterior, medium texture, waterproofing
Waterproofing, clear hydro sealer (material #34)

Brush 1st coat

| | | | | | | | | | |
|---|---|---|---|---|---|---|---|---|---|
| Slow | 125 | 175 | 40.60 | 16.20 | 4.78 | 23.20 | 8.39 | 8.41 | 60.98 |
| Medium | 150 | 163 | 35.50 | 17.17 | 6.09 | 21.78 | 11.26 | 6.75 | 63.05 |
| Fast | 175 | 150 | 30.40 | 18.00 | 7.32 | 20.27 | 14.14 | 4.18 | 63.91 |

Brush 2nd or additional coats

| | | | | | | | | | |
|---|---|---|---|---|---|---|---|---|---|
| Slow | 175 | 200 | 40.60 | 11.57 | 3.40 | 20.30 | 6.70 | 6.72 | 48.69 |
| Medium | 200 | 188 | 35.50 | 12.88 | 4.56 | 18.88 | 9.08 | 5.45 | 50.85 |
| Fast | 225 | 175 | 30.40 | 14.00 | 5.69 | 17.37 | 11.49 | 3.40 | 51.95 |

Roll 1st coat

| | | | | | | | | | |
|---|---|---|---|---|---|---|---|---|---|
| Slow | 325 | 150 | 40.60 | 6.23 | 1.85 | 27.07 | 6.68 | 6.69 | 48.52 |
| Medium | 363 | 138 | 35.50 | 7.09 | 2.50 | 25.72 | 8.83 | 5.30 | 49.44 |
| Fast | 400 | 125 | 30.40 | 7.88 | 3.21 | 24.32 | 10.98 | 3.25 | 49.64 |

Roll 2nd or additional coats

| | | | | | | | | | |
|---|---|---|---|---|---|---|---|---|---|
| Slow | 400 | 175 | 40.60 | 5.06 | 1.50 | 23.20 | 5.65 | 5.66 | 41.07 |
| Medium | 425 | 163 | 35.50 | 6.06 | 2.13 | 21.78 | 7.50 | 4.50 | 41.97 |
| Fast | 450 | 150 | 30.40 | 7.00 | 2.85 | 20.27 | 9.34 | 2.76 | 42.22 |

Spray 1st coat

| | | | | | | | | | |
|---|---|---|---|---|---|---|---|---|---|
| Slow | 650 | 125 | 40.60 | 3.12 | .92 | 32.48 | 6.94 | 6.95 | 50.41 |
| Medium | 700 | 113 | 35.50 | 3.68 | 1.31 | 31.42 | 9.10 | 5.46 | 50.97 |
| Fast | 750 | 100 | 30.40 | 4.20 | 1.70 | 30.40 | 11.26 | 3.33 | 50.89 |

Spray 2nd or additional coats

| | | | | | | | | | |
|---|---|---|---|---|---|---|---|---|---|
| Slow | 750 | 150 | 40.60 | 2.70 | .79 | 27.07 | 5.81 | 5.82 | 42.19 |
| Medium | 825 | 138 | 35.50 | 3.12 | 1.10 | 25.72 | 7.49 | 4.49 | 41.92 |
| Fast | 900 | 125 | 30.40 | 3.50 | 1.42 | 24.32 | 9.07 | 2.68 | 40.99 |

For heights above 8 feet, use the High Time Difficulty Factors on page 139. For oil base paint and clear hydro sealer, I recommend spraying. For painting interior plaster, see Walls, plaster. "Slow" work is based on an hourly wage of $20.25, "Medium" work on an hourly wage of $25.75, and "Fast" work on an hourly wage of $31.50. Other qualifications that apply to this table are on page 9.

*National Painting Cost Estimator*

### Plaster, interior: see Walls

|  | Labor SF per manhour | Material coverage SF/gallon | Material cost per gallon | Labor cost per 100 SF | Labor burden 100 SF | Material cost per 100 SF | Overhead per 100 SF | Profit per 100 SF | Total price per 100 SF |
|---|---|---|---|---|---|---|---|---|---|

### Plaster or stucco, interior/exterior, medium texture, anti-graffiti stain eliminator

Water base primer and sealer (material #39)
Roll & brush each coat

|  |  |  |  |  |  |  |  |  |  |
|---|---|---|---|---|---|---|---|---|---|
| Slow | 350 | 400 | 50.30 | 5.79 | 1.71 | 12.58 | 3.82 | 3.82 | 27.72 |
| Medium | 375 | 375 | 44.00 | 6.87 | 2.44 | 11.73 | 5.26 | 3.15 | 29.45 |
| Fast | 400 | 350 | 37.80 | 7.88 | 3.21 | 10.80 | 6.79 | 2.01 | 30.69 |

Oil base primer and sealer (material #40)
Roll & brush each coat

|  |  |  |  |  |  |  |  |  |  |
|---|---|---|---|---|---|---|---|---|---|
| Slow | 350 | 375 | 49.90 | 5.79 | 1.71 | 13.31 | 3.95 | 3.96 | 28.72 |
| Medium | 375 | 350 | 43.70 | 6.87 | 2.44 | 12.49 | 5.45 | 3.27 | 30.52 |
| Fast | 400 | 325 | 37.40 | 7.88 | 3.21 | 11.51 | 7.01 | 2.07 | 31.68 |

Polyurethane 2 part system (material #41)
Roll & brush each coat

|  |  |  |  |  |  |  |  |  |  |
|---|---|---|---|---|---|---|---|---|---|
| Slow | 300 | 375 | 157.00 | 6.75 | 1.98 | 41.87 | 9.62 | 9.64 | 69.86 |
| Medium | 325 | 350 | 137.40 | 7.92 | 2.82 | 39.26 | 12.50 | 7.50 | 70.00 |
| Fast | 350 | 325 | 117.80 | 9.00 | 3.68 | 36.25 | 15.17 | 4.49 | 68.59 |

For heights above 8 feet, use the High Time Difficulty Factors on page 139. For oil base paint and clear hydro sealer, I recommend spraying. For painting interior plaster, see Walls, plaster. "Slow" work is based on an hourly wage of $20.25, "Medium" work on an hourly wage of $25.75, and "Fast" work on an hourly wage of $31.50. Other qualifications that apply to this table are on page 9.

|  | Labor LF per manhour | Material coverage LF/gallon | Material cost per gallon | Labor cost per 100 LF | Labor burden 100 LF | Material cost per 100 LF | Overhead per 100 LF | Profit per 100 LF | Total price per 100 LF |
|---|---|---|---|---|---|---|---|---|---|

### Pot shelves, 12" to 18" wide

Solid body or semi-transparent stain, water or oil base (material #18 or #19 or #20 or #21)
Roll & brush each coat

|  |  |  |  |  |  |  |  |  |  |
|---|---|---|---|---|---|---|---|---|---|
| Slow | 50 | 50 | 48.83 | 40.50 | 11.94 | 97.66 | 28.52 | 28.58 | 207.20 |
| Medium | 68 | 45 | 42.73 | 37.87 | 13.42 | 94.96 | 36.56 | 21.94 | 204.75 |
| Fast | 75 | 40 | 36.60 | 42.00 | 17.12 | 91.50 | 46.70 | 13.81 | 211.13 |

These figures are based on painting all sides of exterior or interior pot shelves. "Slow" work is based on an hourly wage of $20.25, "Medium" work on an hourly wage of $25.75, and "Fast" work on an hourly wage of $31.50. Other qualifications that apply to this table are on page 9.

*General Painting Costs*

|  | Labor LF per manhour | Material coverage LF/gallon | Material cost per gallon | Labor cost per 100 LF | Labor burden 100 LF | Material cost per 100 LF | Overhead per 100 LF | Profit per 100 LF | Total price per 100 LF |
|---|---|---|---|---|---|---|---|---|---|

### Railing, exterior, rough sawn or resawn wood
Solid body or semi-transparent stain, water or oil base (material #18 or #19 or #20 or #21)
 Roll & brush each coat

|  | | | | | | | | | |
|---|---|---|---|---|---|---|---|---|---|
| Slow | 16 | 20 | 48.83 | 126.56 | 37.32 | 244.15 | 77.53 | 77.69 | 563.25 |
| Medium | 18 | 18 | 42.73 | 143.06 | 50.68 | 237.39 | 107.77 | 64.66 | 603.56 |
| Fast | 20 | 15 | 36.60 | 157.50 | 64.25 | 244.00 | 144.39 | 42.71 | 652.85 |

Use these costs for finishing railing that's 36" to 42" high and with 2" x 2" verticals spaced 4" to 6" on center. These figures include painting the rail cap, baluster, newels and spindles. "Slow" work is based on an hourly wage of $20.25, "Medium" work on an hourly wage of $25.75, and "Fast" work on an hourly wage of $31.50. Other qualifications that apply to this table are on page 9.

|  | Labor LF per manhour | Material coverage LF/gallon | Material cost per gallon | Labor cost per 100 LF | Labor burden 100 LF | Material cost per 100 LF | Overhead per 100 LF | Profit per 100 LF | Total price per 100 LF |
|---|---|---|---|---|---|---|---|---|---|

### Railing, exterior, stain grade, decorative wood
STEP 1: Sand & putty

|  | | | | | | | | | |
|---|---|---|---|---|---|---|---|---|---|
| Slow | 50 | -- | -- | 40.50 | 11.94 | -- | 9.97 | 9.99 | 72.40 |
| Medium | 60 | -- | -- | 42.92 | 15.21 | -- | 14.53 | 8.72 | 81.38 |
| Fast | 70 | -- | -- | 45.00 | 18.38 | -- | 19.64 | 5.81 | 88.83 |

STEP 2 & 3: Stain (material #30a) & wipe
 Brush & wipe, 1 coat

|  | | | | | | | | | |
|---|---|---|---|---|---|---|---|---|---|
| Slow | 25 | 60 | 53.40 | 81.00 | 23.88 | 89.00 | 36.84 | 36.92 | 267.64 |
| Medium | 30 | 55 | 46.70 | 85.83 | 30.39 | 84.91 | 50.28 | 30.17 | 281.58 |
| Fast | 35 | 50 | 40.00 | 90.00 | 36.71 | 80.00 | 64.08 | 18.96 | 289.75 |

 Spray & wipe, 1 coat

|  | | | | | | | | | |
|---|---|---|---|---|---|---|---|---|---|
| Slow | 75 | 35 | 53.40 | 27.00 | 7.95 | 152.57 | 35.63 | 35.71 | 258.86 |
| Medium | 85 | 30 | 46.70 | 30.29 | 10.72 | 155.67 | 49.17 | 29.50 | 275.35 |
| Fast | 95 | 25 | 40.00 | 33.16 | 13.54 | 160.00 | 64.07 | 18.95 | 289.72 |

STEP 4 & 5: Sanding sealer (material #30b) & light sand
 Brush 1 coat

|  | | | | | | | | | |
|---|---|---|---|---|---|---|---|---|---|
| Slow | 45 | 65 | 52.00 | 45.00 | 13.26 | 80.00 | 26.27 | 26.33 | 190.86 |
| Medium | 50 | 60 | 45.50 | 51.50 | 18.24 | 75.83 | 36.39 | 21.83 | 203.79 |
| Fast | 55 | 55 | 39.00 | 57.27 | 23.36 | 70.91 | 46.98 | 13.90 | 212.42 |

 Spray 1 coat

|  | | | | | | | | | |
|---|---|---|---|---|---|---|---|---|---|
| Slow | 125 | 35 | 52.00 | 16.20 | 4.78 | 148.57 | 32.21 | 32.28 | 234.04 |
| Medium | 138 | 30 | 45.50 | 18.66 | 6.62 | 151.67 | 44.24 | 26.54 | 247.73 |
| Fast | 150 | 25 | 39.00 | 21.00 | 8.58 | 156.00 | 57.53 | 17.02 | 260.13 |

## National Painting Cost Estimator

|  | Labor LF per manhour | Material coverage LF/gallon | Material cost per gallon | Labor cost per 100 LF | Labor burden 100 LF | Material cost per 100 LF | Overhead per 100 LF | Profit per 100 LF | Total price per 100 LF |
|---|---|---|---|---|---|---|---|---|---|
| **STEP 6 & 7: Varnish 2 coats (material #30c)** | | | | | | | | | |
| **Varnish, flat or gloss (material #30c)** | | | | | | | | | |
| Brush 1st coat | | | | | | | | | |
| Slow | 22 | 100 | 81.70 | 92.05 | 27.12 | 81.70 | 38.17 | 38.25 | 277.29 |
| Medium | 24 | 90 | 71.50 | 107.29 | 38.01 | 79.44 | 56.18 | 33.71 | 314.63 |
| Fast | 26 | 80 | 61.30 | 121.15 | 49.42 | 76.63 | 76.64 | 22.67 | 346.51 |
| Brush 2nd or additional coats | | | | | | | | | |
| Slow | 30 | 120 | 81.70 | 67.50 | 19.89 | 68.08 | 29.54 | 29.60 | 214.61 |
| Medium | 32 | 110 | 71.50 | 80.47 | 28.50 | 65.00 | 43.49 | 26.09 | 243.55 |
| Fast | 34 | 100 | 61.30 | 92.65 | 37.78 | 61.30 | 59.44 | 17.58 | 268.75 |
| Spray 1st coat | | | | | | | | | |
| Slow | 65 | 65 | 81.70 | 31.15 | 9.18 | 125.69 | 31.55 | 31.61 | 229.18 |
| Medium | 70 | 60 | 71.50 | 36.79 | 13.04 | 119.17 | 42.25 | 25.35 | 236.60 |
| Fast | 75 | 55 | 61.30 | 42.00 | 17.12 | 111.45 | 52.88 | 15.64 | 239.09 |
| Spray 2nd or additional coats | | | | | | | | | |
| Slow | 65 | 65 | 81.70 | 31.15 | 9.18 | 125.69 | 31.55 | 31.61 | 229.18 |
| Medium | 70 | 60 | 71.50 | 36.79 | 13.04 | 119.17 | 42.25 | 25.35 | 236.60 |
| Fast | 75 | 55 | 61.30 | 42.00 | 17.12 | 111.45 | 52.88 | 15.64 | 239.09 |
| **STEP 8: Steel wool, hand buff** | | | | | | | | | |
| Slow | 100 | -- | -- | 20.25 | 5.97 | -- | 4.98 | 4.99 | 36.19 |
| Medium | 113 | -- | -- | 22.79 | 8.07 | -- | 7.72 | 4.63 | 43.21 |
| Fast | 125 | -- | -- | 25.20 | 10.28 | -- | 11.00 | 3.25 | 49.73 |
| **STEP 9: Wax & polish by hand** | | | | | | | | | |
| Slow | 100 | -- | -- | 20.25 | 5.97 | -- | 4.98 | 4.99 | 36.19 |
| Medium | 113 | -- | -- | 22.79 | 8.07 | -- | 7.72 | 4.63 | 43.21 |
| Fast | 125 | -- | -- | 25.20 | 10.28 | -- | 11.00 | 3.25 | 49.73 |
| **Complete 9 step process** | | | | | | | | | |
| Brush stain, brush sanding sealer, brush varnish | | | | | | | | | |
| Slow | 6 | 40 | 62.40 | 337.50 | 99.51 | 156.00 | 112.68 | 112.92 | 818.61 |
| Medium | 7 | 35 | 54.60 | 367.86 | 130.29 | 156.00 | 163.52 | 98.11 | 915.78 |
| Fast | 8 | 30 | 46.80 | 393.75 | 160.63 | 156.00 | 220.22 | 65.14 | 995.74 |
| Spray stain, spray sanding sealer, brush varnish | | | | | | | | | |
| Slow | 11 | 24 | 62.40 | 184.09 | 54.28 | 260.00 | 94.70 | 94.90 | 687.97 |
| Medium | 14 | 27 | 54.60 | 183.93 | 65.15 | 202.22 | 112.82 | 67.69 | 631.81 |
| Fast | 17 | 30 | 46.80 | 185.29 | 75.58 | 156.00 | 129.24 | 38.23 | 584.34 |

Use these figures to estimate the cost of applying a natural finish on stain grade railing that's from 36" to 42" high and with spindles spaced at 4" to 6" on center. These figures include painting the rail cap, baluster, newels and spindles. "Slow" work is based on an hourly wage of $20.25, "Medium" work on an hourly wage of $25.75, and "Fast" work on an hourly wage of $31.50. Other qualifications that apply to this table are on page 9.

*General Painting Costs*

|  | Labor LF per manhour | Material coverage LF/gallon | Material cost per gallon | Labor cost per 100 LF | Labor burden 100 LF | Material cost per 100 LF | Overhead per 100 LF | Profit per 100 LF | Total price per 100 LF |
|---|---|---|---|---|---|---|---|---|---|

## Railing, interior, handrail, decorative wood
### Paint grade
#### Undercoat or enamel, water or oil base (material #3 or #4 or #9 or #10)
##### Brush each coat

|  | | | | | | | | | |
|---|---|---|---|---|---|---|---|---|---|
| Slow | 30 | 120 | 45.85 | 67.50 | 19.89 | 38.21 | 23.87 | 23.92 | 173.39 |
| Medium | 35 | 110 | 40.13 | 73.57 | 26.05 | 36.48 | 34.02 | 20.41 | 190.53 |
| Fast | 40 | 100 | 34.43 | 78.75 | 32.13 | 34.43 | 45.05 | 13.33 | 203.69 |

### Stain grade, 7 step process
#### Stain, seal and 2 coat lacquer system (material #11)
##### Spray all coats

|  | | | | | | | | | |
|---|---|---|---|---|---|---|---|---|---|
| Slow | 55 | 100 | 46.10 | 36.82 | 10.85 | 46.10 | 17.82 | 17.86 | 129.45 |
| Medium | 60 | 88 | 40.40 | 42.92 | 15.21 | 45.91 | 26.01 | 15.60 | 145.65 |
| Fast | 65 | 75 | 34.60 | 48.46 | 19.75 | 46.13 | 35.45 | 10.49 | 160.28 |

Use these costs for finishing decorative wood, wall mounted handrail. "Slow" work is based on an hourly wage of $20.25, "Medium" work on an hourly wage of $25.75, and "Fast" work on an hourly wage of $31.50. Other qualifications that apply to this table are on page 9.

|  | Labor LF per manhour | Material coverage LF/gallon | Material cost per gallon | Labor cost per 100 LF | Labor burden 100 LF | Material cost per 100 LF | Overhead per 100 LF | Profit per 100 LF | Total price per 100 LF |
|---|---|---|---|---|---|---|---|---|---|

## Railing, interior, stain grade, decorative wood
### Stain, seal and 2 coat lacquer system (7 step process)
#### STEP 1: Sand & putty

|  | | | | | | | | | |
|---|---|---|---|---|---|---|---|---|---|
| Slow | 50 | -- | -- | 40.50 | 11.94 | -- | 9.97 | 9.99 | 72.40 |
| Medium | 60 | -- | -- | 42.92 | 15.21 | -- | 14.53 | 8.72 | 81.38 |
| Fast | 70 | -- | -- | 45.00 | 18.38 | -- | 19.64 | 5.81 | 88.83 |

#### STEP 2 & 3: Stain (material #11a) & wipe
##### Brush & wipe, 1 coat

|  | | | | | | | | | |
|---|---|---|---|---|---|---|---|---|---|
| Slow | 25 | 60 | 51.30 | 81.00 | 23.88 | 85.50 | 36.18 | 36.25 | 262.81 |
| Medium | 30 | 55 | 44.90 | 85.83 | 30.39 | 81.64 | 49.46 | 29.68 | 277.00 |
| Fast | 35 | 50 | 38.50 | 90.00 | 36.71 | 77.00 | 63.15 | 18.68 | 285.54 |

##### Spray & wipe, 1 coat

|  | | | | | | | | | |
|---|---|---|---|---|---|---|---|---|---|
| Slow | 75 | 35 | 51.30 | 27.00 | 7.95 | 146.57 | 34.49 | 34.56 | 250.57 |
| Medium | 85 | 30 | 44.90 | 30.29 | 10.72 | 149.67 | 47.67 | 28.60 | 266.95 |
| Fast | 95 | 25 | 38.50 | 33.16 | 13.54 | 154.00 | 62.21 | 18.40 | 281.31 |

*National Painting Cost Estimator*

|  | Labor LF per manhour | Material coverage LF/gallon | Material cost per gallon | Labor cost per 100 LF | Labor burden 100 LF | Material cost per 100 LF | Overhead per 100 LF | Profit per 100 LF | Total price per 100 LF |
|---|---|---|---|---|---|---|---|---|---|
| **STEP 4 & 5: Sanding sealer (material #11b) & light sand** | | | | | | | | | |
| Brush 1 coat | | | | | | | | | |
| Slow | 45 | 65 | 41.50 | 45.00 | 13.26 | 63.85 | 23.20 | 23.25 | 168.56 |
| Medium | 50 | 60 | 36.30 | 51.50 | 18.24 | 60.50 | 32.56 | 19.53 | 182.33 |
| Fast | 55 | 55 | 31.10 | 57.27 | 23.36 | 56.55 | 42.53 | 12.58 | 192.29 |
| Spray 1 coat | | | | | | | | | |
| Slow | 125 | 35 | 41.50 | 16.20 | 4.78 | 118.57 | 26.51 | 26.57 | 192.63 |
| Medium | 138 | 30 | 36.30 | 18.66 | 6.62 | 121.00 | 36.57 | 21.94 | 204.79 |
| Fast | 150 | 25 | 31.10 | 21.00 | 8.58 | 124.40 | 47.73 | 14.12 | 215.83 |
| **STEP 6 & 7: Lacquer (material #11c), 2 coats** | | | | | | | | | |
| Brush 1st coat | | | | | | | | | |
| Slow | 40 | 65 | 45.90 | 50.63 | 14.92 | 70.62 | 25.88 | 25.93 | 187.98 |
| Medium | 50 | 60 | 40.10 | 51.50 | 18.24 | 66.83 | 34.14 | 20.48 | 191.19 |
| Fast | 60 | 55 | 34.40 | 52.50 | 21.43 | 62.55 | 42.31 | 12.51 | 191.30 |
| Brush 2nd coat | | | | | | | | | |
| Slow | 45 | 70 | 45.90 | 45.00 | 13.26 | 65.57 | 23.53 | 23.58 | 170.94 |
| Medium | 55 | 65 | 40.10 | 46.82 | 16.57 | 61.69 | 31.27 | 18.76 | 175.11 |
| Fast | 65 | 60 | 34.40 | 48.46 | 19.75 | 57.33 | 38.92 | 11.51 | 175.97 |
| Spray 1st coat | | | | | | | | | |
| Slow | 75 | 55 | 45.90 | 27.00 | 7.95 | 83.45 | 22.50 | 22.55 | 163.45 |
| Medium | 85 | 50 | 40.10 | 30.29 | 10.72 | 80.20 | 30.30 | 18.18 | 169.69 |
| Fast | 95 | 45 | 34.40 | 33.16 | 13.54 | 76.44 | 38.17 | 11.29 | 172.60 |
| Spray 2nd coat | | | | | | | | | |
| Slow | 85 | 60 | 45.90 | 23.82 | 7.01 | 76.50 | 20.40 | 20.44 | 148.17 |
| Medium | 95 | 55 | 40.10 | 27.11 | 9.61 | 72.91 | 27.41 | 16.44 | 153.48 |
| Fast | 105 | 50 | 34.40 | 30.00 | 12.22 | 68.80 | 34.42 | 10.18 | 155.62 |
| **Complete stain, seal & 2 coat lacquer system (material #11)** | | | | | | | | | |
| Brush all coats | | | | | | | | | |
| Slow | 8 | 30 | 46.10 | 253.13 | 74.62 | 153.67 | 91.48 | 91.67 | 664.57 |
| Medium | 10 | 25 | 40.40 | 257.50 | 91.20 | 161.60 | 127.57 | 76.54 | 714.41 |
| Fast | 12 | 20 | 34.60 | 262.50 | 107.07 | 173.00 | 168.21 | 49.76 | 760.54 |
| Spray all coats | | | | | | | | | |
| Slow | 16 | 20 | 45.90 | 126.56 | 37.32 | 229.50 | 74.75 | 74.90 | 543.03 |
| Medium | 20 | 15 | 40.10 | 128.75 | 45.60 | 267.33 | 110.42 | 66.25 | 618.35 |
| Fast | 24 | 10 | 34.40 | 131.25 | 53.56 | 344.00 | 163.93 | 48.49 | 741.23 |

Use these costs for applying stain, sanding sealer and lacquer to interior railings. Typical railing is 36" to 42" height with spindles spaced at 4" to 6" on center. These costs include finishing the rail cap, baluster, newels and spindles. The typical application is one coat of stain, one coat of sanding sealer, sand, putty, and two coats of lacquer. For rough sawn wood railing with 2" x 2" spindles spaced at 4" to 6" on center, see the tables for Exterior wood railing. "Slow" work is based on an hourly wage of $20.25, "Medium" work on an hourly wage of $25.75, and "Fast" work on an hourly wage of $31.50. Other qualifications that apply to this table are on page 9.

*General Painting Costs*

|  | Labor LF per manhour | Material coverage LF/gallon | Material cost per gallon | Labor cost per 100 LF | Labor burden 100 LF | Material cost per 100 LF | Overhead per 100 LF | Profit per 100 LF | Total price per 100 LF |
|---|---|---|---|---|---|---|---|---|---|

## Railing, interior, wood, paint grade, brush application

Undercoat, water or oil base (material #3 or #4)
  Brush 1 coat

| | | | | | | | | | |
|---|---|---|---|---|---|---|---|---|---|
| Slow | 11 | 50 | 37.45 | 184.09 | 54.28 | 74.90 | 59.53 | 59.65 | 432.45 |
| Medium | 14 | 45 | 32.75 | 183.93 | 65.15 | 72.78 | 80.46 | 48.27 | 450.59 |
| Fast | 17 | 40 | 28.15 | 185.29 | 75.58 | 70.38 | 102.69 | 30.38 | 464.32 |

Split coat (1/2 undercoat + 1/2 enamel), water or oil base (material #3 and #9, or material #4 and #10)
  Brush 1 coat

| | | | | | | | | | |
|---|---|---|---|---|---|---|---|---|---|
| Slow | 15 | 70 | 45.85 | 135.00 | 39.81 | 65.50 | 45.66 | 45.76 | 331.73 |
| Medium | 18 | 65 | 40.13 | 143.06 | 50.68 | 61.74 | 63.86 | 38.32 | 357.66 |
| Fast | 21 | 60 | 34.43 | 150.00 | 61.19 | 57.38 | 83.26 | 24.63 | 376.46 |

Enamel, water or oil base (material #9 or #10)
  Brush 1st finish coat

| | | | | | | | | | |
|---|---|---|---|---|---|---|---|---|---|
| Slow | 13 | 60 | 54.25 | 155.77 | 45.91 | 90.42 | 55.51 | 55.62 | 403.23 |
| Medium | 16 | 55 | 47.50 | 160.94 | 57.00 | 86.36 | 76.07 | 45.64 | 426.01 |
| Fast | 18 | 50 | 40.70 | 175.00 | 71.41 | 81.40 | 101.62 | 30.06 | 459.49 |

  Brush 2nd or additional finish coats

| | | | | | | | | | |
|---|---|---|---|---|---|---|---|---|---|
| Slow | 15 | 70 | 54.25 | 135.00 | 39.81 | 77.50 | 47.94 | 48.04 | 348.29 |
| Medium | 18 | 65 | 47.50 | 143.06 | 50.68 | 73.08 | 66.70 | 40.02 | 373.54 |
| Fast | 21 | 60 | 40.70 | 150.00 | 61.19 | 67.83 | 86.50 | 25.59 | 391.11 |

Use these costs for applying undercoat or enamel to interior railings. Railing is based on a 36" to 42" height and with spindles spaced at 4" to 6" on center. These costs include painting the rail cap, baluster, newels and spindles. For rough sawn wood railing with 2" x 2" spindles spaced at 6" on center, see the tables for Exterior wood railing. "Slow" work is based on an hourly wage of $20.25, "Medium" work on an hourly wage of $25.75, and "Fast" work on an hourly wage of $31.50. Other qualifications that apply to this table are on page 9.

*National Painting Cost Estimator*

|  | Labor LF per manhour | Material coverage LF/gallon | Material cost per gallon | Labor cost per 100 LF | Labor burden 100 LF | Material cost per 100 LF | Overhead per 100 LF | Profit per 100 LF | Total price per 100 LF |
|---|---|---|---|---|---|---|---|---|---|
| **Railing, interior, wood, paint grade, spray application** | | | | | | | | | |
| Undercoat, water or oil base (material #3 or #4) | | | | | | | | | |
|   Spray 1 coat | | | | | | | | | |
|     Slow | 50 | 40 | 37.45 | 40.50 | 11.94 | 93.63 | 27.76 | 27.81 | 201.64 |
|     Medium | 60 | 35 | 32.75 | 42.92 | 15.21 | 93.57 | 37.92 | 22.75 | 212.37 |
|     Fast | 70 | 30 | 28.15 | 45.00 | 18.38 | 93.83 | 48.73 | 14.41 | 220.35 |
| Split coat (1/2 undercoat + 1/2 enamel), water or oil base (material #3 and #9, or material #4 and #10) | | | | | | | | | |
|   Spray 1 coat | | | | | | | | | |
|     Slow | 65 | 50 | 45.85 | 31.15 | 9.18 | 91.70 | 25.09 | 25.14 | 182.26 |
|     Medium | 75 | 45 | 40.13 | 34.33 | 12.15 | 89.18 | 33.92 | 20.35 | 189.93 |
|     Fast | 85 | 40 | 34.43 | 37.06 | 15.10 | 86.08 | 42.86 | 12.68 | 193.78 |
| Enamel, water or oil base (material #9 or #10) | | | | | | | | | |
|   Spray 1st finish coat | | | | | | | | | |
|     Slow | 55 | 45 | 54.25 | 36.82 | 10.85 | 120.56 | 31.97 | 32.03 | 232.23 |
|     Medium | 65 | 40 | 47.50 | 39.62 | 14.01 | 118.75 | 43.10 | 25.86 | 241.34 |
|     Fast | 75 | 35 | 40.70 | 42.00 | 17.12 | 116.29 | 54.38 | 16.09 | 245.88 |
|   Spray 2nd or additional finish coats | | | | | | | | | |
|     Slow | 65 | 50 | 54.25 | 31.15 | 9.18 | 108.50 | 28.28 | 28.34 | 205.45 |
|     Medium | 75 | 45 | 47.50 | 34.33 | 12.15 | 105.56 | 38.01 | 22.81 | 212.86 |
|     Fast | 85 | 40 | 40.70 | 37.06 | 15.10 | 101.75 | 47.72 | 14.12 | 215.75 |

Use these costs for applying undercoat or enamel to interior railings. Railing is based on a 36" to 42" height and with spindles spaced at 4" to 6" on center. These costs include painting the rail cap, baluster, newels and spindles. For rough sawn wood railing with 2" x 2" spindles spaced at 6" on center, see the tables for Exterior wood railing. "Slow" work is based on an hourly wage of $20.25, "Medium" work on an hourly wage of $25.75, and "Fast" work on an hourly wage of $31.50. Other qualifications that apply to this table are on page 9.

## General Painting Costs

|  | Labor LF per manhour | Material coverage LF/gallon | Material cost per gallon | Labor cost per 100 LF | Labor burden 100 LF | Material cost per 100 LF | Overhead per 100 LF | Profit per 100 LF | Total price per 100 LF |
|---|---|---|---|---|---|---|---|---|---|

### Railing, wrought iron, 36" to 42" high bars with wood cap

Metal primer, rust inhibitor, clean metal (material #35)
Brush 1 coat

| | | | | | | | | | |
|---|---|---|---|---|---|---|---|---|---|
| Slow | 15 | 90 | 59.70 | 135.00 | 39.81 | 66.33 | 45.82 | 45.92 | 332.88 |
| Medium | 18 | 85 | 52.20 | 143.06 | 50.68 | 61.41 | 63.78 | 38.27 | 357.20 |
| Fast | 20 | 80 | 44.80 | 157.50 | 64.25 | 56.00 | 86.11 | 25.47 | 389.33 |

Metal primer, rust inhibitor, rusty metal (material #36)
Brush 1 coat

| | | | | | | | | | |
|---|---|---|---|---|---|---|---|---|---|
| Slow | 15 | 90 | 72.30 | 135.00 | 39.81 | 80.33 | 48.48 | 48.58 | 352.20 |
| Medium | 18 | 85 | 63.30 | 143.06 | 50.68 | 74.47 | 67.04 | 40.23 | 375.48 |
| Fast | 20 | 80 | 54.20 | 157.50 | 64.25 | 67.75 | 89.75 | 26.55 | 405.80 |

Metal finish, synthetic enamel, off white, gloss, interior or exterior - (material #37)
Brush 1st finish coat

| | | | | | | | | | |
|---|---|---|---|---|---|---|---|---|---|
| Slow | 20 | 110 | 59.70 | 101.25 | 29.85 | 54.27 | 35.22 | 35.30 | 255.89 |
| Medium | 23 | 100 | 52.20 | 111.96 | 39.65 | 52.20 | 50.95 | 30.57 | 285.33 |
| Fast | 26 | 90 | 44.80 | 121.15 | 49.42 | 49.78 | 68.31 | 20.21 | 308.87 |

Brush 2nd or additional finish coats

| | | | | | | | | | |
|---|---|---|---|---|---|---|---|---|---|
| Slow | 30 | 125 | 59.70 | 67.50 | 19.89 | 47.76 | 25.68 | 25.74 | 186.57 |
| Medium | 35 | 120 | 52.20 | 73.57 | 26.05 | 43.50 | 35.78 | 21.47 | 200.37 |
| Fast | 40 | 115 | 44.80 | 78.75 | 32.13 | 38.96 | 46.45 | 13.74 | 210.03 |

Metal finish, synthetic enamel, colors (except orange/red), gloss, interior or exterior - (material #38)
Brush 1st finish coat

| | | | | | | | | | |
|---|---|---|---|---|---|---|---|---|---|
| Slow | 20 | 110 | 65.20 | 101.25 | 29.85 | 59.27 | 36.17 | 36.25 | 262.79 |
| Medium | 23 | 100 | 57.00 | 111.96 | 39.65 | 57.00 | 52.15 | 31.29 | 292.05 |
| Fast | 26 | 90 | 48.90 | 121.15 | 49.42 | 54.33 | 69.72 | 20.62 | 315.24 |

Brush 2nd or additional finish coats

| | | | | | | | | | |
|---|---|---|---|---|---|---|---|---|---|
| Slow | 30 | 125 | 65.20 | 67.50 | 19.89 | 52.16 | 26.52 | 26.57 | 192.64 |
| Medium | 35 | 120 | 57.00 | 73.57 | 26.05 | 47.50 | 36.78 | 22.07 | 205.97 |
| Fast | 40 | 115 | 48.90 | 78.75 | 32.13 | 42.52 | 47.55 | 14.07 | 215.02 |

Use these figures for painting prefabricated preprimed wrought iron railing which is 36" to 42" high with 1/2" square vertical bars at 4" to 6" on center with a stain grade wood cap supported by a 1/2" by 1-1/2" top rail, and 1" square support posts at 6' to 10' on center and with a 1/2" by 1-1/2" bottom rail, unless otherwise noted. The metal finish figures include only minor touchup of pre-primed steel or wrought iron prefabricated railings. Note: A two coat system, prime and finish, using oil base material is recommended for any metal surface. Although water base material is often used, it may cause oxidation, corrosion and rust. Using one coat of oil base paint on exterior metal may result in cracking, peeling, or chipping without the proper prime coat application. If off white or another light colored finish paint is specified, make sure the prime coat is a light color also, or more than one finish coat will be necessary. "Slow" work is based on an hourly wage of $20.25, "Medium" work on an hourly wage of $25.75, and "Fast" work on an hourly wage of $31.50. Other qualifications that apply to this table are on page 9.

|  | Labor LF per manhour | Material coverage LF/gallon | Material cost per gallon | Labor cost per 100 LF | Labor burden 100 LF | Material cost per 100 LF | Overhead per 100 LF | Profit per 100 LF | Total price per 100 LF |
|---|---|---|---|---|---|---|---|---|---|

### Railing, wrought iron, 36" to 42" high bars with wrought iron cap

Metal primer, rust inhibitor, clean metal (material #35)
  Brush 1 coat

|  | | | | | | | | | |
|---|---|---|---|---|---|---|---|---|---|
| Slow | 20 | 110 | 59.70 | 101.25 | 29.85 | 54.27 | 35.22 | 35.30 | 255.89 |
| Medium | 25 | 105 | 52.20 | 103.00 | 36.48 | 49.71 | 47.29 | 28.38 | 264.86 |
| Fast | 30 | 100 | 44.80 | 105.00 | 42.82 | 44.80 | 59.72 | 17.67 | 270.01 |

Metal primer, rust inhibitor, rusty metal (material #36)
  Brush 1 coat

|  | | | | | | | | | |
|---|---|---|---|---|---|---|---|---|---|
| Slow | 20 | 110 | 72.30 | 101.25 | 29.85 | 65.73 | 37.40 | 37.48 | 271.71 |
| Medium | 25 | 105 | 63.30 | 103.00 | 36.48 | 60.29 | 49.94 | 29.96 | 279.67 |
| Fast | 30 | 100 | 54.20 | 105.00 | 42.82 | 54.20 | 62.63 | 18.53 | 283.18 |

Metal finish, synthetic enamel, off white, gloss, interior or exterior - (material #37)
  Brush 1st finish coat

|  | | | | | | | | | |
|---|---|---|---|---|---|---|---|---|---|
| Slow | 25 | 120 | 59.70 | 81.00 | 23.88 | 49.75 | 29.38 | 29.44 | 213.45 |
| Medium | 30 | 115 | 52.20 | 85.83 | 30.39 | 45.39 | 40.40 | 24.24 | 226.25 |
| Fast | 35 | 110 | 44.80 | 90.00 | 36.71 | 40.73 | 51.91 | 15.36 | 234.71 |

  Brush 2nd or additional finish coats

|  | | | | | | | | | |
|---|---|---|---|---|---|---|---|---|---|
| Slow | 35 | 135 | 59.70 | 57.86 | 17.05 | 44.22 | 22.64 | 22.69 | 164.46 |
| Medium | 40 | 130 | 52.20 | 64.38 | 22.80 | 40.15 | 31.83 | 19.10 | 178.26 |
| Fast | 45 | 125 | 44.80 | 70.00 | 28.55 | 35.84 | 41.66 | 12.32 | 188.37 |

Metal finish, synthetic enamel, colors (except orange/red), gloss, interior or exterior - (material #38)
  Brush 1st finish coat

|  | | | | | | | | | |
|---|---|---|---|---|---|---|---|---|---|
| Slow | 25 | 120 | 65.20 | 81.00 | 23.88 | 54.33 | 30.25 | 30.32 | 219.78 |
| Medium | 30 | 115 | 57.00 | 85.83 | 30.39 | 49.57 | 41.45 | 24.87 | 232.11 |
| Fast | 35 | 110 | 48.90 | 90.00 | 36.71 | 44.45 | 53.06 | 15.70 | 239.92 |

  Brush 2nd or additional finish coats

|  | | | | | | | | | |
|---|---|---|---|---|---|---|---|---|---|
| Slow | 35 | 135 | 65.20 | 57.86 | 17.05 | 48.30 | 23.41 | 23.46 | 170.08 |
| Medium | 40 | 130 | 57.00 | 64.38 | 22.80 | 43.85 | 32.76 | 19.65 | 183.44 |
| Fast | 45 | 125 | 48.90 | 70.00 | 28.55 | 39.12 | 42.68 | 12.63 | 192.98 |

Use these figures for painting prefabricated preprimed wrought iron railing which is 36" to 42" high with 1/2" square vertical bars at 4" to 6" on center and a 1/2" by 1-1/2" wrought iron cap with 1" square support posts at 6' to 10' on center, and a 1/2" by 1-1/2" bottom rail, unless otherwise noted. The metal finish figures include only minor touchup of pre-primed steel or wrought iron prefabricated railings. Note: A two coat system, prime and finish, using oil base material is recommended for any metal surface. Although water base material is often used, it may cause oxidation, corrosion and rust. Using one coat of oil base paint on exterior metal may result in cracking, peeling, or chipping without the proper prime coat application. If off white or another light colored finish paint is specified, make sure the prime coat is also a light color, or more than one finish coat will be necessary. "Slow" work is based on an hourly wage of $20.25, "Medium" work on an hourly wage of $25.75, and "Fast" work on an hourly wage of $31.50. Other qualifications that apply to this table are on page 9.

*General Painting Costs*

|  | Labor LF per manhour | Material coverage LF/gallon | Material cost per gallon | Labor cost per 100 LF | Labor burden 100 LF | Material cost per 100 LF | Overhead per 100 LF | Profit per 100 LF | Total price per 100 LF |
|---|---|---|---|---|---|---|---|---|---|

### Railing, wrought iron, 60" to 72" high bars with wrought iron cap

Metal primer, rust inhibitor, clean metal (material #35)
  Brush 1 coat

| | | | | | | | | | |
|---|---|---|---|---|---|---|---|---|---|
| Slow | 10 | 90 | 59.70 | 202.50 | 59.70 | 66.33 | 62.43 | 62.56 | 453.52 |
| Medium | 15 | 85 | 52.20 | 171.67 | 60.81 | 61.41 | 73.46 | 44.08 | 411.43 |
| Fast | 20 | 80 | 44.80 | 157.50 | 64.25 | 56.00 | 86.11 | 25.47 | 389.33 |

Metal primer, rust inhibitor, rusty metal (material #36)
  Brush 1 coat

| | | | | | | | | | |
|---|---|---|---|---|---|---|---|---|---|
| Slow | 10 | 90 | 72.30 | 202.50 | 59.70 | 80.33 | 65.09 | 65.23 | 472.85 |
| Medium | 15 | 85 | 63.30 | 171.67 | 60.81 | 74.47 | 76.73 | 46.04 | 429.72 |
| Fast | 20 | 80 | 54.20 | 157.50 | 64.25 | 67.75 | 89.75 | 26.55 | 405.80 |

Metal finish, synthetic enamel, off white, gloss, interior or exterior - (material #37)
  Brush 1st finish coat

| | | | | | | | | | |
|---|---|---|---|---|---|---|---|---|---|
| Slow | 15 | 120 | 59.70 | 135.00 | 39.81 | 49.75 | 42.67 | 42.76 | 309.99 |
| Medium | 20 | 115 | 52.20 | 128.75 | 45.60 | 45.39 | 54.93 | 32.96 | 307.63 |
| Fast | 25 | 110 | 44.80 | 126.00 | 51.40 | 40.73 | 67.62 | 20.00 | 305.75 |

  Brush 2nd or additional finish coats

| | | | | | | | | | |
|---|---|---|---|---|---|---|---|---|---|
| Slow | 25 | 135 | 59.70 | 81.00 | 23.88 | 44.22 | 28.33 | 28.39 | 205.82 |
| Medium | 30 | 130 | 52.20 | 85.83 | 30.39 | 40.15 | 39.09 | 23.45 | 218.91 |
| Fast | 35 | 125 | 44.80 | 90.00 | 36.71 | 35.84 | 50.39 | 14.91 | 227.85 |

Metal finish, synthetic enamel, colors (except orange/red), gloss, interior or exterior - (material #38)
  Brush 1st finish coat

| | | | | | | | | | |
|---|---|---|---|---|---|---|---|---|---|
| Slow | 15 | 120 | 65.20 | 135.00 | 39.81 | 54.33 | 43.54 | 43.63 | 316.31 |
| Medium | 20 | 115 | 57.00 | 128.75 | 45.60 | 49.57 | 55.98 | 33.59 | 313.49 |
| Fast | 25 | 110 | 48.90 | 126.00 | 51.40 | 44.45 | 68.78 | 20.34 | 310.97 |

  Brush 2nd or additional finish coats

| | | | | | | | | | |
|---|---|---|---|---|---|---|---|---|---|
| Slow | 25 | 135 | 65.20 | 81.00 | 23.88 | 48.30 | 29.11 | 29.17 | 211.46 |
| Medium | 30 | 130 | 57.00 | 85.83 | 30.39 | 43.85 | 40.02 | 24.01 | 224.10 |
| Fast | 35 | 125 | 48.90 | 90.00 | 36.71 | 39.12 | 51.41 | 15.21 | 232.45 |

Use these figures for painting prefabricated preprimed wrought iron railing which is 60" to 72" high with 1/2" square vertical bars at 4" to 6" on center with 1" square support posts at 6' to 10' on center and with a 1/2" by 1-1/2" bottom rail, unless otherwise noted. The metal finish figures include only minor touchup of pre-primed steel or wrought iron prefabricated railings. Note: A two coat system, prime and finish, using oil base material is recommended for any metal surface. Although water base material is often used, it may cause oxidation, corrosion and rust. Using one coat of oil base paint on exterior metal may result in cracking, peeling, or chipping without the proper prime coat application. If off white or another light colored finish paint is specified, make sure the prime coat is also light color, or more than one finish coat will be necessary. "Slow" work is based on an hourly wage of $20.25, "Medium" work on an hourly wage of $25.75, and "Fast" work on an hourly wage of $31.50. Other qualifications that apply to this table are on page 9.

*National Painting Cost Estimator*

|  | SF floor per manhour | Material SF floor per can | Material cost per can | Labor per 100 SF floor | Labor burden 100 SF | Material per 100 SF floor | Overhead per 100 SF floor | Profit per 100 SF floor | Total per 100 SF floor |
|---|---|---|---|---|---|---|---|---|---|
| **Registers, HVAC, per 100 square feet of floor area** | | | | | | | | | |
| Repaint jobs, spray cans (material #17) | | | | | | | | | |
| Spray 1 coat | | | | | | | | | |
| Slow | 900 | 700 | 9.10 | 2.25 | .66 | 1.30 | .80 | .80 | 5.81 |
| Medium | 950 | 650 | 8.00 | 2.71 | .95 | 1.23 | 1.23 | .74 | 6.86 |
| Fast | 1000 | 600 | 6.90 | 3.15 | 1.29 | 1.15 | 1.73 | .51 | 7.83 |
| New construction projects, spray cans (material #17) | | | | | | | | | |
| Spray 1 coat | | | | | | | | | |
| Slow | 2500 | 800 | 9.10 | .81 | .24 | 1.14 | .42 | .42 | 3.03 |
| Medium | 2750 | 750 | 8.00 | .94 | .32 | 1.07 | .59 | .35 | 3.27 |
| Fast | 3000 | 700 | 6.90 | 1.05 | .41 | .99 | .77 | .23 | 3.45 |

These costs assume HVAC registers are painted with spray cans (bombs) to match the adjacent walls. Costs are based on square footage of the floor area of the building. These rates include time to remove, paint and replace the HVAC registers. Use the square feet of floor area divided by these rates to find manhours and the number of spray bombs needed to paint all the heat registers in a building. *Rule of Thumb*: 2 minutes per 100 square feet of floor is for new construction projects. "Slow" work is based on an hourly wage of $20.25, "Medium" work on an hourly wage of $25.75, and "Fast" work on an hourly wage of $31.50. Other qualifications that apply to this table are on page 9.

*General Painting Costs*

|  | Manhours per 1500 SF roof | Material gallons 1500 SF | Material cost per gallon | Labor per 1500 SF roof | Labor burden 1500 SF | Material per 1500 SF roof | Overhead per 1500 SF roof | Profit per 1500 SF roof | Total per 1500 SF roof |
|---|---|---|---|---|---|---|---|---|---|

## Roof jacks, per 1500 square feet of roof area

Metal primer, clean metal (material #35)
  1 story building, brush prime coat

| | | | | | | | | | |
|---|---|---|---|---|---|---|---|---|---|
| Slow | 0.40 | 0.30 | 59.70 | 8.10 | 2.39 | 17.91 | 5.40 | 5.41 | 39.21 |
| Medium | 0.35 | 0.33 | 52.20 | 9.01 | 3.19 | 17.23 | 7.36 | 4.41 | 41.20 |
| Fast | 0.30 | 0.35 | 44.80 | 9.45 | 3.86 | 15.68 | 8.99 | 2.66 | 40.64 |

  2 story building, brush prime coat

| | | | | | | | | | |
|---|---|---|---|---|---|---|---|---|---|
| Slow | 0.50 | 0.40 | 59.70 | 10.13 | 2.98 | 23.88 | 7.03 | 7.04 | 51.06 |
| Medium | 0.45 | 0.43 | 52.20 | 11.59 | 4.10 | 22.45 | 9.54 | 5.72 | 53.40 |
| Fast | 0.40 | 0.45 | 44.80 | 12.60 | 5.14 | 20.16 | 11.75 | 3.48 | 53.13 |

Metal primer, rusty metal (material #36)
  1 story building, brush prime coat

| | | | | | | | | | |
|---|---|---|---|---|---|---|---|---|---|
| Slow | 0.40 | 0.30 | 72.30 | 8.10 | 2.39 | 21.69 | 6.11 | 6.13 | 44.42 |
| Medium | 0.35 | 0.33 | 63.30 | 9.01 | 3.19 | 20.89 | 8.27 | 4.96 | 46.32 |
| Fast | 0.30 | 0.35 | 54.20 | 9.45 | 3.86 | 18.97 | 10.01 | 2.96 | 45.25 |

  2 story building, brush prime coat

| | | | | | | | | | |
|---|---|---|---|---|---|---|---|---|---|
| Slow | 0.50 | 0.40 | 72.30 | 10.13 | 2.98 | 28.92 | 7.99 | 8.00 | 58.02 |
| Medium | 0.45 | 0.43 | 63.30 | 11.59 | 4.10 | 27.22 | 10.73 | 6.44 | 60.08 |
| Fast | 0.40 | 0.45 | 54.20 | 12.60 | 5.14 | 24.39 | 13.06 | 3.86 | 59.05 |

Metal finish, synthetic enamel - off white, gloss, interior or exterior (material #37)
  1 story building, brush each coat

| | | | | | | | | | |
|---|---|---|---|---|---|---|---|---|---|
| Slow | 0.30 | 0.20 | 59.70 | 6.08 | 1.79 | 11.94 | 3.76 | 3.77 | 27.34 |
| Medium | 0.25 | 0.25 | 52.20 | 6.44 | 2.27 | 13.05 | 5.44 | 3.27 | 30.47 |
| Fast | 0.20 | 0.30 | 44.80 | 6.30 | 2.57 | 13.44 | 6.92 | 2.05 | 31.28 |

  2 story building, brush each coat

| | | | | | | | | | |
|---|---|---|---|---|---|---|---|---|---|
| Slow | 0.40 | 0.30 | 59.70 | 8.10 | 2.39 | 17.91 | 5.40 | 5.41 | 39.21 |
| Medium | 0.35 | 0.33 | 52.20 | 9.01 | 3.19 | 17.23 | 7.36 | 4.41 | 41.20 |
| Fast | 0.30 | 0.35 | 44.80 | 9.45 | 3.86 | 15.68 | 8.99 | 2.66 | 40.64 |

|  | Manhours per 1500 SF roof | Material gallons 1500 SF | Material cost per gallon | Labor per 1500 SF roof | Labor burden 1500 SF | Material per 1500 SF roof | Overhead per 1500 SF roof | Profit per 1500 SF roof | Total per 1500 SF roof |
|---|---|---|---|---|---|---|---|---|---|

Metal finish, synthetic enamel, colors (except orange/red), gloss, interior or exterior - (material #38)
1 story building, brush each coat

| | | | | | | | | | |
|---|---|---|---|---|---|---|---|---|---|
| Slow | 0.30 | 0.20 | 65.20 | 6.08 | 1.79 | 13.04 | 3.97 | 3.98 | 28.86 |
| Medium | 0.25 | 0.25 | 57.00 | 6.44 | 2.27 | 14.25 | 5.74 | 3.45 | 32.15 |
| Fast | 0.20 | 0.30 | 48.90 | 6.30 | 2.57 | 14.67 | 7.30 | 2.16 | 33.00 |

2 story building, brush each coat

| | | | | | | | | | |
|---|---|---|---|---|---|---|---|---|---|
| Slow | 0.40 | 0.30 | 65.20 | 8.10 | 2.39 | 19.56 | 5.71 | 5.72 | 41.48 |
| Medium | 0.35 | 0.33 | 57.00 | 9.01 | 3.19 | 18.81 | 7.75 | 4.65 | 43.41 |
| Fast | 0.30 | 0.35 | 48.90 | 9.45 | 3.86 | 17.12 | 9.43 | 2.79 | 42.65 |

Production rates and coverage figures are minimum values based on 1 or 2 story roof areas of up to 1500 square feet. For example, to apply metal primer on clean metal roof jacks on a 3000 SF one-story building at a medium rate, use two times the cost of $41.20 or $82.40. This figure includes ladder time. See the paragraphs below on Roof pitch difficulty factors and Roof area conversion factors to adjust for roof slope and type. Note: A two coat system, prime and finish, using oil base material is recommended for any metal surface. Although water base material is often used, it may cause oxidation, corrosion and rust. One coat of oil base solid body stain is often used on exterior metal but it may crack, peel or chip without the proper prime coat application. "Slow" work is based on an hourly wage of $20.25, "Medium" work on an hourly wage of $25.75, and "Fast" work on an hourly wage of $31.50. Other qualifications that apply to this table are on page 9.

## Roof area conversion factors
For an arched roof, multiply the building length by the building width, then multiply by 1.5.
For a gambrel roof, multiply the building length by the building width, then multiply by 1.33.

## Roof pitch difficulty factors
It's harder to paint on a sloped surface than on a flat surface. The steeper the slope, the more difficult the work. Roof slope is usually measured in inches of rise per inch of horizontal run. For example, a 3 in 12 pitch means the roof rises 3 inches for each 12 inches of run, measuring horizontally. Use the difficulty factors that follow when estimating the time needed to paint on a sloping roof.

On a flat roof, or roof with a pitch of less than 3 in 12, calculate the roof area without modification.
If the pitch is 3 in 12, multiply the surface area by 1.1.
If the pitch is 4 in 12, multiply the surface area by 1.2.
If the pitch is 6 in 12, multiply the surface area by 1.3.

*General Painting Costs*

|  | Labor SF per manhour | Material coverage SF/gallon | Material cost per gallon | Labor cost per 100 SF | Labor burden 100 SF | Material cost per 100 SF | Overhead per 100 SF | Profit per 100 SF | Total price per 100 SF |
|---|---|---|---|---|---|---|---|---|---|

## Roofing, composition shingles, brush application

**Solid body stain, water base (material #18)**

Brush 1st coat
| | | | | | | | | | |
|---|---|---|---|---|---|---|---|---|---|
| Slow | 45 | 220 | 45.00 | 45.00 | 13.26 | 20.45 | 14.96 | 14.99 | 108.66 |
| Medium | 60 | 200 | 39.40 | 42.92 | 15.21 | 19.70 | 19.45 | 11.67 | 108.95 |
| Fast | 80 | 180 | 33.80 | 39.38 | 16.06 | 18.78 | 23.01 | 6.81 | 104.04 |

Brush 2nd coat
| | | | | | | | | | |
|---|---|---|---|---|---|---|---|---|---|
| Slow | 65 | 330 | 45.00 | 31.15 | 9.18 | 13.64 | 10.26 | 10.28 | 74.51 |
| Medium | 80 | 210 | 39.40 | 32.19 | 11.40 | 18.76 | 15.59 | 9.35 | 87.29 |
| Fast | 100 | 290 | 33.80 | 31.50 | 12.85 | 11.66 | 17.36 | 5.14 | 78.51 |

Brush 3rd or additional coats
| | | | | | | | | | |
|---|---|---|---|---|---|---|---|---|---|
| Slow | 85 | 405 | 45.00 | 23.82 | 7.01 | 11.11 | 7.97 | 7.99 | 57.90 |
| Medium | 100 | 385 | 39.40 | 25.75 | 9.12 | 10.23 | 11.28 | 6.77 | 63.15 |
| Fast | 120 | 365 | 33.80 | 26.25 | 10.69 | 9.26 | 14.33 | 4.24 | 64.77 |

**Solid body stain, oil base (material #19)**

Brush 1st coat
| | | | | | | | | | |
|---|---|---|---|---|---|---|---|---|---|
| Slow | 45 | 270 | 54.10 | 45.00 | 13.26 | 20.04 | 14.88 | 14.91 | 108.09 |
| Medium | 60 | 250 | 47.30 | 42.92 | 15.21 | 18.92 | 19.26 | 11.55 | 107.86 |
| Fast | 80 | 230 | 40.50 | 39.38 | 16.06 | 17.61 | 22.65 | 6.70 | 102.40 |

Brush 2nd coat
| | | | | | | | | | |
|---|---|---|---|---|---|---|---|---|---|
| Slow | 65 | 360 | 54.10 | 31.15 | 9.18 | 15.03 | 10.52 | 10.54 | 76.42 |
| Medium | 80 | 345 | 47.30 | 32.19 | 11.40 | 13.71 | 14.33 | 8.60 | 80.23 |
| Fast | 100 | 330 | 40.50 | 31.50 | 12.85 | 12.27 | 17.55 | 5.19 | 79.36 |

Brush 3rd or additional coats
| | | | | | | | | | |
|---|---|---|---|---|---|---|---|---|---|
| Slow | 85 | 425 | 54.10 | 23.82 | 7.01 | 12.73 | 8.28 | 8.30 | 60.14 |
| Medium | 100 | 405 | 47.30 | 25.75 | 9.12 | 11.68 | 11.64 | 6.98 | 65.17 |
| Fast | 120 | 385 | 40.50 | 26.25 | 10.69 | 10.52 | 14.72 | 4.35 | 66.53 |

Use these figures for repaint jobs only. Some older composition shingles may contain asbestos. It has been established that asbestos fibers are a known carcinogen (cancer causing) and it is likely that no new construction projects will specify materials or products which contain asbestos. Furthermore, roofing materials for a new construction project would not need painting. Roofing and siding products usually contain very little asbestos and are typically non-friable (hand pressure can not crumble, pulverize or reduce to a powder when dry). There is danger when asbestos is being removed because of exposure to airborne particulate matter. Apparently, there is little danger when painting asbestos roofing or siding, but it is a good idea to have your painters wear respirators or particle masks for their safety. Coverage figures are based on shingles or shakes with average moisture content. See the paragraphs on Roof pitch difficulty factors and Roof area conversion factors to adjust for roof slope and type. "Slow" work is based on an hourly wage of $20.25, "Medium" work on an hourly wage of $25.75, and "Fast" work on an hourly wage of $31.50. Other qualifications that apply to this table are on page 9.

|  | Labor SF per manhour | Material coverage SF/gallon | Material cost per gallon | Labor cost per 100 SF | Labor burden 100 SF | Material cost per 100 SF | Overhead per 100 SF | Profit per 100 SF | Total price per 100 SF |
|---|---|---|---|---|---|---|---|---|---|

## Roofing, composition shingles, roll application

Solid body stain, water base (material #18)

Roll 1st coat
| | | | | | | | | | |
|---|---|---|---|---|---|---|---|---|---|
| Slow | 150 | 190 | 45.00 | 13.50 | 3.99 | 23.68 | 7.82 | 7.84 | 56.83 |
| Medium | 170 | 180 | 39.40 | 15.15 | 5.35 | 21.89 | 10.60 | 6.36 | 59.35 |
| Fast | 200 | 170 | 33.80 | 15.75 | 6.43 | 19.88 | 13.04 | 3.86 | 58.96 |

Roll 2nd coat
| | | | | | | | | | |
|---|---|---|---|---|---|---|---|---|---|
| Slow | 250 | 300 | 45.00 | 8.10 | 2.39 | 15.00 | 4.84 | 4.85 | 35.18 |
| Medium | 305 | 290 | 39.40 | 8.44 | 3.00 | 13.59 | 6.26 | 3.75 | 35.04 |
| Fast | 360 | 280 | 33.80 | 8.75 | 3.58 | 12.07 | 7.56 | 2.24 | 34.20 |

Roll 3rd or additional coats
| | | | | | | | | | |
|---|---|---|---|---|---|---|---|---|---|
| Slow | 360 | 385 | 45.00 | 5.63 | 1.66 | 11.69 | 3.61 | 3.61 | 26.20 |
| Medium | 385 | 375 | 39.40 | 6.69 | 2.38 | 10.51 | 4.89 | 2.94 | 27.41 |
| Fast | 420 | 365 | 33.80 | 7.50 | 3.06 | 9.26 | 6.14 | 1.82 | 27.78 |

Solid body stain, oil base (material #19)

Roll 1st coat
| | | | | | | | | | |
|---|---|---|---|---|---|---|---|---|---|
| Slow | 150 | 220 | 54.10 | 13.50 | 3.99 | 24.59 | 7.99 | 8.01 | 58.08 |
| Medium | 170 | 205 | 47.30 | 15.15 | 5.35 | 23.07 | 10.90 | 6.54 | 61.01 |
| Fast | 200 | 190 | 40.50 | 15.75 | 6.43 | 21.32 | 13.49 | 3.99 | 60.98 |

Roll 2nd coat
| | | | | | | | | | |
|---|---|---|---|---|---|---|---|---|---|
| Slow | 250 | 330 | 54.10 | 8.10 | 2.39 | 16.39 | 5.11 | 5.12 | 37.11 |
| Medium | 305 | 320 | 47.30 | 8.44 | 3.00 | 14.78 | 6.55 | 3.93 | 36.70 |
| Fast | 360 | 310 | 40.50 | 8.75 | 3.58 | 13.06 | 7.87 | 2.33 | 35.59 |

Roll 3rd or additional coats
| | | | | | | | | | |
|---|---|---|---|---|---|---|---|---|---|
| Slow | 360 | 405 | 54.10 | 5.63 | 1.66 | 13.36 | 3.92 | 3.93 | 28.50 |
| Medium | 385 | 395 | 47.30 | 6.69 | 2.38 | 11.97 | 5.26 | 3.15 | 29.45 |
| Fast | 420 | 385 | 40.50 | 7.50 | 3.06 | 10.52 | 6.53 | 1.93 | 29.54 |

*General Painting Costs*

|  | Labor SF per manhour | Material coverage SF/gallon | Material cost per gallon | Labor cost per 100 SF | Labor burden 100 SF | Material cost per 100 SF | Overhead per 100 SF | Profit per 100 SF | Total price per 100 SF |
|---|---|---|---|---|---|---|---|---|---|
| **Waterproofing, clear hydro sealer (material #34)** | | | | | | | | | |
| Roll 1st coat | | | | | | | | | |
| Slow | 100 | 300 | 40.60 | 20.25 | 5.97 | 13.53 | 7.55 | 7.57 | 54.87 |
| Medium | 200 | 275 | 35.50 | 12.88 | 4.56 | 12.91 | 7.59 | 4.55 | 42.49 |
| Fast | 300 | 250 | 30.40 | 10.50 | 4.27 | 12.16 | 8.35 | 2.47 | 37.75 |
| Roll 2nd or additional coats | | | | | | | | | |
| Slow | 150 | 350 | 40.60 | 13.50 | 3.99 | 11.60 | 5.53 | 5.54 | 40.16 |
| Medium | 250 | 325 | 35.50 | 10.30 | 3.65 | 10.92 | 6.22 | 3.73 | 34.82 |
| Fast | 350 | 300 | 30.40 | 9.00 | 3.68 | 10.13 | 7.07 | 2.09 | 31.97 |

Use these figures for repaint jobs only. Some older composition shingles may contain asbestos. It has been established that asbestos fibers are a known carcinogen (cancer causing) and it is likely that no new construction projects will specify materials or products which contain asbestos. Furthermore, roofing materials for a new construction project would not need painting. Roofing and siding products usually contain very little asbestos and are typically non-friable (hand pressure can not crumble, pulverize or reduce to a powder when dry). There is danger when asbestos is being removed because of exposure to airborne particulate matter. Apparently, there is little danger when painting asbestos roofing or siding, but it is a good idea to have your painters wear respirators or particle masks for their safety. Coverage figures are based on shingles or shakes with average moisture content. See the paragraphs on Roof pitch difficulty factors and Roof area conversion factors to adjust for roof slope and type. "Slow" work is based on an hourly wage of $20.25, "Medium" work on an hourly wage of $25.75, and "Fast" work on an hourly wage of $31.50. Other qualifications that apply to this table are on page 9.

|  | Labor SF per manhour | Material coverage SF/gallon | Material cost per gallon | Labor cost per 100 SF | Labor burden 100 SF | Material cost per 100 SF | Overhead per 100 SF | Profit per 100 SF | Total price per 100 SF |
|---|---|---|---|---|---|---|---|---|---|

## Roofing, composition shingles, spray application

**Solid body stain, water base (material #18)**

Spray 1st coat
| | | | | | | | | | |
|---|---|---|---|---|---|---|---|---|---|
| Slow | 325 | 200 | 45.00 | 6.23 | 1.85 | 22.50 | 5.81 | 5.82 | 42.21 |
| Medium | 350 | 180 | 39.40 | 7.36 | 2.61 | 21.89 | 7.97 | 4.78 | 44.61 |
| Fast | 375 | 160 | 33.80 | 8.40 | 3.44 | 21.13 | 10.22 | 3.02 | 46.21 |

Spray 2nd coat
| | | | | | | | | | |
|---|---|---|---|---|---|---|---|---|---|
| Slow | 425 | 290 | 45.00 | 4.76 | 1.40 | 15.52 | 4.12 | 4.13 | 29.93 |
| Medium | 450 | 280 | 39.40 | 5.72 | 2.02 | 14.07 | 5.45 | 3.27 | 30.53 |
| Fast | 475 | 270 | 33.80 | 6.63 | 2.73 | 12.52 | 6.78 | 2.00 | 30.66 |

Spray 3rd or additional coats
| | | | | | | | | | |
|---|---|---|---|---|---|---|---|---|---|
| Slow | 500 | 365 | 45.00 | 4.05 | 1.19 | 12.33 | 3.34 | 3.35 | 24.26 |
| Medium | 538 | 355 | 39.40 | 4.79 | 1.70 | 11.10 | 4.40 | 2.64 | 24.63 |
| Fast | 575 | 345 | 33.80 | 5.48 | 2.24 | 9.80 | 5.43 | 1.61 | 24.56 |

**Solid body stain, oil base (material #19)**

Spray 1st coat
| | | | | | | | | | |
|---|---|---|---|---|---|---|---|---|---|
| Slow | 325 | 230 | 54.10 | 6.23 | 1.85 | 23.52 | 6.00 | 6.01 | 43.61 |
| Medium | 350 | 205 | 47.30 | 7.36 | 2.61 | 23.07 | 8.26 | 4.96 | 46.26 |
| Fast | 375 | 180 | 40.50 | 8.40 | 3.44 | 22.50 | 10.64 | 3.15 | 48.13 |

Spray 2nd coat
| | | | | | | | | | |
|---|---|---|---|---|---|---|---|---|---|
| Slow | 425 | 310 | 54.10 | 4.76 | 1.40 | 17.45 | 4.49 | 4.50 | 32.60 |
| Medium | 450 | 300 | 47.30 | 5.72 | 2.02 | 15.77 | 5.88 | 3.53 | 32.92 |
| Fast | 475 | 290 | 40.50 | 6.63 | 2.73 | 13.97 | 7.23 | 2.14 | 32.70 |

Spray 3rd or additional coats
| | | | | | | | | | |
|---|---|---|---|---|---|---|---|---|---|
| Slow | 500 | 380 | 54.10 | 4.05 | 1.19 | 14.24 | 3.70 | 3.71 | 26.89 |
| Medium | 538 | 370 | 47.30 | 4.79 | 1.70 | 12.78 | 4.82 | 2.89 | 26.98 |
| Fast | 575 | 360 | 40.50 | 5.48 | 2.24 | 11.25 | 5.88 | 1.74 | 26.59 |

## General Painting Costs

|  | Labor SF per manhour | Material coverage SF/gallon | Material cost per gallon | Labor cost per 100 SF | Labor burden 100 SF | Material cost per 100 SF | Overhead per 100 SF | Profit per 100 SF | Total price per 100 SF |
|---|---|---|---|---|---|---|---|---|---|
| **Waterproofing, clear hydro sealer (material #34)** | | | | | | | | | |
| Spray 1st coat | | | | | | | | | |
| Slow | 550 | 100 | 40.60 | 3.68 | 1.09 | 40.60 | 8.62 | 8.64 | 62.63 |
| Medium | 600 | 88 | 35.50 | 4.29 | 1.53 | 40.34 | 11.54 | 6.92 | 64.62 |
| Fast | 650 | 75 | 30.40 | 4.85 | 1.98 | 40.53 | 14.68 | 4.34 | 66.38 |
| Spray 2nd or additional coats | | | | | | | | | |
| Slow | 600 | 150 | 40.60 | 3.38 | 1.00 | 27.07 | 5.98 | 5.99 | 43.42 |
| Medium | 650 | 138 | 35.50 | 3.96 | 1.41 | 25.72 | 7.77 | 4.66 | 43.52 |
| Fast | 700 | 125 | 30.40 | 4.50 | 1.84 | 24.32 | 9.50 | 2.81 | 42.97 |

Use these figures for repaint jobs only. Some older composition shingles may contain asbestos. It has been established that asbestos fibers are a known carcinogen (cancer causing) and it is likely that no new construction projects will specify materials or products which contain asbestos. Furthermore, roofing materials for a new construction project would not need painting. Roofing and siding products usually contain very little asbestos and are typically non-friable (hand pressure can not crumble, pulverize or reduce to a powder when dry). There is danger when asbestos is being removed because of exposure to airborne particulate matter. Apparently, there is little danger when painting asbestos roofing or siding, but it is a good idea to have your painters wear respirators or particle masks for their safety. Coverage figures are based on shingles or shakes with average moisture content. See the paragraphs on Roof pitch difficulty factors and Roof area conversion factors to adjust for roof slope and type. "Slow" work is based on an hourly wage of $20.25, "Medium" work on an hourly wage of $25.75, and "Fast" work on an hourly wage of $31.50. Other qualifications that apply to this table are on page 9.

|  | Labor SF per manhour | Material coverage SF/gallon | Material cost per gallon | Labor cost per 100 SF | Labor burden 100 SF | Material cost per 100 SF | Overhead per 100 SF | Profit per 100 SF | Total price per 100 SF |
|---|---|---|---|---|---|---|---|---|---|
| **Roofing, wood shingles or shakes, brush application** | | | | | | | | | |
| Solid body stain, water base (material #18) | | | | | | | | | |
| Brush 1st coat | | | | | | | | | |
|   Slow | 100 | 240 | 45.00 | 20.25 | 5.97 | 18.75 | 8.54 | 8.56 | 62.07 |
|   Medium | 155 | 228 | 39.40 | 16.61 | 5.88 | 17.28 | 9.94 | 5.97 | 55.68 |
|   Fast | 210 | 215 | 33.80 | 15.00 | 6.11 | 15.72 | 11.42 | 3.38 | 51.63 |
| Brush 2nd or additional coats | | | | | | | | | |
|   Slow | 150 | 290 | 45.00 | 13.50 | 3.99 | 15.52 | 6.27 | 6.28 | 45.56 |
|   Medium | 195 | 278 | 39.40 | 13.21 | 4.68 | 14.17 | 8.02 | 4.81 | 44.89 |
|   Fast | 240 | 265 | 33.80 | 13.13 | 5.36 | 12.75 | 9.68 | 2.86 | 43.78 |
| Solid body stain, oil base (material #19) | | | | | | | | | |
| Brush 1st coat | | | | | | | | | |
|   Slow | 100 | 160 | 54.10 | 20.25 | 5.97 | 33.81 | 11.41 | 11.43 | 82.87 |
|   Medium | 155 | 150 | 47.30 | 16.61 | 5.88 | 31.53 | 13.51 | 8.10 | 75.63 |
|   Fast | 210 | 140 | 40.50 | 15.00 | 6.11 | 28.93 | 15.52 | 4.59 | 70.15 |
| Brush 2nd or additional coats | | | | | | | | | |
|   Slow | 150 | 260 | 54.10 | 13.50 | 3.99 | 20.81 | 7.28 | 7.29 | 52.87 |
|   Medium | 195 | 250 | 47.30 | 13.21 | 4.68 | 18.92 | 9.20 | 5.52 | 51.53 |
|   Fast | 240 | 240 | 40.50 | 13.13 | 5.36 | 16.88 | 10.96 | 3.24 | 49.57 |
| Semi-transparent stain, water base (material #20) | | | | | | | | | |
| Brush 1st coat | | | | | | | | | |
|   Slow | 120 | 260 | 47.50 | 16.88 | 4.96 | 18.27 | 7.62 | 7.64 | 55.37 |
|   Medium | 175 | 248 | 41.60 | 14.71 | 5.20 | 16.77 | 9.17 | 5.50 | 51.35 |
|   Fast | 230 | 235 | 35.60 | 13.70 | 5.59 | 15.15 | 10.68 | 3.16 | 48.28 |
| Brush 2nd or additional coats | | | | | | | | | |
|   Slow | 160 | 300 | 47.50 | 12.66 | 3.73 | 15.83 | 6.12 | 6.13 | 44.47 |
|   Medium | 205 | 288 | 41.60 | 12.56 | 4.46 | 14.44 | 7.86 | 4.72 | 44.04 |
|   Fast | 250 | 275 | 35.60 | 12.60 | 5.14 | 12.95 | 9.51 | 2.81 | 43.01 |
| Semi-transparent stain, oil base (material #21) | | | | | | | | | |
| Brush 1st coat | | | | | | | | | |
|   Slow | 120 | 180 | 48.70 | 16.88 | 4.96 | 27.06 | 9.29 | 9.31 | 67.50 |
|   Medium | 175 | 170 | 42.60 | 14.71 | 5.20 | 25.06 | 11.25 | 6.75 | 62.97 |
|   Fast | 230 | 160 | 36.50 | 13.70 | 5.59 | 22.81 | 13.05 | 3.86 | 59.01 |
| Brush 2nd or additional coats | | | | | | | | | |
|   Slow | 160 | 280 | 48.70 | 12.66 | 3.73 | 17.39 | 6.42 | 6.43 | 46.63 |
|   Medium | 205 | 270 | 42.60 | 12.56 | 4.46 | 15.78 | 8.20 | 4.92 | 45.92 |
|   Fast | 250 | 260 | 36.50 | 12.60 | 5.14 | 14.04 | 9.85 | 2.91 | 44.54 |

*General Painting Costs*

|  | Labor SF per manhour | Material coverage SF/gallon | Material cost per gallon | Labor cost per 100 SF | Labor burden 100 SF | Material cost per 100 SF | Overhead per 100 SF | Profit per 100 SF | Total price per 100 SF |
|---|---|---|---|---|---|---|---|---|---|
| **Penetrating oil stain (material #13)** | | | | | | | | | |
| Brush 1st coat | | | | | | | | | |
| Slow | 100 | 160 | 54.50 | 20.25 | 5.97 | 34.06 | 11.45 | 11.48 | 83.21 |
| Medium | 155 | 150 | 47.70 | 16.61 | 5.88 | 31.80 | 13.57 | 8.14 | 76.00 |
| Fast | 210 | 140 | 40.90 | 15.00 | 6.11 | 29.21 | 15.60 | 4.62 | 70.54 |
| Brush 2nd or additional coats | | | | | | | | | |
| Slow | 150 | 205 | 54.50 | 13.50 | 3.99 | 26.59 | 8.37 | 8.39 | 60.84 |
| Medium | 195 | 195 | 47.70 | 13.21 | 4.68 | 24.46 | 10.59 | 6.35 | 59.29 |
| Fast | 240 | 185 | 40.90 | 13.13 | 5.36 | 22.11 | 12.59 | 3.72 | 56.91 |

Coverage figures are based on shingles or shakes with average moisture content. See the paragraphs on Roof pitch difficulty factors and Roof area conversion factors to adjust for roof slope and type. "Slow" work is based on an hourly wage of $20.25, "Medium" work on an hourly wage of $25.75, and "Fast" work on an hourly wage of $31.50. Other qualifications that apply to this table are on page 9.

*National Painting Cost Estimator*

|  | Labor SF per manhour | Material coverage SF/gallon | Material cost per gallon | Labor cost per 100 SF | Labor burden 100 SF | Material cost per 100 SF | Overhead per 100 SF | Profit per 100 SF | Total price per 100 SF |
|---|---|---|---|---|---|---|---|---|---|
| **Roofing, wood shingles or shakes, roll application** | | | | | | | | | |
| Solid body stain, water base (material #18) | | | | | | | | | |
| Roll 1st coat | | | | | | | | | |
| Slow | 210 | 225 | 45.00 | 9.64 | 2.84 | 20.00 | 6.17 | 6.18 | 44.83 |
| Medium | 258 | 213 | 39.40 | 9.98 | 3.55 | 18.50 | 8.00 | 4.80 | 44.83 |
| Fast | 305 | 200 | 33.80 | 10.33 | 4.22 | 16.90 | 9.75 | 2.88 | 44.08 |
| Roll 2nd or additional coats | | | | | | | | | |
| Slow | 250 | 275 | 45.00 | 8.10 | 2.39 | 16.36 | 5.10 | 5.11 | 37.06 |
| Medium | 300 | 263 | 39.40 | 8.58 | 3.03 | 14.98 | 6.65 | 3.99 | 37.23 |
| Fast | 350 | 250 | 33.80 | 9.00 | 3.68 | 13.52 | 8.12 | 2.40 | 36.72 |
| Solid body stain, oil base (material #19) | | | | | | | | | |
| Roll 1st coat | | | | | | | | | |
| Slow | 210 | 150 | 54.10 | 9.64 | 2.84 | 36.07 | 9.22 | 9.24 | 67.01 |
| Medium | 255 | 140 | 47.30 | 10.10 | 3.57 | 33.79 | 11.87 | 7.12 | 66.45 |
| Fast | 305 | 130 | 40.50 | 10.33 | 4.22 | 31.15 | 14.16 | 4.19 | 64.05 |
| Roll 2nd or additional coats | | | | | | | | | |
| Slow | 250 | 245 | 54.10 | 8.10 | 2.39 | 22.08 | 6.19 | 6.20 | 44.96 |
| Medium | 300 | 235 | 47.30 | 8.58 | 3.03 | 20.13 | 7.94 | 4.76 | 44.44 |
| Fast | 350 | 225 | 40.50 | 9.00 | 3.68 | 18.00 | 9.51 | 2.81 | 43.00 |
| Semi-transparent stain, water base (material #20) | | | | | | | | | |
| Roll 1st coat | | | | | | | | | |
| Slow | 240 | 250 | 47.50 | 8.44 | 2.49 | 19.00 | 5.69 | 5.70 | 41.32 |
| Medium | 288 | 238 | 41.60 | 8.94 | 3.16 | 17.48 | 7.40 | 4.44 | 41.42 |
| Fast | 335 | 225 | 35.60 | 9.40 | 3.86 | 15.82 | 9.01 | 2.66 | 40.75 |
| Roll 2nd or additional coats | | | | | | | | | |
| Slow | 270 | 290 | 47.50 | 7.50 | 2.20 | 16.38 | 4.96 | 4.97 | 36.01 |
| Medium | 320 | 278 | 41.60 | 8.05 | 2.86 | 14.96 | 6.47 | 3.88 | 36.22 |
| Fast | 370 | 255 | 35.60 | 8.51 | 3.46 | 13.96 | 8.04 | 2.38 | 36.35 |
| Semi-transparent stain, oil base (material #21) | | | | | | | | | |
| Roll 1st coat | | | | | | | | | |
| Slow | 240 | 175 | 48.70 | 8.44 | 2.49 | 27.83 | 7.36 | 7.38 | 53.50 |
| Medium | 288 | 165 | 42.60 | 8.94 | 3.16 | 25.82 | 9.48 | 5.69 | 53.09 |
| Fast | 335 | 155 | 36.50 | 9.40 | 3.86 | 23.55 | 11.40 | 3.37 | 51.58 |
| Roll 2nd or additional coats | | | | | | | | | |
| Slow | 270 | 260 | 48.70 | 7.50 | 2.20 | 18.73 | 5.40 | 5.41 | 39.24 |
| Medium | 320 | 250 | 42.60 | 8.05 | 2.86 | 17.04 | 6.99 | 4.19 | 39.13 |
| Fast | 370 | 240 | 36.50 | 8.51 | 3.46 | 15.21 | 8.43 | 2.49 | 38.10 |

*General Painting Costs*

|  | Labor SF per manhour | Material coverage SF/gallon | Material cost per gallon | Labor cost per 100 SF | Labor burden 100 SF | Material cost per 100 SF | Overhead per 100 SF | Profit per 100 SF | Total price per 100 SF |
|---|---|---|---|---|---|---|---|---|---|
| **Penetrating oil stain (material #13)** | | | | | | | | | |
| *Roll 1st coat* | | | | | | | | | |
| Slow | 210 | 200 | 54.50 | 9.64 | 2.84 | 27.25 | 7.55 | 7.56 | 54.84 |
| Medium | 258 | 190 | 47.70 | 9.98 | 3.55 | 25.11 | 9.66 | 5.79 | 54.09 |
| Fast | 305 | 180 | 40.90 | 10.33 | 4.22 | 22.72 | 11.55 | 3.42 | 52.24 |
| *Roll 2nd or additional coats* | | | | | | | | | |
| Slow | 250 | 295 | 54.50 | 8.10 | 2.39 | 18.47 | 5.50 | 5.51 | 39.97 |
| Medium | 300 | 285 | 47.70 | 8.58 | 3.03 | 16.74 | 7.09 | 4.25 | 39.69 |
| Fast | 350 | 275 | 40.90 | 9.00 | 3.68 | 14.87 | 8.54 | 2.53 | 38.62 |
| **Waterproofing, clear hydro sealer (material #34)** | | | | | | | | | |
| *Roll 1st coat* | | | | | | | | | |
| Slow | 80 | 225 | 40.60 | 25.31 | 7.47 | 18.04 | 9.66 | 9.68 | 70.16 |
| Medium | 160 | 195 | 35.50 | 16.09 | 5.70 | 18.21 | 10.00 | 6.00 | 56.00 |
| Fast | 230 | 165 | 30.40 | 13.70 | 5.59 | 18.42 | 11.69 | 3.46 | 52.86 |
| *Roll 2nd or additional coats* | | | | | | | | | |
| Slow | 125 | 150 | 40.60 | 16.20 | 4.78 | 27.07 | 9.13 | 9.15 | 66.33 |
| Medium | 190 | 138 | 35.50 | 13.55 | 4.79 | 25.72 | 11.02 | 6.61 | 61.69 |
| Fast | 255 | 125 | 30.40 | 12.35 | 5.04 | 24.32 | 12.93 | 3.82 | 58.46 |

Coverage figures are based on shingles or shakes with average moisture content. See the paragraphs on Roof pitch difficulty factors and Roof area conversion factors to adjust for roof slope and type. "Slow" work is based on an hourly wage of $20.25, "Medium" work on an hourly wage of $25.75, and "Fast" work on an hourly wage of $31.50. Other qualifications that apply to this table are on page 9.

National Painting Cost Estimator

|  | Labor SF per manhour | Material coverage SF/gallon | Material cost per gallon | Labor cost per 100 SF | Labor burden 100 SF | Material cost per 100 SF | Overhead per 100 SF | Profit per 100 SF | Total price per 100 SF |
|---|---|---|---|---|---|---|---|---|---|

## Roofing, wood shingles or shakes, spray application

Solid body stain, water base (material #18)
  Spray 1st coat

| | | | | | | | | | |
|---|---|---|---|---|---|---|---|---|---|
| Slow | 600 | 230 | 45.00 | 3.38 | 1.00 | 19.57 | 4.55 | 4.56 | 33.06 |
| Medium | 700 | 220 | 39.40 | 3.68 | 1.31 | 17.91 | 5.72 | 3.43 | 32.05 |
| Fast | 800 | 200 | 33.80 | 3.94 | 1.60 | 16.90 | 6.96 | 2.06 | 31.46 |

  Spray 2nd or additional coats

| | | | | | | | | | |
|---|---|---|---|---|---|---|---|---|---|
| Slow | 700 | 250 | 45.00 | 2.89 | .86 | 18.00 | 4.13 | 4.14 | 30.02 |
| Medium | 800 | 235 | 39.40 | 3.22 | 1.14 | 16.77 | 5.28 | 3.17 | 29.58 |
| Fast | 900 | 220 | 33.80 | 3.50 | 1.42 | 15.36 | 6.29 | 1.86 | 28.43 |

Solid body stain, oil base (material #19)
  Spray 1st coat

| | | | | | | | | | |
|---|---|---|---|---|---|---|---|---|---|
| Slow | 600 | 170 | 54.10 | 3.38 | 1.00 | 31.82 | 6.88 | 6.89 | 49.97 |
| Medium | 700 | 150 | 47.30 | 3.68 | 1.31 | 31.53 | 9.13 | 5.48 | 51.13 |
| Fast | 800 | 130 | 40.50 | 3.94 | 1.60 | 31.15 | 11.38 | 3.37 | 51.44 |

  Spray 2nd or additional coats

| | | | | | | | | | |
|---|---|---|---|---|---|---|---|---|---|
| Slow | 700 | 230 | 54.10 | 2.89 | .86 | 23.52 | 5.18 | 5.19 | 37.64 |
| Medium | 800 | 215 | 47.30 | 3.22 | 1.14 | 22.00 | 6.59 | 3.95 | 36.90 |
| Fast | 900 | 200 | 40.50 | 3.50 | 1.42 | 20.25 | 7.81 | 2.31 | 35.29 |

Semi-transparent stain, water base (material #20)
  Spray 1st coat

| | | | | | | | | | |
|---|---|---|---|---|---|---|---|---|---|
| Slow | 650 | 265 | 47.50 | 3.12 | .92 | 17.92 | 4.17 | 4.18 | 30.31 |
| Medium | 750 | 253 | 41.60 | 3.43 | 1.21 | 16.44 | 5.27 | 3.16 | 29.51 |
| Fast | 850 | 240 | 35.60 | 3.71 | 1.52 | 14.83 | 6.22 | 1.84 | 28.12 |

  Spray 2nd or additional coats

| | | | | | | | | | |
|---|---|---|---|---|---|---|---|---|---|
| Slow | 750 | 305 | 47.50 | 2.70 | .79 | 15.57 | 3.62 | 3.63 | 26.31 |
| Medium | 850 | 293 | 41.60 | 3.03 | 1.08 | 14.20 | 4.58 | 2.75 | 25.64 |
| Fast | 950 | 270 | 35.60 | 3.32 | 1.34 | 13.19 | 5.54 | 1.64 | 25.03 |

Semi-transparent stain, oil base (material #21)
  Spray 1st coat

| | | | | | | | | | |
|---|---|---|---|---|---|---|---|---|---|
| Slow | 650 | 190 | 48.70 | 3.12 | .92 | 25.63 | 5.64 | 5.65 | 40.96 |
| Medium | 750 | 180 | 42.60 | 3.43 | 1.21 | 23.67 | 7.08 | 4.25 | 39.64 |
| Fast | 850 | 170 | 36.50 | 3.71 | 1.52 | 21.47 | 8.27 | 2.45 | 37.42 |

  Spray 2nd or additional coats

| | | | | | | | | | |
|---|---|---|---|---|---|---|---|---|---|
| Slow | 750 | 275 | 48.70 | 2.70 | .79 | 17.71 | 4.03 | 4.04 | 29.27 |
| Medium | 850 | 265 | 42.60 | 3.03 | 1.08 | 16.08 | 5.05 | 3.03 | 28.27 |
| Fast | 950 | 255 | 36.50 | 3.32 | 1.34 | 14.31 | 5.88 | 1.74 | 26.59 |

## General Painting Costs

|  | Labor SF per manhour | Material coverage SF/gallon | Material cost per gallon | Labor cost per 100 SF | Labor burden 100 SF | Material cost per 100 SF | Overhead per 100 SF | Profit per 100 SF | Total price per 100 SF |
|---|---|---|---|---|---|---|---|---|---|
| **Penetrating oil stain (material #13)** | | | | | | | | | |
| *Spray 1st coat* | | | | | | | | | |
| Slow | 600 | 200 | 54.50 | 3.38 | 1.00 | 27.25 | 6.01 | 6.02 | 43.66 |
| Medium | 700 | 170 | 47.70 | 3.68 | 1.31 | 28.06 | 8.26 | 4.96 | 46.27 |
| Fast | 800 | 140 | 40.90 | 3.94 | 1.60 | 29.21 | 10.78 | 3.19 | 48.72 |
| *Spray 2nd or additional coats* | | | | | | | | | |
| Slow | 700 | 300 | 54.50 | 2.89 | .86 | 18.17 | 4.16 | 4.17 | 30.25 |
| Medium | 800 | 260 | 47.70 | 3.22 | 1.14 | 18.35 | 5.68 | 3.41 | 31.80 |
| Fast | 900 | 240 | 40.90 | 3.50 | 1.42 | 17.04 | 6.81 | 2.01 | 30.78 |
| **Waterproofing, clear hydro sealer (material #34)** | | | | | | | | | |
| *Spray 1st coat* | | | | | | | | | |
| Slow | 450 | 75 | 40.60 | 4.50 | 1.32 | 54.13 | 11.39 | 11.42 | 82.76 |
| Medium | 475 | 63 | 35.50 | 5.42 | 1.94 | 56.35 | 15.92 | 9.55 | 89.18 |
| Fast | 500 | 50 | 30.40 | 6.30 | 2.57 | 60.80 | 21.60 | 6.39 | 97.66 |
| *Spray 2nd or additional coats* | | | | | | | | | |
| Slow | 500 | 150 | 40.60 | 4.05 | 1.19 | 27.07 | 6.14 | 6.15 | 44.60 |
| Medium | 525 | 138 | 35.50 | 4.90 | 1.73 | 25.72 | 8.09 | 4.85 | 45.29 |
| Fast | 550 | 125 | 30.40 | 5.73 | 2.34 | 24.32 | 10.04 | 2.97 | 45.40 |

Coverage figures are based on shingles or shakes with average moisture content. See the paragraphs on Roof pitch difficulty factors and Roof area conversion factors to adjust for roof slope and type. "Slow" work is based on an hourly wage of $20.25, "Medium" work on an hourly wage of $25.75, and "Fast" work on an hourly wage of $31.50. Other qualifications that apply to this table are on page 9.

|  | Labor LF per manhour | Material coverage LF/gallon | Material cost per gallon | Labor cost per 100 LF | Labor burden 100 LF | Material cost per 100 LF | Overhead per 100 LF | Profit per 100 LF | Total price per 100 LF |
|---|---|---|---|---|---|---|---|---|---|

## Sheet metal cap or flashing

3" to 8" wide:
  Metal primer, clean metal (material #35)
    Brush prime coat

| | | | | | | | | | |
|---|---|---|---|---|---|---|---|---|---|
| Slow | 215 | 525 | 59.70 | 9.42 | 2.77 | 11.37 | 4.48 | 4.49 | 32.53 |
| Medium | 228 | 500 | 52.20 | 11.29 | 4.02 | 10.44 | 6.43 | 3.86 | 36.04 |
| Fast | 240 | 475 | 44.80 | 13.13 | 5.36 | 9.43 | 8.66 | 2.56 | 39.14 |

  Metal primer, rusty metal (material #36)
    Brush prime coat

| | | | | | | | | | |
|---|---|---|---|---|---|---|---|---|---|
| Slow | 215 | 525 | 72.30 | 9.42 | 2.77 | 13.77 | 4.93 | 4.94 | 35.83 |
| Medium | 228 | 500 | 63.30 | 11.29 | 4.02 | 12.66 | 6.99 | 4.19 | 39.15 |
| Fast | 240 | 475 | 54.20 | 13.13 | 5.36 | 11.41 | 9.27 | 2.74 | 41.91 |

  Metal finish, synthetic enamel - off white, gloss, interior or exterior (material #37)
    Brush 1st or additional finish coats

| | | | | | | | | | |
|---|---|---|---|---|---|---|---|---|---|
| Slow | 275 | 550 | 59.70 | 7.36 | 2.18 | 10.85 | 3.87 | 3.88 | 28.14 |
| Medium | 288 | 525 | 52.20 | 8.94 | 3.16 | 9.94 | 5.51 | 3.31 | 30.86 |
| Fast | 300 | 500 | 44.80 | 10.50 | 4.27 | 8.96 | 7.36 | 2.18 | 33.27 |

  Metal finish, synthetic enamel, colors (except orange/red), gloss, interior or exterior (material #38)
    Brush 1st or additional finish coats

| | | | | | | | | | |
|---|---|---|---|---|---|---|---|---|---|
| Slow | 275 | 550 | 65.20 | 7.36 | 2.18 | 11.85 | 4.06 | 4.07 | 29.52 |
| Medium | 288 | 525 | 57.00 | 8.94 | 3.16 | 10.86 | 5.74 | 3.44 | 32.14 |
| Fast | 300 | 500 | 48.90 | 10.50 | 4.27 | 9.78 | 7.61 | 2.25 | 34.41 |

This table is based on a two coat system, prime and finish, using oil base material which is recommended for any metal surface. Although water base material is often used, it may cause oxidation, corrosion and rust. One coat of oil base solid body stain is often used on exterior metal but it may crack, peel or chip without the proper prime coat application. If off white or another light colored finish paint is specified, make sure the prime coat is also a light color, or more than one finish coat will be necessary. "Slow" work is based on an hourly wage of $20.25, "Medium" work on an hourly wage of $25.75, and "Fast" work on an hourly wage of $31.50. Other qualifications that apply to this table are on page 9.

*General Painting Costs*

|  | Labor LF per manhour | Material coverage LF/gallon | Material cost per gallon | Labor cost per 100 LF | Labor burden 100 LF | Material cost per 100 LF | Overhead per 100 LF | Profit per 100 LF | Total price per 100 LF |
|---|---|---|---|---|---|---|---|---|---|

### Sheet metal cap or flashing
8" to 12" wide:
  Metal primer, clean metal (material #35)
    Brush prime coat

|  |  |  |  |  |  |  |  |  |  |
|---|---|---|---|---|---|---|---|---|---|
| Slow | 200 | 500 | 59.70 | 10.13 | 2.98 | 11.94 | 4.76 | 4.77 | 34.58 |
| Medium | 215 | 475 | 52.20 | 11.98 | 4.23 | 10.99 | 6.80 | 4.08 | 38.08 |
| Fast | 230 | 450 | 44.80 | 13.70 | 5.59 | 9.96 | 9.07 | 2.68 | 41.00 |

  Metal primer, rusty metal (material #36)
    Brush prime coat

|  |  |  |  |  |  |  |  |  |  |
|---|---|---|---|---|---|---|---|---|---|
| Slow | 200 | 500 | 72.30 | 10.13 | 2.98 | 14.46 | 5.24 | 5.25 | 38.06 |
| Medium | 215 | 475 | 63.30 | 11.98 | 4.23 | 13.33 | 7.39 | 4.43 | 41.36 |
| Fast | 230 | 450 | 54.20 | 13.70 | 5.59 | 12.04 | 9.71 | 2.87 | 43.91 |

  Metal finish, synthetic enamel - off white, gloss, interior or exterior (material #37)
    Brush 1st or additional finish coats

|  |  |  |  |  |  |  |  |  |  |
|---|---|---|---|---|---|---|---|---|---|
| Slow | 250 | 525 | 59.70 | 8.10 | 2.39 | 11.37 | 4.15 | 4.16 | 30.17 |
| Medium | 265 | 500 | 52.20 | 9.72 | 3.43 | 10.44 | 5.90 | 3.54 | 33.03 |
| Fast | 280 | 475 | 44.80 | 11.25 | 4.58 | 9.43 | 7.83 | 2.32 | 35.41 |

  Metal finish, synthetic enamel, colors (except orange/red), gloss, interior or exterior (material #38)
    Brush 1st or additional finish coats

|  |  |  |  |  |  |  |  |  |  |
|---|---|---|---|---|---|---|---|---|---|
| Slow | 250 | 525 | 65.20 | 8.10 | 2.39 | 12.42 | 4.35 | 4.36 | 31.62 |
| Medium | 265 | 500 | 57.00 | 9.72 | 3.43 | 11.40 | 6.14 | 3.68 | 34.37 |
| Fast | 280 | 475 | 48.90 | 11.25 | 4.58 | 10.29 | 8.10 | 2.40 | 36.62 |

This table is based on a two coat system, prime and finish, using oil base material which is recommended for any metal surface. Although water base material is often used, it may cause oxidation, corrosion and rust. One coat of oil base solid body stain is often used on exterior metal but it may crack, peel or chip without the proper prime coat application. If off white or another light colored finish paint is specified, make sure the prime coat is also a light color, or more than one finish coat will be necessary. "Slow" work is based on an hourly wage of $20.25, "Medium" work on an hourly wage of $25.75, and "Fast" work on an hourly wage of $31.50. Other qualifications that apply to this table are on page 9.

*National Painting Cost Estimator*

|  | Labor LF per manhour | Material coverage LF/gallon | Material cost per gallon | Labor cost per 100 LF | Labor burden 100 LF | Material cost per 100 LF | Overhead per 100 LF | Profit per 100 LF | Total price per 100 LF |
|---|---|---|---|---|---|---|---|---|---|

### Sheet metal, diverters or gravel stop

Up to 3" wide:
  Metal primer, clean metal (material #35)
    Brush prime coat

| | | | | | | | | | |
|---|---|---|---|---|---|---|---|---|---|
| Slow | 230 | 600 | 59.70 | 8.80 | 2.61 | 9.95 | 4.06 | 4.07 | 29.49 |
| Medium | 240 | 550 | 52.20 | 10.73 | 3.81 | 9.49 | 6.01 | 3.60 | 33.64 |
| Fast | 250 | 500 | 44.80 | 12.60 | 5.14 | 8.96 | 8.28 | 2.45 | 37.43 |

  Metal primer, rusty metal (material #36)
    Brush prime coat

| | | | | | | | | | |
|---|---|---|---|---|---|---|---|---|---|
| Slow | 230 | 600 | 72.30 | 8.80 | 2.61 | 12.05 | 4.46 | 4.47 | 32.39 |
| Medium | 240 | 550 | 63.30 | 10.73 | 3.81 | 11.51 | 6.51 | 3.91 | 36.47 |
| Fast | 250 | 500 | 54.20 | 12.60 | 5.14 | 10.84 | 8.86 | 2.62 | 40.06 |

  Metal finish, synthetic enamel - off white, gloss, interior or exterior (material #37)
    Brush 1st or additional finish coats

| | | | | | | | | | |
|---|---|---|---|---|---|---|---|---|---|
| Slow | 300 | 650 | 59.70 | 6.75 | 1.98 | 9.18 | 3.40 | 3.41 | 24.72 |
| Medium | 313 | 600 | 52.20 | 8.23 | 2.89 | 8.70 | 4.96 | 2.98 | 27.76 |
| Fast | 325 | 550 | 44.80 | 9.69 | 3.97 | 8.15 | 6.75 | 2.00 | 30.56 |

  Metal finish, synthetic enamel, colors (except orange/red), gloss, interior or exterior (material #38)
    Brush 1st or additional finish coats

| | | | | | | | | | |
|---|---|---|---|---|---|---|---|---|---|
| Slow | 300 | 650 | 65.20 | 6.75 | 1.98 | 10.03 | 3.57 | 3.57 | 25.90 |
| Medium | 313 | 600 | 57.00 | 8.23 | 2.89 | 9.50 | 5.16 | 3.10 | 28.88 |
| Fast | 325 | 550 | 48.90 | 9.69 | 3.97 | 8.89 | 6.98 | 2.07 | 31.60 |

This table is based on a two coat system, prime and finish, using oil base material which is recommended for any metal surface. Although water base material is often used, it may cause oxidation, corrosion and rust. One coat of oil base solid body stain is often used on exterior metal but it may crack, peel or chip without the proper prime coat application. If off white or another light colored finish paint is specified, make sure the prime coat is also a light color, or more than one finish coat will be necessary. "Slow" work is based on an hourly wage of $20.25, "Medium" work on an hourly wage of $25.75, and "Fast" work on an hourly wage of $31.50. Other qualifications that apply to this table are on page 9.

*General Painting Costs*

|  | Manhours per home | Material gallons per home | Material cost per gallon | Labor cost per home | Labor burden per home | Material cost per home | Overhead per home | Profit per home | Total price per home |
|---|---|---|---|---|---|---|---|---|---|

## Sheet metal vents & flashing
### Metal primer, clean metal (material #35)
#### 1 story home, brush prime coat
| | | | | | | | | | |
|---|---|---|---|---|---|---|---|---|---|
| Slow | 0.7 | 0.40 | 59.70 | 14.18 | 4.17 | 23.88 | 8.03 | 8.04 | 58.30 |
| Medium | 0.6 | 0.45 | 52.20 | 15.45 | 5.47 | 23.49 | 11.10 | 6.66 | 62.17 |
| Fast | 0.5 | 0.50 | 44.80 | 15.75 | 6.43 | 22.40 | 13.82 | 4.09 | 62.49 |

#### 2 story home, brush prime coat
| | | | | | | | | | |
|---|---|---|---|---|---|---|---|---|---|
| Slow | 0.9 | 0.50 | 59.70 | 18.23 | 5.37 | 29.85 | 10.16 | 10.18 | 73.79 |
| Medium | 0.8 | 0.55 | 52.20 | 20.60 | 7.30 | 28.71 | 14.15 | 8.49 | 79.25 |
| Fast | 0.7 | 0.60 | 44.80 | 22.05 | 9.00 | 26.88 | 17.96 | 5.31 | 81.20 |

#### Multiple units with attached roofs (per unit or 900 SF of roof area), brush 1st or additional finish coats
| | | | | | | | | | |
|---|---|---|---|---|---|---|---|---|---|
| Slow | 0.6 | 0.40 | 59.70 | 12.15 | 3.58 | 23.88 | 7.53 | 7.54 | 54.68 |
| Medium | 0.5 | 0.45 | 52.20 | 12.88 | 4.56 | 23.49 | 10.23 | 6.14 | 57.30 |
| Fast | 0.4 | 0.50 | 44.80 | 12.60 | 5.14 | 22.40 | 12.44 | 3.68 | 56.26 |

### Metal primer, rusty metal (material #36)
#### 1 story home, brush prime coat
| | | | | | | | | | |
|---|---|---|---|---|---|---|---|---|---|
| Slow | 0.7 | 0.40 | 72.30 | 14.18 | 4.17 | 28.92 | 8.98 | 9.00 | 65.25 |
| Medium | 0.6 | 0.45 | 63.30 | 15.45 | 5.47 | 28.49 | 12.35 | 7.41 | 69.17 |
| Fast | 0.5 | 0.50 | 54.20 | 15.75 | 6.43 | 27.10 | 15.28 | 4.52 | 69.08 |

#### 2 story home, brush prime coat
| | | | | | | | | | |
|---|---|---|---|---|---|---|---|---|---|
| Slow | 0.9 | 0.50 | 72.30 | 18.23 | 5.37 | 36.15 | 11.35 | 11.38 | 82.48 |
| Medium | 0.8 | 0.55 | 63.30 | 20.60 | 7.30 | 34.82 | 15.68 | 9.41 | 87.81 |
| Fast | 0.7 | 0.60 | 54.20 | 22.05 | 9.00 | 32.52 | 19.71 | 5.83 | 89.11 |

#### Multiple units with attached roofs (per unit or 900 SF of roof area), brush 1st or additional finish coats
| | | | | | | | | | |
|---|---|---|---|---|---|---|---|---|---|
| Slow | 0.6 | 0.40 | 72.30 | 12.15 | 3.58 | 28.92 | 8.48 | 8.50 | 61.63 |
| Medium | 0.5 | 0.45 | 63.30 | 12.88 | 4.56 | 28.49 | 11.48 | 6.89 | 64.30 |
| Fast | 0.4 | 0.50 | 54.20 | 12.60 | 5.14 | 27.10 | 13.90 | 4.11 | 62.85 |

### Metal finish, synthetic enamel - off white, gloss, interior or exterior (material #37)
#### 1 story home, brush 1st or additional finish coats
| | | | | | | | | | |
|---|---|---|---|---|---|---|---|---|---|
| Slow | 0.7 | 0.40 | 59.70 | 14.18 | 4.17 | 23.88 | 8.03 | 8.04 | 58.30 |
| Medium | 0.6 | 0.45 | 52.20 | 15.45 | 5.47 | 23.49 | 11.10 | 6.66 | 62.17 |
| Fast | 0.5 | 0.50 | 44.80 | 15.75 | 6.43 | 22.40 | 13.82 | 4.09 | 62.49 |

#### 2 story home, brush 1st or additional finish coats
| | | | | | | | | | |
|---|---|---|---|---|---|---|---|---|---|
| Slow | 0.9 | 0.50 | 59.70 | 18.23 | 5.37 | 29.85 | 10.16 | 10.18 | 73.79 |
| Medium | 0.8 | 0.55 | 52.20 | 20.60 | 7.30 | 28.71 | 14.15 | 8.49 | 79.25 |
| Fast | 0.7 | 0.60 | 44.80 | 22.05 | 9.00 | 26.88 | 17.96 | 5.31 | 81.20 |

*National Painting Cost Estimator*

|  | Manhours per home | Material gallons per home | Material cost per gallon | Labor cost per home | Labor burden per home | Material cost per home | Overhead per home | Profit per home | Total price per home |
|---|---|---|---|---|---|---|---|---|---|
| Multiple units with attached roofs (per unit or 900 SF of roof area), brush 1st or additional finish coats | | | | | | | | | |
| Slow | 0.6 | 0.40 | 59.70 | 12.15 | 3.58 | 23.88 | 7.53 | 7.54 | 54.68 |
| Medium | 0.5 | 0.45 | 52.20 | 12.88 | 4.56 | 23.49 | 10.23 | 6.14 | 57.30 |
| Fast | 0.4 | 0.50 | 44.80 | 12.60 | 5.14 | 22.40 | 12.44 | 3.68 | 56.26 |
| Metal finish, synthetic enamel - colors (except orange/red), gloss, interior or exterior (material #38) | | | | | | | | | |
| 1 story home, brush 1st or additional finish coats | | | | | | | | | |
| Slow | 0.7 | 0.40 | 65.20 | 14.18 | 4.17 | 26.08 | 8.44 | 8.46 | 61.33 |
| Medium | 0.6 | 0.45 | 57.00 | 15.45 | 5.47 | 25.65 | 11.64 | 6.99 | 65.20 |
| Fast | 0.5 | 0.50 | 48.90 | 15.75 | 6.43 | 24.45 | 14.46 | 4.28 | 65.37 |
| 2 story home, brush 1st or additional finish coats | | | | | | | | | |
| Slow | 0.9 | 0.50 | 65.20 | 18.23 | 5.37 | 32.60 | 10.68 | 10.70 | 77.58 |
| Medium | 0.8 | 0.55 | 57.00 | 20.60 | 7.30 | 31.35 | 14.81 | 8.89 | 82.95 |
| Fast | 0.7 | 0.60 | 48.90 | 22.05 | 9.00 | 29.34 | 18.72 | 5.54 | 84.65 |
| Multiple units with attached roofs (per unit or 900 SF of roof area), brush 1st or additional finish coats | | | | | | | | | |
| Slow | 0.6 | 0.40 | 65.20 | 12.15 | 3.58 | 26.08 | 7.94 | 7.96 | 57.71 |
| Medium | 0.5 | 0.45 | 57.00 | 12.88 | 4.56 | 25.65 | 10.77 | 6.46 | 60.32 |
| Fast | 0.4 | 0.50 | 48.90 | 12.60 | 5.14 | 24.45 | 13.08 | 3.87 | 59.14 |

Use this table with metal prime and finish paints only. This table shows the time needed to paint sheet metal vents on an average home or attached dwelling unit. Use it to estimate the costs for residential units without having to take off each vent or piece of flashing. Use the "attached units" section based on 900 square feet of roof area to estimate commercial buildings. Note: A two coat system, prime and finish, using oil base material is recommended for any metal surface. Although water base material is often used, it may cause oxidation, corrosion and rust. One coat of oil base solid body stain is often used on exterior metal but it may crack, peel or chip without the proper prime coat application. If off white or another light colored finish paint is specified, make sure the prime coat is also a light color, or more than one finish coat will be necessary. "Slow" work is based on an hourly wage of $20.25, "Medium" work on an hourly wage of $25.75, and "Fast" work on an hourly wage of $31.50. Other qualifications that apply to this table are on page 9.

*General Painting Costs*

|  | Shutters per manhour | Shutters per gallon | Material cost per gallon | Labor cost per shutter | Labor burden per shutter | Material cost per shutter | Overhead per shutter | Profit per shutter | Total price per shutter |
|---|---|---|---|---|---|---|---|---|---|
| **Shutters or blinds, 2' x 4' average size** | | | | | | | | | |
| Brush each coat | | | | | | | | | |
| Undercoat, water or oil base (material #3 or #4) | | | | | | | | | |
| Slow | 2.5 | 12 | 37.45 | 8.10 | 2.39 | 3.12 | 2.59 | 2.59 | 18.79 |
| Medium | 3.0 | 11 | 32.75 | 8.58 | 3.03 | 2.98 | 3.65 | 2.19 | 20.43 |
| Fast | 3.5 | 10 | 28.15 | 9.00 | 3.68 | 2.82 | 4.80 | 1.42 | 21.72 |
| Split coat (1/2 undercoat + 1/2 enamel), water or oil base (material #3 and #24, or material #4 and #25) | | | | | | | | | |
| Slow | 3.0 | 15 | 45.50 | 6.75 | 1.98 | 3.03 | 2.24 | 2.24 | 16.24 |
| Medium | 3.5 | 14 | 39.83 | 7.36 | 2.61 | 2.85 | 3.21 | 1.92 | 17.95 |
| Fast | 4.0 | 13 | 34.15 | 7.88 | 3.21 | 2.63 | 4.26 | 1.26 | 19.24 |
| Exterior enamel, water or oil base (material #24 or #25) | | | | | | | | | |
| Slow | 2.0 | 15 | 53.55 | 10.13 | 2.98 | 3.57 | 3.17 | 3.18 | 23.03 |
| Medium | 2.5 | 14 | 46.90 | 10.30 | 3.65 | 3.35 | 4.33 | 2.60 | 24.23 |
| Fast | 3.0 | 13 | 40.15 | 10.50 | 4.27 | 3.09 | 5.54 | 1.64 | 25.04 |
| Spray each coat | | | | | | | | | |
| Undercoat, water or oil base (material #3 or #4) | | | | | | | | | |
| Slow | 8 | 10 | 37.45 | 2.53 | .75 | 3.75 | 1.34 | 1.34 | 9.71 |
| Medium | 9 | 9 | 32.75 | 2.86 | 1.01 | 3.64 | 1.88 | 1.13 | 10.52 |
| Fast | 10 | 8 | 28.15 | 3.15 | 1.29 | 3.52 | 2.47 | .73 | 11.16 |
| Split coat (1/2 undercoat + 1/2 enamel), water or oil base (material #3 and #24, or material #4 and #25) | | | | | | | | | |
| Slow | 8 | 12 | 45.50 | 2.53 | .75 | 3.79 | 1.34 | 1.35 | 9.76 |
| Medium | 10 | 11 | 39.83 | 2.58 | .91 | 3.62 | 1.78 | 1.07 | 9.96 |
| Fast | 12 | 10 | 34.15 | 2.63 | 1.05 | 3.42 | 2.21 | .65 | 9.96 |
| Exterior enamel, water or oil base (material #24 or #25) | | | | | | | | | |
| Slow | 7 | 12 | 53.55 | 2.89 | .86 | 4.46 | 1.56 | 1.56 | 11.33 |
| Medium | 8 | 11 | 46.90 | 3.22 | 1.14 | 4.26 | 2.16 | 1.29 | 12.07 |
| Fast | 9 | 10 | 40.15 | 3.50 | 1.42 | 4.02 | 2.77 | .82 | 12.53 |

Use these figures to estimate the costs to paint all six sides of solid face, paint grade, interior or exterior, "false" plant-on type shutters or blinds. Costs are based on the number of single-panel 2' x 4' false (solid) shutters or blinds that can be painted in one hour (manhour). For real louvered shutters, multiply the quantity of shutters by a difficulty factor of 1.5 and then use this table. "Slow" work is based on an hourly wage of $20.25, "Medium" work on an hourly wage of $25.75, and "Fast" work on an hourly wage of $31.50. Other qualifications that apply to this table are on page 9.

*National Painting Cost Estimator*

|  | Labor SF per manhour | Material coverage SF/gallon | Material cost per gallon | Labor cost per 100 SF | Labor burden 100 SF | Material cost per 100 SF | Overhead per 100 SF | Profit per 100 SF | Total price per 100 SF |
|---|---|---|---|---|---|---|---|---|---|
| **Siding, aluminum** | | | | | | | | | |
| Metal primer, clean metal (material #35) | | | | | | | | | |
| Brush prime coat | | | | | | | | | |
| Slow | 215 | 440 | 59.70 | 9.42 | 2.77 | 13.57 | 4.90 | 4.91 | 35.57 |
| Medium | 235 | 420 | 52.20 | 10.96 | 3.89 | 12.43 | 6.82 | 4.09 | 38.19 |
| Fast | 255 | 400 | 44.80 | 12.35 | 5.04 | 11.20 | 8.86 | 2.62 | 40.07 |
| Metal primer, rusty metal (material #36) | | | | | | | | | |
| Brush prime coat | | | | | | | | | |
| Slow | 215 | 440 | 72.30 | 9.42 | 2.77 | 16.43 | 5.44 | 5.45 | 39.51 |
| Medium | 235 | 420 | 63.30 | 10.96 | 3.89 | 15.07 | 7.48 | 4.49 | 41.89 |
| Fast | 255 | 400 | 54.20 | 12.35 | 5.04 | 13.55 | 9.59 | 2.84 | 43.37 |
| Metal finish, synthetic enamel - off white, gloss, interior or exterior (material #37) | | | | | | | | | |
| Brush 1st or additional finish coats | | | | | | | | | |
| Slow | 265 | 480 | 59.70 | 7.64 | 2.24 | 12.44 | 4.24 | 4.25 | 30.81 |
| Medium | 285 | 465 | 52.20 | 9.04 | 3.20 | 11.23 | 5.87 | 3.52 | 32.86 |
| Fast | 305 | 450 | 44.80 | 10.33 | 4.22 | 9.96 | 7.60 | 2.25 | 34.36 |
| Metal finish, synthetic enamel - colors (except orange/red), gloss, interior or exterior (material #38) | | | | | | | | | |
| Brush 1st or additional finish coats | | | | | | | | | |
| Slow | 265 | 480 | 65.20 | 7.64 | 2.24 | 13.58 | 4.46 | 4.47 | 32.39 |
| Medium | 285 | 465 | 57.00 | 9.04 | 3.20 | 12.26 | 6.13 | 3.68 | 34.31 |
| Fast | 305 | 450 | 48.90 | 10.33 | 4.22 | 10.87 | 7.88 | 2.33 | 35.63 |

Don't deduct for openings under 100 square feet. For heights above 8 feet, use the High Time Difficulty Factors on page 139. Note: A two coat system, prime and finish, using oil base material is recommended for any metal surface. Although water base material is often used, it may cause oxidation, corrosion and rust. One coat of oil base solid body stain is often used on exterior metal but it may crack, peel or chip without the proper prime coat application. If off white or another light colored finish paint is specified, make sure the prime coat is also a light color, or more than one finish coat will be necessary. "Slow" work is based on an hourly wage of $20.25, "Medium" work on an hourly wage of $25.75, and "Fast" work on an hourly wage of $31.50. Other qualifications that apply to this table are on page 9.

*General Painting Costs*

|  | Labor SF per manhour | Material coverage SF/gallon | Material cost per gallon | Labor cost per 100 SF | Labor burden 100 SF | Material cost per 100 SF | Overhead per 100 SF | Profit per 100 SF | Total price per 100 SF |
|---|---|---|---|---|---|---|---|---|---|
| **Siding, composition shingle, brush application** | | | | | | | | | |
| Solid body stain, water base (material #18) | | | | | | | | | |
| Brush 1st coat | | | | | | | | | |
| Slow | 65 | 240 | 45.00 | 31.15 | 9.18 | 18.75 | 11.23 | 11.25 | 81.56 |
| Medium | 85 | 220 | 39.40 | 30.29 | 10.72 | 17.91 | 14.73 | 8.84 | 82.49 |
| Fast | 105 | 200 | 33.80 | 30.00 | 12.22 | 16.90 | 18.33 | 5.42 | 82.87 |
| Brush 2nd coat | | | | | | | | | |
| Slow | 90 | 350 | 45.00 | 22.50 | 6.63 | 12.86 | 7.98 | 8.00 | 57.97 |
| Medium | 110 | 335 | 39.40 | 23.41 | 8.29 | 11.76 | 10.87 | 6.52 | 60.85 |
| Fast | 130 | 320 | 33.80 | 24.23 | 9.88 | 10.56 | 13.85 | 4.10 | 62.62 |
| Brush 3rd or additional coats | | | | | | | | | |
| Slow | 110 | 425 | 45.00 | 18.41 | 5.42 | 10.59 | 6.54 | 6.56 | 47.52 |
| Medium | 130 | 405 | 39.40 | 19.81 | 7.01 | 9.73 | 9.14 | 5.48 | 51.17 |
| Fast | 150 | 385 | 33.80 | 21.00 | 8.58 | 8.78 | 11.89 | 3.52 | 53.77 |
| Solid body stain, oil base (material #19) | | | | | | | | | |
| Brush 1st coat | | | | | | | | | |
| Slow | 65 | 290 | 54.10 | 31.15 | 9.18 | 18.66 | 11.21 | 11.23 | 81.43 |
| Medium | 85 | 270 | 47.30 | 30.29 | 10.72 | 17.52 | 14.63 | 8.78 | 81.94 |
| Fast | 105 | 250 | 40.50 | 30.00 | 12.22 | 16.20 | 18.12 | 5.36 | 81.90 |
| Brush 2nd coat | | | | | | | | | |
| Slow | 90 | 390 | 54.10 | 22.50 | 6.63 | 13.87 | 8.17 | 8.19 | 59.36 |
| Medium | 110 | 375 | 47.30 | 23.41 | 8.29 | 12.61 | 11.08 | 6.65 | 62.04 |
| Fast | 130 | 360 | 40.50 | 24.23 | 9.88 | 11.25 | 14.06 | 4.16 | 63.58 |
| Brush 3rd or additional coats | | | | | | | | | |
| Slow | 110 | 445 | 54.10 | 18.41 | 5.42 | 12.16 | 6.84 | 6.85 | 49.68 |
| Medium | 130 | 425 | 47.30 | 19.81 | 7.01 | 11.13 | 9.49 | 5.69 | 53.13 |
| Fast | 150 | 405 | 40.50 | 21.00 | 8.58 | 10.00 | 12.27 | 3.63 | 55.48 |

Use these figures for repaint jobs only. Don't deduct for openings under 100 square feet. For heights above 8 feet, use the High Time Difficulty Factors on page 139. It has been established that asbestos fibers are known carcinogens (cancer causing) and it is likely that materials or products which contain asbestos will not be specified on any new construction projects in the future. Siding and roofing products usually contain very little asbestos and are typically non-friable (hand pressure can not crumble, pulverize or reduce to powder when dry). There is danger when asbestos is being removed because of exposure to airborne particulate matter. Apparently, there is little danger when painting asbestos siding or roofing, but it is a good idea to have your painters wear respirators or particle masks for their safety. "Slow" work is based on an hourly wage of $20.25, "Medium" work an hourly wage of $25.75, and "Fast" work on an hourly wage of $31.50. Other qualifications that apply to this table are on page 9.

*National Painting Cost Estimator*

|  | Labor SF per manhour | Material coverage SF/gallon | Material cost per gallon | Labor cost per 100 SF | Labor burden 100 SF | Material cost per 100 SF | Overhead per 100 SF | Profit per 100 SF | Total price per 100 SF |
|---|---|---|---|---|---|---|---|---|---|
| **Siding, composition shingle, roll application** | | | | | | | | | |
| Solid body stain, water base (material #18) | | | | | | | | | |
| Roll 1st coat | | | | | | | | | |
| Slow | 140 | 230 | 45.00 | 14.46 | 4.26 | 19.57 | 7.28 | 7.29 | 52.86 |
| Medium | 160 | 215 | 39.40 | 16.09 | 5.70 | 18.33 | 10.03 | 6.02 | 56.17 |
| Fast | 180 | 200 | 33.80 | 17.50 | 7.16 | 16.90 | 12.88 | 3.81 | 58.25 |
| Roll 2nd coat | | | | | | | | | |
| Slow | 190 | 330 | 45.00 | 10.66 | 3.13 | 13.64 | 5.21 | 5.22 | 37.86 |
| Medium | 210 | 315 | 39.40 | 12.26 | 4.34 | 12.51 | 7.28 | 4.37 | 40.76 |
| Fast | 230 | 300 | 33.80 | 13.70 | 5.59 | 11.27 | 9.47 | 2.80 | 42.83 |
| Roll 3rd or additional coats | | | | | | | | | |
| Slow | 250 | 395 | 45.00 | 8.10 | 2.39 | 11.39 | 4.16 | 4.17 | 30.21 |
| Medium | 280 | 385 | 39.40 | 9.20 | 3.25 | 10.23 | 5.67 | 3.40 | 31.75 |
| Fast | 300 | 375 | 33.80 | 10.50 | 4.27 | 9.01 | 7.37 | 2.18 | 33.33 |
| Solid body stain, oil base (material #19) | | | | | | | | | |
| Roll 1st coat | | | | | | | | | |
| Slow | 140 | 260 | 54.10 | 14.46 | 4.26 | 20.81 | 7.51 | 7.53 | 54.57 |
| Medium | 160 | 240 | 47.30 | 16.09 | 5.70 | 19.71 | 10.38 | 6.23 | 58.11 |
| Fast | 180 | 220 | 40.50 | 17.50 | 7.16 | 18.41 | 13.35 | 3.95 | 60.37 |
| Roll 2nd coat | | | | | | | | | |
| Slow | 190 | 360 | 54.10 | 10.66 | 3.13 | 15.03 | 5.48 | 5.49 | 39.79 |
| Medium | 210 | 345 | 47.30 | 12.26 | 4.34 | 13.71 | 7.58 | 4.55 | 42.44 |
| Fast | 230 | 330 | 40.50 | 13.70 | 5.59 | 12.27 | 9.78 | 2.89 | 44.23 |
| Roll 3rd or additional coats | | | | | | | | | |
| Slow | 250 | 420 | 54.10 | 8.10 | 2.39 | 12.88 | 4.44 | 4.45 | 32.26 |
| Medium | 280 | 408 | 47.30 | 9.20 | 3.25 | 11.59 | 6.01 | 3.61 | 33.66 |
| Fast | 300 | 395 | 40.50 | 10.50 | 4.27 | 10.25 | 7.76 | 2.30 | 35.08 |

*General Painting Costs*

|  | Labor SF per manhour | Material coverage SF/gallon | Material cost per gallon | Labor cost per 100 SF | Labor burden 100 SF | Material cost per 100 SF | Overhead per 100 SF | Profit per 100 SF | Total price per 100 SF |
|---|---|---|---|---|---|---|---|---|---|
| Waterproofing, clear hydro seal, oil base (material #34) | | | | | | | | | |
| Roll 1st coat | | | | | | | | | |
| Slow | 75 | 275 | 40.60 | 27.00 | 7.95 | 14.76 | 9.45 | 9.47 | 68.63 |
| Medium | 150 | 250 | 35.50 | 17.17 | 6.09 | 14.20 | 9.36 | 5.62 | 52.44 |
| Fast | 225 | 225 | 30.40 | 14.00 | 5.69 | 13.51 | 10.30 | 3.05 | 46.55 |
| Roll 2nd or additional coats | | | | | | | | | |
| Slow | 125 | 325 | 40.60 | 16.20 | 4.78 | 12.49 | 6.36 | 6.37 | 46.20 |
| Medium | 200 | 300 | 35.50 | 12.88 | 4.56 | 11.83 | 7.32 | 4.39 | 40.98 |
| Fast | 275 | 275 | 30.40 | 11.45 | 4.69 | 11.05 | 8.42 | 2.49 | 38.10 |

Use these figures for repaint jobs only. Don't deduct for openings under 100 square feet. For heights above 8 feet, use the High Time Difficulty Factors on page 139. It has been established that asbestos fibers are known carcinogens (cancer causing) and it is likely that materials or products which contain asbestos will not be specified on any new construction projects in the future. Siding and roofing products usually contain very little asbestos and are typically non-friable (hand pressure can not crumble, pulverize or reduce to powder when dry). There is danger when asbestos is being removed because of exposure to airborne particulate matter. Apparently, there is little danger when painting asbestos siding or roofing, but it is a good idea to have your painters wear respirators or particle masks for their safety. "Slow" work is based on an hourly wage of $20.25, "Medium" work an hourly wage of $25.75, and "Fast" work on an hourly wage of $31.50. Other qualifications that apply to this table are on page 9.

|  | Labor SF per manhour | Material coverage SF/gallon | Material cost per gallon | Labor cost per 100 SF | Labor burden 100 SF | Material cost per 100 SF | Overhead per 100 SF | Profit per 100 SF | Total price per 100 SF |
|---|---|---|---|---|---|---|---|---|---|

## Siding, composition shingle, spray application

Solid body stain, water base (material #18)
  Spray 1st coat

| | | | | | | | | | |
|---|---|---|---|---|---|---|---|---|---|
| Slow | 325 | 160 | 45.00 | 6.23 | 1.85 | 28.13 | 6.88 | 6.89 | 49.98 |
| Medium | 350 | 150 | 39.40 | 7.36 | 2.61 | 26.27 | 9.06 | 5.44 | 50.74 |
| Fast | 375 | 140 | 33.80 | 8.40 | 3.44 | 24.14 | 11.15 | 3.30 | 50.43 |

  Spray 2nd coat

| | | | | | | | | | |
|---|---|---|---|---|---|---|---|---|---|
| Slow | 350 | 240 | 45.00 | 5.79 | 1.71 | 18.75 | 4.99 | 5.00 | 36.24 |
| Medium | 375 | 228 | 39.40 | 6.87 | 2.44 | 17.28 | 6.65 | 3.99 | 37.23 |
| Fast | 400 | 215 | 33.80 | 7.88 | 3.21 | 15.72 | 8.31 | 2.46 | 37.58 |

  Spray 3rd or additional coats

| | | | | | | | | | |
|---|---|---|---|---|---|---|---|---|---|
| Slow | 425 | 300 | 45.00 | 4.76 | 1.40 | 15.00 | 4.02 | 4.03 | 29.21 |
| Medium | 450 | 288 | 39.40 | 5.72 | 2.02 | 13.68 | 5.36 | 3.21 | 29.99 |
| Fast | 475 | 275 | 33.80 | 6.63 | 2.73 | 12.29 | 6.71 | 1.98 | 30.34 |

Solid body stain, oil base (material #19)
  Spray 1st coat

| | | | | | | | | | |
|---|---|---|---|---|---|---|---|---|---|
| Slow | 325 | 190 | 54.10 | 6.23 | 1.85 | 28.47 | 6.94 | 6.96 | 50.45 |
| Medium | 350 | 180 | 47.30 | 7.36 | 2.61 | 26.28 | 9.06 | 5.44 | 50.75 |
| Fast | 375 | 170 | 40.50 | 8.40 | 3.44 | 23.82 | 11.05 | 3.27 | 49.98 |

  Spray 2nd coat

| | | | | | | | | | |
|---|---|---|---|---|---|---|---|---|---|
| Slow | 350 | 270 | 54.10 | 5.79 | 1.71 | 20.04 | 5.23 | 5.24 | 38.01 |
| Medium | 375 | 258 | 47.30 | 6.87 | 2.44 | 18.33 | 6.91 | 4.14 | 38.69 |
| Fast | 400 | 245 | 40.50 | 7.88 | 3.21 | 16.53 | 8.57 | 2.53 | 38.72 |

  Spray 3rd or additional coats

| | | | | | | | | | |
|---|---|---|---|---|---|---|---|---|---|
| Slow | 425 | 320 | 54.10 | 4.76 | 1.40 | 16.91 | 4.38 | 4.39 | 31.84 |
| Medium | 450 | 308 | 47.30 | 5.72 | 2.02 | 15.36 | 5.78 | 3.47 | 32.35 |
| Fast | 475 | 295 | 40.50 | 6.63 | 2.73 | 13.73 | 7.15 | 2.12 | 32.36 |

*General Painting Costs*

| | Labor SF per manhour | Material coverage SF/gallon | Material cost per gallon | Labor cost per 100 SF | Labor burden 100 SF | Material cost per 100 SF | Overhead per 100 SF | Profit per 100 SF | Total price per 100 SF |
|---|---|---|---|---|---|---|---|---|---|
| **Waterproofing, clear hydro seal, oil base (material #34)** | | | | | | | | | |
| *Spray 1st coat* | | | | | | | | | |
| Slow | 475 | 100 | 40.60 | 4.26 | 1.27 | 40.60 | 8.76 | 8.78 | 63.67 |
| Medium | 525 | 88 | 35.50 | 4.90 | 1.73 | 40.34 | 11.74 | 7.05 | 65.76 |
| Fast | 575 | 75 | 30.40 | 5.48 | 2.24 | 40.53 | 14.96 | 4.42 | 67.63 |
| *Spray 2nd or additional coats* | | | | | | | | | |
| Slow | 500 | 150 | 40.60 | 4.05 | 1.19 | 27.07 | 6.14 | 6.15 | 44.60 |
| Medium | 550 | 125 | 35.50 | 4.68 | 1.67 | 28.40 | 8.69 | 5.21 | 48.65 |
| Fast | 600 | 100 | 30.40 | 5.25 | 2.16 | 30.40 | 11.71 | 3.47 | 52.99 |

Use these figures for repaint jobs only. Don't deduct for openings under 100 square feet. For heights above 8 feet, use the High Time Difficulty Factors on page 139. It has been established that asbestos fibers are known carcinogens (cancer causing) and it is likely that materials or products which contain asbestos will not be specified on any new construction projects in the future. Siding and roofing products usually contain very little asbestos and are typically non-friable (hand pressure can not crumble, pulverize or reduce to powder when dry). There is danger when asbestos is being removed because of exposure to airborne particulate matter. Apparently, there is little danger when painting asbestos siding or roofing, but it is a good idea to have your painters wear respirators or particle masks for their safety. "Slow" work is based on an hourly wage of $20.25, "Medium" work an hourly wage of $25.75, and "Fast" work on an hourly wage of $31.50. Other qualifications that apply to this table are on page 9.

*National Painting Cost Estimator*

|  | Labor SF per manhour | Material coverage SF/gallon | Material cost per gallon | Labor cost per 100 SF | Labor burden 100 SF | Material cost per 100 SF | Overhead per 100 SF | Profit per 100 SF | Total price per 100 SF |
|---|---|---|---|---|---|---|---|---|---|

## Siding, rough sawn or resawn wood, brush

**Solid body or semi-transparent stain, water base (material #18 or #20)**

Brush 1st coat
| | | | | | | | | | |
|---|---|---|---|---|---|---|---|---|---|
| Slow | 100 | 250 | 46.25 | 20.25 | 5.97 | 18.50 | 8.50 | 8.52 | 61.74 |
| Medium | 135 | 238 | 40.50 | 19.07 | 6.77 | 17.02 | 10.71 | 6.43 | 60.00 |
| Fast | 170 | 225 | 34.70 | 18.53 | 7.55 | 15.42 | 12.87 | 3.81 | 58.18 |

Brush 2nd coat
| | | | | | | | | | |
|---|---|---|---|---|---|---|---|---|---|
| Slow | 135 | 300 | 46.25 | 15.00 | 4.43 | 15.42 | 6.62 | 6.64 | 48.11 |
| Medium | 168 | 288 | 40.50 | 15.33 | 5.42 | 14.06 | 8.71 | 5.22 | 48.74 |
| Fast | 200 | 275 | 34.70 | 15.75 | 6.43 | 12.62 | 10.79 | 3.19 | 48.78 |

Brush 3rd or additional coats
| | | | | | | | | | |
|---|---|---|---|---|---|---|---|---|---|
| Slow | 150 | 335 | 46.25 | 13.50 | 3.99 | 13.81 | 5.95 | 5.96 | 43.21 |
| Medium | 183 | 323 | 40.50 | 14.07 | 4.97 | 12.54 | 7.90 | 4.74 | 44.22 |
| Fast | 215 | 310 | 34.70 | 14.65 | 5.97 | 11.19 | 9.86 | 2.92 | 44.59 |

**Solid body or semi-transparent stain, oil base (material #19 or #21)**

Brush 1st coat
| | | | | | | | | | |
|---|---|---|---|---|---|---|---|---|---|
| Slow | 100 | 275 | 51.40 | 20.25 | 5.97 | 18.69 | 8.53 | 8.55 | 61.99 |
| Medium | 135 | 250 | 44.95 | 19.07 | 6.77 | 17.98 | 10.95 | 6.57 | 61.34 |
| Fast | 170 | 225 | 38.50 | 18.53 | 7.55 | 17.11 | 13.39 | 3.96 | 60.54 |

Brush 2nd coat
| | | | | | | | | | |
|---|---|---|---|---|---|---|---|---|---|
| Slow | 135 | 350 | 51.40 | 15.00 | 4.43 | 14.69 | 6.48 | 6.50 | 47.10 |
| Medium | 168 | 325 | 44.95 | 15.33 | 5.42 | 13.83 | 8.65 | 5.19 | 48.42 |
| Fast | 200 | 300 | 38.50 | 15.75 | 6.43 | 12.83 | 10.85 | 3.21 | 49.07 |

Brush 3rd or additional coats
| | | | | | | | | | |
|---|---|---|---|---|---|---|---|---|---|
| Slow | 150 | 400 | 51.40 | 13.50 | 3.99 | 12.85 | 5.76 | 5.77 | 41.87 |
| Medium | 183 | 375 | 44.95 | 14.07 | 4.97 | 11.99 | 7.76 | 4.66 | 43.45 |
| Fast | 215 | 350 | 38.50 | 14.65 | 5.97 | 11.00 | 9.81 | 2.90 | 44.33 |

**Penetrating oil stain (material #13)**

Brush 1st coat
| | | | | | | | | | |
|---|---|---|---|---|---|---|---|---|---|
| Slow | 100 | 230 | 54.50 | 20.25 | 5.97 | 23.70 | 9.48 | 9.50 | 68.90 |
| Medium | 135 | 210 | 47.70 | 19.07 | 6.77 | 22.71 | 12.13 | 7.28 | 67.96 |
| Fast | 170 | 190 | 40.90 | 18.53 | 7.55 | 21.53 | 14.76 | 4.37 | 66.74 |

## General Painting Costs

|  | Labor SF per manhour | Material coverage SF/gallon | Material cost per gallon | Labor cost per 100 SF | Labor burden 100 SF | Material cost per 100 SF | Overhead per 100 SF | Profit per 100 SF | Total price per 100 SF |
|---|---|---|---|---|---|---|---|---|---|
| **Brush 2nd coat** | | | | | | | | | |
| Slow | 135 | 275 | 54.50 | 15.00 | 4.43 | 19.82 | 7.46 | 7.47 | 54.18 |
| Medium | 168 | 255 | 47.70 | 15.33 | 5.42 | 18.71 | 9.87 | 5.92 | 55.25 |
| Fast | 200 | 235 | 40.90 | 15.75 | 6.43 | 17.40 | 12.27 | 3.63 | 55.48 |
| **Brush 3rd or additional coats** | | | | | | | | | |
| Slow | 150 | 350 | 54.50 | 13.50 | 3.99 | 15.57 | 6.28 | 6.29 | 45.63 |
| Medium | 183 | 330 | 47.70 | 14.07 | 4.97 | 14.45 | 8.38 | 5.03 | 46.90 |
| Fast | 215 | 310 | 40.90 | 14.65 | 5.97 | 13.19 | 10.48 | 3.10 | 47.39 |

Use this table to estimate the cost of painting shingle, shake, resawn or rough sawn wood or plywood siding with average moisture content. Don't deduct for openings under 100 square feet. For heights above 8 feet, use the High Time Difficulty Factors on page 139. For wood or composition drop siding with exposed bevel edges, multiply the surface area by 1.12 to allow for the extra time and material needed to paint the underside of each board. "Slow" work is based on an hourly wage of $20.25, "Medium" work on an hourly wage of $25.75, and "Fast" work on an hourly wage of $31.50. Other qualifications that apply to this table are on page 9.

*National Painting Cost Estimator*

|  | Labor SF per manhour | Material coverage SF/gallon | Material cost per gallon | Labor cost per 100 SF | Labor burden 100 SF | Material cost per 100 SF | Overhead per 100 SF | Profit per 100 SF | Total price per 100 SF |
|---|---|---|---|---|---|---|---|---|---|

## Siding, rough sawn or resawn wood, roll

### Solid body or semi-transparent stain, water base (material #18 or #20)

**Roll 1st coat**

| | | | | | | | | | |
|---|---|---|---|---|---|---|---|---|---|
| Slow | 150 | 235 | 46.25 | 13.50 | 3.99 | 19.68 | 7.06 | 7.08 | 51.31 |
| Medium | 200 | 213 | 40.50 | 12.88 | 4.56 | 19.01 | 9.11 | 5.47 | 51.03 |
| Fast | 250 | 210 | 34.70 | 12.60 | 5.14 | 16.52 | 10.62 | 3.14 | 48.02 |

**Roll 2nd coat**

| | | | | | | | | | |
|---|---|---|---|---|---|---|---|---|---|
| Slow | 200 | 285 | 46.25 | 10.13 | 2.98 | 16.23 | 5.58 | 5.59 | 40.51 |
| Medium | 250 | 273 | 40.50 | 10.30 | 3.65 | 14.84 | 7.20 | 4.32 | 40.31 |
| Fast | 300 | 260 | 34.70 | 10.50 | 4.27 | 13.35 | 8.72 | 2.58 | 39.42 |

**Roll 3rd or additional coats**

| | | | | | | | | | |
|---|---|---|---|---|---|---|---|---|---|
| Slow | 225 | 335 | 46.25 | 9.00 | 2.64 | 13.81 | 4.84 | 4.85 | 35.14 |
| Medium | 288 | 323 | 40.50 | 8.94 | 3.16 | 12.54 | 6.16 | 3.70 | 34.50 |
| Fast | 350 | 310 | 34.70 | 9.00 | 3.68 | 11.19 | 7.40 | 2.19 | 33.46 |

### Solid body or semi-transparent stain, oil base (material #19 or #21)

**Roll 1st coat**

| | | | | | | | | | |
|---|---|---|---|---|---|---|---|---|---|
| Slow | 150 | 250 | 51.40 | 13.50 | 3.99 | 20.56 | 7.23 | 7.24 | 52.52 |
| Medium | 225 | 225 | 44.95 | 11.44 | 4.04 | 19.98 | 8.87 | 5.32 | 49.65 |
| Fast | 275 | 200 | 38.50 | 11.45 | 4.69 | 19.25 | 10.96 | 3.24 | 49.59 |

**Roll 2nd coat**

| | | | | | | | | | |
|---|---|---|---|---|---|---|---|---|---|
| Slow | 200 | 330 | 51.40 | 10.13 | 2.98 | 15.58 | 5.45 | 5.46 | 39.60 |
| Medium | 275 | 305 | 44.95 | 9.36 | 3.33 | 14.74 | 6.85 | 4.11 | 38.39 |
| Fast | 350 | 280 | 38.50 | 9.00 | 3.68 | 13.75 | 8.19 | 2.42 | 37.04 |

**Roll 3rd or additional coats**

| | | | | | | | | | |
|---|---|---|---|---|---|---|---|---|---|
| Slow | 260 | 415 | 51.40 | 7.79 | 2.30 | 12.39 | 4.27 | 4.28 | 31.03 |
| Medium | 335 | 390 | 44.95 | 7.69 | 2.74 | 11.53 | 5.49 | 3.29 | 30.74 |
| Fast | 410 | 365 | 38.50 | 7.68 | 3.14 | 10.55 | 6.62 | 1.96 | 29.95 |

### Penetrating oil stain (material #13)

**Roll 1st coat**

| | | | | | | | | | |
|---|---|---|---|---|---|---|---|---|---|
| Slow | 150 | 150 | 54.50 | 13.50 | 3.99 | 36.33 | 10.22 | 10.24 | 74.28 |
| Medium | 225 | 125 | 47.70 | 11.44 | 4.04 | 38.16 | 13.41 | 8.05 | 75.10 |
| Fast | 275 | 100 | 40.90 | 11.45 | 4.69 | 40.90 | 17.68 | 5.23 | 79.95 |

*General Painting Costs*

|  | Labor SF per manhour | Material coverage SF/gallon | Material cost per gallon | Labor cost per 100 SF | Labor burden 100 SF | Material cost per 100 SF | Overhead per 100 SF | Profit per 100 SF | Total price per 100 SF |
|---|---|---|---|---|---|---|---|---|---|
| **Roll 2nd coat** | | | | | | | | | |
| Slow | 200 | 280 | 54.50 | 10.13 | 2.98 | 19.46 | 6.19 | 6.20 | 44.96 |
| Medium | 275 | 240 | 47.70 | 9.36 | 3.33 | 19.88 | 8.14 | 4.88 | 45.59 |
| Fast | 350 | 200 | 40.90 | 9.00 | 3.68 | 20.45 | 10.27 | 3.04 | 46.44 |
| **Roll 3rd or additional coats** | | | | | | | | | |
| Slow | 260 | 365 | 54.50 | 7.79 | 2.30 | 14.93 | 4.75 | 4.76 | 34.53 |
| Medium | 335 | 330 | 47.70 | 7.69 | 2.74 | 14.45 | 6.22 | 3.73 | 34.83 |
| Fast | 410 | 295 | 40.90 | 7.68 | 3.14 | 13.86 | 7.65 | 2.26 | 34.59 |

Use this table to estimate the cost of painting shingle, shake, resawn or rough sawn wood or plywood siding with average moisture content. Don't deduct for openings under 100 square feet. For heights above 8 feet, use the High Time Difficulty Factors on page 139. For wood or composition drop siding with exposed bevel edges, multiply the surface area by 1.12 to allow for the extra time and material needed to paint the underside of each board. "Slow" work is based on an hourly wage of $20.25, "Medium" work on an hourly wage of $25.75, and "Fast" work on an hourly wage of $31.50. Other qualifications that apply to this table are on page 9.

|  | Labor SF per manhour | Material coverage SF/gallon | Material cost per gallon | Labor cost per 100 SF | Labor burden 100 SF | Material cost per 100 SF | Overhead per 100 SF | Profit per 100 SF | Total price per 100 SF |
|---|---|---|---|---|---|---|---|---|---|
| **Siding, rough sawn or resawn wood, spray** | | | | | | | | | |
| Solid body or semi-transparent stain, water base (material #18 or #20) | | | | | | | | | |
| Spray 1st coat | | | | | | | | | |
| Slow | 400 | 140 | 46.25 | 5.06 | 1.50 | 33.04 | 7.52 | 7.54 | 54.66 |
| Medium | 500 | 115 | 40.50 | 5.15 | 1.82 | 35.22 | 10.55 | 6.33 | 59.07 |
| Fast | 600 | 90 | 34.70 | 5.25 | 2.16 | 38.56 | 14.24 | 4.21 | 64.42 |
| Spray 2nd coat | | | | | | | | | |
| Slow | 500 | 150 | 46.25 | 4.05 | 1.19 | 30.83 | 6.85 | 6.87 | 49.79 |
| Medium | 600 | 125 | 40.50 | 4.29 | 1.53 | 32.40 | 9.55 | 5.73 | 53.50 |
| Fast | 700 | 100 | 34.70 | 4.50 | 1.84 | 34.70 | 12.72 | 3.76 | 57.52 |
| Spray 3rd or additional coats | | | | | | | | | |
| Slow | 550 | 200 | 46.25 | 3.68 | 1.09 | 23.13 | 5.30 | 5.31 | 38.51 |
| Medium | 650 | 170 | 40.50 | 3.96 | 1.41 | 23.82 | 7.30 | 4.38 | 40.87 |
| Fast | 750 | 140 | 34.70 | 4.20 | 1.70 | 24.79 | 9.52 | 2.82 | 43.03 |
| Solid body or semi-transparent stain, oil base (material #19 or #21) | | | | | | | | | |
| Spray 1st coat | | | | | | | | | |
| Slow | 400 | 170 | 51.40 | 5.06 | 1.50 | 30.24 | 6.99 | 7.00 | 50.79 |
| Medium | 500 | 150 | 44.95 | 5.15 | 1.82 | 29.97 | 9.24 | 5.54 | 51.72 |
| Fast | 600 | 130 | 38.50 | 5.25 | 2.16 | 29.62 | 11.47 | 3.39 | 51.89 |
| Spray 2nd coat | | | | | | | | | |
| Slow | 450 | 255 | 51.40 | 4.50 | 1.32 | 20.16 | 4.94 | 4.95 | 35.87 |
| Medium | 550 | 235 | 44.95 | 4.68 | 1.67 | 19.13 | 6.37 | 3.82 | 35.67 |
| Fast | 650 | 215 | 38.50 | 4.85 | 1.98 | 17.91 | 7.67 | 2.27 | 34.68 |
| Spray 3rd or additional coats | | | | | | | | | |
| Slow | 550 | 355 | 51.40 | 3.68 | 1.09 | 14.48 | 3.66 | 3.67 | 26.58 |
| Medium | 650 | 335 | 44.95 | 3.96 | 1.41 | 13.42 | 4.70 | 2.82 | 26.31 |
| Fast | 750 | 315 | 38.50 | 4.20 | 1.70 | 12.22 | 5.62 | 1.66 | 25.40 |
| Penetrating oil stain (material #13) | | | | | | | | | |
| Spray 1st coat | | | | | | | | | |
| Slow | 400 | 200 | 54.50 | 5.06 | 1.50 | 27.25 | 6.42 | 6.44 | 46.67 |
| Medium | 500 | 180 | 47.70 | 5.15 | 1.82 | 26.50 | 8.37 | 5.02 | 46.86 |
| Fast | 600 | 160 | 40.90 | 5.25 | 2.16 | 25.56 | 10.21 | 3.02 | 46.20 |
| Spray 2nd coat | | | | | | | | | |
| Slow | 450 | 290 | 54.50 | 4.50 | 1.32 | 18.79 | 4.68 | 4.69 | 33.98 |
| Medium | 550 | 245 | 47.70 | 4.68 | 1.67 | 19.47 | 6.45 | 3.87 | 36.14 |
| Fast | 650 | 200 | 40.90 | 4.85 | 1.98 | 20.45 | 8.46 | 2.50 | 38.24 |
| Spray 3rd or additional coats | | | | | | | | | |
| Slow | 550 | 390 | 54.50 | 3.68 | 1.09 | 13.97 | 3.56 | 3.57 | 25.87 |
| Medium | 650 | 360 | 47.70 | 3.96 | 1.41 | 13.25 | 4.65 | 2.79 | 26.06 |
| Fast | 750 | 330 | 40.90 | 4.20 | 1.70 | 12.39 | 5.67 | 1.68 | 25.64 |

*General Painting Costs*

|  | Labor SF per manhour | Material coverage SF/gallon | Material cost per gallon | Labor cost per 100 SF | Labor burden 100 SF | Material cost per 100 SF | Overhead per 100 SF | Profit per 100 SF | Total price per 100 SF |
|---|---|---|---|---|---|---|---|---|---|
| **Waterproofing, clear hydro seal, oil base (material #34)** | | | | | | | | | |
| Spray 1st coat | | | | | | | | | |
| Slow | 500 | 150 | 40.60 | 4.05 | 1.19 | 27.07 | 6.14 | 4.61 | 43.06 |
| Medium | 575 | 113 | 35.50 | 4.48 | 1.59 | 31.42 | 9.37 | 5.62 | 52.48 |
| Fast | 650 | 75 | 30.40 | 4.85 | 1.98 | 40.53 | 14.68 | 4.34 | 66.38 |
| Spray 2nd coat | | | | | | | | | |
| Slow | 575 | 175 | 40.60 | 3.52 | 1.04 | 23.20 | 5.27 | 5.28 | 38.31 |
| Medium | 675 | 150 | 35.50 | 3.81 | 1.35 | 23.67 | 7.21 | 4.32 | 40.36 |
| Fast | 775 | 125 | 30.40 | 4.06 | 1.66 | 24.32 | 9.31 | 2.75 | 42.10 |
| Spray 3rd or additional coats | | | | | | | | | |
| Slow | 650 | 200 | 40.60 | 3.12 | .92 | 20.30 | 4.62 | 4.63 | 33.59 |
| Medium | 750 | 175 | 35.50 | 3.43 | 1.21 | 20.29 | 6.23 | 3.74 | 34.90 |
| Fast | 850 | 150 | 30.40 | 3.71 | 1.52 | 20.27 | 7.90 | 2.34 | 35.74 |

Use this table to estimate the cost of painting shingle, shake, resawn or rough sawn wood or plywood siding with average moisture content. Don't deduct for openings under 100 square feet. For heights above 8 feet, use the High Time Difficulty Factors on page 139. For wood or composition drop siding with exposed beveled edges, multiply the surface area by 1.12 to allow for the extra time and material needed to paint the underside of each board. "Slow" work is based on an hourly wage of $20.25, "Medium" work on an hourly wage of $25.75, and "Fast" work on an hourly wage of $31.50. Other qualifications that apply to this table are on page 9.

*National Painting Cost Estimator*

|  | Labor SF per manhour | Material coverage SF/gallon | Material cost per gallon | Labor cost per 100 SF | Labor burden 100 SF | Material cost per 100 SF | Overhead per 100 SF | Profit per 100 SF | Total price per 100 SF |
|---|---|---|---|---|---|---|---|---|---|

## Siding, smooth wood, brush

### Solid body or semi-transparent stain, water base (material #18 or #20)
**Brush 1st coat**

|  |  |  |  |  |  |  |  |  |  |
|---|---|---|---|---|---|---|---|---|---|
| Slow | 100 | 275 | 46.25 | 20.25 | 5.97 | 16.82 | 8.18 | 8.20 | 59.42 |
| Medium | 125 | 363 | 40.50 | 20.60 | 7.30 | 11.16 | 9.76 | 5.86 | 54.68 |
| Fast | 150 | 250 | 34.70 | 21.00 | 8.58 | 13.88 | 13.47 | 3.98 | 60.91 |

**Brush 2nd coat**

|  |  |  |  |  |  |  |  |  |  |
|---|---|---|---|---|---|---|---|---|---|
| Slow | 135 | 350 | 46.25 | 15.00 | 4.43 | 13.21 | 6.20 | 6.21 | 45.05 |
| Medium | 168 | 325 | 40.50 | 15.33 | 5.42 | 12.46 | 8.31 | 4.98 | 46.50 |
| Fast | 200 | 300 | 34.70 | 15.75 | 6.43 | 11.57 | 10.46 | 3.09 | 47.30 |

**Brush 3rd or additional coats**

|  |  |  |  |  |  |  |  |  |  |
|---|---|---|---|---|---|---|---|---|---|
| Slow | 150 | 425 | 46.25 | 13.50 | 3.99 | 10.88 | 5.39 | 5.40 | 39.16 |
| Medium | 188 | 400 | 40.50 | 13.70 | 4.85 | 10.13 | 7.17 | 4.30 | 40.15 |
| Fast | 215 | 375 | 34.70 | 14.65 | 5.97 | 9.25 | 9.26 | 2.74 | 41.87 |

### Solid body or semi-transparent stain, oil base (material #19 or #21)
**Brush 1st coat**

|  |  |  |  |  |  |  |  |  |  |
|---|---|---|---|---|---|---|---|---|---|
| Slow | 100 | 400 | 51.40 | 20.25 | 5.97 | 12.85 | 7.42 | 7.44 | 53.93 |
| Medium | 125 | 363 | 44.95 | 20.60 | 7.30 | 12.38 | 10.07 | 6.04 | 56.39 |
| Fast | 150 | 325 | 38.50 | 21.00 | 8.58 | 11.85 | 12.84 | 3.80 | 58.07 |

**Brush 2nd coat**

|  |  |  |  |  |  |  |  |  |  |
|---|---|---|---|---|---|---|---|---|---|
| Slow | 135 | 450 | 51.40 | 15.00 | 4.43 | 11.42 | 5.86 | 5.87 | 42.58 |
| Medium | 168 | 408 | 44.95 | 15.33 | 5.42 | 11.02 | 7.95 | 4.77 | 44.49 |
| Fast | 200 | 375 | 38.50 | 15.75 | 6.43 | 10.27 | 10.06 | 2.98 | 45.49 |

**Brush 3rd or additional coats**

|  |  |  |  |  |  |  |  |  |  |
|---|---|---|---|---|---|---|---|---|---|
| Slow | 150 | 525 | 51.40 | 13.50 | 3.99 | 9.79 | 5.18 | 5.19 | 37.65 |
| Medium | 188 | 438 | 44.95 | 13.70 | 4.85 | 10.26 | 7.20 | 4.32 | 40.33 |
| Fast | 215 | 450 | 38.50 | 14.65 | 5.97 | 8.56 | 9.05 | 2.68 | 40.91 |

### Penetrating oil stain (material #13)
**Brush 1st coat**

|  |  |  |  |  |  |  |  |  |  |
|---|---|---|---|---|---|---|---|---|---|
| Slow | 100 | 315 | 54.50 | 20.25 | 5.97 | 17.30 | 8.27 | 8.29 | 60.08 |
| Medium | 125 | 303 | 47.70 | 20.60 | 7.30 | 15.74 | 10.91 | 6.54 | 61.09 |
| Fast | 150 | 290 | 40.90 | 21.00 | 8.58 | 14.10 | 13.54 | 4.00 | 61.22 |

*General Painting Costs*

|  | Labor SF per manhour | Material coverage SF/gallon | Material cost per gallon | Labor cost per 100 SF | Labor burden 100 SF | Material cost per 100 SF | Overhead per 100 SF | Profit per 100 SF | Total price per 100 SF |
|---|---|---|---|---|---|---|---|---|---|
| **Brush 2nd coat** | | | | | | | | | |
| Slow | 135 | 355 | 54.50 | 15.00 | 4.43 | 15.35 | 6.61 | 6.62 | 48.01 |
| Medium | 168 | 343 | 47.70 | 15.33 | 5.42 | 13.91 | 8.67 | 5.20 | 48.53 |
| Fast | 200 | 330 | 40.90 | 15.75 | 6.43 | 12.39 | 10.72 | 3.17 | 48.46 |
| **Brush 3rd or additional coats** | | | | | | | | | |
| Slow | 150 | 430 | 54.50 | 13.50 | 3.99 | 12.67 | 5.73 | 5.74 | 41.63 |
| Medium | 188 | 418 | 47.70 | 13.70 | 4.85 | 11.41 | 7.49 | 4.49 | 41.94 |
| Fast | 215 | 405 | 40.90 | 14.65 | 5.97 | 10.10 | 9.53 | 2.82 | 43.07 |

Use this table for butt or tongue and groove siding, joint lap, drop, beveled or board and batten siding in redwood, plywood, fir, hemlock or pine. Don't deduct for openings under 100 square feet. For heights above 8 feet, use the High Time Difficulty Factors on page 139. For wood or composition drop siding with exposed bevel edges, multiply the surface area by 1.12 to allow for the extra time and material needed to paint the underside of each board. "Slow" work is based on an hourly wage of $20.25, "Medium" work on an hourly wage of $25.75, and "Fast" work on an hourly wage of $31.50. Other qualifications that apply to this table are on page 9.

|  | Labor SF per manhour | Material coverage SF/gallon | Material cost per gallon | Labor cost per 100 SF | Labor burden 100 SF | Material cost per 100 SF | Overhead per 100 SF | Profit per 100 SF | Total price per 100 SF |
|---|---|---|---|---|---|---|---|---|---|
| **Siding, smooth wood, roll** | | | | | | | | | |
| Solid body or semi-transparent stain, water base (material #18 or #20) | | | | | | | | | |
| Roll 1st coat | | | | | | | | | |
| Slow | 175 | 250 | 46.25 | 11.57 | 3.40 | 18.50 | 6.36 | 6.37 | 46.20 |
| Medium | 225 | 238 | 40.50 | 11.44 | 4.04 | 17.02 | 8.13 | 4.88 | 45.51 |
| Fast | 275 | 225 | 34.70 | 11.45 | 4.69 | 15.42 | 9.78 | 2.89 | 44.23 |
| Roll 2nd coat | | | | | | | | | |
| Slow | 225 | 300 | 46.25 | 9.00 | 2.64 | 15.42 | 5.15 | 5.16 | 37.37 |
| Medium | 275 | 288 | 40.50 | 9.36 | 3.33 | 14.06 | 6.68 | 4.01 | 37.44 |
| Fast | 325 | 275 | 34.70 | 9.69 | 3.97 | 12.62 | 8.14 | 2.41 | 36.83 |
| Roll 3rd or additional coats | | | | | | | | | |
| Slow | 260 | 375 | 46.25 | 7.79 | 2.30 | 12.33 | 4.26 | 4.27 | 30.95 |
| Medium | 335 | 338 | 40.50 | 7.69 | 2.74 | 11.98 | 5.60 | 3.36 | 31.37 |
| Fast | 410 | 300 | 34.70 | 7.68 | 3.14 | 11.57 | 6.94 | 2.05 | 31.38 |
| Solid body or semi-transparent stain, oil base (material #19 or #21) | | | | | | | | | |
| Roll 1st coat | | | | | | | | | |
| Slow | 175 | 350 | 51.40 | 11.57 | 3.40 | 14.69 | 5.64 | 5.65 | 40.95 |
| Medium | 225 | 325 | 44.95 | 11.44 | 4.04 | 13.83 | 7.33 | 4.40 | 41.04 |
| Fast | 275 | 300 | 38.50 | 11.45 | 4.69 | 12.83 | 8.97 | 2.65 | 40.59 |
| Roll 2nd coat | | | | | | | | | |
| Slow | 225 | 400 | 51.40 | 9.00 | 2.64 | 12.85 | 4.66 | 4.67 | 33.82 |
| Medium | 275 | 375 | 44.95 | 9.36 | 3.33 | 11.99 | 6.17 | 3.70 | 34.55 |
| Fast | 325 | 350 | 38.50 | 9.69 | 3.97 | 11.00 | 7.64 | 2.26 | 34.56 |
| Roll 3rd or additional coats | | | | | | | | | |
| Slow | 260 | 425 | 51.40 | 7.79 | 2.30 | 12.09 | 4.21 | 4.22 | 30.61 |
| Medium | 335 | 413 | 44.95 | 7.69 | 2.74 | 10.88 | 5.32 | 3.19 | 29.82 |
| Fast | 410 | 400 | 38.50 | 7.68 | 3.14 | 9.63 | 6.34 | 1.87 | 28.66 |
| Penetrating oil stain (material #13) | | | | | | | | | |
| Roll 1st coat | | | | | | | | | |
| Slow | 175 | 200 | 54.50 | 11.57 | 3.40 | 27.25 | 8.02 | 8.04 | 58.28 |
| Medium | 225 | 150 | 47.70 | 11.44 | 4.04 | 31.80 | 11.82 | 7.09 | 66.19 |
| Fast | 275 | 100 | 40.90 | 11.45 | 4.69 | 40.90 | 17.68 | 5.23 | 79.95 |

*General Painting Costs*

|  | Labor SF per manhour | Material coverage SF/gallon | Material cost per gallon | Labor cost per 100 SF | Labor burden 100 SF | Material cost per 100 SF | Overhead per 100 SF | Profit per 100 SF | Total price per 100 SF |
|---|---|---|---|---|---|---|---|---|---|
| **Roll 2nd coat** | | | | | | | | | |
| Slow | 225 | 250 | 54.50 | 9.00 | 2.64 | 21.80 | 6.36 | 6.37 | 46.17 |
| Medium | 275 | 200 | 47.70 | 9.36 | 3.33 | 23.85 | 9.13 | 5.48 | 51.15 |
| Fast | 325 | 150 | 40.90 | 9.69 | 3.97 | 27.27 | 12.68 | 3.75 | 57.36 |
| **Roll 3rd or additional coats** | | | | | | | | | |
| Slow | 260 | 300 | 54.50 | 7.79 | 2.30 | 18.17 | 5.37 | 5.38 | 39.01 |
| Medium | 335 | 250 | 47.70 | 7.69 | 2.74 | 19.08 | 7.37 | 4.42 | 41.30 |
| Fast | 410 | 200 | 40.90 | 7.68 | 3.14 | 20.45 | 9.69 | 2.87 | 43.83 |

Use this table for butt or tongue and groove siding, joint lap, drop, beveled or board and batten siding in redwood, plywood, fir, hemlock or pine. Don't deduct for openings under 100 square feet. For heights above 8 feet, use the High Time Difficulty Factors on page 139. For wood or composition drop siding with exposed beveled edges, multiply the surface area by 1.12 to allow for the extra time and material needed to paint the underside of each board. "Slow" work is based on an hourly wage of $20.25, "Medium" work on an hourly wage of $25.75, and "Fast" work on an hourly wage of $31.50. Other qualifications that apply to this table are on page 9.

*National Painting Cost Estimator*

|  | Labor SF per manhour | Material coverage SF/gallon | Material cost per gallon | Labor cost per 100 SF | Labor burden 100 SF | Material cost per 100 SF | Overhead per 100 SF | Profit per 100 SF | Total price per 100 SF |
|---|---|---|---|---|---|---|---|---|---|

## Siding, smooth wood, spray

### Solid body or semi-transparent stain, water base (material #18 or #20)
**Spray 1st coat**
| | | | | | | | | | |
|---|---|---|---|---|---|---|---|---|---|
| Slow | 450 | 150 | 46.25 | 4.50 | 1.32 | 30.83 | 6.97 | 6.98 | 50.60 |
| Medium | 550 | 125 | 40.50 | 4.68 | 1.67 | 32.40 | 9.69 | 5.81 | 54.25 |
| Fast | 650 | 100 | 34.70 | 4.85 | 1.98 | 34.70 | 12.87 | 3.81 | 58.21 |

**Spray 2nd coat**
| | | | | | | | | | |
|---|---|---|---|---|---|---|---|---|---|
| Slow | 550 | 250 | 46.25 | 3.68 | 1.09 | 18.50 | 4.42 | 4.43 | 32.12 |
| Medium | 650 | 225 | 40.50 | 3.96 | 1.41 | 18.00 | 5.84 | 3.50 | 32.71 |
| Fast | 750 | 200 | 34.70 | 4.20 | 1.70 | 17.35 | 7.21 | 2.13 | 32.59 |

**Spray 3rd or additional coats**
| | | | | | | | | | |
|---|---|---|---|---|---|---|---|---|---|
| Slow | 650 | 350 | 46.25 | 3.12 | .92 | 13.21 | 3.28 | 3.28 | 23.81 |
| Medium | 750 | 325 | 40.50 | 3.43 | 1.21 | 12.46 | 4.28 | 2.57 | 23.95 |
| Fast | 850 | 300 | 34.70 | 3.71 | 1.52 | 11.57 | 5.20 | 1.54 | 23.54 |

### Solid body or semi-transparent stain, oil base (material #19 or #21)
**Spray 1st coat**
| | | | | | | | | | |
|---|---|---|---|---|---|---|---|---|---|
| Slow | 450 | 170 | 51.40 | 4.50 | 1.32 | 30.24 | 6.85 | 6.87 | 49.78 |
| Medium | 550 | 150 | 44.95 | 4.68 | 1.67 | 29.97 | 9.08 | 5.45 | 50.85 |
| Fast | 650 | 130 | 38.50 | 4.85 | 1.98 | 29.62 | 11.30 | 3.34 | 51.09 |

**Spray 2nd coat**
| | | | | | | | | | |
|---|---|---|---|---|---|---|---|---|---|
| Slow | 550 | 300 | 51.40 | 3.68 | 1.09 | 17.13 | 4.16 | 4.17 | 30.23 |
| Medium | 650 | 273 | 44.95 | 3.96 | 1.41 | 16.47 | 5.46 | 3.27 | 30.57 |
| Fast | 750 | 245 | 38.50 | 4.20 | 1.70 | 15.71 | 6.70 | 1.98 | 30.29 |

**Spray 3rd or additional coats**
| | | | | | | | | | |
|---|---|---|---|---|---|---|---|---|---|
| Slow | 650 | 400 | 51.40 | 3.12 | .92 | 12.85 | 3.21 | 3.22 | 23.32 |
| Medium | 750 | 373 | 44.95 | 3.43 | 1.21 | 12.05 | 4.17 | 2.50 | 23.36 |
| Fast | 850 | 345 | 38.50 | 3.71 | 1.52 | 11.16 | 5.08 | 1.50 | 22.97 |

### Penetrating oil stain (material #13)
**Spray 1st coat**
| | | | | | | | | | |
|---|---|---|---|---|---|---|---|---|---|
| Slow | 450 | 150 | 54.50 | 4.50 | 1.32 | 36.33 | 8.01 | 8.03 | 58.19 |
| Medium | 550 | 113 | 47.70 | 4.68 | 1.67 | 42.21 | 12.14 | 7.28 | 67.98 |
| Fast | 650 | 75 | 40.90 | 4.85 | 1.98 | 54.53 | 19.02 | 5.63 | 86.01 |

**Spray 2nd coat**
| | | | | | | | | | |
|---|---|---|---|---|---|---|---|---|---|
| Slow | 550 | 225 | 54.50 | 3.68 | 1.09 | 24.22 | 5.51 | 5.52 | 40.02 |
| Medium | 650 | 188 | 47.70 | 3.96 | 1.41 | 25.37 | 7.68 | 4.61 | 43.03 |
| Fast | 750 | 150 | 40.90 | 4.20 | 1.70 | 27.27 | 10.29 | 3.04 | 46.50 |

**Spray 3rd or additional coats**
| | | | | | | | | | |
|---|---|---|---|---|---|---|---|---|---|
| Slow | 650 | 250 | 54.50 | 3.12 | .92 | 21.80 | 4.91 | 4.92 | 35.67 |
| Medium | 750 | 225 | 47.70 | 3.43 | 1.21 | 21.20 | 6.46 | 3.88 | 36.18 |
| Fast | 850 | 200 | 40.90 | 3.71 | 1.52 | 20.45 | 7.96 | 2.35 | 35.99 |

*General Painting Costs*

|  | Labor SF per manhour | Material coverage SF/gallon | Material cost per gallon | Labor cost per 100 SF | Labor burden 100 SF | Material cost per 100 SF | Overhead per 100 SF | Profit per 100 SF | Total price per 100 SF |
|---|---|---|---|---|---|---|---|---|---|
| **Waterproofing, clear hydro seal, oil base (material #34)** | | | | | | | | | |
| Spray 1st coat | | | | | | | | | |
| Slow | 550 | 250 | 40.60 | 3.68 | 1.09 | 16.24 | 3.99 | 3.00 | 28.00 |
| Medium | 650 | 200 | 35.50 | 3.96 | 1.41 | 17.75 | 5.78 | 3.47 | 32.37 |
| Fast | 750 | 150 | 30.40 | 4.20 | 1.70 | 20.27 | 8.12 | 2.40 | 36.69 |
| Spray 2nd coat | | | | | | | | | |
| Slow | 650 | 300 | 40.60 | 3.12 | .92 | 13.53 | 3.34 | 3.35 | 24.26 |
| Medium | 750 | 250 | 35.50 | 3.43 | 1.21 | 14.20 | 4.71 | 2.83 | 26.38 |
| Fast | 850 | 200 | 30.40 | 3.71 | 1.52 | 15.20 | 6.33 | 1.87 | 28.63 |
| Spray 3rd or additional coats | | | | | | | | | |
| Slow | 700 | 325 | 40.60 | 2.89 | .86 | 12.49 | 3.08 | 3.09 | 22.41 |
| Medium | 800 | 275 | 35.50 | 3.22 | 1.14 | 12.91 | 4.32 | 2.59 | 24.18 |
| Fast | 900 | 225 | 30.40 | 3.50 | 1.42 | 13.51 | 5.72 | 1.69 | 25.84 |

Use this table for butt or tongue and groove siding, joint lap, drop, beveled or board and batten siding in redwood, plywood, fir, hemlock or pine. Don't deduct for openings under 100 square feet. For heights above 8 feet, use the High Time Difficulty Factors on page 139. For wood or composition drop siding with exposed bevel edges, multiply the surface area by 1.12 to allow for the extra time and material needed to paint the underside of each board. "Slow" work is based on an hourly wage of $20.25, "Medium" work on an hourly wage of $25.75, and "Fast" work on an hourly wage of $31.50. Other qualifications that apply to this table are on page 9.

## Stair steps, interior or exterior, wood

To estimate the cost to paint or stain stairs, find the surface area. Then use the tables for wood siding. To find the surface area of each tread and riser, multiply the length by the width. To find the tread length, add the run, the rise, and the tread nosing. For example, a tread with a 12" run, an 8" rise, and 1" nosing, has a 23" surface area (measured one side). For estimating purposes, figure any length from 14" to 26" as 2 feet. Use the actual width of the tread if the stringers are calculated separately. If the tread in the example is 3 feet wide and you use 2 feet for the length, the surface area is 6 feet. If there are 15 treads, the total top surface area is 90 square feet.

If you're calculating the area to paint the stair treads and stringers in one operation, add 2 feet to the actual tread width to include the stringers. That would make the effective width of the tread in the example 5 feet. Then multiply 5 feet by 2 feet to find the area of each tread, 10 square feet. For 15 treads, the total surface area is 150 square feet.

*National Painting Cost Estimator*

|  | Labor LF per manhour | Material coverage LF/gallon | Material cost per gallon | Labor cost per 100 LF | Labor burden 100 LF | Material cost per 100 LF | Overhead per 100 LF | Profit per 100 LF | Total price per 100 LF |
|---|---|---|---|---|---|---|---|---|---|

### Stair stringers, exterior, metal, shapes up to 14" wide, each side

Metal primer - rust inhibitor, clean metal (material #35)
  Roll & brush prime coat

|  | | | | | | | | | |
|---|---|---|---|---|---|---|---|---|---|
| Slow | 50 | 120 | 59.70 | 40.50 | 11.94 | 49.75 | 19.42 | 19.46 | 141.07 |
| Medium | 55 | 115 | 52.20 | 46.82 | 16.57 | 45.39 | 27.20 | 16.32 | 152.30 |
| Fast | 60 | 110 | 44.80 | 52.50 | 21.43 | 40.73 | 35.54 | 10.51 | 160.71 |

Metal primer - rust inhibitor, rusty metal (material #36)
  Roll & brush prime coat

|  | | | | | | | | | |
|---|---|---|---|---|---|---|---|---|---|
| Slow | 50 | 120 | 72.30 | 40.50 | 11.94 | 60.25 | 21.41 | 21.46 | 155.56 |
| Medium | 55 | 115 | 63.30 | 46.82 | 16.57 | 55.04 | 29.61 | 17.76 | 165.80 |
| Fast | 60 | 110 | 54.20 | 52.50 | 21.43 | 49.27 | 38.19 | 11.30 | 172.69 |

Metal finish - synthetic enamel, off white (material #37)
  Roll & brush 1st or additional finish coats

|  | | | | | | | | | |
|---|---|---|---|---|---|---|---|---|---|
| Slow | 50 | 135 | 59.70 | 40.50 | 11.94 | 44.22 | 18.37 | 18.41 | 133.44 |
| Medium | 55 | 130 | 52.20 | 46.82 | 16.57 | 40.15 | 25.89 | 15.53 | 144.96 |
| Fast | 60 | 125 | 44.80 | 52.50 | 21.43 | 35.84 | 34.03 | 10.07 | 153.87 |

Metal finish - synthetic enamel, colors - except orange/red (material #38)
  Roll & brush 1st or additional finish coats

|  | | | | | | | | | |
|---|---|---|---|---|---|---|---|---|---|
| Slow | 50 | 135 | 65.20 | 40.50 | 11.94 | 48.30 | 19.14 | 19.18 | 139.06 |
| Medium | 55 | 130 | 57.00 | 46.82 | 16.57 | 43.85 | 26.81 | 16.09 | 150.14 |
| Fast | 60 | 125 | 48.90 | 52.50 | 21.43 | 39.12 | 35.04 | 10.37 | 158.46 |

Use these figures to paint each side of installed stair stringers. Measurements are based on linear feet of each stringer. Note: A two coat system, prime and finish, using oil base material is recommended for any metal surface. Although water base material is often used, it may cause oxidation, corrosion and rust. Using one coat of oil base paint on exterior metal may result in cracking, peeling or chipping without the proper prime coat application. Pre-primed steel or wrought iron generally requires only one coat to cover. The metal finish figures include minor touchup to the prime coat. If off white or other light colored finish paint is specified, make sure the prime coat is also a light color, or more than one finish coat will be necessary. "Slow" work is based on an hourly wage of $20.25, "Medium" work on an hourly wage of $25.75, and "Fast" work on an hourly wage of $31.50. Other qualifications that apply to this table are on page 9.

|  | Labor LF per manhour | Material coverage LF/gallon | Material cost per gallon | Labor cost per 100 LF | Labor burden 100 LF | Material cost per 100 LF | Overhead per 100 LF | Profit per 100 LF | Total price per 100 LF |
|---|---|---|---|---|---|---|---|---|---|

### Stair stringers, exterior, rough sawn wood up to 4" x 12"

Solid body or semi-transparent stain, water or oil base (material #18, #19, #20 or #21)
  Roll & brush each coat

|  | | | | | | | | | |
|---|---|---|---|---|---|---|---|---|---|
| Slow | 40 | 70 | 48.83 | 50.63 | 14.92 | 69.76 | 25.71 | 25.77 | 186.79 |
| Medium | 45 | 65 | 42.73 | 57.22 | 20.26 | 65.74 | 35.81 | 21.48 | 200.51 |
| Fast | 50 | 60 | 36.60 | 63.00 | 25.70 | 61.00 | 46.41 | 13.73 | 209.84 |

Measurements are based on the linear feet of each stringer. "Slow" work is based on an hourly wage of $20.25, "Medium" work on an hourly wage of $25.75, and "Fast" work on an hourly wage of $31.50. Other qualifications that apply to this table are on page 9.

*General Painting Costs*

|  | Labor LF per manhour | Material coverage LF/gallon | Material cost per gallon | Labor cost per 100 LF | Labor burden 100 LF | Material cost per 100 LF | Overhead per 100 LF | Profit per 100 LF | Total price per 100 LF |
|---|---|---|---|---|---|---|---|---|---|

### Stair stringers, interior, metal, shapes up to 14" wide, each side

Metal primer - rust inhibitor, clean metal (material #35)
  Roll & brush prime coat

| | | | | | | | | | |
|---|---|---|---|---|---|---|---|---|---|
| Slow | 45 | 130 | 59.70 | 45.00 | 13.26 | 45.92 | 19.80 | 19.84 | 143.82 |
| Medium | 50 | 125 | 52.20 | 51.50 | 18.24 | 41.76 | 27.87 | 16.72 | 156.09 |
| Fast | 55 | 120 | 44.80 | 57.27 | 23.36 | 37.33 | 36.57 | 10.82 | 165.35 |

Metal primer - rust inhibitor, rusty metal (material #36)
  Roll & brush prime coat

| | | | | | | | | | |
|---|---|---|---|---|---|---|---|---|---|
| Slow | 45 | 130 | 72.30 | 45.00 | 13.26 | 55.62 | 21.64 | 21.69 | 157.21 |
| Medium | 50 | 125 | 63.30 | 51.50 | 18.24 | 50.64 | 30.09 | 18.06 | 168.53 |
| Fast | 55 | 120 | 54.20 | 57.27 | 23.36 | 45.17 | 39.00 | 11.54 | 176.34 |

Metal finish - synthetic enamel, off white (material #37)
  Roll & brush 1st or additional finish coats

| | | | | | | | | | |
|---|---|---|---|---|---|---|---|---|---|
| Slow | 45 | 145 | 59.70 | 45.00 | 13.26 | 41.17 | 18.90 | 18.94 | 137.27 |
| Medium | 50 | 140 | 52.20 | 51.50 | 18.24 | 37.29 | 26.76 | 16.05 | 149.84 |
| Fast | 55 | 135 | 44.80 | 57.27 | 23.36 | 33.19 | 35.29 | 10.44 | 159.55 |

Metal finish - synthetic enamel, colors - except orange/red (material #38)
  Roll & brush 1st or additional finish coats

| | | | | | | | | | |
|---|---|---|---|---|---|---|---|---|---|
| Slow | 45 | 145 | 65.20 | 45.00 | 13.26 | 44.97 | 19.62 | 19.66 | 142.51 |
| Medium | 50 | 140 | 57.00 | 51.50 | 18.24 | 40.71 | 27.61 | 16.57 | 154.63 |
| Fast | 55 | 135 | 48.90 | 57.27 | 23.36 | 36.22 | 36.23 | 10.72 | 163.80 |

Use these figures to paint each side of installed stair stringers. Measurements are based on linear feet of each stringer. Note: A two coat system, prime and finish, using oil base material is recommended for any metal surface. Although water base material is often used, it may cause oxidation, corrosion and rust. Using one coat of oil base paint on exterior metal may result in cracking, peeling or chipping without the proper prime coat application. Pre-primed steel or wrought iron generally requires only one coat to cover. The metal finish figures include minor touchup to the prime coat. If off white or other light colored finish paint is specified, make sure the prime coat is also a light color, or more than one finish coat will be necessary. "Slow" work is based on an hourly wage of $20.25, "Medium" work on an hourly wage of $25.75, and "Fast" work on an hourly wage of $31.50. Other qualifications that apply to this table are on page 9.

*National Painting Cost Estimator*

|  | Labor LF per manhour | Material coverage LF/gallon | Material cost per gallon | Labor cost per 100 LF | Labor burden 100 LF | Material cost per 100 LF | Overhead per 100 LF | Profit per 100 LF | Total price per 100 LF |
|---|---|---|---|---|---|---|---|---|---|

### Stair stringers, interior, rough sawn wood up to 4" x 12", each side
Solid body or semi-transparent stain, water or oil base (material #18, #19, #20 or #21)
   Roll & brush each coat

| | | | | | | | | | |
|---|---|---|---|---|---|---|---|---|---|
| Slow | 35 | 60 | 48.83 | 57.86 | 17.05 | 81.38 | 29.70 | 29.76 | 215.75 |
| Medium | 40 | 55 | 42.73 | 64.38 | 22.80 | 77.69 | 41.22 | 24.73 | 230.82 |
| Fast | 45 | 50 | 36.60 | 70.00 | 28.55 | 73.20 | 53.25— | 15.75 | 240.75 |

Measurements are based on the linear feet of each side of each stringer. "Slow" work is based on an hourly wage of $20.25, "Medium" work on an hourly wage of $25.75, and "Fast" work on an hourly wage of $31.50. Other qualifications that apply to this table are on page 9.

### Stucco: see Plaster and stucco

### Touchup, brush as required

|  | Percentage of interior manhours | Percentage of interior material costs |
|---|---|---|
| **Interior & exterior** | | |
| Slow | 20.0% | 1.0% |
| Medium | 18.0% | 1.0% |
| Fast | 15.0% | 1.0% |
| **Interior only** | | |
| Slow | 10.0% | 0.5% |
| Medium | 9.0% | 0.5% |
| Fast | 7.5% | 0.5% |

|  | Percentage of exterior manhours | Percentage of exterior material costs |
|---|---|---|
| **Exterior only** | | |
| Slow | 10.0% | 0.5% |
| Medium | 9.0% | 0.5% |
| Fast | 7.5% | 0.5% |

Touchup will be required on nearly all repaint jobs. Using these percentages is an easy but accurate way to calculate touchup costs. When painting both interiors and exteriors, use the appropriate percentage of interior hours only. When painting either the interior or the exterior of a building, use the appropriate figures as indicated for touchup. Multiply the percentages above times the total manhours and material costs as indicated to allow enough time for production and customer service touchup. The skill of your paint crews and the type of job will determine the time and material needed. To calculate an accurate percentage for your company, use your actual time and material costs for touchup on previous projects (historical costs) and convert this figure into a percentage of the total job cost.

*General Painting Costs*

|  | Labor LF per manhour | Material coverage LF/gallon | Material cost per gallon | Labor cost per 100 LF | Labor burden 100 LF | Material cost per 100 LF | Overhead per 100 LF | Profit per 100 LF | Total price per 100 LF |
|---|---|---|---|---|---|---|---|---|---|

### Trellis or lattice, roll and brush

2" x 2" to 2" x 6", roll & brush all sides, each coat
  Solid body or semi-transparent stain, water or oil base (material #18, #19, #20 or #21)

|  |  |  |  |  |  |  |  |  |  |
|---|---|---|---|---|---|---|---|---|---|
| Slow | 120 | 130 | 48.83 | 16.88 | 4.96 | 37.56 | 11.29 | 11.31 | 82.00 |
| Medium | 125 | 120 | 42.73 | 20.60 | 7.30 | 35.61 | 15.88 | 9.53 | 88.92 |
| Fast | 130 | 110 | 36.60 | 24.23 | 9.88 | 33.27 | 20.89 | 6.18 | 94.45 |

2" x 8" to 4" x 12", roll & brush all sides, each coat
  Solid body or semi-transparent stain, water or oil base (material #18, #19, #20 or #21)

|  |  |  |  |  |  |  |  |  |  |
|---|---|---|---|---|---|---|---|---|---|
| Slow | 100 | 100 | 48.83 | 20.25 | 5.97 | 48.83 | 14.26 | 14.29 | 103.60 |
| Medium | 110 | 90 | 42.73 | 23.41 | 8.29 | 47.48 | 19.80 | 11.88 | 110.86 |
| Fast | 120 | 80 | 36.60 | 26.25 | 10.69 | 45.75 | 25.64 | 7.58 | 115.91 |

Measurements are based on accumulated total linear feet of each trellis or lattice member. These figures are based on roll and brush staining of all four sides and the ends of each member per coat. "Slow" work is based on an hourly wage of $20.25, "Medium" work on an hourly wage of $25.75, and "Fast" work on an hourly wage of $31.50. Other qualifications that apply to this table are on page 9.

|  | SF surface area per manhour | SF surface area per gallon | Material cost per gallon | Labor cost per 100 SF | Labor burden 100 SF | Material cost per 100 SF | Overhead per 100 SF | Profit per 100 SF | Total price per 100 SF |
|---|---|---|---|---|---|---|---|---|---|

### Trellis or lattice, spray

2" x 2" at 3" on center with 2" x 8" supports, spray all sides, each coat
  Solid body or semi-transparent stain, water or oil base (material #18, #19, #20 or #21)

|  |  |  |  |  |  |  |  |  |  |
|---|---|---|---|---|---|---|---|---|---|
| Slow | 50 | 60 | 48.83 | 40.50 | 11.94 | 81.38 | 25.43 | 25.48 | 184.73 |
| Medium | 55 | 55 | 42.73 | 46.82 | 16.57 | 77.69 | 35.27 | 21.16 | 197.51 |
| Fast | 60 | 50 | 36.60 | 52.50 | 21.43 | 73.20 | 45.61 | 13.49 | 206.23 |

Measurements are based on the square feet of the surface area footprint of the trellis or lattice structure. (The footprint is the surface area seen from the plan or overhead view.) These figures are based on staining all four sides of each member per coat. "Slow" work is based on an hourly wage of $20.25, "Medium" work on an hourly wage of $25.75, and "Fast" work on an hourly wage of $31.50. Other qualifications that apply to this table are on page 9.

|  | Labor LF per manhour | Material coverage LF/gallon | Material cost per gallon | Labor cost per 100 LF | Labor burden 100 LF | Material cost per 100 LF | Overhead per 100 LF | Profit per 100 LF | Total price per 100 LF |
|---|---|---|---|---|---|---|---|---|---|

## Valances for light fixtures, 2" x 8"
Solid body or semi-transparent stain, water or oil base (material #18, #19, #20 or #21)
  Brush each coat

| | | | | | | | | | |
|---|---|---|---|---|---|---|---|---|---|
| Slow | 30 | 100 | 48.83 | 67.50 | 19.89 | 48.83 | 25.89 | 25.94 | 188.05 |
| Medium | 35 | 95 | 42.73 | 73.57 | 26.05 | 44.98 | 36.15 | 21.69 | 202.44 |
| Fast | 40 | 90 | 36.60 | 78.75 | 32.13 | 40.67 | 46.98 | 13.90 | 212.43 |

Rough sawn or resawn 2" x 8" wood valances are commonly found in baths and kitchens surrounding light fixtures or supporting plastic cracked-ice diffusers. Measurements are based on the linear feet of the valance. "Slow" work is based on an hourly wage of $20.25, "Medium" work on an hourly wage of $25.75, and "Fast" work on an hourly wage of $31.50. Other qualifications that apply to this table are on page 9.

## Walls, Concrete tilt-up: See Industrial, Institutional and Heavy Commercial Painting Costs, page 412

*General Painting Costs*

|  | Labor SF per manhour | Material coverage SF/gallon | Material cost per gallon | Labor cost per 100 SF | Labor burden 100 SF | Material cost per 100 SF | Overhead per 100 SF | Profit per 100 SF | Total price per 100 SF |
|---|---|---|---|---|---|---|---|---|---|
| **Walls, gypsum drywall, anti-graffiti stain eliminator, per 100 SF of wall area** | | | | | | | | | |
| Water base primer and sealer (material #39) | | | | | | | | | |
|   Roll & brush each coat | | | | | | | | | |
|     Slow | 375 | 450 | 50.30 | 5.40 | 1.60 | 11.18 | 3.45 | 3.46 | 25.09 |
|     Medium | 400 | 425 | 44.00 | 6.44 | 2.28 | 10.35 | 4.77 | 2.86 | 26.70 |
|     Fast | 425 | 400 | 37.80 | 7.41 | 3.01 | 9.45 | 6.16 | 1.82 | 27.85 |
| Oil base primer and sealer (material #40) | | | | | | | | | |
|   Roll & brush each coat | | | | | | | | | |
|     Slow | 375 | 400 | 49.90 | 5.40 | 1.60 | 12.48 | 3.70 | 3.71 | 26.89 |
|     Medium | 400 | 388 | 43.70 | 6.44 | 2.28 | 11.26 | 5.00 | 3.00 | 27.98 |
|     Fast | 425 | 375 | 37.40 | 7.41 | 3.01 | 9.97 | 6.32 | 1.87 | 28.58 |
| Polyurethane 2 part system (material #41) | | | | | | | | | |
|   Roll & brush each coat | | | | | | | | | |
|     Slow | 325 | 400 | 157.00 | 6.23 | 1.85 | 39.25 | 8.99 | 9.01 | 65.33 |
|     Medium | 350 | 375 | 137.40 | 7.36 | 2.61 | 36.64 | 11.65 | 6.99 | 65.25 |
|     Fast | 375 | 350 | 117.80 | 8.40 | 3.44 | 33.66 | 14.10 | 4.17 | 63.77 |

Measurements are based on the square feet of wall coated. Do not deduct for openings less than 100 square feet. These figures assume paint products are being applied over a smooth finish. For heights above 8 feet, use the High Time Difficulty Factors on page 139. "Slow" work is based on an hourly wage of $20.25, "Medium" work on an hourly wage of $25.75, and "Fast" work on an hourly wage of $31.50. Other qualifications that apply to this table are on page 9.

National Painting Cost Estimator

|  | Labor SF per manhour | Material coverage SF/gallon | Material cost per gallon | Labor cost per 100 SF | Labor burden 100 SF | Material cost per 100 SF | Overhead per 100 SF | Profit per 100 SF | Total price per 100 SF |
|---|---|---|---|---|---|---|---|---|---|

## Walls, gypsum drywall, orange peel or knock-down, brush, per 100 SF of wall area

Flat latex, water base (material #5)
Brush 1st coat
| | | | | | | | | | |
|---|---|---|---|---|---|---|---|---|---|
| Slow | 150 | 300 | 36.70 | 13.50 | 3.99 | 12.23 | 5.64 | 5.66 | 41.02 |
| Medium | 175 | 288 | 32.10 | 14.71 | 5.20 | 11.15 | 7.77 | 4.66 | 43.49 |
| Fast | 200 | 275 | 27.50 | 15.75 | 6.43 | 10.00 | 9.98 | 2.95 | 45.11 |

Brush 2nd coat
| | | | | | | | | | |
|---|---|---|---|---|---|---|---|---|---|
| Slow | 175 | 350 | 36.70 | 11.57 | 3.40 | 10.49 | 4.84 | 4.85 | 35.15 |
| Medium | 200 | 338 | 32.10 | 12.88 | 4.56 | 9.50 | 6.74 | 4.04 | 37.72 |
| Fast | 225 | 325 | 27.50 | 14.00 | 5.69 | 8.46 | 8.73 | 2.58 | 39.46 |

Brush 3rd or additional coats
| | | | | | | | | | |
|---|---|---|---|---|---|---|---|---|---|
| Slow | 200 | 400 | 36.70 | 10.13 | 2.98 | 9.18 | 4.24 | 4.25 | 30.78 |
| Medium | 225 | 375 | 32.10 | 11.44 | 4.04 | 8.56 | 6.01 | 3.61 | 33.66 |
| Fast | 250 | 350 | 27.50 | 12.60 | 5.14 | 7.86 | 7.94 | 2.35 | 35.89 |

Sealer (drywall), water base (material #1)
Brush prime coat
| | | | | | | | | | |
|---|---|---|---|---|---|---|---|---|---|
| Slow | 125 | 300 | 30.50 | 16.20 | 4.78 | 10.17 | 5.92 | 5.93 | 43.00 |
| Medium | 163 | 288 | 26.70 | 15.80 | 5.58 | 9.27 | 7.67 | 4.60 | 42.92 |
| Fast | 200 | 275 | 22.90 | 15.75 | 6.43 | 8.33 | 9.46 | 2.80 | 42.77 |

Sealer (drywall), oil base (material #2)
Brush prime coat
| | | | | | | | | | |
|---|---|---|---|---|---|---|---|---|---|
| Slow | 125 | 250 | 39.70 | 16.20 | 4.78 | 15.88 | 7.00 | 7.02 | 50.88 |
| Medium | 163 | 238 | 34.80 | 15.80 | 5.58 | 14.62 | 9.00 | 5.40 | 50.40 |
| Fast | 200 | 225 | 29.80 | 15.75 | 6.43 | 13.24 | 10.98 | 3.25 | 49.65 |

Enamel, water base (material #9)
Brush 1st finish coat
| | | | | | | | | | |
|---|---|---|---|---|---|---|---|---|---|
| Slow | 100 | 300 | 46.80 | 20.25 | 5.97 | 15.60 | 7.95 | 7.96 | 57.73 |
| Medium | 150 | 288 | 41.00 | 17.17 | 6.09 | 14.24 | 9.37 | 5.62 | 52.49 |
| Fast | 200 | 275 | 35.10 | 15.75 | 6.43 | 12.76 | 10.83 | 3.20 | 48.97 |

Brush 2nd or additional finish coats
| | | | | | | | | | |
|---|---|---|---|---|---|---|---|---|---|
| Slow | 125 | 350 | 46.80 | 16.20 | 4.78 | 13.37 | 6.53 | 6.54 | 47.42 |
| Medium | 163 | 325 | 41.00 | 15.80 | 5.58 | 12.62 | 8.50 | 5.10 | 47.60 |
| Fast | 200 | 300 | 35.10 | 15.75 | 6.43 | 11.70 | 10.50 | 3.11 | 47.49 |

Enamel, oil base (material #10)
Brush 1st finish coat
| | | | | | | | | | |
|---|---|---|---|---|---|---|---|---|---|
| Slow | 100 | 325 | 61.70 | 20.25 | 5.97 | 18.98 | 8.59 | 8.61 | 62.40 |
| Medium | 150 | 300 | 54.00 | 17.17 | 6.09 | 18.00 | 10.31 | 6.19 | 57.76 |
| Fast | 200 | 275 | 46.30 | 15.75 | 6.43 | 16.84 | 12.10 | 3.58 | 54.70 |

*General Painting Costs*

|  | Labor SF per manhour | Material coverage SF/gallon | Material cost per gallon | Labor cost per 100 SF | Labor burden 100 SF | Material cost per 100 SF | Overhead per 100 SF | Profit per 100 SF | Total price per 100 SF |
|---|---|---|---|---|---|---|---|---|---|
| Brush 2nd or additional finish coats | | | | | | | | | |
| Slow | 125 | 350 | 46.80 | 16.20 | 4.78 | 13.37 | 6.53 | 6.54 | 47.42 |
| Medium | 163 | 325 | 41.00 | 15.80 | 5.58 | 12.62 | 8.50 | 5.10 | 47.60 |
| Fast | 200 | 300 | 35.10 | 15.75 | 6.43 | 11.70 | 10.50 | 3.11 | 47.49 |
| Epoxy coating, 2 part system - white (material #52) | | | | | | | | | |
| Brush 1st coat | | | | | | | | | |
| Slow | 175 | 350 | 177.00 | 11.57 | 3.40 | 50.57 | 12.45 | 12.48 | 90.47 |
| Medium | 200 | 325 | 154.90 | 12.88 | 4.56 | 47.66 | 16.28 | 9.77 | 91.15 |
| Fast | 225 | 300 | 132.70 | 14.00 | 5.69 | 44.23 | 19.82 | 5.86 | 89.60 |
| Brush 2nd or additional coats | | | | | | | | | |
| Slow | 200 | 375 | 177.00 | 10.13 | 2.98 | 47.20 | 11.46 | 11.48 | 83.25 |
| Medium | 225 | 350 | 154.90 | 11.44 | 4.04 | 44.26 | 14.94 | 8.96 | 83.64 |
| Fast | 250 | 325 | 132.70 | 12.60 | 5.14 | 40.83 | 18.16 | 5.37 | 82.10 |

Measurements are based on the square feet of wall coated. Do not deduct for openings less than 100 square feet. These figures assume paint products are being applied over a smooth finish. For heights above 8 feet, use the High Time Difficulty Factors on page 139. These figures include brushing-in at corners when all walls are the same color, and at ceilings that are the same color or finished with acoustic spray-on texture. ADD for cutting-in at ceilings if they're a different color than the walls, or at corners where walls in the same room are painted different colors. Do not include cutting-in time for ceilings unless you're only painting the ceilings, not the walls. "Slow" work is based on an hourly wage of $20.25, "Medium" work on an hourly wage of $25.75, and "Fast" work on an hourly wage of $31.50. Other qualifications that apply to this table are on page 9.

*National Painting Cost Estimator*

|  | Labor SF per manhour | Material coverage SF/gallon | Material cost per gallon | Labor cost per 100 SF | Labor burden 100 SF | Material cost per 100 SF | Overhead per 100 SF | Profit per 100 SF | Total price per 100 SF |
|---|---|---|---|---|---|---|---|---|---|

## Walls, gypsum drywall, orange peel or knock-down, roll, per 100 SF of wall area

Flat latex, water base (material #5)
  Roll 1st coat

| | | | | | | | | | |
|---|---|---|---|---|---|---|---|---|---|
| Slow | 400 | 300 | 36.70 | 5.06 | 1.50 | 12.23 | 3.57 | 3.58 | 25.94 |
| Medium | 538 | 275 | 32.10 | 4.79 | 1.70 | 11.67 | 4.54 | 2.72 | 25.42 |
| Fast | 675 | 250 | 27.50 | 4.67 | 1.89 | 11.00 | 5.45 | 1.61 | 24.62 |

  Roll 2nd coat

| | | | | | | | | | |
|---|---|---|---|---|---|---|---|---|---|
| Slow | 500 | 325 | 36.70 | 4.05 | 1.19 | 11.29 | 3.14 | 3.15 | 22.82 |
| Medium | 600 | 313 | 32.10 | 4.29 | 1.53 | 10.26 | 4.02 | 2.41 | 22.51 |
| Fast | 700 | 300 | 27.50 | 4.50 | 1.84 | 9.17 | 4.81 | 1.42 | 21.74 |

  Roll 3rd or additional coats

| | | | | | | | | | |
|---|---|---|---|---|---|---|---|---|---|
| Slow | 550 | 350 | 36.70 | 3.68 | 1.09 | 10.49 | 2.90 | 2.91 | 21.07 |
| Medium | 650 | 338 | 32.10 | 3.96 | 1.41 | 9.50 | 3.72 | 2.23 | 20.82 |
| Fast | 750 | 325 | 27.50 | 4.20 | 1.70 | 8.46 | 4.45 | 1.32 | 20.13 |

Sealer (drywall), water base (material #1)
  Roll prime coat

| | | | | | | | | | |
|---|---|---|---|---|---|---|---|---|---|
| Slow | 325 | 275 | 30.50 | 6.23 | 1.85 | 11.09 | 3.64 | 3.65 | 26.46 |
| Medium | 500 | 263 | 26.70 | 5.15 | 1.82 | 10.15 | 4.28 | 2.57 | 23.97 |
| Fast | 675 | 250 | 22.90 | 4.67 | 1.89 | 9.16 | 4.88 | 1.44 | 22.04 |

Sealer (drywall), oil base (material #2)
  Roll prime coat

| | | | | | | | | | |
|---|---|---|---|---|---|---|---|---|---|
| Slow | 325 | 275 | 39.70 | 6.23 | 1.85 | 14.44 | 4.28 | 4.29 | 31.09 |
| Medium | 500 | 263 | 34.80 | 5.15 | 1.82 | 13.23 | 5.05 | 3.03 | 28.28 |
| Fast | 675 | 250 | 29.80 | 4.67 | 1.89 | 11.92 | 5.74 | 1.70 | 25.92 |

Enamel, water base (material #9)
  Roll 1st finish coat

| | | | | | | | | | |
|---|---|---|---|---|---|---|---|---|---|
| Slow | 300 | 285 | 46.80 | 6.75 | 1.98 | 16.42 | 4.78 | 4.79 | 34.72 |
| Medium | 450 | 263 | 41.00 | 5.72 | 2.02 | 15.59 | 5.83 | 3.50 | 32.66 |
| Fast | 600 | 240 | 35.10 | 5.25 | 2.16 | 14.63 | 6.83 | 2.02 | 30.89 |

  Roll 2nd finish coat

| | | | | | | | | | |
|---|---|---|---|---|---|---|---|---|---|
| Slow | 325 | 300 | 46.80 | 6.23 | 1.85 | 15.60 | 4.50 | 4.51 | 32.69 |
| Medium | 475 | 288 | 41.00 | 5.42 | 1.94 | 14.24 | 5.40 | 3.24 | 30.24 |
| Fast | 625 | 275 | 35.10 | 5.04 | 2.06 | 12.76 | 6.16 | 1.82 | 27.84 |

Enamel, oil base (material #10)
  Roll 1st finish coat

| | | | | | | | | | |
|---|---|---|---|---|---|---|---|---|---|
| Slow | 300 | 250 | 61.70 | 6.75 | 1.98 | 24.68 | 6.35 | 6.36 | 46.12 |
| Medium | 450 | 238 | 54.00 | 5.72 | 2.02 | 22.69 | 7.61 | 4.56 | 42.60 |
| Fast | 600 | 225 | 46.30 | 5.25 | 2.16 | 20.58 | 8.67 | 2.56 | 39.22 |

*General Painting Costs*

|  | Labor SF per manhour | Material coverage SF/gallon | Material cost per gallon | Labor cost per 100 SF | Labor burden 100 SF | Material cost per 100 SF | Overhead per 100 SF | Profit per 100 SF | Total price per 100 SF |
|---|---|---|---|---|---|---|---|---|---|
| Roll 2nd finish coat |  |  |  |  |  |  |  |  |  |
| Slow | 325 | 275 | 61.70 | 6.23 | 1.85 | 22.44 | 5.80 | 5.81 | 42.13 |
| Medium | 475 | 263 | 54.00 | 5.42 | 1.94 | 20.53 | 6.97 | 4.18 | 39.04 |
| Fast | 625 | 250 | 46.30 | 5.04 | 2.06 | 18.52 | 7.94 | 2.35 | 35.91 |
| Epoxy coating, 2 part system - white (material #52) |  |  |  |  |  |  |  |  |  |
| Roll 1st coat |  |  |  |  |  |  |  |  |  |
| Slow | 325 | 300 | 177.00 | 6.23 | 1.85 | 59.00 | 12.74 | 12.77 | 92.59 |
| Medium | 488 | 288 | 154.90 | 5.28 | 1.87 | 53.78 | 15.23 | 9.14 | 85.30 |
| Fast | 700 | 275 | 132.70 | 4.50 | 1.84 | 48.25 | 16.92 | 5.01 | 76.52 |
| Roll 2nd or additional coats |  |  |  |  |  |  |  |  |  |
| Slow | 400 | 325 | 177.00 | 5.06 | 1.50 | 54.46 | 11.59 | 11.62 | 84.23 |
| Medium | 575 | 313 | 154.90 | 4.48 | 1.59 | 49.49 | 13.89 | 8.33 | 77.78 |
| Fast | 750 | 300 | 132.70 | 4.20 | 1.70 | 44.23 | 15.54 | 4.60 | 70.27 |

Measurements are based on the square feet of wall coated. Do not deduct for openings less than 100 square feet. These figures assume paint products are being applied over an orange peel or knock-down texture finish. For heights above 8 feet, use the High Time Difficulty Factors on page 139. These figures include brushing-in at corners when all walls are the same color, and at ceilings that are the same color or finished with acoustic spray-on texture. ADD for cutting-in at ceilings if they're a different color than the walls, or at corners where walls in the same room are painted different colors. Do not include cutting-in time for ceilings unless you're only painting the ceilings, not the walls. "Slow" work is based on an hourly wage of $20.25, "Medium" work on an hourly wage of $25.75, and "Fast" work on an hourly wage of $31.50. Other qualifications that apply to this table are on page 9.

*National Painting Cost Estimator*

|  | SF of floor area per manhour | SF of floor area per gallon | Material cost per gallon | Labor cost per 100 SF | Labor burden 100 SF | Material cost per 100 SF | Overhead per 100 SF | Profit per 100 SF | Total price per 100 SF |
|---|---|---|---|---|---|---|---|---|---|

## Walls, gypsum drywall, orange peel or knock-down, roll, per 100 SF of floor area

Flat latex, water base (material #5)
Roll 1st coat on *walls only*

| | | | | | | | | | |
|---|---|---|---|---|---|---|---|---|---|
| Slow | 250 | 175 | 36.70 | 8.10 | 2.39 | 20.97 | 5.98 | 5.99 | 43.43 |
| Medium | 325 | 158 | 32.10 | 7.92 | 2.82 | 20.32 | 7.76 | 4.66 | 43.48 |
| Fast | 400 | 140 | 27.50 | 7.88 | 3.21 | 19.64 | 9.53 | 2.82 | 43.08 |

Roll 2nd coat on *walls only*

| | | | | | | | | | |
|---|---|---|---|---|---|---|---|---|---|
| Slow | 300 | 200 | 36.70 | 6.75 | 1.98 | 18.35 | 5.15 | 5.16 | 37.39 |
| Medium | 400 | 188 | 32.10 | 6.44 | 2.28 | 17.07 | 6.45 | 3.87 | 36.11 |
| Fast | 500 | 175 | 27.50 | 6.30 | 2.57 | 15.71 | 7.62 | 2.25 | 34.45 |

Sealer (drywall), water base (material #1) on *walls and ceilings*
Roll prime coat

| | | | | | | | | | |
|---|---|---|---|---|---|---|---|---|---|
| Slow | 100 | 100 | 30.50 | 20.25 | 5.97 | 30.50 | 10.78 | 10.80 | 78.30 |
| Medium | 170 | 88 | 26.70 | 15.15 | 5.35 | 30.34 | 12.71 | 7.63 | 71.18 |
| Fast | 240 | 75 | 22.90 | 13.13 | 5.36 | 30.53 | 15.20 | 4.50 | 68.72 |

Sealer (drywall), oil base (material #2) on *walls and ceilings*
Roll prime coat

| | | | | | | | | | |
|---|---|---|---|---|---|---|---|---|---|
| Slow | 100 | 100 | 39.70 | 20.25 | 5.97 | 39.70 | 12.52 | 12.55 | 90.99 |
| Medium | 170 | 88 | 34.80 | 15.15 | 5.35 | 39.55 | 15.02 | 9.01 | 84.08 |
| Fast | 240 | 75 | 29.80 | 13.13 | 5.36 | 39.73 | 18.05 | 5.34 | 81.61 |

Enamel, water base (material #9) on *walls and ceilings*
Roll 1st finish coat

| | | | | | | | | | |
|---|---|---|---|---|---|---|---|---|---|
| Slow | 70 | 100 | 46.80 | 28.93 | 8.54 | 46.80 | 16.01 | 16.04 | 116.32 |
| Medium | 100 | 90 | 41.00 | 25.75 | 9.12 | 45.56 | 20.11 | 12.06 | 112.60 |
| Fast | 135 | 80 | 35.10 | 23.33 | 9.53 | 43.88 | 23.79 | 7.04 | 107.57 |

Roll 2nd finish coat

| | | | | | | | | | |
|---|---|---|---|---|---|---|---|---|---|
| Slow | 125 | 150 | 46.80 | 16.20 | 4.78 | 31.20 | 9.91 | 9.93 | 72.02 |
| Medium | 175 | 125 | 41.00 | 14.71 | 5.20 | 32.80 | 13.18 | 7.91 | 73.80 |
| Fast | 225 | 100 | 35.10 | 14.00 | 5.69 | 35.10 | 16.99 | 5.03 | 76.81 |

## General Painting Costs

| | SF of floor area per manhour | SF of floor area per gallon | Material cost per gallon | Labor cost per 100 SF | Labor burden 100 SF | Material cost per 100 SF | Overhead per 100 SF | Profit per 100 SF | Total price per 100 SF |
|---|---|---|---|---|---|---|---|---|---|
| **Enamel, oil base (material #10) on walls and ceilings** | | | | | | | | | |
| *Roll 1st finish coat* | | | | | | | | | |
| Slow | 70 | 100 | 61.70 | 28.93 | 8.54 | 61.70 | 18.84 | 18.88 | 136.89 |
| Medium | 100 | 90 | 54.00 | 25.75 | 9.12 | 60.00 | 23.72 | 14.23 | 132.82 |
| Fast | 135 | 80 | 46.30 | 23.33 | 9.53 | 57.88 | 28.13 | 8.32 | 127.19 |
| *Roll 2nd finish coat* | | | | | | | | | |
| Slow | 125 | 150 | 61.70 | 16.20 | 4.78 | 41.13 | 11.80 | 11.83 | 85.74 |
| Medium | 175 | 125 | 54.00 | 14.71 | 5.20 | 43.20 | 15.78 | 9.47 | 88.36 |
| Fast | 225 | 100 | 46.30 | 14.00 | 5.69 | 46.30 | 20.46 | 6.05 | 92.50 |

Measurements for these costs are based on square feet of floor area. The flat wall figures are for painting walls only but the Sealer and Enamel figures are for painting walls and ceilings in wet areas, i.e. kitchens, baths, utility areas, etc. The floor area measurements are from outside wall to outside wall or from the edge of the concrete slab or from the outside edge of an interior wall. This method of figuring the costs to paint the walls and ceilings is not as accurate as measuring the actual surface area of the wall or ceiling area directly, but it is much less time consuming. For heights above 8 feet, use the High Time Difficulty Factors on page 139. These figures include brushing-in at corners when all walls are the same color, and at ceilings that are the same color or finished with acoustic spray-on texture. ADD for cutting-in at ceilings if they're a different color than the walls, or at corners where walls in the same room are painted different colors. Do not include cutting-in time for ceilings unless you're only painting the ceilings, not the walls. "Slow" work is based on an hourly wage of $20.25, "Medium" work on an hourly wage of $25.75, and "Fast" work on an hourly wage of $31.50. Other qualifications that apply to this table are on page 9.

*National Painting Cost Estimator*

|  | Labor SF per manhour | Material coverage SF/gallon | Material cost per gallon | Labor cost per 100 SF | Labor burden 100 SF | Material cost per 100 SF | Overhead per 100 SF | Profit per 100 SF | Total price per 100 SF |
|---|---|---|---|---|---|---|---|---|---|

## Walls, gypsum drywall, orange peel or knock-down, spray, per 100 SF of wall area

Flat latex, water base (material #5)
  Spray 1st coat

| | | | | | | | | | |
|---|---|---|---|---|---|---|---|---|---|
| Slow | 700 | 250 | 36.70 | 2.89 | .86 | 14.68 | 3.50 | 3.51 | 25.44 |
| Medium | 800 | 225 | 32.10 | 3.22 | 1.14 | 14.27 | 4.66 | 2.79 | 26.08 |
| Fast | 900 | 200 | 27.50 | 3.50 | 1.42 | 13.75 | 5.79 | 1.71 | 26.17 |

  Spray 2nd coat

| | | | | | | | | | |
|---|---|---|---|---|---|---|---|---|---|
| Slow | 800 | 300 | 36.70 | 2.53 | .75 | 12.23 | 2.95 | 2.95 | 21.41 |
| Medium | 900 | 275 | 32.10 | 2.86 | 1.01 | 11.67 | 3.89 | 2.33 | 21.76 |
| Fast | 1000 | 250 | 27.50 | 3.15 | 1.29 | 11.00 | 4.79 | 1.42 | 21.65 |

  Spray 3rd or additional coats

| | | | | | | | | | |
|---|---|---|---|---|---|---|---|---|---|
| Slow | 850 | 325 | 36.70 | 2.38 | .71 | 11.29 | 2.73 | 2.74 | 19.85 |
| Medium | 950 | 300 | 32.10 | 2.71 | .95 | 10.70 | 3.59 | 2.16 | 20.11 |
| Fast | 1050 | 275 | 27.50 | 3.00 | 1.21 | 10.00 | 4.41 | 1.30 | 19.92 |

Sealer (drywall), water base (material #1)
  Spray prime coat

| | | | | | | | | | |
|---|---|---|---|---|---|---|---|---|---|
| Slow | 575 | 250 | 30.50 | 3.52 | 1.04 | 12.20 | 3.18 | 3.19 | 23.13 |
| Medium | 738 | 225 | 26.70 | 3.49 | 1.25 | 11.87 | 4.15 | 2.49 | 23.25 |
| Fast | 900 | 200 | 22.90 | 3.50 | 1.42 | 11.45 | 5.08 | 1.50 | 22.95 |

Sealer (drywall), oil base (material #2)
  Spray prime coat

| | | | | | | | | | |
|---|---|---|---|---|---|---|---|---|---|
| Slow | 575 | 250 | 39.70 | 3.52 | 1.04 | 15.88 | 3.88 | 3.89 | 28.21 |
| Medium | 738 | 225 | 34.80 | 3.49 | 1.25 | 15.47 | 5.05 | 3.03 | 28.29 |
| Fast | 900 | 200 | 29.80 | 3.50 | 1.42 | 14.90 | 6.15 | 1.82 | 27.79 |

Enamel, water base (material #9)
  Spray 1st finish coat

| | | | | | | | | | |
|---|---|---|---|---|---|---|---|---|---|
| Slow | 500 | 250 | 46.80 | 4.05 | 1.19 | 18.72 | 4.55 | 4.56 | 33.07 |
| Medium | 675 | 238 | 41.00 | 3.81 | 1.35 | 17.23 | 5.60 | 3.36 | 31.35 |
| Fast | 850 | 225 | 35.10 | 3.71 | 1.52 | 15.60 | 6.45 | 1.91 | 29.19 |

  Spray 2nd finish coat

| | | | | | | | | | |
|---|---|---|---|---|---|---|---|---|---|
| Slow | 525 | 275 | 46.80 | 3.86 | 1.12 | 17.02 | 4.18 | 4.19 | 30.37 |
| Medium | 700 | 263 | 41.00 | 3.68 | 1.31 | 15.59 | 5.14 | 3.09 | 28.81 |
| Fast | 875 | 250 | 35.10 | 3.60 | 1.46 | 14.04 | 5.92 | 1.75 | 26.77 |

  Spray 3rd or additional finish coats

| | | | | | | | | | |
|---|---|---|---|---|---|---|---|---|---|
| Slow | 575 | 300 | 46.80 | 3.52 | 1.04 | 15.60 | 3.83 | 3.84 | 27.83 |
| Medium | 775 | 275 | 41.00 | 3.32 | 1.18 | 14.91 | 4.85 | 2.91 | 27.17 |
| Fast | 925 | 250 | 35.10 | 3.41 | 1.38 | 14.04 | 5.84 | 1.73 | 26.40 |

*General Painting Costs*

|  | Labor SF per manhour | Material coverage SF/gallon | Material cost per gallon | Labor cost per 100 SF | Labor burden 100 SF | Material cost per 100 SF | Overhead per 100 SF | Profit per 100 SF | Total price per 100 SF |
|---|---|---|---|---|---|---|---|---|---|
| **Enamel, oil base (material #10)** | | | | | | | | | |
|   Spray 1st finish coat | | | | | | | | | |
|     Slow | 500 | 250 | 61.70 | 4.05 | 1.19 | 24.68 | 5.68 | 5.70 | 41.30 |
|     Medium | 675 | 225 | 54.00 | 3.81 | 1.35 | 24.00 | 7.29 | 4.37 | 40.82 |
|     Fast | 850 | 200 | 46.30 | 3.71 | 1.52 | 23.15 | 8.79 | 2.60 | 39.77 |
|   Spray 2nd finish coat | | | | | | | | | |
|     Slow | 525 | 275 | 61.70 | 3.86 | 1.12 | 22.44 | 5.21 | 5.22 | 37.85 |
|     Medium | 700 | 250 | 54.00 | 3.68 | 1.31 | 21.60 | 6.65 | 3.99 | 37.23 |
|     Fast | 875 | 225 | 46.30 | 3.60 | 1.46 | 20.58 | 7.95 | 2.35 | 35.94 |
|   Spray 3rd or additional finish coat | | | | | | | | | |
|     Slow | 575 | 300 | 61.70 | 3.52 | 1.04 | 20.57 | 4.77 | 4.78 | 34.68 |
|     Medium | 775 | 275 | 54.00 | 3.32 | 1.18 | 19.64 | 6.04 | 3.62 | 33.80 |
|     Fast | 925 | 250 | 46.30 | 3.41 | 1.38 | 18.52 | 7.23 | 2.14 | 32.68 |

Measurements are based on the square feet of wall coated. Do not deduct for openings less than 100 square feet. These figures assume paint products are being applied over a smooth finish. For heights above 8 feet, use the High Time Difficulty Factors on page 139. These figures include spraying at corners when all walls are the same color, and at ceiling-to-wall intersection when ceilings are the same color. ADD for cutting-in at ceilings and protecting adjacent surfaces from overspray if they're a different color than the walls, or at corners where walls in the same room are painted different colors. Do not include cutting-in time for ceilings unless you're only painting the ceilings, not the walls. "Slow" work is based on an hourly wage of $20.25, "Medium" work on an hourly wage of $25.75, and "Fast" work on hourly wage of $31.50. Other qualifications that apply to this table are on page 9.

*National Painting Cost Estimator*

|  | Labor SF per manhour | Material coverage SF/gallon | Material cost per gallon | Labor cost per 100 SF | Labor burden 100 SF | Material cost per 100 SF | Overhead per 100 SF | Profit per 100 SF | Total price per 100 SF |
|---|---|---|---|---|---|---|---|---|---|
| **Walls, gypsum drywall, skip trowel or sand finish, brush, per 100 SF of wall area** | | | | | | | | | |
| Flat latex, water base (material #5) | | | | | | | | | |
|   Brush 1st coat | | | | | | | | | |
|     Slow | 175 | 325 | 36.70 | 11.57 | 3.40 | 11.29 | 4.99 | 5.00 | 36.25 |
|     Medium | 200 | 313 | 32.10 | 12.88 | 4.56 | 10.26 | 6.93 | 4.16 | 38.79 |
|     Fast | 225 | 300 | 27.50 | 14.00 | 5.69 | 9.17 | 8.95 | 2.65 | 40.46 |
|   Brush 2nd coat | | | | | | | | | |
|     Slow | 200 | 400 | 36.70 | 10.13 | 2.98 | 9.18 | 4.24 | 4.25 | 30.78 |
|     Medium | 225 | 375 | 32.10 | 11.44 | 4.04 | 8.56 | 6.01 | 3.61 | 33.66 |
|     Fast | 250 | 350 | 27.50 | 12.60 | 5.14 | 7.86 | 7.94 | 2.35 | 35.89 |
|   Brush 3rd or additional coats | | | | | | | | | |
|     Slow | 225 | 425 | 36.70 | 9.00 | 2.64 | 8.64 | 3.86 | 3.87 | 28.01 |
|     Medium | 250 | 400 | 32.10 | 10.30 | 3.65 | 8.03 | 5.50 | 3.30 | 30.78 |
|     Fast | 275 | 375 | 27.50 | 11.45 | 4.69 | 7.33 | 7.27 | 2.15 | 32.89 |
| Sealer (drywall), water base (material #1) | | | | | | | | | |
|   Brush prime coat | | | | | | | | | |
|     Slow | 140 | 325 | 30.50 | 14.46 | 4.26 | 9.38 | 5.34 | 5.35 | 38.79 |
|     Medium | 183 | 313 | 26.70 | 14.07 | 4.97 | 8.53 | 6.90 | 4.14 | 38.61 |
|     Fast | 225 | 300 | 22.90 | 14.00 | 5.69 | 7.63 | 8.48 | 2.51 | 38.31 |
| Sealer (drywall), oil base (material #2) | | | | | | | | | |
|   Brush prime coat | | | | | | | | | |
|     Slow | 140 | 350 | 39.70 | 14.46 | 4.26 | 11.34 | 5.71 | 5.72 | 41.49 |
|     Medium | 183 | 338 | 34.80 | 14.07 | 4.97 | 10.30 | 7.34 | 4.40 | 41.08 |
|     Fast | 225 | 325 | 29.80 | 14.00 | 5.69 | 9.17 | 8.95 | 2.65 | 40.46 |
| Enamel, water base (material #9) | | | | | | | | | |
|   Brush 1st finish coat | | | | | | | | | |
|     Slow | 125 | 350 | 46.80 | 16.20 | 4.78 | 13.37 | 6.53 | 6.54 | 47.42 |
|     Medium | 175 | 325 | 41.00 | 14.71 | 5.20 | 12.62 | 8.14 | 4.88 | 45.55 |
|     Fast | 225 | 300 | 35.10 | 14.00 | 5.69 | 11.70 | 9.74 | 2.88 | 44.01 |
|   Brush 2nd or additional finish coats | | | | | | | | | |
|     Slow | 140 | 350 | 46.80 | 14.46 | 4.26 | 13.37 | 6.10 | 6.11 | 44.30 |
|     Medium | 185 | 325 | 41.00 | 13.92 | 4.94 | 12.62 | 7.87 | 4.72 | 44.07 |
|     Fast | 235 | 300 | 35.10 | 13.40 | 5.49 | 11.70 | 9.48 | 2.80 | 42.87 |
| Enamel, oil base (material #10) | | | | | | | | | |
|   Brush 1st finish coat | | | | | | | | | |
|     Slow | 125 | 350 | 61.70 | 16.20 | 4.78 | 17.63 | 7.34 | 7.35 | 53.30 |
|     Medium | 175 | 325 | 54.00 | 14.71 | 5.20 | 16.62 | 9.14 | 5.48 | 51.15 |
|     Fast | 225 | 300 | 46.30 | 14.00 | 5.69 | 15.43 | 10.89 | 3.22 | 49.23 |

*General Painting Costs*

|  | Labor SF per manhour | Material coverage SF/gallon | Material cost per gallon | Labor cost per 100 SF | Labor burden 100 SF | Material cost per 100 SF | Overhead per 100 SF | Profit per 100 SF | Total price per 100 SF |
|---|---|---|---|---|---|---|---|---|---|
| **Brush 2nd or additional finish coats** | | | | | | | | | |
| Slow | 140 | 350 | 61.70 | 14.46 | 4.26 | 17.63 | 6.91 | 6.92 | 50.18 |
| Medium | 185 | 338 | 54.00 | 13.92 | 4.94 | 15.98 | 8.71 | 5.22 | 48.77 |
| Fast | 235 | 325 | 46.30 | 13.40 | 5.49 | 14.25 | 10.27 | 3.04 | 46.45 |
| **Epoxy coating, 2 part system - white (material #52)** | | | | | | | | | |
| Brush 1st coat | | | | | | | | | |
| Slow | 200 | 375 | 177.00 | 10.13 | 2.98 | 47.20 | 11.46 | 11.48 | 83.25 |
| Medium | 225 | 350 | 154.90 | 11.44 | 4.04 | 44.26 | 14.94 | 8.96 | 83.64 |
| Fast | 250 | 325 | 132.70 | 12.60 | 5.14 | 40.83 | 18.16 | 5.37 | 82.10 |
| Brush 2nd or additional coats | | | | | | | | | |
| Slow | 225 | 400 | 177.00 | 9.00 | 2.64 | 44.25 | 10.62 | 10.64 | 77.15 |
| Medium | 250 | 375 | 154.90 | 10.30 | 3.65 | 41.31 | 13.82 | 8.29 | 77.37 |
| Fast | 275 | 350 | 132.70 | 11.45 | 4.69 | 37.91 | 16.75 | 4.95 | 75.75 |

Measurements are based on the square feet of wall coated. Do not deduct for openings less than 100 square feet. These figures assume paint products are being applied over a smooth finish. For heights above 8 feet, use the High Time Difficulty Factors on page 139. These figures include brushing-in at corners when all walls are the same color, and at ceilings that are the same color or finished with acoustic spray-on texture. ADD for cutting-in at ceilings if they're a different color than the walls, or at corners where walls in the same room are painted different colors. Do not include cutting-in time for ceilings unless you're only painting the ceilings, not the walls. "Slow" work is based on an hourly wage of $20.25, "Medium" work on an hourly wage of $25.75, and "Fast" work on an hourly wage of $31.50. Other qualifications that apply to this table are on page 9.

|  | Labor SF per manhour | Material coverage SF/gallon | Material cost per gallon | Labor cost per 100 SF | Labor burden 100 SF | Material cost per 100 SF | Overhead per 100 SF | Profit per 100 SF | Total price per 100 SF |
|---|---|---|---|---|---|---|---|---|---|
| **Walls, gypsum drywall, skip trowel or sand finish, roll, per 100 SF of wall area** | | | | | | | | | |
| *Flat latex, water base (material #5)* | | | | | | | | | |
|   Roll 1st coat | | | | | | | | | |
|     Slow | 275 | 325 | 36.70 | 7.36 | 2.18 | 11.29 | 3.96 | 3.96 | 28.75 |
|     Medium | 488 | 300 | 32.10 | 5.28 | 1.87 | 10.70 | 4.46 | 2.68 | 24.99 |
|     Fast | 700 | 275 | 27.50 | 4.50 | 1.84 | 10.00 | 5.07 | 1.50 | 22.91 |
|   Roll 2nd coat | | | | | | | | | |
|     Slow | 350 | 350 | 36.70 | 5.79 | 1.71 | 10.49 | 3.42 | 3.43 | 24.84 |
|     Medium | 538 | 338 | 32.10 | 4.79 | 1.70 | 9.50 | 4.00 | 2.40 | 22.39 |
|     Fast | 725 | 325 | 27.50 | 4.34 | 1.78 | 8.46 | 4.52 | 1.34 | 20.44 |
|   Roll 3rd or additional coats | | | | | | | | | |
|     Slow | 425 | 350 | 36.70 | 4.76 | 1.40 | 10.49 | 3.16 | 3.17 | 22.98 |
|     Medium | 600 | 338 | 32.10 | 4.29 | 1.53 | 9.50 | 3.83 | 2.30 | 21.45 |
|     Fast | 775 | 325 | 27.50 | 4.06 | 1.66 | 8.46 | 4.40 | 1.30 | 19.88 |
| *Sealer (drywall), water base (material #1)* | | | | | | | | | |
|   Roll prime coat | | | | | | | | | |
|     Slow | 225 | 325 | 30.50 | 9.00 | 2.64 | 9.38 | 4.00 | 4.01 | 29.03 |
|     Medium | 463 | 300 | 26.70 | 5.56 | 1.97 | 8.90 | 4.11 | 2.46 | 23.00 |
|     Fast | 700 | 275 | 22.90 | 4.50 | 1.84 | 8.33 | 4.55 | 1.35 | 20.57 |
| *Sealer (drywall), oil base (material #2)* | | | | | | | | | |
|   Roll prime coat | | | | | | | | | |
|     Slow | 225 | 300 | 39.70 | 9.00 | 2.64 | 13.23 | 4.73 | 4.74 | 34.34 |
|     Medium | 463 | 275 | 34.80 | 5.56 | 1.97 | 12.65 | 5.05 | 3.03 | 28.26 |
|     Fast | 700 | 250 | 29.80 | 4.50 | 1.84 | 11.92 | 5.66 | 1.67 | 25.59 |
| *Enamel, water base (material #9)* | | | | | | | | | |
|   Roll 1st finish coat | | | | | | | | | |
|     Slow | 225 | 300 | 46.80 | 9.00 | 2.64 | 15.60 | 5.18 | 5.19 | 37.61 |
|     Medium | 400 | 288 | 41.00 | 6.44 | 2.28 | 14.24 | 5.74 | 3.44 | 32.14 |
|     Fast | 600 | 275 | 35.10 | 5.25 | 2.16 | 12.76 | 6.25 | 1.85 | 28.27 |
|   Roll 2nd or additional finish coats | | | | | | | | | |
|     Slow | 275 | 300 | 46.80 | 7.36 | 2.18 | 15.60 | 4.77 | 4.78 | 34.69 |
|     Medium | 450 | 288 | 41.00 | 5.72 | 2.02 | 14.24 | 5.50 | 3.30 | 30.78 |
|     Fast | 650 | 275 | 35.10 | 4.85 | 1.98 | 12.76 | 6.07 | 1.80 | 27.46 |
| *Enamel, oil base (material #10)* | | | | | | | | | |
|   Roll 1st finish coat | | | | | | | | | |
|     Slow | 225 | 275 | 61.70 | 9.00 | 2.64 | 22.44 | 6.48 | 6.49 | 47.05 |
|     Medium | 400 | 263 | 54.00 | 6.44 | 2.28 | 20.53 | 7.31 | 4.39 | 40.95 |
|     Fast | 600 | 250 | 46.30 | 5.25 | 2.16 | 18.52 | 8.03 | 2.38 | 36.34 |

*General Painting Costs*

|  | Labor SF per manhour | Material coverage SF/gallon | Material cost per gallon | Labor cost per 100 SF | Labor burden 100 SF | Material cost per 100 SF | Overhead per 100 SF | Profit per 100 SF | Total price per 100 SF |
|---|---|---|---|---|---|---|---|---|---|
| Roll 2nd or additional finish coats | | | | | | | | | |
| Slow | 275 | 300 | 61.70 | 7.36 | 2.18 | 20.57 | 5.72 | 5.73 | 41.56 |
| Medium | 450 | 288 | 54.00 | 5.72 | 2.02 | 18.75 | 6.62 | 3.97 | 37.08 |
| Fast | 650 | 275 | 46.30 | 4.85 | 1.98 | 16.84 | 7.34 | 2.17 | 33.18 |
| Epoxy coating, 2 part system - white (material #52) | | | | | | | | | |
| Roll 1st coat | | | | | | | | | |
| Slow | 350 | 350 | 177.00 | 5.79 | 1.71 | 50.57 | 11.03 | 11.06 | 80.16 |
| Medium | 550 | 325 | 154.90 | 4.68 | 1.67 | 47.66 | 13.50 | 8.10 | 75.61 |
| Fast | 725 | 300 | 132.70 | 4.34 | 1.78 | 44.23 | 15.61 | 4.62 | 70.58 |
| Roll 2nd or additional coats | | | | | | | | | |
| Slow | 425 | 375 | 177.00 | 4.76 | 1.40 | 47.20 | 10.14 | 10.16 | 73.66 |
| Medium | 600 | 350 | 154.90 | 4.29 | 1.53 | 44.26 | 12.52 | 7.51 | 70.11 |
| Fast | 775 | 325 | 132.70 | 4.06 | 1.66 | 40.83 | 14.43 | 4.27 | 65.25 |

Measurements are based on the square feet of wall coated. Do not deduct for openings less than 100 square feet. These figures assume paint products are being applied over a smooth finish. For heights above 8 feet, use the High Time Difficulty Factors on page 139. These figures include brushing-in at corners when all walls are the same color, and at ceilings that are the same color or finished with acoustic spray-on texture. ADD for cutting-in at ceilings if they're a different color than the walls, or at corners where walls in the same room are painted different colors. Do not include cutting-in time for ceilings unless you're only painting the ceilings, not the walls. "Slow" work is based on an hourly wage of $20.25, "Medium" work on an hourly wage of $25.75, and "Fast" work on an hourly wage of $31.50. Other qualifications that apply to this table are on page 9.

*National Painting Cost Estimator*

|  | Labor SF per manhour | Material coverage SF/gallon | Material cost per gallon | Labor cost per 100 SF | Labor burden 100 SF | Material cost per 100 SF | Overhead per 100 SF | Profit per 100 SF | Total price per 100 SF |
|---|---|---|---|---|---|---|---|---|---|
| **Walls, gypsum drywall, skip trowel or sand finish, spray, per 100 SF of wall area** | | | | | | | | | |
| Flat latex, water base (material #5) | | | | | | | | | |
| Spray 1st coat | | | | | | | | | |
| Slow | 700 | 275 | 36.70 | 2.89 | .86 | 13.35 | 3.25 | 3.25 | 23.60 |
| Medium | 800 | 250 | 32.10 | 3.22 | 1.14 | 12.84 | 4.30 | 2.58 | 24.08 |
| Fast | 900 | 225 | 27.50 | 3.50 | 1.42 | 12.22 | 5.32 | 1.57 | 24.03 |
| Spray 2nd coat | | | | | | | | | |
| Slow | 800 | 325 | 36.70 | 2.53 | .75 | 11.29 | 2.77 | 2.77 | 20.11 |
| Medium | 900 | 300 | 32.10 | 2.86 | 1.01 | 10.70 | 3.64 | 2.19 | 20.40 |
| Fast | 1000 | 275 | 27.50 | 3.15 | 1.29 | 10.00 | 4.48 | 1.32 | 20.24 |
| Spray 3rd or additional coats | | | | | | | | | |
| Slow | 850 | 325 | 36.70 | 2.38 | .71 | 11.29 | 2.73 | 2.74 | 19.85 |
| Medium | 950 | 313 | 32.10 | 2.71 | .95 | 10.26 | 3.48 | 2.09 | 19.49 |
| Fast | 1050 | 300 | 27.50 | 3.00 | 1.21 | 9.17 | 4.15 | 1.23 | 18.76 |
| Sealer (drywall), water base (material #1) | | | | | | | | | |
| Spray prime coat | | | | | | | | | |
| Slow | 575 | 275 | 30.50 | 3.52 | 1.04 | 11.09 | 2.97 | 2.98 | 21.60 |
| Medium | 738 | 250 | 26.70 | 3.49 | 1.25 | 10.68 | 3.85 | 2.31 | 21.58 |
| Fast | 900 | 225 | 22.90 | 3.50 | 1.42 | 10.18 | 4.68 | 1.39 | 21.17 |
| Sealer (drywall), oil base (material #2) | | | | | | | | | |
| Spray prime coat | | | | | | | | | |
| Slow | 575 | 275 | 39.70 | 3.52 | 1.04 | 14.44 | 3.61 | 3.62 | 26.23 |
| Medium | 738 | 250 | 34.80 | 3.49 | 1.25 | 13.92 | 4.66 | 2.80 | 26.12 |
| Fast | 900 | 225 | 29.80 | 3.50 | 1.42 | 13.24 | 5.63 | 1.67 | 25.46 |
| Enamel, water base (material #9) | | | | | | | | | |
| Spray 1st finish coat | | | | | | | | | |
| Slow | 500 | 275 | 46.80 | 4.05 | 1.19 | 17.02 | 4.23 | 4.24 | 30.73 |
| Medium | 675 | 250 | 41.00 | 3.81 | 1.35 | 16.40 | 5.39 | 3.23 | 30.18 |
| Fast | 850 | 225 | 35.10 | 3.71 | 1.52 | 15.60 | 6.45 | 1.91 | 29.19 |
| Spray 2nd or additional finish coats | | | | | | | | | |
| Slow | 525 | 275 | 46.80 | 3.86 | 1.12 | 17.02 | 4.18 | 4.19 | 30.37 |
| Medium | 700 | 263 | 41.00 | 3.68 | 1.31 | 15.59 | 5.14 | 3.09 | 28.81 |
| Fast | 900 | 250 | 35.10 | 3.50 | 1.42 | 14.04 | 5.88 | 1.74 | 26.58 |

*General Painting Costs*

|  | Labor SF per manhour | Material coverage SF/gallon | Material cost per gallon | Labor cost per 100 SF | Labor burden 100 SF | Material cost per 100 SF | Overhead per 100 SF | Profit per 100 SF | Total price per 100 SF |
|---|---|---|---|---|---|---|---|---|---|
| **Enamel, oil base (material #10)** | | | | | | | | | |
| *Spray 1st finish coat* | | | | | | | | | |
| Slow | 500 | 250 | 61.70 | 4.05 | 1.19 | 24.68 | 5.68 | 5.70 | 41.30 |
| Medium | 675 | 238 | 54.00 | 3.81 | 1.35 | 22.69 | 6.96 | 4.18 | 38.99 |
| Fast | 850 | 225 | 46.30 | 3.71 | 1.52 | 20.58 | 8.00 | 2.37 | 36.18 |
| *Spray 2nd or additional finish coats* | | | | | | | | | |
| Slow | 525 | 275 | 61.70 | 3.86 | 1.12 | 22.44 | 5.21 | 5.22 | 37.85 |
| Medium | 700 | 263 | 54.00 | 3.68 | 1.31 | 20.53 | 6.38 | 3.83 | 35.73 |
| Fast | 900 | 250 | 46.30 | 3.50 | 1.42 | 18.52 | 7.27 | 2.15 | 32.86 |

Measurements are based on the square feet of wall coated. Do not deduct for openings less than 100 square feet. These figures assume paint products are being applied over a smooth finish. For heights above 8 feet, use the High Time Difficulty Factors on page 139. These figures include spraying at corners when all walls are the same color, and at ceiling-to-wall intersection when ceilings are the same color. ADD for cutting-in at ceilings and protecting adjacent surfaces from overspray if they're a different color than the walls, or at corners where walls in the same room are painted different colors. Do not include cutting-in time for ceilings unless you're only painting the ceilings, not the walls. "Slow" work is based on an hourly wage of $20.25, "Medium" work on an hourly wage of $25.75, and "Fast" work on an hourly wage of $31.50. Other qualifications that apply to this table are on page 9.

*National Painting Cost Estimator*

|  | Labor SF per manhour | Material coverage SF/gallon | Material cost per gallon | Labor cost per 100 SF | Labor burden 100 SF | Material cost per 100 SF | Overhead per 100 SF | Profit per 100 SF | Total price per 100 SF |
|---|---|---|---|---|---|---|---|---|---|

### Walls, gypsum drywall, smooth-wall finish, brush, per 100 SF of wall area

Flat latex, water base (material #5)
  Brush 1st coat

|  |  |  |  |  |  |  |  |  |  |
|---|---|---|---|---|---|---|---|---|---|
| Slow | 175 | 325 | 36.70 | 11.57 | 3.40 | 11.29 | 4.99 | 5.00 | 36.25 |
| Medium | 200 | 313 | 32.10 | 12.88 | 4.56 | 10.26 | 6.93 | 4.16 | 38.79 |
| Fast | 225 | 300 | 27.50 | 14.00 | 5.69 | 9.17 | 8.95 | 2.65 | 40.46 |

  Brush 2nd coat

|  |  |  |  |  |  |  |  |  |  |
|---|---|---|---|---|---|---|---|---|---|
| Slow | 225 | 400 | 36.70 | 9.00 | 2.64 | 9.18 | 3.96 | 3.97 | 28.75 |
| Medium | 250 | 375 | 32.10 | 10.30 | 3.65 | 8.56 | 5.63 | 3.38 | 31.52 |
| Fast | 275 | 350 | 27.50 | 11.45 | 4.69 | 7.86 | 7.43 | 2.20 | 33.63 |

  Brush 3rd or additional coats

|  |  |  |  |  |  |  |  |  |  |
|---|---|---|---|---|---|---|---|---|---|
| Slow | 250 | 425 | 36.70 | 8.10 | 2.39 | 8.64 | 3.63 | 3.64 | 26.40 |
| Medium | 275 | 400 | 32.10 | 9.36 | 3.33 | 8.03 | 5.18 | 3.11 | 29.01 |
| Fast | 300 | 375 | 27.50 | 10.50 | 4.27 | 7.33 | 6.85 | 2.03 | 30.98 |

Sealer (drywall), water base (material #1)
  Brush prime coat

|  |  |  |  |  |  |  |  |  |  |
|---|---|---|---|---|---|---|---|---|---|
| Slow | 150 | 325 | 30.50 | 13.50 | 3.99 | 9.38 | 5.10 | 5.11 | 37.08 |
| Medium | 188 | 313 | 26.70 | 13.70 | 4.85 | 8.53 | 6.77 | 4.06 | 37.91 |
| Fast | 225 | 300 | 22.90 | 14.00 | 5.69 | 7.63 | 8.48 | 2.51 | 38.31 |

Sealer (drywall), oil base (material #2)
  Brush prime coat

|  |  |  |  |  |  |  |  |  |  |
|---|---|---|---|---|---|---|---|---|---|
| Slow | 150 | 350 | 39.70 | 13.50 | 3.99 | 11.34 | 5.48 | 5.49 | 39.80 |
| Medium | 188 | 338 | 34.80 | 13.70 | 4.85 | 10.30 | 7.21 | 4.33 | 40.39 |
| Fast | 225 | 325 | 29.80 | 14.00 | 5.69 | 9.17 | 8.95 | 2.65 | 40.46 |

Enamel, water base (material #9)
  Brush 1st finish coat

|  |  |  |  |  |  |  |  |  |  |
|---|---|---|---|---|---|---|---|---|---|
| Slow | 140 | 350 | 46.80 | 14.46 | 4.26 | 13.37 | 6.10 | 6.11 | 44.30 |
| Medium | 185 | 325 | 41.00 | 13.92 | 4.94 | 12.62 | 7.87 | 4.72 | 44.07 |
| Fast | 235 | 300 | 35.10 | 13.40 | 5.49 | 11.70 | 9.48 | 2.80 | 42.87 |

  Brush 2nd or additional finish coats

|  |  |  |  |  |  |  |  |  |  |
|---|---|---|---|---|---|---|---|---|---|
| Slow | 150 | 350 | 46.80 | 13.50 | 3.99 | 13.37 | 5.86 | 5.87 | 42.59 |
| Medium | 200 | 333 | 41.00 | 12.88 | 4.56 | 12.31 | 7.44 | 4.46 | 41.65 |
| Fast | 250 | 315 | 35.10 | 12.60 | 5.14 | 11.14 | 8.95 | 2.65 | 40.48 |

Enamel, oil base (material #10)
  Brush 1st finish coat

|  |  |  |  |  |  |  |  |  |  |
|---|---|---|---|---|---|---|---|---|---|
| Slow | 140 | 350 | 61.70 | 14.46 | 4.26 | 17.63 | 6.91 | 6.92 | 50.18 |
| Medium | 185 | 338 | 54.00 | 13.92 | 4.94 | 15.98 | 8.71 | 5.22 | 48.77 |
| Fast | 235 | 325 | 46.30 | 13.40 | 5.49 | 14.25 | 10.27 | 3.04 | 46.45 |

*General Painting Costs*

|  | Labor SF per manhour | Material coverage SF/gallon | Material cost per gallon | Labor cost per 100 SF | Labor burden 100 SF | Material cost per 100 SF | Overhead per 100 SF | Profit per 100 SF | Total price per 100 SF |
|---|---|---|---|---|---|---|---|---|---|
| **Brush 2nd or additional finish coats** | | | | | | | | | |
| Slow | 150 | 360 | 61.70 | 13.50 | 3.99 | 17.14 | 6.58 | 6.59 | 47.80 |
| Medium | 200 | 348 | 54.00 | 12.88 | 4.56 | 15.52 | 8.24 | 4.94 | 46.14 |
| Fast | 250 | 335 | 46.30 | 12.60 | 5.14 | 13.82 | 9.78 | 2.89 | 44.23 |
| **Stipple finish** | | | | | | | | | |
| Slow | 225 | -- | -- | 9.00 | 2.64 | -- | 2.22 | 2.22 | 16.08 |
| Medium | 250 | -- | -- | 10.30 | 3.65 | -- | 3.49 | 2.09 | 19.53 |
| Fast | 275 | -- | -- | 11.45 | 4.69 | -- | 5.00 | 1.48 | 22.62 |
| **Epoxy coating, 2 part system - white (material #52)** | | | | | | | | | |
| Brush 1st coat | | | | | | | | | |
| Slow | 225 | 425 | 177.00 | 9.00 | 2.64 | 41.65 | 10.13 | 10.15 | 73.57 |
| Medium | 250 | 400 | 154.90 | 10.30 | 3.65 | 38.73 | 13.17 | 7.90 | 73.75 |
| Fast | 275 | 375 | 132.70 | 11.45 | 4.69 | 35.39 | 15.97 | 4.72 | 72.22 |
| Brush 2nd or additional coats | | | | | | | | | |
| Slow | 250 | 450 | 177.00 | 8.10 | 2.39 | 39.33 | 9.47 | 9.49 | 68.78 |
| Medium | 275 | 425 | 154.90 | 9.36 | 3.33 | 36.45 | 12.28 | 7.37 | 68.79 |
| Fast | 300 | 400 | 132.70 | 10.50 | 4.27 | 33.18 | 14.87 | 4.40 | 67.22 |

Measurements are based on the square feet of wall coated. Do not deduct for openings less than 100 square feet. These figures assume paint products are being applied over a smooth finish. For heights above 8 feet, use the High Time Difficulty Factors on page 139. These figures include brushing-in at corners when all walls are the same color, and at ceilings that are the same color or finished with acoustic spray-on texture. ADD for cutting-in at ceilings if they're a different color than the walls, or at corners where walls in the same room are painted different colors. Do not include cutting-in time for ceilings unless you're only painting the ceilings, not the walls. "Slow" work is based on an hourly wage of $20.25, "Medium" work on an hourly wage of $25.75, and "Fast" work on an hourly wage of $31.50. Other qualifications that apply to this table are on page 9.

*National Painting Cost Estimator*

|  | Labor SF per manhour | Material coverage SF/gallon | Material cost per gallon | Labor cost per 100 SF | Labor burden 100 SF | Material cost per 100 SF | Overhead per 100 SF | Profit per 100 SF | Total price per 100 SF |
|---|---|---|---|---|---|---|---|---|---|

## Walls, gypsum drywall, smooth-wall finish, roll, per 100 SF of wall area

### Flat latex, water base (material #5)
Roll 1st coat
| | | | | | | | | | |
|---|---|---|---|---|---|---|---|---|---|
| Slow | 300 | 325 | 36.70 | 6.75 | 1.98 | 11.29 | 3.81 | 3.81 | 27.64 |
| Medium | 513 | 313 | 32.10 | 5.02 | 1.78 | 10.26 | 4.27 | 2.56 | 23.89 |
| Fast | 725 | 300 | 27.50 | 4.34 | 1.78 | 9.17 | 4.74 | 1.40 | 21.43 |

Roll 2nd coat
| | | | | | | | | | |
|---|---|---|---|---|---|---|---|---|---|
| Slow | 375 | 375 | 36.70 | 5.40 | 1.60 | 9.79 | 3.19 | 3.20 | 23.18 |
| Medium | 563 | 363 | 32.10 | 4.57 | 1.64 | 8.84 | 3.76 | 2.25 | 21.06 |
| Fast | 750 | 350 | 27.50 | 4.20 | 1.70 | 7.86 | 4.27 | 1.26 | 19.29 |

Roll 3rd or additional coats
| | | | | | | | | | |
|---|---|---|---|---|---|---|---|---|---|
| Slow | 450 | 400 | 36.70 | 4.50 | 1.32 | 9.18 | 2.85 | 2.86 | 20.71 |
| Medium | 625 | 388 | 32.10 | 4.12 | 1.46 | 8.27 | 3.46 | 2.08 | 19.39 |
| Fast | 800 | 375 | 27.50 | 3.94 | 1.60 | 7.33 | 3.99 | 1.18 | 18.04 |

### Sealer (drywall), water base (material #1)
Roll prime coat
| | | | | | | | | | |
|---|---|---|---|---|---|---|---|---|---|
| Slow | 245 | 350 | 30.50 | 8.27 | 2.43 | 8.71 | 3.69 | 3.70 | 26.80 |
| Medium | 485 | 325 | 26.70 | 5.31 | 1.87 | 8.22 | 3.85 | 2.31 | 21.56 |
| Fast | 725 | 300 | 22.90 | 4.34 | 1.78 | 7.63 | 4.26 | 1.26 | 19.27 |

### Sealer (drywall), oil base (material #2)
Roll prime coat
| | | | | | | | | | |
|---|---|---|---|---|---|---|---|---|---|
| Slow | 245 | 325 | 39.70 | 8.27 | 2.43 | 12.22 | 4.36 | 4.37 | 31.65 |
| Medium | 485 | 300 | 34.80 | 5.31 | 1.87 | 11.60 | 4.70 | 2.82 | 26.30 |
| Fast | 725 | 275 | 29.80 | 4.34 | 1.78 | 10.84 | 5.25 | 1.55 | 23.76 |

### Enamel, water base (material #9)
Roll 1st finish coat
| | | | | | | | | | |
|---|---|---|---|---|---|---|---|---|---|
| Slow | 235 | 325 | 46.80 | 8.62 | 2.55 | 14.40 | 4.86 | 4.87 | 35.30 |
| Medium | 438 | 313 | 41.00 | 5.88 | 2.07 | 13.10 | 5.27 | 3.16 | 29.48 |
| Fast | 640 | 300 | 35.10 | 4.92 | 2.00 | 11.70 | 5.78 | 1.71 | 26.11 |

Roll 2nd or additional finish coats
| | | | | | | | | | |
|---|---|---|---|---|---|---|---|---|---|
| Slow | 280 | 350 | 46.80 | 7.23 | 2.13 | 13.37 | 4.32 | 4.33 | 31.38 |
| Medium | 465 | 338 | 41.00 | 5.54 | 1.96 | 12.13 | 4.91 | 2.94 | 27.48 |
| Fast | 680 | 325 | 35.10 | 4.63 | 1.89 | 10.80 | 5.37 | 1.59 | 24.28 |

### Enamel, oil base (material #10)
Roll 1st finish coat
| | | | | | | | | | |
|---|---|---|---|---|---|---|---|---|---|
| Slow | 235 | 300 | 61.70 | 8.62 | 2.55 | 20.57 | 6.03 | 6.04 | 43.81 |
| Medium | 438 | 288 | 54.00 | 5.88 | 2.07 | 18.75 | 6.68 | 4.01 | 37.39 |
| Fast | 640 | 275 | 46.30 | 4.92 | 2.00 | 16.84 | 7.37 | 2.18 | 33.31 |

*General Painting Costs*

|  | Labor SF per manhour | Material coverage SF/gallon | Material cost per gallon | Labor cost per 100 SF | Labor burden 100 SF | Material cost per 100 SF | Overhead per 100 SF | Profit per 100 SF | Total price per 100 SF |
|---|---|---|---|---|---|---|---|---|---|
| Roll 2nd or additional finish coats |  |  |  |  |  |  |  |  |  |
| Slow | 280 | 325 | 61.70 | 7.23 | 2.13 | 18.98 | 5.38 | 5.40 | 39.12 |
| Medium | 465 | 313 | 54.00 | 5.54 | 1.96 | 17.25 | 6.19 | 3.71 | 34.65 |
| Fast | 680 | 300 | 46.30 | 4.63 | 1.89 | 15.43 | 6.80 | 2.01 | 30.76 |
| Epoxy coating, 2 part system - white (material #52) |  |  |  |  |  |  |  |  |  |
| Roll 1st coat |  |  |  |  |  |  |  |  |  |
| Slow | 375 | 400 | 177.00 | 5.40 | 1.60 | 44.25 | 9.74 | 9.76 | 70.75 |
| Medium | 550 | 375 | 154.90 | 4.68 | 1.67 | 41.31 | 11.91 | 7.15 | 66.72 |
| Fast | 750 | 350 | 132.70 | 4.20 | 1.70 | 37.91 | 13.58 | 4.02 | 61.41 |
| Roll 2nd or additional coats |  |  |  |  |  |  |  |  |  |
| Slow | 450 | 425 | 177.00 | 4.50 | 1.32 | 41.65 | 9.02 | 9.04 | 65.53 |
| Medium | 625 | 400 | 154.90 | 4.12 | 1.46 | 38.73 | 11.08 | 6.65 | 62.04 |
| Fast | 800 | 375 | 132.70 | 3.94 | 1.60 | 35.39 | 12.69 | 3.75 | 57.37 |

Measurements are based on the square feet of wall coated. Do not deduct for openings less than 100 square feet. These figures assume paint products are being applied over a smooth finish. For heights above 8 feet, use the High Time Difficulty Factors on page 139. These figures include brushing-in at corners when all walls are the same color, and at ceilings that are the same color or finished with acoustic spray-on texture. ADD for cutting-in at ceilings if they're a different color than the walls, or at corners where walls in the same room are painted different colors. Do not include cutting-in time for ceilings unless you're only painting the ceilings, not the walls. "Slow" work is based on an hourly wage of $20.25, "Medium" work on an hourly wage of $25.75, and "Fast" work on an hourly wage of $31.50. Other qualifications that apply to this table are on page 9.

*National Painting Cost Estimator*

|  | Labor SF per manhour | Material coverage SF/gallon | Material cost per gallon | Labor cost per 100 SF | Labor burden 100 SF | Material cost per 100 SF | Overhead per 100 SF | Profit per 100 SF | Total price per 100 SF |
|---|---|---|---|---|---|---|---|---|---|

## Walls, gypsum drywall, smooth-wall finish, spray, per 100 SF of wall area

Flat latex, water base (material #5)
Spray 1st coat
| | | | | | | | | | |
|---|---|---|---|---|---|---|---|---|---|
| Slow | 750 | 300 | 36.70 | 2.70 | .79 | 12.23 | 2.99 | 3.00 | 21.71 |
| Medium | 850 | 275 | 32.10 | 3.03 | 1.08 | 11.67 | 3.94 | 2.37 | 22.09 |
| Fast | 950 | 250 | 27.50 | 3.32 | 1.34 | 11.00 | 4.86 | 1.44 | 21.96 |

Spray 2nd coat
| | | | | | | | | | |
|---|---|---|---|---|---|---|---|---|---|
| Slow | 850 | 350 | 36.70 | 2.38 | .71 | 10.49 | 2.58 | 2.58 | 18.74 |
| Medium | 950 | 325 | 32.10 | 2.71 | .95 | 9.88 | 3.39 | 2.03 | 18.96 |
| Fast | 1050 | 300 | 27.50 | 3.00 | 1.21 | 9.17 | 4.15 | 1.23 | 18.76 |

Spray 3rd or additional coats
| | | | | | | | | | |
|---|---|---|---|---|---|---|---|---|---|
| Slow | 950 | 375 | 36.70 | 2.13 | .62 | 9.79 | 2.38 | 2.39 | 17.31 |
| Medium | 1050 | 350 | 32.10 | 2.45 | .86 | 9.17 | 3.12 | 1.87 | 17.47 |
| Fast | 1150 | 325 | 27.50 | 2.74 | 1.12 | 8.46 | 3.82 | 1.13 | 17.27 |

Sealer (drywall), water base (material #1)
Spray prime coat
| | | | | | | | | | |
|---|---|---|---|---|---|---|---|---|---|
| Slow | 600 | 300 | 30.50 | 3.38 | 1.00 | 10.17 | 2.76 | 2.77 | 20.08 |
| Medium | 775 | 275 | 26.70 | 3.32 | 1.18 | 9.71 | 3.55 | 2.13 | 19.89 |
| Fast | 950 | 250 | 27.50 | 3.32 | 1.34 | 11.00 | 4.86 | 1.44 | 21.96 |

Sealer (drywall), oil base (material #2)
Spray prime coat
| | | | | | | | | | |
|---|---|---|---|---|---|---|---|---|---|
| Slow | 600 | 275 | 39.70 | 3.38 | 1.00 | 14.44 | 3.58 | 3.58 | 25.98 |
| Medium | 775 | 250 | 34.80 | 3.32 | 1.18 | 13.92 | 4.61 | 2.76 | 25.79 |
| Fast | 950 | 225 | 29.80 | 3.32 | 1.34 | 13.24 | 5.55 | 1.64 | 25.09 |

Enamel, water base (material #9)
Spray 1st finish coat
| | | | | | | | | | |
|---|---|---|---|---|---|---|---|---|---|
| Slow | 525 | 300 | 46.80 | 3.86 | 1.12 | 15.60 | 3.91 | 3.92 | 28.41 |
| Medium | 713 | 275 | 41.00 | 3.61 | 1.27 | 14.91 | 4.95 | 2.97 | 27.71 |
| Fast | 900 | 250 | 35.10 | 3.50 | 1.42 | 14.04 | 5.88 | 1.74 | 26.58 |

Spray 2nd or additional finish coats
| | | | | | | | | | |
|---|---|---|---|---|---|---|---|---|---|
| Slow | 600 | 300 | 46.80 | 3.38 | 1.00 | 15.60 | 3.80 | 3.80 | 27.58 |
| Medium | 788 | 288 | 41.00 | 3.27 | 1.16 | 14.24 | 4.67 | 2.80 | 26.14 |
| Fast | 975 | 275 | 35.10 | 3.23 | 1.34 | 12.76 | 5.37 | 1.59 | 24.29 |

*General Painting Costs*

| | Labor SF per manhour | Material coverage SF/gallon | Material cost per gallon | Labor cost per 100 SF | Labor burden 100 SF | Material cost per 100 SF | Overhead per 100 SF | Profit per 100 SF | Total price per 100 SF |
|---|---|---|---|---|---|---|---|---|---|
| **Enamel, oil base (material #10)** | | | | | | | | | |
| *Spray 1st finish coat* | | | | | | | | | |
| Slow | 525 | 275 | 61.70 | 3.86 | 1.12 | 22.44 | 5.21 | 5.22 | 37.85 |
| Medium | 713 | 263 | 54.00 | 3.61 | 1.27 | 20.53 | 6.36 | 3.81 | 35.58 |
| Fast | 900 | 250 | 46.30 | 3.50 | 1.42 | 18.52 | 7.27 | 2.15 | 32.86 |
| *Spray 2nd or additional finish coats* | | | | | | | | | |
| Slow | 600 | 300 | 61.70 | 3.38 | 1.00 | 20.57 | 4.74 | 4.75 | 34.44 |
| Medium | 788 | 288 | 54.00 | 3.27 | 1.16 | 18.75 | 5.80 | 3.48 | 32.46 |
| Fast | 975 | 275 | 46.30 | 3.23 | 1.34 | 16.84 | 6.63 | 1.96 | 30.00 |

Measurements are based on the square feet of wall coated. Do not deduct for openings less than 100 square feet. These figures assume paint products are being applied over a smooth finish. For heights above 8 feet, use the High Time Difficulty Factors on page 139. These figures include spraying at corners when all walls are the same color, and at ceiling-to-wall intersection when ceilings are the same color. ADD for cutting-in at ceilings and protecting adjacent surfaces from overspray if they're a different color than the walls, or at corners where walls in the same room are painted different colors. Do not include cutting-in time for ceilings unless you're only painting the ceilings, not the walls. "Slow" work is based on an hourly wage of $20.25, "Medium" work on an hourly wage of $25.75, and "Fast" work on an hourly wage of $31.50. Other qualifications that apply to this table are on page 9.

## Walls, plaster, exterior: see Plaster and stucco

| | Labor SF per manhour | Material coverage SF/gallon | Material cost per gallon | Labor cost per 100 SF | Labor burden 100 SF | Material cost per 100 SF | Overhead per 100 SF | Profit per 100 SF | Total price per 100 SF |
|---|---|---|---|---|---|---|---|---|---|

## Walls, plaster, interior, medium texture, per 100 SF of wall area

Anti-graffiti stain eliminator
  Water base primer and sealer (material #39)
    Roll & brush each coat

| | | | | | | | | | |
|---|---|---|---|---|---|---|---|---|---|
| Slow | 375 | 425 | 50.30 | 5.40 | 1.60 | 11.84 | 3.58 | 3.59 | 26.01 |
| Medium | 400 | 400 | 44.00 | 6.44 | 2.28 | 11.00 | 4.93 | 2.96 | 27.61 |
| Fast | 425 | 375 | 37.80 | 7.41 | 3.01 | 10.08 | 6.36 | 1.88 | 28.74 |

  Oil base primer and sealer (material #40)
    Roll & brush each coat

| | | | | | | | | | |
|---|---|---|---|---|---|---|---|---|---|
| Slow | 375 | 400 | 49.90 | 5.40 | 1.60 | 12.48 | 3.70 | 3.71 | 26.89 |
| Medium | 400 | 375 | 43.70 | 6.44 | 2.28 | 11.65 | 5.09 | 3.06 | 28.52 |
| Fast | 425 | 350 | 37.40 | 7.41 | 3.01 | 10.69 | 6.55 | 1.94 | 29.60 |

  Polyurethane 2 part system (material #41)
    Roll & brush each coat

| | | | | | | | | | |
|---|---|---|---|---|---|---|---|---|---|
| Slow | 325 | 375 | 157.00 | 6.23 | 1.85 | 41.87 | 9.49 | 9.51 | 68.95 |
| Medium | 350 | 350 | 137.40 | 7.36 | 2.61 | 39.26 | 12.31 | 7.38 | 68.92 |
| Fast | 375 | 325 | 117.80 | 8.40 | 3.44 | 36.25 | 14.90 | 4.41 | 67.40 |

Measurements are based on the square feet of wall coated. Do not deduct for openings less than 100 square feet. These figures assume paint products are being applied over a smooth or medium texture finish. For heights above 8 feet, use the High Time Difficulty Factors on page 139. "Slow" work is based on an hourly wage of $20.25, "Medium" work on an hourly wage of $25.75, and "Fast" work on an hourly wage of $31.50. Other qualifications that apply to this table are on page 9.

*General Painting Costs*

|  | Labor SF per manhour | Material coverage SF/gallon | Material cost per gallon | Labor cost per 100 SF | Labor burden 100 SF | Material cost per 100 SF | Overhead per 100 SF | Profit per 100 SF | Total price per 100 SF |
|---|---|---|---|---|---|---|---|---|---|

## Walls, plaster, interior, medium texture, brush, per 100 SF of wall area

### Flat latex, water base (material #5)
**Brush 1st coat**
| | | | | | | | | | |
|---|---|---|---|---|---|---|---|---|---|
| Slow | 125 | 300 | 36.70 | 16.20 | 4.78 | 12.23 | 6.31 | 6.32 | 45.84 |
| Medium | 150 | 288 | 32.10 | 17.17 | 6.09 | 11.15 | 8.60 | 5.16 | 48.17 |
| Fast | 175 | 275 | 27.50 | 18.00 | 7.32 | 10.00 | 10.96 | 3.24 | 49.52 |

**Brush 2nd coat**
| | | | | | | | | | |
|---|---|---|---|---|---|---|---|---|---|
| Slow | 150 | 325 | 36.70 | 13.50 | 3.99 | 11.29 | 5.47 | 5.48 | 39.73 |
| Medium | 168 | 313 | 32.10 | 15.33 | 5.42 | 10.26 | 7.76 | 4.65 | 43.42 |
| Fast | 185 | 300 | 27.50 | 17.03 | 6.96 | 9.17 | 10.28 | 3.04 | 46.48 |

**Brush 3rd or additional coats**
| | | | | | | | | | |
|---|---|---|---|---|---|---|---|---|---|
| Slow | 160 | 350 | 36.70 | 12.66 | 3.73 | 10.49 | 5.11 | 5.12 | 37.11 |
| Medium | 185 | 338 | 32.10 | 13.92 | 4.94 | 9.50 | 7.09 | 4.25 | 39.70 |
| Fast | 210 | 325 | 27.50 | 15.00 | 6.11 | 8.46 | 9.17 | 2.71 | 41.45 |

### Enamel, water base (material #9)
**Brush 1st finish coat**
| | | | | | | | | | |
|---|---|---|---|---|---|---|---|---|---|
| Slow | 100 | 300 | 46.80 | 20.25 | 5.97 | 15.60 | 7.95 | 7.96 | 57.73 |
| Medium | 125 | 288 | 41.00 | 20.60 | 7.30 | 14.24 | 10.53 | 6.32 | 58.99 |
| Fast | 150 | 275 | 35.10 | 21.00 | 8.58 | 12.76 | 13.12 | 3.88 | 59.34 |

**Brush 2nd finish coat**
| | | | | | | | | | |
|---|---|---|---|---|---|---|---|---|---|
| Slow | 125 | 325 | 46.80 | 16.20 | 4.78 | 14.40 | 6.72 | 6.74 | 48.84 |
| Medium | 143 | 313 | 41.00 | 18.01 | 6.36 | 13.10 | 9.37 | 5.62 | 52.46 |
| Fast | 160 | 300 | 35.10 | 19.69 | 8.03 | 11.70 | 12.22 | 3.61 | 55.25 |

**Brush 3rd or additional finish coats**
| | | | | | | | | | |
|---|---|---|---|---|---|---|---|---|---|
| Slow | 135 | 350 | 46.80 | 15.00 | 4.43 | 13.37 | 6.23 | 6.24 | 45.27 |
| Medium | 160 | 338 | 41.00 | 16.09 | 5.70 | 12.13 | 8.48 | 5.09 | 47.49 |
| Fast | 185 | 325 | 35.10 | 17.03 | 6.96 | 10.80 | 10.78 | 3.19 | 48.76 |

### Enamel, oil base (material #10)
**Brush 1st finish coat**
| | | | | | | | | | |
|---|---|---|---|---|---|---|---|---|---|
| Slow | 100 | 325 | 61.70 | 20.25 | 5.97 | 18.98 | 8.59 | 8.61 | 62.40 |
| Medium | 125 | 313 | 54.00 | 20.60 | 7.30 | 17.25 | 11.29 | 6.77 | 63.21 |
| Fast | 150 | 300 | 46.30 | 21.00 | 8.58 | 15.43 | 13.95 | 4.13 | 63.09 |

**Brush 2nd finish coat**
| | | | | | | | | | |
|---|---|---|---|---|---|---|---|---|---|
| Slow | 125 | 400 | 61.70 | 16.20 | 4.78 | 15.43 | 6.92 | 6.93 | 50.26 |
| Medium | 143 | 375 | 54.00 | 18.01 | 6.36 | 14.40 | 9.70 | 5.82 | 54.29 |
| Fast | 160 | 350 | 46.30 | 19.69 | 8.03 | 13.23 | 12.69 | 3.75 | 57.39 |

## National Painting Cost Estimator

|  | Labor SF per manhour | Material coverage SF/gallon | Material cost per gallon | Labor cost per 100 SF | Labor burden 100 SF | Material cost per 100 SF | Overhead per 100 SF | Profit per 100 SF | Total price per 100 SF |
|---|---|---|---|---|---|---|---|---|---|
| **Brush 3rd or additional finish coats** | | | | | | | | | |
| Slow | 135 | 425 | 61.70 | 15.00 | 4.43 | 14.52 | 6.45 | 6.46 | 46.86 |
| Medium | 160 | 400 | 54.00 | 16.09 | 5.70 | 13.50 | 8.82 | 5.29 | 49.40 |
| Fast | 185 | 375 | 46.30 | 17.03 | 6.96 | 12.35 | 11.26 | 3.33 | 50.93 |
| **Stipple finish** | | | | | | | | | |
| Slow | 125 | -- | -- | 16.20 | 4.78 | -- | 3.99 | 4.00 | 28.97 |
| Medium | 143 | -- | -- | 18.01 | 6.36 | -- | 6.10 | 3.66 | 34.13 |
| Fast | 160 | -- | -- | 19.69 | 8.03 | -- | 8.59 | 2.54 | 38.85 |
| **Epoxy coating, 2 part system - white (material #52)** | | | | | | | | | |
| *Brush 1st coat* | | | | | | | | | |
| Slow | 150 | 400 | 177.00 | 13.50 | 3.99 | 44.25 | 11.73 | 11.75 | 85.22 |
| Medium | 165 | 388 | 154.90 | 15.61 | 5.52 | 39.92 | 15.27 | 9.16 | 85.48 |
| Fast | 185 | 375 | 132.70 | 17.03 | 6.96 | 35.39 | 18.40 | 5.44 | 83.22 |
| *Brush 2nd or additional coats* | | | | | | | | | |
| Slow | 160 | 425 | 177.00 | 12.66 | 3.73 | 41.65 | 11.03 | 11.05 | 80.12 |
| Medium | 185 | 413 | 154.90 | 13.92 | 4.94 | 37.51 | 14.09 | 8.45 | 78.91 |
| Fast | 210 | 400 | 132.70 | 15.00 | 6.11 | 33.18 | 16.83 | 4.98 | 76.10 |
| **Glazing & mottling over enamel (material #16)** | | | | | | | | | |
| *Brush each coat* | | | | | | | | | |
| Slow | 50 | 900 | 71.00 | 40.50 | 11.94 | 7.89 | 11.46 | 11.49 | 83.28 |
| Medium | 65 | 800 | 62.10 | 39.62 | 14.01 | 7.76 | 15.35 | 9.21 | 85.95 |
| Fast | 80 | 700 | 53.30 | 39.38 | 16.06 | 7.61 | 19.55 | 5.78 | 88.38 |
| *Stipple* | | | | | | | | | |
| Slow | 100 | -- | -- | 20.25 | 5.97 | -- | 4.98 | 4.99 | 36.19 |
| Medium | 113 | -- | -- | 22.79 | 8.07 | -- | 7.72 | 4.63 | 43.21 |
| Fast | 125 | -- | -- | 25.20 | 10.28 | -- | 11.00 | 3.25 | 49.73 |

Measurements are based on the square feet of wall coated. Do not deduct for openings less than 100 square feet. These figures assume paint products are being applied over a smooth or medium texture finish. For heights above 8 feet, use the High Time Difficulty Factors on page 139. These figures include brushing-in at corners when all walls are the same color, and at ceilings that are the same color or finished with acoustic spray-on texture. ADD for cutting-in at ceilings if they're a different color than the walls, or at corners where walls in the same room are painted different colors. Do not include cutting-in time for ceilings unless you're only painting the ceilings, not the walls. "Slow" work is based on an hourly wage of $20.25, "Medium" work on an hourly wage of $25.75, and "Fast" work on an hourly wage of $31.50. Other qualifications that apply to this table are on page 9.

*General Painting Costs*

|  | Labor SF per manhour | Material coverage SF/gallon | Material cost per gallon | Labor cost per 100 SF | Labor burden 100 SF | Material cost per 100 SF | Overhead per 100 SF | Profit per 100 SF | Total price per 100 SF |
|---|---|---|---|---|---|---|---|---|---|

## Walls, plaster, interior, medium texture, roll, per 100 SF of wall area

### Flat latex, water base (material #5)

**Roll 1st coat**
| | | | | | | | | | |
|---|---|---|---|---|---|---|---|---|---|
| Slow | 225 | 250 | 36.70 | 9.00 | 2.64 | 14.68 | 5.00 | 5.01 | 36.33 |
| Medium | 438 | 238 | 32.10 | 5.88 | 2.07 | 13.49 | 5.36 | 3.22 | 30.02 |
| Fast | 650 | 225 | 27.50 | 4.85 | 1.98 | 12.22 | 5.91 | 1.75 | 26.71 |

**Roll 2nd coat**
| | | | | | | | | | |
|---|---|---|---|---|---|---|---|---|---|
| Slow | 250 | 300 | 36.70 | 8.10 | 2.39 | 12.23 | 4.32 | 4.33 | 31.37 |
| Medium | 463 | 288 | 32.10 | 5.56 | 1.97 | 11.15 | 4.67 | 2.80 | 26.15 |
| Fast | 675 | 275 | 27.50 | 4.67 | 1.89 | 10.00 | 5.14 | 1.52 | 23.22 |

**Roll 3rd or additional coats**
| | | | | | | | | | |
|---|---|---|---|---|---|---|---|---|---|
| Slow | 275 | 325 | 36.70 | 7.36 | 2.18 | 11.29 | 3.96 | 3.96 | 28.75 |
| Medium | 500 | 313 | 32.10 | 5.15 | 1.82 | 10.26 | 4.31 | 2.58 | 24.12 |
| Fast | 725 | 300 | 27.50 | 4.34 | 1.78 | 9.17 | 4.74 | 1.40 | 21.43 |

### Enamel, water base (material #9)

**Roll 1st finish coat**
| | | | | | | | | | |
|---|---|---|---|---|---|---|---|---|---|
| Slow | 200 | 250 | 46.80 | 10.13 | 2.98 | 18.72 | 6.05 | 6.06 | 43.94 |
| Medium | 413 | 238 | 41.00 | 6.23 | 2.21 | 17.23 | 6.42 | 3.85 | 35.94 |
| Fast | 625 | 225 | 35.10 | 5.04 | 2.06 | 15.60 | 7.04 | 2.08 | 31.82 |

**Roll 2nd finish coat**
| | | | | | | | | | |
|---|---|---|---|---|---|---|---|---|---|
| Slow | 225 | 300 | 46.80 | 9.00 | 2.64 | 15.60 | 5.18 | 5.19 | 37.61 |
| Medium | 438 | 288 | 41.00 | 5.88 | 2.07 | 14.24 | 5.55 | 3.33 | 31.07 |
| Fast | 650 | 275 | 35.10 | 4.85 | 1.98 | 12.76 | 6.07 | 1.80 | 27.46 |

**Roll 3rd or additional finish coats**
| | | | | | | | | | |
|---|---|---|---|---|---|---|---|---|---|
| Slow | 250 | 325 | 46.80 | 8.10 | 2.39 | 14.40 | 4.73 | 4.74 | 34.36 |
| Medium | 475 | 313 | 41.00 | 5.42 | 1.94 | 13.10 | 5.11 | 3.07 | 28.64 |
| Fast | 700 | 300 | 35.10 | 4.50 | 1.84 | 11.70 | 5.59 | 1.65 | 25.28 |

### Enamel, oil base (material #10)

**Roll 1st finish coat**
| | | | | | | | | | |
|---|---|---|---|---|---|---|---|---|---|
| Slow | 200 | 275 | 61.70 | 10.13 | 2.98 | 22.44 | 6.76 | 6.77 | 49.08 |
| Medium | 413 | 263 | 54.00 | 6.23 | 2.21 | 20.53 | 7.24 | 4.35 | 40.56 |
| Fast | 625 | 250 | 46.30 | 5.04 | 2.06 | 18.52 | 7.94 | 2.35 | 35.91 |

**Roll 2nd finish coat**
| | | | | | | | | | |
|---|---|---|---|---|---|---|---|---|---|
| Slow | 225 | 350 | 61.70 | 9.00 | 2.64 | 17.63 | 5.57 | 5.58 | 40.42 |
| Medium | 438 | 325 | 54.00 | 5.88 | 2.07 | 16.62 | 6.15 | 3.69 | 34.41 |
| Fast | 650 | 300 | 46.30 | 4.85 | 1.98 | 15.43 | 6.90 | 2.04 | 31.20 |

|  | Labor SF per manhour | Material coverage SF/gallon | Material cost per gallon | Labor cost per 100 SF | Labor burden 100 SF | Material cost per 100 SF | Overhead per 100 SF | Profit per 100 SF | Total price per 100 SF |
|---|---|---|---|---|---|---|---|---|---|
| Roll 3rd or additional finish coats | | | | | | | | | |
| Slow | 250 | 375 | 61.70 | 8.10 | 2.39 | 16.45 | 5.12 | 5.13 | 37.19 |
| Medium | 475 | 350 | 54.00 | 5.42 | 1.94 | 15.43 | 5.69 | 3.42 | 31.90 |
| Fast | 700 | 325 | 46.30 | 4.50 | 1.84 | 14.25 | 6.38 | 1.89 | 28.86 |
| Epoxy coating, 2 part system - white (material #52) | | | | | | | | | |
| Roll 1st coat | | | | | | | | | |
| Slow | 250 | 350 | 177.00 | 8.10 | 2.39 | 50.57 | 11.60 | 11.63 | 84.29 |
| Medium | 463 | 335 | 154.90 | 5.56 | 1.97 | 46.24 | 13.44 | 8.07 | 75.28 |
| Fast | 675 | 320 | 132.70 | 4.67 | 1.89 | 41.47 | 14.90 | 4.41 | 67.34 |
| Roll 2nd or additional coats | | | | | | | | | |
| Slow | 275 | 400 | 177.00 | 7.36 | 2.18 | 44.25 | 10.22 | 10.24 | 74.25 |
| Medium | 500 | 375 | 154.90 | 5.15 | 1.82 | 41.31 | 12.07 | 7.24 | 67.59 |
| Fast | 725 | 350 | 132.70 | 4.34 | 1.78 | 37.91 | 13.65 | 4.04 | 61.72 |

Measurements are based on the square feet of wall coated. Do not deduct for openings less than 100 square feet. These figures assume paint products are being applied over a smooth or medium texture finish. For heights above 8 feet, use the High Time Difficulty Factors on page 139. These figures include brushing-in at corners when all walls are the same color, and at ceilings that are the same color or finished with acoustic spray-on texture. ADD for cutting-in at ceilings if they're a different color than the walls, or at corners where walls in the same room are painted different colors. Do not include cutting-in time for ceilings unless you're only painting the ceilings, not the walls. "Slow" work is based on an hourly wage of $20.25, "Medium" work on an hourly wage of $25.75, and "Fast" work on an hourly wage of $31.50. Other qualifications that apply to this table are on page 9.

*General Painting Costs*

|  | Labor SF per manhour | Material coverage SF/gallon | Material cost per gallon | Labor cost per 100 SF | Labor burden 100 SF | Material cost per 100 SF | Overhead per 100 SF | Profit per 100 SF | Total price per 100 SF |
|---|---|---|---|---|---|---|---|---|---|

## Walls, plaster, interior, medium texture, spray, per 100 SF of wall area

### Flat latex, water base (material #5)
**Spray 1st coat**

| | | | | | | | | | |
|---|---|---|---|---|---|---|---|---|---|
| Slow | 475 | 350 | 36.70 | 4.26 | 1.27 | 10.49 | 3.04 | 3.05 | 22.11 |
| Medium | 600 | 313 | 32.10 | 4.29 | 1.53 | 10.26 | 4.02 | 2.41 | 22.51 |
| Fast | 725 | 275 | 27.50 | 4.34 | 1.78 | 10.00 | 4.99 | 1.48 | 22.59 |

**Spray 2nd coat**

| | | | | | | | | | |
|---|---|---|---|---|---|---|---|---|---|
| Slow | 525 | 400 | 36.70 | 3.86 | 1.12 | 9.18 | 2.69 | 2.70 | 19.55 |
| Medium | 675 | 350 | 32.10 | 3.81 | 1.35 | 9.17 | 3.58 | 2.15 | 20.06 |
| Fast | 825 | 300 | 27.50 | 3.82 | 1.55 | 9.17 | 4.51 | 1.33 | 20.38 |

**Spray 3rd or additional coats**

| | | | | | | | | | |
|---|---|---|---|---|---|---|---|---|---|
| Slow | 575 | 450 | 36.70 | 3.52 | 1.04 | 8.16 | 2.42 | 2.42 | 17.56 |
| Medium | 750 | 388 | 32.10 | 3.43 | 1.21 | 8.27 | 3.23 | 1.94 | 18.08 |
| Fast | 925 | 325 | 27.50 | 3.41 | 1.38 | 8.46 | 4.11 | 1.22 | 18.58 |

### Enamel, water base (material #9)
**Spray 1st finish coat**

| | | | | | | | | | |
|---|---|---|---|---|---|---|---|---|---|
| Slow | 450 | 350 | 46.80 | 4.50 | 1.32 | 13.37 | 3.65 | 3.66 | 26.50 |
| Medium | 575 | 313 | 41.00 | 4.48 | 1.59 | 13.10 | 4.79 | 2.88 | 26.84 |
| Fast | 700 | 275 | 35.10 | 4.50 | 1.84 | 12.76 | 5.92 | 1.75 | 26.77 |

**Spray 2nd finish coat**

| | | | | | | | | | |
|---|---|---|---|---|---|---|---|---|---|
| Slow | 500 | 400 | 46.80 | 4.05 | 1.19 | 11.70 | 3.22 | 3.23 | 23.39 |
| Medium | 650 | 350 | 41.00 | 3.96 | 1.41 | 11.71 | 4.27 | 2.56 | 23.91 |
| Fast | 800 | 300 | 35.10 | 3.94 | 1.60 | 11.70 | 5.35 | 1.58 | 24.17 |

**Spray 3rd or additional finish coats**

| | | | | | | | | | |
|---|---|---|---|---|---|---|---|---|---|
| Slow | 550 | 450 | 46.80 | 3.68 | 1.09 | 10.40 | 2.88 | 2.89 | 20.94 |
| Medium | 750 | 388 | 41.00 | 3.43 | 1.21 | 10.57 | 3.80 | 2.28 | 21.29 |
| Fast | 900 | 325 | 35.10 | 3.50 | 1.42 | 10.80 | 4.88 | 1.44 | 22.04 |

### Enamel, oil base (material #10)
**Spray 1st finish coat**

| | | | | | | | | | |
|---|---|---|---|---|---|---|---|---|---|
| Slow | 450 | 400 | 61.70 | 4.50 | 1.32 | 15.43 | 4.04 | 4.05 | 29.34 |
| Medium | 575 | 363 | 54.00 | 4.48 | 1.59 | 14.88 | 5.24 | 3.14 | 29.33 |
| Fast | 700 | 325 | 46.30 | 4.50 | 1.84 | 14.25 | 6.38 | 1.89 | 28.86 |

**Spray 2nd finish coat**

| | | | | | | | | | |
|---|---|---|---|---|---|---|---|---|---|
| Slow | 500 | 425 | 61.70 | 4.05 | 1.19 | 14.52 | 3.75 | 3.76 | 27.27 |
| Medium | 650 | 388 | 54.00 | 3.96 | 1.41 | 13.92 | 4.82 | 2.89 | 27.00 |
| Fast | 800 | 350 | 46.30 | 3.94 | 1.60 | 13.23 | 5.82 | 1.72 | 26.31 |

|  | Labor SF per manhour | Material coverage SF/gallon | Material cost per gallon | Labor cost per 100 SF | Labor burden 100 SF | Material cost per 100 SF | Overhead per 100 SF | Profit per 100 SF | Total price per 100 SF |
|---|---|---|---|---|---|---|---|---|---|
| **Spray 3rd or additional finish coats** | | | | | | | | | |
| Slow | 550 | 450 | 61.70 | 3.68 | 1.09 | 13.71 | 3.51 | 3.52 | 25.51 |
| Medium | 725 | 400 | 54.00 | 3.55 | 1.26 | 13.50 | 4.58 | 2.75 | 25.64 |
| Fast | 900 | 375 | 46.30 | 3.50 | 1.42 | 12.35 | 5.36 | 1.58 | 24.21 |
| **Epoxy coating, 2 part system - white (material #52)** | | | | | | | | | |
| *Spray 1st coat* | | | | | | | | | |
| Slow | 525 | 325 | 177.00 | 3.86 | 1.12 | 54.46 | 11.30 | 11.32 | 82.06 |
| Medium | 675 | 300 | 154.90 | 3.81 | 1.35 | 51.63 | 14.20 | 8.52 | 79.51 |
| Fast | 825 | 275 | 132.70 | 3.82 | 1.55 | 48.25 | 16.63 | 4.92 | 75.17 |
| **Spray 2nd or additional coats** | | | | | | | | | |
| Slow | 575 | 350 | 177.00 | 3.52 | 1.04 | 50.57 | 10.47 | 10.50 | 76.10 |
| Medium | 725 | 325 | 154.90 | 3.55 | 1.26 | 47.66 | 13.12 | 7.87 | 73.46 |
| Fast | 875 | 300 | 132.70 | 3.60 | 1.46 | 44.23 | 15.28 | 4.52 | 69.09 |

Measurements are based on the square feet of wall coated. Do not deduct for openings less than 100 square feet. These figures assume paint products are being applied over a smooth or medium texture finish. For heights above 8 feet, use the High Time Difficulty Factors on page 139. These figures include spraying at corners when all walls are the same color, and at ceiling-to-wall intersection when ceilings are the same color. ADD for cutting-in at ceilings and protecting adjacent surfaces from overspray if they're a different color than the walls, or at corners where walls in the same room are painted different colors. "Slow" work is based on an hourly wage of $20.25, "Medium" work on an hourly wage of $25.75, and "Fast" work on an hourly wage of $31.50. Other qualifications that apply to this table are on page 9.

*General Painting Costs*

|  | Labor SF per manhour | Material coverage SF/gallon | Material cost per gallon | Labor cost per 100 SF | Labor burden 100 SF | Material cost per 100 SF | Overhead per 100 SF | Profit per 100 SF | Total price per 100 SF |
|---|---|---|---|---|---|---|---|---|---|

## Walls, plaster, interior, rough texture, per 100 SF of wall area

Anti-graffiti stain eliminator
  Water base primer and sealer (material #39)
    Roll & brush each coat

| | | | | | | | | | |
|---|---|---|---|---|---|---|---|---|---|
| Slow | 350 | 400 | 50.30 | 5.79 | 1.71 | 12.58 | 3.82 | 3.82 | 27.72 |
| Medium | 375 | 375 | 44.00 | 6.87 | 2.44 | 11.73 | 5.26 | 3.15 | 29.45 |
| Fast | 400 | 350 | 37.80 | 7.88 | 3.21 | 10.80 | 6.79 | 2.01 | 30.69 |

  Oil base primer and sealer (material #40)
    Roll & brush each coat

| | | | | | | | | | |
|---|---|---|---|---|---|---|---|---|---|
| Slow | 350 | 375 | 49.90 | 5.79 | 1.71 | 13.31 | 3.95 | 3.96 | 28.72 |
| Medium | 375 | 350 | 43.70 | 6.87 | 2.44 | 12.49 | 5.45 | 3.27 | 30.52 |
| Fast | 400 | 325 | 37.40 | 7.88 | 3.21 | 11.51 | 7.01 | 2.07 | 31.68 |

  Polyurethane 2 part system (material #41)
    Roll & brush each coat

| | | | | | | | | | |
|---|---|---|---|---|---|---|---|---|---|
| Slow | 300 | 350 | 157.00 | 6.75 | 1.98 | 44.86 | 10.18 | 10.20 | 73.97 |
| Medium | 325 | 325 | 137.40 | 7.92 | 2.82 | 42.28 | 13.25 | 7.95 | 74.22 |
| Fast | 350 | 300 | 117.80 | 9.00 | 3.68 | 39.27 | 16.10 | 4.76 | 72.81 |

Measurements are based on the square feet of wall coated. Do not deduct for openings less than 100 square feet. These figures assume paint products are being applied over a rough finish, sand finish, or orange peel texture finish. For heights above 8 feet, use the High Time Difficulty Factors on page 139. "Slow" work is based on an hourly wage of $20.25, "Medium" work on an hourly wage of $25.75, and "Fast" work on an hourly wage of $31.50. Other qualifications that apply to this table are on page 9.

*National Painting Cost Estimator*

|  | Labor SF per manhour | Material coverage SF/gallon | Material cost per gallon | Labor cost per 100 SF | Labor burden 100 SF | Material cost per 100 SF | Overhead per 100 SF | Profit per 100 SF | Total price per 100 SF |
|---|---|---|---|---|---|---|---|---|---|
| **Walls, plaster, interior, rough texture, brush, per 100 SF of wall area** | | | | | | | | | |
| Flat latex, water base (material #5) | | | | | | | | | |
| Brush 1st coat | | | | | | | | | |
| Slow | 115 | 300 | 36.70 | 17.61 | 5.20 | 12.23 | 6.66 | 6.67 | 48.37 |
| Medium | 140 | 275 | 32.10 | 18.39 | 6.51 | 11.67 | 9.14 | 5.49 | 51.20 |
| Fast | 165 | 250 | 27.50 | 19.09 | 7.79 | 11.00 | 11.74 | 3.47 | 53.09 |
| Brush 2nd coat | | | | | | | | | |
| Slow | 125 | 325 | 36.70 | 16.20 | 4.78 | 11.29 | 6.13 | 6.14 | 44.54 |
| Medium | 153 | 300 | 32.10 | 16.83 | 5.97 | 10.70 | 8.37 | 5.02 | 46.89 |
| Fast | 180 | 275 | 27.50 | 17.50 | 7.16 | 10.00 | 10.74 | 3.18 | 48.58 |
| Brush 3rd or additional coats | | | | | | | | | |
| Slow | 135 | 350 | 36.70 | 15.00 | 4.43 | 10.49 | 5.68 | 5.70 | 41.30 |
| Medium | 168 | 325 | 32.10 | 15.33 | 5.42 | 9.88 | 7.66 | 4.60 | 42.89 |
| Fast | 200 | 300 | 27.50 | 15.75 | 6.43 | 9.17 | 9.72 | 2.87 | 43.94 |
| Enamel, water base (material #9) | | | | | | | | | |
| Brush 1st finish coat | | | | | | | | | |
| Slow | 100 | 300 | 46.80 | 20.25 | 5.97 | 15.60 | 7.95 | 7.96 | 57.73 |
| Medium | 125 | 275 | 41.00 | 20.60 | 7.30 | 14.91 | 10.70 | 6.42 | 59.93 |
| Fast | 150 | 250 | 35.10 | 21.00 | 8.58 | 14.04 | 13.52 | 4.00 | 61.14 |
| Brush 2nd finish coat | | | | | | | | | |
| Slow | 115 | 325 | 46.80 | 17.61 | 5.20 | 14.40 | 7.07 | 7.08 | 51.36 |
| Medium | 140 | 300 | 41.00 | 18.39 | 6.51 | 13.67 | 9.64 | 5.79 | 54.00 |
| Fast | 165 | 275 | 35.10 | 19.09 | 7.79 | 12.76 | 12.29 | 3.64 | 55.57 |
| Brush 3rd or additional finish coats | | | | | | | | | |
| Slow | 125 | 350 | 46.80 | 16.20 | 4.78 | 13.37 | 6.53 | 6.54 | 47.42 |
| Medium | 160 | 325 | 41.00 | 16.09 | 5.70 | 12.62 | 8.60 | 5.16 | 48.17 |
| Fast | 185 | 300 | 35.10 | 17.03 | 6.96 | 11.70 | 11.06 | 3.27 | 50.02 |
| Enamel, oil base (material #10) | | | | | | | | | |
| Brush 1st finish coat | | | | | | | | | |
| Slow | 100 | 300 | 61.70 | 20.25 | 5.97 | 20.57 | 8.89 | 8.91 | 64.59 |
| Medium | 125 | 288 | 54.00 | 20.60 | 7.30 | 18.75 | 11.66 | 7.00 | 65.31 |
| Fast | 150 | 275 | 46.30 | 21.00 | 8.58 | 16.84 | 14.39 | 4.26 | 65.07 |
| Brush 2nd finish coat | | | | | | | | | |
| Slow | 115 | 375 | 61.70 | 17.61 | 5.20 | 16.45 | 7.46 | 7.47 | 54.19 |
| Medium | 140 | 350 | 54.00 | 18.39 | 6.51 | 15.43 | 10.08 | 6.05 | 56.46 |
| Fast | 165 | 325 | 46.30 | 19.09 | 7.79 | 14.25 | 12.75 | 3.77 | 57.65 |

*General Painting Costs*

|  | Labor SF per manhour | Material coverage SF/gallon | Material cost per gallon | Labor cost per 100 SF | Labor burden 100 SF | Material cost per 100 SF | Overhead per 100 SF | Profit per 100 SF | Total price per 100 SF |
|---|---|---|---|---|---|---|---|---|---|
| **Brush 3rd or additional finish coats** | | | | | | | | | |
| Slow | 125 | 400 | 61.70 | 16.20 | 4.78 | 15.43 | 6.92 | 6.93 | 50.26 |
| Medium | 160 | 375 | 54.00 | 16.09 | 5.70 | 14.40 | 9.05 | 5.43 | 50.67 |
| Fast | 185 | 350 | 46.30 | 17.03 | 6.96 | 13.23 | 11.54 | 3.41 | 52.17 |
| **Epoxy coating, 2 part system - white (material #52)** | | | | | | | | | |
| Brush 1st coat | | | | | | | | | |
| Slow | 125 | 375 | 177.00 | 16.20 | 4.78 | 47.20 | 12.95 | 12.98 | 94.11 |
| Medium | 160 | 363 | 154.90 | 16.09 | 5.70 | 42.67 | 16.12 | 9.67 | 90.25 |
| Fast | 180 | 350 | 132.70 | 17.50 | 7.16 | 37.91 | 19.39 | 5.74 | 87.70 |
| Brush 2nd or additional coats | | | | | | | | | |
| Slow | 135 | 400 | 177.00 | 15.00 | 4.43 | 44.25 | 12.10 | 12.12 | 87.90 |
| Medium | 175 | 388 | 154.90 | 14.71 | 5.20 | 39.92 | 14.96 | 8.98 | 83.77 |
| Fast | 200 | 375 | 132.70 | 15.75 | 6.43 | 35.39 | 17.85 | 5.28 | 80.70 |
| **Glazing & mottling over enamel (material #16)** | | | | | | | | | |
| Brush each coat | | | | | | | | | |
| Slow | 40 | 875 | 71.00 | 50.63 | 14.92 | 8.11 | 14.00 | 14.03 | 101.69 |
| Medium | 50 | 838 | 62.10 | 51.50 | 18.24 | 7.41 | 19.29 | 11.57 | 108.01 |
| Fast | 60 | 800 | 53.30 | 52.50 | 21.43 | 6.66 | 24.98 | 7.39 | 112.96 |
| **Stipple** | | | | | | | | | |
| Slow | 90 | -- | -- | 22.50 | 6.63 | -- | 5.54 | 5.55 | 40.22 |
| Medium | 103 | -- | -- | 25.00 | 8.86 | -- | 8.46 | 5.08 | 47.40 |
| Fast | 115 | -- | -- | 27.39 | 11.19 | -- | 11.96 | 3.54 | 54.08 |

Measurements are based on the square feet of wall coated. Do not deduct for openings less than 100 square feet. These figures assume paint products are being applied over a rough finish. For heights above 8 feet, use the High Time Difficulty Factors on page 139. These figures include brushing-in at corners when all walls are the same color, and at ceilings that are the same color or finished with acoustic spray-on texture. ADD for cutting-in at ceilings if they're a different color than the walls, or at corners where walls in the same room are painted different colors. Do not include cutting-in time for ceilings unless you're only painting the ceilings, not the walls. "Slow" work is based on an hourly wage of $20.25, "Medium" work on an hourly wage of $25.75, and "Fast" work on an hourly wage of $31.50. Other qualifications that apply to this table are on page 9.

|  | Labor SF per manhour | Material coverage SF/gallon | Material cost per gallon | Labor cost per 100 SF | Labor burden 100 SF | Material cost per 100 SF | Overhead per 100 SF | Profit per 100 SF | Total price per 100 SF |
|---|---|---|---|---|---|---|---|---|---|

## Walls, plaster, interior, rough texture, roll, per 100 SF of wall area

### Flat latex, water base (material #5)

Roll 1st coat
| | | | | | | | | | |
|---|---|---|---|---|---|---|---|---|---|
| Slow | 200 | 250 | 36.70 | 10.13 | 2.98 | 14.68 | 5.28 | 5.29 | 38.36 |
| Medium | 413 | 238 | 32.10 | 6.23 | 2.21 | 13.49 | 5.48 | 3.29 | 30.70 |
| Fast | 625 | 225 | 27.50 | 5.04 | 2.06 | 12.22 | 5.99 | 1.77 | 27.08 |

Roll 2nd coat
| | | | | | | | | | |
|---|---|---|---|---|---|---|---|---|---|
| Slow | 225 | 300 | 36.70 | 9.00 | 2.64 | 12.23 | 4.54 | 4.55 | 32.96 |
| Medium | 438 | 288 | 32.10 | 5.88 | 2.07 | 11.15 | 3.63 | 3.64 | 26.37 |
| Fast | 650 | 275 | 27.50 | 4.85 | 1.98 | 10.00 | 5.22 | 1.54 | 23.59 |

Roll 3rd or additional coats
| | | | | | | | | | |
|---|---|---|---|---|---|---|---|---|---|
| Slow | 250 | 325 | 36.70 | 8.10 | 2.39 | 11.29 | 4.14 | 4.15 | 30.07 |
| Medium | 463 | 313 | 32.10 | 5.56 | 1.97 | 10.26 | 4.45 | 2.67 | 24.91 |
| Fast | 675 | 300 | 27.50 | 4.67 | 1.89 | 9.17 | 4.88 | 1.44 | 22.05 |

### Enamel, water base (material #9)

Roll 1st finish coat
| | | | | | | | | | |
|---|---|---|---|---|---|---|---|---|---|
| Slow | 175 | 250 | 46.80 | 11.57 | 3.40 | 18.72 | 6.40 | 6.42 | 46.51 |
| Medium | 388 | 238 | 41.00 | 6.64 | 2.36 | 17.23 | 6.56 | 3.93 | 36.72 |
| Fast | 600 | 225 | 35.10 | 5.25 | 2.16 | 15.60 | 7.13 | 2.11 | 32.25 |

Roll 2nd finish coat
| | | | | | | | | | |
|---|---|---|---|---|---|---|---|---|---|
| Slow | 200 | 325 | 46.80 | 10.13 | 2.98 | 14.40 | 5.23 | 5.24 | 37.98 |
| Medium | 413 | 313 | 41.00 | 6.23 | 2.21 | 13.10 | 5.39 | 3.23 | 30.16 |
| Fast | 625 | 300 | 35.10 | 5.04 | 2.06 | 11.70 | 5.83 | 1.72 | 26.35 |

Roll 3rd or additional finish coats
| | | | | | | | | | |
|---|---|---|---|---|---|---|---|---|---|
| Slow | 225 | 325 | 46.80 | 9.00 | 2.64 | 14.40 | 4.95 | 4.96 | 35.95 |
| Medium | 438 | 313 | 41.00 | 5.88 | 2.07 | 13.10 | 5.27 | 3.16 | 29.48 |
| Fast | 650 | 300 | 35.10 | 4.85 | 1.98 | 11.70 | 5.74 | 1.70 | 25.97 |

### Enamel, oil base (material #10)

Roll 1st finish coat
| | | | | | | | | | |
|---|---|---|---|---|---|---|---|---|---|
| Slow | 175 | 300 | 61.70 | 11.57 | 3.40 | 20.57 | 6.75 | 6.77 | 49.06 |
| Medium | 388 | 288 | 54.00 | 6.64 | 2.36 | 18.75 | 6.94 | 4.16 | 38.85 |
| Fast | 600 | 275 | 46.30 | 5.25 | 2.16 | 16.84 | 7.51 | 2.22 | 33.98 |

Roll 2nd finish coat
| | | | | | | | | | |
|---|---|---|---|---|---|---|---|---|---|
| Slow | 200 | 350 | 61.70 | 10.13 | 2.98 | 17.63 | 5.84 | 5.85 | 42.43 |
| Medium | 413 | 325 | 54.00 | 6.23 | 2.21 | 16.62 | 6.27 | 3.76 | 35.09 |
| Fast | 625 | 300 | 46.30 | 5.04 | 2.06 | 15.43 | 6.98 | 2.07 | 31.58 |

*General Painting Costs*

|  | Labor SF per manhour | Material coverage SF/gallon | Material cost per gallon | Labor cost per 100 SF | Labor burden 100 SF | Material cost per 100 SF | Overhead per 100 SF | Profit per 100 SF | Total price per 100 SF |
|---|---|---|---|---|---|---|---|---|---|
| Roll 3rd or additional finish coats | | | | | | | | | |
| Slow | 225 | 375 | 61.70 | 9.00 | 2.64 | 16.45 | 5.34 | 5.35 | 38.78 |
| Medium | 438 | 350 | 54.00 | 5.88 | 2.07 | 15.43 | 5.85 | 3.51 | 32.74 |
| Fast | 650 | 325 | 46.30 | 4.85 | 1.98 | 14.25 | 6.53 | 1.93 | 29.54 |
| Epoxy coating, 2 part system - white (material #52) | | | | | | | | | |
| Roll 1st coat | | | | | | | | | |
| Slow | 225 | 350 | 177.00 | 9.00 | 2.64 | 50.57 | 11.82 | 11.85 | 85.88 |
| Medium | 438 | 325 | 154.90 | 5.88 | 2.07 | 47.66 | 13.91 | 8.34 | 77.86 |
| Fast | 650 | 300 | 132.70 | 4.85 | 1.98 | 44.23 | 15.83 | 4.68 | 71.57 |
| Roll 2nd or additional coats | | | | | | | | | |
| Slow | 250 | 400 | 177.00 | 8.10 | 2.39 | 44.25 | 10.40 | 10.42 | 75.56 |
| Medium | 463 | 375 | 154.90 | 5.56 | 1.97 | 41.31 | 12.21 | 7.33 | 68.38 |
| Fast | 675 | 350 | 132.70 | 4.67 | 1.89 | 37.91 | 13.79 | 4.08 | 62.34 |

Measurements are based on the square feet of wall coated. Do not deduct for openings less than 100 square feet. These figures assume paint products are being applied over a rough finish. For heights above 8 feet, use the High Time Difficulty Factors on page 139. These figures include brushing-in at corners when all walls are the same color, and at ceilings that are the same color or finished with acoustic spray-on texture. ADD for cutting-in at ceilings if they're a different color than the walls, or at corners where walls in the same room are painted different colors. Do not include cutting-in time for ceilings unless you're only painting the ceilings, not the walls. "Slow" work is based on an hourly wage of $20.25, "Medium" work on an hourly wage of $25.75, and "Fast" work on an hourly wage of $31.50. Other qualifications that apply to this table are on page 9.

*National Painting Cost Estimator*

|  | Labor SF per manhour | Material coverage SF/gallon | Material cost per gallon | Labor cost per 100 SF | Labor burden 100 SF | Material cost per 100 SF | Overhead per 100 SF | Profit per 100 SF | Total price per 100 SF |
|---|---|---|---|---|---|---|---|---|---|

## Walls, plaster, interior, rough texture, spray, per 100 SF of wall area

### Flat latex, water base (material #5)
**Spray 1st coat**

| | | | | | | | | | |
|---|---|---|---|---|---|---|---|---|---|
| Slow | 500 | 325 | 36.70 | 4.05 | 1.19 | 11.29 | 3.14 | 3.15 | 22.82 |
| Medium | 600 | 288 | 32.10 | 4.29 | 1.53 | 11.15 | 4.24 | 2.54 | 23.75 |
| Fast | 700 | 250 | 27.50 | 4.50 | 1.84 | 11.00 | 5.38 | 1.59 | 24.31 |

**Spray 2nd coat**

| | | | | | | | | | |
|---|---|---|---|---|---|---|---|---|---|
| Slow | 600 | 400 | 36.70 | 3.38 | 1.00 | 9.18 | 2.58 | 2.58 | 18.72 |
| Medium | 700 | 350 | 32.10 | 3.68 | 1.31 | 9.17 | 3.54 | 2.12 | 19.82 |
| Fast | 800 | 300 | 27.50 | 3.94 | 1.60 | 9.17 | 4.56 | 1.35 | 20.62 |

**Spray 3rd or additional coats**

| | | | | | | | | | |
|---|---|---|---|---|---|---|---|---|---|
| Slow | 700 | 425 | 36.70 | 2.89 | .86 | 8.64 | 2.35 | 2.36 | 17.10 |
| Medium | 800 | 375 | 32.10 | 3.22 | 1.14 | 8.56 | 3.23 | 1.94 | 18.09 |
| Fast | 900 | 325 | 27.50 | 3.50 | 1.42 | 8.46 | 4.15 | 1.23 | 18.76 |

### Enamel, water base (material #9)
**Spray 1st finish coat**

| | | | | | | | | | |
|---|---|---|---|---|---|---|---|---|---|
| Slow | 450 | 325 | 46.80 | 4.50 | 1.32 | 14.40 | 3.84 | 3.85 | 27.91 |
| Medium | 550 | 288 | 41.00 | 4.68 | 1.67 | 14.24 | 5.15 | 3.09 | 28.83 |
| Fast | 650 | 250 | 35.10 | 4.85 | 1.98 | 14.04 | 6.47 | 1.91 | 29.25 |

**Spray 2nd finish coat**

| | | | | | | | | | |
|---|---|---|---|---|---|---|---|---|---|
| Slow | 550 | 400 | 46.80 | 3.68 | 1.09 | 11.70 | 3.13 | 3.14 | 22.74 |
| Medium | 650 | 350 | 41.00 | 3.96 | 1.41 | 11.71 | 4.27 | 2.56 | 23.91 |
| Fast | 750 | 300 | 35.10 | 4.20 | 1.70 | 11.70 | 5.46 | 1.61 | 24.67 |

**Spray 3rd or additional finish coats**

| | | | | | | | | | |
|---|---|---|---|---|---|---|---|---|---|
| Slow | 650 | 425 | 46.80 | 3.12 | .92 | 11.01 | 2.86 | 2.87 | 20.78 |
| Medium | 750 | 375 | 41.00 | 3.43 | 1.21 | 10.93 | 3.89 | 2.34 | 21.80 |
| Fast | 850 | 325 | 35.10 | 3.71 | 1.52 | 10.80 | 4.97 | 1.47 | 22.47 |

### Enamel, oil base (material #10)
**Spray 1st finish coat**

| | | | | | | | | | |
|---|---|---|---|---|---|---|---|---|---|
| Slow | 450 | 325 | 61.70 | 4.50 | 1.32 | 18.98 | 4.71 | 4.72 | 34.23 |
| Medium | 550 | 300 | 54.00 | 4.68 | 1.67 | 18.00 | 6.09 | 3.65 | 34.09 |
| Fast | 650 | 275 | 46.30 | 4.85 | 1.98 | 16.84 | 7.34 | 2.17 | 33.18 |

**Spray 2nd finish coat**

| | | | | | | | | | |
|---|---|---|---|---|---|---|---|---|---|
| Slow | 550 | 400 | 61.70 | 3.68 | 1.09 | 15.43 | 3.84 | 3.85 | 27.89 |
| Medium | 650 | 362 | 54.00 | 3.96 | 1.41 | 14.92 | 5.07 | 3.04 | 28.40 |
| Fast | 750 | 325 | 46.30 | 4.20 | 1.70 | 14.25 | 6.25 | 1.85 | 28.25 |

*General Painting Costs*

|  | Labor SF per manhour | Material coverage SF/gallon | Material cost per gallon | Labor cost per 100 SF | Labor burden 100 SF | Material cost per 100 SF | Overhead per 100 SF | Profit per 100 SF | Total price per 100 SF |
|---|---|---|---|---|---|---|---|---|---|
| **Spray 3rd or additional finish coats** | | | | | | | | | |
| Slow | 650 | 425 | 61.70 | 3.12 | .92 | 14.52 | 3.53 | 3.53 | 25.62 |
| Medium | 750 | 388 | 54.00 | 3.43 | 1.21 | 13.92 | 4.64 | 2.78 | 25.98 |
| Fast | 850 | 350 | 46.30 | 3.71 | 1.52 | 13.23 | 5.72 | 1.69 | 25.87 |
| **Epoxy coating, 2 part system - white (material #52)** | | | | | | | | | |
| **Spray 1st coat** | | | | | | | | | |
| Slow | 525 | 325 | 177.00 | 3.86 | 1.12 | 54.46 | 11.30 | 11.32 | 82.06 |
| Medium | 663 | 313 | 154.90 | 3.88 | 1.39 | 49.49 | 13.69 | 8.21 | 76.66 |
| Fast | 800 | 300 | 132.70 | 3.94 | 1.60 | 44.23 | 15.43 | 4.56 | 69.76 |
| **Spray 2nd or additional coats** | | | | | | | | | |
| Slow | 575 | 375 | 177.00 | 3.52 | 1.04 | 47.20 | 9.83 | 9.85 | 71.44 |
| Medium | 713 | 363 | 154.90 | 3.61 | 1.27 | 42.67 | 11.89 | 7.13 | 66.57 |
| Fast | 850 | 350 | 132.70 | 3.71 | 1.52 | 37.91 | 13.37 | 3.96 | 60.47 |

Measurements are based on the square feet of wall coated. Do not deduct for openings less than 100 square feet. These figures assume paint products are being applied over a rough finish. For heights above 8 feet, use the High Time Difficulty Factors on page 139. These figures include spraying at corners when all walls are the same color, and at ceiling-to-wall intersection when ceilings are the same color. ADD for cutting-in at ceilings and protecting adjacent surfaces from overspray if they're a different color than the walls, or at corners where walls in the same room are painted different colors. Do not include cutting-in time for ceilings unless you're only painting the ceilings, not the walls. "Slow" work is based on an hourly wage of $20.25, "Medium" work on an hourly wage of $25.75, and "Fast" work on an hourly wage of $31.50. Other qualifications that apply to this table are on page 9.

|  | Labor SF per manhour | Material coverage SF/gallon | Material cost per gallon | Labor cost per 100 SF | Labor burden 100 SF | Material cost per 100 SF | Overhead per 100 SF | Profit per 100 SF | Total price per 100 SF |
|---|---|---|---|---|---|---|---|---|---|
| **Walls, plaster, interior, smooth finish, per 100 SF of wall area** | | | | | | | | | |
| Anti-graffiti stain eliminator | | | | | | | | | |
| Water base primer and sealer (material #39) | | | | | | | | | |
| Roll & brush each coat | | | | | | | | | |
| Slow | 375 | 425 | 50.30 | 5.40 | 1.60 | 11.84 | 3.58 | 3.59 | 26.01 |
| Medium | 400 | 400 | 44.00 | 6.44 | 2.28 | 11.00 | 4.93 | 2.96 | 27.61 |
| Fast | 425 | 375 | 37.80 | 7.41 | 3.01 | 10.08 | 6.36 | 1.88 | 28.74 |
| Oil base primer and sealer (material #40) | | | | | | | | | |
| Roll & brush each coat | | | | | | | | | |
| Slow | 375 | 400 | 49.90 | 5.40 | 1.60 | 12.48 | 3.70 | 3.71 | 26.89 |
| Medium | 400 | 375 | 43.70 | 6.44 | 2.28 | 11.65 | 5.09 | 3.06 | 28.52 |
| Fast | 425 | 350 | 37.40 | 7.41 | 3.01 | 10.69 | 6.55 | 1.94 | 29.60 |
| Polyurethane 2 part system (material #41) | | | | | | | | | |
| Roll & brush each coat | | | | | | | | | |
| Slow | 325 | 375 | 157.00 | 6.23 | 1.85 | 41.87 | 9.49 | 9.51 | 68.95 |
| Medium | 350 | 350 | 137.40 | 7.36 | 2.61 | 39.26 | 12.31 | 7.38 | 68.92 |
| Fast | 375 | 325 | 117.80 | 8.40 | 3.44 | 36.25 | 14.90 | 4.41 | 67.40 |

Measurements are based on the square feet of wall coated. Do not deduct for openings less than 100 square feet. These figures assume paint products are being applied over a smooth finish. For heights above 8 feet, use the High Time Difficulty Factors on page 139. "Slow" work is based on an hourly wage of $20.25, "Medium" work on an hourly wage of $25.75, and "Fast" work on an hourly wage of $31.50. Other qualifications that apply to this table are on page 9.

*General Painting Costs*

|  | Labor SF per manhour | Material coverage SF/gallon | Material cost per gallon | Labor cost per 100 SF | Labor burden 100 SF | Material cost per 100 SF | Overhead per 100 SF | Profit per 100 SF | Total price per 100 SF |
|---|---|---|---|---|---|---|---|---|---|
| **Walls, plaster, interior, smooth finish, brush, per 100 SF of wall area** |||||||||
| Flat latex, water base (material #5) |||||||||
|   Brush 1st coat |||||||||
|     Slow | 150 | 350 | 36.70 | 13.50 | 3.99 | 10.49 | 5.31 | 5.32 | 38.61 |
|     Medium | 175 | 325 | 32.10 | 14.71 | 5.20 | 9.88 | 7.45 | 4.47 | 41.71 |
|     Fast | 200 | 300 | 27.50 | 15.75 | 6.43 | 9.17 | 9.72 | 2.87 | 43.94 |
|   Brush 2nd coat |||||||||
|     Slow | 175 | 375 | 36.70 | 11.57 | 3.40 | 9.79 | 4.71 | 4.72 | 34.19 |
|     Medium | 200 | 350 | 32.10 | 12.88 | 4.56 | 9.17 | 6.65 | 3.99 | 37.25 |
|     Fast | 225 | 325 | 27.50 | 14.00 | 5.69 | 8.46 | 8.73 | 2.58 | 39.46 |
|   Brush 3rd or additional coats |||||||||
|     Slow | 200 | 400 | 36.70 | 10.13 | 2.98 | 9.18 | 4.24 | 4.25 | 30.78 |
|     Medium | 225 | 375 | 32.10 | 11.44 | 4.04 | 8.56 | 6.01 | 3.61 | 33.66 |
|     Fast | 250 | 350 | 27.50 | 12.60 | 5.14 | 7.86 | 7.94 | 2.35 | 35.89 |
| Enamel, water base (material #9) |||||||||
|   Brush 1st finish coat |||||||||
|     Slow | 125 | 350 | 46.80 | 16.20 | 4.78 | 13.37 | 6.53 | 6.54 | 47.42 |
|     Medium | 163 | 325 | 41.00 | 15.80 | 5.58 | 12.62 | 8.50 | 5.10 | 47.60 |
|     Fast | 200 | 300 | 35.10 | 15.75 | 6.43 | 11.70 | 10.50 | 3.11 | 47.49 |
|   Brush 2nd finish coat |||||||||
|     Slow | 150 | 375 | 46.80 | 13.50 | 3.99 | 12.48 | 5.69 | 5.70 | 41.36 |
|     Medium | 175 | 350 | 41.00 | 14.71 | 5.20 | 11.71 | 7.91 | 4.74 | 44.27 |
|     Fast | 200 | 325 | 35.10 | 15.75 | 6.43 | 10.80 | 10.22 | 3.02 | 46.22 |
|   Brush 3rd or additional finish coats |||||||||
|     Slow | 175 | 400 | 46.80 | 11.57 | 3.40 | 11.70 | 5.07 | 5.08 | 36.82 |
|     Medium | 200 | 375 | 41.00 | 12.88 | 4.56 | 10.93 | 7.09 | 4.26 | 39.72 |
|     Fast | 225 | 350 | 35.10 | 14.00 | 5.69 | 10.03 | 9.22 | 2.73 | 41.67 |
| Enamel, oil base (material #10) |||||||||
|   Brush 1st finish coat |||||||||
|     Slow | 125 | 400 | 61.70 | 16.20 | 4.78 | 15.43 | 6.92 | 6.93 | 50.26 |
|     Medium | 163 | 375 | 54.00 | 15.80 | 5.58 | 14.40 | 8.95 | 5.37 | 50.10 |
|     Fast | 200 | 350 | 46.30 | 15.75 | 6.43 | 13.23 | 10.98 | 3.25 | 49.64 |
|   Brush 2nd finish coat |||||||||
|     Slow | 150 | 425 | 46.80 | 13.50 | 3.99 | 11.01 | 5.41 | 5.42 | 39.33 |
|     Medium | 175 | 400 | 41.00 | 14.71 | 5.20 | 10.25 | 7.54 | 4.53 | 42.23 |
|     Fast | 200 | 375 | 35.10 | 15.75 | 6.43 | 9.36 | 9.78 | 2.89 | 44.21 |

*National Painting Cost Estimator*

|  | Labor SF per manhour | Material coverage SF/gallon | Material cost per gallon | Labor cost per 100 SF | Labor burden 100 SF | Material cost per 100 SF | Overhead per 100 SF | Profit per 100 SF | Total price per 100 SF |
|---|---|---|---|---|---|---|---|---|---|
| **Brush 3rd or additional finish coats** | | | | | | | | | |
| Slow | 175 | 450 | 61.70 | 11.57 | 3.40 | 13.71 | 5.45 | 5.46 | 39.59 |
| Medium | 200 | 425 | 54.00 | 12.88 | 4.56 | 12.71 | 7.54 | 4.52 | 42.21 |
| Fast | 225 | 400 | 46.30 | 14.00 | 5.69 | 11.58 | 9.70 | 2.87 | 43.84 |
| **Epoxy coating, 2 part system - white (material #52)** | | | | | | | | | |
| **Brush 1st coat** | | | | | | | | | |
| Slow | 175 | 400 | 177.00 | 11.57 | 3.40 | 44.25 | 11.25 | 11.28 | 81.75 |
| Medium | 200 | 388 | 154.90 | 12.88 | 4.56 | 39.92 | 14.34 | 8.60 | 80.30 |
| Fast | 225 | 375 | 132.70 | 14.00 | 5.69 | 35.39 | 17.08 | 5.05 | 77.21 |
| **Brush 2nd or additional coats** | | | | | | | | | |
| Slow | 200 | 425 | 177.00 | 10.13 | 2.98 | 41.65 | 10.41 | 10.43 | 75.60 |
| Medium | 225 | 413 | 154.90 | 11.44 | 4.04 | 37.51 | 13.25 | 7.95 | 74.19 |
| Fast | 250 | 400 | 132.70 | 12.60 | 5.14 | 33.18 | 15.79 | 4.67 | 71.38 |
| **Glazing & mottling over enamel (material #16)** | | | | | | | | | |
| **Brush each coat** | | | | | | | | | |
| Slow | 75 | 900 | 71.00 | 27.00 | 7.95 | 7.89 | 8.14 | 8.16 | 59.14 |
| Medium | 98 | 850 | 62.10 | 26.28 | 9.29 | 7.31 | 10.72 | 6.43 | 60.03 |
| Fast | 120 | 800 | 53.30 | 26.25 | 10.69 | 6.66 | 13.52 | 4.00 | 61.12 |
| **Stipple finish** | | | | | | | | | |
| Slow | 100 | -- | -- | 20.25 | 5.97 | -- | 4.98 | 4.99 | 36.19 |
| Medium | 123 | -- | -- | 20.93 | 7.42 | -- | 7.09 | 4.25 | 39.69 |
| Fast | 135 | -- | -- | 23.33 | 9.53 | -- | 10.18 | 3.01 | 46.05 |

Measurements are based on the square feet of wall coated. Do not deduct for openings less than 100 square feet. These figures assume paint products are being applied over a smooth finish. For heights above 8 feet, use the High Time Difficulty Factors on page 139. These figures include brushing-in at corners when all walls are the same color, and at ceilings that are the same color or finished with acoustic spray-on texture. ADD for cutting-in at ceilings if they're a different color than the walls, or at corners where walls in the same room are painted different colors. Do not include cutting-in time for ceilings unless you're only painting the ceilings, not the walls. "Slow" work is based on an hourly wage of $20.25, "Medium" work on an hourly wage of $25.75, and "Fast" work on an hourly wage of $31.50. Other qualifications that apply to this table are on page 9.

## General Painting Costs

|  | Labor SF per manhour | Material coverage SF/gallon | Material cost per gallon | Labor cost per 100 SF | Labor burden 100 SF | Material cost per 100 SF | Overhead per 100 SF | Profit per 100 SF | Total price per 100 SF |
|---|---|---|---|---|---|---|---|---|---|

### Walls, plaster, interior, smooth finish, roll, per 100 SF of wall area

**Flat latex, water base (material #5)**

*Roll 1st coat*

| | | | | | | | | | |
|---|---|---|---|---|---|---|---|---|---|
| Slow | 260 | 350 | 36.70 | 7.79 | 2.30 | 10.49 | 3.91 | 3.92 | 28.41 |
| Medium | 430 | 325 | 32.10 | 5.99 | 2.13 | 9.88 | 4.50 | 2.70 | 25.20 |
| Fast | 640 | 300 | 27.50 | 4.92 | 2.00 | 9.17 | 4.99 | 1.48 | 22.56 |

*Roll 2nd coat*

| | | | | | | | | | |
|---|---|---|---|---|---|---|---|---|---|
| Slow | 300 | 375 | 36.70 | 6.75 | 1.98 | 9.79 | 3.52 | 3.53 | 25.57 |
| Medium | 488 | 350 | 32.10 | 5.28 | 1.87 | 9.17 | 4.08 | 2.45 | 22.85 |
| Fast | 675 | 325 | 27.50 | 4.67 | 1.89 | 8.46 | 4.66 | 1.38 | 21.06 |

*Roll 3rd or additional coats*

| | | | | | | | | | |
|---|---|---|---|---|---|---|---|---|---|
| Slow | 325 | 400 | 36.70 | 6.23 | 1.85 | 9.18 | 3.28 | 3.28 | 23.82 |
| Medium | 513 | 375 | 32.10 | 5.02 | 1.78 | 8.56 | 3.84 | 2.30 | 21.50 |
| Fast | 700 | 350 | 27.50 | 4.50 | 1.84 | 7.86 | 4.40 | 1.30 | 19.90 |

**Enamel, water base (material #9)**

*Roll 1st finish coat*

| | | | | | | | | | |
|---|---|---|---|---|---|---|---|---|---|
| Slow | 235 | 350 | 46.80 | 8.62 | 2.55 | 13.37 | 4.66 | 4.67 | 33.87 |
| Medium | 423 | 325 | 41.00 | 6.09 | 2.14 | 12.62 | 5.22 | 3.13 | 29.20 |
| Fast | 615 | 300 | 35.10 | 5.12 | 2.11 | 11.70 | 5.86 | 1.73 | 26.52 |

*Roll 2nd finish coat*

| | | | | | | | | | |
|---|---|---|---|---|---|---|---|---|---|
| Slow | 275 | 375 | 46.80 | 7.36 | 2.18 | 12.48 | 4.18 | 4.19 | 30.39 |
| Medium | 453 | 350 | 41.00 | 5.68 | 2.03 | 11.71 | 4.85 | 2.91 | 27.18 |
| Fast | 630 | 325 | 35.10 | 5.00 | 2.05 | 10.80 | 5.53 | 1.64 | 25.02 |

*Roll 3rd or additional finish coats*

| | | | | | | | | | |
|---|---|---|---|---|---|---|---|---|---|
| Slow | 300 | 400 | 46.80 | 6.75 | 1.98 | 11.70 | 3.88 | 3.89 | 28.20 |
| Medium | 475 | 375 | 41.00 | 5.42 | 1.94 | 10.93 | 4.57 | 2.74 | 25.60 |
| Fast | 650 | 350 | 35.10 | 4.85 | 1.98 | 10.03 | 5.23 | 1.55 | 23.64 |

**Enamel, oil base (material #10)**

*Roll 1st finish coat*

| | | | | | | | | | |
|---|---|---|---|---|---|---|---|---|---|
| Slow | 235 | 375 | 61.70 | 8.62 | 2.55 | 16.45 | 5.25 | 5.26 | 38.13 |
| Medium | 423 | 350 | 54.00 | 6.09 | 2.14 | 15.43 | 5.92 | 3.55 | 33.13 |
| Fast | 615 | 325 | 46.30 | 5.12 | 2.11 | 14.25 | 6.65 | 1.97 | 30.10 |

*Roll 2nd finish coat*

| | | | | | | | | | |
|---|---|---|---|---|---|---|---|---|---|
| Slow | 275 | 400 | 61.70 | 7.36 | 2.18 | 15.43 | 4.74 | 4.75 | 34.46 |
| Medium | 453 | 375 | 54.00 | 5.68 | 2.03 | 14.40 | 5.52 | 3.31 | 30.94 |
| Fast | 630 | 350 | 46.30 | 5.00 | 2.05 | 13.23 | 6.28 | 1.86 | 28.42 |

*Roll 3rd or additional finish coats*

| | | | | | | | | | |
|---|---|---|---|---|---|---|---|---|---|
| Slow | 300 | 425 | 61.70 | 6.75 | 1.98 | 14.52 | 4.42 | 4.43 | 32.10 |
| Medium | 475 | 400 | 54.00 | 5.42 | 1.94 | 13.50 | 5.21 | 3.13 | 29.20 |
| Fast | 650 | 375 | 46.30 | 4.85 | 1.98 | 12.35 | 5.95 | 1.76 | 26.89 |

## National Painting Cost Estimator

|  | Labor SF per manhour | Material coverage SF/gallon | Material cost per gallon | Labor cost per 100 SF | Labor burden 100 SF | Material cost per 100 SF | Overhead per 100 SF | Profit per 100 SF | Total price per 100 SF |
|---|---|---|---|---|---|---|---|---|---|
| **Stipple finish** | | | | | | | | | |
| Slow | 130 | -- | -- | 15.58 | 4.58 | -- | 3.83 | 3.84 | 27.83 |
| Medium | 150 | -- | -- | 17.17 | 6.09 | -- | 5.81 | 3.49 | 32.56 |
| Fast | 170 | -- | -- | 18.53 | 7.55 | -- | 8.09 | 2.39 | 36.56 |
| **Epoxy coating, 2 part system - white (material #52)** | | | | | | | | | |
| *Roll 1st coat* | | | | | | | | | |
| Slow | 300 | 375 | 177.00 | 6.75 | 1.98 | 47.20 | 10.63 | 10.65 | 77.21 |
| Medium | 488 | 350 | 154.90 | 5.28 | 1.87 | 44.26 | 12.85 | 7.71 | 71.97 |
| Fast | 675 | 325 | 132.70 | 4.67 | 1.89 | 40.83 | 14.70 | 4.35 | 66.44 |
| *Roll 2nd or additional coats* | | | | | | | | | |
| Slow | 325 | 425 | 177.00 | 6.23 | 1.85 | 41.65 | 9.45 | 9.47 | 68.65 |
| Medium | 513 | 400 | 154.90 | 5.02 | 1.78 | 38.73 | 11.38 | 6.83 | 63.74 |
| Fast | 700 | 375 | 132.70 | 4.50 | 1.84 | 35.39 | 12.94 | 3.83 | 58.50 |

Measurements are based on the square feet of wall coated. Do not deduct for openings less than 100 square feet. These figures assume paint products are being applied over a smooth finish. For heights above 8 feet, use the High Time Difficulty Factors on page 139. These figures include brushing-in at corners when all walls are the same color, and at ceilings that are the same color or finished with acoustic spray-on texture. ADD for cutting-in at ceilings if they're a different color than the walls, or at corners where walls in the same room are painted different colors. Do not include cutting-in time for ceilings unless you're only painting the ceilings, not the walls. "Slow" work is based on an hourly wage of $20.25, "Medium" work on an hourly wage of $25.75, and "Fast" work on an hourly wage of $31.50. Other qualifications that apply to this table are on page 9.

*General Painting Costs*

| | Labor SF per manhour | Material coverage SF/gallon | Material cost per gallon | Labor cost per 100 SF | Labor burden 100 SF | Material cost per 100 SF | Overhead per 100 SF | Profit per 100 SF | Total price per 100 SF |
|---|---|---|---|---|---|---|---|---|---|

## Walls, plaster, interior, smooth finish, spray, per 100 SF of wall area

### Flat latex, water base (material #5)
**Spray 1st coat**

| | | | | | | | | | |
|---|---|---|---|---|---|---|---|---|---|
| Slow | 500 | 375 | 36.70 | 4.05 | 1.19 | 9.79 | 2.86 | 2.86 | 20.75 |
| Medium | 625 | 338 | 32.10 | 4.12 | 1.46 | 9.50 | 3.77 | 2.26 | 21.11 |
| Fast | 750 | 300 | 27.50 | 4.20 | 1.70 | 9.17 | 4.67 | 1.38 | 21.12 |

**Spray 2nd coat**

| | | | | | | | | | |
|---|---|---|---|---|---|---|---|---|---|
| Slow | 550 | 400 | 36.70 | 3.68 | 1.09 | 9.18 | 2.65 | 2.66 | 19.26 |
| Medium | 700 | 363 | 32.10 | 3.68 | 1.31 | 8.84 | 3.46 | 2.07 | 19.36 |
| Fast | 850 | 325 | 27.50 | 3.71 | 1.52 | 8.46 | 4.24 | 1.25 | 19.18 |

**Spray 3rd or additional coats**

| | | | | | | | | | |
|---|---|---|---|---|---|---|---|---|---|
| Slow | 600 | 425 | 36.70 | 3.38 | 1.00 | 8.64 | 2.47 | 2.48 | 17.97 |
| Medium | 775 | 388 | 32.10 | 3.32 | 1.18 | 8.27 | 3.19 | 1.92 | 17.88 |
| Fast | 950 | 350 | 27.50 | 3.32 | 1.34 | 7.86 | 3.88 | 1.15 | 17.55 |

### Enamel, water base (material #9)
**Spray 1st finish coat**

| | | | | | | | | | |
|---|---|---|---|---|---|---|---|---|---|
| Slow | 475 | 375 | 46.80 | 4.26 | 1.27 | 12.48 | 3.42 | 3.43 | 24.86 |
| Medium | 600 | 338 | 41.00 | 4.29 | 1.53 | 12.13 | 4.49 | 2.69 | 25.13 |
| Fast | 725 | 300 | 35.10 | 4.34 | 1.78 | 11.70 | 5.52 | 1.63 | 24.97 |

**Spray 2nd finish coat**

| | | | | | | | | | |
|---|---|---|---|---|---|---|---|---|---|
| Slow | 525 | 400 | 46.80 | 3.86 | 1.12 | 11.70 | 3.17 | 3.18 | 23.03 |
| Medium | 675 | 388 | 41.00 | 3.81 | 1.35 | 10.57 | 3.93 | 2.36 | 22.02 |
| Fast | 825 | 325 | 35.10 | 3.82 | 1.55 | 10.80 | 5.02 | 1.48 | 22.67 |

**Spray 3rd or additional finish coats**

| | | | | | | | | | |
|---|---|---|---|---|---|---|---|---|---|
| Slow | 575 | 425 | 46.80 | 3.52 | 1.04 | 11.01 | 2.96 | 2.96 | 21.49 |
| Medium | 775 | 388 | 41.00 | 3.32 | 1.18 | 10.57 | 3.77 | 2.26 | 21.10 |
| Fast | 925 | 350 | 35.10 | 3.41 | 1.38 | 10.03 | 4.60 | 1.36 | 20.78 |

### Enamel, oil base (material #10)
**Spray 1st finish coat**

| | | | | | | | | | |
|---|---|---|---|---|---|---|---|---|---|
| Slow | 475 | 425 | 61.70 | 4.26 | 1.27 | 14.52 | 3.81 | 3.82 | 27.68 |
| Medium | 575 | 388 | 54.00 | 4.48 | 1.59 | 13.92 | 5.00 | 3.00 | 27.99 |
| Fast | 725 | 350 | 46.30 | 4.34 | 1.78 | 13.23 | 6.00 | 1.77 | 27.12 |

**Spray 2nd finish coat**

| | | | | | | | | | |
|---|---|---|---|---|---|---|---|---|---|
| Slow | 525 | 450 | 61.70 | 3.86 | 1.12 | 13.71 | 3.55 | 3.56 | 25.80 |
| Medium | 675 | 413 | 54.00 | 3.81 | 1.35 | 13.08 | 4.56 | 2.74 | 25.54 |
| Fast | 825 | 375 | 46.30 | 3.82 | 1.55 | 12.35 | 5.50 | 1.63 | 24.85 |

*National Painting Cost Estimator*

|  | Labor SF per manhour | Material coverage SF/gallon | Material cost per gallon | Labor cost per 100 SF | Labor burden 100 SF | Material cost per 100 SF | Overhead per 100 SF | Profit per 100 SF | Total price per 100 SF |
|---|---|---|---|---|---|---|---|---|---|
| **Spray 3rd or additional finish coats** | | | | | | | | | |
| Slow | 575 | 475 | 61.70 | 3.52 | 1.04 | 12.99 | 3.33 | 3.34 | 24.22 |
| Medium | 750 | 438 | 54.00 | 3.43 | 1.21 | 12.33 | 4.24 | 2.55 | 23.76 |
| Fast | 925 | 400 | 46.30 | 3.41 | 1.38 | 11.58 | 5.08 | 1.50 | 22.95 |
| **Epoxy coating, 2 part system - white (material #52)** | | | | | | | | | |
| *Spray 1st coat* | | | | | | | | | |
| Slow | 550 | 325 | 177.00 | 3.68 | 1.09 | 54.46 | 11.25 | 11.28 | 81.76 |
| Medium | 700 | 300 | 154.90 | 3.68 | 1.31 | 51.63 | 14.15 | 8.49 | 79.26 |
| Fast | 850 | 275 | 132.70 | 3.71 | 1.52 | 48.25 | 16.58 | 4.90 | 74.96 |
| *Spray 2nd or additional coats* | | | | | | | | | |
| Slow | 600 | 375 | 177.00 | 3.38 | 1.00 | 47.20 | 9.80 | 9.82 | 71.20 |
| Medium | 750 | 350 | 154.90 | 3.43 | 1.21 | 44.26 | 12.23 | 7.34 | 68.47 |
| Fast | 900 | 325 | 132.70 | 3.50 | 1.42 | 40.83 | 14.19 | 4.20 | 64.14 |

Measurements are based on the square feet of wall coated. Do not deduct for openings less than 100 square feet. These figures assume paint products are being applied over a smooth finish. For heights above 8 feet, use the High Time Difficulty Factors on page 139. These figures include spraying at corners when all walls are the same color, and at ceiling-to-wall intersection when ceilings are the same color. ADD for cutting-in at ceilings and protecting adjacent surfaces from overspray if they're a different color than the walls, or at corners where walls in the same room are painted different colors. Do not include cutting-in time for ceilings unless you're only painting the ceilings, not the walls. "Slow" work is based on an hourly wage of $20.25, "Medium" work on an hourly wage of $25.75, and "Fast" work on an hourly wage of $31.50. Other qualifications that apply to this table are on page 9.

*General Painting Costs*

|  | Labor SF per manhour | Material coverage SF/gallon | Material cost per gallon | Labor cost per 100 SF | Labor burden 100 SF | Material cost per 100 SF | Overhead per 100 SF | Profit per 100 SF | Total price per 100 SF |
|---|---|---|---|---|---|---|---|---|---|

**Walls, wood paneled, interior, paint grade, brush, per 100 SF of wall area**

Undercoat, water base (material #3)
 Brush, 1 coat

| | | | | | | | | | |
|---|---|---|---|---|---|---|---|---|---|
| Slow | 65 | 300 | 32.60 | 31.15 | 9.18 | 10.87 | 9.73 | 9.75 | 70.68 |
| Medium | 75 | 288 | 28.50 | 34.33 | 12.15 | 9.90 | 14.10 | 8.46 | 78.94 |
| Fast | 85 | 275 | 24.50 | 37.06 | 15.10 | 8.91 | 18.94 | 5.60 | 85.61 |

Undercoat, oil base (material #4)
 Brush, 1 coat

| | | | | | | | | | |
|---|---|---|---|---|---|---|---|---|---|
| Slow | 65 | 375 | 42.30 | 31.15 | 9.18 | 11.28 | 9.81 | 9.83 | 71.25 |
| Medium | 75 | 363 | 37.00 | 34.33 | 12.15 | 10.19 | 14.17 | 8.50 | 79.34 |
| Fast | 85 | 350 | 31.80 | 37.06 | 15.10 | 9.09 | 18.99 | 5.62 | 85.86 |

Split coat (1/2 undercoat + 1/2 enamel), water base (material #3 & #9)
 Brush, 1 coat

| | | | | | | | | | |
|---|---|---|---|---|---|---|---|---|---|
| Slow | 55 | 300 | 39.70 | 36.82 | 10.85 | 13.23 | 11.57 | 11.60 | 84.07 |
| Medium | 65 | 288 | 34.75 | 39.62 | 14.01 | 12.07 | 16.43 | 9.86 | 91.99 |
| Fast | 75 | 275 | 29.80 | 42.00 | 17.12 | 10.84 | 21.69 | 6.42 | 98.07 |

Split coat (1/2 undercoat + 1/2 enamel), oil base (material #4 & #10)
 Brush, 1 coat

| | | | | | | | | | |
|---|---|---|---|---|---|---|---|---|---|
| Slow | 55 | 375 | 52.00 | 36.82 | 10.85 | 13.87 | 11.69 | 11.72 | 84.95 |
| Medium | 65 | 363 | 45.50 | 39.62 | 14.01 | 12.53 | 16.55 | 9.93 | 92.64 |
| Fast | 75 | 350 | 39.05 | 42.00 | 17.12 | 11.16 | 21.79 | 6.45 | 98.52 |

Enamel, water base (material #9)
 Brush 1st finish coat

| | | | | | | | | | |
|---|---|---|---|---|---|---|---|---|---|
| Slow | 80 | 350 | 46.80 | 25.31 | 7.47 | 13.37 | 8.77 | 8.79 | 63.71 |
| Medium | 95 | 338 | 41.00 | 27.11 | 9.61 | 12.13 | 12.21 | 7.33 | 68.39 |
| Fast | 110 | 325 | 35.10 | 28.64 | 11.67 | 10.80 | 15.85 | 4.69 | 71.65 |

 Brush 2nd or additional finish coats

| | | | | | | | | | |
|---|---|---|---|---|---|---|---|---|---|
| Slow | 100 | 375 | 46.80 | 20.25 | 5.97 | 12.48 | 7.35 | 7.37 | 53.42 |
| Medium | 110 | 363 | 41.00 | 23.41 | 8.29 | 11.29 | 10.75 | 6.45 | 60.19 |
| Fast | 120 | 350 | 35.10 | 26.25 | 10.69 | 10.03 | 14.57 | 4.31 | 65.85 |

*National Painting Cost Estimator*

|  | Labor SF per manhour | Material coverage SF/gallon | Material cost per gallon | Labor cost per 100 SF | Labor burden 100 SF | Material cost per 100 SF | Overhead per 100 SF | Profit per 100 SF | Total price per 100 SF |
|---|---|---|---|---|---|---|---|---|---|
| **Enamel, oil base (material #10)** | | | | | | | | | |
| Brush 1st finish coat | | | | | | | | | |
| Slow | 80 | 400 | 61.70 | 25.31 | 7.47 | 15.43 | 9.16 | 9.18 | 66.55 |
| Medium | 95 | 388 | 54.00 | 27.11 | 9.61 | 13.92 | 12.66 | 7.59 | 70.89 |
| Fast | 110 | 375 | 46.30 | 28.64 | 11.67 | 12.35 | 16.33 | 4.83 | 73.82 |
| Brush 2nd or additional finish coats | | | | | | | | | |
| Slow | 100 | 425 | 61.70 | 20.25 | 5.97 | 14.52 | 7.74 | 7.76 | 56.24 |
| Medium | 110 | 413 | 54.00 | 23.41 | 8.29 | 13.08 | 11.20 | 6.72 | 62.70 |
| Fast | 120 | 400 | 46.30 | 26.25 | 10.69 | 11.58 | 15.05 | 4.45 | 68.02 |

These costs are based on painting interior tongue and groove, wood veneer or plain wainscot wood paneling. Do not deduct for openings less than 100 square feet. For heights above 8 feet, use the High Time Difficulty Factors on page 139. ADD for masking-off or cutting-in at wall-to-ceiling intersections and for protecting adjacent surfaces as necessary. "Slow" work is based on an hourly wage of $20.25, "Medium" work on an hourly wage of $25.75, and "Fast" work on an hourly wage of $31.50. Other qualifications that apply to this table are on page 9.

*General Painting Costs*

|  | Labor SF per manhour | Material coverage SF/gallon | Material cost per gallon | Labor cost per 100 SF | Labor burden 100 SF | Material cost per 100 SF | Overhead per 100 SF | Profit per 100 SF | Total price per 100 SF |
|---|---|---|---|---|---|---|---|---|---|

## Walls, wood paneled, interior, paint grade, roll, per 100 SF of wall area

Undercoat, water base (material #3)
  Roll, 1 coat

| | | | | | | | | | |
|---|---|---|---|---|---|---|---|---|---|
| Slow | 200 | 275 | 32.60 | 10.13 | 2.98 | 11.85 | 4.74 | 4.75 | 34.45 |
| Medium | 300 | 263 | 28.50 | 8.58 | 3.03 | 10.84 | 5.62 | 3.37 | 31.44 |
| Fast | 400 | 250 | 24.50 | 7.88 | 3.21 | 9.80 | 6.48 | 1.92 | 29.29 |

Undercoat, oil base (material #4)
  Roll, 1 coat

| | | | | | | | | | |
|---|---|---|---|---|---|---|---|---|---|
| Slow | 200 | 350 | 42.30 | 10.13 | 2.98 | 12.09 | 4.79 | 4.80 | 34.79 |
| Medium | 300 | 325 | 37.00 | 8.58 | 3.03 | 11.38 | 5.75 | 3.45 | 32.19 |
| Fast | 400 | 300 | 31.80 | 7.88 | 3.21 | 10.60 | 6.73 | 1.99 | 30.41 |

Split coat (1/2 undercoat + 1/2 enamel), water base (material #3 & #9)
  Roll, 1 coat

| | | | | | | | | | |
|---|---|---|---|---|---|---|---|---|---|
| Slow | 175 | 275 | 39.70 | 11.57 | 3.40 | 14.44 | 5.59 | 5.60 | 40.60 |
| Medium | 275 | 263 | 34.75 | 9.36 | 3.33 | 13.21 | 6.47 | 3.88 | 36.25 |
| Fast | 375 | 250 | 29.80 | 8.40 | 3.44 | 11.92 | 7.36 | 2.18 | 33.30 |

Split coat (1/2 undercoat + 1/2 enamel), oil base (material #4 & #10)
  Roll, 1 coat

| | | | | | | | | | |
|---|---|---|---|---|---|---|---|---|---|
| Slow | 175 | 350 | 52.00 | 11.57 | 3.40 | 14.86 | 5.67 | 5.68 | 41.18 |
| Medium | 275 | 325 | 45.50 | 9.36 | 3.33 | 14.00 | 6.67 | 4.00 | 37.36 |
| Fast | 375 | 300 | 39.05 | 8.40 | 3.44 | 13.02 | 7.70 | 2.28 | 34.84 |

Enamel, water base (material #9)
  Roll 1st finish coat

| | | | | | | | | | |
|---|---|---|---|---|---|---|---|---|---|
| Slow | 250 | 325 | 46.80 | 8.10 | 2.39 | 14.40 | 4.73 | 4.74 | 34.36 |
| Medium | 375 | 313 | 41.00 | 6.87 | 2.44 | 13.10 | 5.60 | 3.36 | 31.37 |
| Fast | 500 | 300 | 35.10 | 6.30 | 2.57 | 11.70 | 6.38 | 1.89 | 28.84 |

  Roll 2nd or additional finish coats

| | | | | | | | | | |
|---|---|---|---|---|---|---|---|---|---|
| Slow | 300 | 350 | 46.80 | 6.75 | 1.98 | 13.37 | 4.20 | 4.21 | 30.51 |
| Medium | 425 | 338 | 41.00 | 6.06 | 2.13 | 12.13 | 5.09 | 3.05 | 28.46 |
| Fast | 550 | 325 | 35.10 | 5.73 | 2.34 | 10.80 | 5.85 | 1.73 | 26.45 |

|  | Labor SF per manhour | Material coverage SF/gallon | Material cost per gallon | Labor cost per 100 SF | Labor burden 100 SF | Material cost per 100 SF | Overhead per 100 SF | Profit per 100 SF | Total price per 100 SF |
|---|---|---|---|---|---|---|---|---|---|
| **Enamel, oil base (material #10)** | | | | | | | | | |
| Roll 1st finish coat | | | | | | | | | |
| Slow | 250 | 375 | 61.70 | 8.10 | 2.39 | 16.45 | 5.12 | 5.13 | 37.19 |
| Medium | 375 | 363 | 54.00 | 6.87 | 2.44 | 14.88 | 6.05 | 3.63 | 33.87 |
| Fast | 500 | 350 | 46.30 | 6.30 | 2.57 | 13.23 | 6.85 | 2.03 | 30.98 |
| Roll 2nd or additional finish coats | | | | | | | | | |
| Slow | 300 | 400 | 61.70 | 6.75 | 1.98 | 15.43 | 4.59 | 4.60 | 33.35 |
| Medium | 425 | 388 | 54.00 | 6.06 | 2.13 | 13.92 | 5.53 | 3.32 | 30.96 |
| Fast | 550 | 375 | 46.30 | 5.73 | 2.34 | 12.35 | 6.33 | 1.87 | 28.62 |

These costs are based on painting interior tongue and groove, wood veneer or plain wainscot wood paneling. Do not deduct for openings less than 100 square feet. For heights above 8 feet, use the High Time Difficulty Factors on page 139. ADD for masking-off or cutting-in at wall-to-ceiling intersections and for protecting adjacent surfaces as necessary. "Slow" work is based on an hourly wage of $20.25, "Medium" work on an hourly wage of $25.75, and "Fast" work on an hourly wage of $31.50. Other qualifications that apply to this table are on page 9.

*General Painting Costs*

| | Labor SF per manhour | Material coverage SF/gallon | Material cost per gallon | Labor cost per 100 SF | Labor burden 100 SF | Material cost per 100 SF | Overhead per 100 SF | Profit per 100 SF | Total price per 100 SF |
|---|---|---|---|---|---|---|---|---|---|

## Walls, wood paneled, interior, paint grade, spray, per 100 SF of wall area

Undercoat, water base (material #3)
  Spray, 1 coat

| | | | | | | | | | |
|---|---|---|---|---|---|---|---|---|---|
| Slow | 350 | 175 | 32.60 | 5.79 | 1.71 | 18.63 | 4.96 | 4.97 | 36.06 |
| Medium | 425 | 150 | 28.50 | 6.06 | 2.13 | 19.00 | 6.80 | 4.08 | 38.07 |
| Fast | 500 | 125 | 24.50 | 6.30 | 2.57 | 19.60 | 8.83 | 2.61 | 39.91 |

Undercoat, oil base (material #4)
  Spray, 1 coat

| | | | | | | | | | |
|---|---|---|---|---|---|---|---|---|---|
| Slow | 350 | 200 | 42.30 | 5.79 | 1.71 | 21.15 | 5.44 | 5.45 | 39.54 |
| Medium | 425 | 188 | 37.00 | 6.06 | 2.13 | 19.68 | 6.97 | 4.18 | 39.02 |
| Fast | 500 | 175 | 31.80 | 6.30 | 2.57 | 18.17 | 8.38 | 2.48 | 37.90 |

Split coat (1/2 undercoat + 1/2 enamel), water base (material #3 & #9)
  Spray, 1 coat

| | | | | | | | | | |
|---|---|---|---|---|---|---|---|---|---|
| Slow | 325 | 175 | 39.70 | 6.23 | 1.85 | 22.69 | 5.84 | 5.86 | 42.47 |
| Medium | 400 | 150 | 34.75 | 6.44 | 2.28 | 23.17 | 7.97 | 4.78 | 44.64 |
| Fast | 475 | 125 | 29.80 | 6.63 | 2.73 | 23.84 | 10.29 | 3.04 | 46.53 |

Split coat (1/2 undercoat + 1/2 enamel), oil base (material #4 & #10)
  Spray, 1 coat

| | | | | | | | | | |
|---|---|---|---|---|---|---|---|---|---|
| Slow | 325 | 200 | 52.00 | 6.23 | 1.85 | 26.00 | 6.47 | 6.49 | 47.04 |
| Medium | 400 | 188 | 45.50 | 6.44 | 2.28 | 24.20 | 8.23 | 4.94 | 46.09 |
| Fast | 475 | 175 | 39.05 | 6.63 | 2.73 | 22.31 | 9.81 | 2.90 | 44.38 |

Enamel, water base (material #9)
  Spray 1st finish coat

| | | | | | | | | | |
|---|---|---|---|---|---|---|---|---|---|
| Slow | 500 | 250 | 46.80 | 4.05 | 1.19 | 18.72 | 4.55 | 4.56 | 33.07 |
| Medium | 550 | 225 | 41.00 | 4.68 | 1.67 | 18.22 | 6.14 | 3.68 | 34.39 |
| Fast | 600 | 200 | 35.10 | 5.25 | 2.16 | 17.55 | 7.73 | 2.29 | 34.98 |

  Spray 2nd or additional finish coats

| | | | | | | | | | |
|---|---|---|---|---|---|---|---|---|---|
| Slow | 600 | 350 | 46.80 | 3.38 | 1.00 | 13.37 | 3.37 | 3.38 | 24.50 |
| Medium | 650 | 325 | 41.00 | 3.96 | 1.41 | 12.62 | 4.50 | 2.70 | 25.19 |
| Fast | 700 | 300 | 35.10 | 4.50 | 1.84 | 11.70 | 5.59 | 1.65 | 25.28 |

|  | Labor SF per manhour | Material coverage SF/gallon | Material cost per gallon | Labor cost per 100 SF | Labor burden 100 SF | Material cost per 100 SF | Overhead per 100 SF | Profit per 100 SF | Total price per 100 SF |
|---|---|---|---|---|---|---|---|---|---|
| **Enamel, oil base (material #10)** | | | | | | | | | |
| Spray 1st finish coat | | | | | | | | | |
| Slow | 500 | 300 | 61.70 | 4.05 | 1.19 | 20.57 | 4.90 | 4.91 | 35.62 |
| Medium | 550 | 275 | 54.00 | 4.68 | 1.67 | 19.64 | 6.50 | 3.90 | 36.39 |
| Fast | 600 | 250 | 46.30 | 5.25 | 2.16 | 18.52 | 8.03 | 2.38 | 36.34 |
| Spray 2nd or additional finish coats | | | | | | | | | |
| Slow | 600 | 400 | 61.70 | 3.38 | 1.00 | 15.43 | 3.76 | 3.77 | 27.34 |
| Medium | 650 | 375 | 54.00 | 3.96 | 1.41 | 14.40 | 4.94 | 2.96 | 27.67 |
| Fast | 700 | 350 | 46.30 | 4.50 | 1.84 | 13.23 | 6.07 | 1.79 | 27.43 |

These costs are based on painting interior tongue and groove, wood veneer or plain wainscot wood paneling. Do not deduct for openings less than 100 square feet. For heights above 8 feet, use the High Time Difficulty Factors on page 139. ADD for masking-off or cutting-in at wall-to-ceiling intersections and for protecting adjacent surfaces as necessary. "Slow" work is based on an hourly wage of $20.25, "Medium" work on an hourly wage of $25.75, and "Fast" work on an hourly wage of $31.50. Other qualifications that apply to this table are on page 9.

*General Painting Costs*

|  | Labor SF per manhour | Material coverage SF/gallon | Material cost per gallon | Labor cost per 100 SF | Labor burden 100 SF | Material cost per 100 SF | Overhead per 100 SF | Profit per 100 SF | Total price per 100 SF |
|---|---|---|---|---|---|---|---|---|---|

### Walls, wood paneled, interior, stain grade, per 100 SF of wall area

Solid body or semi-transparent stain, water or oil base (material #18 or #19 or #20 or #21)
Roll & brush each coat

| | | | | | | | | | |
|---|---|---|---|---|---|---|---|---|---|
| Slow | 225 | 500 | 48.83 | 9.00 | 2.64 | 9.77 | 4.07 | 4.08 | 29.56 |
| Medium | 263 | 450 | 42.73 | 9.79 | 3.46 | 9.50 | 5.69 | 3.41 | 31.85 |
| Fast | 300 | 400 | 36.60 | 10.50 | 4.27 | 9.15 | 7.42 | 2.19 | 33.53 |

Solid body or semi-transparent stain, water or oil base (material #18 or #19 or #20 or #21)
Spray each coat

| | | | | | | | | | |
|---|---|---|---|---|---|---|---|---|---|
| Slow | 350 | 300 | 48.83 | 5.79 | 1.71 | 16.28 | 4.52 | 4.53 | 32.83 |
| Medium | 400 | 250 | 42.73 | 6.44 | 2.28 | 17.09 | 6.45 | 3.87 | 36.13 |
| Fast | 450 | 200 | 36.60 | 7.00 | 2.85 | 18.30 | 8.73 | 2.58 | 39.46 |

Use these figures for quantities greater than 100 square feet. For quantities less than 100 square feet, use Fireplace siding. These costs are based on painting interior tongue and groove, wood veneer or plain wainscot wood paneling. Do not deduct for openings less than 100 square feet. For heights above 8 feet, use the High Time Difficulty Factors on page 139. ADD for masking-off or cutting-in at wall-to-ceiling intersections and for protecting adjacent surfaces as necessary. "Slow" work is based on an hourly wage of $20.25, "Medium" work on an hourly wage of $25.75, and "Fast" work on an hourly wage of $31.50. Other qualifications that apply to this table are on page 9.

|  | Labor SF per manhour | Material coverage SF/gallon | Material cost per gallon | Labor cost per 100 SF | Labor burden 100 SF | Material cost per 100 SF | Overhead per 100 SF | Profit per 100 SF | Total price per 100 SF |
|---|---|---|---|---|---|---|---|---|---|

## Walls, wood paneled, interior, stain grade, per 100 SF of wall area, brush

Stain, seal and 2 coat lacquer system (7 step process)
STEP 1: Sand & putty

| | | | | | | | | | |
|---|---|---|---|---|---|---|---|---|---|
| Slow | 175 | -- | -- | 11.57 | 3.40 | -- | 2.85 | 2.85 | 20.67 |
| Medium | 200 | -- | -- | 12.88 | 4.56 | -- | 4.36 | 2.62 | 24.42 |
| Fast | 225 | -- | -- | 14.00 | 5.69 | -- | 6.11 | 1.81 | 27.61 |

STEP 2 & 3: Wiping stain, oil base (material #11a) & wipe
Brush 1 coat & wipe

| | | | | | | | | | |
|---|---|---|---|---|---|---|---|---|---|
| Slow | 100 | 400 | 51.30 | 20.25 | 5.97 | 12.83 | 7.42 | 7.44 | 53.91 |
| Medium | 125 | 375 | 44.90 | 20.60 | 7.30 | 11.97 | 9.97 | 5.98 | 55.82 |
| Fast | 150 | 350 | 38.50 | 21.00 | 8.58 | 11.00 | 12.58 | 3.72 | 56.88 |

STEP 4 & 5: Sanding sealer (material #11b) & sand lightly
Brush 1 coat & wipe

| | | | | | | | | | |
|---|---|---|---|---|---|---|---|---|---|
| Slow | 200 | 450 | 41.50 | 10.13 | 2.98 | 9.22 | 4.24 | 4.25 | 30.82 |
| Medium | 220 | 425 | 36.30 | 11.70 | 4.17 | 8.54 | 6.10 | 3.66 | 34.17 |
| Fast | 240 | 400 | 31.10 | 13.13 | 5.36 | 7.78 | 8.14 | 2.41 | 36.82 |

STEP 6 & 7: Lacquer, 2 coats (material #11c)
Brush 1st coat

| | | | | | | | | | |
|---|---|---|---|---|---|---|---|---|---|
| Slow | 175 | 375 | 45.90 | 11.57 | 3.40 | 12.24 | 5.17 | 5.18 | 37.56 |
| Medium | 225 | 350 | 40.10 | 11.44 | 4.04 | 11.46 | 6.74 | 4.04 | 37.72 |
| Fast | 300 | 325 | 34.40 | 10.50 | 4.27 | 10.58 | 7.86 | 2.33 | 35.54 |

Brush 2nd coat

| | | | | | | | | | |
|---|---|---|---|---|---|---|---|---|---|
| Slow | 225 | 400 | 45.90 | 9.00 | 2.64 | 11.48 | 4.40 | 4.41 | 31.93 |
| Medium | 288 | 388 | 40.10 | 8.94 | 3.16 | 10.34 | 5.61 | 3.37 | 31.42 |
| Fast | 350 | 375 | 34.40 | 9.00 | 3.68 | 9.17 | 6.77 | 2.00 | 30.62 |

Complete 7 step stain, seal & 2 coat lacquer system (material #11)
Brush all coats

| | | | | | | | | | |
|---|---|---|---|---|---|---|---|---|---|
| Slow | 40 | 170 | 46.10 | 50.63 | 14.92 | 27.12 | 17.61 | 17.65 | 127.93 |
| Medium | 45 | 158 | 40.40 | 57.22 | 20.26 | 25.57 | 25.76 | 15.46 | 144.27 |
| Fast | 50 | 145 | 34.60 | 63.00 | 25.70 | 23.86 | 34.89 | 10.32 | 157.77 |

Penetrating stain wax (material #14)
Brush each coat

| | | | | | | | | | |
|---|---|---|---|---|---|---|---|---|---|
| Slow | 300 | 500 | 46.70 | 6.75 | 1.98 | 9.34 | 3.44 | 3.44 | 24.95 |
| Medium | 350 | 475 | 40.90 | 7.36 | 2.61 | 8.61 | 4.65 | 2.79 | 26.02 |
| Fast | 400 | 450 | 35.00 | 7.88 | 3.21 | 7.78 | 5.85 | 1.73 | 26.45 |

These costs are based on painting interior tongue and groove, wood veneer or plain wainscot wood paneling. Do not deduct for openings less than 100 square feet. For heights above 8 feet, use the High Time Difficulty Factors on page 139. ADD for masking-off or cutting-in at wall-to-ceiling intersections and for protecting adjacent surfaces as necessary. "Slow" work is based on an hourly wage of $20.25, "Medium" work on an hourly wage of $25.75, and "Fast" work on an hourly wage of $31.50. Other qualifications that apply to this table are on page 9.

*General Painting Costs*

|  | Labor SF per manhour | Material coverage SF/gallon | Material cost per gallon | Labor cost per 100 SF | Labor burden 100 SF | Material cost per 100 SF | Overhead per 100 SF | Profit per 100 SF | Total price per 100 SF |
|---|---|---|---|---|---|---|---|---|---|

## Walls, wood paneled, interior, stain grade, per 100 SF of wall area, spray

Stain, seal and 2 coat lacquer system (7 step process)

STEP 1: Sand & putty

| | | | | | | | | | |
|---|---|---|---|---|---|---|---|---|---|
| Slow | 175 | -- | -- | 11.57 | 3.40 | -- | 2.85 | 2.85 | 20.67 |
| Medium | 200 | -- | -- | 12.88 | 4.56 | -- | 4.36 | 2.62 | 24.42 |
| Fast | 225 | -- | -- | 14.00 | 5.69 | -- | 6.11 | 1.81 | 27.61 |

STEP 2 & 3: Wiping stain, oil base (material #11a) & wipe
Spray 1 coat & wipe

| | | | | | | | | | |
|---|---|---|---|---|---|---|---|---|---|
| Slow | 350 | 175 | 51.30 | 5.79 | 1.71 | 29.31 | 6.99 | 7.01 | 50.81 |
| Medium | 425 | 150 | 44.90 | 6.06 | 2.13 | 29.93 | 9.54 | 5.72 | 53.38 |
| Fast | 500 | 125 | 38.50 | 6.30 | 2.57 | 30.80 | 12.30 | 3.64 | 55.61 |

STEP 4 & 5: Sanding sealer (material #11b) & sand lightly
Spray 1 coat & wipe

| | | | | | | | | | |
|---|---|---|---|---|---|---|---|---|---|
| Slow | 400 | 175 | 41.50 | 5.06 | 1.50 | 23.71 | 5.75 | 5.76 | 41.78 |
| Medium | 500 | 150 | 36.30 | 5.15 | 1.82 | 24.20 | 7.79 | 4.68 | 43.64 |
| Fast | 600 | 125 | 31.10 | 5.25 | 2.16 | 24.88 | 10.00 | 2.96 | 45.25 |

STEP 6 & 7: Lacquer, 2 coats (material #11c)
Spray 1st coat

| | | | | | | | | | |
|---|---|---|---|---|---|---|---|---|---|
| Slow | 450 | 150 | 45.90 | 4.50 | 1.32 | 30.60 | 6.92 | 6.94 | 50.28 |
| Medium | 550 | 125 | 40.10 | 4.68 | 1.67 | 32.08 | 9.61 | 5.76 | 53.80 |
| Fast | 650 | 100 | 34.40 | 4.85 | 1.98 | 34.40 | 12.78 | 3.78 | 57.79 |

Spray 2nd coat

| | | | | | | | | | |
|---|---|---|---|---|---|---|---|---|---|
| Slow | 450 | 225 | 45.90 | 4.50 | 1.32 | 20.40 | 4.98 | 4.99 | 36.19 |
| Medium | 550 | 200 | 40.10 | 4.68 | 1.67 | 20.05 | 6.60 | 3.96 | 36.96 |
| Fast | 650 | 175 | 34.40 | 4.85 | 1.98 | 19.66 | 8.21 | 2.43 | 37.13 |

Complete 7 step stain, seal & 2 coat lacquer system (material #11)
Spray all coats

| | | | | | | | | | |
|---|---|---|---|---|---|---|---|---|---|
| Slow | 70 | 60 | 46.10 | 28.93 | 8.54 | 76.83 | 21.72 | 21.76 | 157.78 |
| Medium | 80 | 50 | 40.40 | 32.19 | 11.40 | 80.80 | 31.10 | 18.66 | 174.15 |
| Fast | 90 | 40 | 34.60 | 35.00 | 14.27 | 86.50 | 42.09 | 12.45 | 190.31 |

These costs are based on painting interior tongue and groove, wood veneer or plain wainscot wood paneling. Do not deduct for openings less than 100 square feet. For heights above 8 feet, use the High Time Difficulty Factors on page 139. ADD for masking-off or cutting-in at wall-to-ceiling intersections and for protecting adjacent surfaces as necessary. "Slow" work is based on an hourly wage of $20.25, "Medium" work on an hourly wage of $25.75, and "Fast" work on an hourly wage of $31.50. Other qualifications that apply to this table are on page 9.

275

|  | Frames per manhour | Frames per gallon | Material cost per gallon | Labor cost per frame | Labor burden frame | Material cost per frame | Overhead per frame | Profit per frame | Total price per frame |
|---|---|---|---|---|---|---|---|---|---|

### Window screen frames, paint grade, per frame (15 square feet)
Undercoat, water or oil base (material #3 or #4)
  Brush 1 coat

| | | | | | | | | | |
|---|---|---|---|---|---|---|---|---|---|
| Slow | 5 | 50 | 37.45 | 4.05 | 1.19 | .75 | 1.14 | 1.14 | 8.27 |
| Medium | 6 | 45 | 32.75 | 4.29 | 1.53 | .73 | 1.64 | .98 | 9.17 |
| Fast | 7 | 40 | 28.15 | 4.50 | 1.84 | .70 | 2.18 | .65 | 9.87 |

Split coat (1/2 undercoat + 1/2 enamel), water or oil base (material #3 or #4 or #9 or #10)
  Brush 1 coat

| | | | | | | | | | |
|---|---|---|---|---|---|---|---|---|---|
| Slow | 8 | 60 | 45.85 | 2.53 | .75 | .76 | .77 | .77 | 5.58 |
| Medium | 9 | 58 | 40.13 | 2.86 | 1.01 | .69 | 1.14 | .68 | 6.38 |
| Fast | 10 | 55 | 34.43 | 3.15 | 1.29 | .63 | 1.57 | .46 | 7.10 |

Enamel, water or oil base (material #9 or #10)
  Brush each finish coat

| | | | | | | | | | |
|---|---|---|---|---|---|---|---|---|---|
| Slow | 6 | 55 | 54.25 | 3.38 | 1.00 | .99 | 1.02 | 1.02 | 7.41 |
| Medium | 7 | 53 | 47.50 | 3.68 | 1.31 | .90 | 1.47 | .88 | 8.24 |
| Fast | 8 | 50 | 40.70 | 3.94 | 1.60 | .81 | 1.97 | .58 | 8.90 |

These figures will apply when painting all sides of wood window screens up to 15 square feet (length times width). Add: Preparation time for protecting adjacent surfaces with masking tape and paper as required. "Slow" work is based on an hourly wage of $20.25, "Medium" work on an hourly wage of $25.75, and "Fast" work on an hourly wage of $31.50. Other qualifications that apply to this table are on page 9.

*General Painting Costs*

|  | Labor SF per manhour | Material coverage SF/gallon | Material cost per gallon | Labor cost per 100 SF | Labor burden 100 SF | Material cost per 100 SF | Overhead per 100 SF | Profit per 100 SF | Total price per 100 SF |
|---|---|---|---|---|---|---|---|---|---|

### Window seats, wood, paint grade, per 100 square feet coated

Undercoat, water or oil base (material #3 or #4)
  Brush 1 coat

| | | | | | | | | | |
|---|---|---|---|---|---|---|---|---|---|
| Slow | 20 | 45 | 37.45 | 101.25 | 29.85 | 83.22 | 40.72 | 40.81 | 295.85 |
| Medium | 25 | 43 | 32.75 | 103.00 | 36.48 | 76.16 | 53.91 | 32.34 | 301.89 |
| Fast | 30 | 40 | 28.15 | 105.00 | 42.82 | 70.38 | 67.65 | 20.01 | 305.86 |

Split coat (1/2 undercoat + 1/2 enamel), water or oil base (material #3 or #4 or #9 or #10)
  Brush 1 coat

| | | | | | | | | | |
|---|---|---|---|---|---|---|---|---|---|
| Slow | 30 | 60 | 45.85 | 67.50 | 19.89 | 76.42 | 31.13 | 31.19 | 226.13 |
| Medium | 35 | 58 | 40.13 | 73.57 | 26.05 | 69.19 | 42.20 | 25.32 | 236.33 |
| Fast | 40 | 55 | 34.43 | 78.75 | 32.13 | 62.60 | 53.78 | 15.91 | 243.17 |

Enamel, water or oil base (material #9 or #10)
  Brush each finish coat

| | | | | | | | | | |
|---|---|---|---|---|---|---|---|---|---|
| Slow | 25 | 55 | 54.25 | 81.00 | 23.88 | 98.64 | 38.67 | 38.75 | 280.94 |
| Medium | 30 | 53 | 47.50 | 85.83 | 30.39 | 89.62 | 51.46 | 30.87 | 288.17 |
| Fast | 35 | 50 | 40.70 | 90.00 | 36.71 | 81.40 | 64.52 | 19.08 | 291.71 |

Measurements are based on square feet of surface area of each window seat. "Slow" work is based on an hourly wage of $20.25, "Medium" work on an hourly wage of $25.75, and "Fast" work on an hourly wage of $31.50. Other qualifications that apply to this table are on page 9.

|  | Labor LF per manhour | Material coverage LF/gallon | Material cost per gallon | Labor cost per 100 LF | Labor burden 100 LF | Material cost per 100 LF | Overhead per 100 LF | Profit per 100 LF | Total price per 100 LF |
|---|---|---|---|---|---|---|---|---|---|

### Window sills, wood, paint grade, per 100 linear feet coated

Undercoat, water or oil base (material #3 or #4)
  Brush 1 coat

| | | | | | | | | | |
|---|---|---|---|---|---|---|---|---|---|
| Slow | 40 | 140 | 37.45 | 50.63 | 14.92 | 26.75 | 17.54 | 17.58 | 127.42 |
| Medium | 50 | 130 | 32.75 | 51.50 | 18.24 | 25.19 | 23.73 | 14.24 | 132.90 |
| Fast | 60 | 120 | 28.15 | 52.50 | 21.43 | 23.46 | 30.19 | 8.93 | 136.51 |

Split coat (1/2 undercoat + 1/2 enamel), water or oil base (material #3 or #4 or #9 or #10)
  Brush 1 coat

| | | | | | | | | | |
|---|---|---|---|---|---|---|---|---|---|
| Slow | 60 | 180 | 45.85 | 33.75 | 9.96 | 25.47 | 13.14 | 13.17 | 95.49 |
| Medium | 70 | 170 | 40.13 | 36.79 | 13.04 | 23.61 | 18.36 | 11.01 | 102.81 |
| Fast | 80 | 160 | 34.43 | 39.38 | 16.06 | 21.52 | 23.86 | 7.06 | 107.88 |

Enamel, water or oil base (material #9 or #10)
  Brush each finish coat

| | | | | | | | | | |
|---|---|---|---|---|---|---|---|---|---|
| Slow | 50 | 175 | 54.25 | 40.50 | 11.94 | 31.00 | 15.86 | 15.89 | 115.19 |
| Medium | 60 | 163 | 47.50 | 42.92 | 15.21 | 29.14 | 21.81 | 13.09 | 122.17 |
| Fast | 70 | 150 | 40.70 | 45.00 | 18.38 | 27.13 | 28.05 | 8.30 | 126.86 |

Measurements are based on linear feet of each window sill. Add: Preparation time for protecting adjacent surfaces with masking tape and paper as required. "Slow" work is based on an hourly wage of $20.25, "Medium" work on an hourly wage of $25.75, and "Fast" work on an hourly wage of $31.50. Other qualifications that apply to this table are on page 9.

|  | Frames per manhour | Frames per gallon | Material cost per gallon | Labor cost per frame | Labor burden frame | Material cost per frame | Overhead per frame | Profit per frame | Total price per frame |
|---|---|---|---|---|---|---|---|---|---|

### Window storm sash, paint grade, per 15 square feet painted
Undercoat, water or oil base (material #3 or #4)
  Brush 1 coat

|  |  |  |  |  |  |  |  |  |  |
|---|---|---|---|---|---|---|---|---|---|
| Slow | 3 | 25 | 37.45 | 6.75 | 1.98 | 1.50 | 1.95 | 1.95 | 14.13 |
| Medium | 4 | 24 | 32.75 | 6.44 | 2.28 | 1.36 | 2.52 | 1.51 | 14.11 |
| Fast | 5 | 22 | 28.15 | 6.30 | 2.57 | 1.28 | 3.15 | .93 | 14.23 |

Split coat (1/2 undercoat + 1/2 enamel), water or oil base (material #3 or #4 or #9 or #10)
  Brush 1 coat

|  |  |  |  |  |  |  |  |  |  |
|---|---|---|---|---|---|---|---|---|---|
| Slow | 5 | 35 | 45.85 | 4.05 | 1.19 | 1.31 | 1.24 | 1.25 | 9.04 |
| Medium | 6 | 33 | 40.13 | 4.29 | 1.53 | 1.22 | 1.76 | 1.05 | 9.85 |
| Fast | 7 | 30 | 34.43 | 4.50 | 1.84 | 1.15 | 2.32 | .69 | 10.50 |

Enamel, water or oil base (material #9 or #10)
  Brush each finish coat

|  |  |  |  |  |  |  |  |  |  |
|---|---|---|---|---|---|---|---|---|---|
| Slow | 4 | 30 | 54.25 | 5.06 | 1.50 | 1.81 | 1.59 | 1.59 | 11.55 |
| Medium | 5 | 28 | 47.50 | 5.15 | 1.82 | 1.70 | 2.17 | 1.30 | 12.14 |
| Fast | 6 | 25 | 40.70 | 5.25 | 2.16 | 1.63 | 2.80 | .83 | 12.67 |

These figures will apply when painting all sides of two-lite wood storm sash measuring up to 15 square feet overall (length times width). Add: Preparation time for protecting adjacent surfaces with window protective coating or masking tape and paper as required. "Slow" work is based on an hourly wage of $20.25, "Medium" work on an hourly wage of $25.75, and "Fast" work on an hourly wage of $31.50. Other qualifications that apply to this table are on page 9.

## Windows, wood, exterior or interior, *per window basis*
## Windows 15 square feet or smaller

Use the figures in the following tables to estimate the costs for finishing exterior or interior wood windows on a *per window basis* where the windows are 15 square feet or less in area (length times width). For estimating windows larger than 15 square feet, use these same tables and estimate additional time and material proportionately or use the system for windows, wood, exterior or interior *square foot basis* on page 290. Both the *per window basis* and the *square foot basis* include time and material needed to paint the sash (mullions or muntins), trim, frames, jambs, sill and apron on ONE SIDE ONLY. The stain, seal and finish coat systems include one coat of stain sanding sealer, light sanding and one finish coat of either varnish for exterior or lacquer for interior. In addition, finalizing the varnish application usually includes a steel wool buff and wax application with minimum material usage. Add preparation time for sanding, putty and for protecting adjacent surfaces and protecting window panes with window protective coating (wax) or masking tape and paper as required.

For heights above 8 feet, use the High Time Difficulty Factors on page 139. "Slow" work is based on an hourly wage of $20.25, "Medium" work on an hourly wage of $25.75, and "Fast" work on an hourly wage of $31.50. Other qualifications that might apply to the following *per window basis* tables are listed on page 9.

National Painting Cost Estimator

|  | Manhours per window | Windows per gallon | Material cost per gallon | Labor cost per window | Labor burden window | Material cost per window | Overhead per window | Profit per window | Total price per window |
|---|---|---|---|---|---|---|---|---|---|

### Windows, wood, exterior, *per window basis,* 1, 2 and 3 panes, 15 square feet or smaller

Undercoat, water or oil base (material #3 or #4)
  Brush 1 coat

| | | | | | | | | | |
|---|---|---|---|---|---|---|---|---|---|
| Slow | .25 | 15.0 | 37.45 | 5.06 | 1.50 | 2.50 | 1.72 | 1.72 | 12.50 |
| Medium | .20 | 14.5 | 32.75 | 5.15 | 1.82 | 2.26 | 2.31 | 1.38 | 12.92 |
| Fast | .15 | 14.0 | 28.15 | 4.73 | 1.92 | 2.01 | 2.69 | .80 | 12.15 |

Split coat (1/2 undercoat + 1/2 enamel), water or oil base (material #3 or #4 or #9 or #10)
  Brush 1 coat

| | | | | | | | | | |
|---|---|---|---|---|---|---|---|---|---|
| Slow | .30 | 17.0 | 45.85 | 6.08 | 1.79 | 2.70 | 2.01 | 2.01 | 14.59 |
| Medium | .25 | 16.5 | 40.13 | 6.44 | 2.28 | 2.43 | 2.79 | 1.67 | 15.61 |
| Fast | .20 | 16.0 | 34.43 | 6.30 | 2.57 | 2.15 | 3.42 | 1.01 | 15.45 |

Enamel, water or oil base (material #9 or #10)
  Brush each finish coat

| | | | | | | | | | |
|---|---|---|---|---|---|---|---|---|---|
| Slow | .35 | 16.0 | 54.25 | 7.09 | 2.09 | 3.39 | 2.39 | 2.39 | 17.35 |
| Medium | .30 | 15.5 | 47.50 | 7.73 | 2.73 | 3.06 | 3.38 | 2.03 | 18.93 |
| Fast | .25 | 15.0 | 40.70 | 7.88 | 3.21 | 2.71 | 4.28 | 1.27 | 19.35 |

Stain, seal & 1 coat varnish system (material #30)
  Brush each coat

| | | | | | | | | | |
|---|---|---|---|---|---|---|---|---|---|
| Slow | .70 | 11.0 | 62.40 | 14.18 | 4.17 | 5.67 | 4.57 | 4.58 | 33.17 |
| Medium | .65 | 10.0 | 54.60 | 16.74 | 5.93 | 5.46 | 7.03 | 4.22 | 39.38 |
| Fast | .60 | 9.0 | 46.80 | 18.90 | 7.71 | 5.20 | 9.86 | 2.92 | 44.59 |

Varnish (material #30c)
  Brush additional coats of varnish

| | | | | | | | | | |
|---|---|---|---|---|---|---|---|---|---|
| Slow | .25 | 22.0 | 81.70 | 5.06 | 1.50 | 3.71 | 1.95 | 1.95 | 14.17 |
| Medium | .23 | 20.0 | 71.50 | 5.92 | 2.10 | 3.58 | 2.90 | 1.74 | 16.24 |
| Fast | .20 | 18.0 | 61.30 | 6.30 | 2.57 | 3.41 | 3.81 | 1.13 | 17.22 |

Buff & wax after varnish application (material - minimal)
  Steel wool buff

| | | | | | | | | | |
|---|---|---|---|---|---|---|---|---|---|
| Slow | .25 | -- | -- | 5.06 | 1.50 | -- | 1.24 | 1.25 | 9.05 |
| Medium | .20 | -- | -- | 5.15 | 1.82 | -- | 1.74 | 1.05 | 9.76 |
| Fast | .15 | -- | -- | 4.73 | 1.92 | -- | 2.06 | .61 | 9.32 |

  Wax application (material - minimal)

| | | | | | | | | | |
|---|---|---|---|---|---|---|---|---|---|
| Slow | .25 | -- | -- | 5.06 | 1.50 | -- | 1.24 | 1.25 | 9.05 |
| Medium | .20 | -- | -- | 5.15 | 1.82 | -- | 1.74 | 1.05 | 9.76 |
| Fast | .15 | -- | -- | 4.73 | 1.92 | -- | 2.06 | .61 | 9.32 |

For notes on this table, see the note section on page 279 under Windows, wood, exterior or interior, *per window basis.*

*General Painting Costs*

|  | Manhours per window | Windows per gallon | Material cost per gallon | Labor cost per window | Labor burden window | Material cost per window | Overhead per window | Profit per window | Total price per window |
|---|---|---|---|---|---|---|---|---|---|

## Windows, wood, exterior, *per window basis,* 4 to 6 panes

Undercoat, water or oil base (material #3 or #4)
  Brush 1 coat

| | | | | | | | | | |
|---|---|---|---|---|---|---|---|---|---|
| Slow | .35 | 14.0 | 37.45 | 7.09 | 2.09 | 2.68 | 2.25 | 2.26 | 16.37 |
| Medium | .30 | 13.5 | 32.75 | 7.73 | 2.73 | 2.43 | 3.23 | 1.94 | 18.06 |
| Fast | .25 | 13.0 | 28.15 | 7.88 | 3.21 | 2.17 | 4.11 | 1.22 | 18.59 |

Split coat (1/2 undercoat + 1/2 enamel), water or oil base (material #3 or #4 or #9 or #10)
  Brush 1 coat

| | | | | | | | | | |
|---|---|---|---|---|---|---|---|---|---|
| Slow | .40 | 16.0 | 45.85 | 8.10 | 2.39 | 2.87 | 2.54 | 2.54 | 18.44 |
| Medium | .35 | 15.5 | 40.13 | 9.01 | 3.19 | 2.59 | 3.70 | 2.22 | 20.71 |
| Fast | .30 | 15.0 | 34.43 | 9.45 | 3.86 | 2.30 | 4.84 | 1.43 | 21.88 |

Enamel, water or oil base (material #9 or #10)
  Brush each finish coat

| | | | | | | | | | |
|---|---|---|---|---|---|---|---|---|---|
| Slow | .50 | 15.0 | 54.25 | 10.13 | 2.98 | 3.62 | 3.18 | 3.19 | 23.10 |
| Medium | .45 | 14.5 | 47.50 | 11.59 | 4.10 | 3.28 | 4.74 | 2.85 | 26.56 |
| Fast | .40 | 14.0 | 40.70 | 12.60 | 5.14 | 2.91 | 6.40 | 1.89 | 28.94 |

Stain, seal & 1 coat varnish system (material #30)
  Brush each coat

| | | | | | | | | | |
|---|---|---|---|---|---|---|---|---|---|
| Slow | .98 | 10.0 | 62.40 | 19.85 | 5.85 | 6.24 | 6.07 | 6.08 | 44.09 |
| Medium | .88 | 9.0 | 54.60 | 22.66 | 8.03 | 6.07 | 9.19 | 5.51 | 51.46 |
| Fast | .78 | 8.0 | 46.80 | 24.57 | 10.02 | 5.85 | 12.54 | 3.71 | 56.69 |

Varnish (material #30c)
  Brush additional coats of varnish

| | | | | | | | | | |
|---|---|---|---|---|---|---|---|---|---|
| Slow | .33 | 21.0 | 81.70 | 6.68 | 1.97 | 3.89 | 2.38 | 2.39 | 17.31 |
| Medium | .27 | 19.0 | 71.50 | 6.95 | 2.46 | 3.76 | 3.29 | 1.98 | 18.44 |
| Fast | .22 | 17.0 | 61.30 | 6.93 | 2.83 | 3.61 | 4.14 | 1.23 | 18.74 |

Buff & wax after varnish application (material - minimal)
  Steel wool buff

| | | | | | | | | | |
|---|---|---|---|---|---|---|---|---|---|
| Slow | .33 | -- | -- | 6.68 | 1.97 | -- | 1.64 | 1.65 | 11.94 |
| Medium | .27 | -- | -- | 6.95 | 2.46 | -- | 2.35 | 1.41 | 13.17 |
| Fast | .22 | -- | -- | 6.93 | 2.83 | -- | 3.03 | .90 | 13.69 |

Wax application (material - minimal)

| | | | | | | | | | |
|---|---|---|---|---|---|---|---|---|---|
| Slow | .33 | -- | -- | 6.68 | 1.97 | -- | 1.64 | 1.65 | 11.94 |
| Medium | .27 | -- | -- | 6.95 | 2.46 | -- | 2.35 | 1.41 | 13.17 |
| Fast | .22 | -- | -- | 6.93 | 2.83 | -- | 3.03 | .90 | 13.69 |

For notes on this table, see the note section on page 279 under Windows, wood, exterior or interior, *per window basis.*

*National Painting Cost Estimator*

|  | Manhours per window | Windows per gallon | Material cost per gallon | Labor cost per window | Labor burden window | Material cost per window | Overhead per window | Profit per window | Total price per window |
|---|---|---|---|---|---|---|---|---|---|

## Windows, wood, exterior, *per window basis,* 7 to 8 panes

Undercoat, water or oil base (material #3 or #4)
  Brush 1 coat

| | | | | | | | | | |
|---|---|---|---|---|---|---|---|---|---|
| Slow | .45 | 13 | 37.45 | 9.11 | 2.69 | 2.88 | 2.79 | 2.80 | 20.27 |
| Medium | .40 | 13 | 32.75 | 10.30 | 3.65 | 2.52 | 4.12 | 2.47 | 23.06 |
| Fast | .35 | 12 | 28.15 | 11.03 | 4.49 | 2.35 | 5.54 | 1.64 | 25.05 |

Split coat (1/2 undercoat + 1/2 enamel), water or oil base (material #3 or #4 or #9 or #10)
  Brush 1 coat

| | | | | | | | | | |
|---|---|---|---|---|---|---|---|---|---|
| Slow | .55 | 15 | 45.85 | 11.14 | 3.28 | 3.06 | 3.32 | 3.33 | 24.13 |
| Medium | .50 | 15 | 40.13 | 12.88 | 4.56 | 2.68 | 5.03 | 3.02 | 28.17 |
| Fast | .45 | 14 | 34.43 | 14.18 | 5.78 | 2.46 | 6.95 | 2.06 | 31.43 |

Enamel, water or oil base (material #9 or #10)
  Brush each finish coat

| | | | | | | | | | |
|---|---|---|---|---|---|---|---|---|---|
| Slow | .67 | 14 | 54.25 | 13.57 | 4.00 | 3.88 | 4.08 | 4.08 | 29.61 |
| Medium | .62 | 14 | 47.50 | 15.97 | 5.65 | 3.39 | 6.25 | 3.75 | 35.01 |
| Fast | .57 | 13 | 40.70 | 17.96 | 7.32 | 3.13 | 8.81 | 2.61 | 39.83 |

Stain, seal & 1 coat varnish system (material #30)
  Brush each coat

| | | | | | | | | | |
|---|---|---|---|---|---|---|---|---|---|
| Slow | 1.20 | 9 | 62.40 | 24.30 | 7.16 | 6.93 | 7.30 | 7.31 | 53.00 |
| Medium | 1.10 | 8 | 54.60 | 28.33 | 10.03 | 6.83 | 11.30 | 6.78 | 63.27 |
| Fast | 1.00 | 7 | 46.80 | 31.50 | 12.85 | 6.69 | 15.82 | 4.68 | 71.54 |

Varnish (material #30c)
  Brush additional coats of varnish

| | | | | | | | | | |
|---|---|---|---|---|---|---|---|---|---|
| Slow | .38 | 20 | 81.70 | 7.70 | 2.26 | 4.09 | 2.67 | 2.68 | 19.40 |
| Medium | .33 | 18 | 71.50 | 8.50 | 3.01 | 3.97 | 3.87 | 2.32 | 21.67 |
| Fast | .27 | 16 | 61.30 | 8.51 | 3.46 | 3.83 | 4.90 | 1.45 | 22.15 |

Buff & wax after varnish application (material - minimal)
  Steel wool buff

| | | | | | | | | | |
|---|---|---|---|---|---|---|---|---|---|
| Slow | .38 | -- | -- | 7.70 | 2.26 | -- | 1.89 | 1.90 | 13.75 |
| Medium | .33 | -- | -- | 8.50 | 3.01 | -- | 2.88 | 1.73 | 16.12 |
| Fast | .27 | -- | -- | 8.51 | 3.46 | -- | 3.71 | 1.10 | 16.78 |

Wax application (material - minimal)

| | | | | | | | | | |
|---|---|---|---|---|---|---|---|---|---|
| Slow | .38 | -- | -- | 7.70 | 2.26 | -- | 1.89 | 1.90 | 13.75 |
| Medium | .33 | -- | -- | 8.50 | 3.01 | -- | 2.88 | 1.73 | 16.12 |
| Fast | .27 | -- | -- | 8.51 | 3.46 | -- | 3.71 | 1.10 | 16.78 |

For notes on this table, see the note section on page 279 under Windows, wood, exterior or interior, *per window basis.*

*General Painting Costs*

|  | Manhours per window | Windows per gallon | Material cost per gallon | Labor cost per window | Labor burden window | Material cost per window | Overhead per window | Profit per window | Total price per window |
|---|---|---|---|---|---|---|---|---|---|

## Windows, wood, exterior, *per window basis,* 9 to 11 panes

Undercoat, water or oil base (material #3 or #4)
  Brush 1 coat

| | | | | | | | | | |
|---|---|---|---|---|---|---|---|---|---|
| Slow | .55 | 12 | 37.45 | 11.14 | 3.28 | 3.12 | 3.33 | 3.34 | 24.21 |
| Medium | .50 | 12 | 32.75 | 12.88 | 4.56 | 2.73 | 5.04 | 3.03 | 28.24 |
| Fast | .45 | 11 | 28.15 | 14.18 | 5.78 | 2.56 | 6.98 | 2.07 | 31.57 |

Split coat (1/2 undercoat + 1/2 enamel), water or oil base (material #3 or #4 or #9 or #10)
  Brush 1 coat

| | | | | | | | | | |
|---|---|---|---|---|---|---|---|---|---|
| Slow | .67 | 14 | 45.85 | 13.57 | 4.00 | 3.28 | 3.96 | 3.97 | 28.78 |
| Medium | .62 | 14 | 40.13 | 15.97 | 5.65 | 2.87 | 6.12 | 3.67 | 34.28 |
| Fast | .57 | 13 | 34.43 | 17.96 | 7.32 | 2.65 | 8.66 | 2.56 | 39.15 |

Enamel, water or oil base (material #9 or #10)
  Brush each finish coat

| | | | | | | | | | |
|---|---|---|---|---|---|---|---|---|---|
| Slow | .78 | 13 | 54.25 | 15.80 | 4.65 | 4.17 | 4.68 | 4.69 | 33.99 |
| Medium | .73 | 13 | 47.50 | 18.80 | 6.66 | 3.65 | 7.28 | 4.37 | 40.76 |
| Fast | .68 | 12 | 40.70 | 21.42 | 8.74 | 3.39 | 10.40 | 3.08 | 47.03 |

Stain, seal & 1 coat varnish system (material #30)
  Brush each coat

| | | | | | | | | | |
|---|---|---|---|---|---|---|---|---|---|
| Slow | 1.50 | 7 | 62.40 | 30.38 | 8.95 | 8.91 | 9.17 | 9.19 | 66.60 |
| Medium | 1.40 | 6 | 54.60 | 36.05 | 12.77 | 9.10 | 14.48 | 8.69 | 81.09 |
| Fast | 1.30 | 5 | 46.80 | 40.95 | 16.71 | 9.36 | 20.78 | 6.15 | 93.95 |

Varnish (material #30c)
  Brush additional coats of varnish

| | | | | | | | | | |
|---|---|---|---|---|---|---|---|---|---|
| Slow | .45 | 19 | 81.70 | 9.11 | 2.69 | 4.30 | 3.06 | 3.07 | 22.23 |
| Medium | .40 | 17 | 71.50 | 10.30 | 3.65 | 4.21 | 4.54 | 2.72 | 25.42 |
| Fast | .35 | 15 | 61.30 | 11.03 | 4.49 | 4.09 | 6.08 | 1.80 | 27.49 |

Buff & wax after varnish application (material - minimal)
  Steel wool buff

| | | | | | | | | | |
|---|---|---|---|---|---|---|---|---|---|
| Slow | .45 | -- | -- | 9.11 | 2.69 | -- | 2.24 | 2.25 | 16.29 |
| Medium | .40 | -- | -- | 10.30 | 3.65 | -- | 3.49 | 2.09 | 19.53 |
| Fast | .35 | -- | -- | 11.03 | 4.49 | -- | 4.81 | 1.42 | 21.75 |

  Wax application (material - minimal)

| | | | | | | | | | |
|---|---|---|---|---|---|---|---|---|---|
| Slow | .45 | -- | -- | 9.11 | 2.69 | -- | 2.24 | 2.25 | 16.29 |
| Medium | .40 | -- | -- | 10.30 | 3.65 | -- | 3.49 | 2.09 | 19.53 |
| Fast | .35 | -- | -- | 11.03 | 4.49 | -- | 4.81 | 1.42 | 21.75 |

For notes on this table, see the note section on page 279 under Windows, wood, exterior or interior, *per window basis.*

|  | Manhours per window | Windows per gallon | Material cost per gallon | Labor cost per window | Labor burden window | Material cost per window | Overhead per window | Profit per window | Total price per window |
|---|---|---|---|---|---|---|---|---|---|

## Windows, wood, exterior, *per window basis,* 12 pane

Undercoat, water or oil base (material #3 or #4)
Brush 1 coat

|  |  |  |  |  |  |  |  |  |  |
|---|---|---|---|---|---|---|---|---|---|
| Slow | .67 | 11 | 37.45 | 13.57 | 4.00 | 3.40 | 3.98 | 3.99 | 28.94 |
| Medium | .62 | 11 | 32.75 | 15.97 | 5.65 | 2.98 | 6.15 | 3.69 | 34.44 |
| Fast | .57 | 10 | 28.15 | 17.96 | 7.32 | 2.82 | 8.71 | 2.58 | 39.39 |

Split coat (1/2 undercoat + 1/2 enamel), water or oil base (material #3 or #4 or #9 or #10)
Brush 1 coat

|  |  |  |  |  |  |  |  |  |  |
|---|---|---|---|---|---|---|---|---|---|
| Slow | .72 | 13 | 45.85 | 14.58 | 4.30 | 3.53 | 4.26 | 4.27 | 30.94 |
| Medium | .67 | 13 | 40.13 | 17.25 | 6.11 | 3.09 | 6.61 | 3.97 | 37.03 |
| Fast | .62 | 12 | 34.43 | 19.53 | 7.97 | 2.87 | 9.41 | 2.78 | 42.56 |

Enamel, water or oil base (material #9 or #10)
Brush each finish coat

|  |  |  |  |  |  |  |  |  |  |
|---|---|---|---|---|---|---|---|---|---|
| Slow | .85 | 12 | 54.25 | 17.21 | 5.08 | 4.52 | 5.09 | 5.10 | 37.00 |
| Medium | .80 | 12 | 47.50 | 20.60 | 7.30 | 3.96 | 7.96 | 4.78 | 44.60 |
| Fast | .75 | 11 | 40.70 | 23.63 | 9.63 | 3.70 | 11.46 | 3.39 | 51.81 |

Stain, seal & 1 coat varnish system (material #30)
Brush each coat

|  |  |  |  |  |  |  |  |  |  |
|---|---|---|---|---|---|---|---|---|---|
| Slow | 1.70 | 6 | 62.40 | 34.43 | 10.14 | 10.40 | 10.45 | 10.47 | 75.89 |
| Medium | 1.60 | 5 | 54.60 | 41.20 | 14.59 | 10.92 | 16.68 | 10.01 | 93.40 |
| Fast | 1.50 | 4 | 46.80 | 47.25 | 19.28 | 11.70 | 24.25 | 7.17 | 109.65 |

Varnish (material #30c)
Brush additional coats of varnish

|  |  |  |  |  |  |  |  |  |  |
|---|---|---|---|---|---|---|---|---|---|
| Slow | .50 | 18 | 81.70 | 10.13 | 2.98 | 4.54 | 3.36 | 3.36 | 24.37 |
| Medium | .45 | 16 | 71.50 | 11.59 | 4.10 | 4.47 | 5.04 | 3.02 | 28.22 |
| Fast | .40 | 14 | 61.30 | 12.60 | 5.14 | 4.38 | 6.86 | 2.03 | 31.01 |

Buff & wax after varnish application (material - minimal)
Steel wool buff

|  |  |  |  |  |  |  |  |  |  |
|---|---|---|---|---|---|---|---|---|---|
| Slow | .50 | -- | -- | 10.13 | 2.98 | -- | 2.49 | 2.50 | 18.10 |
| Medium | .45 | -- | -- | 11.59 | 4.10 | -- | 3.92 | 2.35 | 21.96 |
| Fast | .40 | -- | -- | 12.60 | 5.14 | -- | 5.50 | 1.63 | 24.87 |

Wax application (material - minimal)

|  |  |  |  |  |  |  |  |  |  |
|---|---|---|---|---|---|---|---|---|---|
| Slow | .50 | -- | -- | 10.13 | 2.98 | -- | 2.49 | 2.50 | 18.10 |
| Medium | .45 | -- | -- | 11.59 | 4.10 | -- | 3.92 | 2.35 | 21.96 |
| Fast | .40 | -- | -- | 12.60 | 5.14 | -- | 5.50 | 1.63 | 24.87 |

For notes on this table, see the note section on page 279 under Windows, wood, exterior or interior, *per window basis.*

*General Painting Costs*

|  | Manhour per window | Windows per gallon | Material cost per gallon | Labor cost per window | Labor burden window | Material cost per window | Overhead per window | Profit per window | Total price per window |
|---|---|---|---|---|---|---|---|---|---|

**Windows, wood, interior, *per window basis*, 1, 2 or 3 panes, 15 square feet or smaller**

Undercoat, water or oil base (material #3 or #4)
  Brush 1 coat

| | | | | | | | | | |
|---|---|---|---|---|---|---|---|---|---|
| Slow | .25 | 15 | 37.45 | 5.06 | 1.50 | 2.50 | 1.72 | 1.72 | 12.50 |
| Medium | .20 | 15 | 32.75 | 5.15 | 1.82 | 2.18 | 2.29 | 1.37 | 12.81 |
| Fast | .15 | 14 | 28.15 | 4.73 | 1.92 | 2.01 | 2.69 | .80 | 12.15 |

Split coat (1/2 undercoat + 1/2 enamel), water or oil base (material #3 or #4 or #9 or #10)
  Brush 1 coat

| | | | | | | | | | |
|---|---|---|---|---|---|---|---|---|---|
| Slow | .30 | 17 | 45.85 | 6.08 | 1.79 | 2.70 | 2.01 | 2.01 | 14.59 |
| Medium | .25 | 17 | 40.13 | 6.44 | 2.28 | 2.36 | 2.77 | 1.66 | 15.51 |
| Fast | .20 | 16 | 34.43 | 6.30 | 2.57 | 2.15 | 3.42 | 1.01 | 15.45 |

Enamel, water or oil base (material #9 or #10)
  Brush each finish coat

| | | | | | | | | | |
|---|---|---|---|---|---|---|---|---|---|
| Slow | .35 | 16 | 54.25 | 7.09 | 2.09 | 3.39 | 2.39 | 2.39 | 17.35 |
| Medium | .30 | 16 | 47.50 | 7.73 | 2.73 | 2.97 | 3.36 | 2.02 | 18.81 |
| Fast | .25 | 15 | 40.70 | 7.88 | 3.21 | 2.71 | 4.28 | 1.27 | 19.35 |

Stain, seal & 1 coat lacquer system, (material #11)
  Brush each coat

| | | | | | | | | | |
|---|---|---|---|---|---|---|---|---|---|
| Slow | .70 | 11 | 46.10 | 14.18 | 4.17 | 4.19 | 4.28 | 4.29 | 31.11 |
| Medium | .65 | 10 | 40.40 | 16.74 | 5.93 | 4.04 | 6.68 | 4.01 | 37.40 |
| Fast | .60 | 9 | 34.60 | 18.90 | 7.71 | 3.84 | 9.44 | 2.79 | 42.68 |

Lacquer (material #11c)
  Brush additional coats of lacquer

| | | | | | | | | | |
|---|---|---|---|---|---|---|---|---|---|
| Slow | .25 | 22 | 45.90 | 5.06 | 1.50 | 2.09 | 1.64 | 1.64 | 11.93 |
| Medium | .23 | 20 | 40.10 | 5.92 | 2.10 | 2.01 | 2.51 | 1.50 | 14.04 |
| Fast | .20 | 18 | 34.40 | 6.30 | 2.57 | 1.91 | 3.34 | .99 | 15.11 |

For notes on this table, see the note section on page 279 under Windows, wood, exterior or interior, *per window basis*.

|  | Manhours per window | Windows per gallon | Material cost per gallon | Labor cost per window | Labor burden window | Material cost per window | Overhead per window | Profit per window | Total price per window |
|---|---|---|---|---|---|---|---|---|---|

## Windows, wood, interior, *per window basis,* 4 to 6 panes

Undercoat, water or oil base (material #3 or #4)
  Brush 1 coat

|  |  |  |  |  |  |  |  |  |  |
|---|---|---|---|---|---|---|---|---|---|
| Slow | .35 | 14 | 37.45 | 7.09 | 2.09 | 2.68 | 2.25 | 2.26 | 16.37 |
| Medium | .30 | 14 | 32.75 | 7.73 | 2.73 | 2.34 | 3.20 | 1.92 | 17.92 |
| Fast | .25 | 13 | 28.15 | 7.88 | 3.21 | 2.17 | 4.11 | 1.22 | 18.59 |

Split coat (1/2 undercoat + 1/2 enamel), water or oil base (material #3 or #4 or #9 or #10)
  Brush 1 coat

|  |  |  |  |  |  |  |  |  |  |
|---|---|---|---|---|---|---|---|---|---|
| Slow | .40 | 16 | 45.85 | 8.10 | 2.39 | 2.87 | 2.54 | 2.54 | 18.44 |
| Medium | .35 | 16 | 40.13 | 9.01 | 3.19 | 2.51 | 3.68 | 2.21 | 20.60 |
| Fast | .30 | 15 | 34.43 | 9.45 | 3.86 | 2.30 | 4.84 | 1.43 | 21.88 |

Enamel, water or oil base (material #9 or #10)
  Brush each finish coat

|  |  |  |  |  |  |  |  |  |  |
|---|---|---|---|---|---|---|---|---|---|
| Slow | .50 | 15 | 54.25 | 10.13 | 2.98 | 3.62 | 3.18 | 3.19 | 23.10 |
| Medium | .45 | 15 | 47.50 | 11.59 | 4.10 | 3.17 | 4.72 | 2.83 | 26.41 |
| Fast | .40 | 14 | 40.70 | 12.60 | 5.14 | 2.91 | 6.40 | 1.89 | 28.94 |

Stain, seal & 1 coat lacquer system, (material #11)
  Brush each coat

|  |  |  |  |  |  |  |  |  |  |
|---|---|---|---|---|---|---|---|---|---|
| Slow | .98 | 10 | 46.10 | 19.85 | 5.85 | 4.61 | 5.76 | 5.77 | 41.84 |
| Medium | .88 | 9 | 40.40 | 22.66 | 8.03 | 4.49 | 8.79 | 5.28 | 49.25 |
| Fast | .78 | 8 | 34.60 | 24.57 | 10.02 | 4.33 | 12.07 | 3.57 | 54.56 |

Lacquer (material #11c)
  Brush additional coats of lacquer

|  |  |  |  |  |  |  |  |  |  |
|---|---|---|---|---|---|---|---|---|---|
| Slow | .33 | 21 | 45.90 | 6.68 | 1.97 | 2.19 | 2.06 | 2.06 | 14.96 |
| Medium | .27 | 19 | 40.10 | 6.95 | 2.46 | 2.11 | 2.88 | 1.73 | 16.13 |
| Fast | .22 | 17 | 34.40 | 6.93 | 2.83 | 2.02 | 3.65 | 1.08 | 16.51 |

For notes on this table, see the note section on page 279 under Windows, wood, exterior or interior, *per window basis.*

*General Painting Costs*

|  | Manhours per window | Windows per gallon | Material cost per gallon | Labor cost per window | Labor burden window | Material cost per window | Overhead per window | Profit per window | Total price per window |
|---|---|---|---|---|---|---|---|---|---|

**Windows, wood, interior, *per window basis,* 7 to 8 panes**
  Undercoat, water or oil base (material #3 or #4)
    Brush 1 coat

| | | | | | | | | | |
|---|---|---|---|---|---|---|---|---|---|
| Slow | .45 | 13 | 37.45 | 9.11 | 2.69 | 2.88 | 2.79 | 2.80 | 20.27 |
| Medium | .40 | 13 | 32.75 | 10.30 | 3.65 | 2.52 | 4.12 | 2.47 | 23.06 |
| Fast | .35 | 12 | 28.15 | 11.03 | 4.49 | 2.35 | 5.54 | 1.64 | 25.05 |

  Split coat (1/2 undercoat + 1/2 enamel), water or oil base (material #3 or #4 or #9 or #10)
    Brush 1 coat

| | | | | | | | | | |
|---|---|---|---|---|---|---|---|---|---|
| Slow | .55 | 15 | 45.85 | 11.14 | 3.28 | 3.06 | 3.32 | 3.33 | 24.13 |
| Medium | .50 | 15 | 40.13 | 12.88 | 4.56 | 2.68 | 5.03 | 3.02 | 28.17 |
| Fast | .45 | 14 | 34.43 | 14.18 | 5.78 | 2.46 | 6.95 | 2.06 | 31.43 |

  Enamel, water or oil base (material #9 or #10)
    Brush each finish coat

| | | | | | | | | | |
|---|---|---|---|---|---|---|---|---|---|
| Slow | .67 | 14 | 54.25 | 13.57 | 4.00 | 3.88 | 4.08 | 4.08 | 29.61 |
| Medium | .62 | 14 | 47.50 | 15.97 | 5.65 | 3.39 | 6.25 | 3.75 | 35.01 |
| Fast | .57 | 13 | 40.70 | 17.96 | 7.32 | 3.13 | 8.81 | 2.61 | 39.83 |

  Stain, seal & 1 coat lacquer system, (material #11)
    Brush each coat

| | | | | | | | | | |
|---|---|---|---|---|---|---|---|---|---|
| Slow | 1.20 | 9 | 46.10 | 24.30 | 7.16 | 5.12 | 6.95 | 6.97 | 50.50 |
| Medium | 1.10 | 8 | 40.40 | 28.33 | 10.03 | 5.05 | 10.85 | 6.51 | 60.77 |
| Fast | 1.00 | 7 | 34.60 | 31.50 | 12.85 | 4.94 | 15.28 | 4.52 | 69.09 |

  Lacquer (material #11c)
    Brush additional coats of lacquer

| | | | | | | | | | |
|---|---|---|---|---|---|---|---|---|---|
| Slow | .38 | 20 | 45.90 | 7.70 | 2.26 | 2.30 | 2.33 | 2.34 | 16.93 |
| Medium | .33 | 18 | 40.10 | 8.50 | 3.01 | 2.23 | 3.44 | 2.06 | 19.24 |
| Fast | .27 | 16 | 34.40 | 8.51 | 3.46 | 2.15 | 4.38 | 1.30 | 19.80 |

For notes on this table, see the note section on page 279 under Windows, wood, exterior or interior, *per window basis.*

*National Painting Cost Estimator*

|  | Manhours per window | Windows per gallon | Material cost per gallon | Labor cost per window | Labor burden window | Material cost per window | Overhead per window | Profit per window | Total price per window |
|---|---|---|---|---|---|---|---|---|---|

## Windows, wood, interior, *per window basis,* 9 to 11 panes

Undercoat, water or oil base (material #3 or #4)
  Brush 1 coat

| | | | | | | | | | |
|---|---|---|---|---|---|---|---|---|---|
| Slow | .55 | 12 | 37.45 | 11.14 | 3.28 | 3.12 | 3.33 | 3.34 | 24.21 |
| Medium | .50 | 12 | 32.75 | 12.88 | 4.56 | 2.73 | 5.04 | 3.03 | 28.24 |
| Fast | .45 | 11 | 28.15 | 14.18 | 5.78 | 2.56 | 6.98 | 2.07 | 31.57 |

Split coat (1/2 undercoat + 1/2 enamel), water or oil base (material #3 or #4 or #9 or #10)
  Brush 1 coat

| | | | | | | | | | |
|---|---|---|---|---|---|---|---|---|---|
| Slow | .67 | 14 | 45.85 | 13.57 | 4.00 | 3.28 | 3.96 | 3.97 | 28.78 |
| Medium | .62 | 14 | 40.13 | 15.97 | 5.65 | 2.87 | 6.12 | 3.67 | 34.28 |
| Fast | .57 | 13 | 34.43 | 17.96 | 7.32 | 2.65 | 8.66 | 2.56 | 39.15 |

Enamel, water or oil base (material #9 or #10)
  Brush each finish coat

| | | | | | | | | | |
|---|---|---|---|---|---|---|---|---|---|
| Slow | .78 | 13 | 54.25 | 15.80 | 4.65 | 4.17 | 4.68 | 4.69 | 33.99 |
| Medium | .73 | 13 | 47.50 | 18.80 | 6.66 | 3.65 | 7.28 | 4.37 | 40.76 |
| Fast | .68 | 12 | 40.70 | 21.42 | 8.74 | 3.39 | 10.40 | 3.08 | 47.03 |

Stain, seal & 1 coat lacquer system, (material #11)
  Brush each coat

| | | | | | | | | | |
|---|---|---|---|---|---|---|---|---|---|
| Slow | 1.50 | 8 | 46.10 | 30.38 | 8.95 | 5.76 | 8.57 | 8.59 | 62.25 |
| Medium | 1.40 | 7 | 40.40 | 36.05 | 12.77 | 5.77 | 13.65 | 8.19 | 76.43 |
| Fast | 1.30 | 6 | 34.60 | 40.95 | 16.71 | 5.77 | 19.66 | 5.82 | 88.91 |

Lacquer (material #11c)
  Brush additional coats of lacquer

| | | | | | | | | | |
|---|---|---|---|---|---|---|---|---|---|
| Slow | .45 | 19 | 45.90 | 9.11 | 2.69 | 2.42 | 2.70 | 2.71 | 19.63 |
| Medium | .40 | 17 | 40.10 | 10.30 | 3.65 | 2.36 | 4.08 | 2.45 | 22.84 |
| Fast | .35 | 15 | 34.40 | 11.03 | 4.49 | 2.29 | 5.52 | 1.63 | 24.96 |

For notes on this table, see the note section on page 279 under Windows, wood, exterior or interior, *per window basis.*

*General Painting Costs*

|  | Manhours per window | Windows per gallon | Material cost per gallon | Labor cost per window | Labor burden window | Material cost per window | Overhead per window | Profit per window | Total price per window |
|---|---|---|---|---|---|---|---|---|---|

## Windows, wood, interior, *per window basis,* 12 pane

Undercoat, water or oil base (material #3 or #4)
  Brush 1 coat
|  |  |  |  |  |  |  |  |  |  |
|---|---|---|---|---|---|---|---|---|---|
| Slow | .67 | 11 | 37.45 | 13.57 | 4.00 | 3.40 | 3.98 | 3.99 | 28.94 |
| Medium | .62 | 11 | 32.75 | 15.97 | 5.65 | 2.98 | 6.15 | 3.69 | 34.44 |
| Fast | .57 | 10 | 28.15 | 17.96 | 7.32 | 2.82 | 8.71 | 2.58 | 39.39 |

Split coat (1/2 undercoat + 1/2 enamel), water or oil base (material #3 or #4 or #9 or #10)
  Brush 1 coat
|  |  |  |  |  |  |  |  |  |  |
|---|---|---|---|---|---|---|---|---|---|
| Slow | .72 | 13 | 45.85 | 14.58 | 4.30 | 3.53 | 4.26 | 4.27 | 30.94 |
| Medium | .67 | 13 | 40.13 | 17.25 | 6.11 | 3.09 | 6.61 | 3.97 | 37.03 |
| Fast | .62 | 12 | 34.43 | 19.53 | 7.97 | 2.87 | 9.41 | 2.78 | 42.56 |

Enamel, water or oil base (material #9 or #10)
  Brush each finish coat
|  |  |  |  |  |  |  |  |  |  |
|---|---|---|---|---|---|---|---|---|---|
| Slow | .85 | 12 | 54.25 | 17.21 | 5.08 | 4.52 | 5.09 | 5.10 | 37.00 |
| Medium | .80 | 12 | 47.50 | 20.60 | 7.30 | 3.96 | 7.96 | 4.78 | 44.60 |
| Fast | .75 | 11 | 40.70 | 23.63 | 9.63 | 3.70 | 11.46 | 3.39 | 51.81 |

Stain, seal & 1 coat lacquer system, (material #11)
  Brush each coat
|  |  |  |  |  |  |  |  |  |  |
|---|---|---|---|---|---|---|---|---|---|
| Slow | 1.70 | 7 | 46.10 | 34.43 | 10.14 | 6.59 | 9.72 | 9.74 | 70.62 |
| Medium | 1.60 | 6 | 40.40 | 41.20 | 14.59 | 6.73 | 15.63 | 9.38 | 87.53 |
| Fast | 1.50 | 5 | 34.60 | 47.25 | 19.28 | 6.92 | 22.77 | 6.74 | 102.96 |

Lacquer (material #11c)
  Brush additional coats of lacquer
|  |  |  |  |  |  |  |  |  |  |
|---|---|---|---|---|---|---|---|---|---|
| Slow | .50 | 18 | 45.90 | 10.13 | 2.98 | 2.55 | 2.98 | 2.98 | 21.62 |
| Medium | .45 | 16 | 40.10 | 11.59 | 4.10 | 2.51 | 4.55 | 2.73 | 25.48 |
| Fast | .40 | 14 | 34.40 | 12.60 | 5.14 | 2.46 | 6.26 | 1.85 | 28.31 |

For notes on this table, see the note section on page 279 under Windows, wood, exterior or interior, *per window basis.*

## Windows, wood, exterior or interior, *square foot basis*
## Windows larger than 15 square feet

Use the figures in the following tables to estimate exterior or interior wood windows on a *square foot basis* where the windows are larger than 15 square feet in area (length times width). For estimating windows 15 square feet or smaller, use the system for windows, wood exterior, or interior on a *per window basis*. Both the square foot basis and the per window basis include time and material needed to paint the sash (mullions or muntins), trim, frames, jambs, sill and apron on ONE SIDE ONLY. The stain, seal and finish coat systems include one coat of stain, sanding sealer, light sanding and one finish coat of either varnish for exterior or lacquer for interior. In addition, finalizing the varnish application usually includes a steel wool buff and wax application with minimum material usage. Add preparation time for sanding, putty, protecting adjacent surfaces and protecting window panes with window protective coating (wax) or masking tape and paper as required. For heights above 8 feet, use the High Time Difficulty Factors on page 139. "Slow" work is based on an hourly wage of $20.25, "Medium" work on an hourly wage of $25.75, and "Fast" work on an hourly wage of $31.50. Other qualifications that might apply to the following *per window basis* tables are listed on page 9.

**Example calculation:** Measure each window and add 1 foot to each dimension before calculating the area. For example, a window measuring 4'0" x 4'0" with 1 foot added to the top, bottom, right side and left side is now a 6 x 6 dimension or 36 square feet. Then, add an additional 2 square feet for each window pane, with allows time to finish the mullions, muntins and sash. The square footage calculation for this six pane window would be 36 + (2 x 6) or 48 square feet. Use this number and apply it to the appropriate manhour and material coverage figures in the table.

|  | Labor SF per manhour | Material coverage SF/gallon | Material cost per gallon | Labor cost per 100 SF | Labor burden 100 SF | Material cost per 100 SF | Overhead per 100 SF | Profit per 100 SF | Total price per 100 SF |
|---|---|---|---|---|---|---|---|---|---|

### Paint grade
Undercoat, water or oil base (material #3 or #4)
  Brush 1 coat

| | | | | | | | | | |
|---|---|---|---|---|---|---|---|---|---|
| Slow | 150 | 460 | 37.45 | 13.50 | 3.99 | 8.14 | 4.87 | 4.88 | 35.38 |
| Medium | 165 | 450 | 32.75 | 15.61 | 5.52 | 7.28 | 7.11 | 4.26 | 39.78 |
| Fast | 180 | 440 | 28.15 | 17.50 | 7.16 | 6.40 | 9.62 | 2.85 | 43.53 |

Split coat (1/2 undercoat + 1/2 enamel), water or oil base (material #3 or #4 or #9 or #10)
  Brush 1 coat

| | | | | | | | | | |
|---|---|---|---|---|---|---|---|---|---|
| Slow | 120 | 520 | 45.85 | 16.88 | 4.96 | 8.82 | 5.83 | 5.84 | 42.33 |
| Medium | 135 | 500 | 40.13 | 19.07 | 6.77 | 8.03 | 8.46 | 5.08 | 47.41 |
| Fast | 150 | 480 | 34.43 | 21.00 | 8.58 | 7.17 | 11.39 | 3.37 | 51.51 |

Enamel, water or oil base (material #9 or #10)
  Brush each finish coat

| | | | | | | | | | |
|---|---|---|---|---|---|---|---|---|---|
| Slow | 100 | 500 | 54.25 | 20.25 | 5.97 | 10.85 | 7.04 | 7.06 | 51.17 |
| Medium | 113 | 480 | 47.50 | 22.79 | 8.07 | 9.90 | 10.19 | 6.11 | 57.06 |
| Fast | 125 | 460 | 40.70 | 25.20 | 10.28 | 8.85 | 13.74 | 4.06 | 62.13 |

*General Painting Costs*

|  | Labor SF per manhour | Material coverage SF/gallon | Material cost per gallon | Labor cost per 100 SF | Labor burden 100 SF | Material cost per 100 SF | Overhead per 100 SF | Profit per 100 SF | Total price per 100 SF |
|---|---|---|---|---|---|---|---|---|---|

## Stain grade, exterior

Stain grade: stain, seal & 1 coat varnish system (material #30)
  Brush all coats

| | | | | | | | | | |
|---|---|---|---|---|---|---|---|---|---|
| Slow | 45 | 335 | 62.40 | 45.00 | 13.26 | 18.63 | 14.61 | 14.64 | 106.14 |
| Medium | 55 | 305 | 54.60 | 46.82 | 16.57 | 17.90 | 20.32 | 12.19 | 113.80 |
| Fast | 65 | 280 | 46.80 | 48.46 | 19.75 | 16.71 | 26.33 | 7.79 | 119.04 |

Brush additional coats of varnish (material #30c)

| | | | | | | | | | |
|---|---|---|---|---|---|---|---|---|---|
| Slow | 140 | 675 | 81.70 | 14.46 | 4.26 | 12.10 | 5.86 | 5.87 | 42.55 |
| Medium | 165 | 620 | 71.50 | 15.61 | 5.52 | 11.53 | 8.17 | 4.90 | 45.73 |
| Fast | 190 | 565 | 61.30 | 16.58 | 6.75 | 10.85 | 10.60 | 3.14 | 47.92 |

Buff & wax after varnish application (material - minimal)
  Steel wool buff

| | | | | | | | | | |
|---|---|---|---|---|---|---|---|---|---|
| Slow | 140 | -- | -- | 14.46 | 4.26 | -- | 3.56 | 3.57 | 25.85 |
| Medium | 165 | -- | -- | 15.61 | 5.52 | -- | 5.29 | 3.17 | 29.59 |
| Fast | 190 | -- | -- | 16.58 | 6.75 | -- | 7.24 | 2.14 | 32.71 |

Wax application

| | | | | | | | | | |
|---|---|---|---|---|---|---|---|---|---|
| Slow | 140 | -- | -- | 14.46 | 4.26 | -- | 3.56 | 3.57 | 25.85 |
| Medium | 165 | -- | -- | 15.61 | 5.52 | -- | 5.29 | 3.17 | 29.59 |
| Fast | 190 | -- | -- | 16.58 | 6.75 | -- | 7.24 | 2.14 | 32.71 |

## Stain grade, interior

Stain, seal & 1 coat lacquer system (material #11)
  Brush all coats

| | | | | | | | | | |
|---|---|---|---|---|---|---|---|---|---|
| Slow | 45 | 335 | 46.10 | 45.00 | 13.26 | 13.76 | 13.69 | 13.72 | 99.43 |
| Medium | 55 | 305 | 40.40 | 46.82 | 16.57 | 13.25 | 19.16 | 11.50 | 107.30 |
| Fast | 65 | 280 | 34.60 | 48.46 | 19.75 | 12.36 | 24.98 | 7.39 | 112.94 |

Brush additional coats of lacquer (material #11c)

| | | | | | | | | | |
|---|---|---|---|---|---|---|---|---|---|
| Slow | 140 | 675 | 45.90 | 14.46 | 4.26 | 6.80 | 4.85 | 4.86 | 35.23 |
| Medium | 165 | 620 | 40.10 | 15.61 | 5.52 | 6.47 | 6.90 | 4.14 | 38.64 |
| Fast | 190 | 565 | 34.40 | 16.58 | 6.75 | 6.09 | 9.12 | 2.70 | 41.24 |

For notes on this table, see page 290 under Windows, wood, exterior or interior, *square foot basis.*

## Window conversion factors -- a window area calculation shortcut

| Panes | Manhours per SF conversion factor | Material per SF conversion factor |
|---|---|---|
| 1, 2 or 3 panes | L x W x 2.0 | L x W x 2.0 |
| 4 to 6 panes | L x W x 3.0 | L x W x 2.2 |
| 7 to 8 panes | L x W x 4.0 | L x W x 2.4 |
| 9 to 11 panes | L x W x 5.0 | L x W x 2.6 |
| 12 panes | L x W x 6.0 | L x W x 2.9 |

Use this table in conjunction with the Windows, exterior or interior, *square foot basis* table on page 290 for a guide to calculating window area on a "square foot basis." To convert the window area, calculate the actual square shortcut footage of a window, say, 4'0" x 4'0" or 16 square feet, and look in the conversion table under the number panes, say 6. The conversion factor of a 6-pane window is 3. Multiply the 16 square feet by 3 to equal 48 which is the number used in the square foot basis tables on pages 290 and 291. To undercoat at a slow rate, divide 48 by 150 to come up with .32 hours. Then divide 48 by 460 to result in .10 gallons to undercoat that window. Divide 1 gallon by .1 to find that you can undercoat 10 windows with 1 gallon of undercoat material.

*General Painting Costs*

|  | Labor SF per manhour | Material coverage SF/gallon | Material cost per gallon | Labor cost per 100 SF | Labor burden 100 SF | Material cost per 100 SF | Overhead per 100 SF | Profit per 100 SF | Total price per 100 SF |
|---|---|---|---|---|---|---|---|---|---|

## Wine racks, paint grade, spray, square feet of face

Undercoat, water base (material #3)
  Spray 1 coat

| | | | | | | | | | |
|---|---|---|---|---|---|---|---|---|---|
| Slow | 50 | 100 | 32.60 | 40.50 | 11.94 | 32.60 | 16.16 | 16.19 | 117.39 |
| Medium | 65 | 88 | 28.50 | 39.62 | 14.01 | 32.39 | 21.51 | 12.91 | 120.44 |
| Fast | 80 | 75 | 24.50 | 39.38 | 16.06 | 32.67 | 27.32 | 8.08 | 123.51 |

Undercoat, oil base (material #4)
  Spray 1 coat

| | | | | | | | | | |
|---|---|---|---|---|---|---|---|---|---|
| Slow | 50 | 100 | 42.30 | 40.50 | 11.94 | 42.30 | 18.00 | 18.04 | 130.78 |
| Medium | 65 | 88 | 37.00 | 39.62 | 14.01 | 42.05 | 23.93 | 14.36 | 133.97 |
| Fast | 80 | 75 | 31.80 | 39.38 | 16.06 | 42.40 | 30.33 | 8.97 | 137.14 |

Split coat (1/2 undercoat + 1/2 enamel), water base (material #3 or #9)
  Spray 1 coat

| | | | | | | | | | |
|---|---|---|---|---|---|---|---|---|---|
| Slow | 75 | 150 | 39.70 | 27.00 | 7.95 | 26.47 | 11.67 | 11.70 | 84.79 |
| Medium | 90 | 138 | 34.75 | 28.61 | 10.13 | 25.18 | 15.98 | 9.59 | 89.49 |
| Fast | 125 | 125 | 29.80 | 25.20 | 10.28 | 23.84 | 18.39 | 5.44 | 83.15 |

Split coat (1/2 undercoat + 1/2 enamel), oil base (material #4 or #10)
  Spray 1 coat

| | | | | | | | | | |
|---|---|---|---|---|---|---|---|---|---|
| Slow | 75 | 150 | 52.00 | 27.00 | 7.95 | 34.67 | 13.23 | 13.26 | 96.11 |
| Medium | 90 | 138 | 45.50 | 28.61 | 10.13 | 32.97 | 17.93 | 10.76 | 100.40 |
| Fast | 125 | 125 | 39.05 | 25.20 | 10.28 | 31.24 | 20.68 | 6.12 | 93.52 |

Enamel, water base (material #9)
  Spray 1st finish coat

| | | | | | | | | | |
|---|---|---|---|---|---|---|---|---|---|
| Slow | 65 | 125 | 46.80 | 31.15 | 9.18 | 37.44 | 14.78 | 14.81 | 107.36 |
| Medium | 88 | 113 | 41.00 | 29.26 | 10.35 | 36.28 | 18.98 | 11.39 | 106.26 |
| Fast | 100 | 100 | 35.10 | 31.50 | 12.85 | 35.10 | 24.63 | 7.29 | 111.37 |

  Spray additional finish coats

| | | | | | | | | | |
|---|---|---|---|---|---|---|---|---|---|
| Slow | 75 | 150 | 46.80 | 27.00 | 7.95 | 31.20 | 12.57 | 12.60 | 91.32 |
| Medium | 100 | 138 | 41.00 | 25.75 | 9.12 | 29.71 | 16.15 | 9.69 | 90.42 |
| Fast | 125 | 125 | 35.10 | 25.20 | 10.28 | 28.08 | 19.70 | 5.83 | 89.09 |

Enamel, oil base (material #10)
  Spray 1st finish coat

| | | | | | | | | | |
|---|---|---|---|---|---|---|---|---|---|
| Slow | 65 | 125 | 61.70 | 31.15 | 9.18 | 49.36 | 17.04 | 17.08 | 123.81 |
| Medium | 88 | 113 | 54.00 | 29.26 | 10.35 | 47.79 | 21.85 | 13.11 | 122.36 |
| Fast | 100 | 100 | 46.30 | 31.50 | 12.85 | 46.30 | 28.10 | 8.31 | 127.06 |

  Spray additional finish coats

| | | | | | | | | | |
|---|---|---|---|---|---|---|---|---|---|
| Slow | 75 | 150 | 61.70 | 27.00 | 7.95 | 41.13 | 14.46 | 14.49 | 105.03 |
| Medium | 100 | 138 | 54.00 | 25.75 | 9.12 | 39.13 | 18.50 | 11.10 | 103.60 |
| Fast | 125 | 125 | 46.30 | 25.20 | 10.28 | 37.04 | 22.48 | 6.65 | 101.65 |

These figures include coating all interior and exterior surfaces and are based on overall dimensions (length times width) of the wine rack face. For heights above 8 feet, use the High Time Difficulty Factors on page 139. "Slow" work is based on an hourly wage of $20.25, "Medium" work on an hourly wage of $25.75, and "Fast" work on an hourly wage of $31.50. Other qualifications that apply to this table are on page 9.

|  | Labor SF per manhour | Material coverage SF/gallon | Material cost per gallon | Labor cost per 100 SF | Labor burden 100 SF | Material cost per 100 SF | Overhead per 100 SF | Profit per 100 SF | Total price per 100 SF |
|---|---|---|---|---|---|---|---|---|---|
| **Wine racks, stain grade, per square feet of face** | | | | | | | | | |
| Stain, seal and 2 coat lacquer system (7 step process) | | | | | | | | | |
| STEP 1: Sand & putty | | | | | | | | | |
| Slow | 50 | -- | -- | 40.50 | 11.94 | -- | 9.97 | 9.99 | 72.40 |
| Medium | 75 | -- | -- | 34.33 | 12.15 | -- | 11.62 | 6.97 | 65.07 |
| Fast | 100 | -- | -- | 31.50 | 12.85 | -- | 13.75 | 4.07 | 62.17 |
| STEP 2 & 3: Wiping stain, oil base (material #11a) & wipe | | | | | | | | | |
| Spray 1 coat & wipe | | | | | | | | | |
| Slow | 100 | 150 | 51.30 | 20.25 | 5.97 | 34.20 | 11.48 | 11.50 | 83.40 |
| Medium | 175 | 113 | 44.90 | 14.71 | 5.20 | 39.73 | 14.91 | 8.95 | 83.50 |
| Fast | 225 | 75 | 38.50 | 14.00 | 5.69 | 51.33 | 22.02 | 6.51 | 99.55 |
| STEP 4: Sanding sealer (material #11b) | | | | | | | | | |
| Spray 1 coat & sand | | | | | | | | | |
| Slow | 130 | 150 | 41.50 | 15.58 | 4.58 | 27.67 | 9.09 | 9.11 | 66.03 |
| Medium | 208 | 113 | 36.30 | 12.38 | 4.39 | 32.12 | 12.22 | 7.33 | 68.44 |
| Fast | 275 | 75 | 31.10 | 11.45 | 4.69 | 41.47 | 17.85 | 5.28 | 80.74 |
| STEP 5: Sand lightly | | | | | | | | | |
| Slow | 75 | -- | -- | 27.00 | 7.95 | -- | 6.64 | 6.66 | 48.25 |
| Medium | 100 | -- | -- | 25.75 | 9.12 | -- | 8.72 | 5.23 | 48.82 |
| Fast | 125 | -- | -- | 25.20 | 10.28 | -- | 11.00 | 3.25 | 49.73 |
| STEP 6 & 7: Lacquer (material #11c) | | | | | | | | | |
| Spray 1st coat | | | | | | | | | |
| Slow | 100 | 100 | 45.90 | 20.25 | 5.97 | 45.90 | 13.70 | 13.73 | 99.55 |
| Medium | 200 | 75 | 40.10 | 12.88 | 4.56 | 53.47 | 17.73 | 10.64 | 99.28 |
| Fast | 300 | 50 | 34.40 | 10.50 | 4.27 | 68.80 | 25.91 | 7.66 | 117.14 |
| Spray 2nd coat | | | | | | | | | |
| Slow | 175 | 100 | 45.90 | 11.57 | 3.40 | 45.90 | 11.57 | 11.59 | 84.03 |
| Medium | 313 | 75 | 40.10 | 8.23 | 2.89 | 53.47 | 16.15 | 9.69 | 90.43 |
| Fast | 450 | 50 | 34.40 | 7.00 | 2.85 | 68.80 | 24.38 | 7.21 | 110.24 |
| Complete 7 step stain, seal & 2 coat lacquer system (material #11) | | | | | | | | | |
| Spray all coats | | | | | | | | | |
| Slow | 20 | 25 | 46.10 | 101.25 | 29.85 | 184.40 | 59.95 | 60.08 | 435.53 |
| Medium | 28 | 20 | 40.40 | 91.96 | 32.56 | 202.00 | 81.63 | 48.98 | 457.13 |
| Fast | 35 | 15 | 34.60 | 90.00 | 36.71 | 230.67 | 110.79 | 32.77 | 500.94 |

These figures include coating all interior and exterior surfaces and are based on overall dimensions (length times width) of the wine rack face. For heights above 8 feet, use the High Time Difficulty Factors on page 139. "Slow" work is based on an hourly wage of $20.25, "Medium" work on an hourly wage of $25.75, and "Fast" work on an hourly wage of $31.50. Other qualifications that apply to this table are on page 9.

# Part II

# Preparation Costs

## National Painting Cost Estimator

|  | Labor LF per manhour | Material coverage LF/gallon | Material cost per gallon | Labor cost per 100 LF | Labor burden 100 LF | Material cost per 100 LF | Overhead per 100 LF | Profit per 100 LF | Total price per 100 LF |
|---|---|---|---|---|---|---|---|---|---|
| **Acid wash gutters & downspouts** | | | | | | | | | |
| Acid wash, muriatic acid (material #49) | | | | | | | | | |
| Brush or mitt 1 coat | | | | | | | | | |
| Slow | 80 | 450 | 11.50 | 25.31 | 7.47 | 2.56 | 6.71 | 6.73 | 48.78 |
| Medium | 95 | 425 | 10.10 | 27.11 | 9.61 | 2.38 | 9.77 | 5.86 | 54.73 |
| Fast | 110 | 400 | 8.60 | 28.64 | 11.67 | 2.15 | 13.17 | 3.90 | 59.53 |

For heights above one story, use the High Time Difficulty Factors on page 139. "Slow" work is based on an hourly wage of $20.25, "Medium" work on an hourly wage of $25.75, and "Fast" work on an hourly wage of $31.50. Other qualifications that apply to this table are on page 9.

|  | Labor SF per manhour | Material coverage SF/gallon | Material cost per gallon | Labor cost per 100 SF | Labor burden 100 SF | Material cost per 100 SF | Overhead per 100 SF | Profit per 100 SF | Total price per 100 SF |
|---|---|---|---|---|---|---|---|---|---|
| **Airblast, compressed air** | | | | | | | | | |
| Average production | | | | | | | | | |
| Slow | 150 | -- | -- | 13.50 | 3.99 | -- | 3.32 | 3.33 | 24.14 |
| Medium | 175 | -- | -- | 14.71 | 5.20 | -- | 4.98 | 2.99 | 27.88 |
| Fast | 200 | -- | -- | 15.75 | 6.43 | -- | 6.88 | 2.03 | 31.09 |

All widths less than 12", consider as 1 square foot per linear foot. Add equipment rental costs with Overhead and Profit. For heights above 8 feet, use the High Time Difficulty Factors on page 139. "Slow" work is based on an hourly wage of $20.25, "Medium" work on an hourly wage of $25.75, and "Fast" work on an hourly wage of $31.50. Other qualifications that apply to this table are on page 9.

*Preparation Costs*

|  | Labor SF per manhour | Material coverage SF/gallon | Material cost per gallon | Labor cost per 100 SF | Labor burden 100 SF | Material cost per 100 SF | Overhead per 100 SF | Profit per 100 SF | Total price per 100 SF |
|---|---|---|---|---|---|---|---|---|---|
| **Burn off paint** | | | | | | | | | |
| Exterior: | | | | | | | | | |
|   Exterior trim | | | | | | | | | |
|     Slow | 15 | -- | -- | 135.00 | 39.81 | -- | 33.22 | 33.29 | 241.32 |
|     Medium | 20 | -- | -- | 128.75 | 45.60 | -- | 43.58 | 26.15 | 244.08 |
|     Fast | 25 | -- | -- | 126.00 | 51.40 | -- | 55.00 | 16.27 | 248.67 |
|   Plain surfaces | | | | | | | | | |
|     Slow | 30 | -- | -- | 67.50 | 19.89 | -- | 16.61 | 16.64 | 120.64 |
|     Medium | 40 | -- | -- | 64.38 | 22.80 | -- | 21.79 | 13.08 | 122.05 |
|     Fast | 50 | -- | -- | 63.00 | 25.70 | -- | 27.50 | 8.13 | 124.33 |
|   Beveled wood siding | | | | | | | | | |
|     Slow | 20 | -- | -- | 101.25 | 29.85 | -- | 24.91 | 24.96 | 180.97 |
|     Medium | 30 | -- | -- | 85.83 | 30.39 | -- | 29.05 | 17.43 | 162.70 |
|     Fast | 40 | -- | -- | 78.75 | 32.13 | -- | 34.37 | 10.17 | 155.42 |
| Interior: | | | | | | | | | |
|   Interior trim | | | | | | | | | |
|     Slow | 10 | -- | -- | 202.50 | 59.70 | -- | 49.83 | 49.93 | 361.96 |
|     Medium | 15 | -- | -- | 171.67 | 60.81 | -- | 58.11 | 34.87 | 325.46 |
|     Fast | 20 | -- | -- | 157.50 | 64.25 | -- | 68.75 | 20.34 | 310.84 |
|   Plain surfaces | | | | | | | | | |
|     Slow | 15 | -- | -- | 135.00 | 39.81 | -- | 33.22 | 33.29 | 241.32 |
|     Medium | 25 | -- | -- | 103.00 | 36.48 | -- | 34.87 | 20.92 | 195.27 |
|     Fast | 35 | -- | -- | 90.00 | 36.71 | -- | 39.28 | 11.62 | 177.61 |

All widths less than 12", consider as 1 square foot per linear foot. Note: Because surfaces and the material being removed vary widely, it's best to quote prices for burning-off existing finishes on a Time and Material or Cost Plus Fee basis at a preset hourly rate. "Slow" work is based on an hourly wage of $20.25, "Medium" work on an hourly wage of $25.75, and "Fast" work on an hourly wage of $31.50. Other qualifications that apply to this table are on page 9.

National Painting Cost Estimator

|  | Labor LF per manhour | Material LF/fluid oz ounce | Material cost per ounce | Labor cost per 100 LF | Labor burden 100 LF | Material cost per 100 LF | Overhead per 100 LF | Profit per 100 LF | Total price per 100 LF |
|---|---|---|---|---|---|---|---|---|---|
| **Caulk** | | | | | | | | | |
| 1/8" gap (material #42) | | | | | | | | | |
| Slow | 60 | 14 | .36 | 33.75 | 9.96 | 2.57 | 8.79 | 8.81 | 63.88 |
| Medium | 65 | 13 | .30 | 39.62 | 14.01 | 2.31 | 13.99 | 8.39 | 78.32 |
| Fast | 70 | 12 | .26 | 45.00 | 18.38 | 2.17 | 20.31 | 6.01 | 91.87 |
| 1/4" gap (material #42) | | | | | | | | | |
| Slow | 50 | 3.5 | .36 | 40.50 | 11.94 | 10.29 | 11.92 | 11.95 | 86.60 |
| Medium | 55 | 3.3 | .30 | 46.82 | 16.57 | 9.09 | 18.12 | 10.87 | 101.47 |
| Fast | 60 | 3.0 | .26 | 52.50 | 21.43 | 8.67 | 25.60 | 7.57 | 115.77 |
| 3/8" gap (material #42) | | | | | | | | | |
| Slow | 40 | 1.5 | .36 | 50.63 | 14.92 | 24.00 | 17.02 | 17.05 | 123.62 |
| Medium | 45 | 1.4 | .30 | 57.22 | 20.26 | 21.43 | 24.73 | 14.84 | 138.48 |
| Fast | 50 | 1.3 | .26 | 63.00 | 25.70 | 20.00 | 33.70 | 9.97 | 152.37 |
| 1/2" gap (material #42) | | | | | | | | | |
| Slow | 33 | 1.0 | .36 | 61.36 | 18.09 | 36.00 | 21.94 | 21.98 | 159.37 |
| Medium | 38 | 0.9 | .30 | 67.76 | 24.02 | 33.33 | 31.27 | 18.76 | 175.14 |
| Fast | 43 | 0.8 | .26 | 73.26 | 29.90 | 32.50 | 42.05 | 12.44 | 190.15 |

Caulking that's part of normal surface preparation is included in the painting cost tables. When extra caulking is required, use this cost guide. It's based on oil or latex base, silicone or urethane caulk in 10 ounce tubes. "Slow" work is based on an hourly wage of $20.25, "Medium" work on an hourly wage of $25.75, and "Fast" work on an hourly wage of $31.50. Other qualifications that apply to this table are on page 9.

|  | Labor SF per manhour | Material coverage SF/gallon | Material cost per gallon | Labor cost per 100 SF | Labor burden 100 SF | Material cost per 100 SF | Overhead per 100 SF | Profit per 100 SF | Total price per 100 SF |
|---|---|---|---|---|---|---|---|---|---|
| **Cut cracks** | | | | | | | | | |
| Varnish or hard oil and repair cracks | | | | | | | | | |
| Slow | 120 | -- | -- | 16.88 | 4.96 | -- | 4.15 | 4.16 | 30.15 |
| Medium | 130 | -- | -- | 19.81 | 7.01 | -- | 6.71 | 4.02 | 37.55 |
| Fast | 140 | -- | -- | 22.50 | 9.17 | -- | 9.82 | 2.91 | 44.40 |
| Gloss painted walls and fix cracks | | | | | | | | | |
| Slow | 125 | -- | -- | 16.20 | 4.78 | -- | 3.99 | 4.00 | 28.97 |
| Medium | 135 | -- | -- | 19.07 | 6.77 | -- | 6.46 | 3.87 | 36.17 |
| Fast | 145 | -- | -- | 21.72 | 8.88 | -- | 9.48 | 2.80 | 42.88 |

All widths less than 12", consider as 1 square foot per linear foot. "Slow" work is based on an hourly wage of $20.25, "Medium" work on an hourly wage of $25.75, and "Fast" work on an hourly wage of $31.50. Other qualifications that apply to this table are on page 9.

*Preparation Costs*

|  | Labor SF per manhour | Material coverage SF/gallon | Material cost per gallon | Labor cost per 100 SF | Labor burden 100 SF | Material cost per 100 SF | Overhead per 100 SF | Profit per 100 SF | Total price per 100 SF |
|---|---|---|---|---|---|---|---|---|---|

## Fill wood floors
Fill and wipe wood floors (material #48)
| | | | | | | | | | |
|---|---|---|---|---|---|---|---|---|---|
| Slow | 45 | 155 | 41.40 | 45.00 | 13.26 | 26.71 | 16.15 | 16.18 | 117.30 |
| Medium | 60 | 145 | 36.20 | 42.92 | 15.21 | 24.97 | 20.77 | 12.46 | 116.33 |
| Fast | 75 | 135 | 31.10 | 42.00 | 17.12 | 23.04 | 25.48 | 7.54 | 115.18 |

All widths less than 12", consider as 1 square foot per linear foot. "Slow" work is based on an hourly wage of $20.25, "Medium" work on an hourly wage of $25.75, and "Fast" work on an hourly wage of $31.50. Other qualifications that apply to this table are on page 9.

|  | Labor SF per manhour | Material coverage SF/pound | Material cost per pound | Labor cost per 100 SF | Labor burden 100 SF | Material cost per 100 SF | Overhead per 100 SF | Profit per 100 SF | Total price per 100 SF |
|---|---|---|---|---|---|---|---|---|---|

## Putty application
Good condition, 1 coat (material #45)
| | | | | | | | | | |
|---|---|---|---|---|---|---|---|---|---|
| Slow | 60 | 150 | 6.90 | 33.75 | 9.96 | 4.60 | 9.18 | 9.20 | 66.69 |
| Medium | 90 | 135 | 6.10 | 28.61 | 10.13 | 4.52 | 10.82 | 6.49 | 60.57 |
| Fast | 120 | 120 | 5.20 | 26.25 | 10.69 | 4.33 | 12.80 | 3.79 | 57.86 |

Average condition, 1 coat (material #45)
| | | | | | | | | | |
|---|---|---|---|---|---|---|---|---|---|
| Slow | 35 | 90 | 6.90 | 57.86 | 17.05 | 7.67 | 15.69 | 15.73 | 114.00 |
| Medium | 65 | 75 | 6.10 | 39.62 | 14.01 | 8.13 | 15.45 | 9.27 | 86.48 |
| Fast | 95 | 60 | 5.20 | 33.16 | 13.54 | 8.67 | 17.16 | 5.08 | 77.61 |

Poor condition, 1 coat (material #45)
| | | | | | | | | | |
|---|---|---|---|---|---|---|---|---|---|
| Slow | 15 | 40 | 6.90 | 135.00 | 39.81 | 17.25 | 36.50 | 36.57 | 265.13 |
| Medium | 30 | 30 | 6.10 | 85.83 | 30.39 | 20.33 | 34.14 | 20.48 | 191.17 |
| Fast | 45 | 20 | 5.20 | 70.00 | 28.55 | 26.00 | 38.61 | 11.42 | 174.58 |

These figures apply to either spackle or Swedish putty. All widths less than 12", consider as 1 square foot per linear foot. For heights above 8 feet, use the High Time Difficulty Factors on page 139. For flat trim or sash: Estimate 1 linear foot of trim as 1 square foot of surface. "Slow" work is based on an hourly wage of $20.25, "Medium" work on an hourly wage of $25.75, and "Fast" work on an hourly wage of $31.50. Other qualifications that apply to this table are on page 9.

|  | Labor SF per manhour | Material coverage SF/gallon | Material cost per gallon | Labor cost per 100 SF | Labor burden 100 SF | Material cost per 100 SF | Overhead per 100 SF | Profit per 100 SF | Total price per 100 SF |
|---|---|---|---|---|---|---|---|---|---|

## Sand, medium (before first coat)
Interior flatwall areas
| | | | | | | | | | |
|---|---|---|---|---|---|---|---|---|---|
| Slow | 275 | -- | -- | 7.36 | 2.18 | -- | 2.38 | 1.91 | 13.83 |
| Medium | 300 | -- | -- | 8.58 | 3.03 | -- | 2.91 | 1.74 | 16.26 |
| Fast | 325 | -- | -- | 9.69 | 3.97 | -- | 4.23 | 1.25 | 19.14 |

Interior enamel areas
| | | | | | | | | | |
|---|---|---|---|---|---|---|---|---|---|
| Slow | 250 | -- | -- | 8.10 | 2.39 | -- | 1.99 | 2.00 | 14.48 |
| Medium | 275 | -- | -- | 9.36 | 3.33 | -- | 3.17 | 1.90 | 17.76 |
| Fast | 300 | -- | -- | 10.50 | 4.27 | -- | 4.58 | 1.36 | 20.71 |

All widths less than 12", consider as 1 square foot per linear foot. For heights above 8 feet, use the High Time Difficulty Factors on page 139. "Slow" work is based on an hourly wage of $20.25, "Medium" work on an hourly wage of $25.75, and "Fast" work on an hourly wage of $31.50. Other qualifications that apply to this table are on page 9.

*National Painting Cost Estimator*

|  | Labor SF per manhour | Material coverage SF/gallon | Material cost per gallon | Labor cost per 100 SF | Labor burden 100 SF | Material cost per 100 SF | Overhead per 100 SF | Profit per 100 SF | Total price per 100 SF |
|---|---|---|---|---|---|---|---|---|---|
| **Sand & putty (before second coat)** | | | | | | | | | |
| Interior flatwall areas | | | | | | | | | |
| Slow | 190 | -- | -- | 10.66 | 3.13 | -- | 2.62 | 2.63 | 19.04 |
| Medium | 200 | -- | -- | 12.88 | 4.56 | -- | 4.36 | 2.62 | 24.42 |
| Fast | 210 | -- | -- | 15.00 | 6.11 | -- | 6.55 | 1.94 | 29.60 |
| Interior enamel areas | | | | | | | | | |
| Slow | 110 | -- | -- | 18.41 | 5.42 | -- | 4.53 | 4.54 | 32.90 |
| Medium | 125 | -- | -- | 20.60 | 7.30 | -- | 6.97 | 4.18 | 39.05 |
| Fast | 140 | -- | -- | 22.50 | 9.17 | -- | 9.82 | 2.91 | 44.40 |
| Exterior siding & trim - plain | | | | | | | | | |
| Slow | 180 | -- | -- | 11.25 | 3.33 | -- | 2.77 | 2.77 | 20.12 |
| Medium | 200 | -- | -- | 12.88 | 4.56 | -- | 4.36 | 2.62 | 24.42 |
| Fast | 220 | -- | -- | 14.32 | 5.86 | -- | 6.25 | 1.85 | 28.28 |
| Exterior trim only | | | | | | | | | |
| Slow | 100 | -- | -- | 20.25 | 5.97 | -- | 4.98 | 4.99 | 36.19 |
| Medium | 110 | -- | -- | 23.41 | 8.29 | -- | 7.93 | 4.76 | 44.39 |
| Fast | 120 | -- | -- | 26.25 | 10.69 | -- | 11.46 | 3.39 | 51.79 |
| Bookshelves | | | | | | | | | |
| Slow | 100 | -- | -- | 20.25 | 5.97 | -- | 4.98 | 4.99 | 36.19 |
| Medium | 125 | -- | -- | 20.60 | 7.30 | -- | 6.97 | 4.18 | 39.05 |
| Fast | 150 | -- | -- | 21.00 | 8.58 | -- | 9.17 | 2.71 | 41.46 |
| Cabinets | | | | | | | | | |
| Slow | 125 | -- | -- | 16.20 | 4.78 | -- | 3.99 | 4.00 | 28.97 |
| Medium | 150 | -- | -- | 17.17 | 6.09 | -- | 5.81 | 3.49 | 32.56 |
| Fast | 175 | -- | -- | 18.00 | 7.32 | -- | 7.86 | 2.32 | 35.50 |

All trim which is less than 12" wide, consider to be 12" wide. For heights above 8 feet, use the High Time Difficulty Factors on page 139. High grade work - Use the manhours equal to 1 coat of paint. For medium grade work - Use half (50%) of the manhours for 1 coat of paint. "Slow" work is based on an hourly wage of $20.25, "Medium" work on an hourly wage of $25.75, and "Fast" work on an hourly wage of $31.50. Other qualifications that apply to this table are on page 9.

*Preparation Costs*

|  | Labor SF per manhour | Material coverage SF/gallon | Material cost per gallon | Labor cost per 100 SF | Labor burden 100 SF | Material cost per 100 SF | Overhead per 100 SF | Profit per 100 SF | Total price per 100 SF |
|---|---|---|---|---|---|---|---|---|---|
| **Sand, light (before third coat)** | | | | | | | | | |
| Interior flatwall areas | | | | | | | | | |
| Slow | 335 | -- | -- | 6.04 | 1.80 | -- | 1.49 | 1.49 | 10.82 |
| Medium | 345 | -- | -- | 7.46 | 2.65 | -- | 2.53 | 1.52 | 14.16 |
| Fast | 355 | -- | -- | 8.87 | 3.64 | -- | 3.87 | 1.15 | 17.53 |
| Interior enamel areas | | | | | | | | | |
| Slow | 130 | -- | -- | 15.58 | 4.58 | -- | 3.83 | 3.84 | 27.83 |
| Medium | 140 | -- | -- | 18.39 | 6.51 | -- | 6.23 | 3.74 | 34.87 |
| Fast | 150 | -- | -- | 21.00 | 8.58 | -- | 9.17 | 2.71 | 41.46 |
| Exterior siding & trim - plain | | | | | | | | | |
| Slow | 250 | -- | -- | 8.10 | 2.39 | -- | 1.99 | 2.00 | 14.48 |
| Medium | 275 | -- | -- | 9.36 | 3.33 | -- | 3.17 | 1.90 | 17.76 |
| Fast | 300 | -- | -- | 10.50 | 4.27 | -- | 4.58 | 1.36 | 20.71 |
| Exterior trim only | | | | | | | | | |
| Slow | 150 | -- | -- | 13.50 | 3.99 | -- | 3.32 | 3.33 | 24.14 |
| Medium | 175 | -- | -- | 14.71 | 5.20 | -- | 4.98 | 2.99 | 27.88 |
| Fast | 200 | -- | -- | 15.75 | 6.43 | -- | 6.88 | 2.03 | 31.09 |
| Bookshelves | | | | | | | | | |
| Slow | 175 | -- | -- | 11.57 | 3.40 | -- | 2.85 | 2.85 | 20.67 |
| Medium | 225 | -- | -- | 11.44 | 4.04 | -- | 3.87 | 2.32 | 21.67 |
| Fast | 275 | -- | -- | 11.45 | 4.69 | -- | 5.00 | 1.48 | 22.62 |
| Cabinets | | | | | | | | | |
| Slow | 200 | -- | -- | 10.13 | 2.98 | -- | 2.49 | 2.50 | 18.10 |
| Medium | 250 | -- | -- | 10.30 | 3.65 | -- | 3.49 | 2.09 | 19.53 |
| Fast | 300 | -- | -- | 10.50 | 4.27 | -- | 4.58 | 1.36 | 20.71 |

All widths less than 12", consider 1 square foot per linear foot. For heights above 8 feet, use the High Time Difficulty Factors on page 139. "Slow" work is based on an hourly wage of $20.25, "Medium" work on an hourly wage of $25.75, and "Fast" work on an hourly wage of $31.50. Other qualifications that apply to this table are on page 9.

|  | Labor SF per manhour | Material coverage SF/gallon | Material cost per gallon | Labor cost per 100 SF | Labor burden 100 SF | Material cost per 100 SF | Overhead per 100 SF | Profit per 100 SF | Total price per 100 SF |
|---|---|---|---|---|---|---|---|---|---|
| **Sand, extra fine, flat surfaces, varnish** | | | | | | | | | |
| Sand or steel wool | | | | | | | | | |
| Slow | 50 | -- | -- | 40.50 | 11.94 | -- | 9.97 | 9.99 | 72.40 |
| Medium | 88 | -- | -- | 29.26 | 10.35 | -- | 9.91 | 5.94 | 55.46 |
| Fast | 125 | -- | -- | 25.20 | 10.28 | -- | 11.00 | 3.25 | 49.73 |

All widths less than 12", consider as 1 square foot per linear foot. For heights above 8 feet, use the High Time Difficulty Factors on page 139. "Slow" work is based on an hourly wage of $20.25, "Medium" work on an hourly wage of $25.75, and "Fast" work on an hourly wage of $31.50. Other qualifications that apply to this table are on page 9.

## Sandblast, general

Sandblasting production rates may vary widely. Use the following figures as a reference for estimating and to establish performance data for your company. The abrasive material used in sandblasting is usually white silica sand although slags have recently gained in popularity. Material consumption varies with several factors:

1) Type of finish required
2) Condition of the surface
3) Quality of abrasive material (sharpness, cleanliness and hardness)
4) Nozzle size
5) Equipment arrangement and placement
6) Operator skill

All material consumption values are based on three uses of a 25 to 35 mesh white silica sand abrasive at a cost of $40 to $60 per ton. (Check the current price in your area.) Note: See the Structural Steel Conversion table at Figure 23 on pages 391 through 399 for converting linear feet or tons of structural steel to square feet.

*Preparation Costs*

|  | Labor SF per manhour | Material coverage pounds/SF | Material cost per pound | Labor cost per 100 SF | Labor burden 100 SF | Material cost per 100 SF | Overhead per 100 SF | Profit per 100 SF | Total price per 100 SF |
|---|---|---|---|---|---|---|---|---|---|

## Sandblast, brush-off blast

### Surface condition basis - large projects & surface areas (material #46)

**Remove cement base paint**

| | | | | | | | | | |
|---|---|---|---|---|---|---|---|---|---|
| Slow | 150 | 2.0 | .43 | 13.50 | 3.99 | 86.00 | 19.66 | 19.70 | 142.85 |
| Medium | 175 | 2.5 | .38 | 14.71 | 5.20 | 95.00 | 28.73 | 17.24 | 160.88 |
| Fast | 200 | 3.0 | .32 | 15.75 | 6.43 | 96.00 | 36.64 | 10.84 | 165.66 |

**Remove oil or latex base paint**

| | | | | | | | | | |
|---|---|---|---|---|---|---|---|---|---|
| Slow | 100 | 3.0 | .43 | 20.25 | 5.97 | 129.00 | 29.49 | 29.55 | 214.26 |
| Medium | 125 | 3.5 | .38 | 20.60 | 7.30 | 133.00 | 40.22 | 24.13 | 225.25 |
| Fast | 150 | 4.0 | .32 | 21.00 | 8.58 | 128.00 | 48.85 | 14.45 | 220.88 |

### Surface area basis - large projects & surface areas (material #46)

**Pipe up to 12" O/D**

| | | | | | | | | | |
|---|---|---|---|---|---|---|---|---|---|
| Slow | 125 | 4.0 | .43 | 16.20 | 4.78 | 172.00 | 36.67 | 36.74 | 266.39 |
| Medium | 150 | 4.5 | .38 | 17.17 | 6.09 | 171.00 | 48.56 | 29.14 | 271.96 |
| Fast | 175 | 5.0 | .32 | 18.00 | 7.32 | 160.00 | 57.46 | 17.00 | 259.78 |

### Structural steel

**Sizes up to 2 SF/LF**

| | | | | | | | | | |
|---|---|---|---|---|---|---|---|---|---|
| Slow | 150 | 4.0 | .43 | 13.50 | 3.99 | 172.00 | 36.00 | 36.08 | 261.57 |
| Medium | 175 | 4.5 | .38 | 14.71 | 5.20 | 171.00 | 47.73 | 28.64 | 267.28 |
| Fast | 200 | 5.0 | .32 | 15.75 | 6.43 | 160.00 | 56.48 | 16.71 | 255.37 |

**Sizes from 2 to 5 SF/LF**

| | | | | | | | | | |
|---|---|---|---|---|---|---|---|---|---|
| Slow | 200 | 3.0 | .43 | 10.13 | 2.98 | 129.00 | 27.00 | 27.06 | 196.17 |
| Medium | 225 | 3.5 | .38 | 11.44 | 4.04 | 133.00 | 37.12 | 22.27 | 207.87 |
| Fast | 250 | 4.0 | .32 | 12.60 | 5.14 | 128.00 | 45.18 | 13.36 | 204.28 |

**Sizes over 5 SF/LF**

| | | | | | | | | | |
|---|---|---|---|---|---|---|---|---|---|
| Slow | 250 | 2.0 | .43 | 8.10 | 2.39 | 86.00 | 18.33 | 18.37 | 133.19 |
| Medium | 275 | 3.0 | .38 | 9.36 | 3.33 | 114.00 | 31.67 | 19.00 | 177.36 |
| Fast | 300 | 4.0 | .32 | 10.50 | 4.27 | 128.00 | 44.26 | 13.09 | 200.12 |

### Tanks and vessels

**Sizes up to 12'0" O/D**

| | | | | | | | | | |
|---|---|---|---|---|---|---|---|---|---|
| Slow | 200 | 3.0 | .43 | 10.13 | 2.98 | 129.00 | 27.00 | 27.06 | 196.17 |
| Medium | 225 | 3.5 | .38 | 11.44 | 4.04 | 133.00 | 37.12 | 22.27 | 207.87 |
| Fast | 250 | 4.0 | .32 | 12.60 | 5.14 | 128.00 | 45.18 | 13.36 | 204.28 |

**Sizes over 12'0" O/D**

| | | | | | | | | | |
|---|---|---|---|---|---|---|---|---|---|
| Slow | 250 | 2.0 | .43 | 8.10 | 2.39 | 86.00 | 18.33 | 18.37 | 133.19 |
| Medium | 275 | 3.0 | .38 | 9.36 | 3.33 | 114.00 | 31.67 | 19.00 | 177.36 |
| Fast | 300 | 4.0 | .32 | 10.50 | 4.27 | 128.00 | 44.26 | 13.09 | 200.12 |

For heights above 8 feet, use the High Time Difficulty Factors on page 139. "Slow" work is based on an hourly wage of $20.25, "Medium" work on an hourly wage of $25.75, and "Fast" work on an hourly wage of $31.50. Other qualifications that apply to this table are on page 9.

*National Painting Cost Estimator*

|  | Labor SF per manhour | Material coverage pounds/SF | Material cost per pound | Labor cost per 100 SF | Labor burden 100 SF | Material cost per 100 SF | Overhead per 100 SF | Profit per 100 SF | Total price per 100 SF |
|---|---|---|---|---|---|---|---|---|---|

## Sandblast, commercial blast (67% white)

Surface condition basis - large projects & surface areas (material #46)

Loose mill scale & fine powder rust

| | | | | | | | | | |
|---|---|---|---|---|---|---|---|---|---|
| Slow | 150 | 4.0 | .43 | 13.50 | 3.99 | 172.00 | 36.00 | 36.08 | 261.57 |
| Medium | 175 | 4.5 | .38 | 14.71 | 5.20 | 171.00 | 47.73 | 28.64 | 267.28 |
| Fast | 200 | 5.0 | .32 | 15.75 | 6.43 | 160.00 | 56.48 | 16.71 | 255.37 |

Tight mill scale & little or no rust

| | | | | | | | | | |
|---|---|---|---|---|---|---|---|---|---|
| Slow | 125 | 5.0 | .43 | 16.20 | 4.78 | 215.00 | 44.84 | 44.93 | 325.75 |
| Medium | 150 | 5.5 | .38 | 17.17 | 6.09 | 209.00 | 58.06 | 34.84 | 325.16 |
| Fast | 175 | 6.0 | .32 | 18.00 | 7.32 | 192.00 | 67.38 | 19.93 | 304.63 |

Hard scale, blistered, rusty surface

| | | | | | | | | | |
|---|---|---|---|---|---|---|---|---|---|
| Slow | 75 | 6.0 | .43 | 27.00 | 7.95 | 258.00 | 55.66 | 55.78 | 404.39 |
| Medium | 100 | 7.0 | .38 | 25.75 | 9.12 | 266.00 | 75.22 | 45.13 | 421.22 |
| Fast | 125 | 8.0 | .32 | 25.20 | 10.28 | 256.00 | 90.36 | 26.73 | 408.57 |

Rust nodules and pitted surface

| | | | | | | | | | |
|---|---|---|---|---|---|---|---|---|---|
| Slow | 50 | 8.0 | .43 | 40.50 | 11.94 | 344.00 | 75.33 | 75.48 | 547.25 |
| Medium | 60 | 9.5 | .38 | 42.92 | 15.21 | 361.00 | 104.78 | 62.87 | 586.78 |
| Fast | 70 | 11.0 | .32 | 45.00 | 18.38 | 352.00 | 128.76 | 38.09 | 582.23 |

Surface area basis - large projects & surface areas (material #46)

Pipe up to 12" O/D

| | | | | | | | | | |
|---|---|---|---|---|---|---|---|---|---|
| Slow | 45 | 5.0 | .43 | 45.00 | 13.26 | 215.00 | 51.92 | 52.03 | 377.21 |
| Medium | 60 | 6.0 | .38 | 42.92 | 15.21 | 228.00 | 71.53 | 42.92 | 400.58 |
| Fast | 75 | 7.0 | .32 | 42.00 | 17.12 | 224.00 | 87.77 | 25.96 | 396.85 |

Structural steel

Sizes up to 2 SF/LF

| | | | | | | | | | |
|---|---|---|---|---|---|---|---|---|---|
| Slow | 70 | 5.0 | .43 | 28.93 | 8.54 | 215.00 | 47.97 | 48.07 | 348.51 |
| Medium | 85 | 6.0 | .38 | 30.29 | 10.72 | 228.00 | 67.25 | 40.35 | 376.61 |
| Fast | 100 | 7.0 | .32 | 31.50 | 12.85 | 224.00 | 83.19 | 24.61 | 376.15 |

Sizes from 2 to 5 SF/LF

| | | | | | | | | | |
|---|---|---|---|---|---|---|---|---|---|
| Slow | 80 | 5.0 | .43 | 25.31 | 7.47 | 215.00 | 47.08 | 47.18 | 342.04 |
| Medium | 95 | 5.5 | .38 | 27.11 | 9.61 | 209.00 | 61.43 | 36.86 | 344.01 |
| Fast | 110 | 6.0 | .32 | 28.64 | 11.67 | 192.00 | 72.02 | 21.30 | 325.63 |

Sizes over 5 SF/LF

| | | | | | | | | | |
|---|---|---|---|---|---|---|---|---|---|
| Slow | 85 | 5.0 | .43 | 23.82 | 7.01 | 215.00 | 46.71 | 46.81 | 339.35 |
| Medium | 100 | 5.5 | .38 | 25.75 | 9.12 | 209.00 | 60.97 | 36.58 | 341.42 |
| Fast | 115 | 6.0 | .32 | 27.39 | 11.19 | 192.00 | 71.48 | 21.14 | 323.20 |

*Preparation Costs*

|  | Labor SF per manhour | Material coverage pounds/SF | Material cost per pound | Labor cost per 100 SF | Labor burden 100 SF | Material cost per 100 SF | Overhead per 100 SF | Profit per 100 SF | Total price per 100 SF |
|---|---|---|---|---|---|---|---|---|---|
| Tanks and vessels |  |  |  |  |  |  |  |  |  |
| Sizes up to 12'0" O/D |  |  |  |  |  |  |  |  |  |
| Slow | 80 | 6.0 | .43 | 25.31 | 7.47 | 258.00 | 55.25 | 55.36 | 401.39 |
| Medium | 95 | 6.5 | .38 | 27.11 | 9.61 | 247.00 | 70.93 | 42.56 | 397.21 |
| Fast | 110 | 7.0 | .32 | 28.64 | 11.67 | 224.00 | 81.94 | 24.24 | 370.49 |
| Sizes over 12'0" O/D |  |  |  |  |  |  |  |  |  |
| Slow | 75 | 6.0 | .43 | 27.00 | 7.95 | 258.00 | 55.66 | 55.78 | 404.39 |
| Medium | 100 | 6.3 | .38 | 25.75 | 9.12 | 239.40 | 68.57 | 41.14 | 383.98 |
| Fast | 125 | 6.5 | .32 | 25.20 | 10.28 | 208.00 | 75.48 | 22.33 | 341.29 |

For heights above 8 feet, use the High Time Difficulty Factors on page 139. "Slow" work is based on an hourly wage of $20.25, "Medium" work on an hourly wage of $25.75, and "Fast" work on an hourly wage of $31.50. Other qualifications that apply to this table are on page 9.

|  | Labor SF per manhour | Material coverage pounds/SF | Material cost per pound | Labor cost per 100 SF | Labor burden 100 SF | Material cost per 100 SF | Overhead per 100 SF | Profit per 100 SF | Total price per 100 SF |
|---|---|---|---|---|---|---|---|---|---|

## Sandblast, near white blast (95% white)

### Surface condition basis - large projects & surface areas (material #46)

**Loose mill scale & fine powder rust**

| | | | | | | | | | |
|---|---|---|---|---|---|---|---|---|---|
| Slow | 125 | 5.0 | .43 | 16.20 | 4.78 | 215.00 | 44.84 | 44.93 | 325.75 |
| Medium | 150 | 6.0 | .38 | 17.17 | 6.09 | 228.00 | 62.81 | 37.69 | 351.76 |
| Fast | 175 | 7.0 | .32 | 18.00 | 7.32 | 224.00 | 77.30 | 22.86 | 349.48 |

**Tight mill scale & little or no rust**

| | | | | | | | | | |
|---|---|---|---|---|---|---|---|---|---|
| Slow | 75 | 7.0 | .43 | 27.00 | 7.95 | 301.00 | 63.83 | 63.97 | 463.75 |
| Medium | 100 | 8.0 | .38 | 25.75 | 9.12 | 304.00 | 84.72 | 50.83 | 474.42 |
| Fast | 125 | 9.0 | .32 | 25.20 | 10.28 | 288.00 | 100.28 | 29.66 | 453.42 |

**Hard scale, blistered, rusty surface**

| | | | | | | | | | |
|---|---|---|---|---|---|---|---|---|---|
| Slow | 50 | 9.0 | .43 | 40.50 | 11.94 | 387.00 | 83.50 | 83.67 | 606.61 |
| Medium | 75 | 11.0 | .38 | 34.33 | 12.15 | 418.00 | 116.12 | 69.67 | 650.27 |
| Fast | 100 | 13.0 | .32 | 31.50 | 12.85 | 416.00 | 142.71 | 42.21 | 645.27 |

**Rust nodules and pitted surface**

| | | | | | | | | | |
|---|---|---|---|---|---|---|---|---|---|
| Slow | 35 | 12.0 | .43 | 57.86 | 17.05 | 516.00 | 112.28 | 112.51 | 815.70 |
| Medium | 50 | 14.5 | .38 | 51.50 | 18.24 | 551.00 | 155.18 | 93.11 | 869.03 |
| Fast | 65 | 17.0 | .32 | 48.46 | 19.75 | 544.00 | 189.79 | 56.14 | 858.14 |

### Surface area basis - large projects & surface areas (material #46)

**Pipe up to 12" O/D**

| | | | | | | | | | |
|---|---|---|---|---|---|---|---|---|---|
| Slow | 30 | 8.0 | .43 | 67.50 | 19.89 | 344.00 | 81.97 | 82.14 | 595.50 |
| Medium | 45 | 9.0 | .38 | 57.22 | 20.26 | 342.00 | 104.87 | 62.92 | 587.27 |
| Fast | 60 | 10.0 | .32 | 52.50 | 21.43 | 320.00 | 122.12 | 36.12 | 552.17 |

**Structural steel**

Sizes up to 2 SF/LF

| | | | | | | | | | |
|---|---|---|---|---|---|---|---|---|---|
| Slow | 40 | 7.0 | .43 | 50.63 | 14.92 | 301.00 | 69.65 | 69.80 | 506.00 |
| Medium | 55 | 8.5 | .38 | 46.82 | 16.57 | 323.00 | 96.60 | 57.96 | 540.95 |
| Fast | 70 | 10.0 | .32 | 45.00 | 18.38 | 320.00 | 118.84 | 35.15 | 537.37 |

Sizes from 2 to 5 SF/LF

| | | | | | | | | | |
|---|---|---|---|---|---|---|---|---|---|
| Slow | 45 | 7.0 | .43 | 45.00 | 13.26 | 301.00 | 68.26 | 68.41 | 495.93 |
| Medium | 60 | 8.0 | .38 | 42.92 | 15.21 | 304.00 | 90.53 | 54.32 | 506.98 |
| Fast | 75 | 9.0 | .32 | 42.00 | 17.12 | 288.00 | 107.61 | 31.83 | 486.56 |

Sizes over 5 SF/LF

| | | | | | | | | | |
|---|---|---|---|---|---|---|---|---|---|
| Slow | 55 | 8.0 | .43 | 36.82 | 10.85 | 344.00 | 74.42 | 74.58 | 540.67 |
| Medium | 70 | 8.5 | .38 | 36.79 | 13.04 | 323.00 | 93.20 | 55.92 | 521.95 |
| Fast | 85 | 9.0 | .32 | 37.06 | 15.10 | 288.00 | 105.46 | 31.19 | 476.81 |

*Preparation Costs*

|  | Labor SF per manhour | Material coverage pounds/SF | Material cost per pound | Labor cost per 100 SF | Labor burden 100 SF | Material cost per 100 SF | Overhead per 100 SF | Profit per 100 SF | Total price per 100 SF |
|---|---|---|---|---|---|---|---|---|---|
| **Tanks and vessels** | | | | | | | | | |
| Sizes up to 12'0" O/D | | | | | | | | | |
|   Slow | 65 | 6.0 | .43 | 31.15 | 9.18 | 258.00 | 56.68 | 56.80 | 411.81 |
|   Medium | 80 | 7.0 | .38 | 32.19 | 11.40 | 266.00 | 77.40 | 46.44 | 433.43 |
|   Fast | 95 | 8.0 | .32 | 33.16 | 13.54 | 256.00 | 93.83 | 27.76 | 424.29 |
| Sizes over 12'0" O/D | | | | | | | | | |
|   Slow | 70 | 6.0 | .43 | 28.93 | 8.54 | 258.00 | 56.14 | 56.26 | 407.87 |
|   Medium | 85 | 7.0 | .38 | 30.29 | 10.72 | 266.00 | 76.75 | 46.05 | 429.81 |
|   Fast | 100 | 8.0 | .32 | 31.50 | 12.85 | 256.00 | 93.11 | 27.54 | 421.00 |

For heights above 8 feet, use the High Time Difficulty Factors on page 139. "Slow" work is based on an hourly wage of $20.25, "Medium" work on an hourly wage of $25.75, and "Fast" work on an hourly wage of $31.50. Other qualifications that apply to this table are on page 9.

*National Painting Cost Estimator*

|  | Labor SF per manhour | Material coverage pounds/SF | Material cost per pound | Labor cost per 100 SF | Labor burden 100 SF | Material cost per 100 SF | Overhead per 100 SF | Profit per 100 SF | Total price per 100 SF |
|---|---|---|---|---|---|---|---|---|---|

## Sandblast, white blast (100% uniform white stage)

Surface condition basis - large projects & surface areas (material #46)

Loose mill scale & fine powder rust

| | | | | | | | | | |
|---|---|---|---|---|---|---|---|---|---|
| Slow | 50 | 7.0 | .43 | 40.50 | 11.94 | 301.00 | 67.16 | 67.30 | 487.90 |
| Medium | 75 | 8.5 | .38 | 34.33 | 12.15 | 323.00 | 92.37 | 55.42 | 517.27 |
| Fast | 100 | 10.0 | .32 | 31.50 | 12.85 | 320.00 | 112.95 | 33.41 | 510.71 |

Tight mill scale & little or no rust

| | | | | | | | | | |
|---|---|---|---|---|---|---|---|---|---|
| Slow | 40 | 8.0 | .43 | 50.63 | 14.92 | 344.00 | 77.82 | 77.98 | 565.35 |
| Medium | 60 | 9.5 | .38 | 42.92 | 15.21 | 361.00 | 104.78 | 62.87 | 586.78 |
| Fast | 80 | 11.0 | .32 | 39.38 | 16.06 | 352.00 | 126.31 | 37.36 | 571.11 |

Hard scale, blistered, rusty surface

| | | | | | | | | | |
|---|---|---|---|---|---|---|---|---|---|
| Slow | 30 | 10.0 | .43 | 67.50 | 19.89 | 430.00 | 98.31 | 98.52 | 714.22 |
| Medium | 45 | 12.5 | .38 | 57.22 | 20.26 | 475.00 | 138.12 | 82.87 | 773.47 |
| Fast | 60 | 15.0 | .32 | 52.50 | 21.43 | 480.00 | 171.72 | 50.79 | 776.44 |

Rust nodules and pitted surface

| | | | | | | | | | |
|---|---|---|---|---|---|---|---|---|---|
| Slow | 25 | 15.0 | .43 | 81.00 | 23.88 | 645.00 | 142.48 | 142.78 | 1035.14 |
| Medium | 35 | 17.5 | .38 | 73.57 | 26.05 | 665.00 | 191.15 | 114.69 | 1070.46 |
| Fast | 45 | 20.0 | .32 | 70.00 | 28.55 | 640.00 | 228.95 | 67.73 | 1035.23 |

Surface area basis - large projects & surface areas (material #46)

Pipe up to 12" O/D

| | | | | | | | | | |
|---|---|---|---|---|---|---|---|---|---|
| Slow | 30 | 10.0 | .43 | 67.50 | 19.89 | 430.00 | 98.31 | 98.52 | 714.22 |
| Medium | 40 | 11.5 | .38 | 64.38 | 22.80 | 437.00 | 131.04 | 78.63 | 733.85 |
| Fast | 50 | 13.0 | .32 | 63.00 | 25.70 | 416.00 | 156.46 | 46.28 | 707.44 |

Structural steel

Sizes up to 2 SF/LF

| | | | | | | | | | |
|---|---|---|---|---|---|---|---|---|---|
| Slow | 40 | 9.0 | .43 | 50.63 | 14.92 | 387.00 | 85.99 | 86.17 | 624.71 |
| Medium | 50 | 10.5 | .38 | 51.50 | 18.24 | 399.00 | 117.18 | 70.31 | 656.23 |
| Fast | 60 | 12.0 | .32 | 52.50 | 21.43 | 384.00 | 141.96 | 41.99 | 641.88 |

Sizes from 2 to 5 SF/LF

| | | | | | | | | | |
|---|---|---|---|---|---|---|---|---|---|
| Slow | 45 | 8.0 | .43 | 45.00 | 13.26 | 344.00 | 76.43 | 76.59 | 555.28 |
| Medium | 55 | 9.5 | .38 | 46.82 | 16.57 | 361.00 | 106.10 | 63.66 | 594.15 |
| Fast | 65 | 11.0 | .32 | 48.46 | 19.75 | 352.00 | 130.27 | 38.54 | 589.02 |

Sizes over 5 SF/LF

| | | | | | | | | | |
|---|---|---|---|---|---|---|---|---|---|
| Slow | 50 | 8.0 | .43 | 40.50 | 11.94 | 344.00 | 75.33 | 75.48 | 547.25 |
| Medium | 60 | 9.5 | .38 | 42.92 | 15.21 | 361.00 | 104.78 | 62.87 | 586.78 |
| Fast | 70 | 11.0 | .32 | 45.00 | 18.38 | 352.00 | 128.76 | 38.09 | 582.23 |

*Preparation Costs*

|  | Labor SF per manhour | Material coverage pounds/SF | Material cost per pound | Labor cost per 100 SF | Labor burden 100 SF | Material cost per 100 SF | Overhead per 100 SF | Profit per 100 SF | Total price per 100 SF |
|---|---|---|---|---|---|---|---|---|---|
| **Tanks and vessels** | | | | | | | | | |
| Sizes up to 12'0" O/D | | | | | | | | | |
|    Slow | 60 | 8.0 | .43 | 33.75 | 9.96 | 344.00 | 73.66 | 73.82 | 535.19 |
|    Medium | 70 | 9.5 | .38 | 36.79 | 13.04 | 361.00 | 102.70 | 61.62 | 575.15 |
|    Fast | 80 | 11.0 | .32 | 39.38 | 16.06 | 352.00 | 126.31 | 37.36 | 571.11 |
| Sizes over 12'0" O/D | | | | | | | | | |
|    Slow | 70 | 8.0 | .43 | 28.93 | 8.54 | 344.00 | 72.48 | 72.63 | 526.58 |
|    Medium | 80 | 9.5 | .38 | 32.19 | 11.40 | 361.00 | 101.15 | 60.69 | 566.43 |
|    Fast | 90 | 11.0 | .32 | 35.00 | 14.27 | 352.00 | 124.40 | 36.80 | 562.47 |

For heights above 8 feet, use the High Time Difficulty Factors on page 139. "Slow" work is based on an hourly wage of $20.25, "Medium" work on an hourly wage of $25.75, and "Fast" work on an hourly wage of $31.50. Other qualifications that apply to this table are on page 9.

|  | Labor SF per manhour | Material coverage pounds/SF | Material cost per pound | Labor cost per 100 SF | Labor burden 100 SF | Material cost per 100 SF | Overhead per 100 SF | Profit per 100 SF | Total price per 100 SF |
|---|---|---|---|---|---|---|---|---|---|

## Scribing (edge scraping) and back-painting, horizontal, interior or exterior

Scribing, horizontal, heights up to 6'8"
  Five point tool scribing (edge scraping)

|  | | | | | | | | | |
|---|---|---|---|---|---|---|---|---|---|
|    Slow | 25 | -- | -- | 81.00 | 23.88 | -- | 19.93 | 19.97 | 144.78 |
|    Medium | 34 | -- | -- | 74.91 | 26.53 | -- | 25.36 | 15.21 | 142.01 |
|    Fast | 44 | -- | -- | 72.00 | 29.38 | -- | 31.43 | 9.30 | 142.11 |

Scribing, horizontal, heights from 6'8" to 9'0"   (1.3 High Time Difficulty Factor included)
  Five point tool scribing (edge scraping)

|  | | | | | | | | | |
|---|---|---|---|---|---|---|---|---|---|
|    Slow | 19 | -- | -- | 106.58 | 31.42 | -- | 26.22 | 26.28 | 190.50 |
|    Medium | 26 | -- | -- | 99.04 | 35.07 | -- | 33.53 | 20.12 | 187.76 |
|    Fast | 34 | -- | -- | 92.65 | 37.78 | -- | 40.44 | 11.96 | 182.83 |

Scribing, horizontal, heights from 9'0" to 13'0"   (1.6 High Time Difficulty Factor included)
  Five point tool scribing (edge scraping)

|  | | | | | | | | | |
|---|---|---|---|---|---|---|---|---|---|
|    Slow | 16 | -- | -- | 129.60 | 38.21 | -- | 31.89 | 31.96 | 231.66 |
|    Medium | 21 | -- | -- | 119.85 | 42.47 | -- | 40.57 | 24.34 | 227.23 |
|    Fast | 27 | -- | -- | 115.20 | 46.99 | -- | 50.28 | 14.87 | 227.34 |

Scribing, horizontal, heights from 13'0" to 17'0"   (1.9 High Time Difficulty Factor included)
  Five point tool scribing (edge scraping)

|  | | | | | | | | | |
|---|---|---|---|---|---|---|---|---|---|
|    Slow | 13 | -- | -- | 155.77 | 45.91 | -- | 38.33 | 38.41 | 278.42 |
|    Medium | 18 | -- | -- | 143.06 | 50.68 | -- | 48.43 | 29.06 | 271.23 |
|    Fast | 23 | -- | -- | 136.96 | 55.87 | -- | 59.78 | 17.68 | 270.29 |

Scribing, horizontal, heights from 17'0" to 19'0"   (2.2 High Time Difficulty Factor included)
  Five point tool scribing (edge scraping)

|  | | | | | | | | | |
|---|---|---|---|---|---|---|---|---|---|
|    Slow | 11 | -- | -- | 184.09 | 54.28 | -- | 45.30 | 45.39 | 329.06 |
|    Medium | 16 | -- | -- | 164.80 | 58.37 | -- | 55.79 | 33.47 | 312.43 |
|    Fast | 20 | -- | -- | 157.50 | 64.25 | -- | 68.75 | 20.34 | 310.84 |

*National Painting Cost Estimator*

|  | Labor SF per manhour | Material coverage pounds/SF | Material cost per pound | Labor cost per 100 SF | Labor burden 100 SF | Material cost per 100 SF | Overhead per 100 SF | Profit per 100 SF | Total price per 100 SF |
|---|---|---|---|---|---|---|---|---|---|

**Scribing, horizontal, heights from 19'0" to 21'0"**   (2.5 High Time Difficulty Factor included)
  Five point tool scribing (edge scraping)

| | | | | | | | | | |
|---|---|---|---|---|---|---|---|---|---|
| Slow | 10 | -- | -- | 202.50 | 59.70 | -- | 49.83 | 49.93 | 361.96 |
| Medium | 14 | -- | -- | 187.27 | 66.34 | -- | 63.39 | 38.03 | 355.03 |
| Fast | 18 | -- | -- | 180.00 | 73.42 | -- | 78.57 | 23.24 | 355.23 |

|  | Labor SF per manhour | Material coverage pounds/SF | Material cost per pound | Labor cost per 100 SF | Labor burden 100 SF | Material cost per 100 SF | Overhead per 100 SF | Profit per 100 SF | Total price per 100 SF |
|---|---|---|---|---|---|---|---|---|---|

## Scribing (edge scraping) and back-painting, vertical, interior or exterior

Scribing and back-painting, vertical, heights up to 6'8"
  Five point tool scribing (edge scraping)

| | | | | | | | | | |
|---|---|---|---|---|---|---|---|---|---|
| Slow | 31 | -- | -- | 65.32 | 19.27 | -- | 16.07 | 16.11 | 116.77 |
| Medium | 40 | -- | -- | 63.90 | 22.61 | -- | 21.63 | 12.98 | 121.12 |
| Fast | 50 | -- | -- | 63.51 | 25.90 | -- | 27.72 | 8.20 | 125.33 |

Scribing and back-painting, vertical, heights from 6'8" to 9'0"   (1.3 High Time Difficulty Factor included)
  Five point tool scribing (edge scraping)

| | | | | | | | | | |
|---|---|---|---|---|---|---|---|---|---|
| Slow | 24 | -- | -- | 84.38 | 24.88 | -- | 20.76 | 20.80 | 150.82 |
| Medium | 31 | -- | -- | 83.06 | 29.43 | -- | 28.12 | 16.87 | 157.48 |
| Fast | 38 | -- | -- | 82.89 | 33.84 | -- | 36.18 | 10.70 | 163.61 |

Scribing and back-painting, vertical, heights from 9'0" to 13'0"   (1.6 High Time Difficulty Factor included)
  Five point tool scribing (edge scraping)

| | | | | | | | | | |
|---|---|---|---|---|---|---|---|---|---|
| Slow | 19 | -- | -- | 104.52 | 30.80 | -- | 25.72 | 25.77 | 186.81 |
| Medium | 25 | -- | -- | 102.23 | 36.20 | -- | 34.61 | 20.76 | 193.80 |
| Fast | 31 | -- | -- | 101.61 | 41.46 | -- | 44.35 | 13.12 | 200.54 |

Scribing and back-painting, vertical, heights from 13'0" to 17'0"   (1.9 High Time Difficulty Factor included)
  Five point tool scribing (edge scraping)

| | | | | | | | | | |
|---|---|---|---|---|---|---|---|---|---|
| Slow | 16 | -- | -- | 126.56 | 37.32 | -- | 31.14 | 31.21 | 226.23 |
| Medium | 21 | -- | -- | 122.62 | 43.43 | -- | 41.51 | 24.90 | 232.46 |
| Fast | 26 | -- | -- | 121.15 | 49.42 | -- | 52.88 | 15.64 | 239.09 |

Scribing and back-painting, vertical, heights from 17'0" to 19'0"   (2.2 High Time Difficulty Factor included)
  Five point tool scribing (edge scraping)

| | | | | | | | | | |
|---|---|---|---|---|---|---|---|---|---|
| Slow | 14 | -- | -- | 144.64 | 42.65 | -- | 35.59 | 35.66 | 258.54 |
| Medium | 18 | -- | -- | 143.06 | 50.68 | -- | 48.43 | 29.06 | 271.23 |
| Fast | 23 | -- | -- | 136.96 | 55.87 | -- | 59.78 | 17.68 | 270.29 |

Scribing and back-painting, vertical, heights from 19'0" to 21'0"   (2.5 High Time Difficulty Factor included)
  Five point tool scribing (edge scraping)

| | | | | | | | | | |
|---|---|---|---|---|---|---|---|---|---|
| Slow | 12 | -- | -- | 163.31 | 48.15 | -- | 40.18 | 40.27 | 291.91 |
| Medium | 16 | -- | -- | 159.74 | 56.56 | -- | 54.07 | 32.44 | 302.81 |
| Fast | 20 | -- | -- | 158.77 | 64.75 | -- | 69.30 | 20.50 | 313.32 |

## Preparation Costs

Use these figures in combination with the cutting-in figures to achieve a clean edge on textured surfaces prior to the cutting-in operation. Scribing or edge scraping by hand with a five point tool, then back-painting, is common and necessary where medium to heavy texture has been applied to vertical walls, horizontal ceilings, etc., in preparation for cutting-in at walls and ceilings where different colors or different sheens (i.e. flat vs. semi-gloss) are used on the adjacent surfaces. For example, assume a medium or heavy texture has been applied to the walls and ceiling - the ceiling is painted white and the walls painted an earth tone color. The first step is to scrape or scribe the texture off the wall, down to the drywall tape (approximately 5/16" to 1/2" from the ceiling), to create a smooth surface for cutting-in. Then, the white ceiling color would be painted back (back-painted) on the wall and ceiling where the texture was removed. Now, with this surface smooth and repainted, cut-in the earth tone wall color to the ceiling. "Slow" work is based on an hourly wage of $20.25, "Medium" work on an hourly wage of $25.75, and "Fast" work on an hourly wage of $31.50. "Slow" applies to residential repaints with heavy texture. "Medium" applies to residential or commercial repaints with light-to-medium texture. "Fast" applies to new construction with a light textured surface.

**Notes:**

1 - Material consumption for back-painting is minimal or zero (0) since the material cost is actually calculated in the wall painting or ceiling painting line item.

2 - High Time Difficulty Factors are built into these figures to allow for up and down time and moving ladders or scaffolding.

3 - Horizontal scribing is typically more difficult and consumes more time than vertical scribing, as the figures indicate.

4 - In new construction, it's best to have the drywall texture applicators scribe the edges where different colors occur while the texture is still wet, thus eliminating this painting operation.

|  | Labor SF per manhour | Material coverage SF/gallon | Material cost per gallon | Labor cost per 100 SF | Labor burden 100 SF | Material cost per 100 SF | Overhead per 100 SF | Profit per 100 SF | Total price per 100 SF |
|---|---|---|---|---|---|---|---|---|---|
| **Strip, remove, or bleach** | | | | | | | | | |
| Remove wallcover by hand | | | | | | | | | |
| Slow | 50 | -- | -- | 40.50 | 11.94 | -- | 9.97 | 9.99 | 72.40 |
| Medium | 70 | -- | -- | 36.79 | 13.04 | -- | 12.45 | 7.47 | 69.75 |
| Fast | 90 | -- | -- | 35.00 | 14.27 | -- | 15.28 | 4.52 | 69.07 |
| Stripping flat, vertical, varnished surfaces | | | | | | | | | |
| Light duty liquid remover (material #43) | | | | | | | | | |
| Slow | 25 | 175 | 37.30 | 81.00 | 23.88 | 21.31 | 31.55 | 25.24 | 182.98 |
| Medium | 35 | 158 | 32.60 | 73.57 | 26.05 | 20.63 | 30.06 | 18.04 | 168.35 |
| Fast | 45 | 140 | 28.00 | 70.00 | 28.55 | 20.00 | 36.75 | 10.87 | 166.17 |
| Heavy duty liquid remover (material #44) | | | | | | | | | |
| Slow | 20 | 150 | 41.90 | 101.25 | 29.85 | 27.93 | 39.76 | 31.81 | 230.60 |
| Medium | 30 | 138 | 36.70 | 85.83 | 30.39 | 26.59 | 35.70 | 21.42 | 199.93 |
| Fast | 40 | 125 | 31.40 | 78.75 | 32.13 | 25.12 | 42.16 | 12.47 | 190.63 |
| Stripping flat, horizontal floor surfaces | | | | | | | | | |
| Paint removal with light duty liquid remover (material #43) | | | | | | | | | |
| Slow | 20 | 180 | 37.30 | 101.25 | 29.85 | 20.72 | 37.96 | 30.37 | 220.15 |
| Medium | 30 | 175 | 32.60 | 85.83 | 30.39 | 18.63 | 33.71 | 20.23 | 188.79 |
| Fast | 40 | 170 | 28.00 | 78.75 | 32.13 | 16.47 | 39.48 | 11.68 | 178.51 |

*National Painting Cost Estimator*

|  | Labor SF per manhour | Material coverage SF/gallon | Material cost per gallon | Labor cost per 100 SF | Labor burden 100 SF | Material cost per 100 SF | Overhead per 100 SF | Profit per 100 SF | Total price per 100 SF |
|---|---|---|---|---|---|---|---|---|---|
| **Paint removal with heavy duty liquid remover (material #44)** | | | | | | | | | |
| Slow | 15 | 170 | 41.90 | 135.00 | 39.81 | 24.65 | 49.87 | 39.90 | 289.23 |
| Medium | 25 | 160 | 36.70 | 103.00 | 36.48 | 22.94 | 40.60 | 24.36 | 227.38 |
| Fast | 35 | 150 | 31.40 | 90.00 | 36.71 | 20.93 | 45.77 | 13.54 | 206.95 |
| **Varnish removal with light duty liquid remover (material #43)** | | | | | | | | | |
| Slow | 30 | 185 | 37.30 | 67.50 | 19.89 | 20.16 | 26.89 | 21.51 | 155.95 |
| Medium | 40 | 180 | 32.60 | 64.38 | 22.80 | 18.11 | 26.32 | 15.79 | 147.40 |
| Fast | 50 | 175 | 28.00 | 63.00 | 25.70 | 16.00 | 32.46 | 9.60 | 146.76 |
| **Varnish removal with heavy duty liquid remover (material #44)** | | | | | | | | | |
| Slow | 25 | 180 | 41.90 | 81.00 | 23.88 | 23.28 | 32.05 | 25.64 | 185.85 |
| Medium | 35 | 170 | 36.70 | 73.57 | 26.05 | 21.59 | 30.30 | 18.18 | 169.69 |
| Fast | 45 | 160 | 31.40 | 70.00 | 28.55 | 19.63 | 36.64 | 10.84 | 165.66 |

All widths less than 12", consider as 1 square foot per linear foot. For heights above 8 feet, use the High Time Difficulty Factors on page 139. "Slow" work is based on an hourly wage of $20.25, "Medium" work on an hourly wage of $25.75, and "Fast" work on an hourly wage of $31.50. Other qualifications that apply to this table are on page 9.

|  | Labor LF per manhour | Material coverage LF/gallon | Material cost per gallon | Labor cost per 100 LF | Labor burden 100 LF | Material cost per 100 LF | Overhead per 100 LF | Profit per 100 LF | Total price per 100 LF |
|---|---|---|---|---|---|---|---|---|---|
| **Tape gypsum wallboard** | | | | | | | | | |
| Preparation | | | | | | | | | |
| Bead, spot nail heads & sand | | | | | | | | | |
| Slow | 85 | -- | -- | 23.82 | 7.01 | -- | 5.86 | 5.87 | 42.56 |
| Medium | 100 | -- | -- | 25.75 | 9.12 | -- | 8.72 | 5.23 | 48.82 |
| Fast | 115 | -- | -- | 27.39 | 11.19 | -- | 11.96 | 3.54 | 54.08 |
| Taping | | | | | | | | | |
| Hand operation | | | | | | | | | |
| Slow | 125 | -- | -- | 16.20 | 4.78 | -- | 3.99 | 4.00 | 28.97 |
| Medium | 150 | -- | -- | 17.17 | 6.09 | -- | 5.81 | 3.49 | 32.56 |
| Fast | 175 | -- | -- | 18.00 | 7.32 | -- | 7.86 | 2.32 | 35.50 |
| Mechanical tools | | | | | | | | | |
| Slow | 200 | -- | -- | 10.13 | 2.98 | -- | 2.49 | 2.50 | 18.10 |
| Medium | 225 | -- | -- | 11.44 | 4.04 | -- | 3.87 | 2.32 | 21.67 |
| Fast | 250 | -- | -- | 12.60 | 5.14 | -- | 5.50 | 1.63 | 24.87 |
| Joint cement (premixed) per 75 lb bag | | | | | | | | | |
| Slow | -- | 650 | 10.00 | -- | -- | 1.54 | -- | -- | 1.54 |
| Medium | -- | 600 | 10.00 | -- | -- | 1.67 | -- | -- | 1.67 |
| Fast | -- | 550 | 10.00 | -- | -- | 1.82 | -- | -- | 1.82 |

For heights above 8 feet, use the High Time Difficulty Factors on page 139.

## Unstick windows

On repaint jobs, test all windows during your estimating walk-through and allow approximately 15 minutes (.25 hours) for each stuck window. But don't price yourself out of the job with this extra time.

*Preparation Costs*

| | Labor SF per manhour | Material coverage SF/gallon | Material cost per gallon | Labor cost per 100 SF | Labor burden 100 SF | Material cost per 100 SF | Overhead per 100 SF | Profit per 100 SF | Total price per 100 SF |
|---|---|---|---|---|---|---|---|---|---|
| **Wash** | | | | | | | | | |
| Interior flatwall (smooth surfaces) | | | | | | | | | |
| Wash only | | | | | | | | | |
|   Slow | 175 | -- | -- | 11.57 | 3.40 | -- | 2.85 | 2.85 | 20.67 |
|   Medium | 200 | -- | -- | 12.88 | 4.56 | -- | 4.36 | 2.62 | 24.42 |
|   Fast | 225 | -- | -- | 14.00 | 5.69 | -- | 6.11 | 1.81 | 27.61 |
| Wash & touchup | | | | | | | | | |
|   Slow | 135 | -- | -- | 15.00 | 4.43 | -- | 3.69 | 3.70 | 26.82 |
|   Medium | 160 | -- | -- | 16.09 | 5.70 | -- | 5.45 | 3.27 | 30.51 |
|   Fast | 185 | -- | -- | 17.03 | 6.96 | -- | 7.43 | 2.20 | 33.62 |
| Interior flatwall (rough surfaces) | | | | | | | | | |
| Wash only | | | | | | | | | |
|   Slow | 125 | -- | -- | 16.20 | 4.78 | -- | 3.99 | 4.00 | 28.97 |
|   Medium | 150 | -- | -- | 17.17 | 6.09 | -- | 5.81 | 3.49 | 32.56 |
|   Fast | 175 | -- | -- | 18.00 | 7.32 | -- | 7.86 | 2.32 | 35.50 |
| Wash & touchup | | | | | | | | | |
|   Slow | 55 | -- | -- | 36.82 | 10.85 | -- | 9.06 | 9.08 | 65.81 |
|   Medium | 95 | -- | -- | 27.11 | 9.61 | -- | 9.18 | 5.51 | 51.41 |
|   Fast | 135 | -- | -- | 23.33 | 9.53 | -- | 10.18 | 3.01 | 46.05 |
| Interior enamel (wall surfaces) | | | | | | | | | |
| Wash only | | | | | | | | | |
|   Slow | 190 | -- | -- | 10.66 | 3.13 | -- | 2.62 | 2.63 | 19.04 |
|   Medium | 215 | -- | -- | 11.98 | 4.23 | -- | 4.06 | 2.43 | 22.70 |
|   Fast | 240 | -- | -- | 13.13 | 5.36 | -- | 5.73 | 1.70 | 25.92 |
| Wash & touchup | | | | | | | | | |
|   Slow | 85 | -- | -- | 23.82 | 7.01 | -- | 5.86 | 5.87 | 42.56 |
|   Medium | 113 | -- | -- | 22.79 | 8.07 | -- | 7.72 | 4.63 | 43.21 |
|   Fast | 140 | -- | -- | 22.50 | 9.17 | -- | 9.82 | 2.91 | 44.40 |
| Interior enamel trim | | | | | | | | | |
| Wash only | | | | | | | | | |
|   Slow | 100 | -- | -- | 20.25 | 5.97 | -- | 4.98 | 4.99 | 36.19 |
|   Medium | 150 | -- | -- | 17.17 | 6.09 | -- | 5.81 | 3.49 | 32.56 |
|   Fast | 200 | -- | -- | 15.75 | 6.43 | -- | 6.88 | 2.03 | 31.09 |
| Wash & touchup | | | | | | | | | |
|   Slow | 90 | -- | -- | 22.50 | 6.63 | -- | 5.54 | 5.55 | 40.22 |
|   Medium | 120 | -- | -- | 21.46 | 7.59 | -- | 7.27 | 4.36 | 40.68 |
|   Fast | 150 | -- | -- | 21.00 | 8.58 | -- | 9.17 | 2.71 | 41.46 |

*National Painting Cost Estimator*

|  | Labor SF per manhour | Material coverage SF/gallon | Material cost per gallon | Labor cost per 100 SF | Labor burden 100 SF | Material cost per 100 SF | Overhead per 100 SF | Profit per 100 SF | Total price per 100 SF |
|---|---|---|---|---|---|---|---|---|---|
| **Interior varnish trim** | | | | | | | | | |
| Wash only | | | | | | | | | |
| Slow | 150 | -- | -- | 13.50 | 3.99 | -- | 3.32 | 3.33 | 24.14 |
| Medium | 195 | -- | -- | 13.21 | 4.68 | -- | 4.47 | 2.68 | 25.04 |
| Fast | 240 | -- | -- | 13.13 | 5.36 | -- | 5.73 | 1.70 | 25.92 |
| Wash & touchup | | | | | | | | | |
| Slow | 120 | -- | -- | 16.88 | 4.96 | -- | 4.15 | 4.16 | 30.15 |
| Medium | 140 | -- | -- | 18.39 | 6.51 | -- | 6.23 | 3.74 | 34.87 |
| Fast | 160 | -- | -- | 19.69 | 8.03 | -- | 8.59 | 2.54 | 38.85 |
| **Interior varnish floors** | | | | | | | | | |
| Wash only | | | | | | | | | |
| Slow | 160 | -- | -- | 12.66 | 3.73 | -- | 3.11 | 3.12 | 22.62 |
| Medium | 210 | -- | -- | 12.26 | 4.34 | -- | 4.15 | 2.49 | 23.24 |
| Fast | 260 | -- | -- | 12.12 | 4.95 | -- | 5.29 | 1.56 | 23.92 |
| Wash & touchup | | | | | | | | | |
| Slow | 130 | -- | -- | 15.58 | 4.58 | -- | 3.83 | 3.84 | 27.83 |
| Medium | 153 | -- | -- | 16.83 | 5.97 | -- | 5.70 | 3.42 | 31.92 |
| Fast | 175 | -- | -- | 18.00 | 7.32 | -- | 7.86 | 2.32 | 35.50 |
| **Interior plaster (smooth)** | | | | | | | | | |
| Wash only | | | | | | | | | |
| Slow | 150 | -- | -- | 13.50 | 3.99 | -- | 3.32 | 3.33 | 24.14 |
| Medium | 175 | -- | -- | 14.71 | 5.20 | -- | 4.98 | 2.99 | 27.88 |
| Fast | 200 | -- | -- | 15.75 | 6.43 | -- | 6.88 | 2.03 | 31.09 |
| Wash & touchup | | | | | | | | | |
| Slow | 125 | -- | -- | 16.20 | 4.78 | -- | 3.99 | 4.00 | 28.97 |
| Medium | 140 | -- | -- | 18.39 | 6.51 | -- | 6.23 | 3.74 | 34.87 |
| Fast | 155 | -- | -- | 20.32 | 8.29 | -- | 8.87 | 2.62 | 40.10 |
| **Interior plaster (sand finish)** | | | | | | | | | |
| Wash only | | | | | | | | | |
| Slow | 110 | -- | -- | 18.41 | 5.42 | -- | 4.53 | 4.54 | 32.90 |
| Medium | 135 | -- | -- | 19.07 | 6.77 | -- | 6.46 | 3.87 | 36.17 |
| Fast | 160 | -- | -- | 19.69 | 8.03 | -- | 8.59 | 2.54 | 38.85 |
| Wash & touchup | | | | | | | | | |
| Slow | 85 | -- | -- | 23.82 | 7.01 | -- | 5.86 | 5.87 | 42.56 |
| Medium | 110 | -- | -- | 23.41 | 8.29 | -- | 7.93 | 4.76 | 44.39 |
| Fast | 140 | -- | -- | 22.50 | 9.17 | -- | 9.82 | 2.91 | 44.40 |

Because the type of surface and type of material being removed will alter rates, it is best to wash surfaces with calcium deposits, excess debris or other unusual surface markings on a Time and Material or a Cost Plus Fee basis at a pre-set hourly rate. Consider all trim which is less than 12" wide to be 12" wide and figured as 1 square foot per linear foot. For heights above 8 feet, use the High Time Difficulty Factors on page 139. "Slow" work is based on an hourly wage of $20.25, "Medium" work on an hourly wage of $25.75, and "Fast" work on an hourly wage of $31.50. Other qualifications that apply to this table are on page 9.

*Preparation Costs*

|  | Labor SF per manhour | Material coverage SF/gallon | Material cost per gallon | Labor cost per 100 SF | Labor burden 100 SF | Material cost per 100 SF | Overhead per 100 SF | Profit per 100 SF | Total price per 100 SF |
|---|---|---|---|---|---|---|---|---|---|
| **Waterblast (Power wash)** | | | | | | | | | |
| Power wash | | | | | | | | | |
|   Slow | 700 | -- | -- | 2.89 | .86 | -- | .71 | .71 | 5.17 |
|   Medium | 1000 | -- | -- | 2.58 | .91 | -- | .87 | .52 | 4.88 |
|   Fast | 1500 | -- | -- | 2.10 | .87 | -- | .92 | .27 | 4.16 |

Power wash to clean surfaces prior to painting and to remove deteriorated, cracked, flaking paint from accessible wood, concrete, brick, block, plaster or stucco surfaces. Use the above rates for larger jobs, such as apartments or commercial buildings and large homes. For heights above 8 feet, use the High Time Difficulty Factors on page 139. For average-sized single-family homes, a half-day minimum might apply for move on, set up, power wash, clean up and move off. Rates assume a 1/4" diameter nozzle with 2500 lbs. pressure. "Slow" work is based on an hourly wage of $20.25, "Medium" work on an hourly wage of $25.75, and "Fast" work on an hourly wage of $31.50. Other qualifications that apply to this table are on page 9.

|  | Labor SF per manhour | Material coverage SF/roll | Material cost per roll | Labor cost per 100 SF | Labor burden 100 SF | Material cost per 100 SF | Overhead per 100 SF | Profit per 100 SF | Total price per 100 SF |
|---|---|---|---|---|---|---|---|---|---|
| **Window protection (visqueen, 1.5 mil)** | | | | | | | | | |
| Window protection - visqueen (material #47) | | | | | | | | | |
|   Hand application | | | | | | | | | |
|     Slow | 90 | 2400 | 40.60 | 22.50 | 6.63 | 1.69 | 5.86 | 5.87 | 42.55 |
|     Medium | 100 | 2400 | 35.50 | 25.75 | 9.12 | 1.48 | 9.09 | 5.45 | 50.89 |
|     Fast | 110 | 2400 | 30.40 | 28.64 | 11.67 | 1.27 | 12.90 | 3.82 | 58.30 |

Masking tape is included in the sundry (15%) and escalation (10%) allowances within the material pricing columns in Figure 9. For heights above 8 feet, use the High Time Difficulty Factors on page 139. "Slow" work is based on an hourly wage of $20.25, "Medium" work on an hourly wage of $25.75, and "Fast" work on an hourly wage of $31.50. Other qualifications that apply to this table are on page 9.

*National Painting Cost Estimator*

|  | Labor SF per manhour | Material coverage SF/gallon | Material cost per gallon | Labor cost per 100 SF | Labor burden 100 SF | Material cost per 100 SF | Overhead per 100 SF | Profit per 100 SF | Total price per 100 SF |
|---|---|---|---|---|---|---|---|---|---|

## Wire brush

### Surface area basis - large projects & surface areas

**Pipe up to 12" O/D**

| | | | | | | | | | |
|---|---|---|---|---|---|---|---|---|---|
| Slow | 50 | -- | -- | 40.50 | 11.94 | -- | 9.97 | 9.99 | 72.40 |
| Medium | 75 | -- | -- | 34.33 | 12.15 | -- | 11.62 | 6.97 | 65.07 |
| Fast | 100 | -- | -- | 31.50 | 12.85 | -- | 13.75 | 4.07 | 62.17 |

**Structural steel**

*Sizes up to 2 SF/LF*

| | | | | | | | | | |
|---|---|---|---|---|---|---|---|---|---|
| Slow | 90 | -- | -- | 22.50 | 6.63 | -- | 5.54 | 5.55 | 40.22 |
| Medium | 110 | -- | -- | 23.41 | 8.29 | -- | 7.93 | 4.76 | 44.39 |
| Fast | 125 | -- | -- | 25.20 | 10.28 | -- | 11.00 | 3.25 | 49.73 |

*Sizes from 2 to 5 SF/LF*

| | | | | | | | | | |
|---|---|---|---|---|---|---|---|---|---|
| Slow | 100 | -- | -- | 20.25 | 5.97 | -- | 4.98 | 4.99 | 36.19 |
| Medium | 120 | -- | -- | 21.46 | 7.59 | -- | 7.27 | 4.36 | 40.68 |
| Fast | 140 | -- | -- | 22.50 | 9.17 | -- | 9.82 | 2.91 | 44.40 |

*Sizes over 5 SF/LF*

| | | | | | | | | | |
|---|---|---|---|---|---|---|---|---|---|
| Slow | 110 | -- | -- | 18.41 | 5.42 | -- | 4.53 | 4.54 | 32.90 |
| Medium | 130 | -- | -- | 19.81 | 7.01 | -- | 6.71 | 4.02 | 37.55 |
| Fast | 150 | -- | -- | 21.00 | 8.58 | -- | 9.17 | 2.71 | 41.46 |

**Tanks and vessels**

*Sizes up to 12'0" O/D*

| | | | | | | | | | |
|---|---|---|---|---|---|---|---|---|---|
| Slow | 110 | -- | -- | 18.41 | 5.42 | -- | 4.53 | 4.54 | 32.90 |
| Medium | 130 | -- | -- | 19.81 | 7.01 | -- | 6.71 | 4.02 | 37.55 |
| Fast | 150 | -- | -- | 21.00 | 8.58 | -- | 9.17 | 2.71 | 41.46 |

*Sizes over 12'0" O/D*

| | | | | | | | | | |
|---|---|---|---|---|---|---|---|---|---|
| Slow | 120 | -- | -- | 16.88 | 4.96 | -- | 4.15 | 4.16 | 30.15 |
| Medium | 140 | -- | -- | 18.39 | 6.51 | -- | 6.23 | 3.74 | 34.87 |
| Fast | 160 | -- | -- | 19.69 | 8.03 | -- | 8.59 | 2.54 | 38.85 |

For heights above 8 feet, use the High Time Difficulty Factors on page 139. "Slow" work is based on an hourly wage of $20.25, "Medium" work on an hourly wage of $25.75, and "Fast" work on an hourly wage of $31.50. Other qualifications that apply to this table are on page 9.

# Part III

- INDUSTRIAL
- INSTITUTIONAL
- HEAVY COMMERCIAL

# Painting Costs

National Painting Cost Estimator

|  | Labor SF per manhour | Material coverage SF/gallon | Material cost per gallon | Labor cost per 100 SF | Labor burden 100 SF | Material cost per 100 SF | Overhead per 100 SF | Profit per 100 SF | Total price per 100 SF |
|---|---|---|---|---|---|---|---|---|---|
| **Conduit, electric, brush application** | | | | | | | | | |
| Acid wash coat, muriatic acid (material #49) | | | | | | | | | |
|   Brush each coat | | | | | | | | | |
|     Slow | 60 | 700 | 11.50 | 33.75 | 9.96 | 1.64 | 8.62 | 8.64 | 62.61 |
|     Medium | 80 | 650 | 10.10 | 32.19 | 11.40 | 1.55 | 11.29 | 6.77 | 63.20 |
|     Fast | 100 | 600 | 8.60 | 31.50 | 12.85 | 1.43 | 14.19 | 4.20 | 64.17 |
| Metal primer, rust inhibitor - clean metal (material #35) | | | | | | | | | |
|   Brush prime coat | | | | | | | | | |
|     Slow | 60 | 450 | 59.70 | 33.75 | 9.96 | 13.27 | 10.83 | 10.85 | 78.66 |
|     Medium | 80 | 425 | 52.20 | 32.19 | 11.40 | 12.28 | 13.97 | 8.38 | 78.22 |
|     Fast | 100 | 400 | 44.80 | 31.50 | 12.85 | 11.20 | 17.22 | 5.09 | 77.86 |
| Metal primer, rust inhibitor - rusty metal (material #36) | | | | | | | | | |
|   Brush prime coat | | | | | | | | | |
|     Slow | 60 | 400 | 72.30 | 33.75 | 9.96 | 18.08 | 11.74 | 11.76 | 85.29 |
|     Medium | 80 | 375 | 63.30 | 32.19 | 11.40 | 16.88 | 15.12 | 9.07 | 84.66 |
|     Fast | 100 | 350 | 54.20 | 31.50 | 12.85 | 15.49 | 18.55 | 5.49 | 83.88 |
| Industrial enamel, oil base, high gloss - light colors (material #56) | | | | | | | | | |
|   Brush 1st or additional finish coats | | | | | | | | | |
|     Slow | 100 | 450 | 61.00 | 20.25 | 5.97 | 13.56 | 7.56 | 7.57 | 54.91 |
|     Medium | 125 | 425 | 53.40 | 20.60 | 7.30 | 12.56 | 10.11 | 6.07 | 56.64 |
|     Fast | 150 | 400 | 45.80 | 21.00 | 8.58 | 11.45 | 12.72 | 3.76 | 57.51 |
| Industrial enamel, oil base, high gloss - dark (OSHA) colors (material #57) | | | | | | | | | |
|   Brush 1st or additional finish coats | | | | | | | | | |
|     Slow | 100 | 500 | 67.60 | 20.25 | 5.97 | 13.52 | 7.55 | 7.57 | 54.86 |
|     Medium | 125 | 475 | 59.10 | 20.60 | 7.30 | 12.44 | 10.08 | 6.05 | 56.47 |
|     Fast | 150 | 450 | 50.70 | 21.00 | 8.58 | 11.27 | 12.66 | 3.75 | 57.26 |
| Epoxy coating, 2 part system - clear (material #51) | | | | | | | | | |
|   Brush 1st coat | | | | | | | | | |
|     Slow | 60 | 425 | 146.90 | 33.75 | 9.96 | 34.56 | 14.87 | 14.90 | 108.04 |
|     Medium | 80 | 400 | 128.60 | 32.19 | 11.40 | 32.15 | 18.94 | 11.36 | 106.04 |
|     Fast | 100 | 375 | 110.20 | 31.50 | 12.85 | 29.39 | 22.86 | 6.76 | 103.36 |
|   Brush 2nd or additional finish coats | | | | | | | | | |
|     Slow | 100 | 475 | 146.90 | 20.25 | 5.97 | 30.93 | 10.86 | 10.88 | 78.89 |
|     Medium | 125 | 450 | 128.60 | 20.60 | 7.30 | 28.58 | 14.12 | 8.47 | 79.07 |
|     Fast | 150 | 425 | 110.20 | 21.00 | 8.58 | 25.93 | 17.21 | 5.09 | 77.81 |

*Industrial, Institutional and Heavy Commercial Costs*

| | Labor SF per manhour | Material coverage SF/gallon | Material cost per gallon | Labor cost per 100 SF | Labor burden 100 SF | Material cost per 100 SF | Overhead per 100 SF | Profit per 100 SF | Total price per 100 SF |
|---|---|---|---|---|---|---|---|---|---|
| **Epoxy coating, 2 part system - white (material #52)** | | | | | | | | | |
| Brush 1st coat | | | | | | | | | |
|   Slow | 60 | 425 | 177.00 | 33.75 | 9.96 | 41.65 | 16.22 | 16.25 | 117.83 |
|   Medium | 80 | 400 | 154.90 | 32.19 | 11.40 | 38.73 | 20.58 | 12.35 | 115.25 |
|   Fast | 100 | 375 | 132.70 | 31.50 | 12.85 | 35.39 | 24.72 | 7.31 | 111.77 |
| Brush 2nd or additional finish coats | | | | | | | | | |
|   Slow | 100 | 475 | 177.00 | 20.25 | 5.97 | 37.26 | 12.06 | 12.09 | 87.63 |
|   Medium | 125 | 450 | 154.90 | 20.60 | 7.30 | 34.42 | 15.58 | 9.35 | 87.25 |
|   Fast | 150 | 425 | 132.70 | 21.00 | 8.58 | 31.22 | 18.84 | 5.57 | 85.21 |

This table is based on square feet of conduit surface area. See Figure 21 on page 325 to convert from linear feet of various conduit or pipe sizes to square feet of surface area. For heights above 8 feet, use the High Time Difficulty Factors on page 139. Note: A two coat system, prime and finish, using oil base material is recommended for any metal surface. Using water base material may cause oxidation, corrosion and rust. Using one coat of oil base paint on metal surfaces may result in cracking, peeling or chipping without the proper prime coat application. If off white or another light colored finish paint is specified, make sure the prime coat is also a light color, or more than one finish coat will be necessary. "Slow" work is based on an hourly wage of $20.25, "Medium" work on an hourly wage of $25.75, and "Fast" work on an hourly wage of $31.50. Other qualifications that apply to this table are on page 9.

*National Painting Cost Estimator*

|  | Labor SF per manhour | Material coverage SF/gallon | Material cost per gallon | Labor cost per 100 SF | Labor burden 100 SF | Material cost per 100 SF | Overhead per 100 SF | Profit per 100 SF | Total price per 100 SF |
|---|---|---|---|---|---|---|---|---|---|
| **Conduit, electric, roll application** | | | | | | | | | |
| Acid wash coat, muriatic acid (material #49) | | | | | | | | | |
| Roll each coat | | | | | | | | | |
| Slow | 175 | 700 | 11.50 | 11.57 | 3.40 | 1.64 | 3.16 | 3.16 | 22.93 |
| Medium | 200 | 650 | 10.10 | 12.88 | 4.56 | 1.55 | 4.75 | 2.85 | 26.59 |
| Fast | 225 | 600 | 8.60 | 14.00 | 5.69 | 1.43 | 6.55 | 1.94 | 29.61 |
| Metal primer, rust inhibitor - clean metal (material #35) | | | | | | | | | |
| Roll prime coat | | | | | | | | | |
| Slow | 175 | 425 | 59.70 | 11.57 | 3.40 | 14.05 | 5.52 | 5.53 | 40.07 |
| Medium | 200 | 400 | 52.20 | 12.88 | 4.56 | 13.05 | 7.62 | 4.57 | 42.68 |
| Fast | 225 | 375 | 44.80 | 14.00 | 5.69 | 11.95 | 9.81 | 2.90 | 44.35 |
| Metal primer, rust inhibitor - rusty metal (material #36) | | | | | | | | | |
| Roll prime coat | | | | | | | | | |
| Slow | 175 | 375 | 72.30 | 11.57 | 3.40 | 19.28 | 6.51 | 6.52 | 47.28 |
| Medium | 200 | 350 | 63.30 | 12.88 | 4.56 | 18.09 | 8.88 | 5.33 | 49.74 |
| Fast | 225 | 325 | 54.20 | 14.00 | 5.69 | 16.68 | 11.28 | 3.34 | 50.99 |
| Industrial enamel, oil base, high gloss - light colors (material #56) | | | | | | | | | |
| Roll 1st or additional finish coats | | | | | | | | | |
| Slow | 225 | 425 | 61.00 | 9.00 | 2.64 | 14.35 | 4.94 | 4.95 | 35.88 |
| Medium | 250 | 400 | 53.40 | 10.30 | 3.65 | 13.35 | 6.83 | 4.10 | 38.23 |
| Fast | 275 | 375 | 45.80 | 11.45 | 4.69 | 12.21 | 8.78 | 2.60 | 39.73 |
| Industrial enamel, oil base, high gloss - dark (OSHA) colors (material #57) | | | | | | | | | |
| Roll 1st or additional finish coats | | | | | | | | | |
| Slow | 225 | 475 | 67.60 | 9.00 | 2.64 | 14.23 | 4.92 | 4.93 | 35.72 |
| Medium | 250 | 450 | 59.10 | 10.30 | 3.65 | 13.13 | 6.77 | 4.06 | 37.91 |
| Fast | 275 | 425 | 50.70 | 11.45 | 4.69 | 11.93 | 8.70 | 2.57 | 39.34 |
| Epoxy coating, 2 part system - clear (material #51) | | | | | | | | | |
| Roll 1st coat | | | | | | | | | |
| Slow | 175 | 400 | 146.90 | 11.57 | 3.40 | 36.73 | 9.82 | 9.84 | 71.36 |
| Medium | 200 | 375 | 128.60 | 12.88 | 4.56 | 34.29 | 12.93 | 7.76 | 72.42 |
| Fast | 225 | 350 | 110.20 | 14.00 | 5.69 | 31.49 | 15.87 | 4.69 | 71.74 |
| Roll 2nd or additional finish coats | | | | | | | | | |
| Slow | 225 | 450 | 146.90 | 9.00 | 2.64 | 32.64 | 8.42 | 8.44 | 61.14 |
| Medium | 250 | 425 | 128.60 | 10.30 | 3.65 | 30.26 | 11.05 | 6.63 | 61.89 |
| Fast | 275 | 400 | 110.20 | 11.45 | 4.69 | 27.55 | 13.54 | 4.00 | 61.23 |

*Industrial, Institutional and Heavy Commercial Costs*

| | Labor SF per manhour | Material coverage SF/gallon | Material cost per gallon | Labor cost per 100 SF | Labor burden 100 SF | Material cost per 100 SF | Overhead per 100 SF | Profit per 100 SF | Total price per 100 SF |
|---|---|---|---|---|---|---|---|---|---|
| **Epoxy coating, 2 part system - white (material #52)** | | | | | | | | | |
| Roll 1st coat | | | | | | | | | |
| Slow | 175 | 400 | 177.00 | 11.57 | 3.40 | 44.25 | 11.25 | 11.28 | 81.75 |
| Medium | 200 | 375 | 154.90 | 12.88 | 4.56 | 41.31 | 14.69 | 8.81 | 82.25 |
| Fast | 225 | 350 | 132.70 | 14.00 | 5.69 | 37.91 | 17.86 | 5.28 | 80.74 |
| Roll 2nd or additional finish coats | | | | | | | | | |
| Slow | 225 | 450 | 177.00 | 9.00 | 2.64 | 39.33 | 9.69 | 9.71 | 70.37 |
| Medium | 250 | 425 | 154.90 | 10.30 | 3.65 | 36.45 | 12.60 | 7.56 | 70.56 |
| Fast | 275 | 400 | 132.70 | 11.45 | 4.69 | 33.18 | 15.28 | 4.52 | 69.12 |

This table is based on square feet of conduit surface area. See Figure 21 on page 325 to convert from linear feet of various conduit or pipe sizes to square feet of surface area. For heights above 8 feet, use the High Time Difficulty Factors on page 139. Note: A two coat system, prime and finish, using oil base material is recommended for any metal surface. Using water base material may cause oxidation, corrosion and rust. Using one coat of oil base paint on metal surfaces may result in cracking, peeling or chipping without the proper prime coat application. If off white or another light colored finish paint is specified, make sure the prime coat is also a light color, or more than one finish coat will be necessary. "Slow" work is based on an hourly wage of $20.25, "Medium" work on an hourly wage of $25.75, and "Fast" work on an hourly wage of $31.50. Other qualifications that apply to this table are on page 9.

|  | Labor SF per manhour | Material coverage SF/gallon | Material cost per gallon | Labor cost per 100 SF | Labor burden 100 SF | Material cost per 100 SF | Overhead per 100 SF | Profit per 100 SF | Total price per 100 SF |
|---|---|---|---|---|---|---|---|---|---|
| **Conduit, electric, spray application** | | | | | | | | | |
| Acid wash coat, muriatic acid (material #49) | | | | | | | | | |
|   Spray each coat | | | | | | | | | |
|     Slow | 350 | 350 | 11.50 | 5.79 | 1.71 | 3.29 | 2.05 | 2.05 | 14.89 |
|     Medium | 400 | 325 | 10.10 | 6.44 | 2.28 | 3.11 | 2.96 | 1.77 | 16.56 |
|     Fast | 450 | 300 | 8.60 | 7.00 | 2.85 | 2.87 | 3.95 | 1.17 | 17.84 |
| Metal primer, rust inhibitor - clean metal (material #35) | | | | | | | | | |
|   Spray prime coat | | | | | | | | | |
|     Slow | 350 | 275 | 59.70 | 5.79 | 1.71 | 21.71 | 5.55 | 5.56 | 40.32 |
|     Medium | 400 | 263 | 52.20 | 6.44 | 2.28 | 19.85 | 7.14 | 4.29 | 40.00 |
|     Fast | 450 | 250 | 44.80 | 7.00 | 2.85 | 17.92 | 8.61 | 2.55 | 38.93 |
| Metal primer, rust inhibitor - rusty metal (material #36) | | | | | | | | | |
|   Spray prime coat | | | | | | | | | |
|     Slow | 350 | 225 | 72.30 | 5.79 | 1.71 | 32.13 | 7.53 | 7.55 | 54.71 |
|     Medium | 400 | 213 | 63.30 | 6.44 | 2.28 | 29.72 | 9.61 | 5.77 | 53.82 |
|     Fast | 450 | 200 | 54.20 | 7.00 | 2.85 | 27.10 | 11.46 | 3.39 | 51.80 |
| Industrial enamel, oil base, high gloss - light colors (material #56) | | | | | | | | | |
|   Spray 1st or additional finish coats | | | | | | | | | |
|     Slow | 450 | 275 | 61.00 | 4.50 | 1.32 | 22.18 | 5.32 | 5.33 | 38.65 |
|     Medium | 500 | 263 | 53.40 | 5.15 | 1.82 | 20.30 | 6.82 | 4.09 | 38.18 |
|     Fast | 550 | 250 | 45.80 | 5.73 | 2.34 | 18.32 | 8.18 | 2.42 | 36.99 |
| Industrial enamel, oil base, high gloss - dark (OSHA) colors (material #57) | | | | | | | | | |
|   Spray 1st or additional finish coats | | | | | | | | | |
|     Slow | 450 | 300 | 67.60 | 4.50 | 1.32 | 22.53 | 5.39 | 5.40 | 39.14 |
|     Medium | 500 | 288 | 59.10 | 5.15 | 1.82 | 20.52 | 6.87 | 4.12 | 38.48 |
|     Fast | 550 | 275 | 50.70 | 5.73 | 2.34 | 18.44 | 8.22 | 2.43 | 37.16 |
| Epoxy coating, 2 part system - clear (material #51) | | | | | | | | | |
|   Spray 1st coat | | | | | | | | | |
|     Slow | 350 | 250 | 146.90 | 5.79 | 1.71 | 58.76 | 12.59 | 12.62 | 91.47 |
|     Medium | 400 | 238 | 128.60 | 6.44 | 2.28 | 54.03 | 15.69 | 9.41 | 87.85 |
|     Fast | 450 | 225 | 110.20 | 7.00 | 2.85 | 48.98 | 18.24 | 5.40 | 82.47 |
|   Spray 2nd or additional finish coats | | | | | | | | | |
|     Slow | 450 | 285 | 146.90 | 4.50 | 1.32 | 51.54 | 10.90 | 10.92 | 79.18 |
|     Medium | 500 | 273 | 128.60 | 5.15 | 1.82 | 47.11 | 13.52 | 8.11 | 75.71 |
|     Fast | 550 | 260 | 110.20 | 5.73 | 2.34 | 42.38 | 15.64 | 4.63 | 70.72 |

*Industrial, Institutional and Heavy Commercial Costs*

|  | Labor SF per manhour | Material coverage SF/gallon | Material cost per gallon | Labor cost per 100 SF | Labor burden 100 SF | Material cost per 100 SF | Overhead per 100 SF | Profit per 100 SF | Total price per 100 SF |
|---|---|---|---|---|---|---|---|---|---|
| **Epoxy coating, 2 part system - white (material #52)** | | | | | | | | | |
| Spray 1st coat | | | | | | | | | |
|   Slow | 350 | 250 | 177.00 | 5.79 | 1.71 | 70.80 | 14.88 | 14.91 | 108.09 |
|   Medium | 400 | 238 | 154.90 | 6.44 | 2.28 | 65.08 | 18.45 | 11.07 | 103.32 |
|   Fast | 450 | 225 | 132.70 | 7.00 | 2.85 | 58.98 | 21.34 | 6.31 | 96.48 |
| Spray 2nd or additional finish coats | | | | | | | | | |
|   Slow | 450 | 285 | 177.00 | 4.50 | 1.32 | 62.11 | 12.91 | 12.94 | 93.78 |
|   Medium | 500 | 273 | 154.90 | 5.15 | 1.82 | 56.74 | 15.93 | 9.56 | 89.20 |
|   Fast | 550 | 260 | 132.70 | 5.73 | 2.34 | 51.04 | 18.32 | 5.42 | 82.85 |

This table is based on square feet of conduit surface area. See Figure 21 on page 325 to convert from linear feet of various conduit or pipe sizes to square feet of surface area. For heights above 8 feet, use the High Time Difficulty Factors on page 139. Note: A two coat system, prime and finish, using oil base material is recommended for any metal surface. Using water base material may cause oxidation, corrosion and rust. Using one coat of oil base paint on metal surfaces may result in cracking, peeling or chipping without the proper prime coat application. If off white or another light colored finish paint is specified, make sure the prime coat is also a light color, or more than one finish coat will be necessary. "Slow" work is based on an hourly wage of $20.25, "Medium" work on an hourly wage of $25.75, and "Fast" work on an hourly wage of $31.50. Other qualifications that apply to this table are on page 9.

|  | Labor SF per manhour | Material coverage SF/gallon | Material cost per gallon | Labor cost per 100 SF | Labor burden 100 SF | Material cost per 100 SF | Overhead per 100 SF | Profit per 100 SF | Total price per 100 SF |
|---|---|---|---|---|---|---|---|---|---|
| **Conduit, electric, mitt or glove application** | | | | | | | | | |
| Acid wash coat, muriatic acid (material #49) | | | | | | | | | |
|   Mitt or glove each coat | | | | | | | | | |
|     Slow | 175 | 700 | 11.50 | 11.57 | 3.40 | 1.64 | 3.16 | 3.16 | 22.93 |
|     Medium | 200 | 650 | 10.10 | 12.88 | 4.56 | 1.55 | 4.75 | 2.85 | 26.59 |
|     Fast | 225 | 600 | 8.60 | 14.00 | 5.69 | 1.43 | 6.55 | 1.94 | 29.61 |
| Metal primer, rust inhibitor - clean metal (material #35) | | | | | | | | | |
|   Mitt or glove prime coat | | | | | | | | | |
|     Slow | 175 | 450 | 59.70 | 11.57 | 3.40 | 13.27 | 5.37 | 5.38 | 38.99 |
|     Medium | 200 | 438 | 52.20 | 12.88 | 4.56 | 11.92 | 7.34 | 4.40 | 41.10 |
|     Fast | 225 | 425 | 44.80 | 14.00 | 5.69 | 10.54 | 9.38 | 2.77 | 42.38 |
| Metal primer, rust inhibitor - rusty metal (material #36) | | | | | | | | | |
|   Mitt or glove prime coat | | | | | | | | | |
|     Slow | 175 | 400 | 72.30 | 11.57 | 3.40 | 18.08 | 6.28 | 6.29 | 45.62 |
|     Medium | 200 | 388 | 63.30 | 12.88 | 4.56 | 16.31 | 8.44 | 5.06 | 47.25 |
|     Fast | 225 | 375 | 54.20 | 14.00 | 5.69 | 14.45 | 10.59 | 3.13 | 47.86 |
| Industrial enamel, oil base, high gloss - light colors (material #56) | | | | | | | | | |
|   Mitt or glove 1st or additional finish coats | | | | | | | | | |
|     Slow | 225 | 450 | 61.00 | 9.00 | 2.64 | 13.56 | 4.79 | 4.80 | 34.79 |
|     Medium | 250 | 438 | 53.40 | 10.30 | 3.65 | 12.19 | 6.54 | 3.92 | 36.60 |
|     Fast | 275 | 425 | 45.80 | 11.45 | 4.69 | 10.78 | 8.34 | 2.47 | 37.73 |
| Industrial enamel, oil base, high gloss - dark (OSHA) colors (material #57) | | | | | | | | | |
|   Mitt or glove 1st or additional finish coats | | | | | | | | | |
|     Slow | 225 | 500 | 67.60 | 9.00 | 2.64 | 13.52 | 4.78 | 4.79 | 34.73 |
|     Medium | 250 | 488 | 59.10 | 10.30 | 3.65 | 12.11 | 6.52 | 3.91 | 36.49 |
|     Fast | 275 | 475 | 50.70 | 11.45 | 4.69 | 10.67 | 8.30 | 2.46 | 37.57 |
| Epoxy coating, 2 part system - clear (material #51) | | | | | | | | | |
|   Mitt or glove 1st coat | | | | | | | | | |
|     Slow | 175 | 425 | 146.90 | 11.57 | 3.40 | 34.56 | 9.41 | 9.43 | 68.37 |
|     Medium | 200 | 413 | 128.60 | 12.88 | 4.56 | 31.14 | 12.15 | 7.29 | 68.02 |
|     Fast | 225 | 400 | 110.20 | 14.00 | 5.69 | 27.55 | 14.65 | 4.33 | 66.22 |
|   Mitt or glove 2nd or additional finish coats | | | | | | | | | |
|     Slow | 225 | 475 | 146.90 | 9.00 | 2.64 | 30.93 | 8.09 | 8.11 | 58.77 |
|     Medium | 250 | 463 | 128.60 | 10.30 | 3.65 | 27.78 | 10.43 | 6.26 | 58.42 |
|     Fast | 275 | 450 | 110.20 | 11.45 | 4.69 | 24.49 | 12.59 | 3.72 | 56.94 |

*Industrial, Institutional and Heavy Commercial Costs*

|  | Labor SF per manhour | Material coverage SF/gallon | Material cost per gallon | Labor cost per 100 SF | Labor burden 100 SF | Material cost per 100 SF | Overhead per 100 SF | Profit per 100 SF | Total price per 100 SF |
|---|---|---|---|---|---|---|---|---|---|
| **Epoxy coating, 2 part system - white (material #52)** | | | | | | | | | |
| Mitt or glove 1st coat | | | | | | | | | |
| Slow | 175 | 425 | 177.00 | 11.57 | 3.40 | 41.65 | 10.76 | 10.78 | 78.16 |
| Medium | 200 | 413 | 154.90 | 12.88 | 4.56 | 37.51 | 13.74 | 8.24 | 76.93 |
| Fast | 225 | 400 | 132.70 | 14.00 | 5.69 | 33.18 | 16.40 | 4.85 | 74.12 |
| Mitt or glove 2nd or additional finish coats | | | | | | | | | |
| Slow | 225 | 475 | 177.00 | 9.00 | 2.64 | 37.26 | 9.29 | 9.31 | 67.50 |
| Medium | 250 | 463 | 154.90 | 10.30 | 3.65 | 33.46 | 11.85 | 7.11 | 66.37 |
| Fast | 275 | 450 | 132.70 | 11.45 | 4.69 | 29.49 | 14.14 | 4.18 | 63.95 |

This table is based on square feet of conduit surface area. See Figure 21 below to convert from linear feet of various conduit or pipe sizes to square feet of surface area. For heights above 8 feet, use the High Time Difficulty Factors on page 139. Note: A two coat system, prime and finish, using oil base material is recommended for any metal surface. Using water base material may cause oxidation, corrosion and rust. Using one coat of oil base paint on metal surfaces may result in cracking, peeling or chipping without the proper prime coat application. If off white or another light colored finish paint is specified, make sure the prime coat is also a light color, or more than one finish coat will be necessary. "Slow" work is based on an hourly wage of $20.25, "Medium" work on an hourly wage of $25.75, and "Fast" work on an hourly wage of $31.50. Other qualifications that apply to this table are on page 9.

| Pipe O/D (inches) | Conversion Factor (SF per measured LF) |
|---|---|
| 1" to 3" | 1 SF for each 1 LF |
| 4" to 7" | 2 SF for each 1 LF |
| 8" to 11" | 3 SF for each 1 LF |
| 12" to 15" | 4 SF for each 1 LF |
| 16" to 19" | 5 SF for each 1 LF |
| 20" to 22" | 6 SF for each 1 LF |
| 23" to 26" | 7 SF for each 1 LF |
| 27" to 30" | 8 SF for each 1 LF |

**Figure 21**
Conduit/pipe area conversions

*National Painting Cost Estimator*

|  | Labor SF per manhour | Material coverage SF/gallon | Material cost per gallon | Labor cost per 100 SF | Labor burden 100 SF | Material cost per 100 SF | Overhead per 100 SF | Profit per 100 SF | Total price per 100 SF |
|---|---|---|---|---|---|---|---|---|---|
| **Decking and siding, metal, corrugated metal** | | | | | | | | | |
| Acid wash coat, muriatic acid (material #49) | | | | | | | | | |
|   Spray each coat | | | | | | | | | |
|     Slow | 700 | 500 | 11.50 | 2.89 | .86 | 2.30 | 1.15 | 1.15 | 8.35 |
|     Medium | 750 | 450 | 10.10 | 3.43 | 1.21 | 2.24 | 1.72 | 1.03 | 9.63 |
|     Fast | 800 | 400 | 8.60 | 3.94 | 1.60 | 2.15 | 2.39 | .71 | 10.79 |
| Metal primer, rust inhibitor - clean metal (material #35) | | | | | | | | | |
|   Spray prime coat | | | | | | | | | |
|     Slow | 700 | 325 | 59.70 | 2.89 | .86 | 18.37 | 4.20 | 4.21 | 30.53 |
|     Medium | 750 | 300 | 52.20 | 3.43 | 1.21 | 17.40 | 5.51 | 3.31 | 30.86 |
|     Fast | 800 | 275 | 44.80 | 3.94 | 1.60 | 16.29 | 6.77 | 2.00 | 30.60 |
| Metal primer, rust inhibitor - rusty metal (material #36) | | | | | | | | | |
|   Spray prime coat | | | | | | | | | |
|     Slow | 700 | 275 | 72.30 | 2.89 | .86 | 26.29 | 5.71 | 5.72 | 41.47 |
|     Medium | 750 | 250 | 63.30 | 3.43 | 1.21 | 25.32 | 7.49 | 4.49 | 41.94 |
|     Fast | 800 | 225 | 54.20 | 3.94 | 1.60 | 24.09 | 9.19 | 2.72 | 41.54 |
| Industrial enamel, oil base, high gloss - light colors (material #56) | | | | | | | | | |
|   Spray 1st or additional finish coats | | | | | | | | | |
|     Slow | 850 | 325 | 61.00 | 2.38 | .71 | 18.77 | 4.15 | 4.16 | 30.17 |
|     Medium | 900 | 300 | 53.40 | 2.86 | 1.01 | 17.80 | 5.42 | 3.25 | 30.34 |
|     Fast | 950 | 275 | 45.80 | 3.32 | 1.34 | 16.65 | 6.61 | 1.96 | 29.88 |
| Industrial enamel, oil base, high gloss - dark (OSHA) colors (material #57) | | | | | | | | | |
|   Spray 1st or additional finish coats | | | | | | | | | |
|     Slow | 850 | 425 | 67.60 | 2.38 | .71 | 15.91 | 3.61 | 3.62 | 26.23 |
|     Medium | 900 | 400 | 59.10 | 2.86 | 1.01 | 14.78 | 4.66 | 2.80 | 26.11 |
|     Fast | 950 | 375 | 50.70 | 3.32 | 1.34 | 13.52 | 5.64 | 1.67 | 25.49 |
| Epoxy coating, 2 part system - clear (material #51) | | | | | | | | | |
|   Spray 1st coat | | | | | | | | | |
|     Slow | 700 | 300 | 146.90 | 2.89 | .86 | 48.97 | 10.01 | 10.04 | 72.77 |
|     Medium | 750 | 275 | 128.60 | 3.43 | 1.21 | 46.76 | 12.85 | 7.71 | 71.96 |
|     Fast | 800 | 250 | 110.20 | 3.94 | 1.60 | 44.08 | 15.39 | 4.55 | 69.56 |
|   Spray 2nd or additional finish coats | | | | | | | | | |
|     Slow | 850 | 400 | 146.90 | 2.38 | .71 | 36.73 | 7.56 | 7.58 | 54.96 |
|     Medium | 900 | 375 | 128.60 | 2.86 | 1.01 | 34.29 | 9.54 | 5.72 | 53.42 |
|     Fast | 950 | 350 | 110.20 | 3.32 | 1.34 | 31.49 | 11.21 | 3.32 | 50.68 |

*Industrial, Institutional and Heavy Commercial Costs*

|  | Labor SF per manhour | Material coverage SF/gallon | Material cost per gallon | Labor cost per 100 SF | Labor burden 100 SF | Material cost per 100 SF | Overhead per 100 SF | Profit per 100 SF | Total price per 100 SF |
|---|---|---|---|---|---|---|---|---|---|
| **Epoxy coating, 2 part system - white (material #52)** | | | | | | | | | |
| Spray 1st coat | | | | | | | | | |
| Slow | 700 | 300 | 177.00 | 2.89 | .86 | 59.00 | 11.92 | 11.95 | 86.62 |
| Medium | 750 | 275 | 154.90 | 3.43 | 1.21 | 56.33 | 15.24 | 9.15 | 85.36 |
| Fast | 800 | 250 | 132.70 | 3.94 | 1.60 | 53.08 | 18.18 | 5.38 | 82.18 |
| Spray 2nd or additional finish coats | | | | | | | | | |
| Slow | 850 | 400 | 177.00 | 2.38 | .71 | 44.25 | 8.99 | 9.01 | 65.34 |
| Medium | 900 | 375 | 154.90 | 2.86 | 1.01 | 41.31 | 11.30 | 6.78 | 63.26 |
| Fast | 950 | 350 | 132.70 | 3.32 | 1.34 | 37.91 | 13.20 | 3.90 | 59.67 |

The figures in the table above are based on overall dimensions (length times width). But all decking and siding has corrugations, peaks and valleys that increase the surface that has to be painted. For example, corrugated siding with 2-1/2" center to center corrugations has a surface area 10% greater than the width times length dimension. For corrugated siding with 1-1/4" center to center corrugations, increase the surface area by 15%. For square corner decking, Figure 22 below shows how much area must be added to allow for peaks and valleys. For heights above 8 feet, use the High Time Difficulty Factors on page 139. Note: A two coat system, prime and finish, using oil base material is recommended for any metal surface. Using water base material may cause oxidation, corrosion and rust. Using one coat of oil base paint on metal surfaces may result in cracking, peeling or chipping without the proper prime coat application. If off white or another light colored finish paint is specified, make sure the prime coat is also a light color, or more than one finish coat will be necessary. "Slow" work is based on an hourly wage of $20.25, "Medium" work on an hourly wage of $25.75, and "Fast" work on an hourly wage of $31.50. Other qualifications that apply to this table are on page 9.

| C | 2C | D | PW | VW | Factor |
|---|---|---|---|---|---|
| -- | 12" | 4-1/2" | 3" | 2" | 2.50 |
| -- | 12" | 1-1/2" | 3-1/8" | 2" | 1.50 |
| -- | 12" | 1-1/2" | 5-1/16" | 1" | 1.45 |
| 12" | -- | 3" | 9-5/8" | 1" | 1.50 |
| 12" | -- | 4-1/2" | 9-5/8" | 1" | 1.75 |
| 24" | -- | 4-1/2" | 12" | 12" | 1.60 |
| 24" | -- | 6" | 12" | 12" | 1.75 |
| 24" | -- | 8" | 12" | 12" | 1.95 |

For square corner decking, calculate the overall (length times width) deck area. Then measure the peaks and valleys on the deck. Select the row in the table above that most nearly matches the deck you're painting. Multiply the overall deck area by the number listed in the column headed "factor" to find the actual area you're painting. Use this actual area when calculating labor and material requirements. In the table above, figures in the column headed C show the distance between the center of the peaks. Column 2C shows the distance between every second center of peak (2 centers). Column D shows the depth of corrugation. Column PW shows the peak width. Column VW shows the valley width. If the deck you're painting doesn't match any deck listed in this table, use the factor for the most similar deck in the table.

**Figure 22**
Square corner decking factors

National Painting Cost Estimator

|  | Labor SF per manhour | Material coverage SF/gallon | Material cost per gallon | Labor cost per 100 SF | Labor burden 100 SF | Material cost per 100 SF | Overhead per 100 SF | Profit per 100 SF | Total price per 100 SF |
|---|---|---|---|---|---|---|---|---|---|

### Decking and siding, metal, flat pan metal

Acid wash coat, muriatic acid (material #49)
  Spray each coat

| | | | | | | | | | |
|---|---|---|---|---|---|---|---|---|---|
| Slow | 800 | 600 | 11.50 | 2.53 | .75 | 1.92 | .99 | .99 | 7.18 |
| Medium | 850 | 550 | 10.10 | 3.03 | 1.08 | 1.84 | 1.49 | .89 | 8.33 |
| Fast | 900 | 500 | 8.60 | 3.50 | 1.42 | 1.72 | 2.06 | .61 | 9.31 |

Metal primer, rust inhibitor - clean metal (material #35)
  Spray prime coat

| | | | | | | | | | |
|---|---|---|---|---|---|---|---|---|---|
| Slow | 800 | 375 | 59.70 | 2.53 | .75 | 15.92 | 3.65 | 3.66 | 26.51 |
| Medium | 850 | 350 | 52.20 | 3.03 | 1.08 | 14.91 | 4.75 | 2.85 | 26.62 |
| Fast | 900 | 325 | 44.80 | 3.50 | 1.42 | 13.78 | 5.80 | 1.72 | 26.22 |

Metal primer, rust inhibitor - rusty metal (material #36)
  Spray prime coat

| | | | | | | | | | |
|---|---|---|---|---|---|---|---|---|---|
| Slow | 800 | 300 | 72.30 | 2.53 | .75 | 24.10 | 5.20 | 5.21 | 37.79 |
| Medium | 850 | 275 | 63.30 | 3.03 | 1.08 | 23.02 | 6.78 | 4.07 | 37.98 |
| Fast | 900 | 250 | 54.20 | 3.50 | 1.42 | 21.68 | 8.25 | 2.44 | 37.29 |

Industrial enamel, oil base, high gloss - light colors (material #56)
  Spray 1st or additional finish coats

| | | | | | | | | | |
|---|---|---|---|---|---|---|---|---|---|
| Slow | 1000 | 375 | 61.00 | 2.03 | .59 | 16.27 | 3.59 | 3.60 | 26.08 |
| Medium | 1050 | 350 | 53.40 | 2.45 | .86 | 15.26 | 4.65 | 2.79 | 26.01 |
| Fast | 1100 | 325 | 45.80 | 2.86 | 1.18 | 14.09 | 5.62 | 1.66 | 25.41 |

Industrial enamel, oil base, high gloss - dark (OSHA) colors (material #57)
  Spray 1st or additional finish coats

| | | | | | | | | | |
|---|---|---|---|---|---|---|---|---|---|
| Slow | 1000 | 425 | 67.60 | 2.03 | .59 | 15.91 | 3.52 | 3.53 | 25.58 |
| Medium | 1050 | 400 | 59.10 | 2.45 | .86 | 14.78 | 4.53 | 2.72 | 25.34 |
| Fast | 1100 | 375 | 50.70 | 2.86 | 1.18 | 13.52 | 5.44 | 1.61 | 24.61 |

Epoxy coating, 2 part system - clear (material #51)
  Spray 1st coat

| | | | | | | | | | |
|---|---|---|---|---|---|---|---|---|---|
| Slow | 800 | 350 | 146.90 | 2.53 | .75 | 41.97 | 8.60 | 8.62 | 62.47 |
| Medium | 850 | 325 | 128.60 | 3.03 | 1.08 | 39.57 | 10.92 | 6.55 | 61.15 |
| Fast | 900 | 300 | 110.20 | 3.50 | 1.42 | 36.73 | 12.91 | 3.82 | 58.38 |

  Spray 2nd or additional finish coats

| | | | | | | | | | |
|---|---|---|---|---|---|---|---|---|---|
| Slow | 1000 | 400 | 146.90 | 2.03 | .59 | 36.73 | 7.48 | 7.49 | 54.32 |
| Medium | 1050 | 375 | 128.60 | 2.45 | .86 | 34.29 | 9.40 | 5.64 | 52.64 |
| Fast | 1100 | 350 | 110.20 | 2.86 | 1.18 | 31.49 | 11.01 | 3.26 | 49.80 |

*Industrial, Institutional and Heavy Commercial Costs*

|  | Labor SF per manhour | Material coverage SF/gallon | Material cost per gallon | Labor cost per 100 SF | Labor burden 100 SF | Material cost per 100 SF | Overhead per 100 SF | Profit per 100 SF | Total price per 100 SF |
|---|---|---|---|---|---|---|---|---|---|
| **Epoxy coating, 2 part system - white (material #52)** | | | | | | | | | |
| Spray 1st coat | | | | | | | | | |
| Slow | 800 | 350 | 177.00 | 2.53 | .75 | 50.57 | 10.23 | 10.25 | 74.33 |
| Medium | 850 | 325 | 154.90 | 3.03 | 1.08 | 47.66 | 12.94 | 7.76 | 72.47 |
| Fast | 900 | 300 | 132.70 | 3.50 | 1.42 | 44.23 | 15.24 | 4.51 | 68.90 |
| Spray 2nd or additional coats | | | | | | | | | |
| Slow | 1000 | 400 | 177.00 | 2.03 | .59 | 44.25 | 8.91 | 8.93 | 64.71 |
| Medium | 1050 | 375 | 154.90 | 2.45 | .86 | 41.31 | 11.16 | 6.69 | 62.47 |
| Fast | 1100 | 350 | 132.70 | 2.86 | 1.18 | 37.91 | 13.00 | 3.85 | 58.80 |

The figures in the table above are based on overall dimensions (length times width). But all decking and siding has corrugations, peaks and valleys that increase the surface that has to be painted. For example, corrugated siding with 2-1/2" center to center corrugations has a surface area 10% greater than the width times length dimension. For corrugated siding with 1-1/4" center to center corrugations, increase the surface area by 15%. For square corner decking, Figure 22 on page 327 shows how much area must be added to allow for peaks and valleys. For heights above 8 feet, use the High Time Difficulty Factors on page 139. Note: A two coat system, prime and finish, using oil base material is recommended for any metal surface. Using water base material may cause oxidation, corrosion and rust. Using one coat of oil base paint on metal surfaces may result in cracking, peeling or chipping without the proper prime coat application. If off white or another light colored finish paint is specified, make sure the prime coat is also a light color, or more than one finish coat will be necessary. "Slow" work is based on an hourly wage of $20.25, "Medium" work on an hourly wage of $25.75, and "Fast" work on an hourly wage of $31.50. Other qualifications that apply to this table are on page 9.

|  | Labor SF per manhour | Material coverage SF/gallon | Material cost per gallon | Labor cost per 100 SF | Labor burden 100 SF | Material cost per 100 SF | Overhead per 100 SF | Profit per 100 SF | Total price per 100 SF |
|---|---|---|---|---|---|---|---|---|---|

### Doors, hollow metal, brush application, square foot basis
Metal primer, rust inhibitor - clean metal (material #35)
   Roll and brush prime coat

|  |  |  |  |  |  |  |  |  |  |
|---|---|---|---|---|---|---|---|---|---|
| Slow | 160 | 450 | 59.70 | 12.66 | 3.73 | 13.27 | 5.64 | 5.65 | 40.95 |
| Medium | 180 | 438 | 52.20 | 14.31 | 5.08 | 11.92 | 7.83 | 4.70 | 43.84 |
| Fast | 200 | 425 | 44.80 | 15.75 | 6.43 | 10.54 | 10.14 | 3.00 | 45.86 |

Metal primer, rust inhibitor - rusty metal (material #36)
   Roll and brush prime coat

|  |  |  |  |  |  |  |  |  |  |
|---|---|---|---|---|---|---|---|---|---|
| Slow | 160 | 425 | 72.30 | 12.66 | 3.73 | 17.01 | 6.35 | 6.36 | 46.11 |
| Medium | 180 | 413 | 63.30 | 14.31 | 5.08 | 15.33 | 8.68 | 5.21 | 48.61 |
| Fast | 200 | 400 | 54.20 | 15.75 | 6.43 | 13.55 | 11.08 | 3.28 | 50.09 |

Metal finish - synthetic enamel, gloss, interior or exterior - off white (material #37)
   Roll and brush 1st or additional finish coats

|  |  |  |  |  |  |  |  |  |  |
|---|---|---|---|---|---|---|---|---|---|
| Slow | 175 | 450 | 59.70 | 11.57 | 3.40 | 13.27 | 5.37 | 5.38 | 38.99 |
| Medium | 195 | 438 | 52.20 | 13.21 | 4.68 | 11.92 | 7.45 | 4.47 | 41.73 |
| Fast | 215 | 425 | 44.80 | 14.65 | 5.97 | 10.54 | 9.66 | 2.86 | 43.68 |

Metal finish - synthetic enamel, gloss, interior or exterior - colors, except orange & red (material #38)
   Roll and brush 1st or additional finish coats

|  |  |  |  |  |  |  |  |  |  |
|---|---|---|---|---|---|---|---|---|---|
| Slow | 175 | 475 | 65.20 | 11.57 | 3.40 | 13.73 | 5.45 | 5.47 | 39.62 |
| Medium | 195 | 463 | 57.00 | 13.21 | 4.68 | 12.31 | 7.55 | 4.53 | 42.28 |
| Fast | 215 | 450 | 48.90 | 14.65 | 5.97 | 10.87 | 9.77 | 2.89 | 44.15 |

To calculate the cost per door, figure the square feet for each side based on a 3 x 7 door. Add 3 feet to the width and 1 foot to the top of the door to allow for the time and material necessary to finish the door edges, frame and jamb. The result is a 6 x 8 door or 48 square feet per side, times 2 is 96 square feet per door. The cost per door is simply the 96 square feet times the cost per square foot indicated in the table above. Typically, hollow metal doors are pre-primed by the manufacturer and shipped ready to install and paint. These doors usually require only one coat of finish paint to cover. The metal finish figures include minor touchup of the prime coat. Note: A two coat system, prime and finish, using oil base material is recommended for any metal surface. Using water base material may cause oxidation, corrosion and rust. Using one coat of oil base paint on exterior metal may result in cracking, peeling or chipping without the proper prime coat application. If off white or other light colored finish paint is specified, make sure the prime coat is a light color also, or more than one finish coat will be necessary. "Slow" work is based on an hourly wage of $20.25, "Medium" work on an hourly wage of $25.75, and "Fast" work on an hourly wage of $31.50. Other qualifications that apply to this table are on page 9.

*Industrial, Institutional and Heavy Commercial Costs*

|  | Labor SF per manhour | Material coverage SF/gallon | Material cost per gallon | Labor cost per 100 SF | Labor burden 100 SF | Material cost per 100 SF | Overhead per 100 SF | Profit per 100 SF | Total price per 100 SF |
|---|---|---|---|---|---|---|---|---|---|

## Ductwork, bare duct, brush application

### Acid wash coat, muriatic acid (material #49)
#### Brush each coat
| | | | | | | | | | |
|---|---|---|---|---|---|---|---|---|---|
| Slow | 80 | 750 | 11.50 | 25.31 | 7.47 | 1.53 | 6.52 | 6.53 | 47.36 |
| Medium | 100 | 700 | 10.10 | 25.75 | 9.12 | 1.44 | 9.08 | 5.45 | 50.84 |
| Fast | 120 | 650 | 8.60 | 26.25 | 10.69 | 1.32 | 11.87 | 3.51 | 53.64 |

### Metal primer, rust inhibitor - clean metal (material #35)
#### Brush prime coat
| | | | | | | | | | |
|---|---|---|---|---|---|---|---|---|---|
| Slow | 80 | 400 | 59.70 | 25.31 | 7.47 | 14.93 | 9.06 | 9.08 | 65.85 |
| Medium | 100 | 375 | 52.20 | 25.75 | 9.12 | 13.92 | 12.20 | 7.32 | 68.31 |
| Fast | 120 | 350 | 44.80 | 26.25 | 10.69 | 12.80 | 15.43 | 4.56 | 69.73 |

### Metal primer, rust inhibitor - rusty metal (material #36)
#### Brush prime coat
| | | | | | | | | | |
|---|---|---|---|---|---|---|---|---|---|
| Slow | 80 | 350 | 72.30 | 25.31 | 7.47 | 20.66 | 10.15 | 10.17 | 73.76 |
| Medium | 100 | 325 | 63.30 | 25.75 | 9.12 | 19.48 | 13.59 | 8.15 | 76.09 |
| Fast | 120 | 300 | 54.20 | 26.25 | 10.69 | 18.07 | 17.06 | 5.05 | 77.12 |

### Industrial enamel, oil base, high gloss - light colors (material #56)
#### Brush 1st or additional finish coats
| | | | | | | | | | |
|---|---|---|---|---|---|---|---|---|---|
| Slow | 90 | 400 | 61.00 | 22.50 | 6.63 | 15.25 | 8.43 | 8.45 | 61.26 |
| Medium | 115 | 375 | 53.40 | 22.39 | 7.95 | 14.24 | 11.14 | 6.68 | 62.40 |
| Fast | 140 | 350 | 45.80 | 22.50 | 9.17 | 13.09 | 13.88 | 4.11 | 62.75 |

### Industrial enamel, oil base, high gloss - dark (OSHA) colors (material #57)
#### Brush 1st or additional finish coats
| | | | | | | | | | |
|---|---|---|---|---|---|---|---|---|---|
| Slow | 90 | 450 | 67.60 | 22.50 | 6.63 | 15.02 | 8.39 | 8.41 | 60.95 |
| Medium | 115 | 425 | 59.10 | 22.39 | 7.95 | 13.91 | 11.06 | 6.63 | 61.94 |
| Fast | 140 | 400 | 50.70 | 22.50 | 9.17 | 12.68 | 13.75 | 4.07 | 62.17 |

### Epoxy coating, 2 part system - clear (material #51)
#### Brush 1st coat
| | | | | | | | | | |
|---|---|---|---|---|---|---|---|---|---|
| Slow | 80 | 350 | 146.90 | 25.31 | 7.47 | 41.97 | 14.20 | 14.23 | 103.18 |
| Medium | 100 | 325 | 128.60 | 25.75 | 9.12 | 39.57 | 18.61 | 11.17 | 104.22 |
| Fast | 120 | 300 | 110.20 | 26.25 | 10.69 | 36.73 | 22.84 | 6.76 | 103.27 |

#### Brush 2nd or additional finish coats
| | | | | | | | | | |
|---|---|---|---|---|---|---|---|---|---|
| Slow | 90 | 425 | 146.90 | 22.50 | 6.63 | 34.56 | 12.10 | 12.13 | 87.92 |
| Medium | 115 | 400 | 128.60 | 22.39 | 7.95 | 32.15 | 15.62 | 9.37 | 87.48 |
| Fast | 140 | 375 | 110.20 | 22.50 | 9.17 | 29.39 | 18.93 | 5.60 | 85.59 |

*National Painting Cost Estimator*

|  | Labor SF per manhour | Material coverage SF/gallon | Material cost per gallon | Labor cost per 100 SF | Labor burden 100 SF | Material cost per 100 SF | Overhead per 100 SF | Profit per 100 SF | Total price per 100 SF |
|---|---|---|---|---|---|---|---|---|---|
| **Epoxy coating, 2 part system - white (material #52)** | | | | | | | | | |
| Brush 1st coat | | | | | | | | | |
| Slow | 80 | 350 | 177.00 | 25.31 | 7.47 | 50.57 | 15.84 | 15.87 | 115.06 |
| Medium | 100 | 325 | 154.90 | 25.75 | 9.12 | 47.66 | 20.63 | 12.38 | 115.54 |
| Fast | 120 | 300 | 132.70 | 26.25 | 10.69 | 44.23 | 25.17 | 7.45 | 113.79 |
| Brush 2nd or additional finish coats | | | | | | | | | |
| Slow | 90 | 425 | 177.00 | 22.50 | 6.63 | 41.65 | 13.45 | 13.48 | 97.71 |
| Medium | 115 | 400 | 154.90 | 22.39 | 7.95 | 38.73 | 17.26 | 10.36 | 96.69 |
| Fast | 140 | 375 | 132.70 | 22.50 | 9.17 | 35.39 | 20.79 | 6.15 | 94.00 |

For heights over 8 feet, use the High Time Difficulty Factors on page 139. Note: A two coat system, prime and finish, using oil base material is recommended for any metal surface. Using water base material may cause oxidation, corrosion and rust. Using one coat of oil base paint on metal surfaces may result in cracking, peeling or chipping without the proper prime coat application. If off white or another light colored finish paint is specified, make sure the prime coat is also a light color, or more than one finish coat will be necessary. "Slow" work is based on an hourly wage of $20.25, "Medium" work on an hourly wage of $25.75, and "Fast" work on an hourly wage of $31.50. Other qualifications that apply to this table are on page 9.

*Industrial, Institutional and Heavy Commercial Costs*

|  | Labor SF per manhour | Material coverage SF/gallon | Material cost per gallon | Labor cost per 100 SF | Labor burden 100 SF | Material cost per 100 SF | Overhead per 100 SF | Profit per 100 SF | Total price per 100 SF |
|---|---|---|---|---|---|---|---|---|---|

## Ductwork, bare duct, roll application

### Acid wash coat, muriatic acid (material #49)
**Roll each coat**

| | | | | | | | | | |
|---|---|---|---|---|---|---|---|---|---|
| Slow | 225 | 700 | 11.50 | 9.00 | 2.64 | 1.64 | 2.53 | 2.53 | 18.34 |
| Medium | 250 | 650 | 10.10 | 10.30 | 3.65 | 1.55 | 3.88 | 2.33 | 21.71 |
| Fast | 275 | 600 | 8.60 | 11.45 | 4.69 | 1.43 | 5.44 | 1.61 | 24.62 |

### Metal primer, rust inhibitor - clean metal (material #35)
**Roll prime coat**

| | | | | | | | | | |
|---|---|---|---|---|---|---|---|---|---|
| Slow | 225 | 375 | 59.70 | 9.00 | 2.64 | 15.92 | 5.24 | 5.25 | 38.05 |
| Medium | 250 | 350 | 52.20 | 10.30 | 3.65 | 14.91 | 7.22 | 4.33 | 40.41 |
| Fast | 275 | 325 | 44.80 | 11.45 | 4.69 | 13.78 | 9.27 | 2.74 | 41.93 |

### Metal primer, rust inhibitor - rusty metal (material #36)
**Roll prime coat**

| | | | | | | | | | |
|---|---|---|---|---|---|---|---|---|---|
| Slow | 225 | 325 | 72.30 | 9.00 | 2.64 | 22.25 | 6.44 | 6.46 | 46.79 |
| Medium | 250 | 300 | 63.30 | 10.30 | 3.65 | 21.10 | 8.76 | 5.26 | 49.07 |
| Fast | 275 | 275 | 54.20 | 11.45 | 4.69 | 19.71 | 11.11 | 3.29 | 50.25 |

### Industrial enamel, oil base, high gloss - light colors (material #56)
**Roll 1st or additional finish coats**

| | | | | | | | | | |
|---|---|---|---|---|---|---|---|---|---|
| Slow | 275 | 425 | 61.00 | 7.36 | 2.18 | 14.35 | 4.54 | 4.55 | 32.98 |
| Medium | 300 | 400 | 53.40 | 8.58 | 3.03 | 13.35 | 6.24 | 3.75 | 34.95 |
| Fast | 325 | 375 | 45.80 | 9.69 | 3.97 | 12.21 | 8.01 | 2.37 | 36.25 |

### Industrial enamel, oil base, high gloss - dark (OSHA) colors (material #57)
**Roll 1st or additional finish coats**

| | | | | | | | | | |
|---|---|---|---|---|---|---|---|---|---|
| Slow | 275 | 475 | 67.60 | 7.36 | 2.18 | 14.23 | 4.51 | 4.52 | 32.80 |
| Medium | 300 | 450 | 59.10 | 8.58 | 3.03 | 13.13 | 6.19 | 3.71 | 34.64 |
| Fast | 325 | 425 | 50.70 | 9.69 | 3.97 | 11.93 | 7.93 | 2.35 | 35.87 |

### Epoxy coating, 2 part system - clear (material #51)
**Roll 1st coat**

| | | | | | | | | | |
|---|---|---|---|---|---|---|---|---|---|
| Slow | 225 | 350 | 146.90 | 9.00 | 2.64 | 41.97 | 10.19 | 10.21 | 74.01 |
| Medium | 250 | 325 | 128.60 | 10.30 | 3.65 | 39.57 | 13.38 | 8.03 | 74.93 |
| Fast | 275 | 300 | 110.20 | 11.45 | 4.69 | 36.73 | 16.38 | 4.85 | 74.10 |

**Roll 2nd or additional finish coats**

| | | | | | | | | | |
|---|---|---|---|---|---|---|---|---|---|
| Slow | 275 | 450 | 146.90 | 7.36 | 2.18 | 32.64 | 8.01 | 8.03 | 58.22 |
| Medium | 300 | 425 | 128.60 | 8.58 | 3.03 | 30.26 | 10.47 | 6.28 | 58.62 |
| Fast | 325 | 400 | 110.20 | 9.69 | 3.97 | 27.55 | 12.77 | 3.78 | 57.76 |

*National Painting Cost Estimator*

|  | Labor SF per manhour | Material coverage SF/gallon | Material cost per gallon | Labor cost per 100 SF | Labor burden 100 SF | Material cost per 100 SF | Overhead per 100 SF | Profit per 100 SF | Total price per 100 SF |
|---|---|---|---|---|---|---|---|---|---|
| **Epoxy coating, 2 part system - white (material #52)** | | | | | | | | | |
| Roll 1st coat | | | | | | | | | |
| Slow | 225 | 350 | 177.00 | 9.00 | 2.64 | 50.57 | 11.82 | 11.85 | 85.88 |
| Medium | 250 | 325 | 154.90 | 10.30 | 3.65 | 47.66 | 15.40 | 9.24 | 86.25 |
| Fast | 275 | 300 | 132.70 | 11.45 | 4.69 | 44.23 | 18.71 | 5.53 | 84.61 |
| Roll 2nd or additional finish coats | | | | | | | | | |
| Slow | 275 | 450 | 177.00 | 7.36 | 2.18 | 39.33 | 9.28 | 9.30 | 67.45 |
| Medium | 300 | 425 | 154.90 | 8.58 | 3.03 | 36.45 | 12.02 | 7.21 | 67.29 |
| Fast | 325 | 400 | 132.70 | 9.69 | 3.97 | 33.18 | 14.51 | 4.29 | 65.64 |

For heights over 8 feet, use the High Time Difficulty Factors on page 139. Note: A two coat system, prime and finish, using oil base material is recommended for any metal surface. Using water base material may cause oxidation, corrosion and rust. Using one coat of oil base paint on metal surfaces may result in cracking, peeling or chipping without the proper prime coat application. If off white or another light colored finish paint is specified, make sure the prime coat is also a light color, or more than one finish coat will be necessary. "Slow" work is based on an hourly wage of $20.25, "Medium" work on an hourly wage of $25.75, and "Fast" work on an hourly wage of $31.50. Other qualifications that apply to this table are on page 9.

*Industrial, Institutional and Heavy Commercial Costs*

|  | Labor SF per manhour | Material coverage SF/gallon | Material cost per gallon | Labor cost per 100 SF | Labor burden 100 SF | Material cost per 100 SF | Overhead per 100 SF | Profit per 100 SF | Total price per 100 SF |
|---|---|---|---|---|---|---|---|---|---|
| **Ductwork, bare duct, spray application** | | | | | | | | | |
| Acid wash coat, muriatic acid (material #49) | | | | | | | | | |
|   Spray each coat | | | | | | | | | |
|     Slow | 550 | 450 | 11.50 | 3.68 | 1.09 | 2.56 | 1.39 | 1.40 | 10.12 |
|     Medium | 600 | 400 | 10.10 | 4.29 | 1.53 | 2.53 | 2.09 | 1.25 | 11.69 |
|     Fast | 650 | 350 | 8.60 | 4.85 | 1.98 | 2.46 | 2.88 | .85 | 13.02 |
| Metal primer, rust inhibitor - clean metal (material #35) | | | | | | | | | |
|   Spray prime coat | | | | | | | | | |
|     Slow | 550 | 250 | 59.70 | 3.68 | 1.09 | 23.88 | 5.44 | 5.45 | 39.54 |
|     Medium | 600 | 225 | 52.20 | 4.29 | 1.53 | 23.20 | 7.25 | 4.35 | 40.62 |
|     Fast | 650 | 200 | 44.80 | 4.85 | 1.98 | 22.40 | 9.06 | 2.68 | 40.97 |
| Metal primer, rust inhibitor - rusty metal (material #36) | | | | | | | | | |
|   Spray prime coat | | | | | | | | | |
|     Slow | 550 | 200 | 72.30 | 3.68 | 1.09 | 36.15 | 7.77 | 7.79 | 56.48 |
|     Medium | 600 | 188 | 63.30 | 4.29 | 1.53 | 33.67 | 9.87 | 5.92 | 55.28 |
|     Fast | 650 | 175 | 54.20 | 4.85 | 1.98 | 30.97 | 11.72 | 3.47 | 52.99 |
| Industrial enamel, oil base, high gloss - light colors (material #56) | | | | | | | | | |
|   Spray 1st or additional finish coats | | | | | | | | | |
|     Slow | 700 | 225 | 61.00 | 2.89 | .86 | 27.11 | 5.86 | 5.87 | 42.59 |
|     Medium | 750 | 213 | 53.40 | 3.43 | 1.21 | 25.07 | 7.43 | 4.46 | 41.60 |
|     Fast | 800 | 200 | 45.80 | 3.94 | 1.60 | 22.90 | 8.82 | 2.61 | 39.87 |
| Industrial enamel, oil base, high gloss - dark (OSHA) colors (material #57) | | | | | | | | | |
|   Spray 1st or additional finish coats | | | | | | | | | |
|     Slow | 700 | 275 | 67.60 | 2.89 | .86 | 24.58 | 5.38 | 5.39 | 39.10 |
|     Medium | 750 | 250 | 59.10 | 3.43 | 1.21 | 23.64 | 7.07 | 4.24 | 39.59 |
|     Fast | 800 | 225 | 50.70 | 3.94 | 1.60 | 22.53 | 8.70 | 2.57 | 39.34 |
| Epoxy coating, 2 part system - clear (material #51) | | | | | | | | | |
|   Spray 1st coat | | | | | | | | | |
|     Slow | 550 | 225 | 146.90 | 3.68 | 1.09 | 65.29 | 13.31 | 13.34 | 96.71 |
|     Medium | 600 | 213 | 128.60 | 4.29 | 1.53 | 60.38 | 16.55 | 9.93 | 92.68 |
|     Fast | 650 | 200 | 110.20 | 4.85 | 1.98 | 55.10 | 19.20 | 5.68 | 86.81 |
|   Spray 2nd or additional finish coats | | | | | | | | | |
|     Slow | 700 | 250 | 146.90 | 2.89 | .86 | 58.76 | 11.88 | 11.90 | 86.29 |
|     Medium | 750 | 238 | 128.60 | 3.43 | 1.21 | 54.03 | 14.67 | 8.80 | 82.14 |
|     Fast | 800 | 225 | 110.20 | 3.94 | 1.60 | 48.98 | 16.90 | 5.00 | 76.42 |

|  | Labor SF per manhour | Material coverage SF/gallon | Material cost per gallon | Labor cost per 100 SF | Labor burden 100 SF | Material cost per 100 SF | Overhead per 100 SF | Profit per 100 SF | Total price per 100 SF |
|---|---|---|---|---|---|---|---|---|---|
| **Epoxy coating, 2 part system - white (material #52)** | | | | | | | | | |
| Spray 1st coat | | | | | | | | | |
| Slow | 550 | 225 | 177.00 | 3.68 | 1.09 | 78.67 | 15.85 | 15.89 | 115.18 |
| Medium | 600 | 213 | 154.90 | 4.29 | 1.53 | 72.72 | 19.63 | 11.78 | 109.95 |
| Fast | 650 | 200 | 132.70 | 4.85 | 1.98 | 66.35 | 22.69 | 6.71 | 102.58 |
| Spray 2nd or additional finish coats | | | | | | | | | |
| Slow | 700 | 250 | 177.00 | 2.89 | .86 | 70.80 | 14.16 | 14.19 | 102.90 |
| Medium | 750 | 238 | 154.90 | 3.43 | 1.21 | 65.08 | 17.43 | 10.46 | 97.61 |
| Fast | 800 | 225 | 132.70 | 3.94 | 1.60 | 58.98 | 20.00 | 5.92 | 90.44 |

For heights over 8 feet, use the High Time Difficulty Factors on page 139. Note: A two coat system, prime and finish, using oil base material is recommended for any metal surface. Using water base material may cause oxidation, corrosion and rust. Using one coat of oil base paint on metal surfaces may result in cracking, peeling or chipping without the proper prime coat application. If off white or another light colored finish paint is specified, make sure the prime coat is also a light color, or more than one finish coat will be necessary. "Slow" work is based on an hourly wage of $20.25, "Medium" work on an hourly wage of $25.75, and "Fast" work on an hourly wage of $31.50. Other qualifications that apply to this table are on page 9.

*Industrial, Institutional and Heavy Commercial Costs*

|  | Labor SF per manhour | Material coverage SF/gallon | Material cost per gallon | Labor cost per 100 SF | Labor burden 100 SF | Material cost per 100 SF | Overhead per 100 SF | Profit per 100 SF | Total price per 100 SF |
|---|---|---|---|---|---|---|---|---|---|

## Ductwork, bare duct, mitt or glove application

**Acid wash coat, muriatic acid (material #49)**
*Mitt or glove each coat*

| | | | | | | | | | |
|---|---|---|---|---|---|---|---|---|---|
| Slow | 175 | 700 | 11.50 | 11.57 | 3.40 | 1.64 | 3.16 | 3.16 | 22.93 |
| Medium | 200 | 650 | 10.10 | 12.88 | 4.56 | 1.55 | 4.75 | 2.85 | 26.59 |
| Fast | 225 | 600 | 8.60 | 14.00 | 5.69 | 1.43 | 6.55 | 1.94 | 29.61 |

**Metal primer, rust inhibitor - clean metal (material #35)**
*Mitt or glove prime coat*

| | | | | | | | | | |
|---|---|---|---|---|---|---|---|---|---|
| Slow | 175 | 400 | 59.70 | 11.57 | 3.40 | 14.93 | 5.68 | 5.69 | 41.27 |
| Medium | 200 | 388 | 52.20 | 12.88 | 4.56 | 13.45 | 7.72 | 4.63 | 43.24 |
| Fast | 225 | 375 | 44.80 | 14.00 | 5.69 | 11.95 | 9.81 | 2.90 | 44.35 |

**Metal primer, rust inhibitor - rusty metal (material #36)**
*Mitt or glove prime coat*

| | | | | | | | | | |
|---|---|---|---|---|---|---|---|---|---|
| Slow | 175 | 400 | 72.30 | 11.57 | 3.40 | 18.08 | 6.28 | 6.29 | 45.62 |
| Medium | 200 | 350 | 63.30 | 12.88 | 4.56 | 18.09 | 8.88 | 5.33 | 49.74 |
| Fast | 225 | 325 | 54.20 | 14.00 | 5.69 | 16.68 | 11.28 | 3.34 | 50.99 |

**Industrial enamel, oil base, high gloss - light colors (material #56)**
*Mitt or glove 1st or additional finish coats*

| | | | | | | | | | |
|---|---|---|---|---|---|---|---|---|---|
| Slow | 225 | 425 | 61.00 | 9.00 | 2.64 | 14.35 | 4.94 | 4.95 | 35.88 |
| Medium | 250 | 400 | 53.40 | 10.30 | 3.65 | 13.35 | 6.83 | 4.10 | 38.23 |
| Fast | 275 | 375 | 45.80 | 11.45 | 4.69 | 12.21 | 8.78 | 2.60 | 39.73 |

**Industrial enamel, oil base, high gloss - dark (OSHA) colors (material #57)**
*Mitt or glove 1st or additional finish coats*

| | | | | | | | | | |
|---|---|---|---|---|---|---|---|---|---|
| Slow | 225 | 475 | 67.60 | 9.00 | 2.64 | 14.23 | 4.92 | 4.93 | 35.72 |
| Medium | 250 | 450 | 59.10 | 10.30 | 3.65 | 13.13 | 6.77 | 4.06 | 37.91 |
| Fast | 275 | 425 | 50.70 | 11.45 | 4.69 | 11.93 | 8.70 | 2.57 | 39.34 |

**Epoxy coating, 2 part system - clear (material #51)**
*Mitt or glove 1st coat*

| | | | | | | | | | |
|---|---|---|---|---|---|---|---|---|---|
| Slow | 175 | 400 | 146.90 | 11.57 | 3.40 | 36.73 | 9.82 | 9.84 | 71.36 |
| Medium | 200 | 375 | 128.60 | 12.88 | 4.56 | 34.29 | 12.93 | 7.76 | 72.42 |
| Fast | 225 | 350 | 110.20 | 14.00 | 5.69 | 31.49 | 15.87 | 4.69 | 71.74 |

*Mitt or glove 2nd or additional finish coats*

| | | | | | | | | | |
|---|---|---|---|---|---|---|---|---|---|
| Slow | 225 | 425 | 146.90 | 9.00 | 2.64 | 34.56 | 8.78 | 8.80 | 63.78 |
| Medium | 250 | 400 | 128.60 | 10.30 | 3.65 | 32.15 | 11.53 | 6.92 | 64.55 |
| Fast | 275 | 375 | 110.20 | 11.45 | 4.69 | 29.39 | 14.11 | 4.17 | 63.81 |

*National Painting Cost Estimator*

|  | Labor SF per manhour | Material coverage SF/gallon | Material cost per gallon | Labor cost per 100 SF | Labor burden 100 SF | Material cost per 100 SF | Overhead per 100 SF | Profit per 100 SF | Total price per 100 SF |
|---|---|---|---|---|---|---|---|---|---|
| **Epoxy coating, 2 part system - white (material #52)** | | | | | | | | | |
| Mitt or glove 1st coat | | | | | | | | | |
|   Slow | 175 | 400 | 177.00 | 11.57 | 3.40 | 44.25 | 11.25 | 11.28 | 81.75 |
|   Medium | 200 | 375 | 154.90 | 12.88 | 4.56 | 41.31 | 14.69 | 8.81 | 82.25 |
|   Fast | 225 | 350 | 132.70 | 14.00 | 5.69 | 37.91 | 17.86 | 5.28 | 80.74 |
| Mitt or glove 2nd or additional finish coats | | | | | | | | | |
|   Slow | 225 | 425 | 177.00 | 9.00 | 2.64 | 41.65 | 10.13 | 10.15 | 73.57 |
|   Medium | 250 | 400 | 154.90 | 10.30 | 3.65 | 38.73 | 13.17 | 7.90 | 73.75 |
|   Fast | 275 | 375 | 132.70 | 11.45 | 4.69 | 35.39 | 15.97 | 4.72 | 72.22 |

For heights over 8 feet, use the High Time Difficulty Factors on page 139. Note: A two coat system, prime and finish, using oil base material is recommended for any metal surface. Using water base material may cause oxidation, corrosion and rust. Using one coat of oil base paint on metal surfaces may result in cracking, peeling or chipping without the proper prime coat application. If off white or another light colored finish paint is specified, make sure the prime coat is also a light color, or more than one finish coat will be necessary. "Slow" work is based on an hourly wage of $20.25, "Medium" work on an hourly wage of $25.75, and "Fast" work on an hourly wage of $31.50. Other qualifications that apply to this table are on page 9.

*Industrial, Institutional and Heavy Commercial Costs*

|  | Labor SF per manhour | Material coverage SF/gallon | Material cost per gallon | Labor cost per 100 SF | Labor burden 100 SF | Material cost per 100 SF | Overhead per 100 SF | Profit per 100 SF | Total price per 100 SF |
|---|---|---|---|---|---|---|---|---|---|
| **Ductwork, canvas insulated, brush application** | | | | | | | | | |
| Flat latex, water base (material #5) | | | | | | | | | |
|   Brush 1st coat | | | | | | | | | |
|     Slow | 60 | 250 | 36.70 | 33.75 | 9.96 | 14.68 | 11.09 | 11.12 | 80.60 |
|     Medium | 75 | 238 | 32.10 | 34.33 | 12.15 | 13.49 | 14.99 | 9.00 | 83.96 |
|     Fast | 90 | 225 | 27.50 | 35.00 | 14.27 | 12.22 | 19.07 | 5.64 | 86.20 |
|   Brush 2nd coat | | | | | | | | | |
|     Slow | 85 | 275 | 36.70 | 23.82 | 7.01 | 13.35 | 8.40 | 8.42 | 61.00 |
|     Medium | 105 | 238 | 32.10 | 24.52 | 8.68 | 13.49 | 11.67 | 7.00 | 65.36 |
|     Fast | 125 | 250 | 27.50 | 25.20 | 10.28 | 11.00 | 14.41 | 4.26 | 65.15 |
|   Brush 3rd or additional coats | | | | | | | | | |
|     Slow | 100 | 325 | 36.70 | 20.25 | 5.97 | 11.29 | 7.13 | 7.14 | 51.78 |
|     Medium | 125 | 313 | 32.10 | 20.60 | 7.30 | 10.26 | 9.54 | 5.72 | 53.42 |
|     Fast | 150 | 300 | 27.50 | 21.00 | 8.58 | 9.17 | 12.01 | 3.55 | 54.31 |
| Sealer, off white, water base (material #1) | | | | | | | | | |
|   Brush 1 coat | | | | | | | | | |
|     Slow | 60 | 250 | 30.50 | 33.75 | 9.96 | 12.20 | 10.62 | 10.64 | 77.17 |
|     Medium | 75 | 238 | 26.70 | 34.33 | 12.15 | 11.22 | 14.43 | 8.66 | 80.79 |
|     Fast | 90 | 225 | 22.90 | 35.00 | 14.27 | 10.18 | 18.43 | 5.45 | 83.33 |
| Sealer, off white, oil base (material #2) | | | | | | | | | |
|   Brush 1 coat | | | | | | | | | |
|     Slow | 60 | 275 | 39.70 | 33.75 | 9.96 | 14.44 | 11.05 | 11.07 | 80.27 |
|     Medium | 75 | 263 | 34.80 | 34.33 | 12.15 | 13.23 | 14.93 | 8.96 | 83.60 |
|     Fast | 90 | 250 | 29.80 | 35.00 | 14.27 | 11.92 | 18.97 | 5.61 | 85.77 |
| Enamel, water base (material #9) | | | | | | | | | |
|   Brush 1st finish coat | | | | | | | | | |
|     Slow | 85 | 275 | 46.80 | 23.82 | 7.01 | 17.02 | 9.10 | 9.12 | 66.07 |
|     Medium | 105 | 238 | 41.00 | 24.52 | 8.68 | 17.23 | 12.61 | 7.56 | 70.60 |
|     Fast | 125 | 250 | 35.10 | 25.20 | 10.28 | 14.04 | 15.35 | 4.54 | 69.41 |
|   Brush 2nd or additional finish coats | | | | | | | | | |
|     Slow | 100 | 325 | 46.80 | 20.25 | 5.97 | 14.40 | 7.72 | 7.73 | 56.07 |
|     Medium | 125 | 313 | 41.00 | 20.60 | 7.30 | 13.10 | 10.25 | 6.15 | 57.40 |
|     Fast | 150 | 300 | 35.10 | 21.00 | 8.58 | 11.70 | 12.79 | 3.78 | 57.85 |
| Industrial enamel, oil base, high gloss - light colors (material #56) | | | | | | | | | |
|   Brush 1st finish coat | | | | | | | | | |
|     Slow | 85 | 300 | 61.00 | 23.82 | 7.01 | 20.33 | 9.72 | 9.74 | 70.62 |
|     Medium | 105 | 288 | 53.40 | 24.52 | 8.68 | 18.54 | 12.94 | 7.76 | 72.44 |
|     Fast | 125 | 275 | 45.80 | 25.20 | 10.28 | 16.65 | 16.16 | 4.78 | 73.07 |

*National Painting Cost Estimator*

|  | Labor SF per manhour | Material coverage SF/gallon | Material cost per gallon | Labor cost per 100 SF | Labor burden 100 SF | Material cost per 100 SF | Overhead per 100 SF | Profit per 100 SF | Total price per 100 SF |
|---|---|---|---|---|---|---|---|---|---|
| **Brush 2nd or additional finish coats** | | | | | | | | | |
| Slow | 100 | 350 | 61.00 | 20.25 | 5.97 | 17.43 | 8.29 | 8.31 | 60.25 |
| Medium | 125 | 338 | 53.40 | 20.60 | 7.30 | 15.80 | 10.92 | 6.55 | 61.17 |
| Fast | 150 | 325 | 45.80 | 21.00 | 8.58 | 14.09 | 13.53 | 4.00 | 61.20 |

**Industrial enamel, oil base, high gloss - dark (OSHA) colors (material #57)**

| Brush 1st finish coat | | | | | | | | | |
|---|---|---|---|---|---|---|---|---|---|
| Slow | 85 | 300 | 67.60 | 23.82 | 7.01 | 22.53 | 10.14 | 10.16 | 73.66 |
| Medium | 105 | 288 | 59.10 | 24.52 | 8.68 | 20.52 | 13.43 | 8.06 | 75.21 |
| Fast | 125 | 275 | 50.70 | 25.20 | 10.28 | 18.44 | 16.72 | 4.94 | 75.58 |

| Brush 2nd or additional finish coats | | | | | | | | | |
|---|---|---|---|---|---|---|---|---|---|
| Slow | 100 | 350 | 67.60 | 20.25 | 5.97 | 19.31 | 8.65 | 8.67 | 62.85 |
| Medium | 125 | 338 | 59.10 | 20.60 | 7.30 | 17.49 | 11.35 | 6.81 | 63.55 |
| Fast | 150 | 325 | 50.70 | 21.00 | 8.58 | 15.60 | 14.00 | 4.14 | 63.32 |

**Epoxy coating, 2 part system - clear (material #51)**

| Brush 1st coat | | | | | | | | | |
|---|---|---|---|---|---|---|---|---|---|
| Slow | 60 | 260 | 146.90 | 33.75 | 9.96 | 56.50 | 19.04 | 19.08 | 138.33 |
| Medium | 75 | 243 | 128.60 | 34.33 | 12.15 | 52.92 | 24.85 | 14.91 | 139.16 |
| Fast | 90 | 235 | 110.20 | 35.00 | 14.27 | 46.89 | 29.81 | 8.82 | 134.79 |

| Brush 2nd coat | | | | | | | | | |
|---|---|---|---|---|---|---|---|---|---|
| Slow | 85 | 285 | 146.90 | 23.82 | 7.01 | 51.54 | 15.65 | 15.69 | 113.71 |
| Medium | 105 | 273 | 128.60 | 24.52 | 8.68 | 47.11 | 20.08 | 12.05 | 112.44 |
| Fast | 125 | 260 | 110.20 | 25.20 | 10.28 | 42.38 | 24.14 | 7.14 | 109.14 |

| Brush 3rd or additional coats | | | | | | | | | |
|---|---|---|---|---|---|---|---|---|---|
| Slow | 100 | 335 | 146.90 | 20.25 | 5.97 | 43.85 | 13.31 | 13.34 | 96.72 |
| Medium | 125 | 323 | 128.60 | 20.60 | 7.30 | 39.81 | 16.93 | 10.16 | 94.80 |
| Fast | 150 | 310 | 110.20 | 21.00 | 8.58 | 35.55 | 20.19 | 5.97 | 91.29 |

*Industrial, Institutional and Heavy Commercial Costs*

|  | Labor SF per manhour | Material coverage SF/gallon | Material cost per gallon | Labor cost per 100 SF | Labor burden 100 SF | Material cost per 100 SF | Overhead per 100 SF | Profit per 100 SF | Total price per 100 SF |
|---|---|---|---|---|---|---|---|---|---|
| **Epoxy coating, 2 part system - white (material #52)** | | | | | | | | | |
| Brush 1st coat | | | | | | | | | |
| Slow | 60 | 260 | 177.00 | 33.75 | 9.96 | 68.08 | 21.24 | 21.28 | 154.31 |
| Medium | 75 | 243 | 154.90 | 34.33 | 12.15 | 63.74 | 27.56 | 16.53 | 154.31 |
| Fast | 90 | 235 | 132.70 | 35.00 | 14.27 | 56.47 | 32.78 | 9.70 | 148.22 |
| Brush 2nd coat | | | | | | | | | |
| Slow | 85 | 285 | 177.00 | 23.82 | 7.01 | 62.11 | 17.66 | 17.70 | 128.30 |
| Medium | 100 | 273 | 154.90 | 25.75 | 9.12 | 56.74 | 22.90 | 13.74 | 128.25 |
| Fast | 125 | 260 | 132.70 | 25.20 | 10.28 | 51.04 | 26.82 | 7.93 | 121.27 |
| Brush 3rd or additional coats | | | | | | | | | |
| Slow | 100 | 335 | 177.00 | 20.25 | 5.97 | 52.84 | 15.02 | 15.05 | 109.13 |
| Medium | 125 | 323 | 154.90 | 20.60 | 7.30 | 47.96 | 18.96 | 11.38 | 106.20 |
| Fast | 150 | 310 | 132.70 | 21.00 | 8.58 | 42.81 | 22.44 | 6.64 | 101.47 |

For heights over 8 feet, use the High Time Difficulty Factors on page 139. "Slow" work is based on an hourly wage of $20.25, "Medium" work on an hourly wage of $25.75, and "Fast" work on an hourly wage of $31.50. Other qualifications that apply to this table are on page 9.

*National Painting Cost Estimator*

|  | Labor SF per manhour | Material coverage SF/gallon | Material cost per gallon | Labor cost per 100 SF | Labor burden 100 SF | Material cost per 100 SF | Overhead per 100 SF | Profit per 100 SF | Total price per 100 SF |
|---|---|---|---|---|---|---|---|---|---|
| **Ductwork, canvas insulated, roll application** | | | | | | | | | |
| Flat latex, water base (material #5) | | | | | | | | | |
| Roll 1st coat | | | | | | | | | |
| Slow | 125 | 250 | 36.70 | 16.20 | 4.78 | 14.68 | 6.78 | 6.79 | 49.23 |
| Medium | 150 | 238 | 32.10 | 17.17 | 6.09 | 13.49 | 9.19 | 5.51 | 51.45 |
| Fast | 175 | 225 | 27.50 | 18.00 | 7.32 | 12.22 | 11.64 | 3.44 | 52.62 |
| Roll 2nd coat | | | | | | | | | |
| Slow | 175 | 350 | 36.70 | 11.57 | 3.40 | 10.49 | 4.84 | 4.85 | 35.15 |
| Medium | 200 | 325 | 32.10 | 12.88 | 4.56 | 9.88 | 6.83 | 4.10 | 38.25 |
| Fast | 225 | 300 | 27.50 | 14.00 | 5.69 | 9.17 | 8.95 | 2.65 | 40.46 |
| Roll 3rd or additional coats | | | | | | | | | |
| Slow | 225 | 400 | 36.70 | 9.00 | 2.64 | 9.18 | 3.96 | 3.97 | 28.75 |
| Medium | 250 | 388 | 32.10 | 10.30 | 3.65 | 8.27 | 5.56 | 3.33 | 31.11 |
| Fast | 275 | 375 | 27.50 | 11.45 | 4.69 | 7.33 | 7.27 | 2.15 | 32.89 |
| Sealer, off white, water base (material #1) | | | | | | | | | |
| Roll 1 coat | | | | | | | | | |
| Slow | 125 | 250 | 30.50 | 16.20 | 4.78 | 12.20 | 6.30 | 6.32 | 45.80 |
| Medium | 150 | 238 | 26.70 | 17.17 | 6.09 | 11.22 | 8.62 | 5.17 | 48.27 |
| Fast | 175 | 225 | 22.90 | 18.00 | 7.32 | 10.18 | 11.01 | 3.26 | 49.77 |
| Sealer, off white, oil base (material #2) | | | | | | | | | |
| Roll 1 coat | | | | | | | | | |
| Slow | 125 | 275 | 39.70 | 16.20 | 4.78 | 14.44 | 6.73 | 6.74 | 48.89 |
| Medium | 150 | 263 | 34.80 | 17.17 | 6.09 | 13.23 | 9.12 | 5.47 | 51.08 |
| Fast | 175 | 250 | 29.80 | 18.00 | 7.32 | 11.92 | 11.55 | 3.42 | 52.21 |
| Enamel, water base (material #9) | | | | | | | | | |
| Roll 1st finish coat | | | | | | | | | |
| Slow | 175 | 350 | 46.80 | 11.57 | 3.40 | 13.37 | 5.39 | 5.40 | 39.13 |
| Medium | 200 | 325 | 41.00 | 12.88 | 4.56 | 12.62 | 7.52 | 4.51 | 42.09 |
| Fast | 225 | 300 | 35.10 | 14.00 | 5.69 | 11.70 | 9.74 | 2.88 | 44.01 |
| Roll 2nd or additional finish coats | | | | | | | | | |
| Slow | 225 | 400 | 46.80 | 9.00 | 2.64 | 11.70 | 4.44 | 4.45 | 32.23 |
| Medium | 250 | 388 | 41.00 | 10.30 | 3.65 | 10.57 | 6.13 | 3.68 | 34.33 |
| Fast | 275 | 375 | 35.10 | 11.45 | 4.69 | 9.36 | 7.90 | 2.34 | 35.74 |

*Industrial, Institutional and Heavy Commercial Costs*

|  | Labor SF per manhour | Material coverage SF/gallon | Material cost per gallon | Labor cost per 100 SF | Labor burden 100 SF | Material cost per 100 SF | Overhead per 100 SF | Profit per 100 SF | Total price per 100 SF |
|---|---|---|---|---|---|---|---|---|---|
| **Industrial enamel, oil base, high gloss - light colors (material #56)** | | | | | | | | | |
| Roll 1st finish coat | | | | | | | | | |
| Slow | 175 | 375 | 61.00 | 11.57 | 3.40 | 16.27 | 5.94 | 5.95 | 43.13 |
| Medium | 200 | 350 | 53.40 | 12.88 | 4.56 | 15.26 | 8.18 | 4.91 | 45.79 |
| Fast | 225 | 325 | 45.80 | 14.00 | 5.69 | 14.09 | 10.48 | 3.10 | 47.36 |
| Roll 2nd or additional finish coats | | | | | | | | | |
| Slow | 225 | 450 | 61.00 | 9.00 | 2.64 | 13.56 | 4.79 | 4.80 | 34.79 |
| Medium | 250 | 438 | 53.40 | 10.30 | 3.65 | 12.19 | 6.54 | 3.92 | 36.60 |
| Fast | 275 | 425 | 45.80 | 11.45 | 4.69 | 10.78 | 8.34 | 2.47 | 37.73 |
| **Industrial enamel, oil base, high gloss - dark (OSHA) colors (material #57)** | | | | | | | | | |
| Roll 1st finish coat | | | | | | | | | |
| Slow | 175 | 300 | 67.60 | 11.57 | 3.40 | 22.53 | 7.13 | 7.14 | 51.77 |
| Medium | 200 | 288 | 59.10 | 12.88 | 4.56 | 20.52 | 9.49 | 5.69 | 53.14 |
| Fast | 225 | 275 | 50.70 | 14.00 | 5.69 | 18.44 | 11.83 | 3.50 | 53.46 |
| Roll 2nd or additional finish coats | | | | | | | | | |
| Slow | 225 | 450 | 67.60 | 9.00 | 2.64 | 15.02 | 5.07 | 5.08 | 36.81 |
| Medium | 250 | 438 | 59.10 | 10.30 | 3.65 | 13.49 | 6.86 | 4.12 | 38.42 |
| Fast | 275 | 425 | 50.70 | 11.45 | 4.69 | 11.93 | 8.70 | 2.57 | 39.34 |
| **Epoxy coating, 2 part system - clear (material #51)** | | | | | | | | | |
| Roll 1st coat | | | | | | | | | |
| Slow | 125 | 250 | 146.90 | 16.20 | 4.78 | 58.76 | 15.15 | 15.18 | 110.07 |
| Medium | 150 | 238 | 128.60 | 17.17 | 6.09 | 54.03 | 19.32 | 11.59 | 108.20 |
| Fast | 175 | 225 | 110.20 | 18.00 | 7.32 | 48.98 | 23.04 | 6.82 | 104.16 |
| Roll 2nd coat | | | | | | | | | |
| Slow | 175 | 350 | 146.90 | 11.57 | 3.40 | 41.97 | 10.82 | 10.84 | 78.60 |
| Medium | 200 | 325 | 128.60 | 12.88 | 4.56 | 39.57 | 14.25 | 8.55 | 79.81 |
| Fast | 225 | 300 | 110.20 | 14.00 | 5.69 | 36.73 | 17.50 | 5.18 | 79.10 |
| Roll 3rd or additional coats | | | | | | | | | |
| Slow | 225 | 425 | 146.90 | 9.00 | 2.64 | 34.56 | 8.78 | 8.80 | 63.78 |
| Medium | 250 | 413 | 128.60 | 10.30 | 3.65 | 31.14 | 11.27 | 6.76 | 63.12 |
| Fast | 275 | 400 | 110.20 | 11.45 | 4.69 | 27.55 | 13.54 | 4.00 | 61.23 |

*National Painting Cost Estimator*

|  | Labor SF per manhour | Material coverage SF/gallon | Material cost per gallon | Labor cost per 100 SF | Labor burden 100 SF | Material cost per 100 SF | Overhead per 100 SF | Profit per 100 SF | Total price per 100 SF |
|---|---|---|---|---|---|---|---|---|---|
| **Epoxy coating, 2 part system - white (material #52)** | | | | | | | | | |
| Roll 1st coat | | | | | | | | | |
| Slow | 125 | 250 | 177.00 | 16.20 | 4.78 | 70.80 | 17.44 | 17.48 | 126.70 |
| Medium | 150 | 238 | 154.90 | 17.17 | 6.09 | 65.08 | 22.08 | 13.25 | 123.67 |
| Fast | 175 | 225 | 132.70 | 18.00 | 7.32 | 58.98 | 26.14 | 7.73 | 118.17 |
| Roll 2nd coat | | | | | | | | | |
| Slow | 175 | 375 | 177.00 | 11.57 | 3.40 | 47.20 | 11.81 | 11.84 | 85.82 |
| Medium | 200 | 338 | 154.90 | 12.88 | 4.56 | 45.83 | 15.82 | 9.49 | 88.58 |
| Fast | 225 | 300 | 132.70 | 14.00 | 5.69 | 44.23 | 19.82 | 5.86 | 89.60 |
| Roll 3rd or additional coats | | | | | | | | | |
| Slow | 225 | 425 | 177.00 | 9.00 | 2.64 | 41.65 | 10.13 | 10.15 | 73.57 |
| Medium | 250 | 413 | 154.90 | 10.30 | 3.65 | 37.51 | 12.87 | 7.72 | 72.05 |
| Fast | 275 | 400 | 132.70 | 11.45 | 4.69 | 33.18 | 15.28 | 4.52 | 69.12 |

For heights over 8 feet, use the High Time Difficulty Factors on page 139. "Slow" work is based on an hourly wage of $20.25, "Medium" work on an hourly wage of $25.75, and "Fast" work on an hourly wage of $31.50. Other qualifications that apply to this table are on page 9.

*Industrial, Institutional and Heavy Commercial Costs*

|  | Labor SF per manhour | Material coverage SF/gallon | Material cost per gallon | Labor cost per 100 SF | Labor burden 100 SF | Material cost per 100 SF | Overhead per 100 SF | Profit per 100 SF | Total price per 100 SF |
|---|---|---|---|---|---|---|---|---|---|

## Ductwork, canvas insulated, spray application

### Flat latex, water base (material #5)
Spray prime coat

| | | | | | | | | | |
|---|---|---|---|---|---|---|---|---|---|
| Slow | 450 | 200 | 36.70 | 4.50 | 1.32 | 18.35 | 4.59 | 4.60 | 33.36 |
| Medium | 500 | 188 | 32.10 | 5.15 | 1.82 | 17.07 | 6.01 | 3.61 | 33.66 |
| Fast | 550 | 175 | 27.50 | 5.73 | 2.34 | 15.71 | 7.37 | 2.18 | 33.33 |

Spray 1st finish coat

| | | | | | | | | | |
|---|---|---|---|---|---|---|---|---|---|
| Slow | 550 | 225 | 36.70 | 3.68 | 1.09 | 16.31 | 4.01 | 4.01 | 29.10 |
| Medium | 625 | 213 | 32.10 | 4.12 | 1.46 | 15.07 | 5.16 | 3.10 | 28.91 |
| Fast | 700 | 200 | 27.50 | 4.50 | 1.84 | 13.75 | 6.23 | 1.84 | 28.16 |

Spray 2nd or additional finish coats

| | | | | | | | | | |
|---|---|---|---|---|---|---|---|---|---|
| Slow | 700 | 250 | 36.70 | 2.89 | .86 | 14.68 | 3.50 | 3.51 | 25.44 |
| Medium | 750 | 238 | 32.10 | 3.43 | 1.21 | 13.49 | 4.53 | 2.72 | 25.38 |
| Fast | 800 | 225 | 27.50 | 3.94 | 1.60 | 12.22 | 5.51 | 1.63 | 24.90 |

### Sealer, off white, water base (material #1)
Spray 1 coat

| | | | | | | | | | |
|---|---|---|---|---|---|---|---|---|---|
| Slow | 450 | 200 | 30.50 | 4.50 | 1.32 | 15.25 | 4.01 | 4.01 | 29.09 |
| Medium | 500 | 188 | 26.70 | 5.15 | 1.82 | 14.20 | 5.29 | 3.18 | 29.64 |
| Fast | 550 | 175 | 22.90 | 5.73 | 2.34 | 13.09 | 6.56 | 1.94 | 29.66 |

### Sealer, off white, oil base (material #2)
Spray 1 coat

| | | | | | | | | | |
|---|---|---|---|---|---|---|---|---|---|
| Slow | 450 | 225 | 39.70 | 4.50 | 1.32 | 17.64 | 4.46 | 4.47 | 32.39 |
| Medium | 500 | 213 | 34.80 | 5.15 | 1.82 | 16.34 | 5.83 | 3.50 | 32.64 |
| Fast | 550 | 200 | 29.80 | 5.73 | 2.34 | 14.90 | 7.12 | 2.11 | 32.20 |

### Enamel, water base (material #9)
Spray 1st finish coat

| | | | | | | | | | |
|---|---|---|---|---|---|---|---|---|---|
| Slow | 550 | 225 | 46.80 | 3.68 | 1.09 | 20.80 | 4.86 | 4.87 | 35.30 |
| Medium | 625 | 213 | 41.00 | 4.12 | 1.46 | 19.25 | 6.21 | 3.72 | 34.76 |
| Fast | 700 | 200 | 35.10 | 4.50 | 1.84 | 17.55 | 7.41 | 2.19 | 33.49 |

Spray 2nd or additional finish coats

| | | | | | | | | | |
|---|---|---|---|---|---|---|---|---|---|
| Slow | 700 | 250 | 46.80 | 2.89 | .86 | 18.72 | 4.27 | 4.28 | 31.02 |
| Medium | 750 | 238 | 41.00 | 3.43 | 1.21 | 17.23 | 5.47 | 3.28 | 30.62 |
| Fast | 800 | 225 | 35.10 | 3.94 | 1.60 | 15.60 | 6.56 | 1.94 | 29.64 |

## National Painting Cost Estimator

|  | Labor SF per manhour | Material coverage SF/gallon | Material cost per gallon | Labor cost per 100 SF | Labor burden 100 SF | Material cost per 100 SF | Overhead per 100 SF | Profit per 100 SF | Total price per 100 SF |
|---|---|---|---|---|---|---|---|---|---|
| **Industrial enamel, oil base, high gloss - light colors (material #56)** | | | | | | | | | |
| Spray 1st finish coat | | | | | | | | | |
| Slow | 700 | 250 | 61.00 | 2.89 | .86 | 24.40 | 5.35 | 5.36 | 38.86 |
| Medium | 625 | 238 | 53.40 | 4.12 | 1.46 | 22.44 | 7.01 | 4.20 | 39.23 |
| Fast | 550 | 225 | 45.80 | 5.73 | 2.34 | 20.36 | 8.81 | 2.61 | 39.85 |
| Spray 2nd or additional finish coats | | | | | | | | | |
| Slow | 800 | 275 | 61.00 | 2.53 | .75 | 22.18 | 4.84 | 4.85 | 35.15 |
| Medium | 750 | 263 | 53.40 | 3.43 | 1.21 | 20.30 | 6.24 | 3.74 | 34.92 |
| Fast | 700 | 250 | 45.80 | 4.50 | 1.84 | 18.32 | 7.64 | 2.26 | 34.56 |
| **Industrial enamel, oil base, high gloss - dark (OSHA) colors (material #57)** | | | | | | | | | |
| Spray 1st finish coat | | | | | | | | | |
| Slow | 700 | 250 | 67.60 | 2.89 | .86 | 27.04 | 5.85 | 5.86 | 42.50 |
| Medium | 625 | 238 | 59.10 | 4.12 | 1.46 | 24.83 | 7.60 | 4.56 | 42.57 |
| Fast | 550 | 225 | 50.70 | 5.73 | 2.34 | 22.53 | 9.49 | 2.81 | 42.90 |
| Spray 2nd or additional finish coats | | | | | | | | | |
| Slow | 800 | 275 | 67.60 | 2.53 | .75 | 24.58 | 5.29 | 5.30 | 38.45 |
| Medium | 750 | 263 | 59.10 | 3.43 | 1.21 | 22.47 | 6.78 | 4.07 | 37.96 |
| Fast | 700 | 250 | 50.70 | 4.50 | 1.84 | 20.28 | 8.25 | 2.44 | 37.31 |
| **Epoxy coating, 2 part system - clear (material #51)** | | | | | | | | | |
| Spray prime coat | | | | | | | | | |
| Slow | 450 | 200 | 146.90 | 4.50 | 1.32 | 73.45 | 15.06 | 15.09 | 109.42 |
| Medium | 500 | 188 | 128.60 | 5.15 | 1.82 | 68.40 | 18.84 | 11.31 | 105.52 |
| Fast | 550 | 175 | 110.20 | 5.73 | 2.34 | 62.97 | 22.02 | 6.51 | 99.57 |
| Spray 1st finish coat | | | | | | | | | |
| Slow | 550 | 235 | 146.90 | 3.68 | 1.09 | 62.51 | 12.78 | 12.81 | 92.87 |
| Medium | 625 | 225 | 128.60 | 4.12 | 1.46 | 57.16 | 15.69 | 9.41 | 87.84 |
| Fast | 700 | 215 | 110.20 | 4.50 | 1.84 | 51.26 | 17.86 | 5.28 | 80.74 |
| Spray 2nd or additional finish coats | | | | | | | | | |
| Slow | 700 | 265 | 146.90 | 2.89 | .86 | 55.43 | 11.24 | 11.27 | 81.69 |
| Medium | 750 | 253 | 128.60 | 3.43 | 1.21 | 50.83 | 13.87 | 8.32 | 77.66 |
| Fast | 800 | 240 | 110.20 | 3.94 | 1.60 | 45.92 | 15.96 | 4.72 | 72.14 |

*Industrial, Institutional and Heavy Commercial Costs*

|  | Labor SF per manhour | Material coverage SF/gallon | Material cost per gallon | Labor cost per 100 SF | Labor burden 100 SF | Material cost per 100 SF | Overhead per 100 SF | Profit per 100 SF | Total price per 100 SF |
|---|---|---|---|---|---|---|---|---|---|
| **Epoxy coating, 2 part system - white (material #52)** | | | | | | | | | |
| Spray prime coat | | | | | | | | | |
| Slow | 450 | 200 | 177.00 | 4.50 | 1.32 | 88.50 | 17.92 | 17.96 | 130.20 |
| Medium | 500 | 188 | 154.90 | 5.15 | 1.82 | 82.39 | 22.34 | 13.40 | 125.10 |
| Fast | 550 | 175 | 132.70 | 5.73 | 2.34 | 75.83 | 26.01 | 7.69 | 117.60 |
| Spray 1st finish coat | | | | | | | | | |
| Slow | 550 | 235 | 177.00 | 3.68 | 1.09 | 75.32 | 15.22 | 15.25 | 110.56 |
| Medium | 625 | 225 | 154.90 | 4.12 | 1.46 | 68.84 | 18.61 | 11.16 | 104.19 |
| Fast | 700 | 215 | 132.70 | 4.50 | 1.84 | 61.72 | 21.10 | 6.24 | 95.40 |
| Spray 2nd or additional finish coats | | | | | | | | | |
| Slow | 700 | 265 | 177.00 | 2.89 | .86 | 66.79 | 13.40 | 13.43 | 97.37 |
| Medium | 750 | 253 | 154.90 | 3.43 | 1.21 | 61.23 | 16.47 | 9.88 | 92.22 |
| Fast | 800 | 240 | 132.70 | 3.94 | 1.60 | 55.29 | 18.86 | 5.58 | 85.27 |

For heights over 8 feet, use the High Time Difficulty Factors on page 139. "Slow" work is based on an hourly wage of $20.25, "Medium" work on an hourly wage of $25.75, and "Fast" work on an hourly wage of $31.50. Other qualifications that apply to this table are on page 9.

*National Painting Cost Estimator*

|  | Manhours per flight | Flights per gallon | Material cost per gallon | Labor cost per flight | Labor burden flight | Material cost per flight | Overhead per flight | Profit per flight | Total price per flight |
|---|---|---|---|---|---|---|---|---|---|

## Fire escapes
### Solid (plain) deck
#### Spray each coat
##### Metal primer, rust inhibitor - clean metal (material #35)
| | | | | | | | | | |
|---|---|---|---|---|---|---|---|---|---|
| Slow | 2.0 | 1.25 | 59.70 | 40.50 | 11.94 | 47.76 | 19.04 | 19.08 | 138.32 |
| Medium | 1.5 | 1.00 | 52.20 | 38.63 | 13.68 | 52.20 | 26.13 | 15.68 | 146.32 |
| Fast | 1.0 | 0.75 | 44.80 | 31.50 | 12.85 | 59.73 | 32.26 | 9.54 | 145.88 |

##### Metal primer, rust inhibitor - rusty metal (material #36)
| | | | | | | | | | |
|---|---|---|---|---|---|---|---|---|---|
| Slow | 2.0 | 1.25 | 72.30 | 40.50 | 11.94 | 57.84 | 20.96 | 21.00 | 152.24 |
| Medium | 1.5 | 1.00 | 63.30 | 38.63 | 13.68 | 63.30 | 28.90 | 17.34 | 161.85 |
| Fast | 1.0 | 0.75 | 54.20 | 31.50 | 12.85 | 72.27 | 36.15 | 10.69 | 163.46 |

##### Industrial enamel, oil base, high gloss - light colors (material #56)
| | | | | | | | | | |
|---|---|---|---|---|---|---|---|---|---|
| Slow | 2.25 | 1.50 | 61.00 | 45.56 | 13.44 | 40.67 | 18.94 | 18.98 | 137.59 |
| Medium | 1.75 | 1.25 | 53.40 | 45.06 | 15.96 | 42.72 | 25.93 | 15.56 | 145.23 |
| Fast | 1.25 | 1.00 | 45.80 | 39.38 | 16.06 | 45.80 | 31.39 | 9.28 | 141.91 |

##### Industrial enamel, oil base, high gloss - dark (OSHA) colors (material #57)
| | | | | | | | | | |
|---|---|---|---|---|---|---|---|---|---|
| Slow | 2.25 | 1.50 | 67.60 | 45.56 | 13.44 | 45.07 | 19.77 | 19.81 | 143.65 |
| Medium | 1.75 | 1.25 | 59.10 | 45.06 | 15.96 | 47.28 | 27.07 | 16.24 | 151.61 |
| Fast | 1.25 | 1.00 | 50.70 | 39.38 | 16.06 | 50.70 | 32.91 | 9.73 | 148.78 |

### Grating deck
#### Spray each coat
##### Metal primer, rust inhibitor - clean metal (material #35)
| | | | | | | | | | |
|---|---|---|---|---|---|---|---|---|---|
| Slow | 3.0 | 1.75 | 59.70 | 60.75 | 17.91 | 34.11 | 21.43 | 21.47 | 155.67 |
| Medium | 2.5 | 1.50 | 52.20 | 64.38 | 22.80 | 34.80 | 30.49 | 18.30 | 170.77 |
| Fast | 2.0 | 1.25 | 44.80 | 63.00 | 25.70 | 35.84 | 38.61 | 11.42 | 174.57 |

##### Metal primer, rust inhibitor - rusty metal (material #36)
| | | | | | | | | | |
|---|---|---|---|---|---|---|---|---|---|
| Slow | 3.0 | 1.75 | 72.30 | 60.75 | 17.91 | 41.31 | 22.80 | 22.84 | 165.61 |
| Medium | 2.5 | 1.50 | 63.30 | 64.38 | 22.80 | 42.20 | 32.34 | 19.41 | 181.13 |
| Fast | 2.0 | 1.25 | 54.20 | 63.00 | 25.70 | 43.36 | 40.94 | 12.11 | 185.11 |

*Industrial, Institutional and Heavy Commercial Costs*

|  | Manhours per flight | Flights per gallon | Material cost per gallon | Labor cost per flight | Labor burden flight | Material cost per flight | Overhead per flight | Profit per flight | Total price per flight |
|---|---|---|---|---|---|---|---|---|---|
| Industrial enamel, oil base, high gloss - light colors (material #56) | | | | | | | | | |
| Slow | 3.25 | 2.00 | 61.00 | 65.81 | 19.41 | 30.50 | 21.99 | 22.03 | 159.74 |
| Medium | 2.75 | 1.75 | 53.40 | 70.81 | 25.08 | 30.51 | 31.60 | 18.96 | 176.96 |
| Fast | 2.25 | 1.50 | 45.80 | 70.88 | 28.91 | 30.53 | 40.40 | 11.95 | 182.67 |
| Industrial enamel, oil base, high gloss - dark (OSHA) colors (material #57) | | | | | | | | | |
| Slow | 3.25 | 2.00 | 67.60 | 65.81 | 19.41 | 33.80 | 22.61 | 22.66 | 164.29 |
| Medium | 2.75 | 1.75 | 59.10 | 70.81 | 25.08 | 33.77 | 32.41 | 19.45 | 181.52 |
| Fast | 2.25 | 1.50 | 50.70 | 70.88 | 28.91 | 33.80 | 41.42 | 12.25 | 187.26 |

Fire escapes can also be estimated by the square foot. Calculate the actual area to be coated. For continuous solid (plain) deck, use the rates listed under Decking and siding. For continuous grating deck, use the rates listed under Grates, steel. Note: A two coat system, prime and finish, using oil base material is recommended for any metal surface. Using water base material may cause oxidation, corrosion and rust. Using one coat of oil base paint on metal surfaces may result cracking, peeling or chipping without the proper prime coat application. If off white or another light colored finish paint is specified, make sure the prime coat is also a light color, or more than one finish coat will be necessary. "Slow" work is based on an hourly wage of $20.25, "Medium" work on an hourly wage of $25.75, and "Fast" work on an hourly wage of $31.50. Other qualifications that apply to this table are on page 9.

## Fire sprinkler systems

Use the costs listed for 1" to 4" pipe. For painting sprinkler heads at 12 feet on center at a ceiling height of 12 feet, figure 3 minutes per head (20 per hour). Very little paint is needed. Your material estimate for the sprinkler pipe will include enough to cover the heads. Note: A two coat system, prime and finish, using oil base material is recommended for any metal surface. Using water base material may cause oxidation, corrosion and rust. One coat of oil base paint on metal surfaces may result in cracking, peeling or chipping without the proper prime coat application. If off white or another light colored finish paint is specified, make sure the prime coat is also a light color, or more than one finish coat will be necessary.

*National Painting Cost Estimator*

|  | Labor SF per manhour | Material coverage SF/gallon | Material cost per gallon | Labor cost per 100 SF | Labor burden 100 SF | Material cost per 100 SF | Overhead per 100 SF | Profit per 100 SF | Total price per 100 SF |
|---|---|---|---|---|---|---|---|---|---|

## Grates, steel, over 1" thick
### Without supports
#### Brush each coat
##### Metal primer, rust inhibitor - clean metal (material #35)
| | | | | | | | | | |
|---|---|---|---|---|---|---|---|---|---|
| Slow | 60 | 175 | 59.70 | 33.75 | 9.96 | .34 | 8.37 | 8.39 | 60.81 |
| Medium | 85 | 150 | 52.20 | 30.29 | 10.72 | .35 | 10.34 | 6.20 | 57.90 |
| Fast | 110 | 125 | 44.80 | 28.64 | 11.67 | .36 | 12.61 | 3.73 | 57.01 |

##### Metal primer, rust inhibitor - rusty metal (material #36)
| | | | | | | | | | |
|---|---|---|---|---|---|---|---|---|---|
| Slow | 60 | 175 | 72.30 | 33.75 | 9.96 | .41 | 8.38 | 8.40 | 60.90 |
| Medium | 85 | 150 | 63.30 | 30.29 | 10.72 | .42 | 10.36 | 6.21 | 58.00 |
| Fast | 110 | 125 | 54.20 | 28.64 | 11.67 | .43 | 12.64 | 3.74 | 57.12 |

##### Industrial enamel, oil base, high gloss - light colors (material #56)
| | | | | | | | | | |
|---|---|---|---|---|---|---|---|---|---|
| Slow | 75 | 225 | 61.00 | 27.00 | 7.95 | .27 | 6.70 | 6.71 | 48.63 |
| Medium | 100 | 200 | 53.40 | 25.75 | 9.12 | .27 | 8.79 | 5.27 | 49.20 |
| Fast | 125 | 175 | 45.80 | 25.20 | 10.28 | .26 | 11.08 | 3.28 | 50.10 |

##### Industrial enamel, oil base, high gloss - dark (OSHA) colors (material #57)
| | | | | | | | | | |
|---|---|---|---|---|---|---|---|---|---|
| Slow | 75 | 225 | 67.60 | 27.00 | 7.95 | .30 | 6.70 | 6.72 | 48.67 |
| Medium | 100 | 200 | 59.10 | 25.75 | 9.12 | .30 | 8.79 | 5.28 | 49.24 |
| Fast | 125 | 175 | 50.70 | 25.20 | 10.28 | .29 | 11.09 | 3.28 | 50.14 |

#### Spray each coat
##### Metal primer, rust inhibitor - clean metal (material #35)
| | | | | | | | | | |
|---|---|---|---|---|---|---|---|---|---|
| Slow | 190 | 125 | 59.70 | 10.66 | 3.13 | .48 | 2.71 | 2.72 | 19.70 |
| Medium | 208 | 113 | 52.20 | 12.38 | 4.39 | .46 | 4.31 | 2.58 | 24.12 |
| Fast | 225 | 100 | 44.80 | 14.00 | 5.69 | .45 | 6.25 | 1.85 | 28.24 |

##### Metal primer, rust inhibitor - rusty metal (material #36)
| | | | | | | | | | |
|---|---|---|---|---|---|---|---|---|---|
| Slow | 190 | 125 | 72.30 | 10.66 | 3.13 | .58 | 2.73 | 2.74 | 19.84 |
| Medium | 208 | 113 | 63.30 | 12.38 | 4.39 | .56 | 4.33 | 2.60 | 24.26 |
| Fast | 225 | 100 | 54.20 | 14.00 | 5.69 | .54 | 6.28 | 1.86 | 28.37 |

##### Industrial enamel, oil base, high gloss - light colors (material #56)
| | | | | | | | | | |
|---|---|---|---|---|---|---|---|---|---|
| Slow | 215 | 160 | 61.00 | 9.42 | 2.77 | .38 | 2.39 | 2.40 | 17.36 |
| Medium | 233 | 148 | 53.40 | 11.05 | 3.91 | .36 | 3.83 | 2.30 | 21.45 |
| Fast | 250 | 135 | 45.80 | 12.60 | 5.14 | .34 | 5.60 | 1.66 | 25.34 |

##### Industrial enamel, oil base, high gloss - dark (OSHA) colors (material #57)
| | | | | | | | | | |
|---|---|---|---|---|---|---|---|---|---|
| Slow | 215 | 160 | 67.60 | 9.42 | 2.77 | .42 | 2.40 | 2.40 | 17.41 |
| Medium | 233 | 148 | 59.10 | 11.05 | 3.91 | .40 | 3.84 | 2.30 | 21.50 |
| Fast | 250 | 135 | 50.70 | 12.60 | 5.14 | .38 | 5.62 | 1.66 | 25.40 |

*Industrial, Institutional and Heavy Commercial Costs*

|  | Labor SF per manhour | Material coverage SF/gallon | Material cost per gallon | Labor cost per 100 SF | Labor burden 100 SF | Material cost per 100 SF | Overhead per 100 SF | Profit per 100 SF | Total price per 100 SF |
|---|---|---|---|---|---|---|---|---|---|
| **Including typical supports** | | | | | | | | | |
| Brush each coat | | | | | | | | | |
| Metal primer, rust inhibitor - clean metal (material #35) | | | | | | | | | |
| Slow | 40 | 125 | 59.70 | 50.63 | 14.92 | .48 | 12.55 | 12.58 | 91.16 |
| Medium | 55 | 113 | 52.20 | 46.82 | 16.57 | .46 | 15.96 | 9.58 | 89.39 |
| Fast | 70 | 100 | 44.80 | 45.00 | 18.38 | .45 | 19.78 | 5.85 | 89.46 |
| Metal primer, rust inhibitor - rusty metal (material #36) | | | | | | | | | |
| Slow | 40 | 125 | 72.30 | 50.63 | 14.92 | .58 | 12.57 | 12.60 | 91.30 |
| Medium | 55 | 113 | 63.30 | 46.82 | 16.57 | .56 | 15.99 | 9.59 | 89.53 |
| Fast | 70 | 100 | 54.20 | 45.00 | 18.38 | .54 | 19.81 | 5.86 | 89.59 |
| Industrial enamel, oil base, high gloss - light colors (material #56) | | | | | | | | | |
| Slow | 50 | 160 | 61.00 | 40.50 | 11.94 | .38 | 10.04 | 10.06 | 72.92 |
| Medium | 75 | 148 | 53.40 | 34.33 | 12.15 | .36 | 11.71 | 7.03 | 65.58 |
| Fast | 100 | 135 | 45.80 | 31.50 | 12.85 | .34 | 13.85 | 4.10 | 62.64 |
| Industrial enamel, oil base, high gloss - dark (OSHA) colors (material #57) | | | | | | | | | |
| Slow | 50 | 160 | 67.60 | 40.50 | 11.94 | .42 | 10.05 | 10.07 | 72.98 |
| Medium | 75 | 148 | 59.10 | 34.33 | 12.15 | .40 | 11.72 | 7.03 | 65.63 |
| Fast | 100 | 135 | 50.70 | 31.50 | 12.85 | .38 | 13.87 | 4.10 | 62.70 |
| Spray each coat | | | | | | | | | |
| Metal primer, rust inhibitor - clean metal (material #35) | | | | | | | | | |
| Slow | 120 | 100 | 59.70 | 16.88 | 4.96 | .60 | 4.27 | 4.28 | 30.99 |
| Medium | 135 | 88 | 52.20 | 19.07 | 6.77 | .59 | 6.60 | 3.96 | 36.99 |
| Fast | 150 | 75 | 44.80 | 21.00 | 8.58 | .60 | 9.35 | 2.77 | 42.30 |
| Metal primer, rust inhibitor - rusty metal (material #36) | | | | | | | | | |
| Slow | 120 | 100 | 72.30 | 16.88 | 4.96 | .72 | 4.29 | 4.30 | 31.15 |
| Medium | 135 | 88 | 63.30 | 19.07 | 6.77 | .72 | 6.64 | 3.98 | 37.18 |
| Fast | 150 | 75 | 54.20 | 21.00 | 8.58 | .72 | 9.39 | 2.78 | 42.47 |
| Industrial enamel, oil base, high gloss - light colors (material #56) | | | | | | | | | |
| Slow | 150 | 125 | 61.00 | 13.50 | 3.99 | .49 | 3.41 | 3.42 | 24.81 |
| Medium | 163 | 113 | 53.40 | 15.80 | 5.58 | .47 | 5.47 | 3.28 | 30.60 |
| Fast | 175 | 100 | 45.80 | 18.00 | 7.32 | .46 | 8.00 | 2.37 | 36.15 |
| Industrial enamel, oil base, high gloss - dark (OSHA) colors (material #57) | | | | | | | | | |
| Slow | 150 | 125 | 67.60 | 13.50 | 3.99 | .54 | 3.42 | 3.43 | 24.88 |
| Medium | 163 | 113 | 59.10 | 15.80 | 5.58 | .52 | 5.48 | 3.29 | 30.67 |
| Fast | 175 | 100 | 50.70 | 18.00 | 7.32 | .51 | 8.01 | 2.37 | 36.21 |

Use these figures when estimating steel grates over 1" thick. The figures will apply when both sides are painted with oil or water base paint. Square feet calculations for grates are based on overall (length times width) dimensions. For grilles under 1" thick, see the following table. Note: A two coat system, prime and finish, using oil base material is recommended for any metal surface. Water base material may cause oxidation, corrosion and rust. Using one coat of oil base paint on metal surfaces may result in cracking, peeling, or chipping without the proper prime coat application. If off white or another light colored finish paint is specified, make sure the prime coat is also a light color, or more than one finish coat will be necessary. "Slow" work is based on an hourly wage of $20.25, "Medium" work on an hourly wage of $25.75, and "Fast" work on an hourly wage of $31.50. Other qualifications that apply to this table are on page 9.

*National Painting Cost Estimator*

|  | Labor SF per manhour | Material coverage SF/gallon | Material cost per gallon | Labor cost per 100 SF | Labor burden 100 SF | Material cost per 100 SF | Overhead per 100 SF | Profit per 100 SF | Total price per 100 SF |
|---|---|---|---|---|---|---|---|---|---|

## Grilles, steel, under 1" thick
### Without supports
#### Brush each coat

Metal primer, rust inhibitor, clean metal (material #35)
| | | | | | | | | | |
|---|---|---|---|---|---|---|---|---|---|
| Slow | 175 | 200 | 59.70 | 11.57 | 3.40 | 29.85 | 8.52 | 8.54 | 61.88 |
| Medium | 200 | 175 | 52.20 | 12.88 | 4.56 | 29.83 | 11.82 | 7.09 | 66.18 |
| Fast | 225 | 150 | 44.80 | 14.00 | 5.69 | 29.87 | 15.37 | 4.55 | 69.48 |

Metal primer, rust inhibitor, rusty metal (material #36)
| | | | | | | | | | |
|---|---|---|---|---|---|---|---|---|---|
| Slow | 175 | 200 | 72.30 | 11.57 | 3.40 | 36.15 | 9.71 | 9.73 | 70.56 |
| Medium | 200 | 175 | 63.30 | 12.88 | 4.56 | 36.17 | 13.40 | 8.04 | 75.05 |
| Fast | 225 | 150 | 54.20 | 14.00 | 5.69 | 36.13 | 17.31 | 5.12 | 78.25 |

Industrial enamel, oil base, high gloss, light colors (material #56)
| | | | | | | | | | |
|---|---|---|---|---|---|---|---|---|---|
| Slow | 200 | 250 | 61.00 | 10.13 | 2.98 | 24.40 | 7.13 | 7.14 | 51.78 |
| Medium | 225 | 225 | 53.40 | 11.44 | 4.04 | 23.73 | 9.81 | 5.88 | 54.90 |
| Fast | 250 | 200 | 45.80 | 12.60 | 5.14 | 22.90 | 12.60 | 3.73 | 56.97 |

Industrial enamel, oil base, high gloss, dark (OSHA) colors (material #57)
| | | | | | | | | | |
|---|---|---|---|---|---|---|---|---|---|
| Slow | 200 | 250 | 67.60 | 10.13 | 2.98 | 27.04 | 7.63 | 7.65 | 55.43 |
| Medium | 225 | 225 | 59.10 | 11.44 | 4.04 | 26.27 | 10.44 | 6.26 | 58.45 |
| Fast | 250 | 200 | 50.70 | 12.60 | 5.14 | 25.35 | 13.36 | 3.95 | 60.40 |

#### Spray each coat

Metal primer, rust inhibitor, clean metal (material #35)
| | | | | | | | | | |
|---|---|---|---|---|---|---|---|---|---|
| Slow | 400 | 150 | 59.70 | 5.06 | 1.50 | 39.80 | 8.81 | 8.83 | 64.00 |
| Medium | 450 | 138 | 52.20 | 5.72 | 2.02 | 37.83 | 11.39 | 6.84 | 63.80 |
| Fast | 500 | 125 | 44.80 | 6.30 | 2.57 | 35.84 | 13.86 | 4.10 | 62.67 |

Metal primer, rust inhibitor, rusty metal (material #36)
| | | | | | | | | | |
|---|---|---|---|---|---|---|---|---|---|
| Slow | 400 | 150 | 72.30 | 5.06 | 1.50 | 48.20 | 10.40 | 10.42 | 75.58 |
| Medium | 450 | 138 | 63.30 | 5.72 | 2.02 | 45.87 | 13.40 | 8.04 | 75.05 |
| Fast | 500 | 125 | 54.20 | 6.30 | 2.57 | 43.36 | 16.19 | 4.79 | 73.21 |

Industrial enamel, oil base, high gloss, light colors (material #56)
| | | | | | | | | | |
|---|---|---|---|---|---|---|---|---|---|
| Slow | 425 | 175 | 61.00 | 4.76 | 1.40 | 34.86 | 7.79 | 7.81 | 56.62 |
| Medium | 475 | 163 | 53.40 | 5.42 | 1.94 | 32.76 | 10.03 | 6.02 | 56.17 |
| Fast | 525 | 150 | 45.80 | 6.00 | 2.43 | 30.53 | 12.08 | 3.57 | 54.61 |

Industrial enamel, oil base, high gloss, dark (OSHA) colors (material #57)
| | | | | | | | | | |
|---|---|---|---|---|---|---|---|---|---|
| Slow | 425 | 175 | 67.60 | 4.76 | 1.40 | 38.63 | 8.51 | 8.53 | 61.83 |
| Medium | 475 | 163 | 59.10 | 5.42 | 1.94 | 36.26 | 10.90 | 6.54 | 61.06 |
| Fast | 525 | 150 | 50.70 | 6.00 | 2.43 | 33.80 | 13.10 | 3.87 | 59.20 |

*Industrial, Institutional and Heavy Commercial Costs*

|  | Labor SF per manhour | Material coverage SF/gallon | Material cost per gallon | Labor cost per 100 SF | Labor burden 100 SF | Material cost per 100 SF | Overhead per 100 SF | Profit per 100 SF | Total price per 100 SF |
|---|---|---|---|---|---|---|---|---|---|
| **Including typical supports** | | | | | | | | | |
| Brush each coat | | | | | | | | | |
| Metal primer, rust inhibitor, clean metal (material #35) | | | | | | | | | |
| Slow | 125 | 150 | 59.70 | 16.20 | 4.78 | 39.80 | 11.55 | 11.57 | 83.90 |
| Medium | 150 | 135 | 52.20 | 17.17 | 6.09 | 38.67 | 15.48 | 9.29 | 86.70 |
| Fast | 175 | 120 | 44.80 | 18.00 | 7.32 | 37.33 | 19.43 | 5.75 | 87.83 |
| Metal primer, rust inhibitor, rusty metal (material #36) | | | | | | | | | |
| Slow | 125 | 150 | 72.30 | 16.20 | 4.78 | 48.20 | 13.14 | 13.17 | 95.49 |
| Medium | 150 | 135 | 63.30 | 17.17 | 6.09 | 46.89 | 17.54 | 10.52 | 98.21 |
| Fast | 175 | 120 | 54.20 | 18.00 | 7.32 | 45.17 | 21.86 | 6.47 | 98.82 |
| Industrial enamel, oil base, high gloss, light colors (material #56) | | | | | | | | | |
| Slow | 150 | 200 | 61.00 | 13.50 | 3.99 | 30.50 | 9.12 | 9.14 | 66.25 |
| Medium | 175 | 175 | 53.40 | 14.71 | 5.20 | 30.51 | 12.61 | 7.56 | 70.59 |
| Fast | 200 | 150 | 45.80 | 15.75 | 6.43 | 30.53 | 16.34 | 4.83 | 73.88 |
| Industrial enamel, oil base, high gloss, dark (OSHA) colors (material #57) | | | | | | | | | |
| Slow | 150 | 200 | 67.60 | 13.50 | 3.99 | 33.80 | 9.74 | 9.76 | 70.79 |
| Medium | 175 | 175 | 59.10 | 14.71 | 5.20 | 33.77 | 13.42 | 8.05 | 75.15 |
| Fast | 200 | 150 | 50.70 | 15.75 | 6.43 | 33.80 | 17.35 | 5.13 | 78.46 |
| Spray each coat | | | | | | | | | |
| Metal primer, rust inhibitor, clean metal (material #35) | | | | | | | | | |
| Slow | 325 | 125 | 59.70 | 6.23 | 1.85 | 47.76 | 10.61 | 10.63 | 77.08 |
| Medium | 375 | 113 | 52.20 | 6.87 | 2.44 | 46.19 | 13.87 | 8.32 | 77.69 |
| Fast | 425 | 100 | 44.80 | 7.41 | 3.01 | 44.80 | 17.12 | 5.06 | 77.40 |
| Metal primer, rust inhibitor, rusty metal (material #36) | | | | | | | | | |
| Slow | 325 | 125 | 72.30 | 6.23 | 1.85 | 57.84 | 12.52 | 12.55 | 90.99 |
| Medium | 375 | 113 | 63.30 | 6.87 | 2.44 | 56.02 | 16.33 | 9.80 | 91.46 |
| Fast | 425 | 100 | 54.20 | 7.41 | 3.01 | 54.20 | 20.04 | 5.93 | 90.59 |
| Industrial enamel, oil base, high gloss, light colors (material #56) | | | | | | | | | |
| Slow | 350 | 150 | 61.00 | 5.79 | 1.71 | 40.67 | 9.15 | 9.17 | 66.49 |
| Medium | 400 | 138 | 53.40 | 6.44 | 2.28 | 38.70 | 11.86 | 7.11 | 66.39 |
| Fast | 450 | 125 | 45.80 | 7.00 | 2.85 | 36.64 | 14.42 | 4.26 | 65.17 |
| Industrial enamel, oil base, high gloss, dark (OSHA) colors (material #57) | | | | | | | | | |
| Slow | 350 | 150 | 67.60 | 5.79 | 1.71 | 45.07 | 9.99 | 10.01 | 72.57 |
| Medium | 400 | 138 | 59.10 | 6.44 | 2.28 | 42.83 | 12.89 | 7.73 | 72.17 |
| Fast | 450 | 125 | 50.70 | 7.00 | 2.85 | 40.56 | 15.63 | 4.62 | 70.66 |

Use these figures to estimate steel grilles under 1" thick. The figures will apply when both sides are painted with oil or water base paint. Square foot calculations for grates are based on overall (length times width) dimensions. For grates over 1" thick, see the previous table. Note: A two coat system, prime and finish, using oil base material is recommended for any metal surface. Water base material may cause oxidation, corrosion and rust. Using one coat of oil base paint on metal surfaces may result in cracking, peeling, or chipping without the proper prime coat application. If off white or another light colored finish paint is specified, make sure the prime coat is also a light color, or more than one finish coat will be necessary. "Slow" work is based on an hourly wage of $20.25, "Medium" work on an hourly wage of $25.75, and "Fast" work on an hourly wage of $31.50. Other qualifications that apply to this table are on page 9.

## Ladders

Measure the length of the ladder rungs and vertical members. Then multiply by a difficulty factor of 1.5 (Length x 1.5) to allow for limited access to the back of the ladder. Then use the rates in the Bare Pipe tables to figure the labor and material costs.

|   | Labor SF per manhour | Material coverage SF/gallon | Material cost per gallon | Labor cost per 100 SF | Labor burden 100 SF | Material cost per 100 SF | Overhead per 100 SF | Profit per 100 SF | Total price per 100 SF |
|---|---|---|---|---|---|---|---|---|---|

### Masonry, Concrete Masonry Units (CMU), rough, porous surface

Industrial bonding & penetrating oil paint (material #55)

Brush 1st coat

| | | | | | | | | | |
|---|---|---|---|---|---|---|---|---|---|
| Slow | 225 | 200 | 48.70 | 9.00 | 2.64 | 24.35 | 6.84 | 6.86 | 49.69 |
| Medium | 250 | 188 | 42.60 | 10.30 | 3.65 | 22.66 | 9.15 | 5.49 | 51.25 |
| Fast | 275 | 175 | 36.50 | 11.45 | 4.69 | 20.86 | 11.46 | 3.39 | 51.85 |

Brush 2nd coat

| | | | | | | | | | |
|---|---|---|---|---|---|---|---|---|---|
| Slow | 230 | 275 | 48.70 | 8.80 | 2.61 | 17.71 | 5.53 | 5.54 | 40.19 |
| Medium | 260 | 250 | 42.60 | 9.90 | 3.52 | 17.04 | 7.61 | 4.57 | 42.64 |
| Fast | 290 | 225 | 36.50 | 10.86 | 4.44 | 16.22 | 9.77 | 2.89 | 44.18 |

Industrial waterproofing (material #58)

Brush 1st coat

| | | | | | | | | | |
|---|---|---|---|---|---|---|---|---|---|
| Slow | 65 | 65 | 42.10 | 31.15 | 9.18 | 64.77 | 19.97 | 20.01 | 145.08 |
| Medium | 90 | 55 | 36.80 | 28.61 | 10.13 | 66.91 | 26.41 | 15.85 | 147.91 |
| Fast | 115 | 45 | 31.60 | 27.39 | 11.19 | 70.22 | 33.72 | 9.98 | 152.50 |

Brush 2nd or additional coats

| | | | | | | | | | |
|---|---|---|---|---|---|---|---|---|---|
| Slow | 90 | 150 | 42.10 | 22.50 | 6.63 | 28.07 | 10.87 | 10.89 | 78.96 |
| Medium | 115 | 125 | 36.80 | 22.39 | 7.95 | 29.44 | 14.94 | 8.96 | 83.68 |
| Fast | 145 | 100 | 31.60 | 21.72 | 8.88 | 31.60 | 19.28 | 5.70 | 87.18 |

Roll 1st coat

| | | | | | | | | | |
|---|---|---|---|---|---|---|---|---|---|
| Slow | 100 | 125 | 42.10 | 20.25 | 5.97 | 33.68 | 11.38 | 11.40 | 82.68 |
| Medium | 125 | 108 | 36.80 | 20.60 | 7.30 | 34.07 | 15.49 | 9.29 | 86.75 |
| Fast | 150 | 90 | 31.60 | 21.00 | 8.58 | 35.11 | 20.05 | 5.93 | 90.67 |

Roll 2nd or additional coats

| | | | | | | | | | |
|---|---|---|---|---|---|---|---|---|---|
| Slow | 150 | 175 | 42.10 | 13.50 | 3.99 | 24.06 | 7.89 | 7.91 | 57.35 |
| Medium | 180 | 150 | 36.80 | 14.31 | 5.08 | 24.53 | 10.98 | 6.59 | 61.49 |
| Fast | 210 | 125 | 31.60 | 15.00 | 6.11 | 25.28 | 14.38 | 4.25 | 65.02 |

Use these figures for Concrete Masonry Units (CMU) where the block surfaces are rough, porous or unfilled, with joints struck to average depth. The more porous the surface, the rougher the texture, the more time and material will be required. For heights above 8 feet, use the High Time Difficulty Factors on page 139. Also refer to other masonry applications under Masonry in the "General Painting Operations" section of this book. "Slow" work is based on an hourly wage of $20.25, "Medium" work on an hourly wage of $25.75, "Fast" work on an hourly wage of $31.50. Other qualifications that apply to this table are on page 9.

*Industrial, Institutional and Heavy Commercial Costs*

| | Labor SF per manhour | Material coverage SF/gallon | Material cost per gallon | Labor cost per 100 SF | Labor burden 100 SF | Material cost per 100 SF | Overhead per 100 SF | Profit per 100 SF | Total price per 100 SF |
|---|---|---|---|---|---|---|---|---|---|

## Masonry, Concrete Masonry Units (CMU), smooth surface

Industrial bonding & penetrating oil paint (material #55)

Brush 1st coat

| | | | | | | | | | |
|---|---|---|---|---|---|---|---|---|---|
| Slow | 325 | 240 | 48.70 | 6.23 | 1.85 | 20.29 | 5.39 | 5.40 | 39.16 |
| Medium | 350 | 230 | 42.60 | 7.36 | 2.61 | 18.52 | 7.12 | 4.27 | 39.88 |
| Fast | 375 | 220 | 36.50 | 8.40 | 3.44 | 16.59 | 8.81 | 2.61 | 39.85 |

Brush 2nd coat

| | | | | | | | | | |
|---|---|---|---|---|---|---|---|---|---|
| Slow | 340 | 300 | 48.70 | 5.96 | 1.75 | 16.23 | 4.55 | 4.56 | 33.05 |
| Medium | 370 | 275 | 42.60 | 6.96 | 2.45 | 15.49 | 6.23 | 3.74 | 34.87 |
| Fast | 400 | 250 | 36.50 | 7.88 | 3.21 | 14.60 | 7.97 | 2.36 | 36.02 |

Industrial waterproofing (material #58)

Brush 1st coat

| | | | | | | | | | |
|---|---|---|---|---|---|---|---|---|---|
| Slow | 75 | 100 | 42.10 | 27.00 | 7.95 | 42.10 | 14.64 | 14.67 | 106.36 |
| Medium | 100 | 95 | 36.80 | 25.75 | 9.12 | 38.74 | 18.40 | 11.04 | 103.05 |
| Fast | 125 | 90 | 31.60 | 25.20 | 10.28 | 35.11 | 21.88 | 6.47 | 98.94 |

Brush 2nd or additional coats

| | | | | | | | | | |
|---|---|---|---|---|---|---|---|---|---|
| Slow | 100 | 150 | 42.10 | 20.25 | 5.97 | 28.07 | 10.32 | 10.34 | 74.95 |
| Medium | 125 | 138 | 36.80 | 20.60 | 7.30 | 26.67 | 13.64 | 8.18 | 76.39 |
| Fast | 150 | 125 | 31.60 | 21.00 | 8.58 | 25.28 | 17.00 | 5.03 | 76.89 |

Roll 1st coat

| | | | | | | | | | |
|---|---|---|---|---|---|---|---|---|---|
| Slow | 125 | 150 | 42.10 | 16.20 | 4.78 | 28.07 | 9.32 | 9.34 | 67.71 |
| Medium | 150 | 138 | 36.80 | 17.17 | 6.09 | 26.67 | 12.48 | 7.49 | 69.90 |
| Fast | 175 | 125 | 31.60 | 18.00 | 7.32 | 25.28 | 15.69 | 4.64 | 70.93 |

Roll 2nd or additional coats

| | | | | | | | | | |
|---|---|---|---|---|---|---|---|---|---|
| Slow | 175 | 200 | 42.10 | 11.57 | 3.40 | 21.05 | 6.85 | 6.86 | 49.73 |
| Medium | 200 | 175 | 36.80 | 12.88 | 4.56 | 21.03 | 9.62 | 5.77 | 53.86 |
| Fast | 225 | 150 | 31.60 | 14.00 | 5.69 | 21.07 | 12.64 | 3.74 | 57.14 |

Use these figures for Concrete Masonry Units (CMU), where block surfaces are smooth, as in precision block, filled block or slump stone with joints struck to average depth. The more smooth the surface texture, the less time and material will be required. For heights above 8 feet, use the High Time Difficulty Factors on page 139. Also refer to other masonry applications under Masonry in the "General Painting Operations" section of this book. "Slow" work is based on an hourly wage of $20.25, "Medium" work on an hourly wage of $25.75, "Fast" work on an hourly wage of $31.50. Other qualifications that apply to this table are on page 9.

National Painting Cost Estimator

|  | Labor SF per manhour | Material coverage SF/gallon | Material cost per gallon | Labor cost per 100 SF | Labor burden 100 SF | Material cost per 100 SF | Overhead per 100 SF | Profit per 100 SF | Total price per 100 SF |
|---|---|---|---|---|---|---|---|---|---|
| **Mechanical equipment** | | | | | | | | | |
| Brush each coat | | | | | | | | | |
| Metal primer, rust inhibitor, clean metal (material #35) | | | | | | | | | |
| Slow | 175 | 275 | 59.70 | 11.57 | 3.40 | 21.71 | 6.97 | 6.99 | 50.64 |
| Medium | 200 | 263 | 52.20 | 12.88 | 4.56 | 19.85 | 9.32 | 5.59 | 52.20 |
| Fast | 225 | 250 | 44.80 | 14.00 | 5.69 | 17.92 | 11.67 | 3.45 | 52.73 |
| Metal primer, rust inhibitor, rusty metal (material #36) | | | | | | | | | |
| Slow | 175 | 275 | 72.30 | 11.57 | 3.40 | 26.29 | 7.84 | 7.86 | 56.96 |
| Medium | 200 | 263 | 63.30 | 12.88 | 4.56 | 24.07 | 10.38 | 6.23 | 58.12 |
| Fast | 225 | 250 | 54.20 | 14.00 | 5.69 | 21.68 | 12.83 | 3.80 | 58.00 |
| Industrial enamel, oil base, high gloss, light colors (material #56) | | | | | | | | | |
| Slow | 200 | 375 | 61.00 | 10.13 | 2.98 | 16.27 | 5.58 | 5.60 | 40.56 |
| Medium | 225 | 363 | 53.40 | 11.44 | 4.04 | 14.71 | 7.55 | 4.53 | 42.27 |
| Fast | 250 | 350 | 45.80 | 12.60 | 5.14 | 13.09 | 9.56 | 2.83 | 43.22 |
| Industrial enamel, oil base, high gloss, dark (OSHA) colors (material #57) | | | | | | | | | |
| Slow | 200 | 375 | 67.60 | 10.13 | 2.98 | 18.03 | 5.92 | 5.93 | 42.99 |
| Medium | 225 | 363 | 59.10 | 11.44 | 4.04 | 16.28 | 7.94 | 4.77 | 44.47 |
| Fast | 250 | 350 | 50.70 | 12.60 | 5.14 | 14.49 | 9.99 | 2.96 | 45.18 |
| Spray each coat | | | | | | | | | |
| Metal primer, rust inhibitor, clean metal (material #35) | | | | | | | | | |
| Slow | 350 | 200 | 59.70 | 5.79 | 1.71 | 29.85 | 7.10 | 7.11 | 51.56 |
| Medium | 375 | 175 | 52.20 | 6.87 | 2.44 | 29.83 | 9.78 | 5.87 | 54.79 |
| Fast | 400 | 150 | 44.80 | 7.88 | 3.21 | 29.87 | 12.70 | 3.76 | 57.42 |
| Metal primer, rust inhibitor, rusty metal (material #36) | | | | | | | | | |
| Slow | 350 | 200 | 72.30 | 5.79 | 1.71 | 36.15 | 8.29 | 8.31 | 60.25 |
| Medium | 375 | 175 | 63.30 | 6.87 | 2.44 | 36.17 | 11.37 | 6.82 | 63.67 |
| Fast | 400 | 150 | 54.20 | 7.88 | 3.21 | 36.13 | 14.64 | 4.33 | 66.19 |
| Industrial enamel, oil base, high gloss, light colors (material #56) | | | | | | | | | |
| Slow | 375 | 275 | 61.00 | 5.40 | 1.60 | 22.18 | 5.54 | 5.55 | 40.27 |
| Medium | 400 | 250 | 53.40 | 6.44 | 2.28 | 21.36 | 7.52 | 4.51 | 42.11 |
| Fast | 425 | 225 | 45.80 | 7.41 | 3.01 | 20.36 | 9.54 | 2.82 | 43.14 |
| Industrial enamel, oil base, high gloss, dark (OSHA) colors (material #57) | | | | | | | | | |
| Slow | 375 | 275 | 67.60 | 5.40 | 1.60 | 24.58 | 6.00 | 6.01 | 43.59 |
| Medium | 400 | 250 | 59.10 | 6.44 | 2.28 | 23.64 | 8.09 | 4.85 | 45.30 |
| Fast | 425 | 225 | 50.70 | 7.41 | 3.01 | 22.53 | 10.22 | 3.02 | 46.19 |

Use these figures to estimate the cost of painting mechanical equipment (such as compressors and mixing boxes). Measurements are based on the overall dimension (length times width) of the surface area to be covered in square feet. For heights above 8 feet, use the High Time Difficulty Factors on page 139. Note: A two coat system, prime and finish, using oil base material is recommended for any metal surface. Water base material may cause oxidation, corrosion and rust. Using one coat of oil base paint on metal surfaces may result in cracking, peeling or chipping without the proper prime coat application. If off white or another light colored finish paint is specified, make sure the prime coat is also a light color, or more than one finish coat will be necessary. "Slow" work is based on an hourly wage of $20.25, "Medium" work on an hourly wage of $25.75, "Fast" work on an hourly wage of $31.50. Other qualifications that apply to this table are on page 9.

## Mechanical equipment, boiler room

Don't bother figuring the exact area of boiler room equipment that has to be coated. Instead, take the area as equal to 1/2 the wall height times the ceiling area in the room. Figure a painter will coat 125 square feet per hour and a gallon of paint will cover 300 square feet. This rate does not include time needed to paint walls, ceiling or floor around mechanical equipment. In any case, you'll need to rely on judgment when painting boiler room equipment.

|  | Labor SF per manhour | Material coverage SF/gallon | Material cost per gallon | Labor cost per 100 SF | Labor burden 100 SF | Material cost per 100 SF | Overhead per 100 SF | Profit per 100 SF | Total price per 100 SF |
|---|---|---|---|---|---|---|---|---|---|
| **Piping, bare pipe, brush application** | | | | | | | | | |
| Metal primer, rust inhibitor, clean metal (material #35) | | | | | | | | | |
| Brush prime coat | | | | | | | | | |
| Slow | 75 | 360 | 59.70 | 27.00 | 7.95 | 16.58 | 9.79 | 9.81 | 71.13 |
| Medium | 100 | 335 | 52.20 | 25.75 | 9.12 | 15.58 | 12.61 | 7.57 | 70.63 |
| Fast | 125 | 310 | 44.80 | 25.20 | 10.28 | 14.45 | 15.48 | 4.58 | 69.99 |
| Metal primer, rust inhibitor, rusty metal (material #36) | | | | | | | | | |
| Brush prime coat | | | | | | | | | |
| Slow | 75 | 360 | 72.30 | 27.00 | 7.95 | 20.08 | 10.46 | 10.48 | 75.97 |
| Medium | 100 | 335 | 63.30 | 25.75 | 9.12 | 18.90 | 13.44 | 8.07 | 75.28 |
| Fast | 125 | 310 | 54.20 | 25.20 | 10.28 | 17.48 | 16.42 | 4.86 | 74.24 |
| Industrial enamel, oil base, high gloss, light colors (material #56) | | | | | | | | | |
| Brush 1st finish coat | | | | | | | | | |
| Slow | 90 | 450 | 61.00 | 22.50 | 6.63 | 13.56 | 8.11 | 8.13 | 58.93 |
| Medium | 115 | 425 | 53.40 | 22.39 | 7.95 | 12.56 | 10.72 | 6.43 | 60.05 |
| Fast | 140 | 400 | 45.80 | 22.50 | 9.17 | 11.45 | 13.37 | 3.96 | 60.45 |
| Brush 2nd or additional finish coats | | | | | | | | | |
| Slow | 125 | 500 | 61.00 | 16.20 | 4.78 | 12.20 | 6.30 | 6.32 | 45.80 |
| Medium | 150 | 475 | 53.40 | 17.17 | 6.09 | 11.24 | 8.62 | 5.17 | 48.29 |
| Fast | 175 | 450 | 45.80 | 18.00 | 7.32 | 10.18 | 11.01 | 3.26 | 49.77 |
| Industrial enamel, oil base, high gloss, dark (OSHA) colors (material #57) | | | | | | | | | |
| Brush 1st finish coat | | | | | | | | | |
| Slow | 90 | 450 | 67.60 | 22.50 | 6.63 | 15.02 | 8.39 | 8.41 | 60.95 |
| Medium | 115 | 425 | 59.10 | 22.39 | 7.95 | 13.91 | 11.06 | 6.63 | 61.94 |
| Fast | 140 | 400 | 50.70 | 22.50 | 9.17 | 12.68 | 13.75 | 4.07 | 62.17 |
| Brush 2nd or additional finish coats | | | | | | | | | |
| Slow | 125 | 500 | 67.60 | 16.20 | 4.78 | 13.52 | 6.56 | 6.57 | 47.63 |
| Medium | 150 | 475 | 59.10 | 17.17 | 6.09 | 12.44 | 8.92 | 5.35 | 49.97 |
| Fast | 175 | 450 | 50.70 | 18.00 | 7.32 | 11.27 | 11.35 | 3.36 | 51.30 |

## National Painting Cost Estimator

|  | Labor SF per manhour | Material coverage SF/gallon | Material cost per gallon | Labor cost per 100 SF | Labor burden 100 SF | Material cost per 100 SF | Overhead per 100 SF | Profit per 100 SF | Total price per 100 SF |
|---|---|---|---|---|---|---|---|---|---|
| **Epoxy coating, 2 part system, clear (material #51)** | | | | | | | | | |
| Brush 1st coat | | | | | | | | | |
| Slow | 75 | 375 | 146.90 | 27.00 | 7.95 | 39.17 | 14.09 | 14.12 | 102.33 |
| Medium | 100 | 350 | 128.60 | 25.75 | 9.12 | 36.74 | 17.90 | 10.74 | 100.25 |
| Fast | 125 | 325 | 110.20 | 25.20 | 10.28 | 33.91 | 21.51 | 6.36 | 97.26 |
| Brush 2nd coat | | | | | | | | | |
| Slow | 90 | 425 | 146.90 | 22.50 | 6.63 | 34.56 | 12.10 | 12.13 | 87.92 |
| Medium | 115 | 400 | 128.60 | 22.39 | 7.95 | 32.15 | 15.62 | 9.37 | 87.48 |
| Fast | 140 | 375 | 110.20 | 22.50 | 9.17 | 29.39 | 18.93 | 5.60 | 85.59 |
| Brush 3rd or additional coats | | | | | | | | | |
| Slow | 125 | 475 | 146.90 | 16.20 | 4.78 | 30.93 | 9.86 | 9.88 | 71.65 |
| Medium | 150 | 450 | 128.60 | 17.17 | 6.09 | 28.58 | 12.96 | 7.77 | 72.57 |
| Fast | 175 | 425 | 110.20 | 18.00 | 7.32 | 25.93 | 15.89 | 4.70 | 71.84 |
| **Epoxy coating, 2 part system, white (material #52)** | | | | | | | | | |
| Brush 1st coat | | | | | | | | | |
| Slow | 75 | 375 | 177.00 | 27.00 | 7.95 | 47.20 | 15.61 | 15.64 | 113.40 |
| Medium | 100 | 350 | 154.90 | 25.75 | 9.12 | 44.26 | 19.78 | 11.87 | 110.78 |
| Fast | 125 | 325 | 132.70 | 25.20 | 10.28 | 40.83 | 23.66 | 7.00 | 106.97 |
| Brush 2nd coat | | | | | | | | | |
| Slow | 90 | 425 | 177.00 | 22.50 | 6.63 | 41.65 | 13.45 | 13.48 | 97.71 |
| Medium | 115 | 400 | 154.90 | 22.39 | 7.95 | 38.73 | 17.26 | 10.36 | 96.69 |
| Fast | 140 | 375 | 132.70 | 22.50 | 9.17 | 35.39 | 20.79 | 6.15 | 94.00 |
| Brush 3rd or additional coats | | | | | | | | | |
| Slow | 125 | 475 | 177.00 | 16.20 | 4.78 | 37.26 | 11.07 | 11.09 | 80.40 |
| Medium | 150 | 450 | 154.90 | 17.17 | 6.09 | 34.42 | 14.42 | 8.65 | 80.75 |
| Fast | 175 | 425 | 132.70 | 18.00 | 7.32 | 31.22 | 17.53 | 5.19 | 79.26 |
| **Aluminum base paint (material #50)** | | | | | | | | | |
| Brush each coat | | | | | | | | | |
| Slow | 50 | 600 | 78.40 | 40.50 | 11.94 | 13.07 | 12.45 | 12.48 | 90.44 |
| Medium | 75 | 575 | 68.60 | 34.33 | 12.15 | 11.93 | 14.60 | 8.76 | 81.77 |
| Fast | 100 | 550 | 58.80 | 31.50 | 12.85 | 10.69 | 17.06 | 5.05 | 77.15 |

*Industrial, Institutional and Heavy Commercial Costs*

|  | Labor SF per manhour | Material coverage SF/gallon | Material cost per gallon | Labor cost per 100 SF | Labor burden 100 SF | Material cost per 100 SF | Overhead per 100 SF | Profit per 100 SF | Total price per 100 SF |
|---|---|---|---|---|---|---|---|---|---|
| **Heat resistant enamel, 800 to 1200 degree range (material #53)** | | | | | | | | | |
| Brush each coat | | | | | | | | | |
| Slow | 50 | 600 | 138.10 | 40.50 | 11.94 | 23.02 | 14.34 | 14.37 | 104.17 |
| Medium | 75 | 575 | 120.90 | 34.33 | 12.15 | 21.03 | 16.88 | 10.13 | 94.52 |
| Fast | 100 | 550 | 103.60 | 31.50 | 12.85 | 18.84 | 19.59 | 5.79 | 88.57 |
| **Heat resistant enamel, 300 to 800 degree range (material #54)** | | | | | | | | | |
| Brush each coat | | | | | | | | | |
| Slow | 50 | 600 | 121.40 | 40.50 | 11.94 | 20.23 | 13.81 | 13.84 | 100.32 |
| Medium | 75 | 575 | 106.20 | 34.33 | 12.15 | 18.47 | 16.24 | 9.74 | 90.93 |
| Fast | 100 | 550 | 91.00 | 31.50 | 12.85 | 16.55 | 18.88 | 5.58 | 85.36 |

Use the pipe conversion factors in Figure 21 on page 325 to convert linear feet of pipe to square feet of surface. Vertical pipe runs require 2 to 3 times the manhours plus 10% more material. Solid color coded piping requires 15% to 25% more labor and material. For color bands on piping at 10' to 15' intervals, add the cost of an additional 1st coat. For heights above 8 feet, use the High Time Difficulty Factors on page 139. Note: A two coat system, prime and finish, using oil base material is recommended for any metal surface. Water base material may cause oxidation, corrosion and rust. One coat of oil base paint on metal surfaces may result in cracking, peeling or chipping without the proper prime coat application. If off white or another light colored finish paint is specified, make sure the prime coat is also a light color, or more than one finish coat will be necessary. "Slow" work is based on an hourly wage of $20.25, "Medium" work on an hourly wage of $25.75, "Fast" work on an hourly wage of $31.50. Other qualifications that apply to this table are on page 9.

*National Painting Cost Estimator*

|  | Labor SF per manhour | Material coverage SF/gallon | Material cost per gallon | Labor cost per 100 SF | Labor burden 100 SF | Material cost per 100 SF | Overhead per 100 SF | Profit per 100 SF | Total price per 100 SF |
|---|---|---|---|---|---|---|---|---|---|

### Piping, bare pipe, roll application

**Metal primer, rust inhibitor, clean metal (material #35)**
Roll prime coat

| | | | | | | | | | |
|---|---|---|---|---|---|---|---|---|---|
| Slow | 175 | 400 | 59.70 | 11.57 | 3.40 | 14.93 | 5.68 | 5.69 | 41.27 |
| Medium | 200 | 375 | 52.20 | 12.88 | 4.56 | 13.92 | 7.84 | 4.70 | 43.90 |
| Fast | 225 | 350 | 44.80 | 14.00 | 5.69 | 12.80 | 10.08 | 2.98 | 45.55 |

**Metal primer, rust inhibitor, rusty metal (material #36)**
Roll prime coat

| | | | | | | | | | |
|---|---|---|---|---|---|---|---|---|---|
| Slow | 175 | 400 | 72.30 | 11.57 | 3.40 | 18.08 | 6.28 | 6.29 | 45.62 |
| Medium | 200 | 375 | 63.30 | 12.88 | 4.56 | 16.88 | 8.58 | 5.15 | 48.05 |
| Fast | 225 | 350 | 54.20 | 14.00 | 5.69 | 15.49 | 10.91 | 3.23 | 49.32 |

**Industrial enamel, oil base, high gloss, light colors (material #56)**
Roll 1st finish coat

| | | | | | | | | | |
|---|---|---|---|---|---|---|---|---|---|
| Slow | 200 | 450 | 61.00 | 10.13 | 2.98 | 13.56 | 5.07 | 5.08 | 36.82 |
| Medium | 225 | 425 | 53.40 | 11.44 | 4.04 | 12.56 | 7.01 | 4.21 | 39.26 |
| Fast | 250 | 400 | 45.80 | 12.60 | 5.14 | 11.45 | 9.05 | 2.68 | 40.92 |

Roll 2nd or additional finish coats

| | | | | | | | | | |
|---|---|---|---|---|---|---|---|---|---|
| Slow | 275 | 500 | 61.00 | 7.36 | 2.18 | 12.20 | 4.13 | 4.14 | 30.01 |
| Medium | 300 | 475 | 53.40 | 8.58 | 3.03 | 11.24 | 5.72 | 3.43 | 32.00 |
| Fast | 325 | 450 | 45.80 | 9.69 | 3.97 | 10.18 | 7.38 | 2.18 | 33.40 |

**Industrial enamel, oil base, high gloss, dark (OSHA) colors (material #57)**
Roll 1st finish coat

| | | | | | | | | | |
|---|---|---|---|---|---|---|---|---|---|
| Slow | 200 | 450 | 67.60 | 10.13 | 2.98 | 15.02 | 5.35 | 5.36 | 38.84 |
| Medium | 225 | 425 | 59.10 | 11.44 | 4.04 | 13.91 | 7.35 | 4.41 | 41.15 |
| Fast | 250 | 400 | 50.70 | 12.60 | 5.14 | 12.68 | 9.43 | 2.79 | 42.64 |

Roll 2nd or additional finish coats

| | | | | | | | | | |
|---|---|---|---|---|---|---|---|---|---|
| Slow | 275 | 500 | 67.60 | 7.36 | 2.18 | 13.52 | 4.38 | 4.39 | 31.83 |
| Medium | 300 | 475 | 59.10 | 8.58 | 3.03 | 12.44 | 6.02 | 3.61 | 33.68 |
| Fast | 325 | 450 | 50.70 | 9.69 | 3.97 | 11.27 | 7.72 | 2.28 | 34.93 |

Use the pipe conversion factors in Figure 21 on page 325 to convert linear feet of pipe to square feet of surface. Vertical pipe runs require 2 to 3 times the manhours plus 10% more material. Solid color coded piping requires 15% to 25% more labor and material. For color bands on piping at 10' to 15' intervals, add the cost of an additional 1st coat. For heights above 8 feet, use the High Time Difficulty Factors on page 139. Note: A two coat system, prime and finish, using oil base material is recommended for any metal surface. Water base material may cause oxidation, corrosion and rust. One coat of oil base paint on metal surfaces may result in cracking, peeling or chipping without the proper prime coat application. If off white or another light colored finish paint is specified, make sure the prime coat is also a light color, or more than one finish coat will be necessary. "Slow" work is based on an hourly wage of $20.25, "Medium" work on an hourly wage of $25.75, "Fast" work on an hourly wage of $31.50. Other qualifications that apply to this table are on page 9.

*Industrial, Institutional and Heavy Commercial Costs*

|  | Labor SF per manhour | Material coverage SF/gallon | Material cost per gallon | Labor cost per 100 SF | Labor burden 100 SF | Material cost per 100 SF | Overhead per 100 SF | Profit per 100 SF | Total price per 100 SF |
|---|---|---|---|---|---|---|---|---|---|
| **Piping, bare pipe, spray application** | | | | | | | | | |
| Metal primer, rust inhibitor, clean metal (material #35) | | | | | | | | | |
|   Spray prime coat | | | | | | | | | |
|     Slow | 300 | 175 | 59.70 | 6.75 | 1.98 | 34.11 | 8.14 | 8.16 | 59.14 |
|     Medium | 350 | 163 | 52.20 | 7.36 | 2.61 | 32.02 | 10.50 | 6.30 | 58.79 |
|     Fast | 400 | 150 | 44.80 | 7.88 | 3.21 | 29.87 | 12.70 | 3.76 | 57.42 |
| Metal primer, rust inhibitor, rusty metal (material #36) | | | | | | | | | |
|   Spray prime coat | | | | | | | | | |
|     Slow | 300 | 175 | 72.30 | 6.75 | 1.98 | 41.31 | 9.51 | 9.53 | 69.08 |
|     Medium | 350 | 163 | 63.30 | 7.36 | 2.61 | 38.83 | 12.20 | 7.32 | 68.32 |
|     Fast | 400 | 150 | 54.20 | 7.88 | 3.21 | 36.13 | 14.64 | 4.33 | 66.19 |
| Industrial enamel, oil base, high gloss, light colors (material #56) | | | | | | | | | |
|   Spray 1st finish coat | | | | | | | | | |
|     Slow | 375 | 210 | 61.00 | 5.40 | 1.60 | 29.05 | 6.85 | 6.86 | 49.76 |
|     Medium | 425 | 198 | 53.40 | 6.06 | 2.13 | 26.97 | 8.80 | 5.28 | 49.24 |
|     Fast | 475 | 185 | 45.80 | 6.63 | 2.73 | 24.76 | 10.57 | 3.13 | 47.82 |
|   Spray 2nd or additional finish coats | | | | | | | | | |
|     Slow | 425 | 300 | 61.00 | 4.76 | 1.40 | 20.33 | 5.03 | 5.04 | 36.56 |
|     Medium | 475 | 288 | 53.40 | 5.42 | 1.94 | 18.54 | 6.47 | 3.88 | 36.25 |
|     Fast | 525 | 275 | 45.80 | 6.00 | 2.43 | 16.65 | 7.78 | 2.30 | 35.16 |
| Industrial enamel, oil base, high gloss, dark (OSHA) colors (material #57) | | | | | | | | | |
|   Spray 1st finish coat | | | | | | | | | |
|     Slow | 375 | 210 | 67.60 | 5.40 | 1.60 | 32.19 | 7.44 | 7.46 | 54.09 |
|     Medium | 425 | 198 | 59.10 | 6.06 | 2.13 | 29.85 | 9.52 | 5.71 | 53.27 |
|     Fast | 475 | 185 | 50.70 | 6.63 | 2.73 | 27.41 | 11.39 | 3.37 | 51.53 |
|   Spray 2nd or additional finish coats | | | | | | | | | |
|     Slow | 425 | 300 | 67.60 | 4.76 | 1.40 | 22.53 | 5.45 | 5.46 | 39.60 |
|     Medium | 475 | 288 | 59.10 | 5.42 | 1.94 | 20.52 | 6.97 | 4.18 | 39.03 |
|     Fast | 525 | 275 | 50.70 | 6.00 | 2.43 | 18.44 | 8.34 | 2.47 | 37.68 |
| Epoxy coating, 2 part system, clear (material #51) | | | | | | | | | |
|   Spray 1st coat | | | | | | | | | |
|     Slow | 300 | 185 | 146.90 | 6.75 | 1.98 | 79.41 | 16.75 | 16.78 | 121.67 |
|     Medium | 350 | 173 | 128.60 | 7.36 | 2.61 | 74.34 | 21.08 | 12.65 | 118.04 |
|     Fast | 400 | 160 | 110.20 | 7.88 | 3.21 | 68.88 | 24.79 | 7.33 | 112.09 |
|   Spray 2nd coat | | | | | | | | | |
|     Slow | 375 | 200 | 146.90 | 5.40 | 1.60 | 73.45 | 15.28 | 15.32 | 111.05 |
|     Medium | 425 | 188 | 128.60 | 6.06 | 2.13 | 68.40 | 19.15 | 11.49 | 107.23 |
|     Fast | 475 | 175 | 110.20 | 6.63 | 2.73 | 62.97 | 22.42 | 6.63 | 101.38 |

## National Painting Cost Estimator

|  | Labor SF per manhour | Material coverage SF/gallon | Material cost per gallon | Labor cost per 100 SF | Labor burden 100 SF | Material cost per 100 SF | Overhead per 100 SF | Profit per 100 SF | Total price per 100 SF |
|---|---|---|---|---|---|---|---|---|---|
| Spray 3rd or additional coats | | | | | | | | | |
| Slow | 425 | 275 | 146.90 | 4.76 | 1.40 | 53.42 | 11.32 | 11.34 | 82.24 |
| Medium | 475 | 263 | 128.60 | 5.42 | 1.94 | 48.90 | 14.06 | 8.44 | 78.76 |
| Fast | 525 | 250 | 110.20 | 6.00 | 2.43 | 44.08 | 16.28 | 4.82 | 73.61 |
| Epoxy coating, 2 part system, white (material #52) | | | | | | | | | |
| Spray 1st coat | | | | | | | | | |
| Slow | 300 | 185 | 177.00 | 6.75 | 1.98 | 95.68 | 19.84 | 19.88 | 144.13 |
| Medium | 350 | 173 | 154.90 | 7.36 | 2.61 | 89.54 | 24.88 | 14.93 | 139.32 |
| Fast | 400 | 160 | 132.70 | 7.88 | 3.21 | 82.94 | 29.15 | 8.62 | 131.80 |
| Spray 2nd coat | | | | | | | | | |
| Slow | 375 | 200 | 177.00 | 5.40 | 1.60 | 88.50 | 18.14 | 18.18 | 131.82 |
| Medium | 425 | 188 | 154.90 | 6.06 | 2.13 | 82.39 | 22.65 | 13.59 | 126.82 |
| Fast | 475 | 175 | 132.70 | 6.63 | 2.73 | 75.83 | 26.40 | 7.81 | 119.40 |
| Spray 3rd or additional coats | | | | | | | | | |
| Slow | 425 | 275 | 177.00 | 4.76 | 1.40 | 64.36 | 13.40 | 13.43 | 97.35 |
| Medium | 475 | 263 | 154.90 | 5.42 | 1.94 | 58.90 | 16.56 | 9.94 | 92.76 |
| Fast | 525 | 250 | 132.70 | 6.00 | 2.43 | 53.08 | 19.07 | 5.64 | 86.22 |

Use the pipe conversion factors in Figure 21 on page 325 to convert linear feet of pipe to square feet of surface. Vertical pipe runs require 2 to 3 times the manhours plus 10% more material. Solid color coded piping requires 15% to 25% more labor and material. For color bands on piping at 10' to 15' intervals, add the cost of an additional 1st coat. For heights above 8 feet, use the High Time Difficulty Factors on page 139. Note: A two coat system, prime and finish, using oil base material is recommended for any metal surface. Water base material may cause oxidation, corrosion and rust. One coat of oil base paint on metal surfaces may result in cracking, peeling or chipping without the proper prime coat application. If off white or another light colored finish paint is specified, make sure the prime coat is also a light color, or more than one finish coat will be necessary. "Slow" work is based on an hourly wage of $20.25, "Medium" work on an hourly wage of $25.75, "Fast" work on an hourly wage of $31.50. Other qualifications that apply to this table are on page 9.

*Industrial, Institutional and Heavy Commercial Costs*

|  | Labor SF per manhour | Material coverage SF/gallon | Material cost per gallon | Labor cost per 100 SF | Labor burden 100 SF | Material cost per 100 SF | Overhead per 100 SF | Profit per 100 SF | Total price per 100 SF |
|---|---|---|---|---|---|---|---|---|---|

## Piping, bare pipe, mitt or glove application

**Metal primer, rust inhibitor, clean metal (material #35)**
Mitt or glove prime coat

| | | | | | | | | | |
|---|---|---|---|---|---|---|---|---|---|
| Slow | 175 | 325 | 59.70 | 11.57 | 3.40 | 18.37 | 6.34 | 6.35 | 46.03 |
| Medium | 200 | 313 | 52.20 | 12.88 | 4.56 | 16.68 | 8.53 | 5.12 | 47.77 |
| Fast | 225 | 300 | 44.80 | 14.00 | 5.69 | 14.93 | 10.74 | 3.18 | 48.54 |

**Metal primer, rust inhibitor, rusty metal (material #36)**
Mitt or glove prime coat

| | | | | | | | | | |
|---|---|---|---|---|---|---|---|---|---|
| Slow | 175 | 325 | 72.30 | 11.57 | 3.40 | 22.25 | 7.07 | 7.09 | 51.38 |
| Medium | 200 | 313 | 63.30 | 12.88 | 4.56 | 20.22 | 9.42 | 5.65 | 52.73 |
| Fast | 225 | 300 | 54.20 | 14.00 | 5.69 | 18.07 | 11.71 | 3.46 | 52.93 |

**Industrial enamel, oil base, high gloss, light colors (material #56)**
Mitt or glove 1st finish coat

| | | | | | | | | | |
|---|---|---|---|---|---|---|---|---|---|
| Slow | 200 | 375 | 61.00 | 10.13 | 2.98 | 16.27 | 5.58 | 5.60 | 40.56 |
| Medium | 225 | 363 | 53.40 | 11.44 | 4.04 | 14.71 | 7.55 | 4.53 | 42.27 |
| Fast | 250 | 350 | 45.80 | 12.60 | 5.14 | 13.09 | 9.56 | 2.83 | 43.22 |

Mitt or glove 2nd or additional finish coats

| | | | | | | | | | |
|---|---|---|---|---|---|---|---|---|---|
| Slow | 275 | 400 | 61.00 | 7.36 | 2.18 | 15.25 | 4.71 | 4.72 | 34.22 |
| Medium | 300 | 388 | 53.40 | 8.58 | 3.03 | 13.76 | 6.35 | 3.81 | 35.53 |
| Fast | 325 | 375 | 45.80 | 9.69 | 3.97 | 12.21 | 8.01 | 2.37 | 36.25 |

**Industrial enamel, oil base, high gloss, dark (OSHA) colors (material #57)**
Mitt or glove 1st finish coat

| | | | | | | | | | |
|---|---|---|---|---|---|---|---|---|---|
| Slow | 200 | 375 | 67.60 | 10.13 | 2.98 | 18.03 | 5.92 | 5.93 | 42.99 |
| Medium | 225 | 363 | 59.10 | 11.44 | 4.04 | 16.28 | 7.94 | 4.77 | 44.47 |
| Fast | 250 | 350 | 50.70 | 12.60 | 5.14 | 14.49 | 9.99 | 2.96 | 45.18 |

Mitt or glove 2nd or additional finish coats

| | | | | | | | | | |
|---|---|---|---|---|---|---|---|---|---|
| Slow | 275 | 400 | 67.60 | 7.36 | 2.18 | 16.90 | 5.02 | 5.03 | 36.49 |
| Medium | 300 | 388 | 59.10 | 8.58 | 3.03 | 15.23 | 6.71 | 4.03 | 37.58 |
| Fast | 325 | 375 | 50.70 | 9.69 | 3.97 | 13.52 | 8.42 | 2.49 | 38.09 |

**Epoxy coating, 2 part system, clear (material #51)**
Mitt or glove 1st coat

| | | | | | | | | | |
|---|---|---|---|---|---|---|---|---|---|
| Slow | 175 | 360 | 146.90 | 11.57 | 3.40 | 40.81 | 10.60 | 10.62 | 77.00 |
| Medium | 200 | 348 | 128.60 | 12.88 | 4.56 | 36.95 | 13.60 | 8.16 | 76.15 |
| Fast | 225 | 335 | 110.20 | 14.00 | 5.69 | 32.90 | 16.31 | 4.82 | 73.72 |

Mitt or glove 2nd coat

| | | | | | | | | | |
|---|---|---|---|---|---|---|---|---|---|
| Slow | 200 | 375 | 146.90 | 10.13 | 2.98 | 39.17 | 9.94 | 9.96 | 72.18 |
| Medium | 225 | 363 | 128.60 | 11.44 | 4.04 | 35.43 | 12.73 | 7.64 | 71.28 |
| Fast | 250 | 350 | 110.20 | 12.60 | 5.14 | 31.49 | 15.26 | 4.51 | 69.00 |

## National Painting Cost Estimator

|  | Labor SF per manhour | Material coverage SF/gallon | Material cost per gallon | Labor cost per 100 SF | Labor burden 100 SF | Material cost per 100 SF | Overhead per 100 SF | Profit per 100 SF | Total price per 100 SF |
|---|---|---|---|---|---|---|---|---|---|
| **Mitt or glove 3rd or additional coats** | | | | | | | | | |
| Slow | 275 | 390 | 146.90 | 7.36 | 2.18 | 37.67 | 8.97 | 8.99 | 65.17 |
| Medium | 300 | 378 | 128.60 | 8.58 | 3.03 | 34.02 | 11.41 | 6.85 | 63.89 |
| Fast | 325 | 365 | 110.20 | 9.69 | 3.97 | 30.19 | 13.59 | 4.02 | 61.46 |
| **Epoxy coating, 2 part system, white (material #52)** | | | | | | | | | |
| **Mitt or glove 1st coat** | | | | | | | | | |
| Slow | 175 | 360 | 177.00 | 11.57 | 3.40 | 49.17 | 12.19 | 12.21 | 88.54 |
| Medium | 200 | 348 | 154.90 | 12.88 | 4.56 | 44.51 | 15.49 | 9.29 | 86.73 |
| Fast | 225 | 335 | 132.70 | 14.00 | 5.69 | 39.61 | 18.39 | 5.44 | 83.13 |
| **Mitt or glove 2nd coat** | | | | | | | | | |
| Slow | 200 | 375 | 177.00 | 10.13 | 2.98 | 47.20 | 11.46 | 11.48 | 83.25 |
| Medium | 225 | 363 | 154.90 | 11.44 | 4.04 | 42.67 | 14.54 | 8.72 | 81.41 |
| Fast | 250 | 350 | 132.70 | 12.60 | 5.14 | 37.91 | 17.25 | 5.10 | 78.00 |
| **Mitt or glove 3rd or additional coats** | | | | | | | | | |
| Slow | 275 | 390 | 177.00 | 7.36 | 2.18 | 45.38 | 10.43 | 10.45 | 75.80 |
| Medium | 300 | 378 | 154.90 | 8.58 | 3.03 | 40.98 | 13.15 | 7.89 | 73.63 |
| Fast | 325 | 365 | 132.70 | 9.69 | 3.97 | 36.36 | 15.50 | 4.59 | 70.11 |

Use the pipe conversion factors in Figure 21 on page 325 to convert linear feet of pipe to square feet of surface. Vertical pipe runs require 2 to 3 times the manhours plus 10% more material. Solid color coded piping requires 15% to 25% more labor and material. For color bands on piping at 10' to 15' intervals, add the cost of an additional 1st coat. For heights above 8 feet, use the High Time Difficulty Factors on page 139. Note: A two coat system, prime and finish, using oil base material is recommended for any metal surface. Water base material may cause oxidation, corrosion and rust. One coat of oil base paint on metal surfaces may result in cracking, peeling or chipping without the proper prime coat application. If off white or another light colored finish paint is specified, make sure the prime coat is also a light color, or more than one finish coat will be necessary. "Slow" work is based on an hourly wage of $20.25, "Medium" work on an hourly wage of $25.75, "Fast" work on an hourly wage of $31.50. Other qualifications that apply to this table are on page 9.

*Industrial, Institutional and Heavy Commercial Costs*

|  | Labor SF per manhour | Material coverage SF/gallon | Material cost per gallon | Labor cost per 100 SF | Labor burden 100 SF | Material cost per 100 SF | Overhead per 100 SF | Profit per 100 SF | Total price per 100 SF |
|---|---|---|---|---|---|---|---|---|---|
| **Piping, insulated, canvas jacket, brush** | | | | | | | | | |
| Flat latex, water base (material #5) | | | | | | | | | |
|   Brush 1st coat | | | | | | | | | |
|     Slow | 60 | 150 | 36.70 | 33.75 | 9.96 | 24.47 | 12.95 | 12.98 | 94.11 |
|     Medium | 80 | 138 | 32.10 | 32.19 | 11.40 | 23.26 | 16.71 | 10.03 | 93.59 |
|     Fast | 100 | 125 | 27.50 | 31.50 | 12.85 | 22.00 | 20.57 | 6.08 | 93.00 |
|   Brush 2nd coat | | | | | | | | | |
|     Slow | 75 | 300 | 36.70 | 27.00 | 7.95 | 12.23 | 8.97 | 8.99 | 65.14 |
|     Medium | 100 | 288 | 32.10 | 25.75 | 9.12 | 11.15 | 11.51 | 6.90 | 64.43 |
|     Fast | 125 | 275 | 27.50 | 25.20 | 10.28 | 10.00 | 14.10 | 4.17 | 63.75 |
|   Brush 3rd or additional coats | | | | | | | | | |
|     Slow | 100 | 400 | 36.70 | 20.25 | 5.97 | 9.18 | 6.73 | 6.74 | 48.87 |
|     Medium | 138 | 375 | 32.10 | 18.66 | 6.62 | 8.56 | 8.46 | 5.07 | 47.37 |
|     Fast | 175 | 350 | 27.50 | 18.00 | 7.32 | 7.86 | 10.29 | 3.04 | 46.51 |
| Sealer, off white, water base (material #1) | | | | | | | | | |
|   Brush 1 coat | | | | | | | | | |
|     Slow | 60 | 150 | 30.50 | 33.75 | 9.96 | 20.33 | 12.17 | 12.19 | 88.40 |
|     Medium | 80 | 138 | 26.70 | 32.19 | 11.40 | 19.35 | 15.74 | 9.44 | 88.12 |
|     Fast | 100 | 125 | 22.90 | 31.50 | 12.85 | 18.32 | 19.43 | 5.75 | 87.85 |
| Sealer, off white, oil base (material #2) | | | | | | | | | |
|   Brush 1 coat | | | | | | | | | |
|     Slow | 60 | 200 | 39.70 | 33.75 | 9.96 | 19.85 | 12.08 | 12.10 | 87.74 |
|     Medium | 80 | 188 | 34.80 | 32.19 | 11.40 | 18.51 | 15.53 | 9.32 | 86.95 |
|     Fast | 100 | 175 | 29.80 | 31.50 | 12.85 | 17.03 | 19.03 | 5.63 | 86.04 |
| Enamel, water base latex (material #9) | | | | | | | | | |
|   Brush 1st finish coat | | | | | | | | | |
|     Slow | 75 | 300 | 46.80 | 27.00 | 7.95 | 15.60 | 9.61 | 9.63 | 69.79 |
|     Medium | 100 | 288 | 41.00 | 25.75 | 9.12 | 14.24 | 12.28 | 7.37 | 68.76 |
|     Fast | 125 | 275 | 35.10 | 25.20 | 10.28 | 12.76 | 14.95 | 4.42 | 67.61 |
|   Brush 2nd or additional finish coats | | | | | | | | | |
|     Slow | 100 | 400 | 46.80 | 20.25 | 5.97 | 11.70 | 7.20 | 7.22 | 52.34 |
|     Medium | 138 | 375 | 41.00 | 18.66 | 6.62 | 10.93 | 9.05 | 5.43 | 50.69 |
|     Fast | 175 | 350 | 35.10 | 18.00 | 7.32 | 10.03 | 10.96 | 3.24 | 49.55 |
| Industrial enamel, oil base, high gloss, light colors (material #56) | | | | | | | | | |
|   Brush 1st finish coat | | | | | | | | | |
|     Slow | 75 | 335 | 61.00 | 27.00 | 7.95 | 18.21 | 10.10 | 10.12 | 73.38 |
|     Medium | 100 | 323 | 53.40 | 25.75 | 9.12 | 16.53 | 12.85 | 7.71 | 71.96 |
|     Fast | 125 | 310 | 45.80 | 25.20 | 10.28 | 14.77 | 15.58 | 4.61 | 70.44 |

## National Painting Cost Estimator

| | Labor SF per manhour | Material coverage SF/gallon | Material cost per gallon | Labor cost per 100 SF | Labor burden 100 SF | Material cost per 100 SF | Overhead per 100 SF | Profit per 100 SF | Total price per 100 SF |
|---|---|---|---|---|---|---|---|---|---|
| Brush 2nd or additional finish coats | | | | | | | | | |
| Slow | 100 | 450 | 61.00 | 20.25 | 5.97 | 13.56 | 7.56 | 7.57 | 54.91 |
| Medium | 150 | 438 | 53.40 | 17.17 | 6.09 | 12.19 | 8.86 | 5.32 | 49.63 |
| Fast | 175 | 425 | 45.80 | 18.00 | 7.32 | 10.78 | 11.20 | 3.31 | 50.61 |
| **Industrial enamel, oil base, high gloss, dark (OSHA) colors (material #57)** | | | | | | | | | |
| Brush 1st finish coat | | | | | | | | | |
| Slow | 75 | 335 | 67.60 | 27.00 | 7.95 | 20.18 | 10.48 | 10.50 | 76.11 |
| Medium | 100 | 323 | 59.10 | 25.75 | 9.12 | 18.30 | 13.29 | 7.98 | 74.44 |
| Fast | 125 | 310 | 50.70 | 25.20 | 10.28 | 16.35 | 16.07 | 4.75 | 72.65 |
| Brush 2nd or additional finish coats | | | | | | | | | |
| Slow | 100 | 450 | 67.60 | 20.25 | 5.97 | 15.02 | 7.84 | 7.85 | 56.93 |
| Medium | 150 | 438 | 59.10 | 17.17 | 6.09 | 13.49 | 9.19 | 5.51 | 51.45 |
| Fast | 175 | 425 | 50.70 | 18.00 | 7.32 | 11.93 | 11.55 | 3.42 | 52.22 |
| **Epoxy coating, 2 part system, clear (material #51)** | | | | | | | | | |
| Brush 1st coat | | | | | | | | | |
| Slow | 75 | 325 | 146.90 | 27.00 | 7.95 | 45.20 | 15.23 | 15.26 | 110.64 |
| Medium | 100 | 313 | 128.60 | 25.75 | 9.12 | 41.09 | 18.99 | 11.39 | 106.34 |
| Fast | 125 | 300 | 110.20 | 25.20 | 10.28 | 36.73 | 22.39 | 6.62 | 101.22 |
| Brush 2nd or additional coats | | | | | | | | | |
| Slow | 100 | 450 | 146.90 | 20.25 | 5.97 | 32.64 | 11.18 | 11.21 | 81.25 |
| Medium | 150 | 438 | 128.60 | 17.17 | 6.09 | 29.36 | 13.15 | 7.89 | 73.66 |
| Fast | 175 | 425 | 110.20 | 18.00 | 7.32 | 25.93 | 15.89 | 4.70 | 71.84 |
| **Epoxy coating, 2 part system, white (material #52)** | | | | | | | | | |
| Brush 1st coat | | | | | | | | | |
| Slow | 75 | 325 | 177.00 | 27.00 | 7.95 | 54.46 | 16.99 | 17.03 | 123.43 |
| Medium | 100 | 313 | 154.90 | 25.75 | 9.12 | 49.49 | 21.09 | 12.65 | 118.10 |
| Fast | 125 | 300 | 132.70 | 25.20 | 10.28 | 44.23 | 24.71 | 7.31 | 111.73 |
| Brush 2nd or additional coats | | | | | | | | | |
| Slow | 100 | 450 | 177.00 | 20.25 | 5.97 | 39.33 | 12.45 | 12.48 | 90.48 |
| Medium | 150 | 438 | 154.90 | 17.17 | 6.09 | 35.37 | 14.66 | 8.79 | 82.08 |
| Fast | 175 | 425 | 132.70 | 18.00 | 7.32 | 31.22 | 17.53 | 5.19 | 79.26 |

Use the pipe conversion factors in Figure 21 on page 325 to convert linear feet of pipe to square feet of surface. Vertical pipe runs require 2 to 3 times the manhours plus 10% more material. Solid color coded piping requires 15% to 25% more labor and material. For color bands on piping at 10' to 15' intervals, add the cost of an additional 1st coat. For heights above 8 feet, use the High Time Difficulty Factors on page 139. "Slow" work is based on an hourly wage of $20.25, "Medium" work on an hourly wage of $25.75, "Fast" work on an hourly wage of $31.50. Other qualifications that apply to this table are on page 9.

*Industrial, Institutional and Heavy Commercial Costs*

|  | Labor SF per manhour | Material coverage SF/gallon | Material cost per gallon | Labor cost per 100 SF | Labor burden 100 SF | Material cost per 100 SF | Overhead per 100 SF | Profit per 100 SF | Total price per 100 SF |
|---|---|---|---|---|---|---|---|---|---|
| **Piping, insulated, canvas jacket, roll** | | | | | | | | | |
| Flat latex, water base (material #5) | | | | | | | | | |
|   Roll 1st coat | | | | | | | | | |
|     Slow | 135 | 150 | 36.70 | 15.00 | 4.43 | 24.47 | 8.34 | 8.36 | 60.60 |
|     Medium | 160 | 138 | 32.10 | 16.09 | 5.70 | 23.26 | 11.26 | 6.76 | 63.07 |
|     Fast | 185 | 125 | 27.50 | 17.03 | 6.96 | 22.00 | 14.25 | 4.22 | 64.46 |
|   Roll 2nd coat | | | | | | | | | |
|     Slow | 175 | 300 | 36.70 | 11.57 | 3.40 | 12.23 | 5.17 | 5.18 | 37.55 |
|     Medium | 200 | 288 | 32.10 | 12.88 | 4.56 | 11.15 | 7.15 | 4.29 | 40.03 |
|     Fast | 225 | 275 | 27.50 | 14.00 | 5.69 | 10.00 | 9.21 | 2.72 | 41.62 |
|   Roll 3rd or additional coats | | | | | | | | | |
|     Slow | 275 | 400 | 36.70 | 7.36 | 2.18 | 9.18 | 3.55 | 3.56 | 25.83 |
|     Medium | 300 | 388 | 32.10 | 8.58 | 3.03 | 8.27 | 4.97 | 2.98 | 27.83 |
|     Fast | 325 | 375 | 27.50 | 9.69 | 3.97 | 7.33 | 6.50 | 1.92 | 29.41 |
| Sealer, off white, water base (material #1) | | | | | | | | | |
|   Roll 1 coat | | | | | | | | | |
|     Slow | 135 | 150 | 30.50 | 15.00 | 4.43 | 20.33 | 7.55 | 7.57 | 54.88 |
|     Medium | 160 | 138 | 26.70 | 16.09 | 5.70 | 19.35 | 10.29 | 6.17 | 57.60 |
|     Fast | 185 | 125 | 22.90 | 17.03 | 6.96 | 18.32 | 13.11 | 3.88 | 59.30 |
| Sealer, off white, oil base (material #2) | | | | | | | | | |
|   Roll 1 coat | | | | | | | | | |
|     Slow | 135 | 225 | 39.70 | 15.00 | 4.43 | 17.64 | 7.04 | 7.06 | 51.17 |
|     Medium | 160 | 213 | 34.80 | 16.09 | 5.70 | 16.34 | 9.53 | 5.72 | 53.38 |
|     Fast | 185 | 200 | 29.80 | 17.03 | 6.96 | 14.90 | 12.05 | 3.57 | 54.51 |
| Enamel, water base latex (material #9) | | | | | | | | | |
|   Roll 1st finish coat | | | | | | | | | |
|     Slow | 175 | 300 | 46.80 | 11.57 | 3.40 | 15.60 | 5.81 | 5.82 | 42.20 |
|     Medium | 200 | 288 | 41.00 | 12.88 | 4.56 | 14.24 | 7.92 | 4.75 | 44.35 |
|     Fast | 225 | 275 | 35.10 | 14.00 | 5.69 | 12.76 | 10.07 | 2.98 | 45.50 |
|   Roll 2nd or additional finish coats | | | | | | | | | |
|     Slow | 275 | 400 | 46.80 | 7.36 | 2.18 | 11.70 | 4.03 | 4.04 | 29.31 |
|     Medium | 300 | 388 | 41.00 | 8.58 | 3.03 | 10.57 | 5.55 | 3.33 | 31.06 |
|     Fast | 325 | 375 | 35.10 | 9.69 | 3.97 | 9.36 | 7.13 | 2.11 | 32.26 |
| Industrial enamel, oil base, high gloss, light colors (material #56) | | | | | | | | | |
|   Roll 1st finish coat | | | | | | | | | |
|     Slow | 175 | 335 | 61.00 | 11.57 | 3.40 | 18.21 | 6.31 | 6.32 | 45.81 |
|     Medium | 200 | 323 | 53.40 | 12.88 | 4.56 | 16.53 | 8.49 | 5.10 | 47.56 |
|     Fast | 225 | 310 | 45.80 | 14.00 | 5.69 | 14.77 | 10.69 | 3.16 | 48.31 |

## National Painting Cost Estimator

|  | Labor SF per manhour | Material coverage SF/gallon | Material cost per gallon | Labor cost per 100 SF | Labor burden 100 SF | Material cost per 100 SF | Overhead per 100 SF | Profit per 100 SF | Total price per 100 SF |
|---|---|---|---|---|---|---|---|---|---|
| **Roll 2nd or additional finish coats** | | | | | | | | | |
| Slow | 275 | 450 | 61.00 | 7.36 | 2.18 | 13.56 | 4.39 | 4.40 | 31.89 |
| Medium | 300 | 438 | 53.40 | 8.58 | 3.03 | 12.19 | 5.95 | 3.57 | 33.32 |
| Fast | 325 | 425 | 45.80 | 9.69 | 3.97 | 10.78 | 7.57 | 2.24 | 34.25 |
| **Industrial enamel, oil base, high gloss, dark (OSHA) colors (material #57)** | | | | | | | | | |
| **Roll 1st finish coat** | | | | | | | | | |
| Slow | 175 | 335 | 67.60 | 11.57 | 3.40 | 20.18 | 6.68 | 6.69 | 48.52 |
| Medium | 200 | 323 | 59.10 | 12.88 | 4.56 | 18.30 | 8.94 | 5.36 | 50.04 |
| Fast | 225 | 310 | 50.70 | 14.00 | 5.69 | 16.35 | 11.18 | 3.31 | 50.53 |
| **Roll 2nd or additional finish coats** | | | | | | | | | |
| Slow | 275 | 450 | 67.60 | 7.36 | 2.18 | 15.02 | 4.66 | 4.67 | 33.89 |
| Medium | 300 | 438 | 59.10 | 8.58 | 3.03 | 13.49 | 6.28 | 3.77 | 35.15 |
| Fast | 325 | 425 | 50.70 | 9.69 | 3.97 | 11.93 | 7.93 | 2.35 | 35.87 |
| **Epoxy coating, 2 part system, clear (material #51)** | | | | | | | | | |
| **Roll 1st coat** | | | | | | | | | |
| Slow | 175 | 325 | 146.90 | 11.57 | 3.40 | 45.20 | 11.43 | 11.46 | 83.06 |
| Medium | 200 | 313 | 128.60 | 12.88 | 4.56 | 41.09 | 14.63 | 8.78 | 81.94 |
| Fast | 225 | 300 | 110.20 | 14.00 | 5.69 | 36.73 | 17.50 | 5.18 | 79.10 |
| **Roll 2nd or additional coats** | | | | | | | | | |
| Slow | 275 | 425 | 146.90 | 7.36 | 2.18 | 34.56 | 8.38 | 8.40 | 60.88 |
| Medium | 300 | 413 | 128.60 | 8.58 | 3.03 | 31.14 | 10.69 | 6.41 | 59.85 |
| Fast | 325 | 400 | 110.20 | 9.69 | 3.97 | 27.55 | 12.77 | 3.78 | 57.76 |
| **Epoxy coating, 2 part system, white (material #52)** | | | | | | | | | |
| **Roll 1st coat** | | | | | | | | | |
| Slow | 175 | 325 | 177.00 | 11.57 | 3.40 | 54.46 | 13.19 | 13.22 | 95.84 |
| Medium | 200 | 313 | 154.90 | 12.88 | 4.56 | 49.49 | 16.73 | 10.04 | 93.70 |
| Fast | 225 | 300 | 132.70 | 14.00 | 5.69 | 44.23 | 19.82 | 5.86 | 89.60 |
| **Roll 2nd or additional coats** | | | | | | | | | |
| Slow | 275 | 425 | 177.00 | 7.36 | 2.18 | 41.65 | 9.72 | 9.74 | 70.65 |
| Medium | 300 | 413 | 154.90 | 8.58 | 3.03 | 37.51 | 12.28 | 7.37 | 68.77 |
| Fast | 325 | 400 | 132.70 | 9.69 | 3.97 | 33.18 | 14.51 | 4.29 | 65.64 |

Use the pipe conversion factors in Figure 21 on page 325 to convert linear feet of pipe to square feet of surface. Vertical pipe runs require 2 to 3 times the manhours plus 10% more material. Solid color coded piping requires 15% to 25% more labor and material. For color bands on piping at 10' to 15' intervals, add the cost of an additional 1st coat. For heights above 8 feet, use the High Time Difficulty Factors on page 139. "Slow" work is based on an hourly wage of $20.25, "Medium" work on an hourly wage of $25.75, "Fast" work on an hourly wage of $31.50. Other qualifications that apply to this table are on page 9.

*Industrial, Institutional and Heavy Commercial Costs*

|  | Labor SF per manhour | Material coverage SF/gallon | Material cost per gallon | Labor cost per 100 SF | Labor burden 100 SF | Material cost per 100 SF | Overhead per 100 SF | Profit per 100 SF | Total price per 100 SF |
|---|---|---|---|---|---|---|---|---|---|
| **Piping, insulated, canvas jacket, spray** | | | | | | | | | |
| Flat latex, water base (material #5) | | | | | | | | | |
|   Spray 1st coat | | | | | | | | | |
|     Slow | 225 | 100 | 36.70 | 9.00 | 2.64 | 36.70 | 9.19 | 9.21 | 66.74 |
|     Medium | 250 | 88 | 32.10 | 10.30 | 3.65 | 36.48 | 12.61 | 7.56 | 70.60 |
|     Fast | 275 | 75 | 27.50 | 11.45 | 4.69 | 36.67 | 16.36 | 4.84 | 74.01 |
|   Spray 2nd coat | | | | | | | | | |
|     Slow | 275 | 200 | 36.70 | 7.36 | 2.18 | 18.35 | 5.30 | 5.31 | 38.50 |
|     Medium | 300 | 188 | 32.10 | 8.58 | 3.03 | 17.07 | 7.17 | 4.30 | 40.15 |
|     Fast | 325 | 175 | 27.50 | 9.69 | 3.97 | 15.71 | 9.10 | 2.69 | 41.16 |
|   Spray 3rd or additional coats | | | | | | | | | |
|     Slow | 375 | 300 | 36.70 | 5.40 | 1.60 | 12.23 | 3.65 | 3.66 | 26.54 |
|     Medium | 400 | 288 | 32.10 | 6.44 | 2.28 | 11.15 | 4.97 | 2.98 | 27.82 |
|     Fast | 425 | 275 | 27.50 | 7.41 | 3.01 | 10.00 | 6.33 | 1.87 | 28.62 |
| Sealer, off white, water base (material #1) | | | | | | | | | |
|   Spray 1 coat | | | | | | | | | |
|     Slow | 225 | 100 | 30.50 | 9.00 | 2.64 | 30.50 | 8.01 | 8.03 | 58.18 |
|     Medium | 250 | 88 | 26.70 | 10.30 | 3.65 | 30.34 | 11.07 | 6.64 | 62.00 |
|     Fast | 275 | 75 | 22.90 | 11.45 | 4.69 | 30.53 | 14.46 | 4.28 | 65.41 |
| Sealer, off white, oil base (material #2) | | | | | | | | | |
|   Spray 1 coat | | | | | | | | | |
|     Slow | 225 | 150 | 39.70 | 9.00 | 2.64 | 26.47 | 7.24 | 7.26 | 52.61 |
|     Medium | 250 | 138 | 34.80 | 10.30 | 3.65 | 25.22 | 9.79 | 5.88 | 54.84 |
|     Fast | 275 | 125 | 29.80 | 11.45 | 4.69 | 23.84 | 12.39 | 3.66 | 56.03 |
| Enamel, water base latex (material #9) | | | | | | | | | |
|   Spray 1st finish coat | | | | | | | | | |
|     Slow | 275 | 200 | 46.80 | 7.36 | 2.18 | 23.40 | 6.26 | 6.27 | 45.47 |
|     Medium | 300 | 188 | 41.00 | 8.58 | 3.03 | 21.81 | 8.36 | 5.01 | 46.79 |
|     Fast | 325 | 175 | 35.10 | 9.69 | 3.97 | 20.06 | 10.45 | 3.09 | 47.26 |
|   Spray 2nd or additional finish coats | | | | | | | | | |
|     Slow | 375 | 300 | 46.80 | 5.40 | 1.60 | 15.60 | 4.29 | 4.30 | 31.19 |
|     Medium | 400 | 288 | 41.00 | 6.44 | 2.28 | 14.24 | 5.74 | 3.44 | 32.14 |
|     Fast | 425 | 275 | 35.10 | 7.41 | 3.01 | 12.76 | 7.19 | 2.13 | 32.50 |
| Industrial enamel, oil base, high gloss, light colors (material #56) | | | | | | | | | |
|   Spray 1st finish coat | | | | | | | | | |
|     Slow | 275 | 235 | 61.00 | 7.36 | 2.18 | 25.96 | 6.74 | 6.76 | 49.00 |
|     Medium | 300 | 223 | 53.40 | 8.58 | 3.03 | 23.95 | 8.89 | 5.34 | 49.79 |
|     Fast | 325 | 210 | 45.80 | 9.69 | 3.97 | 21.81 | 10.99 | 3.25 | 49.71 |

## National Painting Cost Estimator

|  | Labor SF per manhour | Material coverage SF/gallon | Material cost per gallon | Labor cost per 100 SF | Labor burden 100 SF | Material cost per 100 SF | Overhead per 100 SF | Profit per 100 SF | Total price per 100 SF |
|---|---|---|---|---|---|---|---|---|---|
| **Spray 2nd or additional finish coats** | | | | | | | | | |
| Slow | 375 | 335 | 61.00 | 5.40 | 1.60 | 18.21 | 4.79 | 4.80 | 34.80 |
| Medium | 400 | 323 | 53.40 | 6.44 | 2.28 | 16.53 | 6.31 | 3.79 | 35.35 |
| Fast | 425 | 310 | 45.80 | 7.41 | 3.01 | 14.77 | 7.81 | 2.31 | 35.31 |
| **Industrial enamel, oil base, high gloss, dark (OSHA) colors (material #57)** | | | | | | | | | |
| *Spray 1st finish coat* | | | | | | | | | |
| Slow | 275 | 235 | 67.60 | 7.36 | 2.18 | 28.77 | 7.28 | 7.29 | 52.88 |
| Medium | 300 | 223 | 59.10 | 8.58 | 3.03 | 26.50 | 9.53 | 5.72 | 53.36 |
| Fast | 325 | 210 | 50.70 | 9.69 | 3.97 | 24.14 | 11.71 | 3.46 | 52.97 |
| *Spray 2nd or additional finish coats* | | | | | | | | | |
| Slow | 375 | 335 | 67.60 | 5.40 | 1.60 | 20.18 | 5.16 | 5.17 | 37.51 |
| Medium | 400 | 323 | 59.10 | 6.44 | 2.28 | 18.30 | 6.76 | 4.05 | 37.83 |
| Fast | 425 | 310 | 50.70 | 7.41 | 3.01 | 16.35 | 8.30 | 2.46 | 37.53 |
| **Epoxy coating, 2 part system, clear (material #51)** | | | | | | | | | |
| *Spray 1st coat* | | | | | | | | | |
| Slow | 275 | 225 | 146.90 | 7.36 | 2.18 | 65.29 | 14.22 | 14.25 | 103.30 |
| Medium | 300 | 213 | 128.60 | 8.58 | 3.03 | 60.38 | 18.00 | 10.80 | 100.79 |
| Fast | 325 | 200 | 110.20 | 9.69 | 3.97 | 55.10 | 21.31 | 6.30 | 96.37 |
| *Spray 2nd or additional coats* | | | | | | | | | |
| Slow | 375 | 325 | 146.90 | 5.40 | 1.60 | 45.20 | 9.92 | 9.94 | 72.06 |
| Medium | 400 | 313 | 128.60 | 6.44 | 2.28 | 41.09 | 12.45 | 7.47 | 69.73 |
| Fast | 425 | 300 | 110.20 | 7.41 | 3.01 | 36.73 | 14.62 | 4.32 | 66.09 |
| **Epoxy coating, 2 part system, white (material #52)** | | | | | | | | | |
| *Spray 1st coat* | | | | | | | | | |
| Slow | 275 | 225 | 177.00 | 7.36 | 2.18 | 78.67 | 16.76 | 16.79 | 121.76 |
| Medium | 300 | 213 | 154.90 | 8.58 | 3.03 | 72.72 | 21.09 | 12.65 | 118.07 |
| Fast | 325 | 200 | 132.70 | 9.69 | 3.97 | 66.35 | 24.80 | 7.34 | 112.15 |
| *Spray 2nd or additional coats* | | | | | | | | | |
| Slow | 375 | 325 | 177.00 | 5.40 | 1.60 | 54.46 | 11.68 | 11.70 | 84.84 |
| Medium | 400 | 313 | 154.90 | 6.44 | 2.28 | 49.49 | 14.55 | 8.73 | 81.49 |
| Fast | 425 | 300 | 132.70 | 7.41 | 3.01 | 44.23 | 16.94 | 5.01 | 76.60 |

Use the pipe conversion factors in Figure 21 on page 325 to convert linear feet of pipe to square feet of surface. Vertical pipe runs require 2 to 3 times the manhours plus 10% more material. Solid color coded piping requires 15% to 25% more labor and material. For color bands on piping at 10' to 15' intervals, add the cost of an additional 1st coat. For heights above 8 feet, use the High Time Difficulty Factors on page 139. "Slow" work is based on an hourly wage of $20.25, "Medium" work on an hourly wage of $25.75, "Fast" work on an hourly wage of $31.50. Other qualifications that apply to this table are on page 9.

*Industrial, Institutional and Heavy Commercial Costs*

|  | Labor SF per manhour | Material coverage SF/gallon | Material cost per gallon | Labor cost per 100 SF | Labor burden 100 SF | Material cost per 100 SF | Overhead per 100 SF | Profit per 100 SF | Total price per 100 SF |
|---|---|---|---|---|---|---|---|---|---|
| **Radiators** | | | | | | | | | |
| Brush each coat | | | | | | | | | |
| Metal primer, rust inhibitor, clean metal (material #35) | | | | | | | | | |
| Slow | 50 | 100 | 59.70 | 40.50 | 11.94 | 59.70 | 21.31 | 21.35 | 154.80 |
| Medium | 70 | 95 | 52.20 | 36.79 | 13.04 | 54.95 | 26.19 | 15.71 | 146.68 |
| Fast | 90 | 90 | 44.80 | 35.00 | 14.27 | 49.78 | 30.71 | 9.08 | 138.84 |
| Metal primer, rust inhibitor, rusty metal (material #36) | | | | | | | | | |
| Slow | 50 | 100 | 72.30 | 40.50 | 11.94 | 72.30 | 23.70 | 23.75 | 172.19 |
| Medium | 70 | 95 | 63.30 | 36.79 | 13.04 | 66.63 | 29.11 | 17.47 | 163.04 |
| Fast | 90 | 90 | 54.20 | 35.00 | 14.27 | 60.22 | 33.95 | 10.04 | 153.48 |
| Industrial enamel, oil base, high gloss, light colors (material #56) | | | | | | | | | |
| Slow | 60 | 150 | 61.00 | 33.75 | 9.96 | 40.67 | 16.03 | 16.07 | 116.48 |
| Medium | 80 | 138 | 53.40 | 32.19 | 11.40 | 38.70 | 20.57 | 12.34 | 115.20 |
| Fast | 100 | 125 | 45.80 | 31.50 | 12.85 | 36.64 | 25.11 | 7.43 | 113.53 |
| Industrial enamel, oil base, high gloss, dark (OSHA) colors (material #57) | | | | | | | | | |
| Slow | 60 | 150 | 67.60 | 33.75 | 9.96 | 45.07 | 16.87 | 16.90 | 122.55 |
| Medium | 80 | 138 | 59.10 | 32.19 | 11.40 | 42.83 | 21.61 | 12.96 | 120.99 |
| Fast | 100 | 125 | 50.70 | 31.50 | 12.85 | 40.56 | 26.32 | 7.79 | 119.02 |
| Spray each coat | | | | | | | | | |
| Metal primer, rust inhibitor, clean metal (material #35) | | | | | | | | | |
| Slow | 225 | 90 | 59.70 | 9.00 | 2.64 | 66.33 | 14.82 | 14.85 | 107.64 |
| Medium | 250 | 83 | 52.20 | 10.30 | 3.65 | 62.89 | 19.21 | 11.53 | 107.58 |
| Fast | 275 | 75 | 44.80 | 11.45 | 4.69 | 59.73 | 23.51 | 6.96 | 106.34 |
| Metal primer, rust inhibitor, rusty metal (material #36) | | | | | | | | | |
| Slow | 225 | 90 | 72.30 | 9.00 | 2.64 | 80.33 | 17.48 | 17.52 | 126.97 |
| Medium | 250 | 83 | 63.30 | 10.30 | 3.65 | 76.27 | 22.56 | 13.53 | 126.31 |
| Fast | 275 | 75 | 54.20 | 11.45 | 4.69 | 72.27 | 27.40 | 8.11 | 123.92 |
| Industrial enamel, oil base, high gloss, light colors (material #56) | | | | | | | | | |
| Slow | 250 | 110 | 61.00 | 8.10 | 2.39 | 55.45 | 12.53 | 12.56 | 91.03 |
| Medium | 275 | 100 | 53.40 | 9.36 | 3.33 | 53.40 | 16.52 | 9.91 | 92.52 |
| Fast | 300 | 90 | 45.80 | 10.50 | 4.27 | 50.89 | 20.36 | 6.02 | 92.04 |
| Industrial enamel, oil base, high gloss, dark (OSHA) colors (material #57) | | | | | | | | | |
| Slow | 250 | 110 | 67.60 | 8.10 | 2.39 | 61.45 | 13.67 | 13.70 | 99.31 |
| Medium | 275 | 100 | 59.10 | 9.36 | 3.33 | 59.10 | 17.94 | 10.77 | 100.50 |
| Fast | 300 | 90 | 50.70 | 10.50 | 4.27 | 56.33 | 22.04 | 6.52 | 99.66 |

Use these figures to estimate the cost of painting both sides of 6" to 18" deep hot water or steam radiators with oil or water base paint. Measurements are per square foot of area measured, one side (length times width). For heights above 8 feet, use the High Time Difficulty Factors on page 139. Note: A two coat system, prime and finish, using oil base material is recommended for any metal surface. Using water base material may cause oxidation, corrosion and rust. Using one coat of oil base paint on metal surfaces may result in cracking, peeling or chipping and rust without the proper prime coat application. If off white or another light colored finish paint is specified, make sure the prime coat is also a light color, or more than one finish coat will be necessary. "Slow" work is based on an hourly wage of $20.25, "Medium" work on an hourly wage of $25.75, "Fast" work on an hourly wage of $31.50. Other qualifications that apply to this table are on page 9.

National Painting Cost Estimator

## Structural steel

Fabrication and erection estimates are usually based on weight of the steel in tons. As a paint estimator you need to convert tons of steel to square feet of surface. Of course, the conversion factor depends on the size of the steel members. On larger jobs and where accuracy is essential, use the Structural Steel conversion table in Figure 23 on pages 391 through 399 at the end of this Structural steel section to make exact conversions. On smaller jobs, a *rule of thumb* is that there are 225 square feet of paintable surface per ton of steel.

| | Labor SF per manhour | Material coverage SF/gallon | Material cost per gallon | Labor cost per 100 SF | Labor burden 100 SF | Material cost per 100 SF | Overhead per 100 SF | Profit per 100 SF | Total price per 100 SF |
|---|---|---|---|---|---|---|---|---|---|

### Structural steel, heavy, brush application

Metal primer, rust inhibitor - clean metal (material #35)
  Brush prime coat

| | | | | | | | | | |
|---|---|---|---|---|---|---|---|---|---|
| Slow | 130 | 400 | 59.70 | 15.58 | 4.58 | 14.93 | 6.67 | 6.68 | 48.44 |
| Medium | 150 | 388 | 52.20 | 17.17 | 6.09 | 13.45 | 9.18 | 5.51 | 51.40 |
| Fast | 170 | 375 | 44.80 | 18.53 | 7.55 | 11.95 | 11.79 | 3.49 | 53.31 |

Metal primer, rust inhibitor - rusty metal (material #36)
  Brush prime coat

| | | | | | | | | | |
|---|---|---|---|---|---|---|---|---|---|
| Slow | 130 | 400 | 72.30 | 15.58 | 4.58 | 18.08 | 7.27 | 7.28 | 52.79 |
| Medium | 150 | 388 | 63.30 | 17.17 | 6.09 | 16.31 | 9.89 | 5.93 | 55.39 |
| Fast | 170 | 375 | 54.20 | 18.53 | 7.55 | 14.45 | 12.57 | 3.72 | 56.82 |

Industrial enamel, oil base, high gloss - light colors (material #56)
  Brush 1st or additional finish coats

| | | | | | | | | | |
|---|---|---|---|---|---|---|---|---|---|
| Slow | 175 | 425 | 61.00 | 11.57 | 3.40 | 14.35 | 5.57 | 5.58 | 40.47 |
| Medium | 200 | 413 | 53.40 | 12.88 | 4.56 | 12.93 | 7.59 | 4.56 | 42.52 |
| Fast | 225 | 400 | 45.80 | 14.00 | 5.69 | 11.45 | 9.66 | 2.86 | 43.66 |

Industrial enamel, oil base, high gloss - dark (OSHA) colors (material #57)
  Brush 1st or additional finish coats

| | | | | | | | | | |
|---|---|---|---|---|---|---|---|---|---|
| Slow | 175 | 475 | 67.60 | 11.57 | 3.40 | 14.23 | 5.55 | 5.56 | 40.31 |
| Medium | 200 | 463 | 59.10 | 12.88 | 4.56 | 12.76 | 7.55 | 4.53 | 42.28 |
| Fast | 225 | 450 | 50.70 | 14.00 | 5.69 | 11.27 | 9.60 | 2.84 | 43.40 |

Epoxy coating, 2 part system, clear (material #51)
  Brush 1st coat

| | | | | | | | | | |
|---|---|---|---|---|---|---|---|---|---|
| Slow | 130 | 425 | 146.90 | 15.58 | 4.58 | 34.56 | 10.40 | 10.42 | 75.54 |
| Medium | 150 | 413 | 128.60 | 17.17 | 6.09 | 31.14 | 13.60 | 8.16 | 76.16 |
| Fast | 170 | 400 | 110.20 | 18.53 | 7.55 | 27.55 | 16.63 | 4.92 | 75.18 |

  Brush 2nd or additional coats

| | | | | | | | | | |
|---|---|---|---|---|---|---|---|---|---|
| Slow | 175 | 450 | 146.90 | 11.57 | 3.40 | 32.64 | 9.05 | 9.07 | 65.73 |
| Medium | 200 | 438 | 128.60 | 12.88 | 4.56 | 29.36 | 11.70 | 7.02 | 65.52 |
| Fast | 225 | 425 | 110.20 | 14.00 | 5.69 | 25.93 | 14.15 | 4.19 | 63.96 |

*Industrial, Institutional and Heavy Commercial Costs*

|  | Labor SF per manhour | Material coverage SF/gallon | Material cost per gallon | Labor cost per 100 SF | Labor burden 100 SF | Material cost per 100 SF | Overhead per 100 SF | Profit per 100 SF | Total price per 100 SF |
|---|---|---|---|---|---|---|---|---|---|
| **Epoxy coating, 2 part system, white (material #52)** | | | | | | | | | |
| Brush 1st coat | | | | | | | | | |
| Slow | 130 | 425 | 177.00 | 15.58 | 4.58 | 41.65 | 11.75 | 11.77 | 85.33 |
| Medium | 150 | 413 | 154.90 | 17.17 | 6.09 | 37.51 | 15.19 | 9.11 | 85.07 |
| Fast | 170 | 400 | 132.70 | 18.53 | 7.55 | 33.18 | 18.37 | 5.43 | 83.06 |
| Brush 2nd or additional coats | | | | | | | | | |
| Slow | 175 | 450 | 177.00 | 11.57 | 3.40 | 39.33 | 10.32 | 10.34 | 74.96 |
| Medium | 200 | 438 | 154.90 | 12.88 | 4.56 | 35.37 | 13.20 | 7.92 | 73.93 |
| Fast | 225 | 425 | 132.70 | 14.00 | 5.69 | 31.22 | 15.79 | 4.67 | 71.37 |

For field painting at heights above 8 feet, use the High Time Difficulty Factors on page 139. Heavy structural steel has from 100 to 150 square feet of surface area per ton. Extra heavy structural steel has from 50 to 100 square feet of surface area per ton. *Rule of thumb*: When coatings are applied by brush, a journeyman painter will apply a first coat on 6 to 7 tons per 8 hour day. When coatings are applied by spray, figure output at 0.2 hours per ton and material use at about 0.2 gallons per ton. Use Figure 23 on pages 391 to 399 to convert structural steel linear feet or tonnage to surface area. Note: A two coat system, prime and finish, using oil base material is recommended for any metal surface. Using water base material may cause oxidation, corrosion and rust. One coat of oil base paint on metal surfaces may result in cracking, peeling or chipping without the proper prime coat application. If off white or another light-color finish paint is specified, make sure the prime coat is also a light color, or more than one finish coat will be necessary. "Slow" work is based on an hourly wage of $20.25, "Medium" work on an hourly wage of $25.75, and "Fast" work on an hourly wage of $31.50. Other qualifications that apply to this table are on page 9.

*National Painting Cost Estimator*

|  | Labor SF per manhour | Material coverage SF/gallon | Material cost per gallon | Labor cost per 100 SF | Labor burden 100 SF | Material cost per 100 SF | Overhead per 100 SF | Profit per 100 SF | Total price per 100 SF |
|---|---|---|---|---|---|---|---|---|---|
| **Structural steel, heavy, roll application** | | | | | | | | | |
| Metal primer, rust inhibitor - clean metal (material #35) | | | | | | | | | |
| Roll prime coat | | | | | | | | | |
| Slow | 250 | 390 | 59.70 | 8.10 | 2.39 | 15.31 | 4.90 | 4.91 | 35.61 |
| Medium | 275 | 378 | 52.20 | 9.36 | 3.33 | 13.81 | 6.62 | 3.97 | 37.09 |
| Fast | 300 | 365 | 44.80 | 10.50 | 4.27 | 12.27 | 8.39 | 2.48 | 37.91 |
| Metal primer, rust inhibitor - rusty metal (material #36) | | | | | | | | | |
| Roll prime coat | | | | | | | | | |
| Slow | 250 | 380 | 72.30 | 8.10 | 2.39 | 19.03 | 5.61 | 5.62 | 40.75 |
| Medium | 275 | 363 | 63.30 | 9.36 | 3.33 | 17.44 | 7.53 | 4.52 | 42.18 |
| Fast | 300 | 355 | 54.20 | 10.50 | 4.27 | 15.27 | 9.32 | 2.76 | 42.12 |
| Industrial enamel, oil base, high gloss - light colors (material #56) | | | | | | | | | |
| Roll 1st or additional finish coats | | | | | | | | | |
| Slow | 275 | 425 | 61.00 | 7.36 | 2.18 | 14.35 | 4.54 | 4.55 | 32.98 |
| Medium | 300 | 413 | 53.40 | 8.58 | 3.03 | 12.93 | 6.14 | 3.68 | 34.36 |
| Fast | 325 | 400 | 45.80 | 9.69 | 3.97 | 11.45 | 7.78 | 2.30 | 35.19 |
| Industrial enamel, oil base, high gloss - dark (OSHA) colors (material #57) | | | | | | | | | |
| Roll 1st or additional finish coats | | | | | | | | | |
| Slow | 275 | 440 | 67.60 | 7.36 | 2.18 | 15.36 | 4.73 | 4.74 | 34.37 |
| Medium | 300 | 428 | 59.10 | 8.58 | 3.03 | 13.81 | 6.36 | 3.81 | 35.59 |
| Fast | 325 | 415 | 50.70 | 9.69 | 3.97 | 12.22 | 8.02 | 2.37 | 36.27 |
| Epoxy coating, 2 part system, clear (material #51) | | | | | | | | | |
| Roll 1st coat | | | | | | | | | |
| Slow | 250 | 400 | 146.90 | 8.10 | 2.39 | 36.73 | 8.97 | 8.99 | 65.18 |
| Medium | 275 | 388 | 128.60 | 9.36 | 3.33 | 33.14 | 11.45 | 6.87 | 64.15 |
| Fast | 300 | 375 | 110.20 | 10.50 | 4.27 | 29.39 | 13.69 | 4.05 | 61.90 |
| Roll 2nd or additional coats | | | | | | | | | |
| Slow | 275 | 425 | 146.90 | 7.36 | 2.18 | 34.56 | 8.38 | 8.40 | 60.88 |
| Medium | 300 | 413 | 128.60 | 8.58 | 3.03 | 31.14 | 10.69 | 6.41 | 59.85 |
| Fast | 325 | 400 | 110.20 | 9.69 | 3.97 | 27.55 | 12.77 | 3.78 | 57.76 |

*Industrial, Institutional and Heavy Commercial Costs*

|  | Labor SF per manhour | Material coverage SF/gallon | Material cost per gallon | Labor cost per 100 SF | Labor burden 100 SF | Material cost per 100 SF | Overhead per 100 SF | Profit per 100 SF | Total price per 100 SF |
|---|---|---|---|---|---|---|---|---|---|
| **Epoxy coating, 2 part system, white (material #52)** | | | | | | | | | |
| Roll 1st coat | | | | | | | | | |
| Slow | 250 | 400 | 177.00 | 8.10 | 2.39 | 44.25 | 10.40 | 10.42 | 75.56 |
| Medium | 275 | 388 | 154.90 | 9.36 | 3.33 | 39.92 | 13.15 | 7.89 | 73.65 |
| Fast | 300 | 375 | 132.70 | 10.50 | 4.27 | 35.39 | 15.55 | 4.60 | 70.31 |
| Roll 2nd or additional coats | | | | | | | | | |
| Slow | 275 | 425 | 177.00 | 7.36 | 2.18 | 41.65 | 9.72 | 9.74 | 70.65 |
| Medium | 300 | 413 | 154.90 | 8.58 | 3.03 | 37.51 | 12.28 | 7.37 | 68.77 |
| Fast | 325 | 400 | 132.70 | 9.69 | 3.97 | 33.18 | 14.51 | 4.29 | 65.64 |

For field painting at heights above 8 feet, use the High Time Difficulty Factors on page 139. Heavy structural steel has from 100 to 150 square feet of surface area per ton. Extra heavy structural steel has from 50 to 100 square feet of surface area per ton. *Rule of thumb*: When coatings are applied by brush, a journeyman painter will apply a first coat on 6 to 7 tons per 8 hour day. When coatings are applied by spray, figure output at 0.2 hours per ton and material use at about 0.2 gallons per ton. Use Figure 23 on pages 391 to 399 to convert structural steel linear feet or tonnage to surface area. Note: A two coat system, prime and finish, using oil base material is recommended for any metal surface. Using water base material may cause oxidation, corrosion and rust. One coat of oil base paint on metal surfaces may result in cracking, peeling or chipping without the proper prime coat application. If off white or another light-color finish paint is specified, make sure the prime coat is also a light color, or more than one finish coat will be necessary. "Slow" work is based on an hourly wage of $20.25, "Medium" work on an hourly wage of $25.75, and "Fast" work on an hourly wage of $31.50. Other qualifications that apply to this table are on page 9.

|  | Labor SF per manhour | Material coverage SF/gallon | Material cost per gallon | Labor cost per 100 SF | Labor burden 100 SF | Material cost per 100 SF | Overhead per 100 SF | Profit per 100 SF | Total price per 100 SF |
|---|---|---|---|---|---|---|---|---|---|
| **Structural steel, heavy, spray application** | | | | | | | | | |
| Metal primer, rust inhibitor - clean metal (material #35) | | | | | | | | | |
| Spray prime coat | | | | | | | | | |
| Slow | 650 | 325 | 59.70 | 3.12 | .92 | 18.37 | 4.26 | 4.27 | 30.94 |
| Medium | 750 | 313 | 52.20 | 3.43 | 1.21 | 16.68 | 5.33 | 3.20 | 29.85 |
| Fast | 850 | 300 | 44.80 | 3.71 | 1.52 | 14.93 | 6.25 | 1.85 | 28.26 |
| Metal primer, rust inhibitor - rusty metal (material #36) | | | | | | | | | |
| Spray prime coat | | | | | | | | | |
| Slow | 650 | 300 | 72.30 | 3.12 | .92 | 24.10 | 5.35 | 5.36 | 38.85 |
| Medium | 750 | 288 | 63.30 | 3.43 | 1.21 | 21.98 | 6.66 | 3.99 | 37.27 |
| Fast | 850 | 275 | 54.20 | 3.71 | 1.52 | 19.71 | 7.73 | 2.29 | 34.96 |
| Industrial enamel, oil base, high gloss - light colors (material #56) | | | | | | | | | |
| Spray 1st or additional finish coats | | | | | | | | | |
| Slow | 750 | 340 | 61.00 | 2.70 | .79 | 17.94 | 4.07 | 4.08 | 29.58 |
| Medium | 850 | 325 | 53.40 | 3.03 | 1.08 | 16.43 | 5.13 | 3.08 | 28.75 |
| Fast | 950 | 310 | 45.80 | 3.32 | 1.34 | 14.77 | 6.03 | 1.78 | 27.24 |
| Industrial enamel, oil base, high gloss - dark (OSHA) colors (material #57) | | | | | | | | | |
| Spray 1st or additional finish coats | | | | | | | | | |
| Slow | 750 | 365 | 67.60 | 2.70 | .79 | 18.52 | 4.18 | 4.19 | 30.38 |
| Medium | 850 | 350 | 59.10 | 3.03 | 1.08 | 16.89 | 5.25 | 3.15 | 29.40 |
| Fast | 950 | 335 | 50.70 | 3.32 | 1.34 | 15.13 | 6.14 | 1.82 | 27.75 |
| Epoxy coating, 2 part system, clear (material #51) | | | | | | | | | |
| Spray 1st coat | | | | | | | | | |
| Slow | 650 | 325 | 146.90 | 3.12 | .92 | 45.20 | 9.36 | 9.38 | 67.98 |
| Medium | 750 | 313 | 128.60 | 3.43 | 1.21 | 41.09 | 11.43 | 6.86 | 64.02 |
| Fast | 850 | 300 | 110.20 | 3.71 | 1.52 | 36.73 | 13.00 | 3.85 | 58.81 |
| Spray 2nd or additional coats | | | | | | | | | |
| Slow | 750 | 350 | 146.90 | 2.70 | .79 | 41.97 | 8.64 | 8.66 | 62.76 |
| Medium | 850 | 338 | 128.60 | 3.03 | 1.08 | 38.05 | 10.54 | 6.32 | 59.02 |
| Fast | 950 | 325 | 110.20 | 3.32 | 1.34 | 33.91 | 11.96 | 3.54 | 54.07 |

*Industrial, Institutional and Heavy Commercial Costs*

|  | Labor SF per manhour | Material coverage SF/gallon | Material cost per gallon | Labor cost per 100 SF | Labor burden 100 SF | Material cost per 100 SF | Overhead per 100 SF | Profit per 100 SF | Total price per 100 SF |
|---|---|---|---|---|---|---|---|---|---|
| **Epoxy coating, 2 part system, white (material #52)** | | | | | | | | | |
| Spray 1st coat | | | | | | | | | |
| Slow | 650 | 325 | 177.00 | 3.12 | .92 | 54.46 | 11.12 | 11.14 | 80.76 |
| Medium | 750 | 313 | 154.90 | 3.43 | 1.21 | 49.49 | 13.53 | 8.12 | 75.78 |
| Fast | 850 | 300 | 132.70 | 3.71 | 1.52 | 44.23 | 15.33 | 4.53 | 69.32 |
| Spray 2nd or additional coats | | | | | | | | | |
| Slow | 750 | 350 | 177.00 | 2.70 | .79 | 50.57 | 10.27 | 10.29 | 74.62 |
| Medium | 850 | 338 | 154.90 | 3.03 | 1.08 | 45.83 | 12.48 | 7.49 | 69.91 |
| Fast | 950 | 325 | 132.70 | 3.32 | 1.34 | 40.83 | 14.11 | 4.17 | 63.77 |

For field painting at heights above 8 feet, use the High Time Difficulty Factors on page 139. Heavy structural steel has from 100 to 150 square feet of surface area per ton. Extra heavy structural steel has from 50 to 100 square feet of surface area per ton. *Rule of thumb*: When coatings are applied by brush, a journeyman painter will apply a first coat on 6 to 7 tons per 8 hour day. When coatings are applied by spray, figure output at 0.2 hours per ton and material use at about 0.2 gallons per ton. Use Figure 23 on pages 391 to 399 to convert structural steel linear feet or tonnage to surface area. Note: A two coat system, prime and finish, using oil base material is recommended for any metal surface. Using water base material may cause oxidation, corrosion and rust. One coat of oil base paint on metal surfaces may result in cracking, peeling or chipping without the proper prime coat application. If off white or another light-color finish paint is specified, make sure the prime coat is also a light color, or more than one finish coat will be necessary. "Slow" work is based on an hourly wage of $20.25, "Medium" work on an hourly wage of $25.75, and "Fast" work on an hourly wage of $31.50. Other qualifications that apply to this table are on page 9.

*National Painting Cost Estimator*

|  | Labor SF per manhour | Material coverage SF/gallon | Material cost per gallon | Labor cost per 100 SF | Labor burden 100 SF | Material cost per 100 SF | Overhead per 100 SF | Profit per 100 SF | Total price per 100 SF |
|---|---|---|---|---|---|---|---|---|---|
| **Structural steel, light, brush application** | | | | | | | | | |
| Metal primer, rust inhibitor, clean metal (material #35) | | | | | | | | | |
| Brush prime coat | | | | | | | | | |
| Slow | 60 | 425 | 59.70 | 33.75 | 9.96 | 14.05 | 10.97 | 11.00 | 79.73 |
| Medium | 80 | 413 | 52.20 | 32.19 | 11.40 | 12.64 | 14.06 | 8.43 | 78.72 |
| Fast | 100 | 400 | 44.80 | 31.50 | 12.85 | 11.20 | 17.22 | 5.09 | 77.86 |
| Metal primer, rust inhibitor, rusty metal (material #36) | | | | | | | | | |
| Brush prime coat | | | | | | | | | |
| Slow | 60 | 400 | 72.30 | 33.75 | 9.96 | 18.08 | 11.74 | 11.76 | 85.29 |
| Medium | 80 | 388 | 63.30 | 32.19 | 11.40 | 16.31 | 14.98 | 8.99 | 83.87 |
| Fast | 100 | 375 | 54.20 | 31.50 | 12.85 | 14.45 | 18.23 | 5.39 | 82.42 |
| Industrial enamel, oil base, high gloss, light colors (material #56) | | | | | | | | | |
| Brush 1st or additional finish coats | | | | | | | | | |
| Slow | 80 | 425 | 61.00 | 25.31 | 7.47 | 14.35 | 8.95 | 8.97 | 65.05 |
| Medium | 100 | 413 | 53.40 | 25.75 | 9.12 | 12.93 | 11.95 | 7.17 | 66.92 |
| Fast | 120 | 400 | 45.80 | 26.25 | 10.69 | 11.45 | 15.01 | 4.44 | 67.84 |
| Industrial enamel, oil base, high gloss, dark (OSHA) colors (material #57) | | | | | | | | | |
| Brush 1st or additional finish coats | | | | | | | | | |
| Slow | 80 | 475 | 67.60 | 25.31 | 7.47 | 14.23 | 8.93 | 8.95 | 64.89 |
| Medium | 100 | 463 | 59.10 | 25.75 | 9.12 | 12.76 | 11.91 | 7.14 | 66.68 |
| Fast | 120 | 450 | 50.70 | 26.25 | 10.69 | 11.27 | 14.95 | 4.42 | 67.58 |
| Epoxy coating, 2 part system, clear (material #51) | | | | | | | | | |
| Brush 1st coat | | | | | | | | | |
| Slow | 60 | 425 | 146.90 | 33.75 | 9.96 | 34.56 | 14.87 | 14.90 | 108.04 |
| Medium | 80 | 413 | 128.60 | 32.19 | 11.40 | 31.14 | 18.68 | 11.21 | 104.62 |
| Fast | 100 | 400 | 110.20 | 31.50 | 12.85 | 27.55 | 22.29 | 6.59 | 100.78 |
| Brush 2nd or additional coats | | | | | | | | | |
| Slow | 80 | 450 | 146.90 | 25.31 | 7.47 | 32.64 | 12.43 | 12.46 | 90.31 |
| Medium | 100 | 438 | 128.60 | 25.75 | 9.12 | 29.36 | 16.06 | 9.63 | 89.92 |
| Fast | 120 | 425 | 110.20 | 26.25 | 10.69 | 25.93 | 19.50 | 5.77 | 88.14 |

*Industrial, Institutional and Heavy Commercial Costs*

|  | Labor SF per manhour | Material coverage SF/gallon | Material cost per gallon | Labor cost per 100 SF | Labor burden 100 SF | Material cost per 100 SF | Overhead per 100 SF | Profit per 100 SF | Total price per 100 SF |
|---|---|---|---|---|---|---|---|---|---|
| **Epoxy coating, 2 part system, white (material #52)** | | | | | | | | | |
| Brush 1st coat | | | | | | | | | |
| Slow | 60 | 425 | 177.00 | 33.75 | 9.96 | 41.65 | 16.22 | 16.25 | 117.83 |
| Medium | 80 | 413 | 154.90 | 32.19 | 11.40 | 37.51 | 20.28 | 12.17 | 113.55 |
| Fast | 100 | 400 | 132.70 | 31.50 | 12.85 | 33.18 | 24.03 | 7.11 | 108.67 |
| Brush 2nd or additional coats | | | | | | | | | |
| Slow | 80 | 450 | 177.00 | 25.31 | 7.47 | 39.33 | 13.70 | 13.73 | 99.54 |
| Medium | 100 | 438 | 154.90 | 25.75 | 9.12 | 35.37 | 17.56 | 10.54 | 98.34 |
| Fast | 120 | 425 | 132.70 | 26.25 | 10.69 | 31.22 | 21.14 | 6.25 | 95.55 |

For field painting at heights above 8 feet, use the High Time Difficulty Factors on page 139. Light structural steel has from 300 to 500 square feet of surface per ton. As a comparison, when coatings are applied by brush, a journeyman painter will apply a first coat on from 2 to 3 tons per 8 hour day. A second and subsequent coats can be applied on 3 to 4 tons per day. Use Figure 23 on pages 391 to 399 to convert structural steel linear feet or tonnage to surface area. Note: A two coat system, prime and finish, using oil base material is recommended for any metal surface. Using water base material may cause oxidation, corrosion and rust. One coat of oil base paint on metal surfaces may result in cracking, peeling or chipping without the proper prime coat application. If off white or another light colored finish paint is specified, make sure the prime coat is also a light color, or more than one finish coat will be necessary. "Slow" work is based on an hourly wage of $20.25, "Medium" work on an hourly wage of $25.75, and "Fast" work on an hourly wage of $31.50. Other qualifications that apply to this table are on page 9.

National Painting Cost Estimator

|  | Labor SF per manhour | Material coverage SF/gallon | Material cost per gallon | Labor cost per 100 SF | Labor burden 100 SF | Material cost per 100 SF | Overhead per 100 SF | Profit per 100 SF | Total price per 100 SF |
|---|---|---|---|---|---|---|---|---|---|
| **Structural steel, light, roll application** | | | | | | | | | |
| Metal primer, rust inhibitor, clean metal (material #35) | | | | | | | | | |
| Roll and brush prime coat | | | | | | | | | |
| Slow | 125 | 390 | 59.70 | 16.20 | 4.78 | 15.31 | 6.90 | 6.91 | 50.10 |
| Medium | 150 | 378 | 52.20 | 17.17 | 6.09 | 13.81 | 9.27 | 5.56 | 51.90 |
| Fast | 175 | 365 | 44.80 | 18.00 | 7.32 | 12.27 | 11.66 | 3.45 | 52.70 |
| Metal primer, rust inhibitor, rusty metal (material #36) | | | | | | | | | |
| Roll and brush prime coat | | | | | | | | | |
| Slow | 125 | 380 | 72.30 | 16.20 | 4.78 | 19.03 | 7.60 | 7.62 | 55.23 |
| Medium | 150 | 368 | 63.30 | 17.17 | 6.09 | 17.20 | 10.11 | 6.07 | 56.64 |
| Fast | 175 | 355 | 54.20 | 18.00 | 7.32 | 15.27 | 12.59 | 3.72 | 56.90 |
| Industrial enamel, oil base, high gloss, light colors (material #56) | | | | | | | | | |
| Roll and brush 1st or additional finish coats | | | | | | | | | |
| Slow | 175 | 390 | 61.00 | 11.57 | 3.40 | 15.64 | 5.82 | 5.83 | 42.26 |
| Medium | 200 | 378 | 53.40 | 12.88 | 4.56 | 14.13 | 7.89 | 4.74 | 44.20 |
| Fast | 225 | 365 | 45.80 | 14.00 | 5.69 | 12.55 | 10.00 | 2.96 | 45.20 |
| Industrial enamel, oil base, high gloss, dark (OSHA) colors (material #57) | | | | | | | | | |
| Roll and brush 1st or additional finish coats | | | | | | | | | |
| Slow | 175 | 440 | 67.60 | 11.57 | 3.40 | 15.36 | 5.76 | 5.78 | 41.87 |
| Medium | 200 | 428 | 59.10 | 12.88 | 4.56 | 13.81 | 7.81 | 4.69 | 43.75 |
| Fast | 225 | 415 | 50.70 | 14.00 | 5.69 | 12.22 | 9.90 | 2.93 | 44.74 |
| Epoxy coating, 2 part system, clear (material #51) | | | | | | | | | |
| Roll and brush 1st coat | | | | | | | | | |
| Slow | 125 | 400 | 146.90 | 16.20 | 4.78 | 36.73 | 10.96 | 10.99 | 79.66 |
| Medium | 150 | 388 | 128.60 | 17.17 | 6.09 | 33.14 | 14.10 | 8.46 | 78.96 |
| Fast | 175 | 375 | 110.20 | 18.00 | 7.32 | 29.39 | 16.97 | 5.02 | 76.70 |
| Roll and brush 2nd or additional coats | | | | | | | | | |
| Slow | 175 | 425 | 146.90 | 11.57 | 3.40 | 34.56 | 9.41 | 9.43 | 68.37 |
| Medium | 200 | 413 | 128.60 | 12.88 | 4.56 | 31.14 | 12.15 | 7.29 | 68.02 |
| Fast | 225 | 400 | 110.20 | 14.00 | 5.69 | 27.55 | 14.65 | 4.33 | 66.22 |

*Industrial, Institutional and Heavy Commercial Costs*

|  | Labor SF per manhour | Material coverage SF/gallon | Material cost per gallon | Labor cost per 100 SF | Labor burden 100 SF | Material cost per 100 SF | Overhead per 100 SF | Profit per 100 SF | Total price per 100 SF |
|---|---|---|---|---|---|---|---|---|---|
| **Epoxy coating, 2 part system, white (material #52)** | | | | | | | | | |
| Roll and brush 1st coat | | | | | | | | | |
| Slow | 125 | 400 | 177.00 | 16.20 | 4.78 | 44.25 | 12.39 | 12.42 | 90.04 |
| Medium | 150 | 388 | 154.90 | 17.17 | 6.09 | 39.92 | 15.79 | 9.48 | 88.45 |
| Fast | 175 | 375 | 132.70 | 18.00 | 7.32 | 35.39 | 18.83 | 5.57 | 85.11 |
| Roll and brush 2nd or additional coats | | | | | | | | | |
| Slow | 175 | 425 | 177.00 | 11.57 | 3.40 | 41.65 | 10.76 | 10.78 | 78.16 |
| Medium | 200 | 413 | 154.90 | 12.88 | 4.56 | 37.51 | 13.74 | 8.24 | 76.93 |
| Fast | 225 | 400 | 132.70 | 14.00 | 5.69 | 33.18 | 16.40 | 4.85 | 74.12 |

For field painting at heights above 8 feet, use the High Time Difficulty Factors on page 139. Light structural steel has from 300 to 500 square feet of surface per ton. As a comparison, when coatings are applied by brush, a journeyman painter will apply a first coat on from 2 to 3 tons per 8 hour day. A second and subsequent coats can be applied on 3 to 4 tons per day. Use Figure 23 on pages 391 to 399 to convert structural steel linear feet or tonnage to surface area. Note: A two coat system, prime and finish, using oil base material is recommended for any metal surface. Using water base material may cause oxidation, corrosion and rust. One coat of oil base paint on metal surfaces may result in cracking, peeling or chipping without the proper prime coat application. If off white or another light colored finish paint is specified, make sure the prime coat is also a light color, or more than one finish coat will be necessary. "Slow" work is based on an hourly wage of $20.25, "Medium" work on an hourly wage of $25.75, and "Fast" work on an hourly wage of $31.50. Other qualifications that apply to this table are on page 9.

|  | Labor SF per manhour | Material coverage SF/gallon | Material cost per gallon | Labor cost per 100 SF | Labor burden 100 SF | Material cost per 100 SF | Overhead per 100 SF | Profit per 100 SF | Total price per 100 SF |
|---|---|---|---|---|---|---|---|---|---|

## Structural steel, light, spray application

Metal primer, rust inhibitor, clean metal (material #35)
  Spray prime coat

| | | | | | | | | | |
|---|---|---|---|---|---|---|---|---|---|
| Slow | 400 | 325 | 59.70 | 5.06 | 1.50 | 18.37 | 4.73 | 4.74 | 34.40 |
| Medium | 500 | 313 | 52.20 | 5.15 | 1.82 | 16.68 | 5.91 | 3.55 | 33.11 |
| Fast | 600 | 300 | 44.80 | 5.25 | 2.16 | 14.93 | 6.92 | 2.05 | 31.31 |

Metal primer, rust inhibitor, rusty metal (material #36)
  Spray prime coat

| | | | | | | | | | |
|---|---|---|---|---|---|---|---|---|---|
| Slow | 400 | 300 | 72.30 | 5.06 | 1.50 | 24.10 | 5.82 | 5.84 | 42.32 |
| Medium | 500 | 288 | 63.30 | 5.15 | 1.82 | 21.98 | 7.24 | 4.34 | 40.53 |
| Fast | 600 | 275 | 54.20 | 5.25 | 2.16 | 19.71 | 8.40 | 2.49 | 38.01 |

Industrial enamel, oil base, high gloss, light colors (material #56)
  Spray 1st or additional finish coats

| | | | | | | | | | |
|---|---|---|---|---|---|---|---|---|---|
| Slow | 500 | 325 | 61.00 | 4.05 | 1.19 | 18.77 | 4.56 | 4.57 | 33.14 |
| Medium | 600 | 313 | 53.40 | 4.29 | 1.53 | 17.06 | 5.72 | 3.43 | 32.03 |
| Fast | 700 | 300 | 45.80 | 4.50 | 1.84 | 15.27 | 6.70 | 1.98 | 30.29 |

Industrial enamel, oil base, high gloss, dark (OSHA) colors (material #57)
  Spray 1st or additional finish coats

| | | | | | | | | | |
|---|---|---|---|---|---|---|---|---|---|
| Slow | 500 | 365 | 67.60 | 4.05 | 1.19 | 18.52 | 4.51 | 4.52 | 32.79 |
| Medium | 600 | 350 | 59.10 | 4.29 | 1.53 | 16.89 | 5.68 | 3.41 | 31.80 |
| Fast | 700 | 335 | 50.70 | 4.50 | 1.84 | 15.13 | 6.66 | 1.97 | 30.10 |

Epoxy coating, 2 part system, clear (material #51)
  Spray 1st coat

| | | | | | | | | | |
|---|---|---|---|---|---|---|---|---|---|
| Slow | 400 | 325 | 146.90 | 5.06 | 1.50 | 45.20 | 9.83 | 9.85 | 71.44 |
| Medium | 500 | 313 | 128.60 | 5.15 | 1.82 | 41.09 | 12.02 | 7.21 | 67.29 |
| Fast | 600 | 300 | 110.20 | 5.25 | 2.16 | 36.73 | 13.68 | 4.05 | 61.87 |

  Spray 2nd or additional coats

| | | | | | | | | | |
|---|---|---|---|---|---|---|---|---|---|
| Slow | 500 | 350 | 146.90 | 4.05 | 1.19 | 41.97 | 8.97 | 8.99 | 65.17 |
| Medium | 600 | 338 | 128.60 | 4.29 | 1.53 | 38.05 | 10.97 | 6.58 | 61.42 |
| Fast | 700 | 325 | 110.20 | 4.50 | 1.84 | 33.91 | 12.48 | 3.69 | 56.42 |

*Industrial, Institutional and Heavy Commercial Costs*

|  | Labor SF per manhour | Material coverage SF/gallon | Material cost per gallon | Labor cost per 100 SF | Labor burden 100 SF | Material cost per 100 SF | Overhead per 100 SF | Profit per 100 SF | Total price per 100 SF |
|---|---|---|---|---|---|---|---|---|---|
| **Epoxy coating, 2 part system, white (material #52)** | | | | | | | | | |
| Spray 1st coat | | | | | | | | | |
|   Slow | 400 | 325 | 177.00 | 5.06 | 1.50 | 54.46 | 11.59 | 11.62 | 84.23 |
|   Medium | 500 | 313 | 154.90 | 5.15 | 1.82 | 49.49 | 14.12 | 8.47 | 79.05 |
|   Fast | 600 | 300 | 132.70 | 5.25 | 2.16 | 44.23 | 16.00 | 4.73 | 72.37 |
| Spray 2nd or additional coats | | | | | | | | | |
|   Slow | 500 | 350 | 177.00 | 4.05 | 1.19 | 50.57 | 10.60 | 10.63 | 77.04 |
|   Medium | 600 | 338 | 154.90 | 4.29 | 1.53 | 45.83 | 12.91 | 7.75 | 72.31 |
|   Fast | 700 | 325 | 132.70 | 4.50 | 1.84 | 40.83 | 14.62 | 4.33 | 66.12 |

For field painting at heights above 8 feet, use the High Time Difficulty Factors on page 139. Light structural steel has from 300 to 500 square feet of surface per ton. The *rule of thumb* for labor output and material usage for spray application on light structural steel is shown in the table on the next page. Use Figure 23 on pages 391 to 399 to convert structural steel linear feet or tonnage to surface area. Note: A two coat system, prime and finish, using oil base material is recommended for any metal surface. Using water base material may cause oxidation, corrosion and rust. One coat of oil base paint on metal surfaces may result in cracking, peeling or chipping without the proper prime coat application. If off white or another light-color finish paint is specified, make sure the prime coat is also a light color, or more than one finish coat will be necessary. "Slow" work is based on an hourly wage of $20.25, "Medium" work on an hourly wage of $25.75, and "Fast" work on an hourly wage of $31.50. Other qualifications that apply to this table are on page 9.

|  | Labor manhours per ton | Material gallons per ton | Material cost per gallon | Labor cost per ton | Labor burden per ton | Material cost per ton | Overhead per ton | Profit per ton | Total price per ton |
|---|---|---|---|---|---|---|---|---|---|

## Structural steel, light, coating *rule of thumb*, spray, per ton

Metal primer, rust inhibitor, clean metal (material #35)
   Spray prime coat
| | | | | | | | | | |
|---|---|---|---|---|---|---|---|---|---|
| Slow | 1.8 | 1.0 | 59.70 | 36.45 | 10.75 | 59.70 | 20.31 | 20.35 | 147.56 |
| Medium | 1.6 | 1.1 | 52.20 | 41.20 | 14.59 | 57.42 | 28.30 | 16.98 | 158.49 |
| Fast | 1.4 | 1.2 | 44.80 | 44.10 | 17.99 | 53.76 | 35.91 | 10.62 | 162.38 |

Metal primer, rust inhibitor, rusty metal (material #36)
   Spray prime coat
| | | | | | | | | | |
|---|---|---|---|---|---|---|---|---|---|
| Slow | 1.8 | 1.0 | 72.30 | 36.45 | 10.75 | 72.30 | 22.71 | 22.75 | 164.96 |
| Medium | 1.6 | 1.1 | 63.30 | 41.20 | 14.59 | 69.63 | 31.35 | 18.81 | 175.58 |
| Fast | 1.4 | 1.2 | 54.20 | 44.10 | 17.99 | 65.04 | 39.41 | 11.66 | 178.20 |

Industrial enamel, oil base, high gloss, light colors (material #56)
   Spray 1st finish coat
| | | | | | | | | | |
|---|---|---|---|---|---|---|---|---|---|
| Slow | 1.5 | 0.9 | 61.00 | 30.38 | 8.95 | 54.90 | 17.91 | 17.94 | 130.08 |
| Medium | 1.3 | 1.0 | 53.40 | 33.48 | 11.85 | 53.40 | 24.68 | 14.81 | 138.22 |
| Fast | 1.1 | 1.1 | 45.80 | 34.65 | 14.14 | 50.38 | 30.74 | 9.09 | 139.00 |

   Spray 2nd or additional finish coats
| | | | | | | | | | |
|---|---|---|---|---|---|---|---|---|---|
| Slow | 1.1 | 0.8 | 61.00 | 22.28 | 6.56 | 48.80 | 14.75 | 14.78 | 107.17 |
| Medium | 1.0 | 0.9 | 53.40 | 25.75 | 9.12 | 48.06 | 20.73 | 12.44 | 116.10 |
| Fast | 0.9 | 1.0 | 45.80 | 28.35 | 11.57 | 45.80 | 26.57 | 7.86 | 120.15 |

Industrial enamel, oil base, high gloss, dark (OSHA) colors (material #57)
   Spray 1st finish coat
| | | | | | | | | | |
|---|---|---|---|---|---|---|---|---|---|
| Slow | 1.5 | 0.9 | 67.60 | 30.38 | 8.95 | 60.84 | 19.03 | 19.07 | 138.27 |
| Medium | 1.3 | 1.0 | 59.10 | 33.48 | 11.85 | 59.10 | 26.11 | 15.66 | 146.20 |
| Fast | 1.1 | 1.1 | 50.70 | 34.65 | 14.14 | 55.77 | 32.41 | 9.59 | 146.56 |

   Spray 2nd or additional finish coats
| | | | | | | | | | |
|---|---|---|---|---|---|---|---|---|---|
| Slow | 1.1 | 0.8 | 67.60 | 22.28 | 6.56 | 54.08 | 15.76 | 15.79 | 114.47 |
| Medium | 1.0 | 0.9 | 59.10 | 25.75 | 9.12 | 53.19 | 22.02 | 13.21 | 123.29 |
| Fast | 0.9 | 1.0 | 50.70 | 28.35 | 11.57 | 50.70 | 28.09 | 8.31 | 127.02 |

For field painting at heights above 8 feet, use the High Time Difficulty Factors on page 139. Note: A two coat system, prime and finish, using oil base material is recommended for any metal surface. Using water base material may cause oxidation, corrosion and rust. One coat of oil base paint on metal surfaces may result in cracking, peeling or chipping without the proper prime coat application. If off white or another light colored finish paint is specified, make sure the prime coat is also a light color, or more than one finish coat will be necessary. "Slow" work is based on an hourly wage of $20.25, "Medium" work on an hourly wage of $25.75, and "Fast" work on an hourly wage of $31.50. Other qualifications that apply to this table are on page 9.

*Industrial, Institutional and Heavy Commercial Costs*

|  | Labor SF per manhour | Material coverage SF/gallon | Material cost per gallon | Labor cost per 100 SF | Labor burden 100 SF | Material cost per 100 SF | Overhead per 100 SF | Profit per 100 SF | Total price per 100 SF |
|---|---|---|---|---|---|---|---|---|---|

## Structural steel, medium, brush application

### Metal primer, rust inhibitor, clean metal (material #35)
#### Brush prime coat
| | | | | | | | | | |
|---|---|---|---|---|---|---|---|---|---|
| Slow | 80 | 425 | 59.70 | 25.31 | 7.47 | 14.05 | 8.90 | 8.92 | 64.65 |
| Medium | 100 | 413 | 52.20 | 25.75 | 9.12 | 12.64 | 11.88 | 7.13 | 66.52 |
| Fast | 120 | 400 | 44.80 | 26.25 | 10.69 | 11.20 | 14.93 | 4.42 | 67.49 |

### Metal primer, rust inhibitor, rusty metal (material #36)
#### Brush prime coat
| | | | | | | | | | |
|---|---|---|---|---|---|---|---|---|---|
| Slow | 80 | 400 | 72.30 | 25.31 | 7.47 | 18.08 | 9.66 | 9.68 | 70.20 |
| Medium | 100 | 388 | 63.30 | 25.75 | 9.12 | 16.31 | 12.80 | 7.68 | 71.66 |
| Fast | 120 | 375 | 54.20 | 26.25 | 10.69 | 14.45 | 15.94 | 4.71 | 72.04 |

### Industrial enamel, oil base, high gloss, light colors (material #56)
#### Brush 1st or additional finish coats
| | | | | | | | | | |
|---|---|---|---|---|---|---|---|---|---|
| Slow | 100 | 425 | 61.00 | 20.25 | 5.97 | 14.35 | 7.71 | 7.72 | 56.00 |
| Medium | 125 | 413 | 53.40 | 20.60 | 7.30 | 12.93 | 10.21 | 6.12 | 57.16 |
| Fast | 150 | 400 | 45.80 | 21.00 | 8.58 | 11.45 | 12.72 | 3.76 | 57.51 |

### Industrial enamel, oil base, high gloss, dark (OSHA) colors (material #57)
#### Brush 1st or additional finish coats
| | | | | | | | | | |
|---|---|---|---|---|---|---|---|---|---|
| Slow | 100 | 475 | 67.60 | 20.25 | 5.97 | 14.23 | 7.69 | 7.70 | 55.84 |
| Medium | 125 | 463 | 59.10 | 20.60 | 7.30 | 12.76 | 10.16 | 6.10 | 56.92 |
| Fast | 150 | 450 | 50.70 | 21.00 | 8.58 | 11.27 | 12.66 | 3.75 | 57.26 |

### Epoxy coating, 2 part system, clear (material #51)
#### Brush 1st coat
| | | | | | | | | | |
|---|---|---|---|---|---|---|---|---|---|
| Slow | 80 | 425 | 146.90 | 25.31 | 7.47 | 34.56 | 12.79 | 12.82 | 92.95 |
| Medium | 100 | 413 | 128.60 | 25.75 | 9.12 | 31.14 | 16.50 | 9.90 | 92.41 |
| Fast | 120 | 400 | 110.20 | 26.25 | 10.69 | 27.55 | 20.00 | 5.92 | 90.41 |

#### Brush 2nd or additional coats
| | | | | | | | | | |
|---|---|---|---|---|---|---|---|---|---|
| Slow | 100 | 450 | 146.90 | 20.25 | 5.97 | 32.64 | 11.18 | 11.21 | 81.25 |
| Medium | 125 | 438 | 128.60 | 20.60 | 7.30 | 29.36 | 14.31 | 8.59 | 80.16 |
| Fast | 150 | 425 | 110.20 | 21.00 | 8.58 | 25.93 | 17.21 | 5.09 | 77.81 |

*National Painting Cost Estimator*

|  | Labor SF per manhour | Material coverage SF/gallon | Material cost per gallon | Labor cost per 100 SF | Labor burden 100 SF | Material cost per 100 SF | Overhead per 100 SF | Profit per 100 SF | Total price per 100 SF |
|---|---|---|---|---|---|---|---|---|---|
| **Epoxy coating, 2 part system, white (material #52)** | | | | | | | | | |
| Brush 1st coat | | | | | | | | | |
| Slow | 80 | 425 | 177.00 | 25.31 | 7.47 | 41.65 | 14.14 | 14.17 | 102.74 |
| Medium | 100 | 413 | 154.90 | 25.75 | 9.12 | 37.51 | 18.10 | 10.86 | 101.34 |
| Fast | 120 | 400 | 132.70 | 26.25 | 10.69 | 33.18 | 21.74 | 6.43 | 98.29 |
| Brush 2nd or additional coats | | | | | | | | | |
| Slow | 100 | 450 | 177.00 | 20.25 | 5.97 | 39.33 | 12.45 | 12.48 | 90.48 |
| Medium | 125 | 438 | 154.90 | 20.60 | 7.30 | 35.37 | 15.82 | 9.49 | 88.58 |
| Fast | 150 | 425 | 132.70 | 21.00 | 8.58 | 31.22 | 18.84 | 5.57 | 85.21 |

For field painting at heights above 8 feet, use the High Time Difficulty Factors on page 139. Medium structural steel has from 150 to 300 square feet of surface per ton. As a comparison, when coatings are applied by brush, a journeyman painter will apply a first coat on 4 to 5 tons per 8 hour day. A second and subsequent coat can be applied on 5 to 6 tons per day. When coatings are applied by spray, figure output at 0.6 hours per ton and material use at about 0.6 gallons per ton. Use Figure 23 on pages 391 to 399 to convert structural steel linear feet or tonnage to surface area. Note: A two coat system, prime and finish, using oil base material is recommended for any metal surface. Using water base material may cause oxidation, corrosion and rust. One coat of oil base paint on metal surfaces may result in cracking, peeling or chipping without the proper prime coat application. If off white or another light colored finish paint is specified, make sure the prime coat is also a light color, or more than one finish coat will be necessary. "Slow" work is based on an hourly wage of $20.25, "Medium" work on an hourly wage of $25.75, and "Fast" work on an hourly wage of $31.50. Other qualifications that apply to this table are on page 9.

*Industrial, Institutional and Heavy Commercial Costs*

|  | Labor SF per manhour | Material coverage SF/gallon | Material cost per gallon | Labor cost per 100 SF | Labor burden 100 SF | Material cost per 100 SF | Overhead per 100 SF | Profit per 100 SF | Total price per 100 SF |
|---|---|---|---|---|---|---|---|---|---|

## Structural steel, medium, roll and brush application

### Metal primer, rust inhibitor, clean metal (material #35)
Roll and brush prime coat

| | | | | | | | | | |
|---|---|---|---|---|---|---|---|---|---|
| Slow | 200 | 390 | 59.70 | 10.13 | 2.98 | 15.31 | 5.40 | 5.41 | 39.23 |
| Medium | 225 | 378 | 52.20 | 11.44 | 4.04 | 13.81 | 7.33 | 4.40 | 41.02 |
| Fast | 250 | 365 | 44.80 | 12.60 | 5.14 | 12.27 | 9.30 | 2.75 | 42.06 |

### Metal primer, rust inhibitor, rusty metal (material #36)
Roll and brush prime coat

| | | | | | | | | | |
|---|---|---|---|---|---|---|---|---|---|
| Slow | 200 | 380 | 72.30 | 10.13 | 2.98 | 19.03 | 6.11 | 6.12 | 44.37 |
| Medium | 225 | 368 | 63.30 | 11.44 | 4.04 | 17.20 | 8.17 | 4.90 | 45.75 |
| Fast | 250 | 355 | 54.20 | 12.60 | 5.14 | 15.27 | 10.23 | 3.03 | 46.27 |

### Industrial enamel, oil base, high gloss, light colors (material #56)
Roll and brush 1st or additional finish coats

| | | | | | | | | | |
|---|---|---|---|---|---|---|---|---|---|
| Slow | 225 | 390 | 61.00 | 9.00 | 2.64 | 15.64 | 5.19 | 5.20 | 37.67 |
| Medium | 250 | 378 | 53.40 | 10.30 | 3.65 | 14.13 | 7.02 | 4.21 | 39.31 |
| Fast | 275 | 365 | 45.80 | 11.45 | 4.69 | 12.55 | 8.89 | 2.63 | 40.21 |

### Industrial enamel, oil base, high gloss, dark (OSHA) colors (material #57)
Roll and brush 1st or additional finish coats

| | | | | | | | | | |
|---|---|---|---|---|---|---|---|---|---|
| Slow | 225 | 440 | 67.60 | 9.00 | 2.64 | 15.36 | 5.13 | 5.14 | 37.27 |
| Medium | 250 | 428 | 59.10 | 10.30 | 3.65 | 13.81 | 6.94 | 4.16 | 38.86 |
| Fast | 275 | 415 | 50.70 | 11.45 | 4.69 | 12.22 | 8.79 | 2.60 | 39.75 |

### Epoxy coating, 2 part system, clear (material #51)
Roll and brush 1st coat

| | | | | | | | | | |
|---|---|---|---|---|---|---|---|---|---|
| Slow | 200 | 400 | 146.90 | 10.13 | 2.98 | 36.73 | 9.47 | 9.49 | 68.80 |
| Medium | 225 | 388 | 128.60 | 11.44 | 4.04 | 33.14 | 12.16 | 7.29 | 68.07 |
| Fast | 250 | 375 | 110.20 | 12.60 | 5.14 | 29.39 | 14.61 | 4.32 | 66.06 |

Roll and brush 2nd or additional coats

| | | | | | | | | | |
|---|---|---|---|---|---|---|---|---|---|
| Slow | 225 | 425 | 146.90 | 9.00 | 2.64 | 34.56 | 8.78 | 8.80 | 63.78 |
| Medium | 250 | 413 | 128.60 | 10.30 | 3.65 | 31.14 | 11.27 | 6.76 | 63.12 |
| Fast | 275 | 400 | 110.20 | 11.45 | 4.69 | 27.55 | 13.54 | 4.00 | 61.23 |

*National Painting Cost Estimator*

|  | Labor SF per manhour | Material coverage SF/gallon | Material cost per gallon | Labor cost per 100 SF | Labor burden 100 SF | Material cost per 100 SF | Overhead per 100 SF | Profit per 100 SF | Total price per 100 SF |
|---|---|---|---|---|---|---|---|---|---|
| **Epoxy coating, 2 part system, white (material #52)** | | | | | | | | | |
| Roll and brush 1st coat | | | | | | | | | |
| Slow | 200 | 400 | 177.00 | 10.13 | 2.98 | 44.25 | 10.90 | 10.92 | 79.18 |
| Medium | 225 | 388 | 154.90 | 11.44 | 4.04 | 39.92 | 13.85 | 8.31 | 77.56 |
| Fast | 250 | 375 | 132.70 | 12.60 | 5.14 | 35.39 | 16.47 | 4.87 | 74.47 |
| Roll and brush 2nd or additional coats | | | | | | | | | |
| Slow | 225 | 425 | 177.00 | 9.00 | 2.64 | 41.65 | 10.13 | 10.15 | 73.57 |
| Medium | 250 | 413 | 154.90 | 10.30 | 3.65 | 37.51 | 12.87 | 7.72 | 72.05 |
| Fast | 275 | 400 | 132.70 | 11.45 | 4.69 | 33.18 | 15.28 | 4.52 | 69.12 |

For field painting at heights above 8 feet, use the High Time Difficulty Factors on page 139. Medium structural steel has from 150 to 300 square feet of surface per ton. As a comparison, when coatings are applied by brush, a journeyman painter will apply a first coat on 4 to 5 tons per 8 hour day. A second and subsequent coat can be applied on 5 to 6 tons per day. When coatings are applied by spray, figure output at 0.6 hours per ton and material use at about 0.6 gallons per ton. Use Figure 23 on pages 391 to 399 to convert structural steel linear feet or tonnage to surface area. Note: A two coat system, prime and finish, using oil base material is recommended for any metal surface. Using water base material may cause oxidation, corrosion and rust. One coat of oil base paint on metal surfaces may result in cracking, peeling or chipping without the proper prime coat application. If off white or another light colored finish paint is specified, make sure the prime coat is also a light color, or more than one finish coat will be necessary. "Slow" work is based on an hourly wage of $20.25, "Medium" work on an hourly wage of $25.75, and "Fast" work on an hourly wage of $31.50. Other qualifications that apply to this table are on page 9.

*Industrial, Institutional and Heavy Commercial Costs*

|  | Labor SF per manhour | Material coverage SF/gallon | Material cost per gallon | Labor cost per 100 SF | Labor burden 100 SF | Material cost per 100 SF | Overhead per 100 SF | Profit per 100 SF | Total price per 100 SF |
|---|---|---|---|---|---|---|---|---|---|

## Structural steel, medium, spray application

**Metal primer, rust inhibitor, clean metal (material #35)**
  Spray prime coat

| | | | | | | | | | |
|---|---|---|---|---|---|---|---|---|---|
| Slow | 500 | 325 | 59.70 | 4.05 | 1.19 | 18.37 | 4.49 | 4.50 | 32.60 |
| Medium | 600 | 313 | 52.20 | 4.29 | 1.53 | 16.68 | 5.62 | 3.37 | 31.49 |
| Fast | 700 | 300 | 44.80 | 4.50 | 1.84 | 14.93 | 6.59 | 1.95 | 29.81 |

**Metal primer, rust inhibitor, rusty metal (material #36)**
  Spray prime coat

| | | | | | | | | | |
|---|---|---|---|---|---|---|---|---|---|
| Slow | 500 | 300 | 72.30 | 4.05 | 1.19 | 24.10 | 5.57 | 5.59 | 40.50 |
| Medium | 600 | 288 | 63.30 | 4.29 | 1.53 | 21.98 | 6.95 | 4.17 | 38.92 |
| Fast | 700 | 275 | 54.20 | 4.50 | 1.84 | 19.71 | 8.08 | 2.39 | 36.52 |

**Industrial enamel, oil base, high gloss, light colors (material #56)**
  Spray 1st or additional finish coats

| | | | | | | | | | |
|---|---|---|---|---|---|---|---|---|---|
| Slow | 600 | 325 | 61.00 | 3.38 | 1.00 | 18.77 | 4.40 | 4.41 | 31.96 |
| Medium | 700 | 313 | 53.40 | 3.68 | 1.31 | 17.06 | 5.51 | 3.31 | 30.87 |
| Fast | 800 | 300 | 45.80 | 3.94 | 1.60 | 15.27 | 6.45 | 1.91 | 29.17 |

**Industrial enamel, oil base, high gloss, dark (OSHA) colors (material #57)**
  Spray 1st or additional finish coats

| | | | | | | | | | |
|---|---|---|---|---|---|---|---|---|---|
| Slow | 600 | 365 | 67.60 | 3.38 | 1.00 | 18.52 | 4.35 | 4.36 | 31.61 |
| Medium | 700 | 350 | 59.10 | 3.68 | 1.31 | 16.89 | 5.47 | 3.28 | 30.63 |
| Fast | 800 | 335 | 50.70 | 3.94 | 1.60 | 15.13 | 6.41 | 1.90 | 28.98 |

**Epoxy coating, 2 part system, clear (material #51)**
  Spray 1st coat

| | | | | | | | | | |
|---|---|---|---|---|---|---|---|---|---|
| Slow | 500 | 325 | 146.90 | 4.05 | 1.19 | 45.20 | 9.58 | 9.60 | 69.62 |
| Medium | 600 | 313 | 128.60 | 4.29 | 1.53 | 41.09 | 11.73 | 7.04 | 65.68 |
| Fast | 700 | 300 | 110.20 | 4.50 | 1.84 | 36.73 | 13.35 | 3.95 | 60.37 |

  Spray 2nd or additional coats

| | | | | | | | | | |
|---|---|---|---|---|---|---|---|---|---|
| Slow | 600 | 350 | 146.90 | 3.38 | 1.00 | 41.97 | 8.81 | 8.83 | 63.99 |
| Medium | 700 | 338 | 128.60 | 3.68 | 1.31 | 38.05 | 10.76 | 6.45 | 60.25 |
| Fast | 800 | 325 | 110.20 | 3.94 | 1.60 | 33.91 | 12.23 | 3.62 | 55.30 |

|  | Labor SF per manhour | Material coverage SF/gallon | Material cost per gallon | Labor cost per 100 SF | Labor burden 100 SF | Material cost per 100 SF | Overhead per 100 SF | Profit per 100 SF | Total price per 100 SF |
|---|---|---|---|---|---|---|---|---|---|
| **Epoxy coating, 2 part system, white (material #52)** | | | | | | | | | |
| Spray 1st coat | | | | | | | | | |
| Slow | 500 | 325 | 177.00 | 4.05 | 1.19 | 54.46 | 11.34 | 11.37 | 82.41 |
| Medium | 600 | 313 | 154.90 | 4.29 | 1.53 | 49.49 | 13.83 | 8.30 | 77.44 |
| Fast | 700 | 300 | 132.70 | 4.50 | 1.84 | 44.23 | 15.68 | 4.64 | 70.89 |
| Spray 2nd or additional coats | | | | | | | | | |
| Slow | 600 | 350 | 177.00 | 3.38 | 1.00 | 50.57 | 10.44 | 10.46 | 75.85 |
| Medium | 700 | 338 | 154.90 | 3.68 | 1.31 | 45.83 | 12.70 | 7.62 | 71.14 |
| Fast | 800 | 325 | 132.70 | 3.94 | 1.60 | 40.83 | 14.38 | 4.25 | 65.00 |

For field painting at heights above 8 feet, use the High Time Difficulty Factors on page 139. Medium structural steel has from 150 to 300 square feet of surface per ton. As a comparison, when coatings are applied by brush, a journeyman painter will apply a first coat on 4 to 5 tons per 8 hour day. A second and subsequent coat can be applied on 5 to 6 tons per day. When coatings are applied by spray, figure output at 0.6 hours per ton and material use at about 0.6 gallons per ton. Use Figure 23 on pages 391 to 399 to convert structural steel linear feet or tonnage to surface area. Note: A two coat system, prime and finish, using oil base material is recommended for any metal surface. Using water base material may cause oxidation, corrosion and rust. One coat of oil base paint on metal surfaces may result in cracking, peeling or chipping without the proper prime coat application. If off white or another light colored finish paint is specified, make sure the prime coat is also a light color, or more than one finish coat will be necessary. "Slow" work is based on an hourly wage of $20.25, "Medium" work on an hourly wage of $25.75, and "Fast" work on an hourly wage of $31.50. Other qualifications that apply to this table are on page 9.

*Industrial, Institutional and Heavy Commercial Costs*

| Section designation | Square feet of surface area per foot of length — Minus one flange side | Square feet of surface area per foot of length — All around | Square feet of surface area per ton — Minus one flange side | Square feet of surface area per ton — All around | Section designation | Square feet of surface area per foot of length — Minus one flange side | Square feet of surface area per foot of length — All around | Square feet of surface area per ton — Minus one flange side | Square feet of surface area per ton — All around |
|---|---|---|---|---|---|---|---|---|---|
| W 30 x 99 | 7.56 | 8.43 | 152.7 | 170.3 | W 14 x 95 | 5.99 | 7.20 | 126.1 | 151.6 |
| W 27 x 94 | 6.99 | 7.81 | 148.7 | 166.2 | x 87 | 5.96 | 7.17 | 137.0 | 164.8 |
| x 84 | 6.99 | 7.79 | 166.4 | 185.5 | x 84 | 5.36 | 6.36 | 127.6 | 151.4 |
| W 24 x 100 | 7.00 | 8.00 | 140.0 | 160.0 | x 78 | 5.33 | 6.33 | 136.7 | 162.3 |
| x 94 | 6.29 | 7.04 | 133.8 | 149.8 | x 74 | 4.92 | 5.77 | 133.0 | 155.9 |
| x 84 | 6.27 | 7.02 | 149.3 | 167.1 | x 68 | 4.83 | 5.67 | 142.1 | 166.8 |
| x 76 | 6.23 | 6.98 | 163.9 | 183.7 | x 61 | 4.81 | 5.65 | 157.7 | 185.2 |
| x 68 | 6.21 | 6.96 | 182.6 | 204.7 | x 53 | 4.33 | 5.00 | 163.4 | 188.7 |
| x 61 | 5.71 | 6.29 | 187.2 | 206.2 | x 48 | 4.29 | 4.96 | 178.8 | 206.7 |
| x 55 | 5.67 | 6.25 | 206.2 | 227.2 | x 43 | 4.27 | 4.94 | 198.6 | 229.8 |
| W 21 x 96 | 5.77 | 6.52 | 120.2 | 135.8 | x 38 | 4.04 | 4.60 | 212.6 | 242.1 |
| x 82 | 5.73 | 6.48 | 139.8 | 158.0 | x 34 | 4.02 | 4.58 | 236.5 | 269.4 |
| x 73 | 5.60 | 6.29 | 153.4 | 172.3 | x 30 | 4.00 | 4.56 | 266.7 | 304.0 |
| x 68 | 5.58 | 6.57 | 164.1 | 184.4 | x 26 | 3.56 | 3.98 | 273.8 | 306.2 |
| x 62 | 5.56 | 6.25 | 179.4 | 201.6 | x 22 | 3.54 | 3.96 | 321.8 | 360.0 |
| x 55 | 5.52 | 6.21 | 200.7 | 225.8 | | | | | |
| x 49 | 5.10 | 5.65 | 208.2 | 230.6 | W 12 x 99 | 5.19 | 6.21 | 104.8 | 125.4 |
| x 44 | 5.08 | 5.63 | 230.9 | 255.9 | x 92 | 5.14 | 6.15 | 111.7 | 133.7 |
| | | | | | x 85 | 5.12 | 6.13 | 120.5 | 144.2 |
| W 18 x 96 | 5.96 | 6.94 | 124.2 | 144.6 | x 79 | 5.09 | 6.10 | 128.9 | 154.4 |
| x 85 | 5.28 | 6.02 | 124.2 | 141.6 | x 72 | 5.04 | 6.04 | 140.0 | 167.8 |
| x 77 | 5.22 | 5.95 | 135.6 | 154.5 | x 65 | 5.02 | 6.02 | 154.5 | 185.2 |
| x 70 | 5.19 | 5.92 | 148.3 | 169.1 | x 58 | 4.54 | 5.38 | 156.6 | 185.5 |
| x 64 | 5.17 | 5.90 | 161.6 | 184.4 | x 53 | 4.50 | 5.33 | 169.8 | 201.1 |
| x 60 | 4.92 | 5.54 | 164.0 | 184.7 | x 50 | 4.07 | 4.75 | 162.8 | 190.0 |
| x 55 | 4.90 | 5.52 | 178.1 | 200.7 | x 45 | 4.00 | 4.67 | 177.8 | 207.6 |
| x 50 | 4.88 | 5.50 | 195.2 | 220.0 | x 40 | 4.00 | 4.67 | 200.0 | 233.5 |
| x 45 | 4.85 | 5.48 | 215.6 | 243.6 | x 36 | 3.70 | 4.25 | 205.6 | 236.1 |
| x 40 | 4.48 | 4.98 | 224.0 | 249.0 | x 31 | 3.65 | 4.19 | 235.5 | 270.3 |
| x 35 | 4.46 | 4.96 | 254.9 | 283.4 | x 27 | 3.63 | 4.17 | 268.9 | 308.9 |
| W 16 x 96 | 5.60 | 6.56 | 116.7 | 136.7 | x 22 | 3.04 | 3.38 | 276.4 | 307.3 |
| x 88 | 5.57 | 6.53 | 126.6 | 148.4 | x 19 | 3.02 | 3.35 | 317.9 | 352.6 |
| x 78 | 4.88 | 5.60 | 125.1 | 143.6 | x 16.5 | 3.00 | 3.33 | 363.6 | 403.6 |
| x 71 | 4.82 | 5.53 | 135.8 | 155.8 | x 14 | 2.98 | 3.31 | 425.7 | 472.9 |
| x 64 | 4.79 | 5.50 | 149.7 | 171.9 | | | | | |
| x 58 | 4.77 | 5.48 | 164.5 | 189.0 | W 10 x 100 | 4.45 | 5.31 | 89.0 | 106.2 |
| x 50 | 4.51 | 5.10 | 180.4 | 204.0 | x 89 | 4.38 | 5.23 | 98.4 | 117.5 |
| x 45 | 4.45 | 5.03 | 197.8 | 223.6 | x 77 | 4.33 | 5.19 | 112.5 | 134.8 |
| x 40 | 4.42 | 5.00 | 221.0 | 250.0 | x 72 | 4.28 | 5.13 | 118.9 | 142.5 |
| x 36 | 4.40 | 4.98 | 244.4 | 276.7 | x 66 | 4.26 | 5.10 | 129.1 | 154.5 |
| x 31 | 4.02 | 4.48 | 259.4 | 289.0 | x 60 | 4.24 | 5.08 | 141.3 | 169.3 |
| x 26 | 3.98 | 4.44 | 306.2 | 341.5 | | | | | |

**Figure 23**
Structural steel conversion table

*National Painting Cost Estimator*

| Section designation | | Square feet of surface area per foot of length — Minus one flange side | Square feet of surface area per foot of length — All around | Square feet of surface area per ton — Minus one flange side | Square feet of surface area per ton — All around | Section designation | | Square feet of surface area per foot of length — Minus one flange side | Square feet of surface area per foot of length — All around | Square feet of surface area per ton — Minus one flange side | Square feet of surface area per ton — All around |
|---|---|---|---|---|---|---|---|---|---|---|---|
| W 10 | x 54 | 4.19 | 5.02 | 155.2 | 185.9 | S-20 | x 95 | 5.15 | 5.75 | 108.4 | 121.1 |
|  | x 49 | 4.17 | 5.00 | 170.2 | 204.0 |  | x 85 | 5.08 | 5.67 | 119.5 | 133.4 |
|  | x 45 | 3.69 | 4.35 | 164.0 | 193.3 |  | x 75 | 4.93 | 5.46 | 131.5 | 145.6 |
|  | x 39 | 3.67 | 4.33 | 188.2 | 222.1 |  | x 65.4 | 4.90 | 5.42 | 149.8 | 165.7 |
|  | x 33 | 3.63 | 4.29 | 220.0 | 260.0 | S-18 | x 70 | 4.56 | 5.08 | 130.3 | 145.1 |
|  | x 29 | 3.15 | 3.63 | 217.2 | 250.3 |  | x 54.7 | 4.50 | 5.00 | 164.5 | 182.8 |
|  | x 25 | 3.13 | 3.60 | 250.4 | 288.0 |  |  |  |  |  |  |
|  | x 21 | 3.08 | 3.56 | 293.3 | 339.0 | S-15 | x 50 | 3.91 | 4.38 | 156.4 | 175.2 |
|  | x 19 | 2.71 | 3.04 | 285.3 | 320.0 |  | x 42.9 | 3.88 | 4.33 | 180.9 | 201.9 |
|  | x 17 | 2.69 | 3.02 | 316.5 | 355.3 | S-12 | x 50 | 3.38 | 3.83 | 135.2 | 153.2 |
|  | x 15 | 2.67 | 3.00 | 356.0 | 400.0 |  | x 40.8 | 3.31 | 3.75 | 162.3 | 183.8 |
|  | x 11.5 | 2.65 | 2.98 | 460.9 | 518.3 |  | x 35 | 3.28 | 3.71 | 187.4 | 212.0 |
|  |  |  |  |  |  |  | x 31.8 | 3.25 | 3.67 | 204.4 | 230.8 |
| W 8 | x 67 | 3.56 | 4.25 | 106.3 | 126.9 |  |  |  |  |  |  |
|  | x 58 | 3.52 | 4.21 | 121.4 | 145.2 | S-10 | x 35 | 2.92 | 3.33 | 166.9 | 190.2 |
|  | x 48 | 3.45 | 4.13 | 143.8 | 172.1 |  | x 25.4 | 2.82 | 3.21 | 222.0 | 252.8 |
|  | x 40 | 3.41 | 4.08 | 170.5 | 204.0 | S-8 | x 23 | 2.36 | 2.71 | 205.2 | 235.7 |
|  | x 35 | 3.35 | 4.02 | 191.4 | 229.7 |  | x 18.4 | 2.33 | 2.67 | 253.3 | 290.2 |
|  | x 31 | 3.33 | 4.00 | 214.8 | 258.1 |  |  |  |  |  |  |
|  | x 28 | 2.96 | 3.50 | 211.4 | 250.0 | S-7 | x 20 | 2.14 | 2.46 | 214.0 | 246.0 |
|  | x 24 | 2.94 | 3.48 | 245.0 | 290.0 |  | x 15.3 | 2.07 | 2.38 | 270.6 | 311.1 |
|  | x 20 | 2.67 | 3.10 | 267.0 | 310.0 |  |  |  |  |  |  |
|  | x 17 | 2.65 | 3.08 | 311.8 | 362.4 | S-6 | x 17.25 | 1.91 | 2.21 | 221.4 | 256.2 |
|  | x 15 | 2.35 | 2.69 | 313.3 | 358.7 |  | x 12.5 | 1.84 | 2.13 | 294.4 | 340.8 |
|  | x 13 | 2.33 | 2.67 | 358.5 | 410.8 | S-5 | x 14.75 | 1.65 | 1.92 | 223.7 | 260.3 |
|  | x 10 | 2.31 | 2.65 | 462.0 | 530.0 |  | x 10 | 1.58 | 1.83 | 316.0 | 366.0 |
| W 6 | x 25 | 2.59 | 3.10 | 207.2 | 248.0 | S-4 | x 9.5 | 1.35 | 1.58 | 284.2 | 332.6 |
|  | x 20 | 2.54 | 3.04 | 254.0 | 304.0 |  | x 7.7 | 1.32 | 1.54 | 342.9 | 400.0 |
|  | x 15.5 | 2.50 | 3.00 | 322.6 | 387.1 |  |  |  |  |  |  |
|  | x 16 | 2.04 | 2.38 | 255.0 | 297.5 | S-3 | x 7.5 | 1.13 | 1.33 | 301.3 | 354.7 |
|  | x 12 | 2.00 | 2.33 | 333.3 | 388.3 |  | x 5.7 | 1.09 | 1.29 | 382.5 | 452.6 |
|  | x 8.5 | 1.98 | 2.31 | 465.9 | 543.5 |  |  |  |  |  |  |
| W 5 | x 18.5 | 2.10 | 2.52 | 227.0 | 272.4 |  |  |  |  |  |  |
|  | x 16 | 2.08 | 2.50 | 260.0 | 312.5 |  |  |  |  |  |  |
| W 4 | x 13 | 1.69 | 2.02 | 260.0 | 310.8 |  |  |  |  |  |  |
| S-24 | x 90 | 5.78 | 6.38 | 128.4 | 141.8 | **Miscellaneous shape** | | | | | |
|  | x 79.9 | 5.75 | 6.33 | 143.9 | 158.4 | M-5 | x 18.9 | 2.08 | 2.50 | 220.1 | 264.6 |

**Figure 23 (cont'd)**
Structural steel conversion table

*Industrial, Institutional and Heavy Commercial Costs*

| Section designation | | Square feet of surface area per foot of length — Minus one flange side | Square feet of surface area per foot of length — All around | Square feet of surface area per ton — Minus one flange side | Square feet of surface area per ton — All around |
|---|---|---|---|---|---|
| C-15 | x 50 | 3.44 | 3.75 | 137.6 | 150.0 |
|  | x 40 | 3.38 | 3.67 | 169.0 | 183.5 |
|  | x 33.9 | 3.34 | 3.63 | 197.1 | 214.2 |
| C-12 | x 30 | 2.78 | 3.04 | 185.3 | 202.7 |
|  | x 25 | 2.75 | 3.00 | 220.0 | 240.0 |
|  | x 20.7 | 2.75 | 3.00 | 265.7 | 289.9 |
| C-10 | x 30 | 2.42 | 2.67 | 161.3 | 178.0 |
|  | x 25 | 2.39 | 2.63 | 191.2 | 210.4 |
|  | x 20 | 2.35 | 2.58 | 235.0 | 258.0 |
|  | x 15.3 | 2.32 | 2.54 | 305.3 | 334.2 |
| C-9 | x 20 | 2.16 | 2.38 | 216.0 | 238.0 |
|  | x 15 | 2.13 | 2.33 | 284.0 | 310.7 |
|  | x 13.4 | 2.09 | 2.29 | 311.9 | 341.8 |
| C-8 | x 18.75 | 1.96 | 2.17 | 209.1 | 231.5 |
|  | x 13.75 | 1.93 | 2.13 | 280.7 | 309.8 |
|  | x 11.5 | 1.90 | 2.08 | 330.4 | 361.7 |
| C-7 | x 14.75 | 1.73 | 1.92 | 234.6 | 260.3 |
|  | x 12.25 | 1.73 | 1.92 | 282.4 | 313.5 |
|  | x 9.8 | 1.70 | 1.88 | 346.9 | 383.7 |
| C-6 | x 13 | 1.53 | 1.71 | 235.4 | 263.1 |
|  | x 10.5 | 1.50 | 1.67 | 285.7 | 318.1 |
|  | x 8.2 | 1.47 | 1.63 | 358.5 | 397.6 |
| C-5 | x 9 | 1.30 | 1.46 | 288.9 | 324.4 |
|  | x 6.7 | 1.27 | 1.42 | 379.1 | 423.9 |
| C-4 | x 7.25 | 1.10 | 1.25 | 295.2 | 344.8 |
|  | x 5.4 | 1.07 | 1.21 | 396.3 | 448.1 |
| C-3 | x 6 | .91 | 1.04 | 303.3 | 346.7 |
|  | x 5 | .88 | 1.00 | 352.0 | 400.0 |
|  | x 4.1 | .84 | .96 | 409.8 | 468.3 |
| MC-18 | x 58 | 4.06 | 4.42 | 140.0 | 152.4 |
|  | x 51.9 | 4.03 | 4.38 | 155.3 | 168.8 |
|  | x 45.8 | 4.00 | 4.33 | 176.7 | 189.1 |
|  | x 42.7 | 4.00 | 4.33 | 187.4 | 202.8 |
| MC-13 | x 50 | 3.26 | 3.63 | 130.4 | 145.2 |
|  | x 40 | 3.20 | 3.54 | 160.0 | 177.0 |
|  | x 35 | 3.20 | 3.54 | 182.9 | 202.3 |
|  | x 31.8 | 3.17 | 3.50 | 199.4 | 220.1 |

| Section designation | | Square feet of surface area per foot of length — Minus one flange side | Square feet of surface area per foot of length — All around | Square feet of surface area per ton — Minus one flange side | Square feet of surface area per ton — All around |
|---|---|---|---|---|---|
| MC-12 | x 50 | 3.03 | 3.38 | 121.2 | 135.2 |
|  | x 45 | 3.00 | 3.33 | 133.3 | 148.0 |
|  | x 40 | 2.97 | 3.29 | 148.5 | 164.5 |
|  | x 35 | 2.94 | 3.25 | 168.0 | 185.7 |
|  | x 37 | 2.91 | 3.21 | 157.3 | 173.5 |
|  | x 32.9 | 2.88 | 3.17 | 175.1 | 192.7 |
|  | x 30.9 | 2.88 | 3.17 | 186.4 | 205.2 |
| MC-10 | x 41.1 | 2.76 | 3.13 | 134.3 | 152.3 |
|  | x 33.6 | 2.70 | 3.04 | 160.7 | 181.0 |
|  | x 28.5 | 2.67 | 3.00 | 187.4 | 210.5 |
|  | x 28.3 | 2.54 | 2.83 | 179.5 | 200.0 |
|  | x 25.3 | 2.54 | 2.83 | 200.8 | 223.7 |
|  | x 24.9 | 2.51 | 2.79 | 201.6 | 224.1 |
|  | x 21.9 | 2.54 | 2.83 | 232.0 | 258.4 |
| MC-9 | x 25.4 | 2.38 | 2.67 | 187.4 | 210.2 |
|  | x 23.9 | 2.38 | 2.67 | 199.2 | 223.4 |
| MC-8 | x 22.8 | 2.21 | 2.50 | 193.9 | 219.3 |
|  | x 21.4 | 2.21 | 2.50 | 206.5 | 233.6 |
|  | x 20 | 2.08 | 2.33 | 208.0 | 233.0 |
|  | x 18.7 | 2.08 | 2.33 | 222.5 | 249.2 |
| MC-7 | x 22.7 | 2.07 | 2.38 | 182.4 | 209.7 |
|  | x 19.1 | 2.04 | 2.33 | 213.6 | 244.0 |
|  | x 17.6 | 1.92 | 2.17 | 218.2 | 246.6 |
| MC-6 | x 18 | 1.88 | 2.17 | 208.9 | 241.1 |
|  | x 15.3 | 1.88 | 2.17 | 245.8 | 283.7 |
|  | x 16.3 | 1.75 | 2.00 | 214.7 | 245.4 |
|  | x 15.1 | 1.75 | 2.00 | 231.8 | 264.9 |
|  | x 12 | 1.63 | 1.83 | 271.7 | 305.0 |
| MC-3 | x 9 | 1.03 | 1.21 | 228.9 | 268.9 |
|  | x 7.1 | 1.00 | 1.17 | 281.7 | 329.6 |

**Figure 23 (cont'd)**
Structural steel conversion table

| Section designation | Surface area per foot of length | Surface area per ton |
|---|---|---|
| ST 18 x 97 | 5.06 | 104.3 |
| x 91 | 5.04 | 110.8 |
| x 85 | 5.02 | 118.1 |
| x 80 | 5.00 | 125.0 |
| x 75 | 4.98 | 132.8 |
| x 67.5 | 4.95 | 147.0 |
| ST 16.5 x 76 | 4.72 | 124.2 |
| x 70.5 | 4.70 | 133.3 |
| x 65 | 4.38 | 144.0 |
| x 59 | 4.65 | 157.6 |
| ST 15 x 95 | 5.02 | 105.7 |
| x 86 | 4.99 | 116.0 |
| x 66 | 4.28 | 129.7 |
| x 62 | 4.27 | 137.7 |
| x 58 | 4.25 | 146.6 |
| x 54 | 4.23 | 156.7 |
| x 49.5 | 4.21 | 170.1 |
| ST 13.5 x 88.5 | 4.63 | 104.6 |
| x 80 | 4.59 | 114.8 |
| x 72.5 | 4.57 | 126.1 |
| x 57 | 3.95 | 138.6 |
| x 51 | 3.93 | 154.1 |
| x 47 | 3.91 | 166.4 |
| x 42 | 3.89 | 185.2 |
| ST 12 x 80 | 4.41 | 110.3 |
| x 72.5 | 4.38 | 120.8 |
| x 65 | 4.36 | 134.1 |
| x 60 | 4.04 | 134.7 |
| x 55 | 4.02 | 146.2 |
| x 50 | 4.00 | 160.0 |
| x 47 | 3.54 | 150.6 |
| x 42 | 3.51 | 167.1 |
| x 38 | 3.49 | 183.7 |
| x 34 | 3.47 | 204.1 |
| x 30.5 | 3.15 | 206.6 |
| x 27.5 | 3.13 | 227.6 |

| Section designation | Surface area per foot of length | Surface area per ton |
|---|---|---|
| ST 10.5 x 71 | 3.97 | 111.8 |
| x 63.5 | 3.95 | 124.4 |
| x 56 | 3.92 | 140.0 |
| x 48 | 3.27 | 136.3 |
| x 41 | 3.23 | 157.6 |
| x 36.5 | 3.15 | 172.6 |
| x 34 | 3.14 | 184.7 |
| x 31 | 3.12 | 201.3 |
| x 27.5 | 3.10 | 225.5 |
| x 24.5 | 2.82 | 230.2 |
| x 22 | 2.81 | 255.5 |
| ST 9 x 57 | 3.51 | 123.2 |
| x 52.5 | 3.49 | 133.0 |
| x 48 | 3.47 | 144.6 |
| x 42.5 | 3.00 | 141.2 |
| x 38.5 | 2.98 | 154.8 |
| x 35 | 2.96 | 169.1 |
| x 32 | 2.94 | 183.8 |
| x 30 | 2.78 | 185.3 |
| x 27.5 | 2.77 | 201.5 |
| x 25 | 2.75 | 220.0 |
| x 22.5 | 2.73 | 242.7 |
| x 20 | 2.49 | 249.0 |
| x 17.5 | 2.48 | 283.4 |
| ST 8 x 48 | 3.28 | 136.7 |
| x 44 | 3.26 | 148.2 |
| x 39 | 2.79 | 143.1 |
| x 35.5 | 2.77 | 156.1 |
| x 32 | 2.76 | 172.5 |
| x 29 | 2.73 | 188.3 |
| x 25 | 2.53 | 202.4 |
| x 22.5 | 2.52 | 224.0 |
| x 20 | 2.50 | 250.0 |
| x 18 | 2.49 | 276.7 |
| x 15.5 | 2.24 | 289.0 |
| x 13 | 2.22 | 341.5 |

**Figure 23 (cont'd)**
Structural steel conversion table

*Industrial, Institutional and Heavy Commercial Costs*

| Section designation | | Surface area per foot of length | Surface area per ton |
|---|---|---|---|
| ST 7 | x 88 | 3.88 | 88.2 |
| | x 83.5 | 3.86 | 92.5 |
| | x 79 | 3.84 | 97.2 |
| | x 75 | 3.83 | 102.1 |
| | x 71 | 3.81 | 107.3 |
| | x 68 | 3.69 | 108.5 |
| | x 63.5 | 3.67 | 115.6 |
| | x 59.5 | 3.65 | 122.7 |
| | x 55.5 | 3.64 | 131.2 |
| | x 51.5 | 3.62 | 140.6 |
| | x 47.5 | 3.60 | 151.6 |
| | x 43.5 | 3.58 | 164.6 |
| | x 42 | 3.19 | 151.9 |
| | x 39 | 3.17 | 162.6 |
| | x 37 | 2.86 | 154.6 |
| | x 34 | 2.85 | 167.6 |
| | x 30.5 | 2.83 | 185.6 |
| | x 26.5 | 2.51 | 189.4 |
| | x 24 | 2.49 | 207.5 |
| | x 21.5 | 2.47 | 229.8 |
| | x 19 | 2.31 | 243.2 |
| | x 17 | 2.29 | 269.4 |
| | x 15 | 2.28 | 304.0 |
| | x 13 | 2.00 | 307.7 |
| | x 11 | 1.98 | 360.0 |
| ST 6 | x 95 | 3.31 | 69.7 |
| | x 80.5 | 3.24 | 80.5 |
| | x 66.5 | 3.18 | 97.8 |
| | x 60 | 3.15 | 105.6 |
| | x 53 | 3.11 | 117.4 |
| | x 49.5 | 3.10 | 125.3 |
| | x 46 | 3.08 | 133.9 |
| | x 42.5 | 3.06 | 144.0 |
| | x 39.5 | 3.05 | 154.4 |
| | x 36 | 3.03 | 168.3 |
| | x 32.5 | 3.01 | 185.2 |
| | x 29 | 2.69 | 185.5 |
| | x 26.5 | 2.67 | 201.5 |
| | x 25 | 2.36 | 188.8 |
| | x 22.5 | 2.35 | 208.9 |

| Section designation | | Surface area per foot of length | Surface area per ton |
|---|---|---|---|
| ST 6 | x 20 | 2.33 | 233.0 |
| | x 18 | 2.11 | 234.4 |
| | x 15.5 | 2.10 | 271.0 |
| | x 13.5 | 2.08 | 308.1 |
| | x 11 | 1.70 | 309.1 |
| | x 9.5 | 1.68 | 353.7 |
| | x 8.25 | 1.67 | 404.8 |
| | x 7 | 1.65 | 471.4 |
| ST 5 | x 56 | 2.68 | 95.7 |
| | x 50 | 2.65 | 106.0 |
| | x 44.5 | 2.62 | 117.8 |
| | x 38.5 | 2.58 | 134.0 |
| | x 36 | 2.57 | 142.8 |
| | x 33 | 2.55 | 154.5 |
| | x 30 | 2.53 | 168.7 |
| | x 27 | 2.51 | 185.9 |
| | x 24.5 | 2.50 | 204.1 |
| | x 22.5 | 2.18 | 193.8 |
| | x 19.5 | 2.16 | 221.5 |
| | x 16.5 | 2.14 | 259.4 |
| | x 14.5 | 1.82 | 251.0 |
| | x 12.5 | 1.80 | 288.0 |
| | x 10.5 | 1.78 | 339.0 |
| | x 9.5 | 1.53 | 322.1 |
| | x 8.5 | 1.51 | 355.3 |
| | x 7.5 | 1.50 | 400.0 |
| | x 5.75 | 1.48 | 514.8 |
| ST 4 | x 33.5 | 2.13 | 127.7 |
| | x 29 | 2.10 | 144.8 |
| | x 24 | 2.06 | 171.7 |
| | x 20 | 2.03 | 203.0 |
| | x 17.5 | 2.01 | 229.7 |
| | x 15.5 | 2.00 | 258.1 |
| | x 14 | 1.76 | 251.4 |
| | x 12 | 1.75 | 291.7 |
| | x 10 | 1.56 | 312.0 |
| | x 8.5 | 1.54 | 362.4 |
| | x 7.5 | 1.35 | 360.0 |
| | x 6.5 | 1.33 | 409.2 |
| | x 5 | 1.31 | 524.0 |

**Figure 23 (cont'd)**
Structural steel conversion table

| Section designation | | Surface area per foot of length | Surface area per ton |
|---|---|---|---|
| ST 3 | x 12.5 | 1.55 | 248.0 |
| | x 10 | 1.52 | 304.0 |
| | x 7.75 | 1.50 | 387.1 |
| | x 8 | 1.19 | 297.5 |
| | x 6 | 1.17 | 390.0 |
| | x 4.25 | 1.14 | 536.5 |
| ST 2.5 | x 9.25 | 1.26 | 272.4 |
| | x 8 | 1.25 | 312.5 |
| ST 2 | x 6.5 | 1.02 | 313.8 |

**Tees cut from American standard shapes**

| Section designation | | Surface area per foot of length | Surface area per ton |
|---|---|---|---|
| ST 12 | x 60 | 3.34 | 111.3 |
| | x 52.95 | 3.31 | 125.0 |
| | x 50 | 3.21 | 128.4 |
| | x 45 | 3.19 | 141.8 |
| | x 39.95 | 3.17 | 158.7 |
| ST 10 | x 47.5 | 2.87 | 120.8 |
| | x 42.5 | 2.84 | 133.6 |
| | x 37.5 | 2.73 | 145.6 |
| | x 32.7 | 2.70 | 165.1 |
| ST 9 | x 35 | 2.54 | 145.1 |
| | x 27.35 | 2.50 | 182.8 |
| ST 7.5 | x 25 | 2.19 | 175.2 |
| | x 21.45 | 2.17 | 202.3 |

| Section designation | | Surface area per foot of length | Surface area per ton |
|---|---|---|---|
| ST 6 | x 25 | 1.91 | 152.8 |
| | x 20.4 | 1.88 | 184.3 |
| | x 17.5 | 1.85 | 211.4 |
| | x 15.9 | 1.83 | 230.2 |
| ST 5 | x 17.5 | 1.66 | 189.7 |
| | x 12.7 | 1.61 | 253.5 |
| ST 4 | x 11.5 | 1.36 | 236.5 |
| | x 9.2 | 1.33 | 289.1 |
| ST 3.5 | x 10 | 1.23 | 246.0 |
| | x 7.65 | 1.19 | 311.0 |
| ST 3 | x 8.625 | 1.09 | 252.8 |
| | x 6.25 | 1.06 | 339.2 |
| ST 2.5 | x 7.375 | .96 | 260.3 |
| | x 5 | .92 | 368.0 |
| ST 2 | x 4.75 | .80 | 336.8 |
| | x 3.85 | .78 | 405.2 |

**Miscellaneous tee (cut from M5 x 18.9)**

| | | | |
|---|---|---|---|
| MT 2.5 | x 9.45 | .83 | 175.7 |

**Figure 23 (cont'd)**
Structural steel conversion table

*Industrial, Institutional and Heavy Commercial Costs*

| Section designation | | | Surface area per foot of length | Surface area per ton |
|---|---|---|---|---|
| L 8 | x 8 | x 1-1/8 | 2.67 | 93.8 |
|  | x 8 | x 1 | 2.67 | 104.7 |
|  | x 8 | x 1 | 2.67 | 118.7 |
|  | x 8 | x 7/8 | 2.67 | 118.7 |
|  | x 8 | x 3/4 | 2.67 | 137.3 |
|  | x 8 | x 5/8 | 2.67 | 163.3 |
|  | x 8 | x 9/16 | 2.67 | 180.4 |
|  | x 8 | x 1/2 | 2.67 | 202.3 |
| L 6 | x 6 | x 1 | 2.00 | 107.0 |
|  | x 6 | x 7/8 | 2.00 | 120.8 |
|  | x 6 | x 3/4 | 2.00 | 139.4 |
|  | x 6 | x 5/8 | 2.00 | 165.3 |
|  | x 6 | x 9/16 | 2.00 | 182.6 |
|  | x 6 | x 1/2 | 2.00 | 204.1 |
|  | x 6 | x 7/16 | 2.00 | 232.6 |
|  | x 6 | x 3/8 | 2.00 | 268.5 |
|  | x 6 | x 5/16 | 2.00 | 322.6 |
| L 5 | x 5 | x 7/8 | 1.67 | 122.8 |
|  | x 5 | x 3/4 | 1.67 | 141.5 |
|  | x 5 | x 5/8 | 1.67 | 167.0 |
|  | x 5 | x 1/2 | 1.67 | 206.2 |
|  | x 5 | x 7/16 | 1.67 | 233.6 |
|  | x 5 | x 3/8 | 1.67 | 271.5 |
|  | x 5 | x 5/16 | 1.67 | 324.3 |
| L 4 | x 4 | x 3/4 | 1.33 | 143.8 |
|  | x 4 | x 5/8 | 1.33 | 169.4 |
|  | x 4 | x 1/2 | 1.33 | 207.8 |
|  | x 4 | x 7/16 | 1.33 | 235.4 |
|  | x 4 | x 3/8 | 1.33 | 271.4 |
|  | x 4 | x 5/16 | 1.33 | 324.4 |
|  | x 4 | x 1/4 | 1.33 | 403.0 |
| L 3-1/2 | x 3/1/2 | x 1/2 | 1.17 | 210.8 |
|  | x 3-1/2 | x 7/16 | 1.17 | 238.8 |
|  | x 3-1/2 | x 3/8 | 1.17 | 275.3 |
|  | x 3-1/2 | x 5/16 | 1.17 | 325.0 |
|  | x 3-1/2 | x 1/4 | 1.17 | 403.4 |

| Section designation | | | Surface area per foot of length | Surface area per ton |
|---|---|---|---|---|
| L 3 | x 3 | x 1/2 | 1.00 | 212.8 |
|  | x 3 | x 7/16 | 1.00 | 241.0 |
|  | x 3 | x 3/8 | 1.00 | 277.8 |
|  | x 3 | x 5/16 | 1.00 | 327.9 |
|  | x 3 | x 1/4 | 1.00 | 408.2 |
|  | x 3 | x 3/16 | 1.00 | 539.1 |
| L 2-1/2 | x 2-1/2 | x 1/2 | .83 | 215.6 |
|  | x 2-1/2 | x 3/8 | .83 | 281.4 |
|  | x 2-1/2 | x 5/16 | .83 | 332.0 |
|  | x 2-1/2 | x 1/4 | .83 | 404.9 |
|  | x 2-1/2 | x 3/16 | .83 | 540.7 |
| L 2 | x 2 | x 3/8 | .67 | 285.1 |
|  | x 2 | x 5/16 | .67 | 341.8 |
|  | x 2 | x 1/4 | .67 | 420.1 |
|  | x 2 | x 3/16 | .67 | 549.2 |
|  | x 2 | x 1/8 | .67 | 812.1 |
| L 1-3/4 | x 1-3/4 | x 1/4 | .58 | 418.8 |
|  | x 1-3/4 | x 3/16 | .58 | 547.2 |
|  | x 1-3/4 | x 1/8 | .58 | 805.6 |
| L 1-1/2 | x 1-1/2 | x 1/4 | .50 | 427.4 |
|  | x 1-1/2 | x 3/16 | .50 | 555.6 |
|  | x 1-1/2 | x 5/32 | .50 | 657.9 |
|  | x 1-1/2 | x 1/8 | .50 | 813.0 |
| L 1-1/4 | x 1-1/4 | x 1/4 | .42 | 437.5 |
|  | x 1-1/4 | x 3/16 | .42 | 567.6 |
|  | x 1-1/4 | x 1/8 | .42 | 831.7 |
| L 1 | x 1 | x 1/4 | .33 | 443.0 |
|  | x 1 | x 3/16 | .33 | 569.0 |
|  | x 1 | x 1/8 | .33 | 825.0 |

**Figure 23 (cont'd)**
Structural steel conversion table

## National Painting Cost Estimator

| Section designation | | | Surface area per foot of length | Surface area per ton |
|---|---|---|---|---|
| L 9 | x 4 | x 1 | 2.17 | 106.4 |
| | x 4 | x 7/8 | 2.17 | 120.2 |
| | x 4 | x 3/4 | 2.17 | 138.7 |
| | x 4 | x 5/8 | 2.17 | 165.0 |
| | x 4 | x 9/16 | 2.17 | 182.4 |
| | x 4 | x 1/2 | 2.17 | 203.8 |
| L 8 | x 6 | x 1 | 2.33 | 105.4 |
| | x 6 | x 7/8 | 2.33 | 119.2 |
| | x 6 | x 3/4 | 2.33 | 137.9 |
| | x 6 | x 5/8 | 2.33 | 163.5 |
| | x 6 | x 9/16 | 2.33 | 181.3 |
| | x 6 | x 1/2 | 2.33 | 202.6 |
| | x 6 | x 7/16 | 2.33 | 230.7 |
| L 8 | x 4 | x 1 | 2.00 | 107.0 |
| | x 4 | x 7/8 | 2.00 | 120.8 |
| | x 4 | x 3/4 | 2.00 | 139.4 |
| | x 4 | x 5/8 | 2.00 | 165.3 |
| | x 4 | x 9/16 | 2.00 | 182.6 |
| | x 4 | x 1/2 | 2.00 | 204.1 |
| | x 4 | x 7/16 | 2.00 | 232.6 |
| L 7 | x 4 | x 7/8 | 1.83 | 121.2 |
| | x 4 | x 3/4 | 1.83 | 139.7 |
| | x 4 | x 5/8 | 1.83 | 165.6 |
| | x 4 | x 9/16 | 1.83 | 183.0 |
| | x 4 | x 1/2 | 1.83 | 204.5 |
| | x 4 | x 7/16 | 1.83 | 231.6 |
| | x 4 | x 3/8 | 1.83 | 269.1 |
| L 6 | x 4 | x 7/8 | 1.67 | 122.8 |
| | x 4 | x 3/4 | 1.67 | 141.5 |
| | x 4 | x 5/8 | 1.67 | 167.0 |
| | x 4 | x 9/16 | 1.67 | 184.5 |
| | x 4 | x 1/2 | 1.67 | 206.2 |
| | x 4 | x 7/16 | 1.67 | 233.6 |
| | x 4 | x 3/8 | 1.67 | 271.5 |
| | x 4 | x 5/16 | 1.67 | 324.3 |
| | x 4 | x 1/4 | 1.67 | 402.4 |
| L 6 | x 3-1/2 | x 1/2 | 1.58 | 206.5 |
| | x 3-1/2 | x 3/8 | 1.58 | 270.1 |
| | x 3-1/2 | x 5/16 | 1.58 | 322.4 |
| | x 3-1/2 | x 1/4 | 1.58 | 400.0 |

| Section designation | | | Surface area per foot of length | Surface area per ton |
|---|---|---|---|---|
| L 5 | x 3-1/2 | x 3/4 | 1.42 | 143.4 |
| | x 3-1/2 | x 5/8 | 1.42 | 169.0 |
| | x 3-1/2 | x 1/2 | 1.42 | 208.8 |
| | x 3-1/2 | x 7/16 | 1.42 | 236.7 |
| | x 3-1/2 | x 3/8 | 1.42 | 273.1 |
| | x 3-1/2 | x 5/16 | 1.42 | 326.4 |
| | x 3-1/2 | x 1/4 | 1.42 | 405.7 |
| L 5 | x 3 | x 1/2 | 1.33 | 207.8 |
| | x 3 | x 7/16 | 1.33 | 235.4 |
| | x 3 | x 3/8 | 1.33 | 271.4 |
| | x 3 | x 5/16 | 1.33 | 324.4 |
| | x 3 | x 1/4 | 1.33 | 403.0 |
| L 4 | x 3-1/2 | x 5/8 | 1.25 | 170.1 |
| | x 3-1/2 | x 1/2 | 1.25 | 210.1 |
| | x 3-1/2 | x 7/16 | 1.25 | 235.8 |
| | x 3-1/2 | x 3/8 | 1.25 | 274.7 |
| | x 3-1/2 | x 5/16 | 1.25 | 324.7 |
| | x 3-1/2 | x 1/4 | 1.25 | 403.2 |
| L 4 | x 3 | x 5/8 | 1.17 | 172.1 |
| | x 3 | x 1/2 | 1.17 | 210.8 |
| | x 3 | x 7/16 | 1.17 | 238.8 |
| | x 3 | x 3/8 | 1.17 | 275.3 |
| | x 3 | x 5/16 | 1.17 | 325.0 |
| | x 3 | x 1/4 | 1.17 | 403.4 |
| L 3-1/2 | x 3 | x 1/2 | 1.08 | 211.8 |
| | x 3 | x 7/16 | 1.08 | 237.4 |
| | x 3 | x 3/8 | 1.08 | 273.4 |
| | x 3 | x 5/16 | 1.08 | 327.3 |
| | x 3 | x 1/4 | 1.08 | 400.0 |
| L 3-1/2 | x 2-1/2 | x 1/2 | 1.00 | 212.8 |
| | x 2-1/2 | x 7/16 | 1.00 | 241.0 |
| | x 2-1/2 | x 3/8 | 1.00 | 277.8 |
| | x 2-1/2 | x 5/16 | 1.00 | 327.9 |
| | x 2-1/2 | x 1/4 | 1.00 | 408.2 |
| L 3 | x 2-1/2 | x 1/2 | .92 | 216.5 |
| | x 2-1/2 | x 7/16 | .92 | 242.1 |
| | x 2-1/2 | x 3/8 | .92 | 278.8 |
| | x 2-1/2 | x 5/16 | .92 | 328.6 |
| | x 2-1/2 | x 1/4 | .92 | 408.9 |
| | x 2-1/2 | x 3/16 | .92 | 542.8 |

**Figure 23 (cont'd)**
Structural steel conversion table

*Industrial, Institutional and Heavy Commercial Costs*

| Section designation | | | Surface area per foot of length | Surface area per ton |
|---|---|---|---|---|
| L 3 | x 2 | x 1/2 | .83 | 215.6 |
| | x 2 | x 7/16 | .83 | 244.1 |
| | x 2 | x 3/8 | .83 | 281.4 |
| | x 2 | x 5/16 | .83 | 332.0 |
| | x 2 | x 1/4 | .83 | 404.9 |
| | x 2 | x 3/16 | .83 | 540.7 |
| L 2-1/2 | x 2 | x 3/8 | .75 | 283.0 |
| | x 2 | x 5/16 | .75 | 333.3 |
| | x 2 | x 1/4 | .75 | 414.4 |
| | x 2 | x 3/16 | .75 | 545.5 |
| L 2-1/2 | x 1-1/2 | x 5/16 | .67 | 341.8 |
| | x 1-1/2 | x 1/4 | .67 | 420.1 |
| | x 1-1/2 | x 3/16 | .67 | 549.2 |

Courtesy: Richardson Engineering Services, Inc.

| Section designation | | | Surface area per foot of length | Surface area per ton |
|---|---|---|---|---|
| L 2 | x 1-1/2 | x 1/4 | .58 | 418.8 |
| | x 1-1/2 | x 3/16 | .58 | 547.2 |
| | x 1-1/2 | x 1/8 | .58 | 805.6 |
| L 2 | x 1-1/4 | x 1/4 | .54 | 423.5 |
| | x 1-1/4 | x 3/16 | .54 | 551.0 |
| L 1-3/4 | x 1-1/4 | x 1/4 | .50 | 427.4 |
| | x 1-1/4 | x 3/16 | .50 | 555.6 |
| | x 1-1/4 | x 1/8 | .50 | 813.0 |

**Figure 23 (cont'd)**
Structural steel conversion table

| Diameter (in feet) | Area (SF) |
|---|---|
| 10 | 314 |
| 15 | 707 |
| 20 | 1,257 |
| 25 | 1,963 |
| 30 | 2,827 |
| 35 | 3,848 |
| 40 | 5,027 |
| 45 | 6,362 |
| 50 | 7,854 |
| 55 | 9,503 |
| 60 | 11,310 |
| 65 | 13,273 |
| 70 | 15,394 |

**Figure 24**
Surface area of spheres

*National Painting Cost Estimator*

|  | Labor SF per manhour | Material coverage SF/gallon | Material cost per gallon | Labor cost per 100 SF | Labor burden 100 SF | Material cost per 100 SF | Overhead per 100 SF | Profit per 100 SF | Total price per 100 SF |
|---|---|---|---|---|---|---|---|---|---|

## Tank, silo, vessel, or hopper, brush, exterior walls only

**Metal primer, rust inhibitor - clean metal (material #35)**
Brush prime coat

| | | | | | | | | | |
|---|---|---|---|---|---|---|---|---|---|
| Slow | 150 | 425 | 59.70 | 13.50 | 3.99 | 14.05 | 5.99 | 6.00 | 43.53 |
| Medium | 175 | 400 | 52.20 | 14.71 | 5.20 | 13.05 | 8.24 | 4.95 | 46.15 |
| Fast | 200 | 375 | 44.80 | 15.75 | 6.43 | 11.95 | 10.58 | 3.13 | 47.84 |

**Metal primer, rust inhibitor - rusty metal (material #36)**
Brush prime coat

| | | | | | | | | | |
|---|---|---|---|---|---|---|---|---|---|
| Slow | 150 | 400 | 72.30 | 13.50 | 3.99 | 18.08 | 6.76 | 6.77 | 49.10 |
| Medium | 175 | 375 | 63.30 | 14.71 | 5.20 | 16.88 | 9.20 | 5.52 | 51.51 |
| Fast | 200 | 350 | 54.20 | 15.75 | 6.43 | 15.49 | 11.68 | 3.45 | 52.80 |

**Industrial enamel, oil base, high gloss - light colors (material #56)**
Brush 1st or additional finish coats

| | | | | | | | | | |
|---|---|---|---|---|---|---|---|---|---|
| Slow | 200 | 450 | 61.00 | 10.13 | 2.98 | 13.56 | 5.07 | 5.08 | 36.82 |
| Medium | 225 | 425 | 53.40 | 11.44 | 4.04 | 12.56 | 7.01 | 4.21 | 39.26 |
| Fast | 250 | 400 | 45.80 | 12.60 | 5.14 | 11.45 | 9.05 | 2.68 | 40.92 |

**Industrial enamel, oil base, high gloss - dark (OSHA) colors (material #57)**
Brush 1st or additional finish coats

| | | | | | | | | | |
|---|---|---|---|---|---|---|---|---|---|
| Slow | 200 | 475 | 67.60 | 10.13 | 2.98 | 14.23 | 5.20 | 5.21 | 37.75 |
| Medium | 225 | 450 | 59.10 | 11.44 | 4.04 | 13.13 | 7.16 | 4.29 | 40.06 |
| Fast | 250 | 425 | 50.70 | 12.60 | 5.14 | 11.93 | 9.20 | 2.72 | 41.59 |

**Epoxy coating, 2 part system, clear (material #51)**
Brush 1st coat

| | | | | | | | | | |
|---|---|---|---|---|---|---|---|---|---|
| Slow | 150 | 425 | 146.90 | 13.50 | 3.99 | 34.56 | 9.89 | 9.91 | 71.85 |
| Medium | 175 | 400 | 128.60 | 14.71 | 5.20 | 32.15 | 13.02 | 7.81 | 72.89 |
| Fast | 200 | 375 | 110.20 | 15.75 | 6.43 | 29.39 | 15.99 | 4.73 | 72.29 |

Brush 2nd or additional coats

| | | | | | | | | | |
|---|---|---|---|---|---|---|---|---|---|
| Slow | 200 | 450 | 146.90 | 10.13 | 2.98 | 32.64 | 8.69 | 8.71 | 63.15 |
| Medium | 225 | 425 | 128.60 | 11.44 | 4.04 | 30.26 | 11.44 | 6.86 | 64.04 |
| Fast | 250 | 400 | 110.20 | 12.60 | 5.14 | 27.55 | 14.04 | 4.15 | 63.48 |

**Epoxy coating, 2 part system, white (material #52)**
Brush 1st coat

| | | | | | | | | | |
|---|---|---|---|---|---|---|---|---|---|
| Slow | 150 | 425 | 177.00 | 13.50 | 3.99 | 41.65 | 11.23 | 11.26 | 81.63 |
| Medium | 175 | 400 | 154.90 | 14.71 | 5.20 | 38.73 | 14.66 | 8.80 | 82.10 |
| Fast | 200 | 375 | 132.70 | 15.75 | 6.43 | 35.39 | 17.85 | 5.28 | 80.70 |

Brush 2nd or additional coats

| | | | | | | | | | |
|---|---|---|---|---|---|---|---|---|---|
| Slow | 200 | 450 | 177.00 | 10.13 | 2.98 | 39.33 | 9.97 | 9.99 | 72.40 |
| Medium | 225 | 425 | 154.90 | 11.44 | 4.04 | 36.45 | 12.99 | 7.79 | 72.71 |
| Fast | 250 | 400 | 132.70 | 12.60 | 5.14 | 33.18 | 15.79 | 4.67 | 71.38 |

*Industrial, Institutional and Heavy Commercial Costs*

| | Labor SF per manhour | Material coverage SF/gallon | Material cost per gallon | Labor cost per 100 SF | Labor burden 100 SF | Material cost per 100 SF | Overhead per 100 SF | Profit per 100 SF | Total price per 100 SF |
|---|---|---|---|---|---|---|---|---|---|
| **Vinyl coating (material #59)** | | | | | | | | | |
| Brush 1st coat | | | | | | | | | |
| Slow | 125 | 250 | 106.40 | 16.20 | 4.78 | 42.56 | 12.07 | 12.10 | 87.71 |
| Medium | 150 | 238 | 93.10 | 17.17 | 6.09 | 39.12 | 15.59 | 9.36 | 87.33 |
| Fast | 175 | 225 | 79.80 | 18.00 | 7.32 | 35.47 | 18.85 | 5.58 | 85.22 |
| Brush 2nd or additional coats | | | | | | | | | |
| Slow | 165 | 150 | 106.40 | 12.27 | 3.62 | 70.93 | 16.50 | 16.53 | 119.85 |
| Medium | 190 | 125 | 93.10 | 13.55 | 4.79 | 74.48 | 23.21 | 13.92 | 129.95 |
| Fast | 215 | 100 | 79.80 | 14.65 | 5.97 | 79.80 | 31.13 | 9.21 | 140.76 |

See Figure 24 on page 399 to find the surface area of a spherical vessel. Use this table when estimating walls only. The cost tables for painting steel tank, silo, vessel or hopper roofs follow those for painting walls. For heights above 8 feet, use the High Time Difficulty Factors on page 139. Note: A two coat system, prime and finish, using oil base material is recommended for any metal surface. Using water base material may cause oxidation, corrosion and rust. One coat of oil base paint on metal surfaces may result in cracking, peeling or chipping without the proper prime coat application. If off-white or another light-colored finish paint is specified, make sure the prime coat is also a light color, or more than one finish coat will be necessary. "Slow" work is based on an hourly wage of $20.25, "Medium" work on an hourly wage of $25.75, and "Fast" work on an hourly wage of $31.50. Other qualifications that apply to this table are on page 9.

|  | Labor SF per manhour | Material coverage SF/gallon | Material cost per gallon | Labor cost per 100 SF | Labor burden 100 SF | Material cost per 100 SF | Overhead per 100 SF | Profit per 100 SF | Total price per 100 SF |
|---|---|---|---|---|---|---|---|---|---|

## Tank, silo, vessel, or hopper, roll, exterior walls only

### Metal primer, rust inhibitor - clean metal (material #35)
#### Roll prime coat

| | | | | | | | | | |
|---|---|---|---|---|---|---|---|---|---|
| Slow | 275 | 400 | 59.70 | 7.36 | 2.18 | 14.93 | 4.65 | 4.66 | 33.78 |
| Medium | 300 | 375 | 52.20 | 8.58 | 3.03 | 13.92 | 6.39 | 3.83 | 35.75 |
| Fast | 325 | 350 | 44.80 | 9.69 | 3.97 | 12.80 | 8.20 | 2.42 | 37.08 |

### Metal primer, rust inhibitor - rusty metal (material #36)
#### Roll prime coat

| | | | | | | | | | |
|---|---|---|---|---|---|---|---|---|---|
| Slow | 275 | 380 | 72.30 | 7.36 | 2.18 | 19.03 | 5.43 | 5.44 | 39.44 |
| Medium | 300 | 355 | 63.30 | 8.58 | 3.03 | 17.83 | 7.36 | 4.42 | 41.22 |
| Fast | 325 | 330 | 54.20 | 9.69 | 3.97 | 16.42 | 9.32 | 2.76 | 42.16 |

### Industrial enamel, oil base, high gloss - light colors (material #56)
#### Roll 1st or additional finish coats

| | | | | | | | | | |
|---|---|---|---|---|---|---|---|---|---|
| Slow | 375 | 425 | 61.00 | 5.40 | 1.60 | 14.35 | 4.05 | 4.06 | 29.46 |
| Medium | 400 | 400 | 53.40 | 6.44 | 2.28 | 13.35 | 5.52 | 3.31 | 30.90 |
| Fast | 425 | 375 | 45.80 | 7.41 | 3.01 | 12.21 | 7.02 | 2.08 | 31.73 |

### Industrial enamel, oil base, high gloss - dark (OSHA) colors (material #57)
#### Roll 1st or additional finish coats

| | | | | | | | | | |
|---|---|---|---|---|---|---|---|---|---|
| Slow | 375 | 450 | 67.60 | 5.40 | 1.60 | 15.02 | 4.18 | 4.19 | 30.39 |
| Medium | 400 | 425 | 59.10 | 6.44 | 2.28 | 13.91 | 5.66 | 3.39 | 31.68 |
| Fast | 425 | 400 | 50.70 | 7.41 | 3.01 | 12.68 | 7.16 | 2.12 | 32.38 |

### Epoxy coating, 2 part system, clear (material #51)
#### Roll 1st coat

| | | | | | | | | | |
|---|---|---|---|---|---|---|---|---|---|
| Slow | 275 | 425 | 146.90 | 7.36 | 2.18 | 34.56 | 8.38 | 8.40 | 60.88 |
| Medium | 300 | 400 | 128.60 | 8.58 | 3.03 | 32.15 | 10.94 | 6.57 | 61.27 |
| Fast | 325 | 375 | 110.20 | 9.69 | 3.97 | 29.39 | 13.34 | 3.95 | 60.34 |

#### Roll 2nd or additional coats

| | | | | | | | | | |
|---|---|---|---|---|---|---|---|---|---|
| Slow | 375 | 450 | 146.90 | 5.40 | 1.60 | 32.64 | 7.53 | 7.55 | 54.72 |
| Medium | 400 | 425 | 128.60 | 6.44 | 2.28 | 30.26 | 9.75 | 5.85 | 54.58 |
| Fast | 425 | 400 | 110.20 | 7.41 | 3.01 | 27.55 | 11.77 | 3.48 | 53.22 |

*Industrial, Institutional and Heavy Commercial Costs*

|  | Labor SF per manhour | Material coverage SF/gallon | Material cost per gallon | Labor cost per 100 SF | Labor burden 100 SF | Material cost per 100 SF | Overhead per 100 SF | Profit per 100 SF | Total price per 100 SF |
|---|---|---|---|---|---|---|---|---|---|
| **Epoxy coating, 2 part system, white (material #52)** | | | | | | | | | |
| Roll 1st coat | | | | | | | | | |
| Slow | 275 | 425 | 177.00 | 7.36 | 2.18 | 41.65 | 9.72 | 9.74 | 70.65 |
| Medium | 300 | 400 | 154.90 | 8.58 | 3.03 | 38.73 | 12.59 | 7.55 | 70.48 |
| Fast | 325 | 375 | 132.70 | 9.69 | 3.97 | 35.39 | 15.20 | 4.50 | 68.75 |
| Roll 2nd or additional coats | | | | | | | | | |
| Slow | 375 | 450 | 177.00 | 5.40 | 1.60 | 39.33 | 8.80 | 8.82 | 63.95 |
| Medium | 400 | 425 | 154.90 | 6.44 | 2.28 | 36.45 | 11.29 | 6.78 | 63.24 |
| Fast | 425 | 400 | 132.70 | 7.41 | 3.01 | 33.18 | 13.52 | 4.00 | 61.12 |

See Figure 24 on page 399 to find the surface area of a spherical vessel. Use this table when estimating walls only. The cost tables for painting steel tank, silo, vessel or hopper roofs follow those for painting walls. For heights above 8 feet, use the High Time Difficulty Factors on page 139. Note: A two coat system, prime and finish, using oil base material is recommended for any metal surface. Using water base material may cause oxidation, corrosion and rust. One coat of oil base paint on metal surfaces may result in cracking, peeling or chipping without the proper prime coat application. If off-white or another light-colored finish paint is specified, make sure the prime coat is also a light color, or more than one finish coat will be necessary. "Slow" work is based on an hourly wage of $20.25, "Medium" work on an hourly wage of $25.75, and "Fast" work on an hourly wage of $31.50. Other qualifications that apply to this table are on page 9.

|  | Labor SF per manhour | Material coverage SF/gallon | Material cost per gallon | Labor cost per 100 SF | Labor burden 100 SF | Material cost per 100 SF | Overhead per 100 SF | Profit per 100 SF | Total price per 100 SF |
|---|---|---|---|---|---|---|---|---|---|

## Tank, silo, vessel, or hopper, spray, exterior walls only

### Metal primer, rust inhibitor - clean metal (material #35)
Spray prime coat
| | | | | | | | | | |
|---|---|---|---|---|---|---|---|---|---|
| Slow | 700 | 325 | 59.70 | 2.89 | .86 | 18.37 | 4.20 | 4.21 | 30.53 |
| Medium | 750 | 300 | 52.20 | 3.43 | 1.21 | 17.40 | 5.51 | 3.31 | 30.86 |
| Fast | 800 | 275 | 44.80 | 3.94 | 1.60 | 16.29 | 6.77 | 2.00 | 30.60 |

### Metal primer, rust inhibitor - rusty metal (material #36)
Spray prime coat
| | | | | | | | | | |
|---|---|---|---|---|---|---|---|---|---|
| Slow | 700 | 300 | 72.30 | 2.89 | .86 | 24.10 | 5.29 | 5.30 | 38.44 |
| Medium | 750 | 275 | 63.30 | 3.43 | 1.21 | 23.02 | 6.92 | 4.15 | 38.73 |
| Fast | 800 | 250 | 54.20 | 3.94 | 1.60 | 21.68 | 8.44 | 2.50 | 38.16 |

### Industrial enamel, oil base, high gloss - light colors (material #56)
Spray 1st or additional finish coats
| | | | | | | | | | |
|---|---|---|---|---|---|---|---|---|---|
| Slow | 850 | 350 | 61.00 | 2.38 | .71 | 17.43 | 3.90 | 3.91 | 28.33 |
| Medium | 900 | 325 | 53.40 | 2.86 | 1.01 | 16.43 | 5.08 | 3.05 | 28.43 |
| Fast | 950 | 300 | 45.80 | 3.32 | 1.34 | 15.27 | 6.18 | 1.83 | 27.94 |

### Industrial enamel, oil base, high gloss - dark (OSHA) colors (material #57)
Spray 1st or additional finish coats
| | | | | | | | | | |
|---|---|---|---|---|---|---|---|---|---|
| Slow | 850 | 375 | 67.60 | 2.38 | .71 | 18.03 | 4.01 | 4.02 | 29.15 |
| Medium | 900 | 350 | 59.10 | 2.86 | 1.01 | 16.89 | 5.19 | 3.11 | 29.06 |
| Fast | 950 | 325 | 50.70 | 3.32 | 1.34 | 15.60 | 6.28 | 1.86 | 28.40 |

### Epoxy coating, 2 part system, clear (material #51)
Spray 1st coat
| | | | | | | | | | |
|---|---|---|---|---|---|---|---|---|---|
| Slow | 700 | 325 | 146.90 | 2.89 | .86 | 45.20 | 9.30 | 9.32 | 67.57 |
| Medium | 750 | 313 | 128.60 | 3.43 | 1.21 | 41.09 | 11.43 | 6.86 | 64.02 |
| Fast | 800 | 300 | 110.20 | 3.94 | 1.60 | 36.73 | 13.11 | 3.88 | 59.26 |

Spray 2nd or additional coats
| | | | | | | | | | |
|---|---|---|---|---|---|---|---|---|---|
| Slow | 850 | 350 | 146.90 | 2.38 | .71 | 41.97 | 8.56 | 8.58 | 62.20 |
| Medium | 900 | 338 | 128.60 | 2.86 | 1.01 | 38.05 | 10.48 | 6.29 | 58.69 |
| Fast | 950 | 325 | 110.20 | 3.32 | 1.34 | 33.91 | 11.96 | 3.54 | 54.07 |

### Epoxy coating, 2 part system, white (material #52)
Spray 1st coat
| | | | | | | | | | |
|---|---|---|---|---|---|---|---|---|---|
| Slow | 700 | 325 | 177.00 | 2.89 | .86 | 54.46 | 11.06 | 11.08 | 80.35 |
| Medium | 750 | 313 | 154.90 | 3.43 | 1.21 | 49.49 | 13.53 | 8.12 | 75.78 |
| Fast | 800 | 300 | 132.70 | 3.94 | 1.60 | 44.23 | 15.43 | 4.56 | 69.76 |

Spray 2nd or additional coats
| | | | | | | | | | |
|---|---|---|---|---|---|---|---|---|---|
| Slow | 850 | 350 | 177.00 | 2.38 | .71 | 50.57 | 10.19 | 10.21 | 74.06 |
| Medium | 900 | 338 | 154.90 | 2.86 | 1.01 | 45.83 | 12.43 | 7.46 | 69.59 |
| Fast | 950 | 325 | 132.70 | 3.32 | 1.34 | 40.83 | 14.11 | 4.17 | 63.77 |

*Industrial, Institutional and Heavy Commercial Costs*

|  | Labor SF per manhour | Material coverage SF/gallon | Material cost per gallon | Labor cost per 100 SF | Labor burden 100 SF | Material cost per 100 SF | Overhead per 100 SF | Profit per 100 SF | Total price per 100 SF |
|---|---|---|---|---|---|---|---|---|---|
| **Vinyl coating (material #59)** | | | | | | | | | |
| Spray 1st coat | | | | | | | | | |
| Slow | 600 | 225 | 106.40 | 3.38 | 1.00 | 47.29 | 9.82 | 9.84 | 71.33 |
| Medium | 625 | 213 | 93.10 | 4.12 | 1.46 | 43.71 | 12.32 | 7.39 | 69.00 |
| Fast | 650 | 200 | 79.80 | 4.85 | 1.98 | 39.90 | 14.49 | 4.29 | 65.51 |
| Spray 2nd or additional coats | | | | | | | | | |
| Slow | 725 | 130 | 106.40 | 2.79 | .83 | 81.85 | 16.24 | 16.27 | 117.98 |
| Medium | 750 | 105 | 93.10 | 3.43 | 1.21 | 88.67 | 23.33 | 14.00 | 130.64 |
| Fast | 775 | 80 | 79.80 | 4.06 | 1.66 | 99.75 | 32.70 | 9.67 | 147.84 |

See Figure 24 on page 399 to find the surface area of a spherical vessel. Use this table when estimating walls only. The cost tables for painting steel tank, silo, vessel or hopper roofs follow those for painting walls. For heights above 8 feet, use the High Time Difficulty Factors on page 139. Note: A two coat system, prime and finish, using oil base material is recommended for any metal surface. Using water base material may cause oxidation, corrosion and rust. One coat of oil base paint on metal surfaces may result in cracking, peeling or chipping without the proper prime coat application. If off-white or another light-colored finish paint is specified, make sure the prime coat is also a light color, or more than one finish coat will be necessary. "Slow" work is based on an hourly wage of $20.25, "Medium" work on an hourly wage of $25.75, and "Fast" work on an hourly wage of $31.50. Other qualifications that apply to this table are on page 9.

National Painting Cost Estimator

|  | Labor SF per manhour | Material coverage SF/gallon | Material cost per gallon | Labor cost per 100 SF | Labor burden 100 SF | Material cost per 100 SF | Overhead per 100 SF | Profit per 100 SF | Total price per 100 SF |
|---|---|---|---|---|---|---|---|---|---|

## Tank, silo, vessel, or hopper, brush, exterior roof only

Metal primer, rust inhibitor - clean metal (material #35)
    Brush prime coat

| | | | | | | | | | |
|---|---|---|---|---|---|---|---|---|---|
| Slow | 175 | 425 | 59.70 | 11.57 | 3.40 | 14.05 | 5.52 | 5.53 | 40.07 |
| Medium | 200 | 400 | 52.20 | 12.88 | 4.56 | 13.05 | 7.62 | 4.57 | 42.68 |
| Fast | 225 | 375 | 44.80 | 14.00 | 5.69 | 11.95 | 9.81 | 2.90 | 44.35 |

Metal primer, rust inhibitor - rusty metal (material #36)
    Brush prime coat

| | | | | | | | | | |
|---|---|---|---|---|---|---|---|---|---|
| Slow | 175 | 400 | 72.30 | 11.57 | 3.40 | 18.08 | 6.28 | 6.29 | 45.62 |
| Medium | 200 | 375 | 63.30 | 12.88 | 4.56 | 16.88 | 8.58 | 5.15 | 48.05 |
| Fast | 225 | 350 | 54.20 | 14.00 | 5.69 | 15.49 | 10.91 | 3.23 | 49.32 |

Industrial enamel, oil base, high gloss - light colors (material #56)
    Brush 1st or additional finish coats

| | | | | | | | | | |
|---|---|---|---|---|---|---|---|---|---|
| Slow | 225 | 450 | 61.00 | 9.00 | 2.64 | 13.56 | 4.79 | 4.80 | 34.79 |
| Medium | 250 | 425 | 53.40 | 10.30 | 3.65 | 12.56 | 6.63 | 3.98 | 37.12 |
| Fast | 275 | 400 | 45.80 | 11.45 | 4.69 | 11.45 | 8.55 | 2.53 | 38.67 |

Industrial enamel, oil base, high gloss - dark (OSHA) colors (material #57)
    Brush 1st or additional finish coats

| | | | | | | | | | |
|---|---|---|---|---|---|---|---|---|---|
| Slow | 225 | 475 | 67.60 | 9.00 | 2.64 | 14.23 | 4.92 | 4.93 | 35.72 |
| Medium | 250 | 450 | 59.10 | 10.30 | 3.65 | 13.13 | 6.77 | 4.06 | 37.91 |
| Fast | 275 | 425 | 50.70 | 11.45 | 4.69 | 11.93 | 8.70 | 2.57 | 39.34 |

Epoxy coating, 2 part system, clear (material #51)
    Brush 1st coat

| | | | | | | | | | |
|---|---|---|---|---|---|---|---|---|---|
| Slow | 175 | 425 | 146.90 | 11.57 | 3.40 | 34.56 | 9.41 | 9.43 | 68.37 |
| Medium | 200 | 400 | 128.60 | 12.88 | 4.56 | 32.15 | 12.40 | 7.44 | 69.43 |
| Fast | 225 | 375 | 110.20 | 14.00 | 5.69 | 29.39 | 15.22 | 4.50 | 68.80 |

    Brush 2nd or additional coats

| | | | | | | | | | |
|---|---|---|---|---|---|---|---|---|---|
| Slow | 225 | 450 | 146.90 | 9.00 | 2.64 | 32.64 | 8.42 | 8.44 | 61.14 |
| Medium | 250 | 425 | 128.60 | 10.30 | 3.65 | 30.26 | 11.05 | 6.63 | 61.89 |
| Fast | 275 | 400 | 110.20 | 11.45 | 4.69 | 27.55 | 13.54 | 4.00 | 61.23 |

Epoxy coating, 2 part system, white (material #52)
    Brush 1st coat

| | | | | | | | | | |
|---|---|---|---|---|---|---|---|---|---|
| Slow | 175 | 425 | 177.00 | 11.57 | 3.40 | 41.65 | 10.76 | 10.78 | 78.16 |
| Medium | 200 | 400 | 154.90 | 12.88 | 4.56 | 38.73 | 14.04 | 8.43 | 78.64 |
| Fast | 225 | 375 | 132.70 | 14.00 | 5.69 | 35.39 | 17.08 | 5.05 | 77.21 |

    Brush 2nd or additional coats

| | | | | | | | | | |
|---|---|---|---|---|---|---|---|---|---|
| Slow | 225 | 450 | 177.00 | 9.00 | 2.64 | 39.33 | 9.69 | 9.71 | 70.37 |
| Medium | 250 | 425 | 154.90 | 10.30 | 3.65 | 36.45 | 12.60 | 7.56 | 70.56 |
| Fast | 275 | 400 | 132.70 | 11.45 | 4.69 | 33.18 | 15.28 | 4.52 | 69.12 |

*Industrial, Institutional and Heavy Commercial Costs*

|  | Labor SF per manhour | Material coverage SF/gallon | Material cost per gallon | Labor cost per 100 SF | Labor burden 100 SF | Material cost per 100 SF | Overhead per 100 SF | Profit per 100 SF | Total price per 100 SF |
|---|---|---|---|---|---|---|---|---|---|
| **Vinyl coating (material #59)** | | | | | | | | | |
| Brush 1st coat | | | | | | | | | |
| Slow | 125 | 250 | 106.40 | 16.20 | 4.78 | 42.56 | 12.07 | 12.10 | 87.71 |
| Medium | 150 | 238 | 93.10 | 17.17 | 6.09 | 39.12 | 15.59 | 9.36 | 87.33 |
| Fast | 175 | 225 | 79.80 | 18.00 | 7.32 | 35.47 | 18.85 | 5.58 | 85.22 |
| Brush 2nd or additional coats | | | | | | | | | |
| Slow | 200 | 150 | 106.40 | 10.13 | 2.98 | 70.93 | 15.97 | 16.00 | 116.01 |
| Medium | 225 | 125 | 93.10 | 11.44 | 4.04 | 74.48 | 22.49 | 13.50 | 125.95 |
| Fast | 250 | 100 | 79.80 | 12.60 | 5.14 | 79.80 | 30.24 | 8.94 | 136.72 |

Use these figures to estimate labor and material costs for painting the exterior surface of a flat roof on a steel tank, silo, vessel or hopper. *Rule of thumb*: For a vaulted, peaked or sloping roof, figure the roof area as though it were flat and add 5%. Note: A two coat system, prime and finish, using oil base material is recommended for any metal surface. Using water base material may cause oxidation, corrosion and rust. One coat of oil base paint on metal surfaces may result in cracking, peeling or chipping without the proper prime coat application. If off-white or another light-colored finish paint is specified, make sure the prime coat is also a light color, or more than one finish coat will be necessary. "Slow" work is based on an hourly wage of $20.25, "Medium" work on an hourly wage of $25.75, and "Fast" work on an hourly wage of $31.50. Other qualifications that apply to this table are on page 9.

*National Painting Cost Estimator*

|  | Labor SF per manhour | Material coverage SF/gallon | Material cost per gallon | Labor cost per 100 SF | Labor burden 100 SF | Material cost per 100 SF | Overhead per 100 SF | Profit per 100 SF | Total price per 100 SF |
|---|---|---|---|---|---|---|---|---|---|

## Tank, silo, vessel, or hopper, roll, exterior roof only

### Metal primer, rust inhibitor - clean metal (material #35)
Roll prime coat

| | | | | | | | | | |
|---|---|---|---|---|---|---|---|---|---|
| Slow | 325 | 400 | 59.70 | 6.23 | 1.85 | 14.93 | 4.37 | 4.38 | 31.76 |
| Medium | 350 | 375 | 52.20 | 7.36 | 2.61 | 13.92 | 5.97 | 3.58 | 33.44 |
| Fast | 375 | 350 | 44.80 | 8.40 | 3.44 | 12.80 | 7.64 | 2.26 | 34.54 |

### Metal primer, rust inhibitor - rusty metal (material #36)
Roll prime coat

| | | | | | | | | | |
|---|---|---|---|---|---|---|---|---|---|
| Slow | 325 | 380 | 72.30 | 6.23 | 1.85 | 19.03 | 5.15 | 5.16 | 37.42 |
| Medium | 350 | 355 | 63.30 | 7.36 | 2.61 | 17.83 | 6.95 | 4.17 | 38.92 |
| Fast | 375 | 330 | 54.20 | 8.40 | 3.44 | 16.42 | 8.76 | 2.59 | 39.61 |

### Industrial enamel, oil base, high gloss - light colors (material #56)
Roll 1st or additional finish coats

| | | | | | | | | | |
|---|---|---|---|---|---|---|---|---|---|
| Slow | 400 | 425 | 61.00 | 5.06 | 1.50 | 14.35 | 3.97 | 3.98 | 28.86 |
| Medium | 425 | 400 | 53.40 | 6.06 | 2.13 | 13.35 | 5.39 | 3.23 | 30.16 |
| Fast | 450 | 375 | 45.80 | 7.00 | 2.85 | 12.21 | 6.84 | 2.02 | 30.92 |

### Industrial enamel, oil base, high gloss - dark (OSHA) colors (material #57)
Roll 1st or additional finish coats

| | | | | | | | | | |
|---|---|---|---|---|---|---|---|---|---|
| Slow | 400 | 450 | 67.60 | 5.06 | 1.50 | 15.02 | 4.10 | 4.11 | 29.79 |
| Medium | 425 | 425 | 59.10 | 6.06 | 2.13 | 13.91 | 5.53 | 3.32 | 30.95 |
| Fast | 450 | 400 | 50.70 | 7.00 | 2.85 | 12.68 | 6.99 | 2.07 | 31.59 |

### Epoxy coating, 2 part system, clear (material #51)
Roll 1st coat

| | | | | | | | | | |
|---|---|---|---|---|---|---|---|---|---|
| Slow | 325 | 425 | 146.90 | 6.23 | 1.85 | 34.56 | 8.10 | 8.12 | 58.86 |
| Medium | 350 | 400 | 128.60 | 7.36 | 2.61 | 32.15 | 10.53 | 6.32 | 58.97 |
| Fast | 375 | 375 | 110.20 | 8.40 | 3.44 | 29.39 | 12.78 | 3.78 | 57.79 |

Roll 2nd or additional coats

| | | | | | | | | | |
|---|---|---|---|---|---|---|---|---|---|
| Slow | 400 | 450 | 146.90 | 5.06 | 1.50 | 32.64 | 7.45 | 7.46 | 54.11 |
| Medium | 425 | 425 | 128.60 | 6.06 | 2.13 | 30.26 | 9.62 | 5.77 | 53.84 |
| Fast | 450 | 400 | 110.20 | 7.00 | 2.85 | 27.55 | 11.60 | 3.43 | 52.43 |

*Industrial, Institutional and Heavy Commercial Costs*

| | Labor SF per manhour | Material coverage SF/gallon | Material cost per gallon | Labor cost per 100 SF | Labor burden 100 SF | Material cost per 100 SF | Overhead per 100 SF | Profit per 100 SF | Total price per 100 SF |
|---|---|---|---|---|---|---|---|---|---|
| **Epoxy coating, 2 part system, white (material #52)** | | | | | | | | | |
| Roll 1st coat | | | | | | | | | |
| Slow | 325 | 425 | 177.00 | 6.23 | 1.85 | 41.65 | 9.45 | 9.47 | 68.65 |
| Medium | 350 | 400 | 154.90 | 7.36 | 2.61 | 38.73 | 12.18 | 7.31 | 68.19 |
| Fast | 375 | 375 | 132.70 | 8.40 | 3.44 | 35.39 | 14.64 | 4.33 | 66.20 |
| Roll 2nd or additional coats | | | | | | | | | |
| Slow | 400 | 450 | 177.00 | 5.06 | 1.50 | 39.33 | 8.72 | 8.74 | 63.35 |
| Medium | 425 | 425 | 154.90 | 6.06 | 2.13 | 36.45 | 11.17 | 6.70 | 62.51 |
| Fast | 450 | 400 | 132.70 | 7.00 | 2.85 | 33.18 | 13.34 | 3.95 | 60.32 |

Use these figures to estimate labor and material costs for painting the exterior surface of a flat roof on a steel tank, silo, vessel or hopper. *Rule of thumb*: For a vaulted, peaked or sloping roof, figure the roof area as though it were flat and add 5%. Note: A two coat system, prime and finish, using oil base material is recommended for any metal surface. Using water base material may cause oxidation, corrosion and rust. One coat of oil base paint on metal surfaces may result in cracking, peeling or chipping without the proper prime coat application. If off-white or another light-colored finish paint is specified, make sure the prime coat is also a light color, or more than one finish coat will be necessary. "Slow" work is based on an hourly wage of $20.25, "Medium" work on an hourly wage of $25.75, and "Fast" work on an hourly wage of $31.50. Other qualifications that apply to this table are on page 9.

*National Painting Cost Estimator*

|  | Labor SF per manhour | Material coverage SF/gallon | Material cost per gallon | Labor cost per 100 SF | Labor burden 100 SF | Material cost per 100 SF | Overhead per 100 SF | Profit per 100 SF | Total price per 100 SF |
|---|---|---|---|---|---|---|---|---|---|
| **Tank, silo, vessel, or hopper, spray, exterior roof only** | | | | | | | | | |
| Metal primer, rust inhibitor - clean metal (material #35) | | | | | | | | | |
|   Spray prime coat | | | | | | | | | |
|     Slow | 850 | 325 | 59.70 | 2.38 | .71 | 18.37 | 4.08 | 4.08 | 29.62 |
|     Medium | 900 | 300 | 52.20 | 2.86 | 1.01 | 17.40 | 5.32 | 3.19 | 29.78 |
|     Fast | 950 | 275 | 44.80 | 3.32 | 1.34 | 16.29 | 6.50 | 1.92 | 29.37 |
| Metal primer, rust inhibitor - rusty metal (material #36) | | | | | | | | | |
|   Spray prime coat | | | | | | | | | |
|     Slow | 850 | 300 | 72.30 | 2.38 | .71 | 24.10 | 5.16 | 5.17 | 37.52 |
|     Medium | 900 | 275 | 63.30 | 2.86 | 1.01 | 23.02 | 6.72 | 4.03 | 37.64 |
|     Fast | 950 | 250 | 54.20 | 3.32 | 1.34 | 21.68 | 8.17 | 2.42 | 36.93 |
| Industrial enamel, oil base, high gloss - light colors (material #56) | | | | | | | | | |
|   Spray 1st or additional finish coats | | | | | | | | | |
|     Slow | 950 | 300 | 61.00 | 2.13 | .62 | 20.33 | 4.39 | 4.40 | 31.87 |
|     Medium | 1025 | 275 | 53.40 | 2.51 | .91 | 19.42 | 5.71 | 3.42 | 31.97 |
|     Fast | 1100 | 250 | 45.80 | 2.86 | 1.18 | 18.32 | 6.93 | 2.05 | 31.34 |
| Industrial enamel, oil base, high gloss - dark (OSHA) colors (material #57) | | | | | | | | | |
|   Spray 1st or additional finish coats | | | | | | | | | |
|     Slow | 950 | 325 | 67.60 | 2.13 | .62 | 20.80 | 4.48 | 4.49 | 32.52 |
|     Medium | 1025 | 300 | 59.10 | 2.51 | .91 | 19.70 | 5.78 | 3.47 | 32.37 |
|     Fast | 1100 | 275 | 50.70 | 2.86 | 1.18 | 18.44 | 6.97 | 2.06 | 31.51 |
| Epoxy coating, 2 part system, clear (material #51) | | | | | | | | | |
|   Spray 1st coat | | | | | | | | | |
|     Slow | 850 | 325 | 146.90 | 2.38 | .71 | 45.20 | 9.17 | 9.19 | 66.65 |
|     Medium | 900 | 313 | 128.60 | 2.86 | 1.01 | 41.09 | 11.24 | 6.74 | 62.94 |
|     Fast | 950 | 300 | 110.20 | 3.32 | 1.34 | 36.73 | 12.83 | 3.80 | 58.02 |
|   Spray 2nd or additional coats | | | | | | | | | |
|     Slow | 950 | 350 | 146.90 | 2.13 | .62 | 41.97 | 8.50 | 8.52 | 61.74 |
|     Medium | 1025 | 338 | 128.60 | 2.51 | .91 | 38.05 | 10.36 | 6.22 | 58.05 |
|     Fast | 1100 | 325 | 110.20 | 2.86 | 1.18 | 33.91 | 11.76 | 3.48 | 53.19 |
| Epoxy coating, 2 part system, white (material #52) | | | | | | | | | |
|   Spray 1st coat | | | | | | | | | |
|     Slow | 850 | 325 | 177.00 | 2.38 | .71 | 54.46 | 10.93 | 10.96 | 79.44 |
|     Medium | 900 | 313 | 154.90 | 2.86 | 1.01 | 49.49 | 13.34 | 8.00 | 74.70 |
|     Fast | 950 | 300 | 132.70 | 3.32 | 1.34 | 44.23 | 15.16 | 4.48 | 68.53 |
|   Spray 2nd or additional coats | | | | | | | | | |
|     Slow | 950 | 350 | 177.00 | 2.13 | .62 | 50.57 | 10.13 | 10.15 | 73.60 |
|     Medium | 1025 | 338 | 154.90 | 2.51 | .91 | 45.83 | 12.31 | 7.38 | 68.94 |
|     Fast | 1100 | 325 | 132.70 | 2.86 | 1.18 | 40.83 | 13.91 | 4.11 | 62.89 |

*Industrial, Institutional and Heavy Commercial Costs*

|  | Labor SF per manhour | Material coverage SF/gallon | Material cost per gallon | Labor cost per 100 SF | Labor burden 100 SF | Material cost per 100 SF | Overhead per 100 SF | Profit per 100 SF | Total price per 100 SF |
|---|---|---|---|---|---|---|---|---|---|
| **Vinyl coating (material #59)** | | | | | | | | | |
| Spray 1st coat | | | | | | | | | |
| Slow | 750 | 225 | 106.40 | 2.70 | .79 | 47.29 | 9.65 | 9.67 | 70.10 |
| Medium | 775 | 213 | 93.10 | 3.32 | 1.18 | 43.71 | 12.05 | 7.23 | 67.49 |
| Fast | 800 | 200 | 79.80 | 3.94 | 1.60 | 39.90 | 14.09 | 4.17 | 63.70 |
| Spray 2nd or additional coats | | | | | | | | | |
| Slow | 900 | 130 | 106.40 | 2.25 | .66 | 81.85 | 16.10 | 16.14 | 117.00 |
| Medium | 950 | 105 | 93.10 | 2.71 | .95 | 88.67 | 23.09 | 13.85 | 129.27 |
| Fast | 1000 | 80 | 79.80 | 3.15 | 1.29 | 99.75 | 32.30 | 9.55 | 146.04 |

Use these figures to estimate labor and material costs for painting the exterior surface of a flat roof on a steel tank, silo, vessel or hopper. *Rule of thumb*: For a vaulted, peaked or sloping roof, figure the roof area as though it were flat and add 5%. Note: A two coat system, prime and finish, using oil base material is recommended for any metal surface. Using water base material may cause oxidation, corrosion and rust. One coat of oil base paint on metal surfaces may result in cracking, peeling or chipping without the proper prime coat application. If off-white or another light-colored finish paint is specified, make sure the prime coat is also a light color, or more than one finish coat will be necessary. "Slow" work is based on an hourly wage of $20.25, "Medium" work on an hourly wage of $25.75, and "Fast" work on an hourly wage of $31.50. Other qualifications that apply to this table are on page 9.

|  | Labor SF per manhour | Material coverage SF/gallon | Material cost per gallon | Labor cost per 100 SF | Labor burden 100 SF | Material cost per 100 SF | Overhead per 100 SF | Profit per 100 SF | Total price per 100 SF |
|---|---|---|---|---|---|---|---|---|---|
| **Walls, concrete tilt-up, brush application** | | | | | | | | | |
| Flat latex, water base (material #5) | | | | | | | | | |
| Brush 1st coat | | | | | | | | | |
| Slow | 150 | 300 | 36.70 | 13.50 | 3.99 | 12.23 | 5.64 | 5.66 | 41.02 |
| Medium | 188 | 263 | 32.10 | 13.70 | 4.85 | 12.21 | 7.69 | 4.61 | 43.06 |
| Fast | 225 | 225 | 27.50 | 14.00 | 5.69 | 12.22 | 9.90 | 2.93 | 44.74 |
| Brush 2nd or additional coats | | | | | | | | | |
| Slow | 200 | 360 | 36.70 | 10.13 | 2.98 | 10.19 | 4.43 | 4.44 | 32.17 |
| Medium | 225 | 305 | 32.10 | 11.44 | 4.04 | 10.52 | 6.50 | 3.90 | 36.40 |
| Fast | 250 | 250 | 27.50 | 12.60 | 5.14 | 11.00 | 8.91 | 2.64 | 40.29 |
| Enamel, water base (material #9) | | | | | | | | | |
| Brush 1st coat | | | | | | | | | |
| Slow | 150 | 275 | 46.80 | 13.50 | 3.99 | 17.02 | 6.56 | 6.57 | 47.64 |
| Medium | 188 | 238 | 41.00 | 13.70 | 4.85 | 17.23 | 8.95 | 5.37 | 50.10 |
| Fast | 225 | 200 | 35.10 | 14.00 | 5.69 | 17.55 | 11.55 | 3.42 | 52.21 |
| Brush 2nd or additional coats | | | | | | | | | |
| Slow | 200 | 360 | 46.80 | 10.13 | 2.98 | 13.00 | 4.96 | 4.97 | 36.04 |
| Medium | 225 | 243 | 41.00 | 11.44 | 4.04 | 16.87 | 8.09 | 4.85 | 45.29 |
| Fast | 250 | 225 | 35.10 | 12.60 | 5.14 | 15.60 | 10.34 | 3.06 | 46.74 |
| Enamel, oil base (material #10) | | | | | | | | | |
| Brush 1st coat | | | | | | | | | |
| Slow | 150 | 300 | 61.70 | 13.50 | 3.99 | 20.57 | 7.23 | 7.24 | 52.53 |
| Medium | 188 | 250 | 54.00 | 13.70 | 4.85 | 21.60 | 10.04 | 6.02 | 56.21 |
| Fast | 225 | 200 | 46.30 | 14.00 | 5.69 | 23.15 | 13.29 | 3.93 | 60.06 |
| Brush 2nd or additional coats | | | | | | | | | |
| Slow | 200 | 400 | 61.70 | 10.13 | 2.98 | 15.43 | 5.42 | 5.44 | 39.40 |
| Medium | 225 | 325 | 54.00 | 11.44 | 4.04 | 16.62 | 8.03 | 4.82 | 44.95 |
| Fast | 250 | 250 | 46.30 | 12.60 | 5.14 | 18.52 | 11.24 | 3.33 | 50.83 |
| Epoxy coating, 2 part system, clear (material #51) | | | | | | | | | |
| Brush 1st coat | | | | | | | | | |
| Slow | 150 | 330 | 146.90 | 13.50 | 3.99 | 44.52 | 11.78 | 11.80 | 85.59 |
| Medium | 188 | 290 | 128.60 | 13.70 | 4.85 | 44.34 | 15.72 | 9.43 | 88.04 |
| Fast | 225 | 250 | 110.20 | 14.00 | 5.69 | 44.08 | 19.77 | 5.85 | 89.39 |
| Brush 2nd or additional coats | | | | | | | | | |
| Slow | 200 | 380 | 146.90 | 10.13 | 2.98 | 38.66 | 9.84 | 9.86 | 71.47 |
| Medium | 225 | 340 | 128.60 | 11.44 | 4.04 | 37.82 | 13.33 | 8.00 | 74.63 |
| Fast | 250 | 300 | 110.20 | 12.60 | 5.14 | 36.73 | 16.89 | 5.00 | 76.36 |

## Industrial, Institutional and Heavy Commercial Costs

| | Labor SF per manhour | Material coverage SF/gallon | Material cost per gallon | Labor cost per 100 SF | Labor burden 100 SF | Material cost per 100 SF | Overhead per 100 SF | Profit per 100 SF | Total price per 100 SF |
|---|---|---|---|---|---|---|---|---|---|
| **Epoxy coating, 2 part system, white (material #52)** | | | | | | | | | |
| Brush 1st coat | | | | | | | | | |
| Slow | 150 | 330 | 177.00 | 13.50 | 3.99 | 53.64 | 13.51 | 13.54 | 98.18 |
| Medium | 188 | 290 | 154.90 | 13.70 | 4.85 | 53.41 | 17.99 | 10.79 | 100.74 |
| Fast | 225 | 250 | 132.70 | 14.00 | 5.69 | 53.08 | 22.56 | 6.67 | 102.00 |
| Brush 2nd or additional coats | | | | | | | | | |
| Slow | 200 | 380 | 177.00 | 10.13 | 2.98 | 46.58 | 11.34 | 11.37 | 82.40 |
| Medium | 225 | 340 | 154.90 | 11.44 | 4.04 | 45.56 | 15.26 | 9.16 | 85.46 |
| Fast | 250 | 300 | 132.70 | 12.60 | 5.14 | 44.23 | 19.21 | 5.68 | 86.86 |
| **Waterproofing, clear hydro sealer (material #34)** | | | | | | | | | |
| Brush 1st coat | | | | | | | | | |
| Slow | 150 | 160 | 40.60 | 13.50 | 3.99 | 25.38 | 8.14 | 8.16 | 59.17 |
| Medium | 175 | 140 | 35.50 | 14.71 | 5.20 | 25.36 | 11.32 | 6.79 | 63.38 |
| Fast | 200 | 120 | 30.40 | 15.75 | 6.43 | 25.33 | 14.73 | 4.36 | 66.60 |
| Brush 2nd or additional coats | | | | | | | | | |
| Slow | 230 | 200 | 40.60 | 8.80 | 2.61 | 20.30 | 6.02 | 6.04 | 43.77 |
| Medium | 275 | 188 | 35.50 | 9.36 | 3.33 | 18.88 | 7.89 | 4.73 | 44.19 |
| Fast | 295 | 175 | 30.40 | 10.68 | 4.35 | 17.37 | 10.05 | 2.97 | 45.42 |
| **Industrial waterproofing (material #58)** | | | | | | | | | |
| Brush 1st coat | | | | | | | | | |
| Slow | 90 | 100 | 42.10 | 22.50 | 6.63 | 42.10 | 13.54 | 13.56 | 98.33 |
| Medium | 100 | 95 | 36.80 | 25.75 | 9.12 | 38.74 | 18.40 | 11.04 | 103.05 |
| Fast | 110 | 90 | 31.60 | 28.64 | 11.67 | 35.11 | 23.39 | 6.92 | 105.73 |
| Brush 2nd or additional coats | | | | | | | | | |
| Slow | 150 | 200 | 42.10 | 13.50 | 3.99 | 21.05 | 7.32 | 7.34 | 53.20 |
| Medium | 180 | 188 | 36.80 | 14.31 | 5.08 | 19.57 | 9.74 | 5.84 | 54.54 |
| Fast | 195 | 175 | 31.60 | 16.15 | 6.60 | 18.06 | 12.65 | 3.74 | 57.20 |

Use these figures to estimate the costs for finishing concrete walls which have a smooth surface (trowel), rough texture, or exposed aggregate finish. For wall heights above 10', increase the computed area by 50%. "Slow" work is based on an hourly wage of $20.25, "Medium" work on an hourly wage of $25.75, and "Fast" work on an hourly wage of $31.50. Other qualifications that apply to this table are on page 9.

*National Painting Cost Estimator*

|  | Labor SF per manhour | Material coverage SF/gallon | Material cost per gallon | Labor cost per 100 SF | Labor burden 100 SF | Material cost per 100 SF | Overhead per 100 SF | Profit per 100 SF | Total price per 100 SF |
|---|---|---|---|---|---|---|---|---|---|

## Walls, concrete tilt-up, roll application

### Flat latex, water base (material #5)
Roll 1st coat

| | | | | | | | | | |
|---|---|---|---|---|---|---|---|---|---|
| Slow | 275 | 275 | 36.70 | 7.36 | 2.18 | 13.35 | 4.35 | 4.36 | 31.60 |
| Medium | 300 | 238 | 32.10 | 8.58 | 3.03 | 13.49 | 6.28 | 3.77 | 35.15 |
| Fast | 325 | 225 | 27.50 | 9.69 | 3.97 | 12.22 | 8.02 | 2.37 | 36.27 |

Roll 2nd or additional coats

| | | | | | | | | | |
|---|---|---|---|---|---|---|---|---|---|
| Slow | 300 | 375 | 36.70 | 6.75 | 1.98 | 9.79 | 3.52 | 3.53 | 25.57 |
| Medium | 338 | 325 | 32.10 | 7.62 | 2.70 | 9.88 | 5.05 | 3.03 | 28.28 |
| Fast | 375 | 275 | 27.50 | 8.40 | 3.44 | 10.00 | 6.77 | 2.00 | 30.61 |

### Enamel, water base (material #9)
Roll 1st coat

| | | | | | | | | | |
|---|---|---|---|---|---|---|---|---|---|
| Slow | 275 | 275 | 46.80 | 7.36 | 2.18 | 17.02 | 5.04 | 5.05 | 36.65 |
| Medium | 300 | 238 | 41.00 | 8.58 | 3.03 | 17.23 | 7.21 | 4.33 | 40.38 |
| Fast | 325 | 200 | 35.10 | 9.69 | 3.97 | 17.55 | 9.67 | 2.86 | 43.74 |

Roll 2nd or additional coats

| | | | | | | | | | |
|---|---|---|---|---|---|---|---|---|---|
| Slow | 300 | 325 | 46.80 | 6.75 | 1.98 | 14.40 | 4.40 | 4.41 | 31.94 |
| Medium | 338 | 275 | 41.00 | 7.62 | 2.70 | 14.91 | 6.31 | 3.78 | 35.32 |
| Fast | 375 | 225 | 35.10 | 8.40 | 3.44 | 15.60 | 8.50 | 2.52 | 38.46 |

### Enamel, oil base (material #10)
Roll 1st coat

| | | | | | | | | | |
|---|---|---|---|---|---|---|---|---|---|
| Slow | 275 | 260 | 61.70 | 7.36 | 2.18 | 23.73 | 6.32 | 6.33 | 45.92 |
| Medium | 300 | 210 | 54.00 | 8.58 | 3.03 | 25.71 | 9.33 | 5.60 | 52.25 |
| Fast | 325 | 160 | 46.30 | 9.69 | 3.97 | 28.94 | 13.20 | 3.90 | 59.70 |

Roll 2nd or additional coats

| | | | | | | | | | |
|---|---|---|---|---|---|---|---|---|---|
| Slow | 300 | 350 | 61.70 | 6.75 | 1.98 | 17.63 | 5.01 | 5.02 | 36.39 |
| Medium | 338 | 300 | 54.00 | 7.62 | 2.70 | 18.00 | 7.08 | 4.25 | 39.65 |
| Fast | 375 | 250 | 46.30 | 8.40 | 3.44 | 18.52 | 9.41 | 2.78 | 42.55 |

### Epoxy coating, 2 part system, clear (material #51)
Roll 1st coat

| | | | | | | | | | |
|---|---|---|---|---|---|---|---|---|---|
| Slow | 275 | 290 | 146.90 | 7.36 | 2.18 | 50.66 | 11.44 | 11.46 | 83.10 |
| Medium | 300 | 250 | 128.60 | 8.58 | 3.03 | 51.44 | 15.77 | 9.46 | 88.28 |
| Fast | 325 | 210 | 110.20 | 9.69 | 3.97 | 52.48 | 20.50 | 6.06 | 92.70 |

Roll 2nd or additional coats

| | | | | | | | | | |
|---|---|---|---|---|---|---|---|---|---|
| Slow | 300 | 380 | 146.90 | 6.75 | 1.98 | 38.66 | 9.01 | 9.03 | 65.43 |
| Medium | 338 | 340 | 128.60 | 7.62 | 2.70 | 37.82 | 12.04 | 7.22 | 67.40 |
| Fast | 375 | 300 | 110.20 | 8.40 | 3.44 | 36.73 | 15.05 | 4.45 | 68.07 |

## Industrial, Institutional and Heavy Commercial Costs

|  | Labor SF per manhour | Material coverage SF/gallon | Material cost per gallon | Labor cost per 100 SF | Labor burden 100 SF | Material cost per 100 SF | Overhead per 100 SF | Profit per 100 SF | Total price per 100 SF |
|---|---|---|---|---|---|---|---|---|---|
| **Epoxy coating, 2 part system, white (material #52)** | | | | | | | | | |
| Roll 1st coat | | | | | | | | | |
| Slow | 275 | 290 | 177.00 | 7.36 | 2.18 | 61.03 | 13.41 | 13.44 | 97.42 |
| Medium | 300 | 250 | 154.90 | 8.58 | 3.03 | 61.96 | 18.40 | 11.04 | 103.01 |
| Fast | 325 | 210 | 132.70 | 9.69 | 3.97 | 63.19 | 23.82 | 7.05 | 107.72 |
| Roll 2nd or additional coats | | | | | | | | | |
| Slow | 300 | 380 | 177.00 | 6.75 | 1.98 | 46.58 | 10.51 | 10.53 | 76.35 |
| Medium | 338 | 340 | 154.90 | 7.62 | 2.70 | 45.56 | 13.97 | 8.38 | 78.23 |
| Fast | 375 | 300 | 132.70 | 8.40 | 3.44 | 44.23 | 17.38 | 5.14 | 78.59 |
| **Waterproofing, clear hydro sealer (material #34)** | | | | | | | | | |
| Roll 1st coat | | | | | | | | | |
| Slow | 170 | 200 | 40.60 | 11.91 | 3.51 | 20.30 | 6.79 | 6.80 | 49.31 |
| Medium | 200 | 165 | 35.50 | 12.88 | 4.56 | 21.52 | 9.74 | 5.84 | 54.54 |
| Fast | 245 | 130 | 30.40 | 12.86 | 5.23 | 23.38 | 12.86 | 3.80 | 58.13 |
| Roll 2nd or additional coats | | | | | | | | | |
| Slow | 275 | 325 | 40.60 | 7.36 | 2.18 | 12.49 | 4.18 | 4.19 | 30.40 |
| Medium | 300 | 275 | 35.50 | 8.58 | 3.03 | 12.91 | 6.13 | 3.68 | 34.33 |
| Fast | 325 | 225 | 30.40 | 9.69 | 3.97 | 13.51 | 8.42 | 2.49 | 38.08 |
| **Industrial waterproofing (material #58)** | | | | | | | | | |
| Roll 1st coat | | | | | | | | | |
| Slow | 100 | 125 | 42.10 | 20.25 | 5.97 | 33.68 | 11.38 | 11.40 | 82.68 |
| Medium | 113 | 113 | 36.80 | 22.79 | 8.07 | 32.57 | 15.86 | 9.51 | 88.80 |
| Fast | 125 | 100 | 31.60 | 25.20 | 10.28 | 31.60 | 20.79 | 6.15 | 94.02 |
| Roll 2nd or additional coats | | | | | | | | | |
| Slow | 180 | 200 | 42.10 | 11.25 | 3.33 | 21.05 | 6.77 | 6.78 | 49.18 |
| Medium | 198 | 188 | 36.80 | 13.01 | 4.60 | 19.57 | 9.30 | 5.58 | 52.06 |
| Fast | 215 | 175 | 31.60 | 14.65 | 5.97 | 18.06 | 11.99 | 3.55 | 54.22 |

Use these figures to estimate the costs for finishing concrete walls which have a smooth surface (trowel), rough texture, or exposed aggregate finish. For wall heights above 10', increase the computed area by 50%. "Slow" work is based on an hourly wage of $20.25, "Medium" work on an hourly wage of $25.75, and "Fast" work on an hourly wage of $31.50. Other qualifications that apply to this table are on page 9.

|  | Labor SF per manhour | Material coverage SF/gallon | Material cost per gallon | Labor cost per 100 SF | Labor burden 100 SF | Material cost per 100 SF | Overhead per 100 SF | Profit per 100 SF | Total price per 100 SF |
|---|---|---|---|---|---|---|---|---|---|

## Walls, concrete tilt-up, spray application

Flat latex, water base (material #5)
Spray 1st coat

| | | | | | | | | | |
|---|---|---|---|---|---|---|---|---|---|
| Slow | 500 | 225 | 36.70 | 4.05 | 1.19 | 16.31 | 4.09 | 4.10 | 29.74 |
| Medium | 600 | 188 | 32.10 | 4.29 | 1.53 | 17.07 | 5.72 | 3.43 | 32.04 |
| Fast | 700 | 150 | 27.50 | 4.50 | 1.84 | 18.33 | 7.65 | 2.26 | 34.58 |

Spray 2nd or additional coats

| | | | | | | | | | |
|---|---|---|---|---|---|---|---|---|---|
| Slow | 600 | 275 | 36.70 | 3.38 | 1.00 | 13.35 | 3.37 | 3.38 | 24.48 |
| Medium | 700 | 238 | 32.10 | 3.68 | 1.31 | 13.49 | 4.62 | 2.77 | 25.87 |
| Fast | 800 | 200 | 27.50 | 3.94 | 1.60 | 13.75 | 5.98 | 1.77 | 27.04 |

Enamel, water base (material #9)
Spray 1st coat

| | | | | | | | | | |
|---|---|---|---|---|---|---|---|---|---|
| Slow | 500 | 225 | 46.80 | 4.05 | 1.19 | 20.80 | 4.95 | 4.96 | 35.95 |
| Medium | 550 | 188 | 41.00 | 4.68 | 1.67 | 21.81 | 7.04 | 4.22 | 39.42 |
| Fast | 600 | 150 | 35.10 | 5.25 | 2.16 | 23.40 | 9.54 | 2.82 | 43.17 |

Spray 2nd or additional coats

| | | | | | | | | | |
|---|---|---|---|---|---|---|---|---|---|
| Slow | 600 | 275 | 46.80 | 3.38 | 1.00 | 17.02 | 4.07 | 4.08 | 29.55 |
| Medium | 700 | 238 | 41.00 | 3.68 | 1.31 | 17.23 | 5.55 | 3.33 | 31.10 |
| Fast | 800 | 200 | 35.10 | 3.94 | 1.60 | 17.55 | 7.16 | 2.12 | 32.37 |

Enamel, oil base (material #10)
Spray 1st coat

| | | | | | | | | | |
|---|---|---|---|---|---|---|---|---|---|
| Slow | 500 | 200 | 61.70 | 4.05 | 1.19 | 30.85 | 6.86 | 6.87 | 49.82 |
| Medium | 550 | 163 | 54.00 | 4.68 | 1.67 | 33.13 | 9.87 | 5.92 | 55.27 |
| Fast | 600 | 125 | 46.30 | 5.25 | 2.16 | 37.04 | 13.77 | 4.07 | 62.29 |

Spray 2nd or additional coats

| | | | | | | | | | |
|---|---|---|---|---|---|---|---|---|---|
| Slow | 600 | 300 | 61.70 | 3.38 | 1.00 | 20.57 | 4.74 | 4.75 | 34.44 |
| Medium | 700 | 243 | 54.00 | 3.68 | 1.31 | 22.22 | 6.80 | 4.08 | 38.09 |
| Fast | 800 | 175 | 46.30 | 3.94 | 1.60 | 26.46 | 9.92 | 2.94 | 44.86 |

Epoxy coating, 2 part system, clear (material #51)
Spray 1st coat

| | | | | | | | | | |
|---|---|---|---|---|---|---|---|---|---|
| Slow | 500 | 270 | 146.90 | 4.05 | 1.19 | 54.41 | 11.33 | 11.36 | 82.34 |
| Medium | 700 | 253 | 128.60 | 3.68 | 1.31 | 50.83 | 13.95 | 8.37 | 78.14 |
| Fast | 900 | 235 | 110.20 | 3.50 | 1.42 | 46.89 | 16.06 | 4.75 | 72.62 |

Spray 2nd or additional coats

| | | | | | | | | | |
|---|---|---|---|---|---|---|---|---|---|
| Slow | 600 | 375 | 146.90 | 3.38 | 1.00 | 39.17 | 8.27 | 8.29 | 60.11 |
| Medium | 800 | 338 | 128.60 | 3.22 | 1.14 | 38.05 | 10.60 | 6.36 | 59.37 |
| Fast | 1000 | 300 | 110.20 | 3.15 | 1.29 | 36.73 | 12.76 | 3.78 | 57.71 |

*Industrial, Institutional and Heavy Commercial Costs*

|  | Labor SF per manhour | Material coverage SF/gallon | Material cost per gallon | Labor cost per 100 SF | Labor burden 100 SF | Material cost per 100 SF | Overhead per 100 SF | Profit per 100 SF | Total price per 100 SF |
|---|---|---|---|---|---|---|---|---|---|
| **Epoxy coating, 2 part system, white (material #52)** | | | | | | | | | |
| Spray 1st coat | | | | | | | | | |
| Slow | 500 | 270 | 177.00 | 4.05 | 1.19 | 65.56 | 13.45 | 13.48 | 97.73 |
| Medium | 700 | 253 | 154.90 | 3.68 | 1.31 | 61.23 | 16.55 | 9.93 | 92.70 |
| Fast | 900 | 235 | 132.70 | 3.50 | 1.42 | 56.47 | 19.03 | 5.63 | 86.05 |
| Spray 2nd or additional coats | | | | | | | | | |
| Slow | 600 | 375 | 177.00 | 3.38 | 1.00 | 47.20 | 9.80 | 9.82 | 71.20 |
| Medium | 800 | 338 | 154.90 | 3.22 | 1.14 | 45.83 | 12.55 | 7.53 | 70.27 |
| Fast | 1000 | 300 | 132.70 | 3.15 | 1.29 | 44.23 | 15.09 | 4.46 | 68.22 |
| **Waterproofing, clear hydro sealer (material #34)** | | | | | | | | | |
| Spray 1st coat | | | | | | | | | |
| Slow | 600 | 125 | 40.60 | 3.38 | 1.00 | 32.48 | 7.00 | 7.02 | 50.88 |
| Medium | 650 | 113 | 35.50 | 3.96 | 1.41 | 31.42 | 9.20 | 5.52 | 51.51 |
| Fast | 700 | 100 | 30.40 | 4.50 | 1.84 | 30.40 | 11.39 | 3.37 | 51.50 |
| Spray 2nd or additional coats | | | | | | | | | |
| Slow | 700 | 200 | 40.60 | 2.89 | .86 | 20.30 | 4.57 | 4.58 | 33.20 |
| Medium | 800 | 170 | 35.50 | 3.22 | 1.14 | 20.88 | 6.31 | 3.79 | 35.34 |
| Fast | 900 | 140 | 30.40 | 3.50 | 1.42 | 21.71 | 8.26 | 2.44 | 37.33 |

Use these figures to estimate the costs for finishing concrete walls which have a smooth surface (trowel), rough texture, or exposed aggregate finish. For wall heights above 10', increase the computed area by 50%. "Slow" work is based on an hourly wage of $20.25, "Medium" work on an hourly wage of $25.75, and "Fast" work on an hourly wage of $31.50. Other qualifications that apply to this table are on page 9.

## Walls, gypsum drywall
## Smooth-wall finish, no texture: See General Painting Costs, page 240

|  | Labor LF per manhour | Material coverage LF/gallon | Material cost per gallon | Labor cost per 100 LF | Labor burden 100 LF | Material cost per 100 LF | Overhead per 100 LF | Profit per 100 LF | Total price per 100 LF |
|---|---|---|---|---|---|---|---|---|---|
| **Windows, steel factory sash, brush application** | | | | | | | | | |
| Metal primer, rust inhibitor - clean metal (material #35) | | | | | | | | | |
| Brush prime coat | | | | | | | | | |
| Slow | 100 | 850 | 59.70 | 20.25 | 5.97 | 7.02 | 6.32 | 6.33 | 45.89 |
| Medium | 125 | 800 | 52.20 | 20.60 | 7.30 | 6.53 | 8.61 | 5.16 | 48.20 |
| Fast | 150 | 750 | 44.80 | 21.00 | 8.58 | 5.97 | 11.02 | 3.26 | 49.83 |
| Metal primer, rust inhibitor - rusty metal (material #36) | | | | | | | | | |
| Brush prime coat | | | | | | | | | |
| Slow | 100 | 800 | 72.30 | 20.25 | 5.97 | 9.04 | 6.70 | 6.71 | 48.67 |
| Medium | 125 | 750 | 63.30 | 20.60 | 7.30 | 8.44 | 9.08 | 5.45 | 50.87 |
| Fast | 150 | 700 | 54.20 | 21.00 | 8.58 | 7.74 | 11.57 | 3.42 | 52.31 |
| Metal finish - synthetic enamel, gloss, interior or exterior, off white (material #37) | | | | | | | | | |
| Brush 1st coat | | | | | | | | | |
| Slow | 125 | 900 | 59.70 | 16.20 | 4.78 | 6.63 | 5.25 | 5.26 | 38.12 |
| Medium | 150 | 850 | 52.20 | 17.17 | 6.09 | 6.14 | 7.35 | 4.41 | 41.16 |
| Fast | 175 | 800 | 44.80 | 18.00 | 7.32 | 5.60 | 9.59 | 2.84 | 43.35 |
| Brush 2nd or additional coats | | | | | | | | | |
| Slow | 150 | 1000 | 59.70 | 13.50 | 3.99 | 5.97 | 4.46 | 4.47 | 32.39 |
| Medium | 175 | 950 | 52.20 | 14.71 | 5.20 | 5.49 | 6.35 | 3.81 | 35.56 |
| Fast | 200 | 900 | 44.80 | 15.75 | 6.43 | 4.98 | 8.42 | 2.49 | 38.07 |
| Metal finish - synthetic enamel, gloss, interior or exterior, colors, except orange & red (material #38) | | | | | | | | | |
| Brush 1st coat | | | | | | | | | |
| Slow | 125 | 950 | 65.20 | 16.20 | 4.78 | 6.86 | 5.29 | 5.30 | 38.43 |
| Medium | 150 | 900 | 57.00 | 17.17 | 6.09 | 6.33 | 7.40 | 4.44 | 41.43 |
| Fast | 175 | 850 | 48.90 | 18.00 | 7.32 | 5.75 | 9.64 | 2.85 | 43.56 |
| Brush 2nd or additional coats | | | | | | | | | |
| Slow | 150 | 1050 | 65.20 | 13.50 | 3.99 | 6.21 | 4.50 | 4.51 | 32.71 |
| Medium | 175 | 1000 | 57.00 | 14.71 | 5.20 | 5.70 | 6.41 | 3.84 | 35.86 |
| Fast | 200 | 950 | 48.90 | 15.75 | 6.43 | 5.15 | 8.47 | 2.51 | 38.31 |

These figures will apply when painting steel factory sash but do not include work on glazing or frame. For heights above 8 feet, use the High Time Difficulty Factors on page 139. Note: A two coat system, prime and finish, using oil base material is recommended for any metal surface. Using water base material may cause oxidation, corrosion and rust. Using one coat of oil base paint on metal surfaces may result in cracking, peeling or chipping without the proper prime coat application. If off-white or another light-colored finish paint is specified, make sure the prime coat is also a light color, or more than one finish coat will be necessary. "Slow" work is based on an hourly wage of $20.25, "Medium" work on an hourly wage of $25.75, and "Fast" work on an hourly wage of $31.50. Other qualifications that apply to this table are on page 9.

## Field Production Times and Rates

| Date / Painter | > | 10-15-13 Operation | Start times | Finish times | Total hours | LF or SF completed | LF or SF per hour | Average rate | Your rate |
|---|---|---|---|---|---|---|---|---|---|
| David H. | 1 | Cutting-in ceiling | 7:05 | 8:35 | 1.5 | 28 LF | 18.67 | | |
| | 2 | 8' 0" height | 8:40 | 9:40 | 1 | 20 LF | 20 | | |
| | 3 | | 9:40 | 11:55 | 2.25 | 38 LF | 16.89 | | |
| | 4 | | 12:45 | 2:00 | 1.25 | 20 LF | 16 | 17.67 | 18 |
| | 5 | | | | | | | | |
| | 6 | | | | | | | | |
| | 7 | | | | | | | | |
| | 8 | | | | | | | | |
| | 9 | | | | | | | | |
| | 10 | | | | | | | | |
| | 11 | | | | | | | | |
| | 12 | | | | | | | | |
| | 13 | | | | | | | | |
| | 14 | | | | | | | | |
| | 15 | | | | | | | | |
| | 16 | | | | | | | | |
| | 17 | | | | | | | | |
| | 18 | | | | | | | | |
| | 19 | | | | | | | | |
| | 20 | | | | | | | | |
| | 21 | | | | | | | | |
| | 22 | | | | | | | | |
| | 23 | | | | | | | | |
| | 24 | | | | | | | | |
| | 25 | | | | | | | | |
| | 26 | | | | | | | | |
| | 27 | | | | | | | | |
| | 28 | | | | | | | | |
| | 29 | | | | | | | | |
| | 30 | | | | | | | | |
| | 31 | | | | | | | | |
| | 32 | | | | | | | | |
| | 33 | | | | | | | | |
| | 34 | | | | | | | | |
| | 35 | | | | | | | | |
| | 36 | | | | | | | | |
| | 37 | | | | | | | | |

**Figure 25**
Sample field production times and rates form

## Field Production Times and Rates

| Date Painter | > | Operation | Start times | Finish times | Total hours | LF or SF completed | LF or SF per hour | Average rate | Your rate |
|---|---|---|---|---|---|---|---|---|---|
| | 1 | | | | | | | | |
| | 2 | | | | | | | | |
| | 3 | | | | | | | | |
| | 4 | | | | | | | | |
| | 5 | | | | | | | | |
| | 6 | | | | | | | | |
| | 7 | | | | | | | | |
| | 8 | | | | | | | | |
| | 9 | | | | | | | | |
| | 10 | | | | | | | | |
| | 11 | | | | | | | | |
| | 12 | | | | | | | | |
| | 13 | | | | | | | | |
| | 14 | | | | | | | | |
| | 15 | | | | | | | | |
| | 16 | | | | | | | | |
| | 17 | | | | | | | | |
| | 18 | | | | | | | | |
| | 19 | | | | | | | | |
| | 20 | | | | | | | | |
| | 21 | | | | | | | | |
| | 22 | | | | | | | | |
| | 23 | | | | | | | | |
| | 24 | | | | | | | | |
| | 25 | | | | | | | | |
| | 26 | | | | | | | | |
| | 27 | | | | | | | | |
| | 28 | | | | | | | | |
| | 29 | | | | | | | | |
| | 30 | | | | | | | | |
| | 31 | | | | | | | | |
| | 32 | | | | | | | | |
| | 33 | | | | | | | | |
| | 34 | | | | | | | | |
| | 35 | | | | | | | | |
| | 36 | | | | | | | | |
| | 37 | | | | | | | | |

**Figure 26**
Blank field production times and rates form

# Part IV

# Wallcovering Costs

|  | American rolls per gallon | Linear yards per gallon | Adhesive cost per gallon |
|---|---|---|---|

## Adhesive coverage, rolls to yards conversion (2.5 yards per roll)
Ready-mix

| | American rolls per gallon | Linear yards per gallon | Adhesive cost per gallon |
|---|---|---|---|
| **Light weight vinyl (material #60)** | | | |
| Slow | 8.0 | 20.0 | 13.20 |
| Medium | 7.5 | 18.8 | 11.60 |
| Fast | 7.0 | 17.5 | 9.90 |
| **Heavy weight vinyl (material #61)** | | | |
| Slow | 6.0 | 15.0 | 14.70 |
| Medium | 5.5 | 13.8 | 12.90 |
| Fast | 5.0 | 12.5 | 11.00 |
| **Cellulose (material #62)** | | | |
| Slow | 8.0 | 20.0 | 16.60 |
| Medium | 7.0 | 17.5 | 14.50 |
| Fast | 6.0 | 15.0 | 12.40 |
| **Vinyl to vinyl (material #63)** | | | |
| Slow | 7.0 | 17.5 | 24.70 |
| Medium | 6.5 | 16.3 | 21.60 |
| Fast | 6.0 | 15.0 | 18.60 |
| **Powdered cellulose (material #64)** | | | |
| Slow | 12.0 | 30.0 | 7.20 |
| Medium | 11.0 | 27.5 | 6.30 |
| Fast | 10.0 | 25.0 | 5.40 |
| **Powdered vinyl (material #65)** | | | |
| Slow | 12.0 | 30.0 | 8.40 |
| Medium | 11.0 | 27.5 | 7.30 |
| Fast | 10.0 | 25.0 | 6.30 |
| **Powdered wheat paste (material #66)** | | | |
| Slow | 13.0 | 32.5 | 6.10 |
| Medium | 12.0 | 30.0 | 5.30 |
| Fast | 11.0 | 27.5 | 4.50 |

These figures are based on rolls or yards per gallon of liquid paste. Vinyl to vinyl ready-mix is usually distributed in pint containers which have been converted to gallons. One pint makes 6 gallons. Powdered adhesive coverage is based on water added to powder to prepare gallon quantities. One pound of powdered vinyl or wheat paste makes 1.75 gallons of liquid paste when mixed with about 1-1/2 gallons of cold water. Two ounces of powdered cellulose makes 1.75 gallons of liquid paste.

## Wallcovering Costs

| | Labor SF per manhour | Material coverage SF/gallon | Material cost per gallon | Labor cost per 100 SF | Labor burden 100 SF | Material cost per 100 SF | Overhead per 100 SF | Profit per 100 SF | Total cost per 100 SF |
|---|---|---|---|---|---|---|---|---|---|

**Adhesive coverage and application rates, square foot basis**
  Ready-mix
    Light weight vinyl (material #60)
      Slow | 350 | 275 | 13.20 | 5.50 | 1.63 | 4.80 | 2.26 | 2.27 | 16.46
      Medium | 375 | 250 | 11.60 | 6.53 | 2.33 | 4.64 | 3.37 | 2.02 | 18.89
      Fast | 400 | 225 | 9.90 | 7.56 | 3.09 | 4.40 | 4.66 | 1.38 | 21.09

    Heavy weight vinyl (material #61)
      Slow | 275 | 200 | 14.70 | 7.00 | 2.07 | 7.35 | 3.12 | 3.13 | 22.67
      Medium | 300 | 175 | 12.90 | 8.17 | 2.88 | 7.37 | 4.61 | 2.76 | 25.79
      Fast | 325 | 150 | 11.00 | 9.31 | 3.81 | 7.33 | 6.34 | 1.87 | 28.66

    Cellulose (material #62)
      Slow | 325 | 250 | 16.60 | 5.92 | 1.76 | 6.64 | 2.72 | 2.72 | 19.76
      Medium | 350 | 225 | 14.50 | 7.00 | 2.49 | 6.44 | 3.98 | 2.39 | 22.30
      Fast | 375 | 200 | 12.40 | 8.07 | 3.30 | 6.20 | 5.44 | 1.61 | 24.62

    Vinyl to vinyl (material #63)
      Slow | 300 | 225 | 24.70 | 6.42 | 1.88 | 10.98 | 3.67 | 3.67 | 26.62
      Medium | 325 | 200 | 21.60 | 7.54 | 2.68 | 10.80 | 5.25 | 3.15 | 29.42
      Fast | 350 | 175 | 18.60 | 8.64 | 3.54 | 10.63 | 7.07 | 2.09 | 31.97

    Powdered cellulose (material #64)
      Slow | 425 | 400 | 7.20 | 4.53 | 1.33 | 1.80 | 1.46 | 1.46 | 10.58
      Medium | 450 | 370 | 6.30 | 5.44 | 1.92 | 1.70 | 2.27 | 1.36 | 12.69
      Fast | 475 | 335 | 5.40 | 6.37 | 2.62 | 1.61 | 3.28 | .97 | 14.85

    Powdered vinyl (material #65)
      Slow | 425 | 400 | 8.40 | 4.53 | 1.33 | 2.10 | 1.51 | 1.52 | 10.99
      Medium | 450 | 370 | 7.30 | 5.44 | 1.92 | 1.97 | 2.34 | 1.40 | 13.07
      Fast | 475 | 335 | 6.30 | 6.37 | 2.62 | 1.88 | 3.36 | .99 | 15.22

    Powdered wheat paste (material #66)
      Slow | 450 | 425 | 6.10 | 4.27 | 1.26 | 1.44 | 13.07 | 1.33 | 9.64
      Medium | 475 | 400 | 5.30 | 5.17 | 1.83 | 1.33 | 13.63 | 1.25 | 11.65
      Fast | 500 | 375 | 4.50 | 6.05 | 2.47 | 1.20 | 14.22 | .89 | 13.62

These figures are based on gallon quantities of liquid paste. Vinyl to vinyl ready-mix is usually distributed in pint containers which have been converted to gallons. Powdered adhesive coverage is based on water added to powder to prepare gallon quantities. Typically, powdered ready-mix material is in 2 to 4 ounce packages which will adhere 6 to 12 rolls of wallcovering. See the Adhesive coverage table on the previous page for conversion to rolls and yards. "Slow" work is based on an hourly rate of $19.25, "Medium" work on an hourly rate of $24.50, and "Fast" work on an hourly rate of $30.25.

*National Painting Cost Estimator*

|  | Labor rolls per day | Material by others | Labor cost per 10 rolls | Labor burden 10 rolls | Overhead per 10 rolls | Profit per 10 rolls | Total cost per 10 rolls | Total price per roll |
|---|---|---|---|---|---|---|---|---|

### Wallcovering application, average labor production, medium rooms
Walls
| | | | | | | | | |
|---|---|---|---|---|---|---|---|---|
| Slow | 17 | -- | 90.59 | 26.73 | 22.29 | 22.34 | 161.95 | 16.19 |
| Medium | 19 | -- | 103.16 | 36.52 | 34.92 | 20.95 | 195.55 | 19.56 |
| Fast | 21 | -- | 115.24 | 47.03 | 50.30 | 14.88 | 227.45 | 22.74 |

Ceilings
| | | | | | | | | |
|---|---|---|---|---|---|---|---|---|
| Slow | 15 | -- | 102.67 | 30.28 | 25.26 | 25.32 | 183.53 | 18.35 |
| Medium | 17 | -- | 115.29 | 40.81 | 39.03 | 23.42 | 218.55 | 21.86 |
| Fast | 19 | -- | 127.37 | 51.98 | 55.60 | 16.45 | 251.40 | 25.14 |

The table above assumes that residential rolls are hand pasted. Add surface preparation time on page 425 as needed. For heights above 8 feet, use the High Time Difficulty Factors on page 139. "Slow" work is based on an hourly wage of $19.25, "Medium" work on an hourly wage of $24.50, and "Fast" work on an hourly wage of $30.25.

|  | Labor rolls per day | Material by others | Labor cost per 10 rolls | Labor burden 10 rolls | Overhead per 10 rolls | Profit per 10 rolls | Total cost per 10 rolls | Total price per roll |
|---|---|---|---|---|---|---|---|---|

### Wallcovering application, average labor production, small rooms
Walls
| | | | | | | | | |
|---|---|---|---|---|---|---|---|---|
| Slow | 7 | -- | 220.00 | 64.92 | 54.13 | 54.24 | 393.29 | 39.33 |
| Medium | 9 | -- | 217.78 | 77.07 | 73.72 | 44.23 | 412.80 | 41.28 |
| Fast | 11 | -- | 220.00 | 89.76 | 96.03 | 28.41 | 434.20 | 43.42 |

Ceilings
| | | | | | | | | |
|---|---|---|---|---|---|---|---|---|
| Slow | 6 | -- | 256.67 | 75.72 | 63.15 | 63.29 | 458.83 | 45.88 |
| Medium | 8 | -- | 245.00 | 86.70 | 82.93 | 49.76 | 464.39 | 46.44 |
| Fast | 10 | -- | 242.00 | 98.72 | 105.63 | 31.25 | 477.60 | 47.76 |

The table above assumes that residential rolls are hand pasted. Add surface preparation time on page 425 as needed. For heights above 8 feet, use the High Time Difficulty Factors on page 139. "Slow" work is based on an hourly wage of $19.25, "Medium" work on an hourly wage of $24.50, and "Fast" work on an hourly wage of $30.25.

|  | Labor LF per manhour | Material by others | Labor cost per 100 LF | Labor burden 100 LF | Overhead per 100 LF | Profit per 100 LF | Total cost per 100 LF | Total price per LF |
|---|---|---|---|---|---|---|---|---|

### Borders 3" to 8" wide, commercial, machine pasted
Medium size rooms (10 x 10 range)
| | | | | | | | | |
|---|---|---|---|---|---|---|---|---|
| Slow | 140 | -- | 13.04 | 3.83 | 3.21 | 3.22 | 23.30 | .23 |
| Medium | 158 | -- | 14.56 | 5.15 | 3.74 | 3.75 | 27.20 | .27 |
| Fast | 175 | -- | 16.14 | 6.57 | 4.32 | 4.33 | 31.36 | .31 |

The table above assumes that commercial rolls are machine pasted. ADD for surface preparation time from page 425 or from the tables in Part II, Preparation costs beginning on page 295, as needed. For heights above 8 feet, use the High Time Difficulty Factors on page 139. "Slow" work is based on an hourly wage of $18.25, "Medium" work on an hourly wage of $23.00, and "Fast" work on an hourly wage of $28.25.

*Wallcovering Costs*

|  | Labor LF per manhour | Material by others | Labor cost per 100 LF | Labor burden 100 LF | Overhead per 100 LF | Profit per 100 LF | Total cost per 100 LF | Total price per LF |
|---|---|---|---|---|---|---|---|---|
| **Borders 3" to 8" wide, residential, hand pasted** | | | | | | | | |
| Medium size rooms (bedrooms, dining rooms) | | | | | | | | |
| Slow | 100 | -- | 19.25 | 5.68 | 4.74 | 4.75 | 34.42 | .34 |
| Medium | 113 | -- | 21.68 | 7.68 | 7.34 | 4.40 | 41.10 | .41 |
| Fast | 125 | -- | 24.20 | 9.87 | 10.56 | 3.12 | 47.75 | .48 |

The table above assumes that residential rolls are hand pasted. ADD for surface preparation time from table at bottom or from the tables in Part II, Preparation costs beginning on page 295, as needed. For heights above 8 feet, use the High Time Difficulty Factors on page 139. "Slow" work is based on an hourly wage of $19.25, "Medium" work on an hourly wage of $24.50, and "Fast" work on an hourly wage of $30.25.

|  | Labor SF per manhour | Material by others | Labor cost per 100 SF | Labor burden 100 SF | Overhead per 100 SF | Profit per 100 SF | Total cost per 100 SF | Total price per SF |
|---|---|---|---|---|---|---|---|---|
| **Flexible wood sheet and veneer** | | | | | | | | |
| Wood veneer flexwood (residential or commercial) | | | | | | | | |
| Medium size rooms (bedrooms, dining rooms, offices, reception areas) | | | | | | | | |
| Slow | 14 | -- | 133.93 | 39.50 | 32.95 | 33.02 | 239.40 | 2.39 |
| Medium | 20 | -- | 118.75 | 42.05 | 40.20 | 24.12 | 225.12 | 2.25 |
| Fast | 26 | -- | 112.50 | 45.88 | 49.10 | 14.53 | 222.01 | 2.22 |
| Flexi-wall systems (residential or commercial) | | | | | | | | |
| Medium size rooms (bedrooms, dining rooms, offices, reception areas) | | | | | | | | |
| Slow | 12 | -- | 156.25 | 46.08 | 38.44 | 38.52 | 279.29 | 2.79 |
| Medium | 18 | -- | 131.94 | 46.74 | 44.66 | 26.80 | 250.14 | 2.50 |
| Fast | 24 | -- | 121.88 | 49.72 | 53.20 | 15.74 | 240.54 | 2.41 |

Flexible wood sheet and veneer appears under section 097416 in the Construction Specifications Institute (CSI) indexing system. For heights above 8 feet, use the High Time Difficulty Factors on page 139. The labor rates in the table above are an average of the residential and commercial rates. Thus, "Slow" work is based on an hourly rate of $18.75, "Medium" work on an hourly rate of $23.75, and "Fast" work on an hourly rate of $29.25.

|  | Labor SF per manhour | Material by others | Labor cost per 100 SF | Labor burden 100 SF | Overhead per 100 SF | Profit per 100 SF | Total cost per 100 SF | Total price per SF |
|---|---|---|---|---|---|---|---|---|
| **Surface preparation, wallcovering** | | | | | | | | |
| Rule of thumb, typical preparation | | | | | | | | |
| Slow | 100 | -- | 19.25 | 5.68 | 7.73 | 2.29 | 34.95 | .35 |
| Medium | 125 | -- | 19.60 | 6.94 | 8.23 | 2.43 | 37.20 | .37 |
| Fast | 150 | -- | 20.17 | 8.24 | 8.80 | 2.60 | 39.81 | .40 |
| Putty cracks, sand and wash | | | | | | | | |
| Slow | 120 | -- | 16.04 | 4.73 | 6.44 | 1.90 | 29.11 | .29 |
| Medium | 135 | -- | 18.15 | 6.43 | 7.62 | 2.25 | 34.45 | .34 |
| Fast | 150 | -- | 20.17 | 8.24 | 8.80 | 2.60 | 39.81 | .40 |

For additional preparation tasks see the Preparation operation tables beginning on page 295. For heights above 8 feet, use the High Time Difficulty Factors on page 139. "Slow" work is based on an hourly rate of $19.25, "Medium" work on an hourly rate of $24.50, and "Fast" work on an hourly rate of $30.25.

National Painting Cost Estimator

|  | Labor yards per day | Material by others | Labor cost per 10 yards | Labor burden 10 yards | Overhead per 10 yards | Profit per 10 yards | Total cost per 10 yards | Total price per yard |
|---|---|---|---|---|---|---|---|---|

## Vinyl wallcover, commercial, machine pasted, yards per day, 48" to 54" width

Cut-up areas (stair halls, landing areas)
  Walls

| | | | | | | | | |
|---|---|---|---|---|---|---|---|---|
| Slow | 40 | -- | 36.50 | 10.76 | 8.98 | 9.00 | 65.24 | 6.53 |
| Medium | 45 | -- | 40.89 | 14.48 | 13.84 | 8.31 | 77.52 | 7.75 |
| Fast | 50 | -- | 45.20 | 18.45 | 19.73 | 5.84 | 89.22 | 8.92 |

  Ceilings

| | | | | | | | | |
|---|---|---|---|---|---|---|---|---|
| Slow | 33 | -- | 44.24 | 13.04 | 10.89 | 10.91 | 79.08 | 7.91 |
| Medium | 38 | -- | 48.42 | 17.13 | 16.39 | 9.83 | 91.77 | 9.18 |
| Fast | 43 | -- | 52.56 | 21.43 | 22.94 | 6.79 | 103.72 | 10.37 |

Small rooms (restrooms, utility rooms)
  Walls

| | | | | | | | | |
|---|---|---|---|---|---|---|---|---|
| Slow | 42 | -- | 34.76 | 10.26 | 8.55 | 8.57 | 62.14 | 6.21 |
| Medium | 50 | -- | 36.80 | 13.02 | 12.46 | 7.47 | 69.75 | 6.98 |
| Fast | 55 | -- | 41.09 | 16.79 | 17.93 | 5.30 | 81.11 | 8.11 |

  Ceilings

| | | | | | | | | |
|---|---|---|---|---|---|---|---|---|
| Slow | 38 | -- | 38.42 | 11.32 | 9.45 | 9.47 | 68.66 | 6.87 |
| Medium | 46 | -- | 40.00 | 14.15 | 13.54 | 8.12 | 75.81 | 7.58 |
| Fast | 51 | -- | 44.31 | 18.10 | 19.34 | 5.72 | 87.47 | 8.75 |

Medium rooms (offices)
  Walls

| | | | | | | | | |
|---|---|---|---|---|---|---|---|---|
| Slow | 60 | -- | 24.33 | 7.17 | 5.99 | 6.00 | 43.49 | 4.35 |
| Medium | 75 | -- | 24.53 | 8.70 | 8.30 | 4.98 | 46.51 | 4.65 |
| Fast | 90 | -- | 25.11 | 10.25 | 10.96 | 3.24 | 49.56 | 4.96 |

  Ceilings

| | | | | | | | | |
|---|---|---|---|---|---|---|---|---|
| Slow | 56 | -- | 26.07 | 7.70 | 6.41 | 6.43 | 46.61 | 4.66 |
| Medium | 69 | -- | 26.67 | 9.42 | 9.03 | 5.42 | 50.54 | 5.06 |
| Fast | 81 | -- | 27.90 | 11.40 | 12.18 | 3.60 | 55.08 | 5.51 |

Large rooms (conference rooms)
  Walls

| | | | | | | | | |
|---|---|---|---|---|---|---|---|---|
| Slow | 76 | -- | 19.21 | 5.67 | 4.73 | 4.74 | 34.35 | 3.44 |
| Medium | 89 | -- | 20.67 | 7.32 | 7.00 | 4.20 | 39.19 | 3.92 |
| Fast | 102 | -- | 22.16 | 9.03 | 9.67 | 2.86 | 43.72 | 4.37 |

  Ceilings

| | | | | | | | | |
|---|---|---|---|---|---|---|---|---|
| Slow | 66 | -- | 22.12 | 6.52 | 5.44 | 5.45 | 39.53 | 3.95 |
| Medium | 79 | -- | 23.29 | 8.25 | 7.88 | 4.73 | 44.15 | 4.41 |
| Fast | 91 | -- | 24.84 | 10.13 | 10.84 | 3.21 | 49.02 | 4.90 |

*Wallcovering Costs*

|  | Labor yards per day | Material by others | Labor cost per 10 yards | Labor burden 10 yards | Overhead per 10 yards | Profit per 10 yards | Total cost per 10 yards | Total price per yard |
|---|---|---|---|---|---|---|---|---|
| **Large wall areas (corridors, long hallways)** | | | | | | | | |
| *Walls* | | | | | | | | |
| Slow | 89 | -- | 16.40 | 4.84 | 4.04 | 4.04 | 29.32 | 2.93 |
| Medium | 102 | -- | 18.04 | 6.37 | 6.11 | 3.66 | 34.18 | 3.42 |
| Fast | 114 | -- | 19.82 | 8.11 | 8.65 | 2.56 | 39.14 | 3.91 |
| *Ceilings* | | | | | | | | |
| Slow | 76 | -- | 19.21 | 5.67 | 4.73 | 4.74 | 34.35 | 3.44 |
| Medium | 89 | -- | 20.67 | 7.32 | 7.00 | 4.20 | 39.19 | 3.92 |
| Fast | 102 | -- | 22.16 | 9.03 | 9.67 | 2.86 | 43.72 | 4.37 |
| **Paper-backed vinyl on medium room walls** | | | | | | | | |
| *Bedrooms, dining rooms* | | | | | | | | |
| Slow | 43 | -- | 33.95 | 10.00 | 8.35 | 8.37 | 60.67 | 6.07 |
| Medium | 53 | -- | 34.72 | 12.27 | 11.75 | 7.05 | 65.79 | 6.58 |
| Fast | 64 | -- | 35.31 | 14.42 | 15.41 | 4.56 | 69.70 | 6.97 |
| **Cork wallcovering on medium room walls** | | | | | | | | |
| *Bedrooms, dining rooms* | | | | | | | | |
| Slow | 43 | -- | 33.95 | 10.00 | 8.35 | 8.37 | 60.67 | 6.07 |
| Medium | 53 | -- | 34.72 | 12.27 | 11.75 | 7.05 | 65.79 | 6.58 |
| Fast | 64 | -- | 35.31 | 14.42 | 15.41 | 4.56 | 69.70 | 6.97 |

Vinyl and vinyl-coated wallcovering appear under section 097216 in the Construction Specifications Institute (CSI) indexing system. Cork wallcovering appears in section 097213. The table above assumes that commercial rolls are machine pasted. ADD for surface preparation time from page 425 or from the tables in Part II, Preparation costs beginning on page 295, as needed. For heights above 8 feet, use the High Time Difficulty Factors on page 139. "Slow" work is based on an hourly wage of $18.25, "Medium" work on an hourly wage of $23.00, and "Fast" work on an hourly wage of $28.25.

*National Painting Cost Estimator*

|  | Labor rolls per day | Material by others | Labor cost per 10 rolls | Labor burden 10 rolls | Overhead per 10 rolls | Profit per 10 rolls | Total cost per 10 rolls | Total price per roll |
|---|---|---|---|---|---|---|---|---|

## Vinyl wallcovering, residential, hand pasted, single rolls per day 18" to 27" wide

Cut-up areas (stair halls, landing areas)
  Walls

| | | | | | | | | |
|---|---|---|---|---|---|---|---|---|
| Slow | 10 | -- | 154.00 | 45.44 | 37.89 | 37.97 | 275.30 | 27.53 |
| Medium | 11 | -- | 178.18 | 63.07 | 60.32 | 36.19 | 337.76 | 33.78 |
| Fast | 12 | -- | 201.67 | 82.28 | 88.02 | 26.04 | 398.01 | 39.80 |

  Ceilings

| | | | | | | | | |
|---|---|---|---|---|---|---|---|---|
| Slow | 7 | -- | 220.00 | 64.92 | 54.13 | 54.24 | 393.29 | 39.33 |
| Medium | 8 | -- | 245.00 | 86.70 | 82.93 | 49.76 | 464.39 | 46.44 |
| Fast | 9 | -- | 268.89 | 109.69 | 117.37 | 34.72 | 530.67 | 53.07 |

Small rooms (baths, utility rooms)
  Walls

| | | | | | | | | |
|---|---|---|---|---|---|---|---|---|
| Slow | 11 | -- | 140.00 | 41.32 | 34.45 | 34.52 | 250.29 | 25.03 |
| Medium | 12 | -- | 163.33 | 57.81 | 55.29 | 33.17 | 309.60 | 30.96 |
| Fast | 13 | -- | 186.15 | 75.95 | 81.25 | 24.03 | 367.38 | 36.74 |

  Ceilings

| | | | | | | | | |
|---|---|---|---|---|---|---|---|---|
| Slow | 9 | -- | 171.11 | 50.49 | 42.10 | 42.19 | 305.89 | 30.59 |
| Medium | 10 | -- | 196.00 | 69.36 | 66.35 | 39.81 | 371.52 | 37.15 |
| Fast | 11 | -- | 220.00 | 89.76 | 96.03 | 28.41 | 434.20 | 43.42 |

Medium rooms (bedrooms, dining rooms)
  Walls

| | | | | | | | | |
|---|---|---|---|---|---|---|---|---|
| Slow | 17 | -- | 90.59 | 26.73 | 22.29 | 22.34 | 161.95 | 16.19 |
| Medium | 19 | -- | 103.16 | 36.52 | 34.92 | 20.95 | 195.55 | 19.56 |
| Fast | 21 | -- | 115.24 | 47.03 | 50.30 | 14.88 | 227.45 | 22.74 |

  Ceilings

| | | | | | | | | |
|---|---|---|---|---|---|---|---|---|
| Slow | 15 | -- | 102.67 | 30.28 | 25.26 | 25.32 | 183.53 | 18.35 |
| Medium | 17 | -- | 115.29 | 40.81 | 39.03 | 23.42 | 218.55 | 21.86 |
| Fast | 19 | -- | 127.37 | 51.98 | 55.60 | 16.45 | 251.40 | 25.14 |

Large rooms (living rooms)
  Walls

| | | | | | | | | |
|---|---|---|---|---|---|---|---|---|
| Slow | 20 | -- | 77.00 | 22.72 | 18.95 | 18.99 | 137.66 | 13.77 |
| Medium | 23 | -- | 85.22 | 30.15 | 28.85 | 17.31 | 161.53 | 16.16 |
| Fast | 26 | -- | 93.08 | 37.97 | 40.63 | 12.02 | 183.70 | 18.37 |

  Ceilings

| | | | | | | | | |
|---|---|---|---|---|---|---|---|---|
| Slow | 18 | -- | 85.56 | 25.23 | 21.05 | 21.10 | 152.94 | 15.30 |
| Medium | 20 | -- | 98.00 | 34.68 | 33.17 | 19.90 | 185.75 | 18.58 |
| Fast | 22 | -- | 110.00 | 44.86 | 48.01 | 14.20 | 217.07 | 21.71 |

*Wallcovering Costs*

|  | Labor rolls per day | Material by others | Labor cost per 10 rolls | Labor burden per 10 rolls | Overhead per 10 rolls | Profit per 10 rolls | Total cost per 10 rolls | Total price per roll |
|---|---|---|---|---|---|---|---|---|
| **Large wall areas (corridors, long hallways)** | | | | | | | | |
|   Walls | | | | | | | | |
|     Slow | 24 | -- | 64.17 | 18.92 | 15.79 | 15.82 | 114.70 | 11.47 |
|     Medium | 27 | -- | 72.59 | 25.69 | 24.57 | 14.74 | 137.59 | 13.76 |
|     Fast | 30 | -- | 80.67 | 32.92 | 35.21 | 10.42 | 159.22 | 15.92 |
|   Ceilings | | | | | | | | |
|     Slow | 21 | -- | 73.33 | 21.65 | 18.04 | 18.08 | 131.10 | 13.11 |
|     Medium | 23 | -- | 85.22 | 30.15 | 28.85 | 17.31 | 161.53 | 16.16 |
|     Fast | 25 | -- | 96.80 | 39.49 | 42.25 | 12.50 | 191.04 | 19.10 |
| **Paper-backed vinyl on medium room walls** | | | | | | | | |
|   Bedrooms, dining rooms | | | | | | | | |
|     Slow | 8 | -- | 192.50 | 56.80 | 47.37 | 47.47 | 344.14 | 34.41 |
|     Medium | 10 | -- | 196.00 | 69.36 | 66.35 | 39.81 | 371.52 | 37.15 |
|     Fast | 12 | -- | 201.67 | 82.28 | 88.02 | 26.04 | 398.01 | 39.80 |
| **Cork wallcovering on medium room walls** | | | | | | | | |
|   Bedrooms, dining rooms | | | | | | | | |
|     Slow | 8 | -- | 192.50 | 56.80 | 47.37 | 47.47 | 344.14 | 34.41 |
|     Medium | 10 | -- | 196.00 | 69.36 | 66.35 | 39.81 | 371.52 | 37.15 |
|     Fast | 12 | -- | 201.67 | 82.28 | 88.02 | 26.04 | 398.01 | 39.80 |

The table above assumes that residential rolls are hand pasted. ADD for surface preparation time from page 425 or from the tables in Part II, Preparation costs beginning on page 295, as needed. For heights above 8 feet, use the High Time Difficulty Factors on page 139. "Slow" work is based on an hourly wage of $19.25, "Medium" work on an hourly wage of $24.50, and "Fast" work on an hourly wage of $30.25. Add for ready-mix paste.

|  | Labor yards per day | Material by others | Labor cost per 10 yards | Labor burden 10 yards | Overhead per 10 yards | Profit per 10 yards | Total cost per 10 yards | Total price per yard |
|---|---|---|---|---|---|---|---|---|

## Wall fabric, commercial, machine pasted, yards per day, 48" to 54" width
Coated fabric
  Cut-up areas (stair halls, landing areas)
    Walls

| | | | | | | | | |
|---|---|---|---|---|---|---|---|---|
| Slow | 58 | -- | 25.17 | 7.42 | 6.19 | 6.21 | 44.99 | 4.50 |
| Medium | 63 | -- | 29.21 | 10.34 | 9.89 | 5.93 | 55.37 | 5.54 |
| Fast | 68 | -- | 33.24 | 13.54 | 14.51 | 4.29 | 65.58 | 6.56 |

    Ceilings

| | | | | | | | | |
|---|---|---|---|---|---|---|---|---|
| Slow | 35 | -- | 41.71 | 12.31 | 10.26 | 10.28 | 74.56 | 7.46 |
| Medium | 40 | -- | 46.00 | 16.28 | 15.57 | 9.34 | 87.19 | 8.72 |
| Fast | 45 | -- | 50.22 | 20.51 | 21.92 | 6.48 | 99.13 | 9.91 |

  Small rooms (restrooms, utility rooms)
    Walls

| | | | | | | | | |
|---|---|---|---|---|---|---|---|---|
| Slow | 60 | -- | 24.33 | 7.17 | 5.99 | 6.00 | 43.49 | 4.35 |
| Medium | 65 | -- | 28.31 | 10.02 | 9.58 | 5.75 | 53.66 | 5.37 |
| Fast | 70 | -- | 32.29 | 13.18 | 14.09 | 4.17 | 63.73 | 6.37 |

    Ceilings

| | | | | | | | | |
|---|---|---|---|---|---|---|---|---|
| Slow | 40 | -- | 36.50 | 10.76 | 8.98 | 9.00 | 65.24 | 6.53 |
| Medium | 48 | -- | 38.33 | 13.58 | 12.98 | 7.79 | 72.68 | 7.27 |
| Fast | 55 | -- | 41.09 | 16.79 | 17.93 | 5.30 | 81.11 | 8.11 |

  Medium rooms (offices)
    Walls

| | | | | | | | | |
|---|---|---|---|---|---|---|---|---|
| Slow | 68 | -- | 21.47 | 6.32 | 5.28 | 5.29 | 38.36 | 3.84 |
| Medium | 80 | -- | 23.00 | 8.14 | 7.79 | 4.67 | 43.60 | 4.36 |
| Fast | 93 | -- | 24.30 | 9.91 | 10.61 | 3.14 | 47.96 | 4.80 |

    Ceilings

| | | | | | | | | |
|---|---|---|---|---|---|---|---|---|
| Slow | 60 | -- | 24.33 | 7.17 | 5.99 | 6.00 | 43.49 | 4.35 |
| Medium | 73 | -- | 25.21 | 8.92 | 8.53 | 5.12 | 47.78 | 4.78 |
| Fast | 85 | -- | 26.59 | 10.84 | 11.61 | 3.43 | 52.47 | 5.25 |

  Large rooms (conference rooms)
    Walls

| | | | | | | | | |
|---|---|---|---|---|---|---|---|---|
| Slow | 85 | -- | 17.18 | 5.06 | 4.23 | 4.24 | 30.71 | 3.07 |
| Medium | 98 | -- | 18.78 | 6.63 | 6.36 | 3.81 | 35.58 | 3.56 |
| Fast | 110 | -- | 20.55 | 8.37 | 8.97 | 2.65 | 40.54 | 4.06 |

    Ceilings

| | | | | | | | | |
|---|---|---|---|---|---|---|---|---|
| Slow | 68 | -- | 21.47 | 6.32 | 5.28 | 5.29 | 38.36 | 3.84 |
| Medium | 80 | -- | 23.00 | 8.14 | 7.79 | 4.67 | 43.60 | 4.36 |
| Fast | 93 | -- | 24.30 | 9.91 | 10.61 | 3.14 | 47.96 | 4.80 |

*Wallcovering Costs*

|  | Labor yards per day | Material by others | Labor cost per 10 yards | Labor burden 10 yards | Overhead per 10 yards | Profit per 10 yards | Total cost per 10 yards | Total price per yard |
|---|---|---|---|---|---|---|---|---|
| **Large wall areas (corridors, long hallways)** | | | | | | | | |
| *Walls* | | | | | | | | |
| Slow | 80 | -- | 18.25 | 5.38 | 4.49 | 4.50 | 32.62 | 3.26 |
| Medium | 110 | -- | 16.73 | 5.91 | 5.66 | 3.40 | 31.70 | 3.17 |
| Fast | 125 | -- | 18.08 | 7.38 | 7.89 | 2.33 | 35.68 | 3.57 |
| *Ceilings* | | | | | | | | |
| Slow | 78 | -- | 18.72 | 5.52 | 4.61 | 4.62 | 33.47 | 3.35 |
| Medium | 90 | -- | 20.44 | 7.24 | 6.92 | 4.15 | 38.75 | 3.88 |
| Fast | 103 | -- | 21.94 | 8.97 | 9.58 | 2.83 | 43.32 | 4.33 |

Canvas sheeting: see Wall fabric, residential, hand pasted

Grasscloth: see Wall fabric, residential, hand pasted

Burlap: see Wall fabric, residential, hand pasted

Natural fabric, silk: see Wall fabric, residential, hand pasted

Natural fabric, felt, linen, cotton: see Wall fabric, residential, hand pasted

The table above assumes that commercial rolls are machine pasted. ADD for surface preparation time from page 425 or from the tables in Part II, Preparation costs beginning on page 295 as needed. For heights above 8 feet, use the High Time Difficulty Factors on page 139.  "Slow" work is based on an hourly wage of $18.25, "Medium" work on an hourly wage of $23.00, and "Fast" work on an hourly wage of $28.25. Add for ready-mix paste.

|  | Labor rolls per day | Material by others | Labor cost per 10 rolls | Labor burden 10 rolls | Overhead per 10 rolls | Profit per 10 rolls | Total cost per 10 rolls | Total price per roll |
|---|---|---|---|---|---|---|---|---|

## Wall fabric, residential, hand pasted, single rolls per day 18" to 27" wide

Coated fabrics
  Cut-up areas (stair halls, landing areas)
    Walls

| | | | | | | | | |
|---|---|---|---|---|---|---|---|---|
| Slow | 12 | -- | 128.33 | 37.88 | 31.58 | 31.64 | 229.43 | 22.94 |
| Medium | 13 | -- | 150.77 | 53.36 | 51.04 | 30.62 | 285.79 | 28.58 |
| Fast | 14 | -- | 172.86 | 70.50 | 75.45 | 22.32 | 341.13 | 34.12 |

    Ceilings

| | | | | | | | | |
|---|---|---|---|---|---|---|---|---|
| Slow | 8 | -- | 192.50 | 56.80 | 47.37 | 47.47 | 344.14 | 34.41 |
| Medium | 9 | -- | 217.78 | 77.07 | 73.72 | 44.23 | 412.80 | 41.28 |
| Fast | 10 | -- | 242.00 | 98.72 | 105.63 | 31.25 | 477.60 | 47.76 |

  Small rooms (baths, utility rooms)
    Walls

| | | | | | | | | |
|---|---|---|---|---|---|---|---|---|
| Slow | 13 | -- | 118.46 | 34.96 | 29.15 | 29.21 | 211.78 | 21.18 |
| Medium | 14 | -- | 140.00 | 49.53 | 47.39 | 28.43 | 265.35 | 26.54 |
| Fast | 15 | -- | 161.33 | 65.80 | 70.42 | 20.83 | 318.38 | 31.84 |

    Ceilings

| | | | | | | | | |
|---|---|---|---|---|---|---|---|---|
| Slow | 10 | -- | 154.00 | 45.44 | 37.89 | 37.97 | 275.30 | 27.53 |
| Medium | 11 | -- | 178.18 | 63.07 | 60.32 | 36.19 | 337.76 | 33.78 |
| Fast | 12 | -- | 201.67 | 82.28 | 88.02 | 26.04 | 398.01 | 39.80 |

  Medium rooms (bedrooms, dining rooms)
    Walls

| | | | | | | | | |
|---|---|---|---|---|---|---|---|---|
| Slow | 18 | -- | 85.56 | 25.23 | 21.05 | 21.10 | 152.94 | 15.30 |
| Medium | 20 | -- | 98.00 | 34.68 | 33.17 | 19.90 | 185.75 | 18.58 |
| Fast | 22 | -- | 110.00 | 44.86 | 48.01 | 14.20 | 217.07 | 21.71 |

    Ceilings

| | | | | | | | | |
|---|---|---|---|---|---|---|---|---|
| Slow | 16 | -- | 96.25 | 28.40 | 23.68 | 23.73 | 172.06 | 17.21 |
| Medium | 18 | -- | 108.89 | 38.52 | 36.86 | 22.12 | 206.39 | 20.64 |
| Fast | 20 | -- | 121.00 | 49.36 | 52.81 | 15.62 | 238.79 | 23.88 |

  Large rooms (living rooms)
    Walls

| | | | | | | | | |
|---|---|---|---|---|---|---|---|---|
| Slow | 22 | -- | 70.00 | 20.65 | 17.22 | 17.26 | 125.13 | 12.51 |
| Medium | 25 | -- | 78.40 | 27.74 | 26.54 | 15.92 | 148.60 | 14.86 |
| Fast | 28 | -- | 86.43 | 35.25 | 37.72 | 11.16 | 170.56 | 17.06 |

    Ceilings

| | | | | | | | | |
|---|---|---|---|---|---|---|---|---|
| Slow | 19 | -- | 81.05 | 23.93 | 19.94 | 19.98 | 144.90 | 14.49 |
| Medium | 21 | -- | 93.33 | 33.05 | 31.59 | 18.96 | 176.93 | 17.69 |
| Fast | 23 | -- | 105.22 | 42.91 | 45.93 | 13.59 | 207.65 | 20.77 |

## Wallcovering Costs

|  | Labor rolls per day | Material by others | Labor cost per 10 rolls | Labor burden per 10 rolls | Overhead per 10 rolls | Profit per 10 rolls | Total cost per 10 rolls | Total price per roll |
|---|---|---|---|---|---|---|---|---|
| **Large wall areas (corridors, long hallways)** | | | | | | | | |
| Walls | | | | | | | | |
| Slow | 26 | -- | 59.23 | 17.48 | 14.57 | 14.60 | 105.88 | 10.59 |
| Medium | 29 | -- | 67.59 | 23.93 | 22.88 | 13.73 | 128.13 | 12.81 |
| Fast | 32 | -- | 75.63 | 30.85 | 33.01 | 9.77 | 149.26 | 14.93 |
| Ceilings | | | | | | | | |
| Slow | 22 | -- | 70.00 | 20.65 | 17.22 | 17.26 | 125.13 | 12.51 |
| Medium | 24 | -- | 81.67 | 28.89 | 27.65 | 16.59 | 154.80 | 15.48 |
| Fast | 26 | -- | 93.08 | 37.97 | 40.63 | 12.02 | 183.70 | 18.37 |
| **Canvas sheeting** | | | | | | | | |
| Medium room walls (bedrooms, dining rooms) | | | | | | | | |
| Walls | | | | | | | | |
| Slow | 14 | -- | 110.00 | 32.45 | 27.07 | 27.12 | 196.64 | 19.66 |
| Medium | 16 | -- | 122.50 | 43.35 | 41.47 | 24.88 | 232.20 | 23.22 |
| Fast | 17 | -- | 142.35 | 58.08 | 62.13 | 18.38 | 280.94 | 28.09 |
| **Grasscloth** | | | | | | | | |
| Medium room walls (bedrooms, dining rooms) | | | | | | | | |
| Walls | | | | | | | | |
| Slow | 15 | -- | 102.67 | 30.28 | 25.26 | 25.32 | 183.53 | 18.35 |
| Medium | 20 | -- | 98.00 | 34.68 | 33.17 | 19.90 | 185.75 | 18.58 |
| Fast | 24 | -- | 100.83 | 41.12 | 44.01 | 13.02 | 198.98 | 19.90 |
| **Burlap** | | | | | | | | |
| Medium rooms (bedrooms, dining rooms) | | | | | | | | |
| Walls | | | | | | | | |
| Slow | 10 | -- | 154.00 | 45.44 | 37.89 | 37.97 | 275.30 | 27.53 |
| Medium | 14 | -- | 140.00 | 49.53 | 47.39 | 28.43 | 265.35 | 26.54 |
| Fast | 18 | -- | 134.44 | 54.83 | 58.68 | 17.36 | 265.31 | 26.53 |
| **Natural fabric, silk** | | | | | | | | |
| Medium rooms (bedrooms, dining rooms) | | | | | | | | |
| Walls | | | | | | | | |
| Slow | 8 | -- | 192.50 | 56.80 | 47.37 | 47.47 | 344.14 | 34.41 |
| Medium | 12 | -- | 163.33 | 57.81 | 55.29 | 33.17 | 309.60 | 30.96 |
| Fast | 15 | -- | 161.33 | 65.80 | 70.42 | 20.83 | 318.38 | 31.84 |
| **Natural fabric, felt, linen, cotton** | | | | | | | | |
| Medium rooms (bedrooms, dining rooms) | | | | | | | | |
| Walls | | | | | | | | |
| Slow | 7 | -- | 220.00 | 64.92 | 54.13 | 54.24 | 393.29 | 39.33 |
| Medium | 9 | -- | 217.78 | 77.07 | 73.72 | 44.23 | 412.80 | 41.28 |
| Fast | 11 | -- | 220.00 | 89.76 | 96.03 | 28.41 | 434.20 | 43.42 |

The table above assumes that residential rolls are hand pasted. ADD for surface preparation time from page 425 or from the tables in Part II, Preparation costs beginning on page 295 as needed. For heights above 8 feet, use the High Time Difficulty Factors on page 139. "Slow" work is based on an hourly wage of $19.25, "Medium" work on an hourly wage of $24.50, and "Fast" work on an hourly wage of $30.25. Add for ready-mix paste.

*National Painting Cost Estimator*

|  | Labor rolls per day | Material by others | Labor cost per 10 rolls | Labor burden 10 rolls | Overhead per 10 rolls | Profit per 10 rolls | Total cost per 10 rolls | Total price per roll |
|---|---|---|---|---|---|---|---|---|

## Wallpaper, commercial, machine pasted, single rolls per day, 27" width

Blind stock (lining)
  Cut-up areas (stair halls, landing areas)
    Walls

| | | | | | | | | |
|---|---|---|---|---|---|---|---|---|
| Slow | 19 | -- | 76.84 | 22.67 | 18.91 | 18.95 | 137.37 | 13.74 |
| Medium | 21 | -- | 87.62 | 31.02 | 29.66 | 17.80 | 166.10 | 16.61 |
| Fast | 23 | -- | 98.26 | 40.09 | 42.89 | 12.69 | 193.93 | 19.39 |

    Ceilings

| | | | | | | | | |
|---|---|---|---|---|---|---|---|---|
| Slow | 16 | -- | 91.25 | 26.90 | 22.45 | 22.50 | 163.10 | 16.31 |
| Medium | 18 | -- | 102.22 | 36.17 | 34.60 | 20.76 | 193.75 | 19.38 |
| Fast | 20 | -- | 113.00 | 46.12 | 49.32 | 14.59 | 223.03 | 22.30 |

  Small rooms (restrooms, utility rooms)
    Walls

| | | | | | | | | |
|---|---|---|---|---|---|---|---|---|
| Slow | 21 | -- | 69.52 | 20.51 | 17.11 | 17.14 | 124.28 | 12.43 |
| Medium | 25 | -- | 73.60 | 26.05 | 24.91 | 14.95 | 139.51 | 13.95 |
| Fast | 29 | -- | 77.93 | 31.82 | 34.02 | 10.06 | 153.83 | 15.38 |

    Ceilings

| | | | | | | | | |
|---|---|---|---|---|---|---|---|---|
| Slow | 17 | -- | 85.88 | 25.32 | 21.13 | 21.17 | 153.50 | 15.35 |
| Medium | 20 | -- | 92.00 | 32.56 | 31.14 | 18.69 | 174.39 | 17.44 |
| Fast | 22 | -- | 102.73 | 41.91 | 44.84 | 13.26 | 202.74 | 20.27 |

  Medium rooms (offices)
    Walls

| | | | | | | | | |
|---|---|---|---|---|---|---|---|---|
| Slow | 29 | -- | 50.34 | 14.86 | 12.39 | 12.41 | 90.00 | 9.00 |
| Medium | 35 | -- | 52.57 | 18.62 | 17.80 | 10.68 | 99.67 | 9.97 |
| Fast | 41 | -- | 55.12 | 22.49 | 24.06 | 7.12 | 108.79 | 10.88 |

    Ceilings

| | | | | | | | | |
|---|---|---|---|---|---|---|---|---|
| Slow | 25 | -- | 58.40 | 17.22 | 14.37 | 14.40 | 104.39 | 10.44 |
| Medium | 30 | -- | 61.33 | 21.72 | 20.76 | 12.46 | 116.27 | 11.63 |
| Fast | 34 | -- | 66.47 | 27.13 | 29.01 | 8.58 | 131.19 | 13.12 |

  Large rooms (conference rooms)
    Walls

| | | | | | | | | |
|---|---|---|---|---|---|---|---|---|
| Slow | 35 | -- | 41.71 | 12.31 | 10.26 | 10.28 | 74.56 | 7.46 |
| Medium | 41 | -- | 44.88 | 15.87 | 15.19 | 9.12 | 85.06 | 8.51 |
| Fast | 47 | -- | 48.09 | 19.62 | 20.99 | 6.21 | 94.91 | 9.49 |

    Ceilings

| | | | | | | | | |
|---|---|---|---|---|---|---|---|---|
| Slow | 29 | -- | 50.34 | 14.86 | 12.39 | 12.41 | 90.00 | 9.00 |
| Medium | 34 | -- | 54.12 | 19.15 | 18.32 | 10.99 | 102.58 | 10.26 |
| Fast | 38 | -- | 59.47 | 24.27 | 25.96 | 7.68 | 117.38 | 11.74 |

## Wallcovering Costs

|  | Labor rolls per day | Material by others | Labor cost per 10 rolls | Labor burden 10 rolls | Overhead per 10 rolls | Profit per 10 rolls | Total cost per 10 rolls | Total price per roll |
|---|---|---|---|---|---|---|---|---|
| **Large wall areas (corridors, long hallways)** | | | | | | | | |
| **Walls** | | | | | | | | |
| Slow | 40 | -- | 36.50 | 10.76 | 8.98 | 9.00 | 65.24 | 6.53 |
| Medium | 45 | -- | 40.89 | 14.48 | 13.84 | 8.31 | 77.52 | 7.75 |
| Fast | 50 | -- | 45.20 | 18.45 | 19.73 | 5.84 | 89.22 | 8.92 |
| **Ceilings** | | | | | | | | |
| Slow | 33 | -- | 44.24 | 13.04 | 10.89 | 10.91 | 79.08 | 7.91 |
| Medium | 38 | -- | 48.42 | 17.13 | 16.39 | 9.83 | 91.77 | 9.18 |
| Fast | 42 | -- | 53.81 | 21.97 | 23.49 | 6.95 | 106.22 | 10.62 |
| **Ordinary pre-trimmed wallpaper or butt joint work** | | | | | | | | |
| **Medium room walls (offices)** | | | | | | | | |
| **Walls** | | | | | | | | |
| Slow | 26 | -- | 56.15 | 16.56 | 13.81 | 13.84 | 100.36 | 10.04 |
| Medium | 31 | -- | 59.35 | 21.02 | 20.09 | 12.05 | 112.51 | 11.25 |
| Fast | 36 | -- | 62.78 | 25.61 | 27.40 | 8.11 | 123.90 | 12.39 |
| **Ceilings** | | | | | | | | |
| Slow | 23 | -- | 63.48 | 18.71 | 15.62 | 15.65 | 113.46 | 11.35 |
| Medium | 28 | -- | 65.71 | 23.26 | 22.24 | 13.35 | 124.56 | 12.46 |
| Fast | 32 | -- | 70.63 | 28.82 | 30.83 | 9.12 | 139.40 | 13.94 |
| **Hand-crafted wallpaper** | | | | | | | | |
| **Medium room walls (offices)** | | | | | | | | |
| **Walls** | | | | | | | | |
| Slow | 20 | -- | 73.00 | 21.52 | 17.96 | 18.00 | 130.48 | 13.05 |
| Medium | 24 | -- | 76.67 | 27.12 | 25.95 | 15.57 | 145.31 | 14.53 |
| Fast | 28 | -- | 80.71 | 32.94 | 35.23 | 10.42 | 159.30 | 15.93 |
| **Ceilings** | | | | | | | | |
| Slow | 18 | -- | 81.11 | 23.90 | 19.96 | 20.00 | 144.97 | 14.50 |
| Medium | 21 | -- | 87.62 | 31.02 | 29.66 | 17.80 | 166.10 | 16.61 |
| Fast | 23 | -- | 98.26 | 40.09 | 42.89 | 12.69 | 193.93 | 19.39 |
| **Flock wallpaper, medium rooms (offices)** | | | | | | | | |
| **Walls** | | | | | | | | |
| Slow | 14 | -- | 104.29 | 30.73 | 25.66 | 25.72 | 186.40 | 18.64 |
| Medium | 17 | -- | 108.24 | 38.30 | 36.64 | 21.98 | 205.16 | 20.52 |
| Fast | 20 | -- | 113.00 | 46.12 | 49.32 | 14.59 | 223.03 | 22.30 |
| **Foil wallpaper, medium rooms (offices)** | | | | | | | | |
| **Walls** | | | | | | | | |
| Slow | 13 | -- | 112.31 | 33.11 | 27.63 | 27.69 | 200.74 | 20.08 |
| Medium | 16 | -- | 115.00 | 40.70 | 38.93 | 23.36 | 217.99 | 21.80 |
| Fast | 19 | -- | 118.95 | 48.56 | 51.92 | 15.36 | 234.79 | 23.48 |

## National Painting Cost Estimator

|  | Labor rolls per day | Material by others | Labor cost per 10 rolls | Labor burden 10 rolls | Overhead per 10 rolls | Profit per 10 rolls | Total cost per 10 rolls | Total price per roll |
|---|---|---|---|---|---|---|---|---|
| **Canvas wallpaper, medium rooms (offices)** | | | | | | | | |
| Walls | | | | | | | | |
| Slow | 12 | -- | 121.67 | 35.87 | 29.94 | 30.00 | 217.48 | 21.75 |
| Medium | 14 | -- | 131.43 | 46.50 | 44.49 | 26.69 | 249.11 | 24.91 |
| Fast | 16 | -- | 141.25 | 57.65 | 61.65 | 18.24 | 278.79 | 27.88 |
| **Scenic wallpaper, medium rooms (offices)** | | | | | | | | |
| Walls | | | | | | | | |
| Slow | 16 | -- | 91.25 | 26.90 | 22.45 | 22.50 | 163.10 | 16.31 |
| Medium | 18 | -- | 102.22 | 36.17 | 34.60 | 20.76 | 193.75 | 19.38 |
| Fast | 20 | -- | 113.00 | 46.12 | 49.32 | 14.59 | 223.03 | 22.30 |

The table above assumes that commercial rolls are machine pasted. ADD for surface preparation time from page 425 or from the tables in Part II, Preparation costs beginning on page 295, as needed. For heights above 8 feet, use the High Time Difficulty Factors on page 139. "Slow" work is based on an hourly wage of $18.25, "Medium" work on an hourly wage of $23.00, and "Fast" work on an hourly wage of $28.25. Add for ready-mix paste.

*Wallcovering Costs*

|  | Labor rolls per day | Material by others | Labor cost per 10 rolls | Labor burden 10 rolls | Overhead per 10 rolls | Profit per 10 rolls | Total cost per 10 rolls | Total price per roll |
|---|---|---|---|---|---|---|---|---|

## Wallpaper, residential, hand pasted, single rolls per day 18" to 27" wide
### Blind stock (lining)
#### Cut-up areas (stair halls, landing areas)
##### Walls
| | | | | | | | | |
|---|---|---|---|---|---|---|---|---|
| Slow | 11 | -- | 140.00 | 41.32 | 34.45 | 34.52 | 250.29 | 25.03 |
| Medium | 13 | -- | 150.77 | 53.36 | 51.04 | 30.62 | 285.79 | 28.58 |
| Fast | 14 | -- | 172.86 | 70.50 | 75.45 | 22.32 | 341.13 | 34.12 |

##### Ceilings
| | | | | | | | | |
|---|---|---|---|---|---|---|---|---|
| Slow | 10 | -- | 154.00 | 45.44 | 37.89 | 37.97 | 275.30 | 27.53 |
| Medium | 11 | -- | 178.18 | 63.07 | 60.32 | 36.19 | 337.76 | 33.78 |
| Fast | 12 | -- | 201.67 | 82.28 | 88.02 | 26.04 | 398.01 | 39.80 |

#### Small rooms (baths, utility rooms)
##### Walls
| | | | | | | | | |
|---|---|---|---|---|---|---|---|---|
| Slow | 12 | -- | 128.33 | 37.88 | 31.58 | 31.64 | 229.43 | 22.94 |
| Medium | 14 | -- | 140.00 | 49.53 | 47.39 | 28.43 | 265.35 | 26.54 |
| Fast | 16 | -- | 151.25 | 61.70 | 66.02 | 19.53 | 298.50 | 29.85 |

##### Ceilings
| | | | | | | | | |
|---|---|---|---|---|---|---|---|---|
| Slow | 11 | -- | 140.00 | 41.32 | 34.45 | 34.52 | 250.29 | 25.03 |
| Medium | 13 | -- | 150.77 | 53.36 | 51.04 | 30.62 | 285.79 | 28.58 |
| Fast | 14 | -- | 172.86 | 70.50 | 75.45 | 22.32 | 341.13 | 34.12 |

#### Medium rooms (bedrooms, dining rooms)
##### Walls
| | | | | | | | | |
|---|---|---|---|---|---|---|---|---|
| Slow | 20 | -- | 77.00 | 22.72 | 18.95 | 18.99 | 137.66 | 13.77 |
| Medium | 23 | -- | 85.22 | 30.15 | 28.85 | 17.31 | 161.53 | 16.16 |
| Fast | 26 | -- | 93.08 | 37.97 | 40.63 | 12.02 | 183.70 | 18.37 |

##### Ceilings
| | | | | | | | | |
|---|---|---|---|---|---|---|---|---|
| Slow | 18 | -- | 85.56 | 25.23 | 21.05 | 21.10 | 152.94 | 15.30 |
| Medium | 20 | -- | 98.00 | 34.68 | 33.17 | 19.90 | 185.75 | 18.58 |
| Fast | 22 | -- | 110.00 | 44.86 | 48.01 | 14.20 | 217.07 | 21.71 |

#### Large rooms (living rooms)
##### Walls
| | | | | | | | | |
|---|---|---|---|---|---|---|---|---|
| Slow | 23 | -- | 66.96 | 19.75 | 16.47 | 16.51 | 119.69 | 11.97 |
| Medium | 27 | -- | 72.59 | 25.69 | 24.57 | 14.74 | 137.59 | 13.76 |
| Fast | 31 | -- | 78.06 | 31.86 | 34.07 | 10.08 | 154.07 | 15.41 |

##### Ceilings
| | | | | | | | | |
|---|---|---|---|---|---|---|---|---|
| Slow | 20 | -- | 77.00 | 22.72 | 18.95 | 18.99 | 137.66 | 13.77 |
| Medium | 22 | -- | 89.09 | 31.52 | 30.16 | 18.09 | 168.86 | 16.89 |
| Fast | 24 | -- | 100.83 | 41.12 | 44.01 | 13.02 | 198.98 | 19.90 |

## National Painting Cost Estimator

|  | Labor rolls per day | Material by others | Labor cost per 10 rolls | Labor burden 10 rolls | Overhead per 10 rolls | Profit per 10 rolls | Total cost per 10 rolls | Total price per roll |
|---|---|---|---|---|---|---|---|---|
| **Large wall areas (corridors, long hallways)** | | | | | | | | |
| *Walls* | | | | | | | | |
| Slow | 29 | -- | 53.10 | 15.68 | 13.06 | 13.09 | 94.93 | 9.49 |
| Medium | 33 | -- | 59.39 | 21.01 | 20.10 | 12.06 | 112.56 | 11.26 |
| Fast | 36 | -- | 67.22 | 27.41 | 29.34 | 8.68 | 132.65 | 13.27 |
| *Ceilings* | | | | | | | | |
| Slow | 23 | -- | 66.96 | 19.75 | 16.47 | 16.51 | 119.69 | 11.97 |
| Medium | 25 | -- | 78.40 | 27.74 | 26.54 | 15.92 | 148.60 | 14.86 |
| Fast | 27 | -- | 89.63 | 36.56 | 39.12 | 11.57 | 176.88 | 17.69 |
| **Ordinary pre-trimmed wallpaper or butt joint work** | | | | | | | | |
| *Medium room walls (bedrooms, dining rooms)* | | | | | | | | |
| *Walls* | | | | | | | | |
| Slow | 18 | -- | 85.56 | 25.23 | 21.05 | 21.10 | 152.94 | 15.30 |
| Medium | 21 | -- | 93.33 | 33.05 | 31.59 | 18.96 | 176.93 | 17.69 |
| Fast | 24 | -- | 100.83 | 41.12 | 44.01 | 13.02 | 198.98 | 19.90 |
| *Ceilings* | | | | | | | | |
| Slow | 16 | -- | 96.25 | 28.40 | 23.68 | 23.73 | 172.06 | 17.21 |
| Medium | 18 | -- | 108.89 | 38.52 | 36.86 | 22.12 | 206.39 | 20.64 |
| Fast | 20 | -- | 121.00 | 49.36 | 52.81 | 15.62 | 238.79 | 23.88 |
| **Hand-crafted wallpaper** | | | | | | | | |
| *Medium room walls (bedrooms, dining rooms)* | | | | | | | | |
| *Walls* | | | | | | | | |
| Slow | 12 | -- | 128.33 | 37.88 | 31.58 | 31.64 | 229.43 | 22.94 |
| Medium | 15 | -- | 130.67 | 46.23 | 44.23 | 26.54 | 247.67 | 24.77 |
| Fast | 18 | -- | 134.44 | 54.83 | 58.68 | 17.36 | 265.31 | 26.53 |
| *Ceilings* | | | | | | | | |
| Slow | 10 | -- | 154.00 | 45.44 | 37.89 | 37.97 | 275.30 | 27.53 |
| Medium | 12 | -- | 163.33 | 57.81 | 55.29 | 33.17 | 309.60 | 30.96 |
| Fast | 14 | -- | 172.86 | 70.50 | 75.45 | 22.32 | 341.13 | 34.12 |
| **Flock wallpaper, medium rooms (bedrooms, dining rooms)** | | | | | | | | |
| *Walls* | | | | | | | | |
| Slow | 10 | -- | 154.00 | 45.44 | 37.89 | 37.97 | 275.30 | 27.53 |
| Medium | 13 | -- | 150.77 | 53.36 | 51.04 | 30.62 | 285.79 | 28.58 |
| Fast | 16 | -- | 151.25 | 61.70 | 66.02 | 19.53 | 298.50 | 29.85 |
| **Foil wallpaper, medium rooms (bedrooms, dining rooms)** | | | | | | | | |
| *Walls* | | | | | | | | |
| Slow | 9 | -- | 171.11 | 50.49 | 42.10 | 42.19 | 305.89 | 30.59 |
| Medium | 12 | -- | 163.33 | 57.81 | 55.29 | 33.17 | 309.60 | 30.96 |
| Fast | 15 | -- | 161.33 | 65.80 | 70.42 | 20.83 | 318.38 | 31.84 |

# Wallcovering Costs

|  | Labor rolls per day | Material by others | Labor cost per 10 rolls | Labor burden 10 rolls | Overhead per 10 rolls | Profit per 10 rolls | Total cost per 10 rolls | Total price per roll |
|---|---|---|---|---|---|---|---|---|
| **Canvas wallpaper, medium rooms (bedrooms, dining rooms)** | | | | | | | | |
| Walls | | | | | | | | |
| Slow | 8 | -- | 192.50 | 56.80 | 47.37 | 47.47 | 344.14 | 34.41 |
| Medium | 10 | -- | 196.00 | 69.36 | 66.35 | 39.81 | 371.52 | 37.15 |
| Fast | 12 | -- | 201.67 | 82.28 | 88.02 | 26.04 | 398.01 | 39.80 |
| **Scenic wallpaper, medium rooms (bedrooms, dining rooms)** | | | | | | | | |
| Walls | | | | | | | | |
| Slow | 12 | -- | 128.33 | 37.88 | 31.58 | 31.64 | 229.43 | 22.94 |
| Medium | 14 | -- | 140.00 | 49.53 | 47.39 | 28.43 | 265.35 | 26.54 |
| Fast | 16 | -- | 151.25 | 61.70 | 66.02 | 19.53 | 298.50 | 29.85 |

The table above assumes that residential rolls are hand pasted. ADD for surface preparation time from page 425 or from the tables in Part II, Preparation costs beginning on page 295, as needed. For heights above 8 feet, use the High Time Difficulty Factors on page 139. "Slow" work is based on an hourly wage of $19.25, "Medium" work on an hourly wage of $24.50, and "Fast" work on an hourly wage of $30.25. Add for ready-mix paste.

# Index

## A

Accessories,
  remove and replace . . . . . . . .9
Acid wash gutters &
  downspouts . . . . . . . . . . . . .296
Acoustic spray-on texture . . .61
Adhesive coverage . . . . . . . .422
Adjustments to costs . . . . . . . .7
Adobe block . . . . . . . . .144-146
Air compressors, rental . . . . .33
Air hose, rental . . . . . . . . . . .33
Airblast . . . . . . . . . . . . . . . .296
Allowance
  for supervision . . . . . . . . . .14
  overhead . . . . . . . . . . . . . . .32
  sundries . . . . . . . . . . . . .10, 26
Aluminum base paint
  . . . . . . . . . . . .19, 22, 25, 358
Aluminum siding . . . . . . . .202
Anti-graffiti stain eliminator
  . . . . .18, 21, 24, 62, 140, 225
Apartments, allowance
  for supervision . . . . . . . . . .14
Application method . . . . . . . .6
Application rate
  . . . . . . . . .5, 13, 15, 30, 424
Arched roof . . . . . . . . . . . . .184

## B

Back-painting . . . . .94, 309-311
Bags, strainer . . . . . . . . . . . .28
Balusters . . . . . . . . . . .173, 177
Banana board . . . . . . . . . . . .33
Bare duct . . . . . . . . . .331-338
Bare piping . . . . . . . .357-365
Bargaining, collective . . . . . .31
Baseboard . . . . . . . . . . . .43-44
  preparation . . . . . . . . . . . .10
Basis for estimates . . . . . . . . .5
Baths, painting . . . . . . . . . .231
Beams . . . . . . . . . . . . . . .45-47
Bender paint pads . . . . . . . .27
Benefits . . . . . . . . . . . . . . . . .8
  employee . . . . . . . . . . .30-31
  fringe . . . . . . . . . . . .7, 30-31
  health . . . . . . . . . . . . . . . .30
Beveled siding . . . . . . .214-219

Bid
  expiration date . . . . . . . . . .29
  standard base . . . . . . . .36-37
  surface preparation . . . . . .10
Bidding variables . . . . . .36-37
Bifold doors . . . . . . . . . . . .102
Blank estimating form . . .40-41
Blank painting estimate . . . .40
Bleach . . . . . . . . . . . . . . . . .311
Blinds and shutters . . . . . . .201
Block filler .18, 21, 24, 140-141
Board and batten siding .214-219
Boiler room . . . . . . . . . . . .357
Bond, performance . . . . . . .31
Bonds . . . . . . . . . . . . . . . . . .9
Boneyard . . . . . . . . . . . .43-44
Bonuses . . . . . . . . . . . . . .9, 35
Bookcases
  paint grade . . . . . . . . . .48-49
  stain grade . . . . . . . . . .50-51
Boomlift, rental . . . . . . . . . .33
Borders, wallpaper . . . .424-425
Bottom line . . . . . . . . . . . . .37
Brick
  masonry . . . . . . . . . .141-146
  sandblasting . . . . . . . . . . . .11
Bridge painters, wages . . . . .30
Brush-off blast . . . . . . .11, 303
Brushes . . . . . . . . . . . . . . . .27
Burden
  employer's . . . . . . . . . . . . .8
  fixed . . . . . . . . . . . . . . . . .30
  labor . . . . . . . . . . . . . . . .5, 6
Burlap . . . . . . . . . . . . . . . .433
Burn off paint . . . . . . . . . .297
Butt joint . . . . . . . . . . . . . .435
Butt siding . . . . . . . . .214-219

## C

Cabinet
  faces . . . . . . . . . . . . . . . . .52
  masking . . . . . . . . . . . . . . .9
  paint grade . . . . . . . . . .52-54
  stain grade . . . . . . . . . .55-56
Calculate
  labor rate . . . . . . . . . . . . .30
  overhead . . . . . . . . . . . . . .32
  paint film thickness . . . . . .15
  profit percentage . . . . . . . .35

Canvas
  insulated ductwork . .339-347
  jacketed piping . . . .365-370
  sheeting . . . . . . . . . .433, 436
Cap
  railing . . . . . . . . . . . . . . .173
  sheet metal . . . . . . . . . . .196
Carport overhang . . . . . . . .159
Casters, scaffolding . . . . . . .33
Categories, labor productivity .13
Caulk . . . . . . . . . . . . . .10, 298
Caulking . . . . . . .19, 22, 25, 27
Caulking gun . . . . . . . . . . . .27
Ceiling panels, suspended.57-59
Ceiling pans . . . . . . . . . . . . .60
Ceilings, drywall
  acoustic spray-on texture . .61
  anti-graffiti stain eliminator.62
  orange peel texture . . . .63-68
  sand finish texture . . . . .67-74
  smooth finish . . . . . . . .75-79
Ceilings, tongue & groove
  paint grade . . . . . . . . . .80-85
  stain grade . . . . . . . . . .86-88
Cellulose, powdered
  . . . . . . . . . .19, 22, 25, 422
Chain link fence . . . . . . . . .123
Clay brick tile . . . . . . .144-146
Cleanup . . . . . . . . . . . . . .9, 10
Closets . . . . . . . . . . . . . . . . .91
  doors . . . . . . . . . . . . . . . .102
  moldings . . . . . . . . . .91, 102
  poles . . . . . . . . . . . .88-89, 102
  shelves . . . . . . . . . .89-90, 102
Coatings, mixing . . . . . . . . . .9
Collective bargaining
  agreement . . . . . . . . . . . .31
Color codes, piping . . .359-370
Color samples . . . . . . . . . . . .9
Colors, OSHA . . . . . .19, 22, 25
Column headings defined . . .13
Commercial
  jobs . . . . . . . . . . . . . . . . . .9
  sandblasting . . . . . . . .11, 304
  supervision, allowance for .14
Commercial blast . . . . . . . .304
Commercial wallcoverings
  fabric . . . . . . . . . . . .430-431
  paper . . . . . . . . . . . .434-436
  vinyl . . . . . . . . . . . .426-427

Commissions . . . . . . . . . .9, 35
Competition between
  manufacturers . . . . . . . . . .26
Competition, bidding . . .35-37
Composition
  roof shingles . . . . . . .185-189
  siding shingles . . . . . .203-207
Compressed air . . . . . . . . .295
Compressors, painting . . . . .356
Computing overhead . . . . . .32
Concrete floors . . . . . .129-132
Concrete Masonry Units
  . . . . . . . . . .147-152, 354-355
Concrete tilt-up walls . .412-417
Condos, allowance for
  supervision . . . . . . . . . . . .14
Conduit . . . . . . . . . . . .318-325
Conduit/pipe area conversion
  table . . . . . . . . . . . . . . . .325
Contingency allowance . . .9, 11
Contractors, remodeling . . . .35
Conversion table,
  conduit/pipe area . . . . . . .325
Converting unit prices . . . . . .9
Corbels . . . . . . . . . . . . . . . .92
Cork wallcovering . . . .427, 429
Cornice, overhang . . . . . . .159
Corrugated metal . . . . . . . .326
Corrugations, estimating
  . . . . . . . . . . . . . . . .326-329
Cost estimates, basis for . . . . .6
Cost overruns . . . . . . . . . . .10
Cost per unit . . . . . . . . . . . .31
Cost Plus Fee . . . . . . . .296, 315
Cost tables, using . . . . . . . . .6
Costs
  customizing . . . . . . . . . . . .7
  delivery . . . . . . . . . . . . . . .9
  equipment purchase & rental. 9
  labor . . . . . . . . . . . . . . .6, 29
  material . . . . . . . .6, 8, 16, 31
  miscellaneous . . . . . . . . . .10
  nonproductive labor . . . . .14
  pavement marking . . . .10, 12
  preparation materials . . . . .10
  rental . . . . . . . . . . . . . .33-34
  sandblasting . . . . . . . . .10-11
  subcontract . . . . . . . . . .9-10
  supervision . . . . . . . . . . . .14

# Index

total, Column 9 . . . . . . . . . . .8
variables . . . . . . . . . . . . . . .7
waterblasting . . . . . . . .11, 13
Cotton wall fabric . . . .433-434
Coverage
  material . . . . . . . . . . . . . .6, 15
  powdered adhesive . . . . . .422
Cracks, repair . . . . . . . . . . .298
Crews
  productivity . . . . . . . . . . . . .13
  skill levels . . . . . . . . . . . . . .6
Custom homes, allowance
  for supervision . . . . . . . . . .14
Customizing cost tables . . . . .7
Cut cracks . . . . . . . . . . . . . .298
Cutting-in . . . . . . . . . . . . .92-94

## D

Dark (OSHA) colors .19, 22, 25
Davis Bacon Act . . . . . . . . . .30
Deck enamel or epoxy
  . . . . . . . . . . . . . . . . .18, 21, 24
Deck overhang and
  surface . . . . . . . . . . . . .94, 161
Decking
  corrugated metal . . . .326-327
  flat pan metal . . . . . .328-329
Decking factors,
  square corner . . . . . . . . . .327
Decorative railing . . . . . . . .173
Deficient working conditions.11
Definitions, column headings .13
Delayed work . . . . . . . . . . . .29
Delivery costs . . . . . . . . . . . . .9
Demobilization . . . . . . . . . . . .9
Direct overhead . . . . .31, 32, 35
Discount tables . . . . . . .17-25
Discounts
  material . . . . . . . . . . . . . . .16
  supplier . . . . . . . . . . . . . . . .26
  volume . . . . . . . . . . . . . . . .16
Diverters, sheet metal . . . . .198
Door
  frames . . . . . . . . .95, 96, 102
  trim . . . . . . . . . . . . . . .95, 96
Doors
  Dutch . . . . . . . . . . . . . . . .102
  exterior . . . . . . . . . . . .97-101
  flush . . . . . . . . . .98, 109-111
  French . . . . . . . . .99, 111-112
  hollow metal . . . . . . . . . . .330
  interior . . .103, 109, 111, 113
  louvered . . . . . . .100, 113-115
  opening count method .102-108
  panel . . . . . . . . . . . . .116-118
  panel, entry . . . . . . . . . . .101
  two-coat system . . . . .98-101
Downspouts
  acid wash . . . . . . . . . . . . .296
  galvanized . . . . . . . . .138-139
Dripowder mixed . . .17, 20, 23
Drop siding . . . . . . . . .214-219
Dry pressed brick . . . .144-146
Drywall ceilings
  acoustic spray-on texture . .61
  orange peel texture . . . .63-68
  sand finish texture . . . .69-74

smooth finish . . . . . . . .75-79
  taping . . . . . . . . . . . . . . . .312
Drywall walls
  orange peel texture . .226-233
  sand finish . . . . . . . .234-239
  smooth finish . . . . . .240-245
  taping . . . . . . . . . . . . . . . .312
Ductwork
  bare duct . . . . . . . . .331-338
  canvas insulated . . . .339-347
Dutch doors . . . . . . . . . . . .102

## E

Eaves, overhang . . . . . .159-161
Edge scraping . . . . . . .309-311
Efficiency, work . . . . . . . . . .14
Electric conduit . . . . . .318-325
Employee benefits . . . . . . . . .30
Employer's burden . . . . . . . . .8
Enamel
  exterior . . . . . . . . . .18, 21, 24
  heat resistant . . . . . . . . . . .19
  oil based . . . . . . . . .17, 20, 23
  water based . . . . . . .17, 20, 23
Entry
  doors . . . . . . . . . . . . . .97-102
  overhang . . . . . . . . . . . . .161
Epoxy coating system
  . . . . . . . . . . . . . . . . .19, 22, 25
Equipment
  costs . . . . . . . . . . . . . . . . . . .9
  field . . . . . . . . . . . . . . . . . .32
  placement . . . . . . . . . . . . . .9
  purchase costs . . . . . . .33-34
  rental . . . . . . . . . . .9, 33-34
  sandblasting . . . . . . . . . . . .33
  spray . . . . . . . . . . . . . . .28, 34
Escalation . . . . . . . . . . . .26, 29
Estimate, sample . . . . . .38-39
Estimating
  accuracy . . . . . . . . . . . . . . .8
  basis for . . . . . . . . . . . . . . .5
  errors . . . . . . . . . . . . . . . . .10
  exterior system . . . .18, 21, 24
  form . . . . . . . . . . . . . . .40-41
  interior system . . . .17, 20, 23
  price escalation . . . . . .26-29
  reliable . . . . . . . . . . . . . . . .5
  unit cost . . . . . . . . . . . . . . .8
Evening work . . . . . . . . . . . . .9
Excluded preparation costs.9-10
Expendable tools and
  supplies . . . . . . . . . . . . . . .26
Expense
  overhead . . . . . . . . . . . .5, 31
  supervision . . . . . . . . . . . .14
Expiration date, bid . . . . . . .29
Exposed aggregate finish
  . . . . . . . . . . . . . . . . . .412-417
Extensive preparation . . . . . .26
Exterior
  enamel . . . . . . . . . .18, 21, 24
  floors . . . . . . . . . . . . .129-136
  preparation . . . . . . . . . . . . .9
  railings . . . . . . . . . . .173-174
  trim . . . . . . . . . . . . . .162-167
Extra heavy structural
  steel . . . . . . . . . . . . . .373-377

## F

Fascia . . . . . . . . . . . . . .118-122
Fast application rate . . . . .6, 13
Federal taxes . . . . . . . . . .30-31
Fees . . . . . . . . . . . . . . . . . . . .9
Felt . . . . . . . . . . . . . . .431, 433
Fences
  chain link . . . . . . . . . . . . .123
  picket . . . . . . . . . . . .124-126
  wire mesh . . . . . . . . . . . .123
  wood . . . . . . . . . . . . . . . .123
Fiber ceiling panels . . . . .57-59
FICA . . . . . . . . . . . . . . . .30-31
Field equipment . . . . . . .32-35
Field production . . . . . . . . . .14
  times & rates form . .419-420
Field superintendent . . . .14, 30
Figures
  Basis for cost estimates . . . .6
  Bidding variables . . . . . . .36
  Blank painting estimate . . .40
  Conduit/pipe area conversion
    table . . . . . . . . . . . . . . . .325
  Customizing the tables . . . . .7
  Equipment purchase & rental
    rates . . . . . . . . . . . . . . . . .33
  Interior opening count
    allowance table . . . . . . .102
  Labor burden percentages . .30
  Material coverage rates . . .15
  Material price discounts . . .16
  Material prices at
    discount . . . . . . . .17, 20, 23
  Pavement marking
    pricing table . . . . . . . . . .12
  Risk factors and profit
    margin . . . . . . . . . . . . . . .36
  Sample painting estimate . .38
  Sandblasting pricing table .11
  Square corner decking
    factors . . . . . . . . . . . . . .327
  Structural steel conversion
    tables . . . . . . . . . . . . . . .391
  Sundry inventory checklist .27
  Surface area of spheres . .399
  Wage rates, wallcovering . .29
  Waterblasting pricing table .13
Fill wood floors . . . . . . . . . .299
Filled block . . . . . . . . . . . . .355
Filler
  block . . . . . . . . . . . .18, 21, 24
  wood . . . . . . . . . . . .19, 22, 25
Film thickness, calculating . .15
Fir siding . . . . . . . . . . .214-219
Fire escapes . . . . . . . . .348-349
Fire sprinkler systems . . . . .349
Fireplace
  masonry . . . . . . . . . . . . . .127
  trim . . . . . . . . . . . . . . . . .128
Firewood boxes . . . . . . . . . .128
Fixed burden . . . . . . . . . . . . .30
Flashing, sheet metal
  . . . . . . . . . . . .196-197, 199-200
Flat latex . . . . . . . . .17, 20, 23
Flat pan metal . . . . . . . . . . .328
Flat roofs . . . . . . . . . . . . . . .184
Flexi-wall systems . . . . . . . .425
Flexible wood sheet and
  veneer . . . . . . . . . . . . . . . .425

Flexwood . . . . . . . . . . . . . . .425
Flock wallpaper . . . . . . . . . .435
Floors
  concrete . . . . . . . . . . .129-132
  wood . . . . . . . . . . . . .133-136
Flush doors . . . . . . . . . . . . . .98
Foil wallpaper . . . . . . . . . . .435
Forced Air Unit doors . . . . .102
Foremen, project . . . . . . .14, 30
Form
  estimating . . . . . . . . . .40-41
  field production times & rates
    . . . . . . . . . . . . . . . . .419-420
Formulation, paint . . . . . . . .16
Frames, door . . . . . . . . . .95-96
French doors . .99, 102, 111-112
Fringe benefits . . . . . . .7, 30-31
FUTA . . . . . . . . . . . . . . .30-31

## G

Gambrel roof . . . . . . . . . . . .184
Garage door backs . . . . . . . .137
General painting costs . .42-293
General qualifications . . . . . .9
Glazing . . . . . . . . . .17, 20, 23
Glove application
  . . . . . .324-325, 337-338, 363
Good neighbor fence . . . . . .123
Graffiti eliminator .62, 140, 225
Granite masonry . . . . . . . . .153
Grasscloth . . . . . . . . . . . . . .433
Grates, steel . . . . . . . .350-353
Grating deck, fire escapes . .348
Gravel stop, sheet metal . . .198
Grilles, steel . . . . . . . .352-353
Guaranteed maximum price .10
Gutters . . . . . . . . . . . .138-139
  acid wash . . . . . . . . . . . . .296
Gypsum drywall ceilings
  acoustic spray-on texture . .61
  orange peel texture . . .68-73
  sand finish texture . . . .74-79
  smooth finish . . . . . . .62-66
  taping . . . . . . . . . . . . . . .312
Gypsum drywall walls .225-245
  orange peel texture . .226-233
  sand finish . . . . . . . .234-239
  smooth finish . . . . . .240-245
  taping . . . . . . . . . . . . . . . .312

## H

Hand-crafted wallpaper.435-436
Hand-pasted wall covering
  . . . . . . . . . .428-429, 432-434
Handling, material . . . . . . . . .9
Handrail, wood . . . . . . . . . .175
Hardware, remove and
  replace . . . . . . . . . . . . .9-10
Headache factor . . . . . . . . . .35
Health benefits . . . . . . . . . . .30
Heat resistant enamel.19, 22, 25
Heavy commercial painting
  costs . . . . . . . . . . . . .317-418
Heavy mastic, sandblasting . .11
Heavy structural steel .372-377
Hemlock siding . . . . . .214-219

441

High time difficulty factors .139
Hollow metal doors . . . . . . .330
Home office overhead . . . . . .31
Homeowner, traits . . . . . . . . .35
Hopper
   roofs, exterior . . . . . .406-411
   walls, exterior . . . . . .400-405
Hot water radiators . . . . . . .371
Hourly wage rate, cost book .10
How to use the tables . . . . . . .6
HVAC registers . . . . . . . . . .182
Hydraulic fluid . . . . . . . . . . .27

## I

Incentives . . . . . . . . . . . . . . .35
Included costs . . . . . . . . . . . .9
Indirect overhead . . . . . . .31-32
Industrial
   allowance for supervision . .14
   bonding . . . . . . . . .19, 22, 25
   enamel . . . . . . . . . .19, 22, 25
   material . . . . . . . . .19, 22, 25
   painting costs . . . . . .317-418
   waterproofing . . . . .19, 22, 25
Inflationary cost increases . .29
Injury, compensation for . . . .30
Institutional painting
   costs . . . . . . . . . . . . .317-418
Institutional work, allowance
   for supervision . . . . . . . . .14
Insulated piping . . . . . .365-370
Insurance . . . . . . . . . . . . .30-31
   additional . . . . . . . . . . . . . .9
   liability . . . . . . . . . . . . . . .31
   medical . . . . . . . . . . . . . . .31
   unemployment . . . . . . .30-31
Interior
   floors . . . . . . . . . . . .129-136
   railings . . . . . . . . . . .175-178
   surface preparation . . . . . . .9
Interior opening count
   allowance table . . . . . . . . .102
Inventory, sundries . . . . . . .26
Iron painters, wages . . . . . . .30

## J

Job conditions, unknown . . .11
Job qualifications . . . . . . . . . .9
Jobs
   commercial . . . . . . . . . . . .9
   private . . . . . . . . . . . . . . .29
   repaint . . . . . . . . . . . . .9, 35
   residential tract . . . . . . . . .9
   time and material . . . . . . .10
Joint lap siding . . . . . . .214-219
Journeyman painters . . . . . . .8
Judgment, using . . . . . . . . . . .8

## K

Kitchens, painting . . . . . . .231

## L

Labor
   burden . . . . . . . . . . . .5, 6, 30

cost . . . . . . . . . . . . . . . .6, 29
rate, calculating . . . . . . . .30
surface preparation . . . . . .10
Labor burden percentages . . .30
Labor productivity categories
    . . . . . . . . . . . . . . . . . . . . .13
Lacquer, semi gloss,
   interior . . . . . . . . . .17, 20, 23
Ladder jack, purchase . . . . . .33
Ladders . . . . . . . . . . .9, 33, 354
   rental . . . . . . . . . . . . . . . .33
Lattice . . . . . . . . . . . . . . . .223
Lemon oil . . . . . . . . . . . . . . .27
Liability insurance . . . . . . . .31
Life insurance . . . . . . . . . . .31
Light fixture valances . . . . .224
Light structural steel . . .378-384
Linen wall fabric . . . . .431, 433
Linen doors . . . . . . . . . . . .102
Liquid paste, wallpaper . . . .423
Lites, window . . . . . . .290-291
Loss, risk of . . . . . . . . . . . . .35
Louvered doors
    . . . . . . . .100, 102, 113-115
Low productivity . . . . . . . . .14

## M

Machine pasted wallcovering
    . . . . . . . . . . . . . . . .426-431
Mail box structures . . . . . .140
Manhour productivity . . . . . .6
Mantel . . . . . . . . . . . . . . . .128
Marble masonry . . . . . . . . .153
Margin of profit . . . . . . .35-36
Marine spar varnish
    . . . . . . . .18, 21, 24, 98-101
Marking table, pavement . . .12
Masking materials . . . . . . . .27
Masking paper dispenser . . .33
Masks, particle . . . . . . . . . .27
Masonry
   anti-graffiti stain
      eliminator . . . . . . . . . . .140
   block filler . . . . . . . . . . .140
   CMU, rough surface
       . . . . . . . . . .147-149, 354
   CMU, smooth surface
       . . . . . . . . . .150-152, 355
   granite . . . . . . . . . . . . . . .153
   marble . . . . . . . . . . . . . . .153
   new brick . . . . . . . . .141-143
   paint . . . . . . . . . .18, 21, 24
   sandblasting . . . . . . . . . . .11
   stone . . . . . . . . . . . . . . . .153
   used brick . . . . . . . . .144-146
Material
   costs . . . . . . . . . . . . .6, 8, 10
   coverage rates . . . . . . .6, 15
   handling . . . . . . . . . . . . . .9
   prices . . . . . . . . . . . . .16, 26
   storage . . . . . . . . . . . . . . .9
   waste . . . . . . . . . . . . . .9, 16
Material cost per unit . . . . . .31
Material formulation,
   changes in . . . . . . . . . . . .16
Material price discounts . .16, 26
20 percent . . . . . . . . . . .17-19

30 percent . . . . . . . . . .20-22
40 percent . . . . . . . . . .23-25
Material pricing tables . . .17-25
   exterior paints . . . . .18, 21, 24
   industrial paints . . .19, 22, 25
   interior paints . . . . .17, 20, 23
   preparation . . . . . .19, 22, 25
   wallcovering . . . . . .19, 22, 25
Maximum price, guaranteed .10
Maximum productivity,
   conditions for . . . . . . . . . .14
Mechanical equipment . . . .356
Medical insurance . . . . . . . .31
Medium application rate . .6, 13
Medium finish,
   plaster walls . . . . . . .246-252
Medium structural steel
    . . . . . . . . . . . . . . . .385-390
Metal
   ceiling pans . . . . . . . . . . .60
   finish-synthetic . . .18, 21, 24
   primer . . . . . . . . .18, 21, 24
   stair stringers . . . . . . . . .220
   surfaces . . . . . . . . . .138-139
Minor price escalation . . . . .29
Miscellaneous costs . . . . . . .10
Mitt application
    . . . . . . .324-325, 337-338, 363
Mixing boxes, painting . . . .356
Mixing coatings . . . . . . . . . . .9
Mobilization . . . . . . . . . . . . .9
Model homes, allowance
   for supervision . . . . . . . . .14
Molding . . . . . . . . . . .153-158
   closet . . . . . . . . .89, 91, 102
   exterior . . . . . . .153, 157-158
   interior . . . . . . . . . . .153-158
Mullions & muntins . . . . .290

## N

National Estimator, installing .5
Natural fabric . . . . . . . . . .433
Near white blast . . . . . .11, 306
New construction preparation .9
Newels . . . . . . . . . . . .173, 177
Non-productive time,
   supervisors . . . . . . . . . . .14
Normal preparation . . . . . . .10
"Not to exceed" bid . . . . . . .10

## O

Office
   home . . . . . . . . . . . . . . . .31
   overhead . . . . . . . . . . .31-32
   rental, portable . . . . . . . . .34
Oil paints, sandblasting . . . .11
Oil-based paint . .16, 17, 20, 23
Opening count method
    . . . . .88, 95-97, 102, 103-108
Orange peel texture
   ceilings . . . . . . . . . . . .63-68
   walls . . . . . . . . . . . .226-234
OSHA colors . . . . . .19, 22, 25,
    . . . . .356-388, 400-408, 410
Overhang . . . . . . . . . . .159-161
Overhang difficulty factors .159

Overhead . . . . . . . . . . .6, 8, 36
   allowance . . . . . . . . . .32, 35
   computing . . . . . . . . .32, 35
   direct . . . . . . . . . . . . . . . .35
   expense . . . . . . . . . . . . . . .5
   indirect . . . . . . . . . . . .31-32
   office . . . . . . . . . . . . . . . .31
   rate . . . . . . . . . . . . . . . . .31
Overtime . . . . . . . . . . . . .9, 14
Owner allowances . . . . . . . . .9

## P

Paint . . . . . . . . . . . . . . . . . .16
   aluminum-based . . .19, 22, 25
   burn off . . . . . . . . . . . . .297
   coverage formula . . . . .15-16
   formulation . . . . . . . . . . .16
   masonry . . . . . . . .18, 21, 24
   oil-based . . . . . . .16, 17, 20, 23
   remover . . . . . . . . .19, 22, 25
   waste factors . . . . . . . . . .16
   water-based . . .16, 17, 20, 23
Paint pads, bender . . . . . . . .27
Paint stripper, rental . . . . . .34
Painters
   bridge . . . . . . . . . . . . . . .30
   journeyman . . . . . . . . . . . .8
   productivity . . . . . . . . . . .13
Panel doors
   exterior . . . . . . . . . . . . .101
   interior . . . . . . . . . . .116-118
Paper-backed vinyl . . .426-429
Paraffin wax . . . . . . . . . . .315
Particle masks . . . . . . . . . . .27
Pass-through shelves . . . . .162
Passage doors . . . . . . . . . .102
Paste . . . . . . . . . . . .19, 22, 25
Pavement marking . . . . . . .10
   pricing table . . . . . . . . . .12
Pay, premium . . . . . . . . . . . .9
Payroll tax . . . . . . . . . . . . . .30
Payroll withholding . . . . . . .30
Penetrating oil paint .19, 22, 25
Penetrating oil stain .17, 20, 23
Penetrating stain wax.17, 20, 23
Pension plans . . . . . . . . .30-31
Per diem . . . . . . . . . . . . . . . .9
Per unit costs . . . . . . . . . . . .31
Performance bonds . . . . . . .31
Performance by painters . . . .14
Permits . . . . . . . . . . . . . . . . .9
Picket fence . . . . . . . . .124-126
Pics . . . . . . . . . . . . . . . . . . .33
Pine siding . . . . . . . . .214-219
Piping
   bare pipe . . . . . . . . .357-363
   insulated, canvas
      jacket . . . . . . . . . . .365-370
Planks, rental . . . . . . . . . . .33
Plant-on trim . . . . . . . .162-167
Plaster walls, interior
   medium texture . . . . .246-252
   rough texture . . . . . .253-259
   smooth texture . . . . .260-266
Plaster, exterior . . . . . .168-172
   anti-graffiti stain
      eliminator . . . . . . . . . . .172
   waterproofing . . . . . . . . .171

# Index

Platform, rolling ..........33
Plywood siding ......208-219
Poles
   closet ..........88-89, 102
   roller ..................28
Polyurethane .......18, 21, 24
Porch & deck enamel
   or epoxy ..........18, 21, 24
Porches, wood ............94
Porous block .............354
Portable office, rental .....34
Pot shelves .............172
Powdered adhesives
   ..........19, 22, 25, 422
   coverage, rolls to yards
   conversion ............422
Power wash .............315
Pre-primed
   metal doors ...........330
   railing ...........179-181
Pre-trimmed wallpaper ....435
Precision block ...........355
Premium pay ..............9
Preparation materials .19, 22, 25
   cost ..................10
Preparation operations ...9, 10
   extensive .............26
Prevailing wage ...........30
Price guide, retail ........26
Price, maximum guaranteed .10
Prices at discount .........26
Pricing
   material ..............16
   sandblasting ..........11
   variables ............7-8
Primer, metal ......18, 21, 24
Private jobs ..............29
Productive time, supervisors .14
Productivity
   categories, labor .......13
   crew .................13
   low ..................14
   manhour ...............6
   rate ............5, 14, 29
   tracking .......14, 419-420
Profit ........6, 8, 26, 35
   margin .............35-37
   percentage ............35
   requirements ...........5
   risk ..................36
   tailoring .............36
Project foreman ..........14
Project variables ..........37
Protection ...............10
Protective window coating
   ........19, 22, 25, 278-290
Public projects ...........29
Pullman cabinets .........102
Putty .9, 10, 22, 25, 27, 299, 300
PVA sealer ...............27

## Q

Qualification statement ......9
Quality tracts, allowance for
   supervision ............14

## R

Radiators ................371
Rags .....................27

Railing
   exterior ..........173-174
   handrail, wood ........175
   interior ..........175-178
   wrought iron .....179-181
Rake, overhang ......160-161
Rate
   coverage ..............15
   hourly ................10
   overhead .............31
   productivity .....5, 14, 29
   wage .................29
Ready-mix paste ....19, 22, 25
Reduced productivity ......14
Redwood siding .....214-219
Registers ...............182
Remodeling contractors ....35
Remove and replace ......9-10
Remove coatings .........311
Remover, paint .....19, 22, 25
Rental equipment ..9, 31-32, 35
Repaint jobs ........9-10, 35
Repaint preparation ........10
Requirements, profit .......5
Resawn
   valances .............224
   wood railing ..........173
   wood siding .....208-214
Residential tract work .....6, 9
Residential wallcovering
   fabric ...........432-434
   vinyl ............428-429
   wallpaper ........437-439
Resin sealer .............27
Respirators ...............27
Retail price guide ........26
Risers ..................219
Risk factors and profit
   margin .............36-37
Roller covers ..........27-28
Rolling equipment,
   rent/purchase .........33
Rolls to yards conversion
   table, adhesive ........422
Roof
   arched ..............184
   flat .........184, 408-411
   gambrel .............184
   hopper ..........408-411
   peaked ..........408-411
   sloping .......184, 408-411
   vaulted ..........408-411
Roof area conversion factors
   ....................184
Roof jacks ..............183
Roof pitch difficulty factors.184
Roofing
   composition shingle .185-189
   waterproofing ....193, 195
   wood shingle or
   shakes ..........190-195
Rough finish plaster walls
   ................253-259
Rough sawn
   railing ..............173
   siding ..........208-214
   valances ............224
Run, stair ..............219

## S

Safety net, purchase ......33
Sales staff ...............35
Sales tax ................26
Sample estimating form ..40-41
Sample estimate ......38-39
Sample preparation .......10
Sand finish texture
   ceilings ............69-74
   walls, drywall ....234-239
Sand, silica .......19, 22, 25
   white silica ..........302
Sandblast
   brick .................11
   brush-off blast .......303
   commercial blast ....304-305
   equipment, rental .....33
   near white blast .....306-307
   rates ................10
   white blast ......308-309
Sandblasters, wages .......30
Sandblasting pricing table ...11
Sanders, rental ...........33
Sanding ............299-301
Sanding sealer ...........27
   exterior .......18, 21, 24
   interior .......17, 20, 23
Sandpaper ...............28
Sash, window .......290, 298
Scaffolding, rental ....9, 33-34
Scenic wallpaper .........436
Scope of work ...........10
Scribing ............309-311
Sealer
   off white .......17, 20, 23
   PVA .................27
   resin ................27
Sealer, sanding ...........27
   exterior .......18, 21, 24
   interior .......17, 20, 23
Semi-transparent stain .......
   ..............18, 21, 24
Setup .................9, 10
Shake siding ........208-213
Shakes, roofing ......190-195
Sheet metal .............196
   caps ............196-197
   diverters ............198
   flashing ...196-197, 199-200
   gravel stops .........198
   vents ...........199-200
Shellac ..........17, 20, 23
Shelves ..............48-51
   closet .........89-90, 102
   paint grade ........48-49
   pass-through .........162
   stain grade ........50-51
   wood ................162
Shift adjustments ..........9
Shingle siding ......208-213
Shingle roofing .....190-195
Shutters ................201
Siding
   aluminum ............202
   composition shingle .203-207
   corrugated metal ....326-327
   flat pan metal .....328-329
   waterproofing
   ..........205, 207, 212, 219

wood, rough or resawn
   ................208-213
wood, smooth ......214-219
Silica sand .....19, 22, 25, 302
Silicone caulk ...........297
Silk wall fabric ..........433
Silo ................400-412
   roofs, exterior ....406-411
   walls, exterior ....400-405
Site variables .............37
Sizing, wallpaper .........425
Skill levels, crew ..........6
Skilled specialists ........30
Slag, sandblasting ........302
Sloped surfaces .........184
Slow application rate ....6, 13
Slump stone .............355
Smooth finish texture
   drywall walls .....240-245
   plaster walls ......260-266
Social security tax .....30-31
Solid body stain ....18, 21, 24
Solid deck fire escapes ....348
Solids, percentage of .......15
Solvent-based paint ........16
Spackle ..................28
Specialist's wages .........30
Spillage ...................9
Spindles ............173, 177
Split coat operation .......102
Spray can .......17, 20, 23
Spray equipment ......28, 34
   rental/purchase .......34
Spray rigs ............9, 34
Spray-on texture ceilings ...61
Sprinklers ...............349
Square corner decking
   factors ..............327
Square foot estimating,
   fire escapes .........349
Staff, sales ..............35
Stain
   eliminator, anti-graffiti
   ..............18, 21, 24
   exterior seal & varnish
   ..............18, 21, 24
   interior seal & lacquer
   ..............17, 20, 23
Stairs
   steps ................219
   stringers .........220-222
   tread length .........219
   wood ............94, 219
Standard base bid .........36
Staples ..................28
State unemployment
   insurance ..........30-31
Steam radiators ..........371
Steel factory sash windows .418
Steel grates .........350-354
Steel painters, wages .....30
Steeplejack ..............30
Steps, wood .........94, 219
Stone, sealing ...........153
Storage
   containers, rental ......34
   material ..............9
   trailer ...............31

Strainer bags . . . . . . . . . . . . . .28
Stringers, stair . . . . . . .220-222
Stripper, rental . . . . . . . . . . . .34
Stripping . . . . . . . . . . . . . . . .311
Structural steel . . . . . . .372-399
   extra heavy . . . . . . . .373-377
   heavy . . . . . . . . . . . . .372-377
   light . . . . . . . . . . . . . .378-384
   medium . . . . . . . . . . .385-390
   sandblasting . . . . . . . . . . .11
Structural steel conversion
   tables . . . . . . . . . . . . .391-399
Stucco, exterior . . . . . .168-172
   anti-graffiti stain
      eliminator . . . . . . . . . . .172
   waterproofing . . . . . . . . .171
Subcontractor bids . . . . . .10-11
Subcontractor costs . . . . .9, 10
SUI . . . . . . . . . . . . . . . . . .30-31
Sundries allowance . . . . . . . .26
Sundry inventory
   checklist . . . . . . . . . . . .27-28
Superintendent, field . . . . . . .30
Supervision expense . . . . . . .14
Supervisor, responsibility . . .14
Supplier discounts . . . . . . . . .26
Surface area of spheres . . . .399
Surface preparation . . . . . .9, 10
   specialists . . . . . . . . . . . . .30
   wallcovering . . . . . . . . . .425
SURRPTUCU . . . . . . . . . .9, 10
Suspended ceilings . . . . .57-59
Swedish putty . . . . . . . . . . .298
Swing stage
   rental . . . . . . . . . . . . . . . .34
   wages . . . . . . . . . . . . . . . .30
System estimates
   exterior . . . . . . . . . .18, 21, 24
   interior . . . . . . . . . .17, 20, 23

## T

T-bar ceiling frames . . . . .57-59
Tables
   adjustments to . . . . . . . . . . .7
   assumptions . . . . . . . . . . . . .7
   compilation methods . . . . . .7
   excluded costs . . . . . . . . . . .9
   how to use . . . . . . . . . . . . . .6
   included costs . . . . . . . . . . .9
   order, defined . . . . . . . . . . .6
   preparation . . . . . . . . . . . . .9
Take-off sheet . . . . . . . . . . . .31
Tanks
   roof exterior . . . . . . .406-411
   vinyl coating, industrial
      . . . . . . . . . . . . . .19, 22, 25
   wall exterior . . . . . . .400-405
Taping wallboard . . . . . . . . .312
Taxes
   payroll . . . . . . . . . . . . .30-31
   sales . . . . . . . . . . . . . . . . .26
Thinner . . . . . . . . . . . . . . . . .28

Tile, clay brick . . . . . . .144-146
Tilt-up walls . . . . . . . . .412-417
Time and Material .10, 296, 314
Tip-off operation . . . . . . . . .102
Tongue & groove
   ceilings . . . . . . . . . . . .80-88
   paneling . . . . . . . . . .267-275
   siding . . . . . . . . . . . .214-219
Tools and supplies,
   expendable . . . . . . . . . . . .26
Total cost . . . . . . . . . . . . .8, 37
Touchup . . . . . . . . . .9, 10, 222
Tower, rolling . . . . . . . . . . . .33
Tract work, residential . . . . . .6
Trailers, rental . . . . . . . . .31, 34
Training fund . . . . . . . . . . . . .31
Travel time . . . . . . . . . . . . . . .9
Treads, stair . . . . . . . . . . . .219
Trellis . . . . . . . . . . . . . . . . .223
Trim, door . . . . . . . . . . . .95-96
Trowel finish, walls . . .412-417

## U

Undercoat . . . . . . . .17, 20, 23
Unemployment insurance.30-31
Unfilled block . . . . . . . . . . .354
Union wage rates . . . . . . . . .29
Unit cost estimate . . . . . . . . .8
Unit prices, converting . . . . .9
Unknown job conditions . . . .11
Unstick windows . . . . . . . .312
Urethane caulk . . . . . . . . .297
Used brick . . . . . . . . .144-146
Utility areas, painting . . . . .231

## V

Vacation pay . . . . . . . . . .30-31
Valances for light fixtures . .224
Variables
   bidding . . . . . . . . . . . .36-37
   pricing . . . . . . . . . . . . . .7-8
   site . . . . . . . . . . . . . . . . .37
Varnish . . . . . . . . . . . . . . . .301
   exterior . . . . . . . . .18, 21, 24
   marine spar . . . . . .18, 21, 24
Veneer, flexible wood sheet .425
Vents, sheet metal . . . .199-200
Vertical pipe runs . . . . . . . .359
Vessels
   roof exterior . . . . . . .406-411
   wall exterior . . . . . . .400-405
Vinyl coating, industrial
   . . . . . . . . . . . . . . .19, 22, 25
Vinyl paste
   powdered . . . . . . .19, 22, 25
   vinyl to vinyl ready-mix . .422
Vinyl wallcovering
   commercial . . . . . . . .426-427
   residential . . . . . . . .428-429
Volume discounts . . . . . . . . .16

## W

Wage rates
   painting . . . . . . . . . . . . . . . .6
   wallcovering . . . . . . . . . . .29
Wages
   overtime . . . . . . . . . . . .9, 14
   prevailing . . . . . . . . . . . . .30
   specialists . . . . . . . . . . . .30
   union, national average . . .29
Wainscot paneling . . . .267-275
Wall fabric
   commercial . . . . . . . .430-431
   residential . . . . . . . .432-433
Wallboard, taping . . . . . . . .312
Wallcovering
   adhesive coverage . . . . . .422
   application rate . . .29, 424
   costs . . . . . . . . . . . .421-439
   fabric . . . . . . . . . . . .430-433
   material pricing . . .19, 22, 25
   surface preparation . . . . .425
   vinyl . . . . . . . . . . . .426-429
Wallpaper . . . . . . . . . .434-436
   borders . . . . . . . . . .424-425
   canvas . . . . . . . . . . . . . .436
   commercial . . . . . . . .434-436
   flock . . . . . . . . . . . . . . . .435
   foil . . . . . . . . . . . . . . . . .435
   hand-crafted . . . . . . . . . .435
   paste . . . . . . . . . . . . . . .423
   residential . . . . . . . .437-439
   scenic . . . . . . . . . . . . . .436
   sizing . . . . . . . . . . . . . . .425
Walls, concrete tilt-up .412-417
Walls, gypsum drywall
   anti-graffiti stain
      eliminator . . . . . . . . . . .225
   orange peel texture . .226-233
   sand finish . . . . . . . .234-239
   smooth finish . . . . . .240-245
Walls, interior plaster
   medium texture . . . . .246-252
   rough texture . . . . . .253-259
   smooth texture . . . . .260-266
Walls, tank, silo,
   vessel or hopper . . . .400-405
Walls, wood panel
   paint grade . . . . . . . .267-272
   stain grade . . . . . . . .273-275
Wardrobe doors . . . . . . . . .102
Wash . . . . . . . . . . . . . . . . .313
Waste factor . . . . . . . . . .15, 16
Waste, material . . . . . . . . . . .9
Water soluble paints,
   sandblasting . . . . . . . . . .11
Water-based paint.16, 17, 20, 23
Waterblasting . . . . . .10-13, 315
   pricing table . . . . . . . . . .13
Waterproofing
   . . . . . . . .18, 21, 24, 193, 195
   industrial . . . . . . . .19, 22, 25
Wax . . . . . . . . . . . .17, 20, 23

WCI . . . . . . . . . . . . . . . .30-31
Wet areas, painting . . . . . .231
Wheat paste, powdered
   . . . . . . . . . . . . . . .19, 22, 25
White blast . . . . . . . . . .11, 308
White silica sand . . . . . . . .302
Window
   frames, screen . . . . . . . .276
   seats . . . . . . . . . . . . . . .277
   sills . . . . . . . . . . . . . . . .277
   storm sash . . . . . . . . . . .278
Window conversion factors .292
Window estimating
   interior opening count . . .102
   square foot basis . . . . . . .290
Window protective
   coating, wax . . .19, 22, 25, 315
Windows
   exterior wood
      . . . . . . . .18, 21, 24, 279-284
   interior wood
      . . . . . . . . . .17, 20, 23, 285-291
   steel factory sash . . . . .418
Wine racks . . . . . . . . .293-294
Wiping stain
   exterior . . . . . . . . .18, 21, 24
   interior . . . . . . . . . . .17, 2029
Wire brush . . . . . . . . . . . . .316
Wire mesh fence . . . . . . . .123
Withheld taxes . . . . . . . .30-31
Wood fence . . . . . . . . . . . .123
Wood filler . . . . . . .19, 22, 25
Wood floors . . . . . . . .133-136
   fill . . . . . . . . . . . . . . . . .299
Wood paneled walls . . . . . .267
Wood shingles or
   shakes . . . . . . . . . . .190-195
Wood siding
   rough sawn or resawn
      . . . . . . . . . . . . . . .208-213
   smooth . . . . . . . . . .214-219
Wood stair stringers . . . . . .222
Wood stairs or steps . . . . .219
Wood trim . . . . . . . . . . . . . .92
Wood veneer
   flexwood . . . . . . . . . . . .425
   paneling . . . . . . . . .267-275
Wood windows . . . . . .279-291
Work
   delayed . . . . . . . . . . . . . .29
   efficiency . . . . . . . . . . . . .14
   evening . . . . . . . . . . . . . . .9
Work pots, plastic . . . . . . . .28
Workers' comp. insurance ..30-31
Working conditions . . . . .11, 29
Wrought iron
   railing . . . . . . . . . . .179-181
   shelf supports . . . . . . . .162

## Z

Zinc chromate . . . . . .18, 21, 24

# Practical References for Builders

## Builder's Guide to Accounting Revised

Step-by-step, easy-to-follow guidelines for setting up and maintaining records for your building business. This practical guide to all accounting methods shows how to meet state and federal accounting requirements, explains the new depreciation rules, and describes how the Tax Reform Act can affect the way you keep records. Full of charts, diagrams, simple directions and examples to help you keep track of where your money is going. Recommended reading for many state contractor's exams. Each chapter ends with a set of test questions, and a CD-ROM included FREE has all the questions in interactive self-test software. Use the Study Mode to make studying for the exam much easier, and Exam Mode to practice your skills. **360 pages, 8½ x 11, $35.50. Also available as an eBook (PDF), $17.75 at www.craftsman-book.com**

## Paint Contractor's Manual

How to start and run a profitable paint contracting company: getting set up and organized to handle volume work, avoiding mistakes, squeezing top production from your crews and the most value from your advertising dollar. Shows how to estimate all prep and painting. Loaded with manhour estimates, sample forms, contracts, charts, tables and examples you can use. **224 pages, 8½ x 11, $34.00**

## Paper Contracting: The How-To of Construction Management Contracting

Risk, and the headaches that go with it, have always been a major part of any construction project — risk of loss, negative cash flow, construction claims, regulations, excessive changes, disputes, slow pay — sometimes you'll make money, and often you won't. But many contractors today are avoiding almost all of that risk by working under a construction management contract, where they are simply a paid consultant to the owner, running the job, but leaving him the risk. This manual is the how-to of construction management contracting. You'll learn how the process works, how to get started as a CM contractor, what the job entails, how to deal with the issues that come up, when to step back, and how to get the job completed on time and on budget. Includes a link to free downloads of CM contracts legal in each state.
**272 pages, 8½ x 11, $55.50. Also available as an eBook (PDF & ePub), $27.75 at www.craftsman-book.com**

## Insurance Restoration Contracting: Startup to Success

Insurance restoration — the repair of buildings damaged by water, fire, smoke, storms, vandalism and other disasters — is an exciting field of construction that provides lucrative work that's immune to economic downturns. And, with insurance companies funding the repairs, your payment is virtually guaranteed. But this type of work requires special knowledge and equipment, and that's what you'll learn about in this book. It covers fire repairs and smoke damage, water losses and specialized drying methods, mold remediation, content restoration, even damage to mobile and manufactured homes. You'll also find information on equipment needs, training classes, estimating books and software, and how restoration leads to lucrative remodeling jobs. It covers all you need to know to start and succeed as the restoration contractor that both homeowners and insurance companies call on first for the best jobs. **640 pages, 8½ x 11, $69.00. Also available as an eBook (PDF), $34.50 at www.craftsman-book.com**

## Estimating Home Building Costs, Revised

Estimate every phase of residential construction from site costs to the profit margin you include in your bid. Shows how to keep track of manhours and make accurate labor cost estimates for site clearing and excavation, footings, foundations, framing and sheathing finishes, electrical, plumbing, and more. Provides and explains sample cost estimate worksheets with complete instructions for each job phase. This practical guide to estimating home construction costs has been updated with digital Excel estimating forms and worksheets that ensure accurate and complete estimates for your residential projects. Enter your project information on the worksheets and Excel automatically totals each material and labor cost from every stage of construction to a final cost estimate worksheet. Load the enclosed CD-ROM into your computer and create your own estimate as you follow along with the step-by-step techniques in this book.
**336 pages, 8½ x 11, $38.00. Also available as an eBook (PDF), $19.00 at www.craftsman-book.com**

## National Renovation & Insurance Repair Estimator

Current prices in dollars and cents for hard-to-find items needed on most insurance, repair, remodeling, and renovation jobs. All price items include labor, material, and equipment breakouts, plus special charts that tell you exactly how these costs are calculated. Includes a free download of an electronic version of the book with *National Estimator*, a stand-alone *Windows*™ estimating program. An interactive multimedia video that shows how to use the software to compile renovation and repair cost estimates is free at www.costbook.com. **488 pages, 8½ x 11, $74.50. Revised annually**

## Working Alone

This unique book shows you how to become a dynamic one-man team as you handle nearly every aspect of house construction, including foundation layout, setting up scaffolding, framing floors, building and erecting walls, squaring up walls, installing sheathing, laying out rafters, raising the ridge, getting the roof square, installing rafters, subfascia, sheathing, finishing eaves, installing windows, hanging drywall, measuring trim, installing cabinets, and building decks. **152 pages, 5½ x 8½, $17.95**

## Drywall, Revised & Updated, 4th Edition with DVD

This revised version of *Drywall* gives readers important information on new tools and materials and techniques that the author has field-tested since the last revision in 2008. For the first time, the book also includes a bound-in DVD with tips and techniques for hassle-free drywall installation. This new edition offers the very latest information with the familiar easy-to-use format that made the first three editions such great successes. In this colorful, informative book you'll find everything you've ever wanted to know about drywall installation — starting from how to plan the job, through estimating materials, to the types of tools and materials available today. **233 pages, $9^{3}/_{4}$ x $10^{7}/_{8}$, $21.95**

## Contractor's Plain-English Legal Guide

For today's contractors, legal problems are like snakes in the swamp — you might not see them, but you know they're there. This book tells you where the snakes are hiding and directs you to the safe path. With the directions in this easy-to-read handbook you're less likely to need a $200-an-hour lawyer. Includes simple directions for starting your business, writing contracts that cover just about any eventuality, collecting what's owed you, filing liens, protecting yourself from unethical subcontractors, and more. For about the price of 15 minutes in a lawyer's office, you'll have a guide that will make many of those visits unnecessary. Includes a CD-ROM with blank copies of all the forms and contracts in the book.
**272 pages, 8½ x 11, $49.50**

## Contractor's Guide to QuickBooks 2012

*QuickBooks* 2012 has many new features that simplify a building contractor's bookkeeping work. You'll wonder how you managed without them. To help you make the most of these new features, or to make getting set up with *QuickBooks* almost painless, this user-friendly manual walks you through *QuickBooks'* detailed setup procedure and explains step-by-step how to create a first-rate accounting system. You'll learn in days, rather than weeks, how to use *QuickBooks* to get your contracting business organized, with simple, fast accounting procedures. But setting up QuickBooks from scratch can be time-consuming. On the free download included with purchase of the book you'll find a *QuickBooks* file preconfigured for a construction company. Open it, enter your company's data, add info on your suppliers, subs and customers, and you're up and running. The setup's done for you. **288 pages, 8½ x 11, $58.50. Also available as an eBook (PDF), $29.25 at www.craftsman-book.com**
See checklist for other available editions.

### Craftsman's Construction Installation Encyclopedia

Step-by-step installation instructions for just about any residential construction, remodeling or repair task, arranged alphabetically, from *Acoustic tile* to *Wood flooring*. Includes hundreds of illustrations that show how to build, install, or remodel each part of the job, as well as manhour tables for each work item so you can estimate and bid with confidence. Also includes a CD-ROM with all the material in the book, handy look-up features, and the ability to capture and print out for your crew the instructions and diagrams for any job. **792 pages, 8½ x 11, $65.00. Also available as an eBook (PDF), $32.50 at www.craftsman-book.com**

### Finish Carpentry: Efficient Techniques for Custom Interiors

Professional finish carpentry demands expert skills, precise tools, and a solid understanding of how to do the work. This new book explains how to install moldings, paneled walls and ceilings, and just about every aspect of interior trim — including doors and windows. Covers built-in bookshelves, coffered ceilings, and skylight wells and soffits, including paneled ceilings with decorative beams. **288 pages, 8½ x 11, $34.95**

### CD Estimator

If your computer has *Windows*™ and a CD-ROM drive, CD Estimator puts at your fingertips over 150,000 construction costs for new construction, remodeling, renovation & insurance repair, home improvement, framing & finish carpentry, electrical, concrete & masonry, painting, earthwork & heavy equipment and plumbing & HVAC. Quarterly cost updates are available at no charge on the Internet. You'll also have the *National Estimator* program — a stand-alone estimating program for *Windows*™ that *Remodeling* magazine called a "computer wiz," and *Job Cost Wizard*, a program that lets you export your estimates to *QuickBooks Pro* for actual job costing. A 60-minute interactive video teaches you how to use this CD-ROM to estimate construction costs. And to top it off, to help you create professional-looking estimates, the disk includes over 40 construction estimating and bidding forms in a format that's perfect for nearly any *Windows*™ word processing or spreadsheet program. **CD Estimator is $108.50**

### Construction Forms for Contractors

This practical guide contains 78 practical forms, letters and checklists, guaranteed to help you streamline your office, organize your jobsites, gather and organize records and documents, keep a handle on your subs, reduce estimating errors, administer change orders and lien issues, monitor crew productivity, track your equipment use, and more. Includes accounting forms, change order forms, forms for customers, estimating forms, field work forms, HR forms, lien forms, office forms, bids and proposals, subcontracts, and more. All are also on the CD-ROM included, in *Excel* spreadsheets, as formatted Rich Text that you can fill out on your computer, and as PDFs. **360 pages, 8½ x 11, $48.50. Also available as an eBook (PDF), $24.25 at www.craftsman-book.com**

### Profits in Buying & Renovating Homes

Step-by-step instructions for selecting, repairing, improving, and selling highly profitable "fixer-uppers." Shows which price ranges offer the highest profit-to-investment ratios, which neighborhoods offer the best return, practical directions for repairs, and tips on dealing with buyers, sellers, and real estate agents. Shows you how to determine your profit before you buy, what "bargains" to avoid, and how to make simple, profitable, inexpensive upgrades. **304 pages, 8½ x 11, $24.75**

### Rough Framing Carpentry

If you'd like to make good money working outdoors as a framer, this is the book for you. Here you'll find shortcuts to laying out studs; speed cutting blocks, trimmers and plates by eye; quickly building and blocking rake walls; installing ceiling backing, ceiling joists, and truss joists; cutting and assembling hip trusses and California fills; arches and drop ceilings — all with production line procedures that save you time and help you make more money. Over 100 on-the-job photos of how to do it right and what can go wrong. **304 pages, 8½ x 11, $26.50**

### National Home Improvement Estimator

Current labor and material prices for home improvement projects. Provides manhours for each job, recommended crew size, and the labor cost for removal and installation work. Material prices are current, with location adjustment factors and free monthly updates on the Web. Gives step-by-step instructions for the work, with helpful diagrams, and home improvement shortcuts and tips from experts. Includes a free download of an electronic version of the book, and *National Estimator*, a stand-alone *Windows*™ estimating program. An interactive multimedia tutorial that shows how to use the software to compile home improvement cost estimates is free at www.costbook.com. **568 pages, 8½ x 11, $73.75. Revised annually**

### Blueprint Reading for the Building Trades

How to read and understand construction documents, blueprints, and schedules. Includes layouts of structural, mechanical, HVAC and electrical drawings. Shows how to interpret sectional views, follow diagrams and schematics, and covers common problems with construction specifications. **192 pages, 5½ x 8½, $16.75**

### Wiring a House

A master electrician gives you the tips and shortcuts he's learned in over 30 years of wiring houses to meet code and to provide years of reliable service. Here you'll learn what materials work best in what application, which tools get the job done in the fastest time, and how to figure out and design the right wiring layout for any residential job, whether the entire house, or just a room. You also see how to install main service panels, ensure that the house is properly grounded, and install receptacles, GFCIs, switches, fixtures and appliances per *NEC* requirements. Dozens of diagrams and full-color illustrations show you exactly how the work goes together. **248 pages, 8½ x 11, $24.95**

### Markup & Profit: A Contractor's Guide, Revisited

In order to succeed in a construction business, you have to be able to price your jobs to cover all labor, material and overhead expenses, and make a decent profit. But calculating markup is only part of the picture. If you're going to beat the odds and stay in business — profitably, you also need to know how to write good contracts, manage your crews, work with subcontractors and collect on your work. This book covers the business basics of running a construction company, whether you're a general or specialty contractor working in remodeling, new construction or commercial work. The principles outlined here apply to all construction-related businesses. You'll find tried and tested formulas to guarantee profits, with step-by-step instructions and easy-to-follow examples to help you learn how to operate your business successfully. Includes a link to free downloads of blank forms and checklists used in this book. **336 pages, 8½ x 11, $47.50. Also available as an eBook (ePub, mobi for Kindle), $39.95 at www.craftsman-book.com**

### National Construction Estimator

Current building costs for residential, commercial, and industrial construction. Estimated prices for every common building material. Provides manhours, recommended crew, and gives the labor cost for installation. Includes a free download of an electronic version of the book with *National Estimator*, a stand-alone *Windows*™ estimating program. An interactive multimedia video that shows how to use the software to compile construction cost estimates is free at www.costbook.com. **672 pages, 8½ x 11, $72.50. Revised annually**

### Estimating Excavation Revised eBook

How to calculate the amount of dirt you'll have to move and the cost of owning and operating the machines you'll do it with. Detailed, step-by-step instructions on how to assign bid prices to each part of the job, including labor and equipment costs. Also, the best ways to set up an organized and logical estimating system, take off from contour maps, estimate quantities in irregular areas, and figure your overhead. This revised edition includes a chapter on earthwork estimating software. As with any tool, you have to pick the right one. Written by an experienced dirt contractor and instructor of computer estimating software, this chapter covers the program types, explains how they work, gives the basics of how to use them, and discusses what will work best for the type of work you handle. This eBook is the download version of the book in text searchable, PDF format. Craftsman eBooks are for use in the freely distributed Adobe Reader and are compatible with Reader 6.0 or above. **550 pages, eBook (PDF), $21.75, available at www.craftsman-book.com**

## Estimating & Bidding for Builders & Remodelers

This 5th edition has all the information you need for estimating and bidding new construction and home improvement projects. It shows how to select jobs that will be profitable, do a labor and materials take-off from the plans, calculate overhead and figure your markup, and schedule the work. Includes a CD with an easy-to-use construction estimating program and a database of 50,000 current labor and material cost estimates for new construction and home improvement work, with area modifiers for every zip code. Price updates on the Web are free and automatic.
**272 pages, 8½ x 11, $89.50. Also available as an eBook (PDF), $44.75 at www.craftsman-book.com**

## Painter's Handbook

Loaded with "how-to" information you'll use every day to get professional results on any job: the best way to prepare a surface for painting or repainting; selecting and using the right materials and tools (including airless spray); tips for repainting kitchens, bathrooms, cabinets, eaves and porches; how to match and blend colors; why coatings fail and what to do about it. Lists 30 profitable specialties in the painting business.
**320 pages, 8½ x 11, $33.00**

## Building Code Compliance for Contractors & Inspectors

An answer book for both contractors and building inspectors, this manual explains what it takes to pass inspections under the 2009 *International Residential Code*. It includes a code checklist for every trade, covering some of the most common reasons why inspectors reject residential work — footings, foundations, slabs, framing, sheathing, plumbing, electrical, HVAC, energy conservation and final inspection. The requirement for each item on the checklist is explained, and the code section cited so you can look it up or show it to the inspector. Knowing in advance what the inspector wants to see gives you an (almost unfair) advantage. To pass inspection, do your own pre-inspection before the inspector arrives. If your work requires getting permits and passing inspections, put this manual to work on your next job. If you're considering a career in code enforcement, this can be your guidebook. **8½ x 11, 232 pages, $32.50. Also available as an eBook (PDF), $16.25 at www.craftsman-book.com**

## Journeyman Electrician's Preparation & Study Guide

This is not only a great study guide filled with sample electrician's exam questions — it teaches you how to quickly turn to the code section that answers the questions. Most electrician's exams give you about 2 minutes per question — not enough time to browse through 800 pages of fine print looking for each answer. This manual, based on the 2008 and 2011 NEC editions, explains how the Code is organized, so you understand where the information you need is located. Then it shows how to rearrange and tab your copy of the Code to streamline your search efforts. Next, you learn a step-by-step search procedure, in which you're shown how to analyze the question to determine its subject, know where to look in the index, find the exact article, then turn right to the Code section that answers your question. **96 pages, 8½ x 11, $34.00. Also available as an eBook (PDF), $17.00 at www.craftsman-book.com**

## JLC Field Guide to Residential Construction

**Volume 1**: The ultimate visual quick-reference guide for construction professionals. Over 400 precisely-detailed drawings with clear concise notes and explanations that show you everything from estimating and selecting lumber to foundations, roofing, siding and exteriors. Explains code requirements for all U.S. building codes. Spiral bound. **386 pages, 11 x 8½, $69.95**

## JLC Field Guide to Residential Construction

**Volume 2**: Over 300 detailed technical drawings, illustrations and tables giving key dimensions and critical details from accessible kitchens to zoned heating systems. This new version of the JLC Field Guide has the field-proven principles, methods and materials on all facets of interior construction and remodeling. Spiral bound. **350 pages, 11 x 8½, $69.95**

## Roofing Construction & Estimating

Installation, repair and estimating for nearly every type of roof covering available today in residential and commercial structures: asphalt shingles, roll roofing, wood shingles and shakes, clay tile, slate, metal, built-up, and elastomeric. Covers sheathing and underlayment techniques, as well as secrets for installing leakproof valleys. Many estimating tips help you minimize waste, as well as insure a profit on every job. Troubleshooting techniques help you identify the true source of most leaks. Over 300 large, clear illustrations help you find the answer to just about all your roofing questions. **432 pages, 8½ x 11, $38.00**

## Estimating Electrical Construction Revised

Estimating the cost of electrical work can be a very detailed and exacting discipline. It takes specialized skills and knowledge to create reliable estimates for electrical work. See how an expert estimates materials and labor for residential and commercial electrical construction. Learn how to use labor units, the plan take-off, and the bid summary to make an accurate estimate, how to deal with suppliers, use pricing sheets, and modify labor units. This book provides extensive labor unit tables and blank forms on a CD for estimating your next electrical job. **272 pages, 8½ x 11, $59.00 Also available as an eBook (PDF), $29.50 at www.craftsman-book.com**

## Construction Spanish

Carry in your pocket over 1000 words and terms and 15 commonly-used phrases in both English to Spanish and Spanish to English for job use on residential, commercial and heavy commercial projects. If you want an inexpensive English-Spanish dictionary that fits in your shirt pocket, you should have a copy of this new book. **120 pages, 3½ x 5, $6.00**

## Drywall Contracting

How to set up and operate a drywall contracting business. Here you'll find how to get set up as a drywall contractor, the tools you'll need, how to do the work, and how to estimate and schedule jobs so that you keep the work flowing and the money coming in. How to prevent drywall problems, spot hidden problems before you begin, and how to install and repair drywall in new construction or remodeling work. Lists the eight essential steps in making a drywall estimate and includes estimating forms and manhour tables for your use. This book is filled with practical tips, illustrations, pictures, tables and forms to help you build your career as a successful drywall contractor. **256 pages, 8½ x 11, $34.95**

## Construction Contract Writer

Relying on a "one-size-fits-all" boilerplate construction contract to fit your jobs can be dangerous — almost as dangerous as a handshake agreement. *Construction Contract Writer* lets you draft a contract in minutes that precisely fits your needs and the particular job, and meets both state and federal requirements. You just answer a series of questions — like an interview — to construct a legal contract for each project you take on. Anticipate where disputes could arise and settle them in the contract before they happen. Include the warranty protection you intend, the payment schedule, and create subcontracts from the prime contract by just clicking a box. Includes a feedback button to an attorney on the Craftsman staff to help should you get stumped — *No extra charge*. **$99.95. Download the *Construction Contract Writer* program at http://www.constructioncontractwriter.com**

## Easy Scheduling

*Easy Scheduling* presents you with a complete set of "real world" scheduling tools that are specifically tailored to meet the needs of small- to medium-sized construction businesses. Step by step, it shows you how to use *Microsoft Project* to build a schedule that will synchronize everyone's efforts into an organized system that becomes the foundation of all planning and communication for all your jobs. You'll see how to establish realistic project goals, set checkpoints, activities, relationships and time estimates for each task, as well as establish priorities. You'll learn how to create a project flowchart to keep everyone focused and on track, and see how to use CSI (Construction Specification Institute) coding to organize and sort tasks, methods, and materials across multiple projects. If you want an easy way to schedule your jobs, *Microsoft Project* and *Easy Scheduling* is the answer for you. (Does not include Microsoft Project.) Published by BNI. **316 pages, 8½ x 11, $59.95**

## Basic Plumbing with Illustrations, Revised

This completely-revised edition brings this comprehensive manual fully up-to-date with all the latest plumbing codes. It is the journeyman's and apprentice's guide to installing plumbing, piping, and fixtures in residential and light commercial buildings: how to select the right materials, lay out the job and do professional-quality plumbing work, use essential tools and materials, make repairs, maintain plumbing systems, install fixtures, and add to existing systems. Includes extensive study questions at the end of each chapter, and a section with all the correct answers.
**384 pages, 8½ x 11, $36.00 Also available as an eBook (PDF), $18.00 at www.craftsman-book.com**

## Renovating & Restyling Older Homes

Any builder can turn a run-down old house into a showcase of perfection — if the customer has unlimited funds to spend. Unfortunately, most customers are on a tight budget. They usually want more improvements than they can afford — and they expect you to deliver. This book shows how to add economical improvements that can increase the property value by two, five or even ten times the cost of the remodel. Sound impossible? Here you'll find the secrets of a builder who has been putting these techniques to work on Victorian and Craftsman-style houses for twenty years. You'll see what to repair, what to replace and what to leave, so you can remodel or restyle older homes for the least amount of money and the greatest increase in value. **416 pages, 8½ x 11, $33.50**

## Concrete Construction

Just when you think you know all there is about concrete, many new innovations create faster, more efficient ways to do the work. This comprehensive concrete manual has both the tried-and-tested methods and materials, and more recent innovations. It covers everything you need to know about concrete, along with Styrofoam forming systems, fiber reinforcing adjuncts, and some architectural innovations, like architectural foam elements, that can help you offer more in the jobs you bid on. Every chapter provides detailed, step-by-step instructions for each task, with hundreds of photographs and drawings that show exactly how the work is done. To keep your jobs organized, there are checklists for each stage of the concrete work, from planning, to finishing and protecting your pours. Whether you're doing residential or commercial work, this manual has the instructions, illustrations, charts, estimating data, rules of thumb and examples every contractor can apply on their concrete jobs.
**288 pages, 8½ x 11, $28.75. Also available as an eBook (PDF), $14.38 at www.craftsman-book.com**

## National Repair & Remodeling Estimator

The complete pricing guide for dwelling reconstruction costs. Reliable, specific data you can apply on every repair and remodeling job. Up-to-date material costs and labor figures based on thousands of jobs across the country. Provides recommended crew sizes; average production rates; exact material, equipment, and labor costs; a total unit cost and a total price including overhead and profit. Separate listings for high- and low-volume builders, so prices shown are specific for any size business. Estimating tips specific to repair and remodeling work to make your bids complete, realistic, and profitable. Includes a free download of an electronic version of the book with National Estimator, a stand-alone Windows™ estimating program. An interactive multimedia video that shows how to use the software to compile repair and remodeling cost estimates is free at www.costbook.com.
**504 pages, 8½ x 11, $73.50. Revised annually**

## Concrete at Home

Build artistic custom concrete floors, cabinets, countertops, sinks, dividers, fireplaces, mantle pieces and more. In the pages of this 216-page, four-color book you'll find hundreds of ideas for ways to use concrete on the job. You'll learn how to custom design, pour, finish, and seal one-of-a-kind custom interior and exterior floors. Includes information on admixtures, crack control, custom finishes, self-leveling compounds, and reinforcement techniques. Shows how to apply inlays, linework, and stamps and finishes to concrete floors. Explains how to create custom concrete countertops and sinks. Illustrates the fundamentals of concrete wall design, including innovative uses for concrete block, applying color and texture on walls, using ties, rebar, and forms for walls. How to design, form and place fireplace surrounds, water pieces, columns, and more from concrete. **216 pages, 8½ x 11, $32.00**

---

**Craftsman Book Company**
6058 Corte del Cedro
Carlsbad, CA 92011

☎ 24 hour order line
**1-800-829-8123**
Fax (760) 438-0398

Name _____
e-mail address (for order tracking and special offers)
Company _____
Address _____
City/State/Zip _____ ○ This is a residence
Total enclosed _____ (In California add 7.25% tax)

*Free Media Mail shipping, within the US, when your check covers your order in full.*

## In A Hurry?

We accept phone orders charged to your
○ Visa, ○ MasterCard, ○ Discover or ○ American Express

Card# _____
Exp. date _____ Initials _____

**Tax Deductible:** Treasury regulations make these references tax deductible when used in your work. Save the canceled check or charge card statement as your receipt.

**Order online** www.craftsman-book.com
**Free on the Internet!** Download any of Craftsman's estimating database for a 30-day free trial! www.craftsman-book.com/downloads

*Download all of Craftsman's most popular costbooks for one low price with the Craftsman Site License. www.craftsmansitelicense.com*

- ○ 36.00 Basic Plumbing with Illustrations, Revised
- ○ 16.75 Blueprint Reading for the Building Trades
- ○ 35.50 Builder's Guide to Accounting Revised
- ○ 32.50 Building Code Compliance for Contractors & Inspectors
- ○ 108.50 CD Estimator
- ○ 32.00 Concrete at Home
- ○ 28.75 Concrete Construction
- ○ 48.50 Construction Forms for Contractors
- ○ 6.00 Construction Spanish
- ○ 58.50 Contractor's Guide to *QuickBooks* 2012
- ○ 57.00 Contractor's Guide to *QuickBooks Pro* 2010
- ○ 56.50 Contractor's Guide to *QuickBooks Pro* 2009
- ○ 49.50 Contractor's Plain-English Legal Guide
- ○ 65.00 Craftsman's Construction Installation Encyclopedia
- ○ 21.95 Drywall, Revised & Updated, 4th Edition with DVD
- ○ 34.95 Drywall Contracting
- ○ 59.95 Easy Scheduling
- ○ 89.50 Estimating & Bidding for Builders & Remodelers
- ○ 59.00 Estimating Electrical Construction, Revised
- ○ 38.00 Estimating Home Building Costs, Revised
- ○ 34.95 Finish Carpentry: Efficient Techniques for Custom Interiors
- ○ 69.00 Insurance Restoration Contracting: Startup to Success
- ○ 69.95 JLC Field Guide to Residential Construction, Volume 1
- ○ 69.95 JLC Field Guide to Residential Construction, Volume 2
- ○ 34.00 Journeyman Electrician's Preparation & Study Guide
- ○ 47.50 Markup & Profit: A Contractor's Guide, Revisited
- ○ 72.50 Natl Construction Est w/FREE *Natl Estimator* Download
- ○ 73.75 Natl Home Improvement Est w/FREE *Natl Estimator* Download
- ○ 74.50 Natl Renovation & Ins Repair Est w/FREE *Natl Estimator* Download
- ○ 73.50 Natl Repair & Remodeling Est w/FREE *Natl Estimator* Download
- ○ 34.00 Paint Contractor's Manual
- ○ 33.00 Painter's Handbook
- ○ 55.50 Paper Contracting: The How-To of Constr Mngt Contracting
- ○ 24.75 Profits in Buying & Renovating Homes
- ○ 33.50 Renovating & Restyling Older Homes
- ○ 38.00 Roofing Construction & Estimating
- ○ 26.50 Rough Framing Carpentry
- ○ 24.95 Wiring a House
- ○ 17.95 Working Alone
- ○ 73.00 National Painting Cost Est w/FREE Download
- ○ FREE Full Color Catalog

**10-Day Money Back Guarantee**     **Prices subject to change without notice**

*Download free construction contracts legal for your state: www.construction-contract.net*